A STUDY OF HISTORY

Arnold Toynbee writes:

IN the first six volumes of this work, I have been looking at human affairs in terms of civilizations. I have been trying to make a comparative study of these in their births, growths, breakdowns, and declines and falls. When a society is disintegrating, each of the factions into which it splits produces a new institution. The dominant minority tries to preserve its threatened power by uniting the disintegrating society politically in a universal state (Vol. 7A). The internal proletariat produces a missionary religion embodied in a universal church (Vol. 7B). The barbarians enjoy a brief heroic age as they break through the universal state's frontiers and overrun its interior (the first subject in Vol. 8).

Regarded from the standpoint of the disintegrating civilization, these institutions are simply products of its last phase; and barbarian heroic ages are in truth no more than that. On the other hand, the universal states of the past—local and ephemeral though they have been—are perhaps foretastes of a future regime in which the whole human race will live together like a single family.

As for the higher religions, the emergence of these marks so important a new departure in human history that they cannot be dealt with adequately in terms of the civilizations whose declines and falls have given rise to them. The higher religions are not just incidents in the histories of civilizations. It would be nearer to the truth to look on the rises and falls of civilizations as being preparatory stages for the births of higher religions. Thus the higher religions carry us beyond the comparative study of civilizations.

We have still to study the reciprocal influence of the civilizations on each other. Encounters between societies that are contemporary with each other are the main subject of Volume 8.

But at my back I always hear
Time's wingèd chariot hurrying near.

ANDREW MARVELL

ποιεῖν τι δεῖ ἆς γόνυ χλωρόν.

THEOCRITUS: Κυνίσκας Ἔρως, l. 70

γηράσκω δ᾽ αἰεὶ πολλὰ διδασκόμενος.

SOLON

My times are in Thy hand.

Ps. xxxi. 15, in the A.V.

But Thou art the same, and Thy
years shall have no end.

Ps. cii. 27, in the A.V.

A STUDY OF HISTORY

7A

Universal States

ARNOLD J. TOYNBEE

A Galaxy Book

New York   OXFORD UNIVERSITY PRESS   1963

A Study of History was first issued under the auspices of the Royal Institute of International Affairs, of which Arnold J. Toynbee was then Director of Studies.

First published, 1954
First published as a Galaxy Book, 1963

The illustration on the cover of this volume is a rendering by Charles Gottlieb of a marble statue of Augustus (detail), *c.* 20 B.C. [Vatican Museum].

PRINTED IN THE UNITED STATES OF AMERICA

THE PLAN OF THE BOOK

PUBLISHER'S NOTE

In order to facilitate paperback publication of the hardcover edition of Volume 7, the two natural sub-sections of that volume, "Universal States" and "Universal Churches," now appear in paper covers as Volume 7A and Volume 7B. Therefore, the tables and annexes referred to in Volume 7A, *Universal States,* will be found in Volume 7B, *Universal Churches.*

1963

PREFACE

THESE four volumes contain Parts VI–XIII of the thirteen parts which are set out in the plan of the book on p.vii above, and their publication brings the book to a close.

I was not able to begin writing these concluding eight parts till I had been released from work as a temporary civil servant during the Second World War. By the summer of A.D. 1946, when I found myself free to return to my normal occupations, more than seven years had passed since the publication of volumes iv–vi in the summer of A.D. 1939, forty-one days before Great Britain had gone to war with Germany, and more than seventeen years had now passed since the latest of the notes for the book, which had all been written between June 1927 and June 1929, had been put on paper.

If these notes had not still been in existence—as they were, thanks to their safe-keeping during the war in the hands of the Council on Foreign Relations in New York—I might have found it beyond my power to take up my work again after a seven years' interruption during which there had been a break in my personal life as well as in the life of the society into which I had been born. On the other hand, I should assuredly have failed at this stage to carry the work to completion if, after having set my thoughts moving again by reacquainting myself with my notes in their original form, I had not thrown them into the melting-pot and recast them.

The world around me and within me had, indeed, met with a number of challenging and transforming experiences in the course of the nineteen years and more that, by the summer of A.D. 1946, had already passed since the first of the original notes for the book had been written. The focus and perspective in which the earlier millennia of the Age of the Civilizations presented themselves to the eyes of our generation had been appreciably modified in the meantime by further discoveries in the field of Archaeology. The prospects of a contemporary Western Civilization, and of an *Oikoumenê* which this civilization had enveloped in its world-encompassing net, had become clearer and graver since the National Socialist movement in Germany had given to Western Man—and to his non-Western contemporaries likewise—a horrifying practical demonstration of the moral depths to which the heirs of a Christian civilization were capable of dragging themselves down. A new dimension of the Spiritual Universe had been brought to light by the psychologists, and a new dimension of the Material Universe by the atomic physicists. An Einstein and a Rutherford, a Freud and a Jung, and a Marshall and a Woolley, as well as a Gandhi, a Stalin, a Hitler, a Churchill, and a Roosevelt, had been changing the face of the Macrocosm; and at the same time my inner world had been undergoing changes which, on the miniature scale of an individual life, were, for me, of proportionate magnitude. The cumulative effect of these divers changes in my universe had been so far-reaching that, when in A.D. 1946 I was once more free to think of resuming and finishing my work,

I found that the reawakening of my original thoughts was only the beginning of my next task. In order to carry out my purpose, I should have to think again in the light of the revolutionary experience which the nineteen intervening years had been thrusting upon me and my contemporaries.

The effort required for performing this act of mental rejuvenation might have been beyond my capacity if I had been left to attempt it in solitude; but at this point I was effectively helped on my way by the timely receipt of a series of invitations to give public lectures on the topics that were the agenda for the still unexecuted parts of the plan of the book. In a set of Edward Cadbury Lectures delivered at the University of Birmingham, England, in the autumn of 1946 I dealt with the subjects of Parts VI–VIII; in a set of Mary Flexner Lectures delivered at Bryn Mawr College, Pennsylvania, in the spring of 1947 I dealt with the subject of Part IX; in a set of Bampton Lectures delivered at Columbia University, New York, in April 1948 I dealt with the subject of Part XII, and, later in the same month, with the subject of Part XIII in a set of Rushton Lectures delivered at Southern College, Birmingham, Alabama. The subject of Part XI was my theme in a set of Chichele Lectures delivered in the autumn of 1948 in the University of Oxford on an invitation from All Souls College. The subject of Part X was broached in a couple of lectures delivered in April 1949 in the University of Chicago on an invitation from the Committee on Social Thought.

I was fortunate in being given these opportunities of feeling my way back into a study of History for the immediate practical purpose of sharing my thoughts and feelings with responsive audiences. The congenial necessity of writing notes for these lectures gave me the stimulus that I needed in order to recast my original notes for the book in a new form answering to the new experiences, public and personal, that I had encountered since the summer of 1927. In the outcome, the original plan of the book still stood and the execution of Parts VI, VIII, X, and XIII was carried out more or less on the lines of the original notes. The subjects of Parts VII, IX, XI, and XII, on the other hand, came, in the event, to be treated very differently from the original design—and the subject of Part XI, in particular, so differently that the title of this Part had to be changed from 'Rhythms in the Histories of Civilizations' to 'Law and Freedom in History'.

When these invitations to lecture had thus given me the impetus required for finishing the book in the light of my experience since 1927, I should have found myself overwhelmed by the accumulation of seven years' arrears of work on the Chatham House *Survey of International Affairs*—work which was the first call on my time and energy —but for the imagination, considerateness, and generosity of the Royal Institute of International Affairs, the Rockefeller Foundation of New York, and the Institute for Advanced Study at Princeton, N.J., in co-operating with one another to release the major part of my time, for a period of five years beginning on the 1st July, 1947, for writing the rest of *A Study of History*, partly in England and partly in America, under ideal conditions. My debt to the Rockefeller Foundation, and to the authorities at Bryn Mawr College who were the Foundation's consultants when it was considering this project, is a greater one than I can put into words.

My acknowledgements and thanks for the help of many kinds, from many quarters, which I have received in the writing of the book as a whole are set out at the end (in volume x, on pp. 213–42), since they run to too great a length to allow of their being included in a preface; but I cannot bring myself to postpone my expression of gratitude for certain essential pieces of help in the production of this last batch of four volumes.

The index to the volumes now published, like the two indexes to the preceding six volumes, has been made by my wife and colleague and co-author of the *Survey of International Affairs*. If the reader ever loses the thread of my thought, he will find it again here—as I know from having often found it, myself, in the indexes to the two previous batches of volumes. My gratitude is not lessened by the happy knowledge that this skilful and exacting task has been a labour of love.

Miss Bridget Reddin has completed the enormous tasks—begun in the winter of 1930–1—of typing from a manuscript that has always been complicated, and of deciphering a handwriting that has not improved in the course of putting on paper some millions of words. Both the printer and I would have been at a loss if Miss Reddin had not returned to give us this help after having served during the Second World War, with my wife and me, in the same department of the Government of the United Kingdom.

The book that I am finishing in the act of writing this preface has had a long history on the Time-scale of an individual human life. Now that I have finished it, I can see in retrospect that, without knowing it, I was already at work on it in rather early days. For instance, the Annex to Part VI C (ii) (c) 3 first found its way on to paper, in the form of a child's coloured illustrations to the text of Herodotus, Book VII, chaps. 61–99, in a drawing-book, dated August 1903, which is on my table at my elbow at this moment. Upon it lies the manuscript—running to sixty-four pages of sermon paper and ending with a quotation from the Book of the Prophet Ezekiel xxxvii. 1–10—of an essay on 'the Philosophy of History' read at Oxford to an undergraduate society at some date in the academic year 1910–11. In the summer of 1920, after the philosophic contemporaneity of the Western and Hellenic civilizations had been borne in on me by the experience of the First World War, I for the first time consciously tried—and, at this first attempt, signally failed—to write the present work in the form (dictated by a Late Medieval Italian education in the Greek and Latin Classics) of a commentary on the second chorus (ll. 332–75) of Sophocles' *Antigone*. I did not succeed in finding my way into my subject till more than a year later.

On Saturday, 17 September, 1921, I was travelling with my school-fellow and life-long friend Theodore Wade-Gery in the Orient Express *en route* from Constantinople to England. Before dawn we had been awakened by the rumbling of our train as it crossed the bridge over the

Maritsa, below Adrianople, and, for the rest of that day, we were travelling on westward up the valley of a river that had once been famous as the
Hebrus. As I stood, hour after hour, at the corridor window, watching
the stream glide by, with an endless fringe of willows and poplars
marking out, as they slid past, the curves of the gently flowing waters'
course, my mind began to dream of historical and legendary events of
which an Hellenic Thrace and an Ottoman Rumili had been the theatre:
the legendary violent death of the Prophet Orpheus; the historic
violent deaths of the Emperors Valens and Nicephorus; the entrench-
ment of the Ottoman Power on the European side of the Straits in the
reign of Sultan Murād I. When a group of inquisitive Bulgarian
peasants clustered round the door of our coach as the train lingered in
a wayside station, my eye was caught by the fox-skin cap that one of
these Thracian contemporaries of mine was wearing; for this was the
headgear in which Herodotus (in Book VII, chap. 75) had paraded the
Asiatic Thracian contingent of Xerxes' expeditionary force, and a
picture of a Thracian fighting-man in just such a cap, which I had copied
into my drawing-book eighteen years ago, had left its imprint on my
memory. These stimulating sights and reminiscences must have released some psychic well-spring at a subconscious level. That evening
I was still standing at the window, overwhelmed by the beauty of the
Bela Palanka Gorge in the light of a full moon, as our train bore down
upon Nish. If I had been cross-examined on my activities during that
day, I should have sworn that my attention had been wholly absorbed
by the entrancing scenes that were passing continually before my outward eye. Yet, before I went to sleep that night, I found that I had put
down on half a sheet of notepaper a list of topics which, in its contents
and in their order, was substantially identical with the plan of this book
as it now stands printed in volumes i, iv, and vii. The path that had thus
unexpectedly—and, as it might seem, casually—opened at last before
my feet was to carry me farther than I then foresaw on a journey that
was to take nearly thirty years to complete; but, once open, the path
went on unfolding itself before me till today I find myself at this long
journey's end.

                                        ARNOLD J. TOYNBEE

LONDON
16 *August* 1951

SINCE writing this preface, I have begun to be able to see ahead to
the next stage of this Study beyond the moment when I shall have
delivered the last proofs of volumes vii–x to the printer.

   While these four volumes have been in the press, I have been co-
operating with my friend Professor E. D. Myers, of Washington and
Lee University, Lexington, Virginia, and with my former colleague
Mrs. Gomme, who was the head of the cartographical section of the
Foreign Office Research Department during the Second World War, in
producing the maps, and compiling the gazetteer of place-names that

are either shown on these maps or are mentioned in the text of volumes i–x, which are to be published together in a forthcoming volume xi. This eleventh volume, which is mostly Professor Myers' and Mrs. Gomme's work, will, I believe, be welcomed by readers of volumes i–x.

On the 26th February, 1953, the Rockefeller Foundation once again came to my aid in a most imaginative and effective way by giving my wife and me a grant to cover the costs of travel with a view eventually to revising this book. Our first use of this kind grant was to pay a visit to Mexico, from the 14th April to the 16th May, 1953, for the three-fold purpose of seeing at first hand some of the monuments of the Middle American Civilization and of the Spanish Empire of the Indies in the former Viceroyalty of New Spain and some of the aspects, in the Mexican field, of the current encounter between the World and the Modern West. Thanks to the hospitality and help of the Federal Ministry of Public Instruction and the Autonomous National University of Mexico, we were able to use our precious time in Mexico to good advantage. We look forward to following up this reconnaissance in Middle America by visiting Japan and Peru in 1956 on a journey to and from Australia which is to take us round the World. When, after that, we settle down to the task of revision, our plan is, first, to produce a volume of 'reconsiderations' (*retractationes* in Saint Augustine's usage of the Latin word). Since the first publication of the first batch of volumes in 1934, there have been additions to our historical knowledge, particularly through the wonderful work of the archaeologists, which have changed the appearance of some tracts of the historical land-scape. There have also been comments and criticisms, both general and particular, on the ideas presented in the book and on some of the citations of facts by which these ideas have been illustrated and suppor-ted. While I have already profited greatly by many of these criticisms in writing the later volumes, I shall not have drawn the full benefit from them till I have taken a synoptic view of them; and this will be the second topic in the volume of *retractationes* that my wife and I are planning to produce.

We also have other books on the stocks, and we should be happy if there could be said of us what Clarendon has said of himself in his autobiography:

'In all this retirement he was very seldom vacant . . . from reading excellent books or writing some animadversions and exercitations of his own. . . . He left so many papers of several kinds, and cut out so many pieces of work, that a man may conclude that he never intended to be idle.'[1]

ARNOLD J. TOYNBEE

LONDON

18 *February* 1954

---

[1] *The Life of Edward Earl of Clarendon*, written by himself, *ad fin.* (Oxford 1817, Clarendon Press), vol. ii, p. 567, quoted in the present Study, III. iii. 321.

SCRIPTORIS VITA NOVA

O silvae, silvae, raptae mihi, non revidendae,
    O mea, Silvani filia, musa dryas,
non dolet: hoc Paeto dictum immortale profata
    Arria procudit mi quoque robur et aes—
mi quoque; non solus tamen exsulo: nonne priores
    clara creaverunt tristi opera exsilio?
Exsul—et immeritus—divom, Florentia, carmen
    edidit, alma intra moenia tale tua
nil orsus, vates. Non iuste expulsus Athenis,
    Pangaei clivis advena Threïciis,
scripsit postnatis in perpetuom relegendam
    vir, bello infelix dux prius, historiam.
His ego par fato: par sim virtute. Fovetur
    acrius aerumnis magnanimum ingenium.
Me patriae excidium stimulat nova quaerere regna.
    Troia, vale! Latium per maria atra peto.
Silvae, musa dryas, praesens Silvane, penates,
    'non' mihi clamanti 'non' reboate 'dolet'.

Quae sibi nil quaerens quaerenti tanta ministrat,
    quae nil accipiens omnia suppeditat,
quae constanter amat non tali robore amata,
    quae dare—et hoc totis viribus—ardet opem,
nonne haec digna suo Beronice nomine sancto?
    Quod patet ante oculos, improbe, nonne vides?

Cui tam cara comes, non exsulat exsul: ubique
    patria qua praesens coniugis adsit amor.

Caece diu, tandem vidisti clarius. Audi:
    Perdita mortali gaudia flere nefas:
non datur humanis in perpetuom esse beatos:
    mox marcent vitae praemia: segnities
Elysii pretiumst: hebetat dulcedo: doloris
    sopitam recreant volnera viva animam.
Haec non quaesitae tibi ianua aperta salutis:
    tu fato felix: te nova vita vocat.

Gavisus iuvenis vitae describere metas,
   ausus eram fatum prospicere ipse meum.
Prospexi triplicem—fauste ducentis Amoris,
   Musarum comitum, coniugis—harmoniam,
amens, qui, vasti peragrans vagus aequora ponti,
   non cavi fulmen, saeva procella, tuom.
Non iterum de me dictabo oracula: nosti,
   qui me servasti, Tu mea fata, Deus.

CONTENTS OF VOLUMES VII–X
VOLUME VII

CONTENTS

VII. UNIVERSAL CHURCHES

ANNEXES

TABLES

VOLUME VIII

CONTENTS

ANNEXES

TABLE

VOLUME IX

X. CONTACTS BETWEEN CIVILIZATIONS IN TIME (RENAISSANCES)

CONTENTS

XII. THE PROSPECTS OF THE WESTERN CIVILIZATION

ANNEXES

TABLES

VOLUME X

XIII. THE INSPIRATIONS OF HISTORIANS

ACKNOWLEDGEMENTS AND THANKS

INDEX TO VOLUMES VII–X, by V. M. TOYNBEE . 243

A KEY TO THE CROSS-REFERENCES

IN THE FOOTNOTES TO VOLS. VII–X

THE final text of this book, like the original notes for it, has been written (except for some of the annexes) in the order in which the chapters appear in the Table of Contents. At each step in both making the notes and writing the text, the writer has always tried to see the particular passage on which he has been working at the moment in its relation to the plan of the whole book; and he has printed in his footnotes to the text the resulting network of cross-references because he believes that a method of continually taking his bearings, which has been an indispensable guide and discipline for the course of his own thought, is likely also to be of some help to his readers.

Since, in the nature of the case, the quantity of these notes of cross-references has increased as one Part of the book after another has been written out in full, the writer has sought, in the printing of this concluding batch of four volumes, to spare the reader's eye—and, in the act, to lighten the printer's labours—by reducing the bulk of his cross-references to a minimum. Accordingly, each reference has been cut down to three entries: a large Roman numeral indicating the Part, a small Roman numeral indicating the volume, and an Arabic numeral giving the page, with an n. to stand for 'footnote' when the reference is to one of these. For example, a reference which in volumes i–vi would have appeared in a footnote in the form 'See IV. C (iii) (c) 2 (γ), Annex, vol. iv, p. 637, above', would appear in the four present volumes as 'See IV. iv. 637'. Neither the printer nor the reader, the writer believes, is likely to regret this compression.

ADDENDA

Vol. vii, p. 529, footnote 1, add (running on):

This derivation of the Christian usage has, however, been disputed, in favour of an alternative derivation from a Greek philosophical expression ἀναχωρεῖν εἰς ἑαυτόν ('to retire into oneself') by Festugière, A.-J.: *Personal Religion among the Greeks* (Berkeley 1954, University of California Press), pp. 57–59, 66–67, 153–4.

Vol. vii, p. 649, footnote 3 carried over from p. 648, add to last paragraph (running on):

A lowland location for the Thataguš, west of the Indus, might, however, perhaps be found along the lower course of the Gumāl River, in the latitude of Dera Isma'il Khan, if 'Gumāl' is derived from Gomatī, meaning, in Sanskrit, 'abounding in cattle' (see Rawlinson, H. G.: *India, A Short Cultural History* (London 1948, Cresset Press), p. 20).

Vol. vii, p. 668, footnote to line 3:

The location of Xerxes' *Ākaufačiyā* in the Caucasus is, of course, uncertain, since this name, like 'Aparytai'—'Parouêtai'—'Parautai', is a descriptive one, meaning 'highlanders' (see vol. vii, p. 616, above). An alternative location would be the hill country south-east of the south-eastern end of the Central Desert of Iran, between Kirmān and Seistan, whose inhabitants were called Kaufaj or Qufs under the 'Abbasid Caliphate (see Spuler, B.: *Iran in Früh-Islamische Zeit* (Wiesbaden 1952, Steiner), pp. 17, &c.).

Vol. x, p. 24, footnote 1, add (running on):

Lord Bryce's own account of this expedition is given in his *Memories of Travel* (London 1923, Macmillan): 'The Altai Mountains (1913).'

Vol. x, p. 57, footnote to line 14:

[1] The writer's sister, Professor J. M. C. Toynbee, points out that the *cucullus* (cowl) and *caracalla* (hooded cloak) were being worn in Western Europe already under the Roman Empire. She finds the ancestors of the Dwarfs in the Celtic *genii cucullati*.

VI

UNIVERSAL STATES

A. ENDS OR MEANS?

THE starting-point of this book was a search for fields of historical study which would be intelligible in themselves within their own limits in Space and Time, without reference to extraneous historical events. An empirical pursuit of this inquiry led us to find the self-contained units for which we were seeking in societies of the species called civilizations,[1] and so far we have been working on the assumption that a comparative study of the geneses, growths, breakdowns, and disintegrations of the twenty-one civilizations that we have succeeded in identifying would comprehend everything of any significance in the history of Mankind since the time when the first civilizations emerged among the primitive societies which had previously been the only existing form of human social organization. Up to the present stage of our investigation this assumption has perhaps on the whole been justified by results; yet from time to time we have stumbled upon indications that our first master-key might not serve to unlock all the doors through which we have to pass in order to reach our mental journey's end.

Near the outset, in the act of identifying as many representatives as possible of the species of society that we had set ourselves to study, we found that certain civilizations were related to one another by a tie that was closer than the mere common characteristic of being representatives of the same species. We described this more intimate relation as one of 'apparentation-and-affiliation';[2] and we found, on analysis,[3] that the evidences of apparentation-and-affiliation were certain characteristic social products of a Dominant Minority, an Internal Proletariat, and an External Proletariat into which the 'apparented' society split up in the course of its disintegration. It appeared that dominant minorities produced philosophies which sometimes gave inspirations to universal states, that internal proletariats produced higher religions which sought to embody themselves in universal churches, and that external proletariats produced heroic ages which were the tragedies of barbarian war-bands.

In the aggregate, these experiences and institutions manifestly constitute a link between an 'apparented' and an 'affiliated' civilization that cannot be ignored. And this link in the Time-dimension between two non-contemporary civilizations is not the only kind of relation between civilizations that a comparative study of universal states, universal churches, and heroic ages brings to light. Though civilizations may be intelligible fields of historical study and self-contained units of social life on the whole—at any rate by comparison with the relatively parochial and ephemeral political communities into which they are apt to articulate themselves in their growth stage—the fractions, in the shape

[1] See I. i. 17-50.   [2] See I. i. 44.   [3] See I. i. 52-62.

of social classes, into which they disintegrate after breaking down acquire a liberty to enter into social and cultural combinations with alien elements derived from other contemporary civilizations.[1] This receptivity of theirs is revealed in the institutions that are their products. Some universal states have been the handiwork of alien empire-builders; some higher religions have been animated by alien inspirations;[2] and some barbarian war-bands have imbibed a tincture of alien culture.[3]

Universal states, universal churches, and heroic ages thus link together contemporary, as well as non-contemporary, civilizations in relations that are closer and more individual than an affinity consisting in the bare fact of their being representatives of the same species of society; and this observation raises the question whether we have been justified in treating these historical phenomena as mere by-products, in each case, of the disintegration of some single civilization and in assuming that the civilizations themselves are the sole objects of historical study which we need to take into account. Now that we have found that universal states, universal churches, and heroic ages cannot, for their part, be studied intelligibly within the framework that the history of a single civilization provides, ought we not to study them on their own respective merits, with a view to testing the validity, or at any rate the sufficiency, of the assumption on which we have been proceeding hitherto? Until we have examined the respective claims of institutions of each of these three kinds to be intelligible fields of study in themselves, and have also considered the alternative possibility that they might be parts of some larger whole embracing them and the civilizations alike, we cannot be sure that we have brought within our purview the whole of human history, above the primitive level, in all its aspects.

This further inquiry was the task that we set ourselves at the end of Part V of this Study.[4] We shall now try to acquit ourselves of it in Parts VI, VII, and VIII; and happily in this case we are in a position to proceed straight from the formulation of our question to an attempt to answer it, without having to go through the laborious process of seeking, sifting, assembling, and comparing those historical facts that are indispensable raw materials for the empirical method of investigation that we are following in this Study. An incidental survey of philosophies and universal states, higher religions and universal churches, heroic ages and war-bands has already been taken in our review of the dominant minorities and the internal and external proletariats of civilizations in disintegration,[5] and the results have been summarized in four tables printed in volume vi[6] and reprinted here.[7]

Accordingly, without further preliminaries, we can now investigate the claims of universal states, and may begin by asking whether they are ends in themselves or means towards something beyond them.

Our best approach to this question may be to remind ourselves of certain salient features of universal states that we have already ascertained.

[1] See V. v. 338–40.   [2] See I. i. 40–41 and 57; II. ii. 213–16; and V. v. 360–1.
[3] See V. v. 351–9.   [4] See V. vi. 325–6.
[5] See V. v. 35–337.   [6] vi. 327–31.
[7] Tables I–III, pp. 769–71 of the present volume, below, and Table I, in vol. viii, pp. 734–5.

In the first place, universal states arise after, and not before, the break-downs of the civilizations to whose bodies social they bring political unity. They are not summers but 'Indian Summers', masking autumn and presaging winter.[1] In the second place, they are the products of dominant minorities: that is, of once creative minorities that have lost their creative power.[2] The negativeness which is the hall-mark of their authorship and also the essential condition of their establishment and maintenance is brought out in the following passages from the works of a nineteenth-century French philosopher and a twentieth-century English satirist.

'The result of the Roman conquest was the destruction of all the city-states in the greater part of the then known world, just as the result of all the partial conquests that merged in the Roman conquest had been already to reduce their numbers. Thereafter one city-state alone, the arch-aggressor, remained standing; but on the very morrow of the establish-ment of the Empire we see Rome herself promptly divesting herself of her original character, gradually losing her power of aggression and with-drawing into herself. Her dominant aim at this stage is no longer conquest but conservation; the Roman city-state, in short, disappears in order to make way for the Roman Empire.

'But what order, what state of society, did this empire stand for? Was the aim of conservation, which we have just attributed to the Roman Empire, expressed in a new dogma, in a corresponding social hierarchy, as the Roman conquest had been expressed and organised by the religious dogmas and the social institutions of the Roman city-state? Unquestion-ably, no: in casting our eyes over this immense empire, we do not find anywhere, in all its vast extent, any sentiments, ideas or habits that do not go back to the preceding institution—that of the city-state. And these sentiments, ideas and habits are deprived of energy, are no longer able to receive any [practical] social application, and therefore no longer provide positive links between individuals. In short, the Roman Empire in no sense constitutes a society; for, in its capacity as an empire, it has no religion, no goal, and no general practical aim whatsoever; it represents merely a vast aggregation of human beings, a shapeless congeries of the débris of societies. The imperial administration—in spite of being so far-flung, so complicated, so meticulous, and of giving so great an appearance of symmetry at first glance—does not constitute a political order or a social hierarchy at all; this administration is in strict truth nothing but a vast office for administering Rome's conquests. . . .

'These are the characteristics and the causes of the demoralisation of Rome that has made so lively an impression on the mind of Posterity. This demoralisation had almost reached full measure before the Empire had completed the first century of its existence. Thereafter, this huge body appears to maintain itself merely by a kind of mechanical equili-brium; and, if it does not actually dissolve, that is not so much because there is any positive reason for it to maintain itself as because there is no positive reason, either, for it to undergo any change.'[3]

The point thus illustrated by Bazard from 'real life' in the instance of

[1] See IV. iv. 56–119, especially 59–60.
[2] See V. v. 35–58.
[3] Bazard, A: 'Exposition de la Doctrine Saint-Simonienne', in Œuvres Complètes de Saint-Simon et d'Enfantin, vol. xlii (Paris 1877, Leroux), pp. 181–5.

the Roman Empire is brought out more wittily by Huxley in his imaginary Anti-Utopia:

' "The Nine Years' War, the great Economic Collapse. There was a choice between World Control and destruction. Between stability and. . . .

' "It's curious . . . to read what people in the time of Our Ford used to write about scientific progress. They seem to have imagined that it could be allowed to go on indefinitely, regardless of everything else. Knowledge was the highest good, truth the supreme value; all the rest was secondary and subordinate. True, ideas were beginning to change even then. Our Ford himself did a great deal to shift the emphasis from truth and beauty to comfort and happiness. Mass production demanded the shift. Universal happiness keeps the wheels steadily turning; truth and beauty can't. And of course, whenever the masses seized political power, then it was happiness rather than truth and beauty that mattered. Still, in spite of everything, unrestricted scientific research was still permitted. People still went on talking about truth and beauty as though they were the sovereign goods. Right up to the time of the Nine Years' War. *That* made them change their tune all right. What's the point of truth or beauty or knowledge when the anthrax bombs are popping all around you? That was when science first began to be controlled—after the Nine Years' War. People were ready to have even their appetites controlled then. Anything for a quiet life. We've gone on controlling ever since. It hasn't been very good for truth, of course. But it's been very good for happiness. One can't have something for nothing. Happiness has got to be paid for. . . ."

' "Art, science—you seem to have paid a fairly high price for your happiness," said the Savage. . . . "Anything else?"

' "Well, religion, of course," replied the Controller: "There used to be something called God—before the Nine Years' War. . . ." '[1]

This, however, is not the whole picture; for, besides being accompaniments of social breakdown and products of dominant minorities, universal states display a third salient feature: they are expressions of a rally—and a particularly notable one—in a process of disintegration that works itself out in successive pulsations of lapse-and-rally followed by relapse;[2] and it is this last feature that strikes the imagination and evokes the gratitude of the generation that lives to see the successful establishment of a universal state set a term at last to a Time of Troubles that had previously been gathering momentum from successive failures of repeated attempts to stem it.[3]

Taken together, these features present a picture of universal states that, at first sight, looks ambiguous. Universal states are symptoms of social disintegration, yet at the same time they are attempts to check this disintegration and to defy it.

The tenacity with which universal states do cling to life, when once established, is revealed by a survey of their endings. The divers types into which these endings can be analysed form an illuminating series when arranged in an ascending order of the obstinacy with which a universal state rebels against being condemned to death. To comprehend,

---

[1] Huxley, Aldous: *Brave New World* (London 1932, Chatto & Windus), pp. 56 and 269–70 and 271.
[2] This rhythm has been analysed and illustrated in V. vi. 278–321.
[3] See V. vi. 181–2 and 191.

and compare with one another, these divers typical endings of universal states, we must view each of them in the setting of its own particular version of the common plot of the tragedy of decline and fall; and an attempt at a survey on these lines will be found in an annex to the present chapter at a later point in this volume.[1] The analysis of the divers types of endings of universal states, which this survey of their histories yields, may be summarized here as follows:

When the establishment of a universal state by indigenous empire-builders has been forestalled by the intrusion of an alien society, the impulse, in the body social of the disintegrating society, to pass through the universal state phase before going into dissolution is powerful enough sometimes to be able to constrain the triumphant alien aggressor to provide his victims with the institution which his very triumph has made it impossible for indigenous hands to set up. The Central American, Chibcha Andean, main Orthodox Christian, and Hindu civilizations all succeeded in exacting this social service from alien intruders; the Hindu Civilization actually succeeded in exacting it from two intruders in succession: first from Mughal representatives of the Iranic Muslim Civilization and then from British representatives of the Western Civilization.

When an indigenous universal state has been overthrown by the intrusion of an alien civilization before the exhaustion of the social rally which the foundation of the universal state has inaugurated, the impulse in the body social of the invaded disintegrating society to complete the universal state phase before going into dissolution is powerful enough sometimes to be able to constrain the triumphant aggressor to provide an alien substitute for the indigenous institution which he himself has destroyed, and sometimes to enable the invaded society to bide its time —for many centuries if need be—until at last it finds its opportunity to expel the intruder, re-establish the long ago overthrown indigenous universal state, and, this time, carry it through to the completion of its natural course. The Andean and the Babylonic Society succeeded in exacting from their alien conquerors the social service that they required—the Andean Society from Spanish representatives of the Western Civilization, the Babylonic actually from two intruders in succession: first from Achaemenid representatives of the Syriac Civilization and then from Seleucid representatives of the Hellenic. The Syriac and the Indic Society succeeded in biding their time and eventually re-establishing their overthrown indigenous universal states.

When an indigenous universal state has collapsed after the exhaustion of the social rally which its foundation has inaugurated, the impulse in the body social of the disintegrating society to complete the universal state phase, before going into dissolution, is powerful enough to be able to achieve the restoration of the prostrate indigenous universal state, sometimes—as the Hellenic, Sinic, and Sumeric civilizations achieved this—by self-help alone, and sometimes—as the Orthodox Christian Civilization in Russia achieved it—by self-help reinforced by the reception of an alien civilization.

[1] On pp. 569–76, below.

After an indigenous universal state has reached the term of its natural expectation of life and has duly given place to the social interregnum in which the dissolution of a moribund civilization is normally consummated, the impulse in the body social of the moribund society to retrieve its life from the jaws of death may be powerful enough—as is witnessed by the Egyptiac Civilization's achievement of this *tour de force*—to be able to restore the defunct universal state and thereafter to maintain it in existence by one means or another until the moribund society, preserved within this institutional mummy-case in an uncanny state of life-in-death, has succeeded, like King Menkaure in the folk-tale,[1] in doubling the span of life allotted to it by the Gods.

Indeed, after a universal state has reached the term of its natural expectation of life, the determination of the body social of the moribund society not to taste of death may be obstinate enough—as is witnessed by the history of the Far Eastern Civilization in China—to be able to maintain the senile universal state in existence, without a break, for an additional term by inducing a vigorous and victorious barbarian invader to shoulder the burden of preserving an institution which he might have been expected to destroy.

These divers endings of universal states bear concordant witness to the craving for life by which these institutions are animated. So strong is this craving of theirs that they refuse to forgo their claims to be brought into existence and to be allowed to live out their normal terms, and sometimes even refuse to pass out of existence after having duly realized their natural expectation of life. In other words, universal states show a strong tendency to behave as though they were ends in themselves, whereas in truth they represent a phase in a process of social disintegration and, if they have any significance beyond that, can only have it in virtue of being a means to some end that is outside and beyond them.

The judgement of History on their idolization of themselves is pronounced in one of the masterpieces of a Modern Western poet:

> It is not growing like a tree
> In bulk, doth make Man better be,
> Or standing long an oak, three hundred year,
> To fall a log at last, dry, bald and sere:
> A lily of a day
> Is fairer far in May,
> Although it fall and die that night—
> It was the plant and flower of light.
> In small proportions we just beauties see,
> And in short measures Life may perfect be.[2]

[1] See IV. iv. 409 and V. v. 2.   [2] Ben Jonson.

B. UNIVERSAL STATES AS ENDS

(I) THE MIRAGE OF IMMORTALITY

A Paradoxical Misapprehension

AS we have seen in the last chapter, the endings of universal states indicate that these institutions are possessed by an almost demonic craving for life; and, if we now look at them, no longer through the eyes of alien observers, but through those of their own citizens, we shall find that these are apt not only to desire with their whole hearts that this earthly commonwealth of theirs may live for ever,[1] but actually to believe that the immortality of this human institution is assured—and this sometimes in the teeth of contemporary events which, to an observer posted at a different standpoint in Time or Space, declare beyond question that this particular universal state is at this very moment in its last agonies. To observers who happen to have been born into the history of their own societies at a time when these have not been passing through the universal state phase, it is manifest that universal states, as a class of polity, are by-products of a process of social disintegration and are stamped by their certificates of origin as being uncreative and ephemeral.[2] Why is it, such observers may well ask, that, in defiance of apparently plain facts, the citizens of a universal state are prone to regard it, not as a night's shelter in the wilderness, but as the Promised Land, the goal of human endeavours? How is it possible for them to mistake this mundane institution for the *Civitas Dei* itself?

This misapprehension is so extreme in its degree that its very occurrence might perhaps be called in question, were this not attested by the incontrovertible evidence of a cloud of witnesses who convict themselves, out of their own mouths, of being victims of this strange hallucination.

The Aftermaths of the Roman Empire[3] and the Arab Caliphate[4]

In the history of the Roman Empire, which was the universal state

[1] This desire appears to be the characteristic sentiment of citizens of universal states that have been established and maintained by indigenous empire-builders, in contrast to the aversion commonly felt for universal states of alien origin (see V. v. 341–51). An indigenous origin is, of course, the rule, and an alien origin the exception. The love and hatred inspired by these two different kinds of universal state both show a tendency to grow stronger with the passage of time.

[2] An imperfection that is transparent in universal states is, of course, characteristic of all states of all kinds in all circumstances, as is pointed out by a Modern Western Christian philosopher in the following passage:

'What men call peace is never anything but a space between two wars: a precarious equilibrium that lasts as long as mutual fear prevents dissension from declaring itself. This parody of true peace, this armed fear, which there is no need to denounce to our contemporaries, may very well support a kind of order, but never can it bring Mankind tranquillity. Not until the social order becomes the spontaneous expression of an interior peace in men's hearts shall we have tranquillity; were all men's minds in accord with themselves, all wills interiorly unified by love of the supreme good, then they would know the absence of internal dissension, unity, order from within, a peace, finally, made of the tranquillity of this order: *pax est tranquillitas ordinis*. But, if each will were in accord with itself, all wills would be in mutual accord, each would find peace in willing what the others will. Then also we should have a true society, based on union in love of one and the same end' (Gilson, E.: *The Spirit of Mediaeval Philosophy*, English translation (London 1936, Sheed & Ward), p. 399).

[3] See xi, map 29.

[4] See xi, map 37.

of the Hellenic World, we find the generation that had witnessed the establishment of the *Pax Augusta* asserting, in evidently sincere good faith, that the Empire and the City that has built it have been endowed with a common immortality.[1]

Tibullus (*vivebat circa* 54–18 B.C.) sings of the 'aeternae urbis moenia',[2] while Virgil (*vivebat* 70–19 B.C.) makes his Iuppiter, speaking of the future Roman scions of Aeneas' race, proclaim: 'His ego nec metas rerum nec tempora pono:/imperium sine fine dedi.'[3] A soldier-historian may show somewhat greater caution than a philosopher-poet by expressing the same expectation in the form, not of a divine communiqué, but of a human hope. In recording the adoption of Tiberius by Augustus, Velleius (*vivebat circa* 19 B.C.–A.D. 31) speaks of a 'spem conceptam perpetuae securitatis aeternitatisque Romani imperii'.[4] An historian-propagandist can perhaps afford to be less circumspect, and Livy (*vivebat* 59 B.C.–A.D. 17) writes with the assurance of Tibullus: 'in aeternum urbe conditâ';[5] 'urbem . . . diis auctoribus in aeternum conditam'.[6] But Horace, who was both a poet and a sceptic, was doubly audacious in claiming immortality for his own verse and in taking, as his concrete measure of eternity, the repetition, *in saecula saeculorum*, of the annual round of the religious ritual of the Roman city-state:

> Exegi monumentum aere perennius
> regalique situ Pyramidum altius,
> quod non imber edax, non Aquilo impotens
> possit diruere aut innumerabilis
> annorum series et fuga temporum.
> non omnis moriar . . . : usque ego posterâ
> crescam laude recens dum Capitolium
> scandet cum tacitâ virgine pontifex.[7]

These lines ring ironically in the ears of a Modern Western student of history as he reflects on the unsuccessful rearguard action that was fought by an outgoing Roman Paganism, only four centuries after Horace's day, to induce a Christian Roman Government to reinstate in the Senate House the statue and altar of Victory that had been placed there by 'Caesar the God' in Horace's lifetime.[8] If some good-natured deity had forewarned Horace, in time, of this not far distant demise of Rome's native religious institutions, we may guess that the poet would have heartily thanked his informant and hastily changed his measure of duration. Whether Horace's poetry was, as its author believed it to be, immortal, Time, in A.D. 1952, had still to show; but this etherial creation of an individual genius had already lasted, *volitans viva per ora virum*, four or five times longer than the rites that are the second term of the poet's unlucky comparison. As a sceptic, the Roman poet Horace finds

1 'The little rivulet of disbelief which runs counter to the main stream of popular faith, and which takes the form of a belief in an "allotted span" for the Roman state', is traced from the last century B.C. to the fifth century of the Christian Era by D. A. Malcolm in 'Urbs Aeterna', in *The University of Birmingham Historical Journal*, vol. iii, No. 1 (1951), pp. 1–15.
2 *Carmina*, Book II, Elegy 5, ll. 24–25.   3 *Aeneid*, Book I, ll. 278–9.
4 Velleius Paterculus, C.: *Historia Romana*, Book II, chap. 103.
5 Book IV, chap. 4, § 4.   6 Book XXVIII, chap. 28, § 11.
7 *Carmina*, Book III, Ode xxx, ll. 1–9.   8 See V. vi. 89, with n. 3.

his match in the English historian Gibbon; yet Gibbon, who was inspired on the 15th October, A.D. 1764, to record 'the triumph of Barbarism and Religion' over the Roman Empire by hearing friars singing Vespers in the Temple of Iuppiter as he sat musing among the ruins of the Capitol[1] nearly 1,772 years after the date of Horace's death on the 17th November, 8 B.C., no doubt believed in the immortality of Horace's verse as confidently as the justifiably conceited poet had believed in it himself.

The same ludicrously inadequate ritual 'yard-stick' that had been taken by Horace as a measure for the duration of his personal literary work was taken by Livy as a measure for the duration of his historical theme the Roman Empire: 'Vestae aedem petitam et aeternos ignes et conditum in penetrali fatale pignus imperii Romani.'[2] The 'guarantee' (*pignus*) of the Roman Empire's survival is the Palladium.[3] In thus reading his modern political symbolism into an archaic religious rite, Livy was perhaps taking a cue from his Imperial patron, and Augustus a cue from his Imperial predecessors on the throne of an earlier universal state which had failed after all to discover the elixir of life. According to an eminent authority,[4] the interpretation of Vesta's undying flame as a symbol of the eternity of an oecumenical ruler was a Roman adaptation of an Achaemenian idea[5] that was adopted by Augustus when, in 12 B.C., he became Pontifex Maximus and consecrated a new temple of Vesta in his house on the Palatine. Augustus's successors, from the Antonines onwards, gave publicity to this idea by making it their practice to have Vesta's fire carried in procession in front of them.[6]

During the century and a quarter that elapsed between the death of Augustus in A.D. 14 and the accession of Pius in A.D. 138, the concept of the eternity of Rome and the Roman Empire had been cherished by two bad emperors who both had met their deserts by coming to untimely personal ends. Nero had instituted games 'quos pro aeternitate imperii susceptos appellari [ludos] maximos voluit'.[7] The *Acta Fratrum Arvalium* record 'aeterni[tati imperi vaccam]' among the proceedings of A.D. 66,[8] and 'vota si custodieris aeternitatem imperii quod [susci]piendo ampliavit (Domitianus)'[9] under the years A.D. 86, 87, and 90.

In the Age of the Antonines we find a Greek man of letters expressing the Augustan belief in the more delicate form of a prayer, without a suspicion that he was living in an 'Indian Summer' and was praying that

---

[1] See IV. iv. 59–60 and XIII. x. 103 and 104.
[2] Book XXVI, chap. 27, § 14. Cp. Book V, chap. 42, § 7.
[3] See Cicero: *Pro Scauro*, chap. xxiii, § 48: 'Palladium illud quod quasi pignus nostrae salutis atque imperi custodiis Vestae continetur'; *Philippicae*, Speech xi, ch. x, § 24: ' signum . . . de caelo delapsum . . . quo salvo salvi sumus futuri', quoted by Malcolm, D. A.: 'Urbs Aeterna', in *The University of Birmingham Historical Journal*, vol. iii, No. 1 (1951), p. 4.
[4] Cumont, Fr.: 'L'Éternité des Empereurs Romains', in *Revue d'Histoire et de Littérature Religieuses*, vol. i (Paris 1896; printed at Macon), pp. 436 and 441–2.
[5] In the Achaemenian *Weltanschauung* the symbolization of eternity by fire was connected with a belief in the divinity and eternity of the heavenly bodies (Cumont, op. cit., pp. 443–4).
[6] See Cumont, op. cit., pp. 437 and 442.
[7] Suetonius Tranquillus, C.: *The Lives of the Caesars*, 'Nero', chap. 11, § 2.
[8] *Acta Fratrum Arvalium Quae Supersunt*, ed. by G. Henzen (Berlin 1874, Reimer), p. lxxxi.   [9] Ibid. pp. cxv, cxix, cxxvi.

a fugitive October might be miraculously transformed into a perpetual June.

'Let us invoke all the gods and all the children of the gods, and let us pray them to grant this empire and this city life and prosperity world without end. May they endure until ingots learn to float on the sea and until trees forget to blossom in the spring. And long live the supreme magistrate and his children likewise. Long may they be with us to carry on their work of dispensing happiness to all their subjects'.[1]

Thereafter, when the touch of winter begins to make itself felt, its victims defy a change of season, which they have not foreseen and cannot face, by insisting more and more emphatically that they have been privileged to enjoy an everlasting midsummer's day.[2] In the Severan Age and its bleaker sequel, the contrast between the official eternity of the emperors[3] and the ephemeralness that was their actual lot makes a painfully strange impression.[4] It is still more strange to hear the watchwords of the Augustan poets being no less confidently repeated, in the same Latin, and this by men of letters whose mother-tongue was Greek,[5] on the eve of the final collapse of all but the easternmost extremity of the Latin-speaking portion of the Empire.[6] And, even after the truth has been proclaimed, in a deed more eloquent than any words, by Alaric's capture and sack of Rome herself, we can hear, above the reverberations of this resounding blow, the high voice of a Gallic poet reasserting the immortality of Rome as he travels back from the no longer inviolate Imperial City to his own war-ravaged native province.

> Erige crinales lauros seniumque sacrati
>   verticis in virides, Roma, refinge comas. . . .
> astrorum flammae renovant occasibus ortus;
>   lunam finiri cernis, ut incipiat.

---

[1] Aristeides, P. Aelius: *In Romam*, edited by Keil, B., *Aelii Aristidis Quae Supersunt Omnia*, vol. ii (Berlin 1898, Weidmann), p. 124 (Or. XXVI, § 109).

[2] See V. vi. 370–5.

[3] In this age of the Roman Empire's decline 'Your Eternity' gradually comes to be used, like 'Your Majesty' in Modern Western Europe, as the stock style and title for a crowned head (Cumont, op. cit., p. 435).

[4] The inscription 'Aeternitas Augusti' first appears on the Senatorial copper coinage of the Roman Empire in the reign of Vespasian (*imperabat* A.D. 69–79), gradually wins its way on to coins of other series, and holds its own till the close of the fourth century of the Christian Era (Cumont, op. cit., p. 438). Severus (*imperabat* A.D. 193–211), whose accession, like Vespasian's, had cost the Empire a disastrous civil war, perhaps had as much—or little—warrant for inscribing on his coinage the motto 'Aeternitas Imperii' and for evoking a dedication 'pro aeternitate imperii et salute Imperatoris Caesaris L. Septimi Severi' (C.I.L., vol. ii (Berlin 1869, Reimer), p. 31, No. 259). But the same motto becomes a bad joke on coins issued in the names of Caracalla and Geta as well as their father; and it makes a farcical effect on coins bearing the name of a Philip or a Carus. (See Cumont, op. cit., p. 437.)

[5] In the *Res Gestae* of the Antiochene historian Ammianus Marcellinus the Tibullan phrase 'urbs aeterna' is used as a stock periphrasis for 'Rome': e.g. in Book XIV. vi. 1: in Book XV. vii. 1 and vii. 10; in Book XVI. x. 14; and in eight other passages, according to Charlesworth, M. P.: 'Providentia and Aeternitas', in the *Harvard Theological Review*, vol. xxix, No. 22 (April 1936). The same conviction is expressed in the circumlocutions 'victura dum erunt homines Roma' (Book XIV, vi. 3) and 'victura cum saeculis Roma' (Book XXVI. i. 14). The Alexandrian poet Claudian, in his *De Consulatu Stilichonis*, Book III, ll. 159–60, declares: 'Nec terminus unquam/Romanae ditionis erit', and spends a dozen further lines on variations on this Virgilian theme.

[6] For the *tracée* of the geographical line of division between the Latin-speaking and Greek-speaking portions of the Roman Empire, see IV. iv. 326, n. 2.

victoris Brenni non distulit Allia poenam;
    Samnis servitio foedera saeva luit.
post multas Pyrrhum clades superata fugasti;
    flevit successus Hannibal ipse suos.
quae mergi nequeunt nisu maiore resurgunt,
    exsiliuntque imis altius acta vadis.
utque novas vires fax inclinata resumit,
    clarior ex humili sorte superna petis.
porrige victuras Romana in saecula leges,
    solaque fatales non vereare colos. . . .
quae restant, nullis obnoxia tempora metis:
    dum stabunt terrae, dum polus astra feret.
illud te reparat quod cetera regna resolvit:
    ordo renascendi est, crescere posse malis.
ergo age, sacrilegae tandem cadat hostia gentis:
    submittant trepidi perfida colla Getae.
ditia pacatae dent vectigalia terrae;
    impleat augustos barbara praeda sinus.
aeternum tibi Rhenus aret, tibi Nilus inundet,
    altricemque suam fertilis orbis alat.[1]

Perhaps the strangest testimony of all is Saint Jerome's description of the shock that he suffered when the news of the fall of Rome reached him in his remote and still secure retreat at Jerusalem. The saint was devoted to the service of a Church that avowedly placed its hopes in the Common-wealth of God, and not in any earthly polity; yet this news, mundane though it might be, affected Jerome so profoundly that for the moment he found himself incapable of proceeding with his literary labours of theological controversy and scriptural exegesis;[2] and the language in which he describes his admiration for what Rome has once been and his grief for the fate that has now overtaken her anticipates the language of Rutilius in verbal correspondences that can hardly be accidental.[3] Their common stupefaction, perhaps even more than their common sorrow, at the break-up of the universal state that was their common social universe was an emotion strong enough to bridge the moral gulf between the would-be exclusively Christian saint and the aggressively pagan *Praefectus Urbi emeritus.*

The shock administered by the fall of Rome in A.D. 410 to the citizens of a transient universal state which they had mistaken for an everlasting habitation[4] has its counterpart in the shock suffered by the subjects of the Arab Caliphate when Baghdad fell to the Mongols in A.D. 1258.[5] In

1 Rutilius Namatianus, C.: *De Reditu Suo*, Book I, ll. 115–16, 123–34, 137–46. The poet's exhortation to his heroine in ll. 141–2 was duly acted upon by her when, a century and more after Rutilius's day, Justinian annihilated the Visigoths' Ostrogothic cousins in a fight to the finish on Italian soil, and even struck some shrewd blows at the Visigoths themselves in the distant retreat that they had found for themselves in Spain after paving sacked Rome *en route*. The sequel, however, was just the opposite of what Rutilius so confidently looks forward to in ll. 143–6. So far from restoring the Empire's revenues, Justinian's reconquest of some of the Empire's lost Latin provinces was achieved at such a cost, in blood and treasure, to the hitherto still sound Greek and Oriental core of the Hellenic universal state that his extravagant régime was quickly followed by a collapse which proved to be irretrievable (see IV. iv. 326–8 and 397–8, and V. vi. 224–5).
2 See Saint Jerome, Ep. cxxvii, cap. 12, quoted in V. v, 223, n. 2.
3 See V. v. 345, n. 4.   4 Luke xvi. 9.
5 A touch of the emotion caused by this catastrophe can be felt in the last words of the passage quoted from Falak-ad-Dín Muhammad b. Aydímir in IV. iv. 446.

the Roman World the shock was felt from Palestine to Gaul; in the Arab World, from Farghānah to Andalusia.

'It is difficult to estimate the bewilderment that Muslims felt when there was no longer a Caliph on whom the blessing of God could be invoked in the *khutbah*; such an event was without precedent throughout the previous history of Islam. Their suffering finds expression in the prayer offered in the great mosque of Baghdad on the Friday following the death of the Caliph: "Praise be to God who has caused exalted personages to perish and has given over to destruction the inhabitants of this city. . . . O God, help us in our misery, the like of which Islam and its children have never witnessed; we are God's, and unto God do we return".'[1]

The intensity of the psychological effect is even more remarkable in this than in the Roman case, for, by the time when Hūlāgū gave the 'Abbasid Caliphate its *coup de grâce*, its sovereignty had been ineffective, for three or four centuries past, over the greater part of the vast domain that was nominally subject to it.[2] It is perhaps comprehensible that, even for that length of time, a shadow should continue to be mistaken, half deliberately, for the substance by a dominant minority for whom the moribund universal state represented their own latest achievement and last hope; a more astonishing testimony to the hold that a universal state can acquire over the hearts and minds of contemporaries is the fascination which it also exerts upon members of the now victoriously insurgent internal and external proletariats, who do not so much refuse to admit as, apparently, fail altogether to realize that they are in the act of pulling down with their own hands an institution which, in their eyes, is so venerable that it would be inconceivably impious even to imagine its disappearance.

On the strength of this widespread and long-lasting hallucination, which is itself a psychological and political fact to be reckoned with by the roughest-handed and hardest-headed carvers-out of indigenous or barbarian successor-states, the holders, in lawful succession, of the sovereign authority in a universal state may retain—for generations or even centuries after their loss of all genuine power over their nominal dominions—a by no means negligible status as the sole dispensers of legitimacy. Indeed, this monopoly of an imponderable political commodity usually counts for so much that it is rare to find a barbarian conqueror of an imperial province allowing himself the satisfaction of openly boasting that he has seized his prize by force and is holding it by right of conquest.[3] The heretic Arian Vandal conquerors of Roman

---

[1] Arnold, Sir T. W.: *The Caliphate* (Oxford 1924, Clarendon Press), pp. 81–82.

[2] For the stages in the progressive decline of the 'Abbasid Caliphate from the ninth century of the Christian Era onwards, see Arnold, op. cit., pp. 57–69.

[3] 'The minister who manages to establish an ascendancy over the ruler . . . appropriates the power without giving an inkling of his desire to usurp the throne; he contents himself with the [substantial] advantages of royalty: that is to say, the power of enjoining and prohibiting, of binding and loosing, of deciding and annulling. By this policy he leads the notables of the empire to believe that he is acting under instructions transmitted to him by the sovereign from his cabinet, and that he is merely executing the prince's orders. Although he has appropriated the whole of the authority, he takes care not to usurp the marks, emblems and titles of sovereignty, in order to avoid exciting any suspicions of his ambitions. The curtain which, since the foundation of the empire, has made the sultan and his ancestors invisible to the public, likewise serves to conceal the encroachments of the minister and to make the public believe that this officer is just the

Africa, and the heretic Shī'ī Katāma Berber conquerors of 'Abbasid Ifrīqīyah and Egypt, did permit themselves this indulgence; indeed the Katāma's self-declared but unauthenticated 'Fāṭimid' leaders were not content with repudiating the authority of the legitimate Sunnī 'Abbasid Caliphs at Baghdad, but pretended to the title of Caliphs themselves. For such presumption these two avowedly usurping war-bands both paid the penalty of being liquidated—the Vandals by Belisarius's Roman expeditionary force, and the Fāṭimids by the Sanhāja Berbers in Ifrī-qīyah and by Saladin in Egypt.[1] These, however, are exceptions that prove a rule. The Amalung leaders of the Arian Ostrogoths and Buwayhid leaders of the Shī'ī Daylamīs[2] were wiser in their generation in seeking title for their conquests by ruling them, in official theory, as vicegerents of the Emperor at Constantinople[3] and the Caliph at Baghdad[4] respectively; and, though this tactful handling of a senile universal state did not avail, in their case, to avert the doom to which both of these war-bands condemned themselves by clinging to their distinctive heresy instead of commending themselves to their subjects by adopting the orthodox faiths of Catholic Christianity and of Sunnī Islam,[5] the same political manœuvre was brilliantly successful when executed by fellow barbarians who had the sagacity or good fortune to be at the same time impeccable in their profession of religious faith. Clovis, for instance, who was the most successful of all founders of bar-barian successor-states of the Roman Empire, found it worth while to follow up his conversion from paganism to Catholicism in A.D. 496 by obtaining in A.D. 510 from Anastasius, the reigning Emperor at Con-stantinople, the title of proconsul with the consular insignia.[6] In the history of the decline of the 'Abbasid Caliphate there are notable ex-amples of a corresponding practice.

'Throughout the whole period of the decline of the Caliphate up to the date of the death of Musta'sim (A.D. 1258), the Caliph was to all orthodox Sunnīs[7] the Commander of the Faithful, and as Successor of the Prophet

prince's lieutenant and nothing more.'—Ibn Khaldūn: *Muqaddamāt*, French translation by de Slane, Baron McG. (Paris 1863–8, Imprimerie Impériale, 3 vols.), vol. i, p. 379.

[1] See V. v. 252 and 358. In the former passage, the Sanhāja have been correctly described as Sunnīs but incorrectly as Murābits. In the latter passage, the deposition of the Fāṭimids in Egypt has been erroneously ascribed to Saladin's uncle and companion in arms Shīrkūh, who died before the process of extinguishing the Fāṭimids was com-pleted by Saladin in A.D. 1171.

[2] For the Buwayhids, see I. i. 356 and V. v. 358.

[3] In this device for saving Roman 'face', Theodoric had been anticipated by his predecessor and victim Odovacer.

[4] See Arnold, op. cit., pp. 60–68, especially the account, on pp. 65–68, of the parti-cularly piquant farce that was played in A.D. 980, at the Caliphial Court of Baghdad, by the Buwayhid 'mayor of the palace' 'Aḍud-ad-Dawlah, who chose the occasion of his presentation of an ambassador from his fellow heretic the Fāṭimid anti-Caliph at Cairo as his moment for obtaining from the 'Abbasid Caliph Ṭā'i' a formal commission to exercise those plenary powers of government in the Caliph's dominions which he had long since usurped *de facto*.

[5] For the contrast between the respective fortunes of barbarian conquerors who retain an heretical form of religion or a tinge of alien culture and those who adopt the culture and faith of the subject population which they have taken over from a derelict universal state, see V. v. 351–8.

[6] See J. B. Bury's footnote in his *editio minor* of Edward Gibbon's *The History of the Decline and Fall of the Roman Empire*, vol. iv (London 1901, Methuen), p. 119.

[7] For the mass-conversion to Islam that accompanied the decline of the 'Abbasid Cali-phate and anticipated the dissolution of the Syriac Society, see pp. 397–400, below.—A.J.T.

he was held to be the source of all authority and the fountain of honour. The Caliph by his very name led men's thoughts back to the founder of their faith, the promulgator of their system of sacred law, and represented to them the principle of established law and authority. Whatever shape the course of external events might take, the faith of the Sunnī theologians and legists in the doctrines expounded in their textbooks remained unshaken, and, even though the Caliph could not give an order outside his own palace, they still went on teaching the faithful that he was the supreme head of the whole body of Muslims. Accordingly, a diploma of investiture sent by the Caliph, or a title of honour conferred by him, would satisfy the demands of the religious law and tranquillise the tender consciences of the subjects of an independent prince, though the ruler himself might remain entirely autonomous and be under no obligation of obedience to the puppet Caliph. . . . Even the Buwayhids, though their occupation of Baghdad was the culmination of the rapid growth of their extensive dominions, and though the Caliph was their pensioner and practically a prisoner in their hands, found it politic to disguise their complete independence under a pretence of subserviency and to give a show of legitimacy to their rule by accepting titles from him.'[1]

The precedent set by the heretical Buwayhids was followed by their Sunnī rivals, supplanters, and successors in the scramble for fragments of the 'Abbasid heritage.[2] Mahmūd of Ghaznah (*dominabatur* A.D. 998–1030)[3] obtained a title from the 'Abbasid Caliph Qādir bi'llāh (*imperabat* A.D. 991–1031) to legitimize the dominion which he had won for himself *de facto* by successful rebellion against a Sāmānid master whose Transoxanian principality was itself the fruit of previous successful usurpation at the 'Abbasid Caliphate's expense.[4] The Saljūq Turkish Nomad supplanters of the Sāmānids and the Buwayhids took over the Buwayhids' ascendancy at Baghdad in A.D. 1055 under the pretext of delivering the 'Abbasids from it. At the opposite extremity of Dār-al-Islām, *circa* A. D. 1086, Yūsuf b. Tāshfīn, the founder of a Murābit Berber principality embracing derelict provinces of both the 'Abbasid Caliphate of Baghdad in North-West Africa and the Umayyad Caliphate of Cordova in the Iberian Peninsula, obtained a title and insignia from the 'Abbasid Caliph Muqtadī (*imperabat* A.D. 1075–94), who, by his complacency in granting his uncouth petitioner a style barely distinguishable from his own,[5] rather easily won the empty distinction of being the first of his House whose Commandership was recognized—though not, of course, obeyed—by the Faithful in Andalusia. In A.D. 1175 Saladin, having appropriated, in the preceding year, the heritage of his own dead master Nūr-ad-Dīn's lawful heir, sought and obtained from the reigning Caliph Mustadī (*imperabat* A.D. 1170–80) a retrospective legitimization of the dominion which he had already acquired *de facto* by his act of usurpation. How could the Caliph refuse this request from an orthodox Sunnī champion who had restored the recitation of the Caliph's name in the bidding prayer (*khutbah*) in the mosques of Egypt after an interval of

---

[1] Arnold op. cit., pp. 77 and 78.   [2] See ibid., pp. 78–88.
[3] For Mahmūd of Ghaznah see I. i. 360, n. 1, and V. v. 303.
[4] For the role of the Sāmānids as wardens of the North-Eastern Marches of the Syriac World, see II. ii. 142.
[5] Yūsuf was now entitled to style himself the Amīr-al-Muslimīn, in the Maghrib, of the Amīr-al-Mu'minīn at Baghdad.

more than two hundred years during which it had been recited there in
the names of heretical pseudo-Fātimids?[1] How could he disappoint a
hero who had broken an aggressive Frankish Power that, by its lodgement in Syria, had almost severed the geographical link between the
Asiatic and the African portion of Dār-al-Islām? And how could he say
'No' to a war-lord whose territories lay next door to the Caliph's own,
and who could march, if provoked, on Baghdad as easily as on Cairo,
Jerusalem, or Damascus?

In the thirteenth century of the Christian Era a special need for the
Caliph's good offices was felt by the 'Slave Kings' of Delhi,[2] who were
masters of a vast new domain that had been added to Dār-al-Islām by
the conquest of Hindustan between the years 1191 and 1204 of the
Christian Era. The rule over this new dominion was transmitted, not by
hereditary succession from father to son, but by acquisition by slave
from slave, and each 'Slave King' who mounted the throne, in his turn,
by this contentious avenue required a personal ablution from the
'Abbasid fount of honour to make his tenure secure. The practice was
initiated by the first ruler of the series, Iltutmysh, who made himself
master of Delhi in A.D. 1211 and obtained a retrospective diploma of
investiture from the Caliph Mustansir (*imperabat* A.D. 1221–42) in A.D.
1229.

'The document was solemnly read out in a vast assembly held in
Delhi, and Iltutmysh from that date put the name of the Caliph on his
coins. His successors followed this pious example. The name of the last
'Abbasid Khalīfah of Baghdad, Musta'sim (*imperabat* A.D. 1242–58)
first appears on the coins of 'Alā-ad-Dīn Mas'ūd Shāh (*dominabatur* A.D.
1241–6); and, though Musta'sim was put to death by the Mongols in A.D.
1258, his name still appears on the coins of successive Kings of Delhi, e.g.
Mahmūd Shāh Nāsir-ad-Dīn (*dominabatur* A.D. 1246–65), Ghiyāth-ad-
Dīn Balban (*dominabatur* A.D. 1265–87), and Mu'izz-ad-Dīn Kayqubād
(*dominabatur* A.D. 1287–90), the last monarch of the so-called 'Slave'
dynasty; and the first of these continued to have the name of Musta'sim
mentioned in the *khutbah*.

'A new dynasty arose, that of the Khaljī [or Khiljī]; the same need for
legitimization was apparently still felt, and the coins of Jalāl-ad-Dīn
Fīrūz Shāh II (*dominabatur* A.D. 1290–5) continued to bear the name of
Musta'sim, though this Caliph had been trampled to death by the
Mongols more than thirty years before.[3]

1 Saladin employed the manœuvre of acting in the name of an august puppet twice
over. He had established himself in Egypt as the Sunnī Wazīr of the Shī'ī Fāṭimid Caliph
whom he deposed (the inverse of the situation at Baghdad two centuries earlier, when
Sunnī 'Abbasid Caliphs had been in the power of Shī'ī Buwayhid 'mayors of the palace'
(see p. 13, n. 4, above)). Saladin now secured legitimization for his acquisitions by holding them, in turn, as the vicegerent of the 'Abbasid Caliph Mustadī.
2 See II. ii. 131; III. iii. 30 and 31, n. 1; IV. iv. 99, with n. 1.
3 Though Hūlāgū Khan was a pagan under the influence of a Nestorian Christian
wife (see II. ii. 238 and 451), he did not take the 'Abbasid Caliph's life without some
searchings of heart:
'The awe with which the institution of the Caliphate was regarded, even in these days
of its weakness, may be realised by the fact that, cruel and bloodthirsty savage though
Hūlāgū was, even he hesitated to put to death the Successor of the Prophet, for the
Muhammadans who accompanied him in his army in the expedition against Baghdad had
warned him that, if the blood of the Khalīfah was shed upon the ground, the World
would be overspread with darkness and the army of the Mongols be swallowed up by an
earthquake' (Arnold, op. cit., p. 81).

'What was an unfortunate Muslim monarch to do, who felt that his title was insecure? He knew that it was only his sword that had set him on the throne, that his own dynasty might at any time be displaced, as he had himself displaced the dynasty that had preceded him, while his legal advisers and religious guides told him that the only legitimate source of authority was the Khalīfah, the Imām; and he realised that all his devout Muslim subjects shared their opinion. So he went on putting the name of the dead Musta'sim on his coins, because he could find no other, and the Muslim theory of the State had not succeeded in adjusting itself to the fact that there was no Khalīfah or Imām in existence. His [Jālāl-ad-Dīn's] successor, 'Alā-ad-Dīn Muhammad Shah I (*dominabatur* A.D. 1295–1315), got out of the difficulty by ceasing to insert Musta'sim's name and by describing himself merely as Yamīn-al-Khilāfat Nāsir Amīri'l-Mu'minīn, "the Right Hand of the Caliphate, the Helper of the Commander of the Faithful", and this was sufficient for the satisfaction of tender consciences, though in reality he was giving no help at all to any Caliph, any more than either of his predecessors had done, who had seen the unhappy Musta'sim trampled to death without moving a finger, though they had gone on making use of his name for their own selfish purposes.'[1]

The Aftermaths of the Manchu,[2] Ottoman,[3] and Mughal[4] Empires

The belief in the immortality of universal states which is attested by their ability to maintain their status as dispensers of legitimacy long after they have lost the realities of power—or even after they have actually ceased altogether to exist—can be illustrated from other histories besides those of the 'Abbasid Caliphate at Baghdad and the Roman Empire at Constantinople.

The Government of the Manchu incarnation of the Far Eastern universal state in China—surrounded, as the Middle Kingdom was accustomed to find itself, by tributary states, such as Korea, Annam, and the Mongol principalities, whose rulers did receive investiture from the Son of Heaven at Peking—affected to believe that all sovereigns, in any part of the World, with whom the Celestial Empire might be drawn into diplomatic relations, derived their title from the same unique source of legitimacy.[5]

In the decline of the Ottoman Empire, during the critical period between the disastrous end of the great Turco-Russian War of A.D. 1768–74 and the ignominious end of Sultan Mahmūd II's final trial of strength with Mehmed 'Alī Pasha in the hostilities of A.D. 1839–40, the ambitious war-lords who were carving out successor-states for themselves *de facto*—a Mehmed 'Alī in Egypt and Syria, an 'Alī of Yannina in Albania and Greece, a Pasvānoghlu of Viddin in the north-western corner of Rumelia—were sedulous in doing in the Pādishāh's name all that they were doing to his detriment in their own private interests; and, even when the greatest and most successful of them all, Mehmed 'Alī, had to submit to seeing the verdict of ordeal by battle between himself and his lawful master reversed by the irresistible decision of the Concert

---

[1] Arnold, op. cit., pp. 86–88. [2] See xi, map 54.
[3] See xi, map 51. [4] See xi, map 52.
[5] See, for example, the letter, addressed in A.D. 1793 by the Emperor Ch'ien Lung to King George III of the United Kingdom of Great Britain and Ireland, that has been quoted in I. i. 161.

of Powers of an infidel Western World, his mortification at being awarded the loss of Syria as the fruit of his victory was tempered by his satisfaction at securing from the Powers, as his *quid pro quo*, a diploma, drawn in the Pādishāh's chancery, which conferred the Pashalyq of Egypt on Mehmed 'Alī and his heirs in perpetuity.

Even when an Ottoman Emperor who had been wont to style himself 'Sultan of the Two Continents, Khāqān of the Two Seas',[1] had thus declined into being the 'Sick Man' of Europe,[2] dependent for his very existence on the infidel Powers finding it convenient still to keep the life in his body for fear of falling out awkwardly among themselves over the disposal of his estate, it became one of the regular practices of Western diplomacy, for the best part of a century, to mitigate, by maintaining the fiction of legitimacy, the shock that was being administered to Muslims, inside and outside the Ottoman Empire, by its progressive break-up. On the model of the Danubian Principalities of Wallachia and Moldavia and the Khanate of the Crimea, the embryos of the Ottoman Empire's Orthodox Christian 'successor-states' were required to serve terms in the transitional status of 'autonomous' principalities or provinces under the 'suzerainty' of a Pādishāh[3] who had emphasized this aspect of his office by changing his style, as was done by Sultan Mahmūd II (*imperabat* A.D. 1808–39), to 'Sultan of the Sultans of the Age'.[4] Serbia served this apprenticeship from A.D. 1830 to A.D. 1878; Samos from A.D. 1832 to A.D. 1913; Bulgaria and Eastern Rumelia from A.D. 1878 to A.D. 1908; Crete from A.D. 1898 to A.D. 1913. The juridical independence of Rumania and Serbia dated only from 1878 and that of Bulgaria only from 1908. The Powers themselves conformed to the formality which they imposed upon their Ottoman Christian creatures and protégés. It was in the name of the Sultan at Constantinople that the Hapsburg Monarchy administered Bosnia-Herzegovina from A.D. 1878 to A.D. 1908 and Great Britain administered Cyprus from A.D. 1878 and Egypt from A.D. 1882 until she found herself at war with Turkey in A.D. 1914.

The Ottoman and Manchu Empires' success in still retaining, in their decline, a monopoly of the prerogative of serving as a fount of legitimacy was not, however, so remarkable as the Mughal Empire's performance of the same diplomatico-psychological *tour de force*; for the Timurid Mughal Dynasty continued to assert this prerogative in its dealings with alien Powers who held the shadow of a *ci-devant* Mughal Empire at their mercy after it had sunk to a degree of impotence to which neither the Ottoman nor the Manchu Empire ever sank until its dying day.

Within half a century of the Emperor Awrangzīb's death in A.D. 1707, an empire which had once exercised an effective sovereignty over by far the greater part of the Indian sub-continent had been whittled down to a

---

[1] See Arnold, op. cit., p. 147.

[2] The phrase seems to have been struck out by the Tsar Nicholas I of Russia in conversation with Lord Aberdeen in A.D. 1844, but the celebrated occasion of its use by its coiner was in A.D. 1853, on the eve of the Crimean War.

[3] 'Pādishāh' was the Persian for 'Foot Shah', meaning a potentate who had his foot on the necks of other potentates. It was thus the equivalent of 'Shāhinshāh' or 'King of Kings'.

[4] See Arnold, op. cit., pp. 147–8.

torso that was no more than some 250 miles long by some 100 miles broad,[1] and within a hundred years of A.D. 1707 this truncated dominion had been reduced to the circuit of the walls of the Red Fort at Delhi; yet, 150 years after A.D. 1707—the date which had marked the palpable beginning of a decline that had been germinating long before that—a descendant of Akbar and Awrangzīb was still squatting on their throne in their imperial palace, and he might have been left undisturbed there for an indefinite time to come, even by British rulers of India who had retorted to 'the Great Mogul's' claim still to be their suzerain by insisting that he had now become their pensioner, if, in A.D. 1857, his apparently fantastic pretension to be still seised *de jure* of his mighty ancestors' imperial authority had not been unexpectedly vindicated by a flagrant act which the Mughal Emperor could not avert and which his British masters could not overlook.

In 1857, to the Emperor's own dismay and to his British masters' indignation, the British East India Company's mutinous sepoy army insisted upon exploiting a puppet Emperor's not yet exhausted prestige by inaugurating in his name[2] the government of a revolutionary counter-rāj which they were seeking to substitute by force of arms for the unconsecrated dominion of their British employers.

'There is much evidence . . . of the King's distrust of and distaste for the Army. . . . But there is also no doubt that he clothed their acts with the mantle of his authority';[3]

and, in insisting upon acting in a now impotent 'Great Mogul's' name, the Mutineers in A.D. 1857 were taking practical account of a persisting state of Indian public opinion with which their predecessors had likewise found it necessary to reckon. This was the consideration that had moved the British East India Company, in acquiescing in the terms of the imperial farmans of A.D. 1764 and 1765, to acknowledge the Emperor's suzerainty as the *quid pro quo* for his formal conferment upon them of the right to conduct the administration and collect the revenue in the imperial provinces of Bihar and Bengal; and the same consideration had moved successive Marāthā war-lords of the House of Sindia, from A.D. 1755 to A.D. 1803, to exercise their offensively asserted *de facto* domination over the remnant of the Mughal Empire in the doubly modest official role of deputies for an absentee regent (in the person of the Marāthā Peshwa at Poona) over a puppet Mughal Emperor's shrunken dominions.[4]

The most striking demonstration that this imponderable remnant of Mughal imperial power did in fact possess a genuine specific gravity that could not be ignored with impunity was afforded by British experience. Though, as early as A.D. 1773, the British had revoked[5] the recognition, accorded by them in A.D. 1765, of the Mughal Emperor's continuing suzerainty over Bihar and Bengal, they were confronted as late as A.D. 1811 with a reassertion of the Emperor's title to a formal sovereignty in

---

[1] See Spear, T. G. P.: *Twilight of the Mughuls* (Cambridge 1951, University Press), p. 5.
[2] See ibid., pp. 205–7.   [3] Ibid., p. 224.
[4] See ibid., pp. 24, 26, 34, 225.   [5] See ibid., pp. 32 and 34.

these long-since ceded provinces which they did not find it altogether easy to quash;[1] and in the Emperor's last stronghold at Delhi within the walls of the Red Fort the controversy over the question whether he was the suzerain or a pensionary of the British East India Company[2] remained unsettled throughout the fifty-five-years' interval between the British military occupation of Delhi in A.D. 1803 and the suppression of the Mutiny in A.D. 1858. The British East India Company's explicit public declaration in A.D. 1811 that it was 'unnecessary to derive from the King of Delhi any additional title to the allegiance of our Indian subjects'[3] was a form of words that, to Indian minds, was less significant than the British Resident's continued performance of a subject's customary visible acts of homage when he attended the Emperor's durbar;[4] and the British thesis was overtly challenged in A.D. 1829, when a new incumbent of the office of Nizām of Hyderabad applied to the Mughal Emperor for investiture,[5] as his predecessor had applied in A.D. 1803.[6]

'Those who took the imperial claims at their face value and those who regarded the Imperial Court as a mere puppet show, alike erred. . . . The British were prone to the latter mistake. But that it was a mistake was shown by the eagerness with which so realistic a man as Madho Rao Sindia sought the cloak of imperial authority for his acts, or a prince like the Nizām solemnly sought confirmation of his accession from Delhi as late as 1803 [and as 1829]. The truth was as nearly expressed as possible by Major Browne when he wrote: "I take the Shah's name to be of as much importance as an Act of Parliament in England if supported by as strong a force."'[7]

The justice of this comparison was to be demonstrated, half a century later, when the British East India Company's own mutinous Indian soldiery followed Sindia's example by cloaking their force under the name of the last occupant of Akbar's imperial throne.

Ghosts of Defunct Universal States

A still more remarkable testimony to the tenacity of the belief in the immortality of universal states is the paradoxical practice of evoking their ghosts after they have proved themselves mortal by expiring. The 'Abbasid Caliphate of Baghdad was thus resuscitated in the shape of the 'Abbasid Caliphate of Cairo,[8] the Roman Empire in the two rival shapes of the Holy Roman Empire of the West[9] and the East Roman Empire of Orthodox Christendom;[10] the Empire of the Ts'in and Han Dynasties in the shape of the Sui and T'ang Empire of the Far Eastern

---

[1] See ibid., pp. 42–43.   [2] See ibid., pp. 37 and 41–45.

[3] Dispatch from the Court of Directors, quoted ibid., p. 44.

[4] See ibid., pp. 38 and 50. When Francis Hawkins, who had succeeded to the Residency in A.D. 1831, sought to break this practice by the flagrant act of riding right into the innermost court of the Mughal imperial palace, he was so far from carrying his principals with him that he 'found himself relieved first of his charge of the palace and then of the Residency altogether' (see ibid., pp. 77–78).

[5] See ibid., p. 49.

[6] See ibid., p. 9.   [7] Ibid., pp. 8–9.

[8] See Arnold, op. cit., chaps vii, viii, and xii, and the present work, I. i, 67, n. 2, 70, 360, and 396; II. ii. 75–76; and X. ix. 15.

[9] See I. i. 343; III. iii. 276; IV. iv. 378–9; V. v. 477, n. 1; and X. ix. 9.

[10] See I. i. 64, n. 3, 65, 66, and 70; IV. iv. 320; and X. ix, 15.

Society in China.[1] Such ghosts of universal states are conspicuous products of the historical phenomenon of 'renaissance' or contact in the
Time-dimension between a civilization of the 'affiliated' class and the
extinct civilization that is related to it by 'apparentation',[2] and, in that
aspect, they are dealt with in a later part of this Study.[3]

The four representatives of this spectral species of polity that are here
in question display wide differences from one another both in the timing
of their evocation and in their subsequent fortunes. Whereas the Sui and
T'ang Empire in the Far East and the Holy Roman Empire in the West
were not evoked till after an interval of more than four hundred years
since the *de facto* break-up of the universal state of which each of them
was respectively a revival,[4] and the East Roman Empire not till after an
interval of some hundred and fifty years,[5] the 'Abbasid Caliphate was
resuscitated at Cairo less than three and a half years after its extinction
at Baghdad.[6] From the date of their prompt installation in A.D. 1261 by
the strong hand of the Mamlūk Sultan Baybars to the date of their almost
unnoticed cessation as a result of the conquest and annexation of Egypt
by Sultan Selīm I 'Osmanli in A.D. 1517, the Cairene 'Abbasid Caliphs
were never anything more than the puppets that they were intended to
be.[7] The Holy Roman Empire, after starting as a mighty power in virtue
of being imposed upon the Austrasian Frankish state at the culminating
moment of its history, shared in the collapse which Charlemagne brought
upon his ambitious political structure by recklessly overstraining
its resources, and was never more than partially rehabilitated by the
successive efforts and sacrifices of Saxon, Franconian, and Swabian
heirs of this fatal incubus; yet it survived, at least as a name—the ghost
of a ghost—for nearly a thousand years after Charlemagne's death.[8] On
the other hand the East Roman Empire in the main body of Orthodox
Christendom and the Sui and T'ang Empire in the Chinese portion of
the Far Eastern World fulfilled the intentions of their respective founders
by becoming and remaining solid political realities—the East Roman
Empire for more than 250 years[9] and the Sui and T'ang Empire for not

---

[1] See II. ii. 376; III. iii. 449; and X. ix. 16.
[2] For this relation of Apparentation-and-Affiliation between civilizations of different
generations, see I. i. 44, 45–6, 51–2.   [3] In X. ix. 7–21.
[4] The Empire of the Posterior Han became impotent *de facto* circa A.D. 175; the Far
Eastern Society in China was united politically under the Sui Dynasty in A.D. 581. The
Roman Empire in the West became impotent *de facto* after the *Clades Gothica* of A.D.
378 or, at latest, after the death of the Emperor Theodosius I in A.D. 395; Charlemagne
was crowned Emperor in St. Peter's at Rome on Christmas Day, A.D. 800.
[5] The Roman Empire in the East ran out between the death of Justinian in A.D. 565
and the overthrow of Maurice in A.D. 602; the East Roman Empire was constructed by
Leo Syrus (*imperabat* A.D. 717–40).
[6] See Arnold, op. cit., p. 82, following Suyūtī: *Husn-al-Muhādarah*, vol. ii, pp. 53
seqq. and 57. The Caliph Musta'sim was put to death at Baghdad in February 1258;
his uncle was installed at Cairo as the Caliph Mustansir in June 1261.
[7] When the first of them, Mustansir, showed signs of taking his office seriously, his
Mamlūk patron Baybars packed him off to his death, on the forlorn hope of reconquering Baghdad from the Mongols, and installed another member of the 'Abbasid House in
his stead. This lesson was not forgotten by Caliph Hākim and his successors (see Arnold,
op. cit., pp. 94–95).
[8] Charlemagne died in A.D. 814; the Emperor Francis II Hapsburg renounced the
title of Roman Emperor in A.D. 1806 (see I. i. 343 and X. ix. 11).
[9] From the raising of the second Arab siege of Constantinople in A.D. 717 to the outbreak of the Great Romano-Bulgarian War in A.D. 977.

much less than 300[1]—but this at the cost, on which their founders certainly never reckoned, of exhausting the strength of the still immature societies on whose life-blood these two lusty vampire-states waxed fat for a season.[2] The common feature, conspicuous above these differences, that concerns us here is the status which these ghosts, like their originals, acquired and retained as founts of legitimacy.

The Haunting of Cairo and Istanbul by the Ghost of the Caliphate

The Mamlūks had been quick to install a refugee 'Abbasid at Cairo because, being themselves usurpers of their Ayyubid masters' heritage, and being faced with the problem of handing it down thereafter from slave to slave, they had the same urgent and recurring need of legitimization as their contemporaries and counterparts the Slave Kings of Delhi. The Mamlūk Sultans and their subjects appear to have treated their 'Abbasid puppets with contempt from first to last,[3] and at Mecca their names were never recited in the *khutbah*.[4] Distance, however, lent them an appearance of dignity, and contemporary Muslim rulers in Hindustan made the same use of the Cairene 'Abbasid Caliphs as their predecessors had made of the last Baghdadī 'Abbasid Caliph Musta'sim. A diploma of investiture was sought and obtained from the Cairene 'Abbasid Caliph of the day not only by the parricide and tyrant Muhammad b. Taghlaq (*dominabatur* A.D. 1324–51) but by his estimable successor Fīrūz Shāh (*dominabatur* A.D. 1351–88), who had not his predecessor's incentive for seeking external sanction for his régime.[5] Even Timur Lenk's grandson Pīr Muhammad seems to have thought of taking the same step as a manœuvre in the contest for Timur's heritage, and the Ottoman Pādishāh Bāyezīd I (*imperabat* A.D. 1389–1402) seems actually to have applied in A.D. 1394 to the reigning Cairene 'Abbasid for a grant of the title of Sultan.[6]

Bāyezīd's descendant Selīm I felt himself in no need of legitimization, and did not covet a title borne by a puppet of his defeated and executed opponent the last Mamlūk Sultan Tūmān Bey.[7] A new generation of *de facto* rulers of a nascent Iranic Muslim World esteemed the blood of the Eurasian Nomad war-lord Chinghis Khan to be a nobler liquid than that of any Meccan Holy Family, and they were also well aware that the strength of their own right arm was their only valid title in the last resort. In these revolutionary circumstances the maintenance of 'Abbasid Shadow-Caliphs at Cairo, and the occasional utilization of these *fainéants'* services as rubber-stamps by other Muslim potentates besides

---

[1] From the foundation of the Sui Empire in A.D. 581 to A.D. 878, when the T'ang régime became impotent *de facto* (see IV. iv. 87–88 and V. vi. 311, n. 3).

[2] For this fatal effect of the success of the East Roman Empire on the fortunes of the main body of the Orthodox Christian Society, see II. ii. 368 and IV. iv. 320–408.

[3] See Arnold, op. cit., pp. 99–102.　　　　　　[4] See ibid., p. 101.

[5] See ibid., pp. 103–5.　　　　　　　　　　　[6] See ibid., pp. 105–6.

[7] See ibid., chap. xii. 'The fiction that the last 'Abbasid Caliph of Egypt handed over his dignity, by a formal act of transfer, to Sultan Selīm, was first enunciated in A.D. 1787 by' the Levantine Christian scholar 'Constantine Mouradgea d'Ohsson in his monumental work *Tableau Général de l'Empire Othoman*' (ibid., p. 146), thirteen years after the negotiation of the Russo-Turkish peace treaty of Küchük Qaynārja, which seems to have been the first occasion on which the Ottoman Pādishāh made any attempt to turn his title of Caliph to any practical account (see p. 23, below).

their own Mamlūk slave-masters, had not deterred ex-barbarian *novi homines* from confidently assuming for themselves, and politely applying to one another, the style of 'Caliph' as a synonym for the effective sovereign of a state that was not oecumenical but was merely a Great Power.[1] This inflationary style had already been accepted by Bāyezīd I 'Osmanli's father and predecessor Murād I (*imperabat* A.D. 1360–89) from the pens of the rulers of neighbouring Turkish principalities in Anatolia.[2] In these circumstances the history of the Khilāfat might have been expected to come to an end with the death, in obscurity, of the last Cairene Caliph in A.D. 1543; yet this was not, after all, the last chapter in this long-protracted story. After having thought nothing of the Caliphate for more than four hundred years after the unwarrantable ascription of the office to Sultan Murād I, the 'Osmanlis discovered belatedly, in the days of their decline, that this long despised and neglected ornament was worth bringing out of their lumber-room and polishing up.

'During the century which began with the negotiation of the Russo-Turkish peace treaty of Küchük Qaynārja in A.D. 1774 and ended with the accession of 'Abd-al-Hamīd II to the Ottoman throne in 1876 the Ottoman Caliphate ceased to be merely titular and became for the first time an active factor in international affairs. This change was the consequence of three new developments: first, the continual transfer of ex-Ottoman provinces, containing Muslim populations, to the rule of Western Governments; second, the successive extinction of all sovereign independent Sunnī Powers of any importance, with the single precarious exception of the fast diminishing Ottoman Empire, and their replacement by the colonial empires of Western Powers (the most conspicuous example of this second development being India, where a large Muslim population passed from the Mughal Rāj to the British Rāj after a short interval of anarchy); and, third, the gradual emergence in Islamic society of a new sense of solidarity and a new desire to express this feeling in some practical form—a development which was a natural and, indeed, almost inevitable reaction to the other two. As a result of these three related developments, interest in the Caliphate revived, and at the same time a confusion of thought arose regarding the character of an office which had been obsolete, in all but name, for many centuries.

'This confusion was due to the misinterpretation of both the history and the theory of the Caliphate by insufficiently instructed Western observers, who drew a false analogy between an Islamic institution which they failed to understand and a Western institution with which they were familiar. They equated the Caliphate with the Papacy; explained it as a "spiritual" office in the Western sense (an abstraction

---

[1] See Arnold, op. cit., chaps. ix and xi. This rapid depreciation of a title connoting a unique oecumenical sovereignty into one applied by courtesy to any sovereign of any consequence in a comity of parochial states has its parallel in the fate of the title of 'Emperor' in the Western World. The usurpation of this title by Napoleon Buonaparte on the 18th May, 1804, was followed—when the last legitimate Holy Roman Emperor Francis II Hapsburg had opened the flood-gates in proclaiming himself 'Hereditary Emperor of Austria' on the 10th August, 1804, and renouncing his own legitimate title of 'Roman Emperor' on the 6th August, 1806—by the crowning of Dom Pedro I as 'Constitutional Emperor of Brazil' on the 12th October, 1822 (see X. ix. 11).

[2] See Arnold, op. cit., pp. 130–1.

which was quite foreign to Islamic thought); assumed that the double title of Sultan-Caliph implied a personal union of the "spiritual" and "temporal" powers in the Ottoman Pādishāh; and inferred that these powers could alternatively be divided between different persons. Their error obtained a wide currency in the West[1] (except among a few scholars without influence in international affairs) and even among Muslims who had received a Modern Western in place of a Classical Islamic education. It was consciously and skilfully exploited by 'Abd-al-Hamīd in his dealings with Western Governments, with Muslim peoples under Western rule, and with his own Muslim subjects.'[2]

In at least three peace treaties signed between the years A.D. 1774 and A.D. 1913[3] the Ottoman negotiators slily took advantage of this Western Christian misconception of the Caliphate as a 'spiritual' office in order to secure, in territories that the Sultan was being compelled to cede as Pādishāh, a recognition of his continuing authority there as Caliph—a concession which, if maintained and fully implemented, would have restored to him under one title the political authority that he was surrendering under another. As it turned out, the Christian parties to two of these treaties quickly detected the ruse and insisted—in the one case within seven years and in the other within eleven years of the date of signature of the original instrument—on the cancellation of the insidious provisions.[4]

Although, however, the Caliphate, thus refurbished and passed off as a 'spiritual' office, did not, after all, prove an effective instrument for staving off, or even attenuating, the loss of Ottoman political control over ex-Ottoman territories that the Sultan-Caliph had been compelled to surrender owing to the turning of the tables in the military and political relations between the Ottoman Empire and its Western or Westernizing neighbours since the close of the seventeenth century of the

---

[1] It seems to have been popularized by M. C. M. d'Ohsson in the first volume of his *Tableau Général de l'Empire Othoman* (Paris 1787), in which 'he speaks of the "sacerdotal authority" of the Sultan and styles him the "Pontiff of the Musulmans" ' (Arnold, op. cit., p. 170).

[2] Toynbee, A. J.: *Survey of International Affairs, 1925*, vol. i (Oxford 1927, University Press): 'The Islamic World since the Peace Settlement', pp. 32–33.

[3] The Russo-Turkish peace treaty signed at Küchük Qaynārja on the 21st July, 1774, Art. 3; the Italo-Ottoman preliminaries of peace signed at Ouchy on the 15th October, 1912; the Turco-Bulgarian peace treaty signed at Constantinople on the 29th September, 1913 (see Toynbee, op. cit., pp. 34–36).

[4] See Toynbee, op. cit., p. 36. The extent to which the minds of the ruling element in Russia had been Westernized by A.D. 1774 is revealed by the success of Ottoman diplomacy in playing this trick upon the representatives of a still officially Orthodox Christian Power; for in Orthodox Christendom the Christian distinction between Church and State had been confounded in the constitution of Leo III's East Roman Empire (see IV. iv. 352–3 and 592–623); and this East Roman 'Caesaro-papism', transmitted to Russia, had been carried a step farther by Peter the Great when, in A.D. 1700, he had allowed the Patriarchate of Moscow to lapse and then, in A.D. 1721, had made the Orthodox Church in his dominions into a department of state in form as well as in fact by placing it under the administration of a 'Holy Synod' (see p. 38 below). Thus, in the post-Petrine Russian Empire of A.D. 1774, Church and State were so nearly fused together into an indistinguishable unity that it ought not to have been difficult for Russian statesmen of that age to appreciate, by analogy, the non-existence, in Islam, of any differentiation of a 'spiritual' from a 'temporal' sphere of social life. The less obvious implications of the status of the Oecumenical Patriarch of Constantinople as a servant of the East Roman Emperor had been realized immediately by the less sophisticated Bulgars upon their conversion to Orthodox Christianity in A.D. 865 (see IV. iv. 377–81).

Christian Era, it did produce psychological effects which were imponderable yet appreciable factors in international politics. It gave pause to aggressive-minded Western or Westernizing Powers which had taken the measure of the Ottoman Empire's present political weakness but still remained in awe of the explosive religious force of Islam. Conversely, it made the Ottoman Empire—shrunken though it was—a moral rallying-point for a Muslim diasporá, not only in ex-Ottoman provinces which had passed under the rule of Orthodox Christian 'successor-states', but in distant regions, on other fringes of Dār-al-Islām, which had never been under the rule of an Ottoman or any other Caliph. By the date of the abolition of the Ottoman Caliphate in A.D. 1924 the Muslim minorities in the British Indian Empire, the Soviet Union, and the Chinese Republic alone numbered considerably more than a hundred million in the aggregate, and these outlying millions—unlike the Arab peoples and others in the solid core of the Islamic World, including the Ottoman Turks themselves—had little prospect of ever being able to attain the current political ideal of a Westernizing World by exchanging the alien rule under which they were living at the time for national states of their own.[1] Their situation was not unlike that of their predecessors in the tenth, eleventh, and twelfth centuries of the Christian Era, when Dār-al-Islām was being overrun by barbarians and partitioned among military adventurers, and in these circumstances the Ottoman Caliphate gave them something of the same cohesion and encouragement that the 'Abbasid Caliphate of Baghdad had given to Muslims of that earlier age.[2]

These psychological effects of the Ottoman Caliphate, as turned to account by Sultan 'Abd-al-Hamīd II (imperabat A.D. 1876–1909), were such manifestly valuable assets for the Ottoman body politic that the 'New 'Osmanli' liberal opponents of a tyrannous Hamidian autocracy sought, not to abolish the Ottoman Caliphate, but to preserve it for manipulation as an instrument of their own Turkish national policy. The sovereign was styled Caliph, as well as Sultan and Pādishāh, in the Ottoman Constitution of A.D. 1876, and the Caliphate survived 'Abd-al-Hamīd's successful coup d'état of 1877 and unsuccessful attempt to repeat it in 1909 after the re-establishment of the Constitution in 1908.[3] It even survived the abolition of the Sultanate and the vesting of the sovereign power in Turkey in the Great National Assembly at Ankara by a law voted by that body on the 1st November, 1922.[4] This drastic piece of legislation was a retort to the hostile action of the last Sultan-Caliph Mehmed VI Vahīd-ad-Dīn (imperabat A.D. 1918–22), who, seeing

---

[1] On this point see Toynbee, op. cit., p. 39. By the time when the present passage was being written, the abolition of the Ottoman Caliphate was already more than a quarter of a century old, and the Indian Muslims had succeeded in establishing a separate national state of their own in the shape of Pakistan; but it would have been premature to assume that this was necessarily the end of the story.

[2] For the alertness of Sultan 'Abd-al-Hamīd II in making use of railways, newspapers, and other Modern Western means of communication and propaganda for keeping in touch with a Muslim clientèle all over the World, see Toynbee, op. cit., pp. 39–40.

[3] See Toynbee, op. cit., pp. 42–43, and the present Study, IX. viii. 261–3.

[4] The text of this law of the 1st November, 1922, is printed in Toynbee, op. cit., pp. 50–51.

the monarch's opportunity in the country's adversity, had thrown in his lot with the Empire's ex-victorious adversaries in the late wars of 1914-22 in the hope of putting back the constitutional clock to the point at which it had been marking time before the Revolution of A.D. 1908. In the same law the Caliphate was declared to reside in the House of 'Osmān, and the right of election to the office to lie with the Turkish Great National Assembly. On the strength of a legal opinion (fetvā), rendered by the Commissary for the Islamic Law (Sherī'ah) in the Government ruling the country in the Assembly's name, to the effect that the office of Caliph had been forfeited by Vahīd-ad-Dīn Efendi, the Assembly voted, on the 18th November, 1922, that the office was now vacant, and on the same day they elected another member of the House of 'Osmān, 'Abd-al-Mejīd Efendi, as Caliph without any other title.[1]

In attempting to draw this distinction between two traditional titles which historically and juridically were, both alike, emblems of political authority, the followers of Ghāzi Mustafā Kemāl Atatürk were unintentionally playing on themselves the trick which their ancestors had deliberately played on the Russians in A.D. 1774,[2] and, once again, the equivocal situation created by a false interpretation of the nature of the Caliph's office proved untenable—notwithstanding the suitably inoffensive character of the Assembly's unlucky nominee. When the law of the 1st November, 1922, was followed by another of the 29th October, 1923, proclaiming Turkey a republic and declaring the President of the Republic to be Chief of the State, the incompatibility between the legal position thus created in Turkey and the prerogatives of the Caliphate according to the Sherī'ah became so glaring that it was bound to be used as ammunition by Turkish opponents of the régime and to cause overt anxiety among Indian Muslims. The premature publication, in opposition newspapers at Constantinople, of a letter from two eminent Indian Muslims, the Agha Khan and Mr. Ameer Ali, to the Prime Minister of Turkey, intimating, in studiously tactful language, the distress that the Turkish Great National Assembly's actions had been producing among Muslims abroad,[3] precipitated the passage by the Turkish Great National Assembly, on the 3rd March, 1924, of a law abolishing the Caliphate and banishing the members of the Ottoman Imperial family from the territories of the Republic of Turkey.[4] When the news reached Delhi—where, as we have seen, the Caliphate had been revered for seven hundred years with a naïveté seldom corrected by first-hand acquaintance—the shock declared itself in a dramatic incident at a Red Crescent tea-party which offers a burlesque counterpart to the

[1] See Toynbee, op. cit., p. 51.
[2] The innocent misapprehension under which the Assembly acted in November 1922 was attested in a speech delivered by Mustafā Kemāl Pasha himself on the 30th October, 1922, in the debate preceding the passage of the Law of the 1st November. To the question 'What becomes of the Caliphate when the temporal power is taken away from it?' the Ghāzi gave the Levantine d'Ohsson's erroneous answer: in the days of the 'Abbasid Caliphs at Baghdad and of their successors at Cairo, 'the spiritual and temporal power existed separately side by side'. The relevant passage of the speech is printed in Toynbee, op. cit., pp. 54–55.
[3] The text is printed in Toynbee, op. cit., pp. 571–2.
[4] Ibid., p. 575.

tragic scene in Saint Jerome's cell at Bethlehem when the Christian scholar received the news of the fall of Rome.[1]

'A mission from the Turkish Red Crescent Society, which was collecting funds in India at the moment when the news of the abolition of the Ottoman Caliphate arrived, found it advisable to cut short its activities and return home. (*The Times*, 5th March, 1924; *Oriente Moderno*, IV, 3, p. 181). The news was actually received during a tea-party at Delhi, where the members of the Turkish mission were being entertained by their Indian co-religionists. Upon the recital of the telegram containing the text of the Turkish Law of the 3rd March, [1924,] all but two of the Indians present immediately left the room.'[2]

At the time when the present chapter was being written, it looked as if this had really been the end of the Caliphate, for an immediate attempt on the part of the Hāshimī King Husayn of the Hijāz to assume the office (on the eve, as it turned out, of his own ejection from his ancestral patrimony by Ibn Saʿūd) was—in spite of the Sharīf's unimpeachable Qurayshī lineage and his sovereignty, at the moment, over the two Holy Cities of Mecca and Medina—as dismal a failure as most of his other enterprises.[3] Nor did any practical action result from a Caliphate Congress held at Cairo on the 13th–19th May, 1926.[4]

Yet, even if this forecast were to prove correct—though, in the light of previous history, it would not be safe to sign a death certificate for so resilient an institution as the Caliphate until it had been in abeyance for at least a quarter of a millennium[5]—the marvel would be, not that the Caliphate should have petered out at last, but that, on the strength of having been an effective sovereignty over a span of less than two hundred years,[6] it should have been able within that time to acquire a prestige sufficient to keep it alive, and twice revive it,[7] for another eleven hundred

---

[1] See the passage quoted in V. v. 223, n. 2.

[2] Toynbee, op. cit., p. 63, n. 7. Indian Muslims might have inoculated themselves against this shock by previously exposing themselves to another. 'The present writer once heard, from a British resident in Constantinople, of one instance in which this ignorance [of realities in Turkey] was cruelly dispelled. His informant had been in commercial relations with an Indian Muslim merchant who was a capable man of business and a loyal subject of the British Indian Government, but who cherished a keen sentimental regret for the lost dominion of Islam in India and consoled himself with the belief that in the Ottoman Caliphate there survived one Islamic Power which was as splendid as the Mughal Empire and as efficient as the British Rāj. After sustaining his self-respect as a Muslim upon this illusion for many years, this Indian merchant saved enough money to make a pilgrimage to the seat of the Caliphate at Constantinople—which meant more to him than the Holy Land of the Hijāz—and there became the guest of his British correspondent. The contrast between his long-cherished dream of the Caliphate and the sordid reality of the Ottoman Empire caused him a distress which it was painful to witness. He was appalled by the vast difference of standard between Muslim government in *Dār-al-Islām* and British government in India; and he went home with his spirit broken' (Toynbee, op. cit., p. 39, n. 1).

[3] See Toynbee, op. cit., pp. 63–66.

[4] See ibid., pp. 81–90.

[5] Its latest interregnum had lasted from the death of the last Cairene ʿAbbasid Caliph Mutawakkil in A.D. 1543 to the drafting of the Russo-Turkish Treaty of Küchük Qaynārja in A.D. 1774.

[6] From the death of the Prophet Muhammad in A.D. 632 to the death of the ʿAbbasid Caliph Amīn (*imperabat* A.D. 809–13), in a civil war with his brother and supplanter Maʾmūn (*imperabat* A.D. 813–33) over the heritage of their father Hārūn-ar-Rashīd (*imperabat* A.D. 786–809).

[7] i.e. at Cairo in A.D. 1261 and at Constantinople in A.D. 1774.

years[1] during which it never emerged from the state of political impotence into which it had begun to decline in the reign of Hārūn-ar-Rashīd's son Ma'mūn (*imperabat* A.D. 813–33).

'The Holy Roman Empire'[2]

This life-curve of the Caliphate, with its successive evocations at Cairo and Istanbul, has its counterpart in the aftermath of the Roman Empire in the West, with its abortive revival there in the shape of the Holy Roman Empire.[3] The Roman Power which Pope Leo III and Charlemagne tried to raise from the dead on Christmas Day, A.D. 800, had been effective in the West for rather more than four hundred years.[4] The Austrasian Power, which thus rashly shouldered the formidable burden of the Roman mantle, was effective for not more than 127 years at the longest reckoning.[5] Yet, on the strength of these two spasmodic 'jet-propulsions', the Holy Roman Empire not only materialized in the heyday of Austrasia's fortunes, but survived thereafter for all but a thousand years more[6] in a state of paralysis into which it fell at the death of Charlemagne, the first holder of the title (*regnabat* A.D. 768–814; *imperabat* A.D. 800–14), and from which it never afterwards more than partially recovered.[7] The shadowy aftermath of the Roman Empire in the West thus attained a span of more than fourteen hundred years in all.[8] A millennium and a half is no doubt an infinitesimally short span of time on the Time-scale of the age, up to date, of the Human Race or of Life or of the Earth or of the Stellar Cosmos,[9] but it is a period of almost Egyptiac longevity on the scale of the six-thousand-years-old history of the species of human societies called civilizations.

[1] Reckoning from the death of the Baghdādī 'Abbasid Caliph Amīn in A.D. 813 to the deposition of the Constantinopolitan 'Osmanli Caliph 'Abd-al-Mejīd in A.D. 1924.

[2] See xi, map 37.

[3] In conformity with our procedure in reckoning back the history of the Caliphate to its inauguration at Mecca in A.D. 632, and not merely to the evocation of its ghost at Cairo in A.D. 1261, we have to reckon back the history of the institution liquidated at Vienna in A.D. 1806 to the foundation of the Roman Empire itself by 'the crafty nephew of Julius' in the year 31 B.C.—as Lord Bryce makes his reckoning in the famous exordium of *The Holy Roman Empire* (quoted in I. i. 343).

[4] Reckoning from the Battle of Actium in 31 B.C. to the Battle of Adrianople in A.D. 378, or at latest to the death of the Emperor Theodosius I in A.D. 395 (see p. 20, n. 4, above, and p. 40, n. 2, below).

[5] Reckoning to the death of Charlemagne in A.D. 814 from the Battle of Textri in A.D. 687 in which Charlemagne's great-grandfather Pepin of Heristal had ended the anarchy let loose by the decay of the Merovingian Power and had brought Neustria as well as Austrasia under the effective rule of the House of Arnulf. The period would be still shorter if its initial date were to be reckoned from Charles Martel's victory over the Arabs at Tours in A.D. 732 or from the crowning of Pepin III in A.D. 754 as King of the Franks (see IV. iv. 488, n. 1), or from the crowning of Charlemagne himself as Emperor on Christmas Day, A.D. 800.

[6] Reckoning from the death of Charlemagne in A.D. 814 to the renunciation of the title by Francis II in A.D. 1806.

[7] In Charlemagne's time, and likewise at each of the successive revivals of the Holy Roman Empire after its first rapid lapse into impotence in the hands of Charlemagne's Carolingian successors, this Western ghost of the Roman Empire was an effective political power only in so far as it played the part of a continental march for Western Christendom. Under Charlemagne and the Saxon Emperors the Holy Roman Empire served as a march against the Continental European barbarians (see II. ii. 166–70); under the Hapsburgs it served as a march against the 'Osmanlis (see II. ii. 177–90).

[8] Reckoning from the death of Theodosius I in A.D. 395 to A.D. 1806.

[9] For time-scales, see Zeuner, F. E.: *Dating the Past* (London 1946, 2nd ed. 1950, Methuen), and the present Study, I. i. 173.

It is noteworthy that, like the 'Abbasid Caliphate, the Holy Roman Empire retained, even at the vanishing-point of its effective power, a certain market value as a unique fount of honour.

'To [the] strange political fiction [that the 'Abbasid Caliphs of Baghdad were still ruling after they had ceased to govern] there is a parallel in the history of the Holy Roman Empire during the fifteenth century [of the Christian Era]. While the unfortunate Emperor Frederick III, having been driven out of Vienna, was wandering about from monastery to monastery as a beggar, making what money he could out of the fees paid by those on whom he conferred titles, a contemporary jurist, Aeneas Piccolomini (afterwards famous as Pope Pius II), could write that the power of the Emperor was eternal and incapable of diminution or injury, and that anyone who denied that the Emperor was lord and monarch of the whole Earth was a heretic, since his authority was ordained by Holy Writ and by the decree of the Church.'[1]

In A.D. 1952, when nearly a century and a half had elapsed since the self-liquidation of the Holy Roman Empire in A.D. 1806 by a voluntary act of the then reigning Emperor, the title of 'Count of the Holy Roman Empire' was still being conferred by the Sovereign Pontiff of the temple-state of the Vatican—who would perhaps have pleaded a victor's right to dispose of the sole remaining spoils of a rival institution which his own predecessors had brought to the ground in the tremendous struggle between Papacy and Empire during the so-called 'Middle Ages' of Western history.[2]

The Haunting of the 'Osmanlis and the Mongols by 'Ghosts of Ghosts'

While the Holy Roman Empire was compensated for the briefness of its effective reign, and the Cairene Caliphate for being cheated of any effective reign at all, by the inordinate length of a dim epilogue, the East Roman Empire in Orthodox Christendom and the Sui and T'ang Empire in the Far East had to pay for a longer spell of full-blooded life by suffering a more swift and drastic liquidation. No milder remedy than this could have saved from an immediate and premature death the societies on whose life-blood these two vampires had been feasting. The collapse, when it came, was in both societies so extreme that the exhausted civilization was fain to receive its respite and rest-cure in the shape of a universal state from the hands of alien empire-builders— the 'Osmanlis performing this unwelcome and indispensable service for the main body of Orthodox Christendom, and the Mongols for China.[3]

These aliens began by filling the social void which they found in their field of reconstruction work with characteristic institutions of their own,[4] and they also eked out their own talents by enlisting ability wherever else they could lay hands on it, rather than from among the demoralized and discredited *ci-devant* dominant minority of the prostrate society for whose government the high-handed conquerors had now made themselves responsible. The Mongols organized their government of China

[1] Arnold, op. cit., pp. 77-78.   [2] See IV. iv. 512-84.
[3] See V. v. 348-51, and pp. 570 and 576, below.
[4] For the institutions that the 'Osmanlis brought with them into Orthodox Christendom from the Eurasian Steppe, see III. iii. 22-50.

with the help of Muslims from the western fringes of their spreading dominion, or of Western Christians from beyond its verge, of whom the most famous was Marco Polo. The 'Osmanlis drew on Western Christian renegades as well as on children of their own Orthodox Christian ra'īyeh whom they had first 'denatured' by a Platonic system of education. In the governments of both these alien universal states it is the more remarkable to observe, on closer inspection, the presence of a number of institutional survivals of the liquidated vampire polities, and to find the evicted native dominant minority stealthily winning their way back into power as the mandarins who inducted Mongol and Manchu war-lords into the arts of Chinese administration, and as the Phanariots who made themselves indispensable to their Ottoman masters as soon as these were driven to enter into serious diplomatic relations with the Powers of the Western World owing to the loss of their own former military ascendancy.[1] Though the institutional survivals, as they catch our eye, present themselves largely in the forms of outward ceremonial and official insignia and costume, we may infer with confidence, from these outward visible signs, an inward psychological legacy from the East Roman Empire to an Ottoman 'Qaysar-i-Rum' and from the Sui and T'ang Empire to a Mongol 'Son of Heaven'.

'The Great Idea' of the Modern Greeks

The legacy that descended on the victorious 'Osmanlis did not cease to weigh upon the discomfited Greeks. Though the East Roman Empire came to grief in A.D. 1071[2] through the nemesis of the suicidal policy of military aggression on all fronts[3] which had preceded, precipitated, and followed the great Romano-Bulgarian war of A.D. 977–1019, and though the rally led by the Emperor Alexius Comnenus (*imperabat* A.D. 1081–1118)[4] brought no more than a passing relief, the Byzantine political incubus that was crushing the life out of the Greek people not only made a profound impression on their imaginations but also secured an enduring hold on their affections. When the Western military adventurers whose enterprise was nicknamed 'the Fourth Crusade' gave the stricken East Roman Empire its *coup de grâce* by storming and sacking Constantinople in A.D. 1204, they found the prestige of the battered Imperial Throne at Constantinople still standing so high among the conquered Greek population that they decided to enthrone one of their own number as a usurping 'Latin Emperor', in the hope—a vain one, yet the only hope that they had—that the double magic of the Imperial City and Name might commend their hated rule to their recalcitrant subjects.

These lures did indeed exercise an irresistible attraction upon the East Roman Empire's refugee Greek 'successor-state' at Nicaea in North-Western Anatolia, which had first successfully defied the invaders and had afterwards anticipated the career of the 'Osmanlis by bestriding the Dardanelles and gathering in fragments of ex-Imperial territory in the Balkan Peninsula.[5] The able princes of Nicaea were

---

[1] For the Phanariots see II. ii. 222–8 and IX. viii. 187–9.
[2] See IV. iv. 392, n. 2.   [3] See IV. iv. 391–404.
[4] See V. vi. 298.   [5] See III. iii. 27.

obsessed from first to last by the ambition of reoccupying Constantinople and there assuming the Imperial style and title; and in A.D. 1261 Michael Palaiológhos duly achieved these Epimethean ambitions at the cost of losing to Turkish interlopers the best part of that precious Anatolian ground from which his principality had drawn its strength. This loss condemned the outwardly restored Empire to impotence from the start. Yet even the two-centuries-long agony of this shadow of a shadow of the Roman Empire, from the reoccupation of Constantinople in A.D. 1261 to its capture by the 'Osmanlis in A.D. 1453, did not cure the Greeks of their infatuation with a polity that had proved their ruin. Year by year, till these years had mounted up to little less than half a millennium,[1] the Greeks of Constantinople continued, under Ottoman rule, to expect the restoration of the East Roman Empire by a miraculous intervention of God.[2] And, in spite of invariable disappointment, 'the Great Idea'[3] had power to entice Hypsilandi into making his fatuous raid across the Pruth in A.D. 1821[4] and Venizelos into embarking in A.D. 1919 on an Anatolian adventure that was to meet with such a tragic ending in 1922. Nothing less than the eviction of a Greek diasporà of some

---

[1] A.D. 1453–1923.

[2] This expectation was sufficiently intense and persistent to find its way into Modern Greek folk-lore, where it expressed itself in the two parallel motifs of the miraculously interrupted service in the Cathedral Church of Ayía Sophía in Constantinople and the miraculously interrupted frying of the fishes.

A folk-song about the miraculous interruption of the service on the eve of the capture of the Imperial City by Sultan Mehmed II Fātih in A.D. 1453 is printed in Politis, N.G.: Ἐκλογαὶ ἀπὸ τὰ Τραγούδια τοῦ Ἑλληνικοῦ Λαοῦ (Athens 1914, Estia), pp. 4–5, and a folk-song about the miraculous interruption of the fish-frying in Passow, A.: Carmina Popularia Graeciae Recentioris (Leipzig 1860, Teubner), p. 147, No. cxcvii. A folk-tale about the fish-frying is published by Politis in two versions in his Μελέται περὶ τοῦ Βίου καὶ τῆς Γλώσσης τοῦ Ἑλληνικοῦ Λαοῦ: Παραδόσεις (Athens 1904, Sakellarios, 2 parts), part i, p. 21 (texts), and part ii, pp. 656–7 (commentary). The writer has been able to run these sources of the legend to earth thanks to the learning and the kindness of Professor R. J. H. Jenkins.

In one of these three pieces of popular Romaic Greek literature—the folk-song about the fishes—the episode of the miracle heralding the fall of Constantinople stands by itself— τὰ ψάρια πεταχτήκανε, τὰ ψάρια ζωντανέψαν, / κι' ὁ ἀμηρᾶς εἰσέβηκεν ἀτός του καβαλάρης —without the promise of an equally miraculous future retrieval of Greek fortunes which is the sequel in both the other two places. The first of the two prose versions of the legend about the fish, as given by Politis, runs as follows:

'At the time when the Turks were besieging the City, a monk was frying seven fishes in a frying-pan. He had already fried them on one side and was just turning them over on to the other when someone comes and tells him that the Turks have taken the City. "Never will the Turks set foot in the City," says the monk. "I will wait to believe that till I see these fried fishes come to life again." The words were not out of his mouth before the fishes leapt out of the frying-pan alive and dropped into a piece of water close by; and, down to this day, those fishes that came alive are in Balyqly [Anglicè 'Fishwych' —A.J.T.] and will continue to be found there, still half-fried yet alive again, until the hour comes for us to take the City. Then, they say, another monk will come and finish frying them.'

'The fishes are pointed out in the holy well of the Zoodhókhos, outside the walls [of Constantinople], not far from the Gate of Silymbria (alias Piyí)', according to Politis, Μελέται, part ii, p. 656. According to a Turkish version of the tale (ibid., n. 1), there were originally seven fishes, but only five are now left.

The writer of this Study visited Balyqly in A.D. 1921, but did not see even a residue of five half-fried fishes swimming there, though, in a year when Eastern Thrace was under Greek military occupation again for the first time since A.D. 1360, the possibility that the Greeks might reoccupy Constantinople too seemed less remote than at any other date, either earlier or later, since A.D. 1453.

[3] Ἡ Μεγάλη Ἰδέα, meaning a conception of Modern Greece as being the heir of the East Roman Empire.

[4] See II. ii. 226–7 for Hypsilandi (in Greek spelling 'Hypsêlantês') and his adventure.

1,280,000 souls from Anatolia and Eastern Thrace[1] availed to banish
from Greek minds the persistent dream of restoring the East Roman
Empire; and the previous potency of the ghost that was thus at last
exorcised is demonstrated by the sequel. Though the Graeco-Turkish
war of A.D. 1919–22 had inflicted greater devastation and suffering on
both sides than any of its predecessors, it was followed within eight years
by a Graeco-Turkish *entente*;[2] and this apparent paradox admits of only
one explanation. The loading of the atmosphere with a new charge of
hate was far outbalanced by the lightening of it through the dissipation
of an old illusion.

'At Ankara, a silent witness of the historic event of October 1930 was
one of the most famous monuments of Classical Antiquity: the longest
extant Latin inscription in the World, in which the first of the Roman
Emperors had recorded his achievements. The Roman Empire had bequeathed its name to its former dominions in the Near East (Rum,
Rum-ili, Romania) and to the peoples which had inherited them. The
'Osmānlīs had been known as Romans (Rūmīs) among their Muslim
neighbours in Iran and Hindustan, while the modern Greeks had called
themselves Romans (Romaioi) until a romantic nationalism, acquired in
the West, had taught them to think of themselves as Hellenes. The hold
of Rome upon the Near Eastern imagination had only relaxed with the
break-up of the Ottoman Empire, which was the Roman Empire's last and
strangest reincarnation. The Greeks really repudiated their Imperial
Roman heritage when they rose in insurrection in A.D. 1821, the Turks
when they signed their National Pact in A.D. 1920. Therewith, the ghost
of the Roman Empire, which had so long haunted the Near East, was
finally exorcised. The Imperial City of Constantine—the New Rome on
the Bosphorus—had ceased to be the capital of an empire or even of a
"successor-state". Indeed it was no longer a bone of contention between
the states into which the defunct empire had been partitioned. The
Oecumenical Patriarch, who had once laid claim, in his very title, to be the
head of the Orthodox Church through all the World, had seen his flock
diminish until now it was merely represented by that Orthodox Christian
minority—less than 100,000 strong—which was recognised as "established" in Constantinople by the terms of the convention of the 10th June,
1930. . . . A meeting, at Constantinople, between the ecclesiastical head of
the ancient Greek Church and the political head of the modern Greek
State had ceased to be an event of political significance. If there were any
statesmen living in 1930 who could claim to have "made history", they
were Mustafā Kemāl and Elefterios Venizelos.'[3]

'Moscow the Third Rome'[4]

While 'the Great Idea' of the Greeks had been a minor tragedy and
major curiosity of history, the sowing of the same seed in Russia had
been big with consequences of historic importance which, at a date
midway through the twentieth century of the Christian Era, had perhaps not yet come to full harvest.

---

[1] See the figures given by V. M. Boulter in *Survey of International Affairs, 1925*, vol.
ii (London 1928, Milford), p. 276.
[2] For this beneficent revolution in Graeco-Turkish relations, see Toynbee, A. J., and
Boulter, V. M.: *Survey of International Affairs, 1930* (Oxford 1931, University Press),
pp. 157–68.
[3] Toynbee and Boulter, op. cit., p. 168. [4] See xi, map 49.

When the lingering shadow of a restored East Roman Empire—the ghost of the ghost of an Hellenic universal state—was finally effaced by the Ottoman conquest of Constantinople in A.D. 1453, the Russian off-shoot of Orthodox Christendom[1] was about to enter into a universal state of its own. The establishment of this Russian universal state may be dated from the annexation of the Republic of Novgorod[2] between

[1] For the relation of Russian Orthodox Christendom to the original home of the Orthodox Christian Civilization in Anatolia and the Balkan Peninsula, see I. i. 132–3.

[2] See IV. iv. 88; V. v. 312; V. vi. 191 and 309; and IX. viii. 126. Prince Dmitrī Obolensky comments:

'Is there not some danger of over-estimating the importance of this union? I would say that the annexation of Novgorod and its dependencies by Ivan III, though of course it vastly increased the territories and economic resources of Muscovy, was in itself only a stage in the lengthy process by which the Muscovite sovereigns succeeded in annexing the greater part of their Kievan predecessors' "patrimony" (except, of course, the south-western regions). This process began circa A.D. 1300 and may be said to have ended in A.D. 1533, with the death of Basil III; and the annexations of Tver, the Chernigov and Seversk lands, Pskov, Smolensk and Ryazan, which took place in the latter part of Ivan III's reign and in the reign of Basil III, were perhaps in the long run as important land-marks in this process of "gathering" as the conquest of the Novgorodian lands.

'It seems to me, moreover, that the term "universal state" is more applicable to the multi-national Empire that arose out of Ivan IV's Eastern conquests than to the still essentially Russian states of Ivan III and Basil III. For the annexation of Smolensk (A.D. 1514) and the incorporation of the Ryazan principality (circa A.D. 1520) into Muscovy mark the final political unification of the Great Russian lands under Muscovite dominion, while the conquest of Qāzān, Astrakhan and Western Siberia in the reign of Ivan IV, which brought into the Muscovite realm large areas of non-Russian population and culture, may perhaps be regarded with greater justification as the opening chapters in the history of the Russian "universal state".'

On consideration of the first of the two points here made by Prince Obolensky, the writer of this Study does not find himself persuaded that the union of Novgorod with Muscovy was not, after all, the crucial event in the process of the political unification of the territorial patrimony of a Russian Orthodox Christendom under Muscovite rule. Among the parochial states that had sprung from the ruins of the ascendancy of the principality of Kiev, Novgorod was surely unique in being a commercial community with a vast economic hinterland extending north-eastwards to the shores of the White Sea and the Arctic Ocean as far as the estuary of the River Obi on the farther side of the Urals, and in maintaining an active intercourse with the Hanseatic states members of a con-temporary Western city-state cosmos on the cultural as well as on the economic plane. In exchange for the furs produced by her north-eastern hinterland, Novgorod had imported from her Western customers the political institution of self-government on the city-state scale. In virtue of this combination of commercial wealth with political liberties, Novgorod was surely the one other Russian parochial state in this age that might perhaps have competed seriously with Moscow for the role of becoming the nucleus of a Russian universal state which, had it crystallized round Novgorod instead of crystallizing round Moscow, would have had a different êthos, as well as a different geographical centre, from the Muscovy that actually performed this historic service for a Russian Orthodox Christendom. On this account the writer remains convinced that, in the building of the Russian universal state, the subjugation of Novgorod by Moscow was the decisive event that may be taken as marking the Russian universal state's establishment (though, of course, the precise dating of the consummation of any historical process is inevitably arbitrary and conventional and consequently open to dispute).

Prince Obolensky's second point turns, as will be seen, on the choice of a different criterion for the epiphany of a universal state from the criterion chosen in the present Study. The term 'universal state' is used here to denote an empire that is 'oecumenical' in the sense of embracing the whole geographical domain of the 'world' constituted by some single civilization, while Prince Obolensky is inclined to appropriate the same term for the different (though, no doubt, equally legitimate) purpose of denoting a state that is universal in the sense of embracing at least parts of the domains of more civilizations than one. In a later chapter (pp. 61–67, below) we shall observe that most of the universal states that had been 'oecumenical' in the sense of embracing the whole domain of some single civilization had also been 'cosmopolitan' in the sense of including parts of the domains of alien civilizations as well; but this feature in the composition of a univer-sal state, though usual, will prove to be neither essential nor indeed invariably present. The essential and never-absent mark of a universal state, in the sense in which the term is used in this Study, is the political unification, within its frontiers, of the whole domain of some single civilization.

A.D. 1471 and A.D. 1479 by the Grand Duke of Moscow, Ivan III (*impera-bat* A.D. 1462–1505). This swift sequence of momentous events in the main body of Orthodox Christendom and in its Russian off-shoot, and the dramatic contrast between the final downfall of Orthodox Constantinople and the definitive triumph of Orthodox Moscow, made a profound effect upon the Russian imagination.

'The expansion of every nation, the growth of every empire, is usually the outward sign of an inward conviction of the people that they have a special mission to perform. The striking transformation of the small Moscow principality into one of the largest states of the World was the result of the deep-rooted belief of her people that they were called upon to defend Eastern Orthodoxy.'[1]

Other Orthodox Slav princes before the Muscovite Ivan III had coveted the dazzling insignia of the East Roman Empire and had audaciously stretched out greedy hands to snatch them from the person of a legitimate Emperor reigning at Constantinople; but, unnerved by their own impiety, they had faltered and failed, with disastrous ulterior consequences for their own principalities. After missing, in A.D. 913, a chance of mounting the Imperial Throne at Constantinople, Khan Symeon of Bulgaria had proclaimed himself 'Emperor of the Romans and Bulgars' in A.D. 925, and the Archbishop of Preslav 'Patriarch' of his hybrid empire in the year after;[2] but within less than a century the Bulgarian state had been erased from the political map of Orthodox Christendom: a war to the death had ended in the outright annexation of all Bulgaria by an East Roman Empire which Khan Symeon had aspired to supplant.[3] The Bulgar Khan had rashly challenged the East Roman Empire at its zenith; at its nadir, when the possession of the beggarly remnant of its domain was being contested between a legitimate Palaiológhos and the pretender John Kandakouzinós, the Serb warlord Stephen Dushan had had himself crowned by the Patriarch of Bulgaria and by his own Serbian Archbishop of Peć on Easter Day, A.D. 1346, as 'King of Serbia . . . Albania and the sea-board, prince of the Empire of Bulgaria, and lord of almost all the Empire of Romania'.[4] The misgivings revealed in this cautiously accurate enumeration had afterwards been veiled in the bolder style and title of 'Emperor and Autocrat of Serbia and Romania';[5] yet the waning shadow of the East Roman Empire had eluded Dushan's grasp, and, within less than half a century, the Serb war-Lands had been scattered like chaff by their 'Osmanli competitors for the prize of becoming the founders of a universal state for the main body of Orthodox Christendom. The Muscovites, who afterwards trod with impunity the perilous path down which a Bulgarian Symeon and a Serbian Stephen had carried their ephemeral empires to destruction, were not even inspired directly by either of these two magnificent failures; they drew their inspiration from a Second

---

[1] Zernov, N.: *The Russians and their Church* (London 1945, S.P.C.K.), p. 49.
[2] See IV. iv. 384 and 386. [3] See IV. iv. 390–2.
[4] 'Serviae . . . Albaniae, maritimae regionis rex, Bulgariae imperii princeps et fere totius imperii Romaniae dominus' (Gibbons, H. A.: *The Foundation of the Ottoman Empire* (Oxford 1916, Clarendon Press), p. 88).
[5] Gibbons, loc. cit.

Bulgarian Empire which had dragged out its undistinguished existence
during the two centuries (A.D. 1186–1393) between the collapse of the
East Roman Empire in South-Eastern Europe and the political unification of the main body of Orthodox Christendom by the 'Osmanlis.

'The Second Bulgarian Empire with its centre at Trnovo had for a time
controlled the Balkans; its rulers had styled themselves Tsar and Auto-
krátôr, and at their court there had been a literary revival when Greek
works were translated into Bulgarian. Among these translated works was
the verse chronicle of Manasses. In this chronicle the decline of the
Roman Power in Western Europe was described: the Old Rome of the
West had failed, but Constantinople had taken its place and still stood
young and vigorous. In the Bulgarian version Constantinople disappears,
and in its stead the chronicler's praise is transferred to "our new Tsari-
grad" and the Bulgarian Tsar. Trnovo claimed for itself the imperial
glory of the city of Constantine. In A.D. 1393 the Bulgarian Empire fell
before the attack of the Turks, and many exiles fled from Bulgaria to
Moscow. A Bulgarian, Kiprian, at this time became Metropolitan of
Moscow. It looks as if these *émigrés* had carried with them the imperial
theory which on Bulgarian soil had been shattered by the Turkish victory.
It was Kiprian who, when a dispute had arisen between Moscow and the
[East Roman] Empire, wrote to the Patriarch of Constantinople: "We
have a church but no Emperor, and we do not recognise him." Byzantium
replied by a re-assertion of its sole claim to imperial sovereignty. In A.D.
1438–9 came the Council of Florence and the union of the Eastern and
Western churches. Orthodoxy had been betrayed by the Greeks: The
Metropolitan Isidor [of Moscow], who had played the traitor's part at the
Council, was cursed as a renegade.[1] In A.D. 1453 Constantinople itself fell
into the hands of the Turks. The lesson thus taught by history was
obvious: here was the hand of God.'[2]

The Muscovites took full advantage of the opportunity that now lay
open to them. In A.D. 1472 the Grand Duke Ivan III married Zoë
(*Russicè* Sophia) Palaiológhos, a niece of the last Constantinopolitan
Orthodox Emperor Constantine,[3] and adopted as his own coat-of-arms
the two-headed East Roman eagle.[4] In A.D. 1480 he repudiated the

---

[1] Isidore was not only discredited; he was ejected and replaced by a successor of
Russian, instead of Greek, nationality; and at the same time the Oecumenical Patriarch's
ecclesiastical suzerainty over the Metropolitan See of Moscow was repudiated. See IX.
viii. 398.—A.J.T.

[2] Baynes, N. H., and Moss, H. St. L. B.: *Byzantium* (Oxford 1948, Clarendon Press),
pp. 383–4. Cp. Zernov, N.: *Moscow the Third Rome*, reprint of 2nd ed. (London 1944,
S.P.C.K.), p. 34: 'This catastrophe, comparable only to the destruction of Jerusalem or
the sack of Rome, required an explanation, and this was found in the apostasy of the
Emperor and the Oecumenical Patriarch.'

[3] The Thirteenth, counting from Constantine the Great, on one reckoning, the
Eleventh on another.

[4] These two events are, however, given a different complexion by Prince Obolensky in
'Russia's Byzantine Heritage', *Oxford Slavonic Papers*, vol. i (Oxford 1950, Clarendon
Press), p. 46:

'Of course there can be no doubt that Russian Tsarism welcomed the theory that the
seat of Imperial sovereignty had migrated to Moscow after the fall of Constantinople;
the Tsar's adoption of Byzantine titles, heraldry and ceremonial can be regarded as a
visible symbol of this claim. But . . . the Christian universalism of East Rome was transformed and distorted within the more narrow framework of Muscovite nationalism. The
really significant fact is that the beginning of Russia's turning away from her Byzantine
heritage in the late fifteenth century coincided with the growth of her connexions with
the West; Ivan III's marriage with Zoë was a harbinger of these connexions; for the

suzerainty of the Tatars of Bātū Khan's Appanage and proclaimed his own independence under the title of Autocrat. His second successor Ivan IV the Terrible (*imperabat* A.D. 1533–84) had himself crowned Emperor in 1547. In A.D. 1551 a Council of the Russian Church asserted the superiority of the Russian version of Orthodoxy over all others.[1] In the reign of Tsar Theodore (*imperabat* A.D. 1584–98), in A.D. 1589, the Metropolitan of Moscow was elevated by the Oecumenical Patriarch of the day to the status of Patriarch of All Russia.[2] In taking these successive steps the Russians were on stronger ground than their Bulgar and Serb precursors whose ventures had ended so ignominiously. They were not usurpers challenging living legitimate bearers of the Imperial title, but residuary legatees taking over a vacant heritage; and, so far from being conscious of sin, they were confidently self-righteous.

'The feeling that the Greeks had betrayed their Orthodoxy, and were therefore punished by God, was particularly strong in the remote Church of Russia, where anti-Latin tendencies were very pronounced. . . . To the Russians it seemed that, if the Greeks were rejected by God for the betrayal of Orthodoxy, they themselves were restored to political independence because of their devotion to the Church. The Russian nation was the last stronghold of the Orthodox Faith, and would thus inherit all the privileges and duties of the Christian Roman Empire.'[3]

This Russian belief in Russia's high destiny was fortified by Biblical and Patristic authority. The four successive universal states that were a prominent motif in the Book of Daniel[4] had been identified by the Christian Father Hippolytus (*florebat circa* A.D. 230)[5] as the Empires of Babylon,[6] the Achaemenidae, Alexander the Great, and Rome.

'During the ascendancy of the Fourth Realm the greatest events in human history were expected to take place, including the Second as well

niece of the last Byzantine Emperor came to Russia from Italy accompanied by a papal legate, and the marriage had been arranged in Rome.'

[1] See Zernov, op. cit., p. 58.

[2] See Zernov, ibid., pp. 69–73. In spite of his assumption of this style and title, the Patriarch of Moscow did not succeed immediately in extending his ecclesiastical domain beyond the previous limits of the Muscovite Metropolitan See. Russian Orthodox Christians who were political subjects of the United Kingdom of Poland-Lithuania and who did not become Uniate ecclesiastical subjects of the Roman Church continued to be ecclesiastical subjects of the Oecumenical Patriarchate of Constantinople until after Kiev had fallen under the political sovereignty of Muscovy—as it fell provisionally in A.D. 1667 and definitively in A.D. 1686. After the death of the reigning Metropolitan of Kiev in A.D. 1671, the Muscovite Government deliberately kept the See vacant; and, when in A.D. 1684 they gave their consent at last to the holding of a new election, they stipulated that the new incumbent should be the ecclesiastical subject of the Patriarch of Moscow, and no longer of the Oecumenical Patriarch of Constantinople. The Metropolitan of Kiev who was elected on the 29th June, 1685, accordingly obtained investiture from the Patriarch of Moscow; and, when the Oecumenical Patriarch refused to recognize the alienation of the See of Kiev from his own ecclesiastical jurisdiction, he was compelled to give way by the Sultan acting at the instance of the Tsar, whom the Porte was eager to appease, in the vain hope of deterring Moscow from joining the Western Christian coalition against the Ottoman Empire (see Doroshenko, D.: *History of the Ukraine*, English translation (Edmonton, Alberta, 1939, The Institute Press), pp. 324–8).

[3] Zernov, op. cit., pp. 34–36.

[4] Daniel ii. 27–49; vii. 1–28; ix. 24–27.

[5] Though Hippolytus lived and worked in Rome, he wrote in Greek—which was the language of the proletariat, and therefore of the Church, in the Imperial City till after his day—and his works were therefore current in Eastern Orthodox Christendom.

[6] i.e. the Neo-Babylonian Empire of Nebuchadnezzar, not the original Babylonian Empire of Hammurabi.

as the First Coming of the Messiah. The collapse of the western part of the Roman Empire in the fifth century did not affect this conviction, for the Eastern Christians believed that Constantinople was the New or Second Rome. They ascribed to her the same promises of indestructibility which were originally made in regard to Rome herself. When Moscow became the only capital among the Eastern Christians free from the control of the Infidels, it was natural that she should be elevated to the position of the Third and Last Rome.'[1]

This belief was given its classical formulation by an elder of a monastery in Pskov, Philotheus, in an epistle addressed to the Grand Duke Basil III (*imperabat* A.D. 1505–33).

'The Church of Old Rome fell [because of] its heresy; the gates of the Second Rome, Constantinople, were hewn down by the axes of the infidel Turks; but the Church of Moscow, the Church of the New Rome, shines brighter than the Sun in the whole Universe. Thou art the one universal sovereign of all Christian folk; thou shouldst hold the reins in awe of God. Fear Him who hath committed them to thee. Two Romes are fallen, but the Third stands fast; a fourth there cannot be. Thy Christian kingdom shall not be given to another.'[2]

Two generations later, a paraphrase of this famous passage was written into the installation charter of the first Patriarch of Moscow[3] over the signature of his creator the Oecumenical Patriarch Jeremiah:

'Because the Old Rome has collapsed on account of the heresy of Apollinarius, and because the Second Rome, which is Constantinople, is now in [the] possession of the godless Turks, thy great kingdom, O pious Tsar, is the Third Rome. It surpasses in devotion every other, and all Christian kingdoms are now merged in thy realm. Thou art the only Christian sovereign in the World, the master of all faithful Christians.'[4]

The Russians' bold application to their own universal state of the belief in the immortality of an oecumenical Roman Empire seems to have moved a Muscovite Government—in so far as this 'great idea' had any practical influence on Muscovite policy—to concentrate its attention and effort more steadily than ever upon working for the Russian aims of saving a still inviolate 'Third Rome' from suffering 'the Second Rome's' and 'the First Rome's' fates and of liberating from Western political and ecclesiastical domination the Russian Orthodox Christian lands and peoples that had fallen under the rule of Poland and Lithuania since the fourteenth century,[5] without allowing itself to be diverted by Western diplomacy into fancying itself in the romantic role of a divinely appointed liberator of non-Russian Orthodox Christians who had fallen under Otto-

---

[1] Zernov, N.: *The Russians and their Church*, p. 50.
[2] Philotheus of Pskov, op. cit., as cited in Zernov, *The Russians and their Church*, p. 5
In this passage, Philotheus has taken his cue from earlier Russian expressions of the same idea. For instance, 'the chronographer of A.D. 1512 writes: "Constantine's city is fallen, but our Russian land through the help of the Mother of God and the Saints grows and is young and exalted. So may it be, O Christ, until the end of Time!" The words which the Bulgarian translator of Manasses had applied to Trnovo are here claimed for Moscow' (Baynes, N. H., and Moss, H. St. L. B.: *Byzantium* (Oxford 1948, Clarendon Press), p. 384).
[3] For the establishment of the Patriarchate of Moscow in A.D. 1589, see p. 35, above.
[4] Text as cited in Zernov, op. cit., p. 71.
[5] See IX. viii. 126–8.

man Muslim rule as a penalty for 'the Second Rome's' apostasy.[1] The political mission of 'the Third Rome' would be neither to rescue nor to reform 'the Second Rome', but to supplant her, as it had been the Christian Church's mission to supplant the Jewish Church. The effect, in Russian souls, of the concept of 'Moscow the Third Rome' seems to have been to precipitate, focus, and express a Russian sense of the uniqueness of Russia's own destiny as the sole surviving repository and citadel of an impeccably orthodox Christianity; and this sense of destiny subsequently demonstrated its strength by surviving some very formidable opposition.

While 'it is an open question whether Jeremiah himself fully understood the Russian text [of his charter] and shared the interpretation given by the Russians to the act committed by him',[2] it is certain that, when the four Greek Patriarchs of Constantinople, Alexandria, Antioch, and Jerusalem jointly accorded recognition to the Patriarchate of Moscow in A.D. 1593, they assigned to the new Patriarch the fifth and not the first place in their order of precedence.[3] Thereafter, in the seventeenth and eighteenth centuries, the ideal of 'Moscow the Third Rome' was signally defeated first by Greek Orthodoxy and then by the secular civilization of the West.

In consequence of a schism within the bosom of the Russian Church, arising from the championship of Greek as against Russian ritual practice[4] by no less a person than the reigning Patriarch of Moscow, Nikon,[5] the four Greek Patriarchs—Ottoman ra'īyeh though they were—became for a moment the arbiters of Russia's ecclesiastical destiny. At a Council held at Moscow in A.D. 1666–7, over which the Patriarchs of Alexandria and Antioch presided, the opponents of Nikon's Graecizing reforms were excommunicated, and the Russian hierarchy were compelled to sign a statement renouncing the pretension, put on record by the Council of A.D. 1551, that Muscovite Orthodoxy was an ensample for the rest of the Orthodox Church. At the same time Nikon himself was deposed and unfrocked.[6]

---

[1] See Prince Dmitri Obolensky in *Oxford Slavonic Papers*, vol. i (Oxford 1950, Clarendon Press), pp. 46 and 62, together with the further observations from him and from B. H. Sumner that are quoted, in an annex, on pp. 577–9, below.

[2] Zernov, op. cit., p. 71.

[3] See Zernov, op. cit., loc. cit.

[4] 'The cause of these differences in ritual, discovered by the Russians in the seventeenth century, was their long separation, under the Tatar yoke, from the rest of Eastern Christendom. For, whilst the Church of Byzantium had gradually altered liturgical customs, the Russians had preserved intact the ritual received by them at the time of their conversion in the tenth century' (Zernov, op. cit., p. 100). It will be seen that the circumstances in which this issue between the Russian and Greek versions of Eastern Orthodoxy arose in the seventeenth century were remarkably similar to those in which the issue between the Irish and Roman versions of Western Catholicism had arisen in the seventh century (see the present Study, I. i. 29 and II. ii. 333–6). There is a singular resemblance between the masterful characters, and parallelism between the chequered careers, of Nikon and Wilfrid. The two prelates won a conspicuous and enduring victory for the causes of Constantinople and Rome respectively, and both of them eventually brought personal discomfiture and downfall on themselves through the intolerable hybris bred in their imperious souls by the brilliance of their previous successes.

[5] Nikon *patriarchico munere fungebatur* A.D. 1652–66.

[6] Zernov, op. cit., pp. 103–4. This Greek ecclesiastical ascendancy in Muscovy proved ephemeral. 'In general, the religious and cultural links between the [Russians and the Greeks], which had been steadily increasing during the first three-quarters of the

In the next generation, Peter the Great applied his extraordinary
genius to a revolutionary attempt to transform Muscovy from a Russian
Orthodox Christian universal state, believing itself to be charged with a
unique oecumenical mission, into an efficient parochial state member of
the contemporary Western comity. Peter transferred the capital of his
dominions from Russian Orthodox Moscow to a new city, founded by
him in the maritime Western March of the Russian World and named
after its founder; and, on the culturally as well as physically virgin soil
of St. Petersburg, a Westernizing Russia was to have a seat of government that would be Western from the start, uncontaminated by any
antecedent deposit of Orthodox tradition.[1] Peter also instilled a tincture
of Westernism into the Muscovite Church by filling the key posts in the
Russian Orthodox hierarchy, hitherto held by Muscovites, with Ukrainian clerics from Kiev and the Ukrainian territories lying east of the
River Dniepr that had been acquired by Muscovy from Poland-
Lithuania in A.D. 1667;[2] for, under a Roman Catholic ascendancy, the
Ukrainian Orthodox clergy, whether they opposed Romanization or
yielded to it, had been constrained to study Roman theology and in the
process had been mentally re-oriented to a partially Western outlook.[3]
Finally, after having left the Patriarchal Throne of Moscow lying vacant
for twenty years, Peter replaced the Patriarchate in A.D. 1721 by a 'Holy
Synod' composed of ecclesiastics appointed by the Emperor himself
and explicitly acknowledging his supremacy; and, to make sure that his
control should be effective, he placed the Synod under the supervision of
a lay Procurator.[4]

This rain of blows might have been expected to be crushing, yet the
ideal once conveyed in the concept of 'Moscow the Third Rome' clung
to life in its traditional religious expression and eventually found for
itself new expressions in terms of the ideologies of a Westernizing World
whose atmosphere the Russians were now constrained to breathe. The

seventeenth-century, had declined in the last quarter, when Kiev [ceded to Muscovy by
Poland-Lithuania in A.D. 1667], not Constantinople, proved itself the leading Orthodox
cultural influence on Russia. When in A.D. 1685–6 the Metropolitanate of Kiev was
placed under the jurisdiction of the Moscow Patriarchate, this was effected without
previous agreement with Constantinople, and the [Oecumenical] Patriarch could do
nothing but register unavailing protests. Ukrainians, not Greeks, became the leading
representatives, in Russia, of new trends in Orthodox thought and education. Constantinople no longer, as in the days of Nikon, represented for Russia the fountainhead of
learning and of Orthodox tradition' (Sumner, B. H.: *Peter the Great and the Ottoman
Empire* (Oxford 1949, Blackwell), p. 64). Both Peter the Great and his ambassador at
Constantinople, P. A. Tolstoi, seem to have disliked and despised the Phanariot Greek
Orthodox Christian prelates (see ibid., pp. 63–65).

[1] A corresponding consideration had been in the mind of Constantine the Great
when he had transferred the capital of the Roman Empire from Old Rome to his own
foundation of New Rome or Constantinople. The seat of Government of a converted
Roman Empire was to be Christian from the outset, unaffected by the archaistic paganism
that was dying so hard in its Senatorial fastness on the banks of the Tiber (see V. vi. 89).
In making the transfer, both Constantine and Peter were, of course, moved by political
and strategic motives in addition to the cultural motive here in question (see II. ii.
157–8 and pp. 221–3, below).

[2] The Zaporozhian Cossacks, who controlled the southern fringe of the Ukraine,
below Kiev (see II. ii. 154–7 and V. v. 283), had transferred their allegiance from Poland-
Lithuania to Muscovy already between the years 1648 and 1667.

[3] See Zernov, N.: *Moscow the Third Rome*, pp. 89–91.

[4] See Zernov, op. cit., pp. 81–82; eundem, *The Russians and their Church*, pp. 122–4;
and the present chapter of the present Study, p. 23, n. 4, above.

excommunicated opponents of Nikon succeeded in establishing and maintaining, under the Petrine régime, the dissident church of the Old Believers,[1] and in a Western Age of Romanticism the Russian faith in Russia's unique destiny and oecumenical mission acclimatized itself to the spiritual temperature of a secular Western culture under the guise of the Slavophil Movement.[2] When the Petrine political régime collapsed in A.D. 1917, the Patriarchate of Moscow was re-established[3] and the political capital was retransferred to Moscow from Petrograd.

It might have been expected, again, that, after this flicker of life, the ideal of 'Moscow the Third Rome' would have received its *coup de grâce* from the Bolshevik régime; for did not Lenin and his companions out-Peter Peter? Was it not the aim of the Communists to complete the Westernization of Russia on a radical futurist pattern? Were they not setting themselves to uproot, not merely Orthodoxy, but the very belief in the existence of God? Did they not deliberately eliminate the name of Russia from the official style of their 'Union of Soviet Socialist Republics'? The answers to these rhetorical questions are necessarily affirmative, yet they leave unsolved the enigma of the ambiguity in the nature of Bolshevism which has been touched on at an earlier point in this Study[4] and which still remained obscure at a time when the Soviet Government had been in existence for a third of a century.

The would-be disciples of Marx might prove to be involuntary disciples of Philotheus. It was they, after all, who had repaired Peter's breach with Muscovite geographical tradition by bringing back to Moscow from Leningrad the capital of the Empire which the Soviet régime had inherited from Peter, and Peter from Ivan III; and, though this deliberate act of theirs had no doubt been prompted by other motives,[5] it was improbable that, once ensconced in the Kremlin, they would be impervious to an atmosphere from which their clear-sighted precursor had taken

---

[1] See V. vi. 120–1 and IX. viii. 131–2.

[2] See Kohn, Hans: 'Dostoevsky's Nationalism', in the *Journal of the History of Ideas*, October 1945, vol. vi, No. 4 (New York 1945, College of the City of New York), pp. 385–414, and the present Study, IX. viii. 131–2.

[3] Tikhon, the Metropolitan of Moscow, was elected Patriarch on the 5th November, 1917 (i.e. after the Bolsheviks had come into power), by a Church Council, including lay as well as ecclesiastical members, which had been convened on the 15th August (Zernov, *The Russians and their Church*, p. 154).

[4] In III. iii. 200–2. See further IX. viii. 133–6 and 607–8.

[5] These motives are discussed, in an annex, on pp. 690–1, below. One motive of the Bolsheviks in retransferring the capital from Leningrad to Moscow on the 12th March, 1918, had been to entrench themselves in a strategic position covering the eastern exit of an overland avenue of attack from Western Europe along which the Germans had marched, in Polish and French footsteps, in two world wars. Another of their motives had been to establish their hold over, and spread their doctrine among, the mass of the people whom they had set out to rule, by planting themselves at a point which, besides covering the most dangerously exposed of all Russia's twentieth-century frontiers, had the second advantage of lying much nearer than Leningrad lay to the heart of the country. This was the motive that likewise led the British Government of India to retransfer the capital of the Indian Empire from Calcutta to Delhi in A.D. 1912, the Kemalist Government of Turkey to remove the capital of Turkey from Constantinople to Ankara in April 1920, and the Kuomintang Government of China to retransfer the capital of China from Peking to Nanking in A.D. 1928. Such moves are likely to have two-way cultural effects. While they may fulfil the migrating Governments' purpose of strengthening their own influence over the interior of their dominions, these Governments will also be exposing themselves, by their migration, to the influence of the traditional culture of the interior. (For transfers of capitals and some of their causes and effects, see II. ii. 112–208 and pp. 193–228, below.)

such pains to extricate the new ruling element in his own anti-traditional régime. The spirit of Moscow was a faith in Russia's destiny;[1] and, at the time of writing, the Russians' consciousness of a unique destiny was sharing with the Americans' possession of a unique weapon the invidious distinction of being one of two titanic facts that, between them, were darkening the horizon of a world which had condemned itself to political unification by its two feats of disintegrating the Atom and 'annihilating distance'. This was an impressive testimony to the strength of the belief in the immortality of a Roman Empire which in reality had ceased to exist not less than thirteen hundred years ago.[2]

The Riddle of the Prestige of the Imperial Office in Japan

A similar testimony to the endurance of the prestige of the Ts'in and Hau Empire is perhaps afforded by the history of the Imperial House of Japan.[3]

At an earlier point in this Study[4] an explanation has been offered for the ebbing away of power from the Imperial Government in Yamato to the feudal nobility in the Kwanto. We have still to explain why an Imperial House which exercised effective authority for less than three hundred years after the reorganization of the Imperial Government on a Chinese model in A.D. 645 should have survived for another thousand years in impotence as the sole fount of honour and dispenser of legitimacy. All the *de facto* rulers of Japan, since the time in the tenth century of the Christian Era when the Imperial Government had lost control, had felt it necessary to do their ruling in the Emperor's name. At the time of writing, an utterly victorious occupying Power was finding it convenient to administer the country through a native Japanese Government acting in the name of the Emperor of the day.

This extraordinary vitality of the prestige of the Japanese Imperial House had been attributed by the Japanese themselves to their own official belief that the Imperial Family were descendants, in unbroken line, from the Sun Goddess Amaterasu. But, though, no doubt, this myth went back to the dawn of Japanese history, the deliberate exploitation of it for a political purpose seemed to be no older than the Meiji Period, when the new masters of Japan, who had wrested the *de facto* power from the last of the Tokugawa shoguns in A.D. 1868 and had appropriated to themselves the manipulation of the indispensable Imperial puppet under pretence of 'restoring' him to the status enjoyed by his forefathers, were concerned to enhance the prestige of the institution in whose name they had to rule. Moreover, the Emperor Hirohito did not seem to have forfeited his hold on the allegiance of the Japanese people by his public declaration to them, on New Year's Day 1946, that he was not a god but a man.[5] It therefore looked as if there were some

---

[1] For the persistence of this faith and the fundamental identity of the Slavophil and the Communist manifestation of it, see Kohn, op. cit., p. 414.

[2] Reckoning that even the relatively tough Greek and Oriental core of the Roman Empire went to pieces within the hundred years following the death of Justinian in A.D. 565. In the West the Empire went to pieces some two hundred years earlier (see p. 20, n. 4, and p. 27, n. 4, above).

[3] For the relation of the offshoot of the Far Eastern Civilization in Japan to the main stem in China, see I. i. 132–3.   [4] In II. ii. 158–9.

[5] In his rescript of that date, the Emperor Hirohito declared: 'The ties between us and

firm foundation, other than the Sun Goddess myth, for the immense esteem which the Imperial House had continued to enjoy through all vicissitudes of their fortunes and Japan's, and this foundation might perhaps be discovered in the historic 'reception', in A.D. 645, of the Chinese Imperial Constitution of that age. This bureaucratic system of administration was far too elaborate and refined to be practicable under the rude conditions of contemporary Japanese society. Yet its exotic character, which doomed it to a speedy failure in the field of practical politics, may have been the very feature that ensured its age-long preservation as a palladium of the Japanese polity; for the Japanese Imperial Constitution of A.D. 645 was modelled on that of the then reigning Chinese dynasty of the T'ang, and the T'ang Empire had been a resuscitation of the Han Empire, which had been the Sinic Society's universal state. On this showing, the Japanese Imperial Office in the twentieth century of the Christian Era was living on political capital that had been accumulated by Han Liu Pang in the second century B.C.

The Grounds of the Illusion

We have perhaps now sufficiently established the fact that the belief in the immortality of universal states survives for centuries and millennia after it has been decisively confuted by plain hard facts. What are the causes of a phenomenon that looks strange at first sight?

One manifest cause is the potency of the personal impression made by the founders of universal states and by their successors who enter into the fruits of their labours[1]—an impression that their contemporaries, who receive it at first hand as the direct beneficiaries of these great men's achievements, hand on to a receptive Posterity with an emphasis which, by the cumulative effect of transmission, exaggerates an imposing truth into an overwhelming legend. From among the many famous testimonies to the impression made by the Emperor Augustus, we have singled out already, in another context, the almost lyrical tribute paid by Philo,[2]

our people have always stood upon mutual trust and affection. They do not depend upon mere legends and myths. They are not predicated on the false conception that the Emperor is divine and that the Japanese people are superior to other races and fated to rule the World' (English text published in *The New York Times*, 1st January, 1946).

[1] A survey of representatives of these two generations of 'saviours with the sword' has been given in V. vi. 189–97. See further V. vi. 370–5.

[2] See V. vi. 181, n. 3. The Alexandrian Jewish man of letters' private and personal tribute to Augustus had an official counterpart in a decree passed—probably in the year 9 B.C.—by the Κοινόν of the Province of Asia, providing that in this province in future Augustus's birthday shall be kept as New Year's Day and that the first month of the new calendar year shall be called 'Caesar'. This inscription (No. 458 in W. Dittenberger: *Orientis Graeci Inscriptiones Selectae*, vol. ii (Leipzig 1905, Hirzel), pp. 48–60) expresses the same sentiments as Philo in outright religious language:

'[The Most Divine Caesar] has re-established a Universe that had everywhere been in disintegration and had degenerated into a lamentable state. He has put a new face on the whole Cosmos—a Cosmos that would have been only too happy to pass out of existence if, at the critical moment, Caesar had not been born to be the Universe's universal blessing. . . . The Providence that has organised every detail of Human Life has exerted and surpassed Itself in order to bring Life to perfection in producing Augustus—whom It has filled with virtue to be the benefactor of Mankind, sending him to us and to Posterity as a saviour whose mission has been to put an end to War and to set the Universe in order.'

This official eulogy is capped by one from Halicarnassus (No. 94 in *The Collection of Ancient Greek Inscriptions in the British Museum*, Part IV, section i (Oxford 1893,

who, as a Jew, a Hellenist, an Alexandrian, and a philosopher, can hardly be suspected of having gone to exceptional lengths in his enthusiasm for the Roman founder of an Hellenic universal state. The prestige to which such tributes gave a flying start can be seen gathering momentum during the next two centuries.

'A very important "virtue", which emerges and takes shape slowly, . . . is the *Providentia* (in Greek πρόνοια) of the ruler. This . . . "foresight" or "forethought" . . . as we meet it in Cicero . . . appears to be a virtue at once of the wise magistrate, who foresees and so forestalls dangers, and of the loving father, who makes provision for the welfare and future of the family of which he is the head. Both these senses tend to blend and come together, as they naturally might in a ruler who was at once a magistrate . . . of the Roman People and a father for the whole Empire.

'Through a hundred years it develops till it reaches its first climax under Trajan, "the most provident prince". . . . This aspect of the rule of Trajan and Hadrian and the Antonine Emperors, stressed as it was on coins, on buildings, by speakers and publicists, was bound to have its effect. Slowly the common people learnt to look for help and aid to the *Providentia* of their all-powerful ruler—he knows, he cares, he can act: he is like some Hercules, who visits all corners of the World putting down injustice and ending misery. Remembering this, we can form for ourselves some faint idea of how tremendous the effect of Hadrian's great journeys must have been on the provincials: here was an Emperor who did not stay in Rome (or, if he left it, leave merely for campaigns), but who visited every part of his realm to put things in order and to restore. . . . As years pass, this *Providentia* of the one ruler becomes more comprehensive. . . . When men are in distress and trouble they turn to the one person of whose help they can be sure: oppressed tenant-farmers on an Imperial estate in Africa appeal for aid to the *Divina Providentia* at Rome, and the harassed colonists of Scaptopara in Thrace beg the Emperor to pity them and help them by his θεία πρόνοια.[1]

'There is something very touching in this faith, this belief in the *providentissimus princeps*: however far away he may be in Rome, he cares for them, he pities them, he cannot be deceived, and he exerts always, to quote the fine phrase of one of Hadrian's officers, "a care that is never tired, with which he watches unrestingly on behalf of the good of Mankind (*infatigabilis cura, per quam adsidue pro humanis utilitatibus excubat*)". . . . Justice, clemency, duty, warlike prowess—these are fine things; but even more important is it that the subject peoples and provincials over this vast area should have believed in a ruler who was not merely a soldier but who cared for them and provided for their needs.'[2]

Clarendon Press), pp. 63–65), which must have been drafted not earlier than the year 2 B.C., since it cites Augustus's title 'Pater Patriae':
'Considering that the eternal and immortal Nature of the Universe has lavished upon Mankind the greatest blessing, redounding to superlative benefactions, in bringing forth Caesar Augustus, who in the blissful life of our generation is the father of his own fatherland the goddess Rome, and is the ancestral Zeus and saviour of the whole Human Race, whose providence has not only fulfilled but has surpassed the prayers of all Mankind—for there is peace on land and sea, the commonwealths flourish in law-abidingness, concord and prosperity, and there is a peak and a fecundity of every blessing: of good hopes for the future and of good cheer in the present, in a world whose inhabitants have been given full measure of matches and monuments and celebrations. . . .'
     [1] 'La notion de l'éternité des Césars est . . . étroitement unie à celle de leur divinité' (Cumont, Fr.: 'L'Éternité des Empereurs Romains', in *Revue d'Histoire et de Littérature Religieuses*, vol. i (Paris 1896; printed at Macon), pp. 439–40).
     [2] Charlesworth, M. P.: *The Virtues of a Roman Emperor: Propaganda and the Creation*

This epiphany of the ruler of a universal state as the one shepherd whose oecumenical monarchy makes one fold for all Mankind[1] appeals to one of the Human Soul's deepest longings, as, in Dostoyevski's fable, the Grand Inquisitor reminds a subversive Christ.

'Thou mightest have taken . . . the sword of Caesar. Why didst Thou reject that last gift? Hadst Thou accepted that last counsel of the mighty spirit, Thou wouldst have accomplished all that Man seeks on Earth—that is, someone to worship, someone to keep his conscience, and some means of uniting all in one unanimous and harmonious ant-heap; for the craving for universal unity is the third and last anguish of men. Mankind as a whole has always striven to organise a universal state. There have been many great nations with great histories, but the more highly they were developed the more unhappy they were, for they felt more acutely than other people the craving for world-wide union. The great conquerors —Timurs and Chingis Khans—whirled like hurricanes over the face of the Earth, striving to subdue its people, and they too were but the unconscious expression of the same craving for universal unity. Hadst Thou taken the World and Caesar's purple, Thou wouldst have founded the universal state and have given universal peace. For who can rule men if not he who holds their conscience and their bread in his hands?'[2]

Another cause of the persistence of the belief in the immortality of universal states is the impressiveness of the institution itself, as distinct from the prestige of the succession of rulers who are its living incarnations. A universal state captivates hearts and minds because it is the embodiment of a rally from the long-unhalted rout of a Time of Troubles, and it was this aspect of the Roman Empire that eventually won the admiration and love of originally hostile Greek men of letters.

'There is no salvation in the exercise of a dominion divorced from power. To find oneself under the dominion of one's superiors is a "second best" alternative; but this "second best" proved to be the best of all in our present experience of a Roman Empire. This happy experience has moved the whole World to cleave to Rome with might and main. The World would no more think of seceding from Rome than a ship's crew would think of parting company with the pilot. You must have seen bats in a cave clinging tight to one another and to the rocks; and this is an apt image of the whole World's dependence on Rome. In every heart to-day the focus of anxiety is the fear of becoming detached from the cluster. The thought of being abandoned by Rome is so appalling that it precludes any thought of wantonly abandoning her.

'There is an end of those disputes over sovereignty and prestige which were the causes of the outbreak of all the wars of the past; and, while some of the nations, like noiselessly flowing water, are delightfully quiet—rejoicing in their release from toil and trouble, and aware at last that all their old struggles were to no purpose—there are other nations which do not even know or remember whether they once sat in the seat of power.

of Belief (London 1937, Milford), pp. 15, 16, 17, and 19–20. Cf. eundem: 'Providentia and Aeternitas', in the Harvard Theological Review, vol. xxix, No. 2, April 1936. See also Cumont, Fr.: 'L'Éternité des Empereurs Romains', in Revue d'Histoire et de Littérature Religieuses, vol. i (1896), pp. 435 seqq., cited by Charlesworth.
    1 John x. 16.
    2 Dostoyevski, F.: The Brothers Karamazov, Part II, Book V, chap. 5: 'The Grand Inquisitor'.

In fact we are witnessing a new version of the Pamphylian's myth (or is it Plato's own?). At a moment when the states of the World were already laid out on the funeral pyre as the victims of their own fratricidal strife and turmoil, they were all at once presented with the [Roman] dominion and straightway came to life again. How they arrived at this condition, they are unable to say. They know nothing about it, and can only marvel at their present well-being. They are like sleepers awakened who have come to themselves and now dismiss from their thoughts the dreams that obsessed them only a moment ago. They no longer find it credible that there were ever such things as wars; and, when the word "war" is mentioned to-day, it has a mythical sound in most peoples' ears. . . .

'The entire Inhabited World now keeps perpetual holiday. It has laid aside the steel which it used to wear of old and has turned, care-free, to festivities and enjoyment of all kinds. All other rivalries have died out, and one form of competition alone now pre-occupies all the cities—a competition in making the finest show of beauty and amenity. The whole World is now full of gymnasiums, fountains, gateways, temples, workshops, academies; and it is now possible to say with scientific certainty that a World which was in its death-agonies has made a recovery and gained a new lease of life. . . . The whole Earth has been laid out like a pleasure park. The smoke of burning villages and the watch fires (lit by friend or foeman) have vanished beyond the horizon, as though some mighty wind had winnowed them away, and their place has been taken by an innumerable multitude and variety of enchanting shows and sports. . . . So that the only people who still need pity for the good things that they are missing are those outside your empire—if there are any such people left. . . .'[1]

If there are, they are hardly worth speaking of in the estimation of those inside, and this is another reason why the belief in their immortality that universal states inspire is so blindly persistent. Universal states are the supreme expressions, on the political plane, of a sense of unity which is one of the psychological products of the process of social disintegration.[2] During the Times of Troubles through which disintegrating civilizations make their rough passage, the vision of unity grows ever clearer and the yearning for it ever more poignant as the reality of it continues to elude the storm-tossed wayfarers; and, when, at the lowest ebb of hope, the long-pursued goal is at last unexpectedly attained, and this in a monumental form, the psychological effect is overwhelming.

'Ahuramazda, the creator of Heaven and Earth, has made the King of the Persians "ruler, far and wide, over this great Earth"—made "him, the one [lord], to be ruler over many"; made him "king over many lands and tongues", "over the mountains and plains this side of the Sea and beyond it" [Babylonian Inscription H]. He can style himself "the lord of all men from sunrise to sunset" [Aeschines, iii. 132]. All the peoples whose representatives are portrayed on the seat of his throne render him obedience, bring him tribute and serve in his armed forces.'[3]

This sense of unity and universality is not a peculiarity of the

[1] Aristeides, P. Aelius: In Romam, edited by Keil, B., in Aelii Aristidis Quae Supersunt Omnia, vol. ii (Berlin 1898, Weidmann), pp. 110–11 (Or. XXVI, §§ 68–70) and p. 120 (Or. XXVI, §§ 97–99).
[2] See V. vi. 1–49.
[3] Meyer, E.: Geschichte des Altertums, vol. iii (Stuttgart 1901, Cotta), pp. 24–25.

Achaemenian Empire;[1] it is the hall-mark of universal states, which stamps those that bear it as authentic representatives of this class of polity. In his eulogy of Rome, the Greek man of letters, quoted above, makes a point of the universality of her rule as well as of the new lease of life that she has brought to a lacerated Hellenic Society.

'Of this city of Rome you could not say either that it was left unfortified with a Lacedaemonian bravado or that it was enclosed in fortifications of a Babylonian magnificence. . . . You have not, however, you Romans, neglected to build walls; only you have run them round your empire and not round your city. You have placed them in the uttermost parts of the Earth; yet they are magnificent walls which are worthy of you and are a sight for the eyes of all who live within their shelter—though it would take an intending sight-seer months or even years to reach them if Rome itself were the starting-point of his journey; for you have pushed your way beyond the outermost circuit of the Inhabited World and there, in no-man's-land, you have drawn a second circuit with a more convenient *tracée* which is easier to defend—for all the world as though you were simply fortifying a city. . . . This circuit is utterly impregnable and indestructible at every point; it outshines all others; and no system of fortifications that was ever constructed before bears any resemblance to it.'[2]

In this passage, a literary contemporary of Marcus Aurelius, in whose anxious reign Rome's magnificent world-wall was beginning to crack, was re-expounding the theme of a writer of the preceding generation, in whose day the World's defences did indeed look impregnably secure. During the last two centuries, says Appian of Alexandria (*vivebat circa* A.D. 90–160) in the preface to his *Studies in Roman History*,

'The [Roman] State has reached its highest point of organisation and the public revenue its highest figure, while a long and stable peace has raised the whole World to a level of secure prosperity. A few more subject nations have been added by the Emperors to those already under the

---

[1] In the sentence immediately preceding the passage quoted above, Eduard Meyer suggests that 'the Empire of the Achaemenidae is the first state known to history to have put forward the claim to universality'. This is surely incorrect. The Sumeric universal state founded by Ur-Engur, *alias* Ur-Nammu (*imperabat circa* 2143–2126 or 2079–2062 B.C.), and re-established by Hammurabi (*imperabat circa* 1792–1750 or 1728–1686 B.C.), advertised a claim to universality by entitling itself 'The Realm of the Four Quarters'; and, though Hammurabi was a contemporary of the epigoni of the Egyptiac Twelfth Dynasty, we may guess that, from the standpoint of 'the Middle Empire', which was the Egyptiac universal state, even the Sumeric 'Realm of the Four Quarters' was an exception, hardly worth speaking of, to Pharaoh's universal rule even at a date when this had in truth fallen into decadence. 'The New Empire's' claim to universality is better attested than 'the Middle Empire's', and also better founded, since, in 'the New Empire's' day, 'the Realm of the Four Quarters' was extinct and its former dominions in Syria and Mesopotamia had become provinces or dependencies of the Emperors who were reigning at Thebes. The Emperor Ikhnaton, who broke so sharply with his predecessors' traditions on so many points, both cherished and accentuated their oecumenicalism. Universality was the leading note of his revolutionary cult of the Aton; and the impartial benevolence with which the Aton showed the light of His countenance to all peoples was symbolized in the foundation of an 'Aton city' in Nubia, and perhaps another in Syria, as counterparts of the original 'Aton city' which Ikhnaton had laid out in Middle Egypt on the site subsequently known as Tall-al-'Amarnah (see Breasted, J. H.: *The Development of Religion and Thought in Ancient Egypt* (London 1912, Hodder & Stoughton), pp. 322–3).

[2] Aristeides, P. Aelius: *In Romam*, edited by Keil, B., in *Aelii Aristidis Quae Supersunt Omnia*, vol. ii (Berlin 1898, Weidmann), pp. 114–15 (Or. XXVI, §§ 79–84).

Roman dominion, and others which have revolted have been reduced to obedience; but, since the Romans already possess the choicest portions of the land and water surface of the globe, they are wise enough to aim at retaining what they hold rather than at extending their empire to infinity over the poverty-stricken and unremunerative territories of uncivilized nations. I myself have seen representatives of such nations attending at Rome on diplomatic missions and offering to become her subjects, and the Emperor refusing to accept the allegiance of peoples who would be of no value to his government. There are other nations innumerable whose kings the Romans appoint themselves, since they feel no necessity to incorporate them into their Empire. There are also certain subject nations to whom they make grants from their treasury, because they are too proud to repudiate them in spite of their being a financial burden. They have garrisoned the frontiers of their Empire with a ring of powerful armies, and keep guard over this vast extent of land and sea as easily as if it were a modest farm.'[1]

In the view of an Appian and an Aelius Aristeides, the Roman Empire was eternal[2]

> sicut summarum summa est aeterna, neque extra
> qui locus est quo dissiliant neque corpora sunt quae
> possint incidere et validâ dissolvere plagâ.[3]

In the lines of the Latin poet, Democritus's argument looks as impregnable as the Roman *limes* itself.

> Nec rerum summam commutare ulla potest vis;
> nam neque quo possit genus ullum materiai
> effugere ex omni, quicquam est [extra], neque in omne
> unde coorta queat nova vis irrumpere et omnem
> naturam rerum mutare et vertere motus.[4]

A universal state has indeed as little to fear from outer barbarians as the Universe has from stray star clusters that are *ex hypothesi* non-existent; yet the argument is a fallacy nevertheless, for, as we have seen in an earlier context, 'things rot through evils native to their selves'.[5] In Physical Nature there are elements whose atoms disintegrate by spontaneous radiation, without requiring any bombardment from extraneous bodies; and, in human social life, universal states 'are betrayed by what is false within'[6] into revealing, for those who have eyes to see through their specious appearance of impregnability, that, so far from being immortal, these are spontaneously fissile polities.

---

[1] Appian of Alexandria: *Studies in Roman History*, Preface.
[2] A modern Western student of the religions that were contemporaries of Christianity traces to Syria the association, in Roman minds, of the idea of the Roman Empire's eternity with the idea of its universality:
'L'origine de cette association des deux idées doit sans doute être cherchée en Syrie, où un seul et même mot '*olmo* signifie *aevum* et *mundus*, de telle sorte que le même titre, qu'on trouve porté par un dieu, peut se traduire aussi bien par "maître du monde" que par "maître de l'éternité" ' (Cumont, Fr.: 'L'Éternité des Empereurs Romains', in *Revue d'Histoire et de Littérature Religieuses*, vol. i (Paris 1896; printed at Macon), p. 450, n. 2).
[3] Lucretius: *De Rerum Natura*, Book V, ll. 361–3.
[4] Lucretius, op. cit., Book II, ll. 303–7.
[5] Menander, fragment 540, quoted in IV. iv, 120, n. 3.
[6] Meredith, George: *Modern Love*, stanza 43, last line, quoted in IV. iv. 120.

(II) THE DOOM OF TITHONUS

If it were the truth—as the course of history had so far invariably indicated it to be—that a universal state is not the goal of human endeavours, the watchword for citizens of universal states should be 'here have we no continuing city'.[1] Yet the impulse to idolize any institution is so strong,[2] and the particular institution with which we are here concerned wears so radiant a halo in the deceptive light cast by the mirage of immortality, that it is not surprising to find its citizens persistently mistaking this Gilead for the Promised Land, and translating their error into action by attempting to settle down there in comfort instead of proceeding manfully on their pilgrimage. Transjordan is indeed a better-watered and more smiling land than Palestine, and its woods and pastures appear to offer to the weary fugitive from the desert of a Time of Troubles a home which he can make his own without having to face the final ordeal of crossing Jordan's stream. The penalty of this intellectual and moral aberration is the doom of Tithonus.

An obscure divinity of the Nubian marches of the Egyptiac universal state[3] was transfigured by the genius of Hellenic mythology into a mortal king of the Ethiopians who had the misfortune to be loved by Eôs, the immortal Goddess of the Dawn. The goddess besought her fellow Olympians to confer on her human lover the immortality which she and her peers enjoyed; and, jealous though they were of their divine privileges, she teased them into yielding at last to her feminine importunity. Yet even this grudging gift was marred by a fatal flaw; for the eager goddess had forgotten that the Olympians' immortality was mated with an everlasting youth, and the other immortals had spitefully taken care to grant her no more than her bare request. The consequence was both ironic and tragic. After a honeymoon that flashed past in the twinkling of an Olympian eye, Eôs and her now immortal but still inexorably aging human mate found themselves condemned for eternity to grieve together over Tithonus's hapless plight. A senility to which the merciful hand of Death could never set a term was an affliction that no mortal man could ever be made to suffer, and an eternal grief was an obsession that left no room for any other thought or feeling.

The tragic irony of the Hellenic myth has been transposed into the realism of a Flemish picture by the sardonic imagination of Jonathan Swift in the character of Gulliver's cicerone on the air-borne island of Laputa.

'He gave me a particular account of the Struldbrugs among them. He said they commonly acted like mortals till about thirty years old, after which by degrees they grew melancholy and dejected, increasing in both till they came to fourscore. . . . When they came to fourscore years, which is reckoned the extremity of living in this country, they had not only all the follies and infirmities of other old men, but many more which arose from the dreadful prospects of never dying. They were not only opinionative,

[1] Heb. xiii. 14.
[2] For the idolization of institutions, see IV. iv. 303–423.
[3] For the authentic god Tetwen, see Meyer, E.: *Geschichte des Altertums*, vol. i, Part II, 3rd ed. (Stuttgart and Berlin 1913, Cotta), p. 210.

peevish, covetous, morose, vain, talkative, but uncapable of friendship and dead to all natural affection. . . . Envy and impotent desires are their prevailing passions. But those objects against which their envy seems principally directed are the vices of the younger sort and the deaths of the old. By reflecting on the former, they find themselves cut off from all possibility of pleasure; and whenever they see a funeral they lament and repine that others are gone to an harbour of rest to which they themselves never can hope to arrive. They have no remembrance of anything but what they learned and observed in their youth and middle age, and even that is very imperfect. And, for the truth or particulars of any fact, it is safer to depend on common traditions than upon their best recollections. . . .

'The language of this country being always upon the flux, the Struldbrugs of one age do not understand those of another, neither are they able after two hundred years to hold any conversation (farther than by a few general words) with their neighbours the mortals; and thus they lie under the disadvantage of living like foreigners in their own country. . . .

'They were the most mortifying sight I ever beheld. . . . Besides the usual deformities in extreme old age, they acquired an additional ghastliness, in proportion to their number of years, which is not to be described; and among half a dozen I soon distinguished which was the eldest, although there was not above a century or two between them.'[1]

For any human soul or human institution, an immortality in This World would prove a martyrdom, even if it were unaccompanied by either physical decrepitude or mental senility.

> Eadem sunt omnia semper.
> si tibi non annis corpus iam marcet et artus
> confecti languent, eadem tamen omnia restant,
> omnia si pergas vivendo vincere saecla,
> atque etiam potius, si nunquam sis moriturus.[2]

'In this sense it would be true to say that any man of forty who is endowed with moderate intelligence has seen—in the light of the uniformity of Nature—the entire Past and Future';[3] and, if this estimate of the capacity of human souls for experience strikes the reader as an inordinately low one, he may find the reason in the character of the age in which the philosopher-emperor happened to live; for an 'Indian Summer' is an age of boredom. The price of the Roman Peace was the forfeiture of Hellenic liberty;[4] and, though that liberty might always have been the privilege of a minority, and this privileged minority might latterly have turned irresponsible and oppressive,[5] it was manifest in retrospect that the turbulent wickedness of the Ciceronian climax of an Hellenic 'Time of Troubles' had provided a wealth of exciting and inspiring themes for Roman public speakers which their epigoni in a smugly ordered Trajanic epoch might conventionally condemn as

---

[1] Swift, Jonathan: *Travels into Several Remote Nations of the World by Lemuel Gulliver*, Part III: 'A Voyage to Laputa, &c.', chap. x.
[2] Lucretius: *De Rerum Natura*, Book III, ll. 945–9.
[3] Aurelius Antoninus, Marcus: *Meditations*, Book XI, ch. 1, quoted in VI. vi. 137.
[4] 'Caesar Augustus . . . dedit . . . iura quis pace et principe uteremur' (Tacitus: *Annals*, Book III, chap. 28).
[5] 'Corruptissimâ re publicâ plurimae leges . . . continua discordia, non mos, non ius; deterrima quaeque impune ac multa honesta exitio fuere' (Tacitus, loc. cit.).

horrors not *nostri saeculi*[1] but must secretly envy as they found themselves perpetually failing in their laborious efforts to substitute far-
fetched artifice for the stimulus of importunate life.[2]

The doom of Tithonus may overtake a whole society as well as an
individual soul.

'Un peuple marche, vit, fonctionne, souvent même grandit après que
le mobile générateur de sa vie et de sa gloire a cessé d'être.'[3]

On the morrow of the breakdown of the Hellenic Society, Plato, seeking
anxiously to safeguard the Hellenic Civilization against a further fall by
pegging it in a securely rigid posture,[4] had idealized the comparative
stability of the Egyptiac culture;[5] and a thousand years later, when this
Egyptiac culture was still in being while the Hellenic Civilization had
arrived at its last agonies, the last of the Neoplatonists pushed their
reputed master's sentimentality to an almost frenzied pitch of uncritical
adoration.[6]

Thanks to the obstinacy of the Egyptiac universal state in again and
again insisting on returning to life after its body, like Êr's, had been duly
laid upon the salutary funeral pyre,[7] the Egyptiac Society lived to see its
contemporaries—the Minoan and Sumeric civilizations and the Indus
Culture—all pass away and give place to successors of a younger generation, some of which passed away in their turn while the Egyptiac Society
still kept alive. Egyptiac students of history could have observed—if they
had had the curiosity to observe—the birth and death of the First Syriac,[8]
Hittite, and Babylonic offspring of the Sumeric Civilization, and the rise
and decline of the Syriac and Hellenic offspring of the Minoan. Yet, even
if they had made the most of this intellectual opportunity, would it have
been worth the spiritual price? The fabulously long-drawn-out epilogue
to the broken-down Egyptiac Society's natural term of life[9] was an
alternation between dull stretches of boredom, in which the victim lay
prone, an ἄχθος ἀρούρης,[10] in a cataleptic trance, and hectic bouts of
demonic energy into which this somnolent society was galvanized by the
impacts of alien bodies social.

The Egyptiac reactions to these impacts of foreign bodies may be
likened to the successive explosions that keep a jet-plane in the air. The
first recurrence of the Egyptiac universal state in the form of 'the New
Empire' was a consequence of Amosis' 'Zealot' reaction against the
tincture of Sumeric culture in the Hyksos barbarians who had swooped

---

[1] Traianus, Marcus Ulpius, in *Correspondence between C. Plinius Secundus and M.
Ulpius Traianus*, Letter xcvii [xcviii].
[2] This point is made by Tacitus in his *Dialogus de Oratoribus*, chap. 36, § 1, chap. 38,
§ 2, and chap. 41, § 5, quoted in V. vi. 80, n. 5.
[3] De Gobineau, J. A.: *Essai sur l'Inégalité des Races Humaines* (Paris 1853–5, Firmin-
Didot, 4 vols.), vol. i, p. 52.
[4] For this practical purpose of the construction of utopias, see III. iii. 88–106.
[5] See, for example, *Timaeus*, 21A–25D, especially the passages quoted in IV. iv. 24–25.
[6] For the êthos of these cranky but not ignoble fighters of Hellenism's last rearguard
action, see V. v. 565–7 and 680–3.
[7] For the myth of Êr the Armenian, see Plato: *Respublica*, Book X, 614B–621D, to
which Aelius Aristeides alludes in the passage cited on p. 44, above.
[8] For this abortive First Syriac Civilization, see II. ii. 388–91.
[9] See I. i. 136–46 and IV. iv. 84–86.
[10] *Iliad*, Book XVIII, l. 104, *et alibi*.

down to batten on the carcass of 'the Middle Empire' after this original Egyptiac universal state had gone into dissolution in due course.[1] The subsequent re-establishment of the Egyptiac universal state in the northern half of the Egyptiac World under the Saïte régime was a consequence of the 'Zealot' reaction of Psammetichus I (*imperabat* 663–609 B.C.)[2] against the Babylonic culture of Assyrian invaders.[3] Psammetichus and his Saïte successors liberated Egypt from the Assyrians, and kept her free from the Assyrians' Neo-Babylonian successors, by employing the prowess of Ionian and Carian mercenaries. The infiltration of Hellenic culture that seeped into Egypt in the wake of these 'brazen men from the sea'[4] produced, within a hundred years, a 'Zealot' reaction against Hellenism in which Amasis (*dominabatur* 566–526 B.C.) usurped the throne of the too complacently xenophile Saïtes with a popular mandate to put the intrusive Hellenes in their place. The Achaemenian conquest of Egypt *circa* 525 B.C.—which the conqueror, Cambyses, rendered doubly odious by persecuting the Egyptiac religion and culture with an un-Achaemenian intolerance[5]—evoked a spate of insurrections, the first in 485–484 B.C., the second lasting from 465 to 449, and the third from 404 to 343, that gave Egypt successive interludes of freedom from alien rule. The Achaemenian reconquest of Egypt in 343 B.C. was final only because it was followed within the next few years by a Macedonian conquest of the whole Achaemenian Empire. Yet the Egyptiac capacity for provocation by alien impacts was not exhausted. The Macedonian conquest of Egypt in 332 B.C. was followed, before the close of the third century B.C., by a fresh spate of insurrections,[6] through which the native Egyptiac community wrung notable concessions from their Hellenic masters. It was not till after the Ptolemaic had given place to a Roman régime that these explosions of xenophobia which had been following one another in the Egyptiac World since the sixteenth century B.C. gave way at last to a counter-movement towards assimilation that culminated in the conversion of the provincial capitals (*metropoleis*) of the 'nomes' into simulacra of Hellenic city-states;[7] and it was not till the fifth century of the Christian Era that this long-delayed liquidation of the petrified Egyptiac culture was completed by a mass-conversion to Christianity.[8]

---

[1] See I. i. 138–9; II. ii. 112; V. v. 351–3; and V. vi. 190.

[2] See II. ii. 116 and IV. iv. 476.

[3] The Psammetichan reaction seems to have surpassed the Amosan in vehemence, if this can be measured in terms of Archaism. The Archaists of the Eighteenth Dynasty, under the mild stimulus of the Sumeric tincture in the Hyksos, sought to leap no farther back up the stream of Egyptiac history than the age of 'the Middle Empire'; the Archaists of the Twenty-Sixth Dynasty, more violently stimulated by the full-blooded Babylonic Civilization of the Assyrians, sought to carry their flying leap right back to the age of 'the Old Kingdom'.

[4] Herodotus, Book II, chap. 152.   [5] See V. v. 704–5.

[6] The first of these native Egyptiac revolts against the Ptolemaic régime broke out *circa* 213/212 B.C. according to *The Cambridge Ancient History*, vol. vii (Cambridge 1928, University Press), pp. 151–2; in 216 B.C. according to Tarn, W. W.: *The Hellenistic Age* (London 1927, Arnold), pp. 161–4. The next insurrection followed *circa* 189–184 B.C.

[7] See IX. viii. 408 and 586.

[8] Even this final apostasy from their ancestral civilization did not cure the Egyptians of a xenophobia which, by that time, had been their breath of life for two thousand years. The Christianity to which they and their Hellenic contemporaries were simultaneously converted did not bridge the gulf between the Egyptians and their alien masters. Before the fifth century was over, the Egyptians had transferred their religious allegiance from the Catholic—or, as they termed it, 'Imperial' (Melchite)—Church (see II. ii. 236, n. 1,

The same rhythm of trance-like somnolence alternating with out-bursts of fanatical xenophobia can be discerned in the epilogue to the history of the Far Eastern Civilization in China.[1] The tincture of Far Eastern Christian culture in the Mongols who had forced upon China an alien universal state evoked a reaction in which the Mongols were evicted and their dominion over China was replaced by the indigenous universal state of the Ming. Even the Manchu barbarians, who stepped into a political vacuum created by the Ming's collapse and whose taint of Far Eastern Christian culture was less noticeable than their receptivity in adopting the Chinese way of life, aroused a popular opposition which, in Southern China at any rate, never ceased to maintain itself underground and broke out into the open again at last in the T'aip'ing insurrection of A.D. 1852–64.[2] The infiltration of the Early Modern Western Civilization, in its Catholic Christian form, in the sixteenth and seventeenth centuries of the Christian Era provoked the proscrip-tion of Catholicism in the first quarter of the eighteenth century. The blasting open of the sea-gates of China for Western trade by military force between A.D. 1839 and A.D. 1861 provoked the retort in kind of the anti-Western 'Boxer' Rising of A.D. 1900; and the Manchu Dynasty was overthrown in A.D. 1911 in retribution for the double crime of being ineradicably alien itself and at the same time showing itself incompetent to keep the now far more formidable alien force of Western penetration at bay.[3]

In the trance-like phases of this ghastly alternating rhythm, the Egyptiac and the Chinese Society recall the figure of Lot's wife trans-formed into a pillar of salt as the retribution for her forbidden back-ward glance at the perishing Cities of the Plain. In the furious bouts in

and IV. iv. 86) to a Monophysitism that could serve them as an expression of their anti-Hellenic feelings. This 'cultural isolationism' survived down to the twentieth century of the Christian Era, some seven centuries after the mass-conversion of all but a small minority of the Egyptian people from Monophysitism to Islam and after the complete replacement of Coptic by Arabic as the living language of Christian and Muslim Egypt-ians alike. In the twentieth century of the Christian Era, when a Westernizing Egyptian intelligentsia was aspiring to make Egypt the cultural and perhaps even the political metropolis of the Arabic World of the day, the Egyptian fallāhīn—Arabic-speaking Muslims though they now were—felt no more at home with their Asiatic Arab co-religionists than their progenitors had felt with the Hyksos, Assyrians, Persians, and Hellenes. The home-sickness of the Egyptian labour corps that had been sent to Palestine and 'Irāq during the war of A.D. 1914–18 was one of the causes of the Egyptian insurrec-tion of A.D. 1919 against a British régime.

  [1] See IV. iv. 86–88; V. v. 3–4, 54, and 348–51.
  [2] For the T'aip'ing insurrection, see V. v. 107 and 112. Since the T'aip'ing move-ment was to some extent stimulated by Western Protestantism, its suppression by the Imperial Government was also in some sense an anti-alien movement, like the con-temporary suppression of the Muslim insurrections in Kansu and Yunnan. But the Imperial Government did not get the upper hand over the Western-stimulated T'aip'ing until it had itself enlisted Western military leadership and organization by placing its own forces under the command of General Gordon (see V. vi. 208).
  [3] The 'Boxer' Rising was anti-Manchu mainly for the reason that the decrepit Manchu régime of the day was only ineffectively anti-Western. From the T'aip'ing in-surrection onwards, all Chinese revolts were directly anti-Manchu were also in-directly anti-Western. We are reminded of the anti-Western impetus of the Wahhābī reaction against the Ottoman Empire of Sultan Selīm III and the Mahdist reaction against the Egypt of Khedive Ismā'īl (see IV. iv. 76–79; V. v. 294–6, 329, and 333–4; and IX. viii. 601–2). The two subsequent counter-movements towards assimilation—to Western culture through the Kuomintang and to Russian culture through Com-munism—were counterparts of the successive conversions of an Egyptiac Society to Hellenism and to Christianity under the Roman Empire.

which these same societies are galvanized into action by the stimulus of
an alien energy that they abhor, they call up the more horrifying image
of Life-in-Death as she displayed herself to the Ancient Mariner.

> The western wave was all aflame,
> The day was wellnigh done!
> Almost upon the western wave
> Rested the broad, bright Sun;
> When that strange shape drove suddenly
> Betwixt us and the Sun. . . .
>
> Are those her ribs through which the Sun
> Did peer, as through a grate?
> And is that woman all her crew?
> Is that a Death? and are there two?
> Is Death that woman's mate?
>
> Her lips were red, her looks were free,
> Her locks were yellow as gold:
> Her skin was as white as leprosy,
> The Nightmare Life-in-Death was she
> Who thicks man's blood with cold.[1]

Happily in this instance life is kinder than legend, for the sentence
of immortality that mythology has passed on Tithonus and the Struldbrugs is commuted in real life to a not interminable longevity. Marcus's
disillusioned man of forty must die at last though he may outlive his
zest for life by fifty or sixty years; and a universal state that kicks again
and again against the pricks of death will weather away, in the course of
ages, like the pillar of salt that was fabled to be the petrified substance of
a once living woman. The struggle for the dreadful prize of immortality
is actually foredoomed to failure.

> Nec prorsum vitam ducendo demimus hilum
> tempore de mortis nec delibare valemus
> quo minus esse diu possimus forte perempti.
> proinde licet quot vis vivendo condere saecla:
> mors aeterna tamen nilo minus illa manebit,
> nec minus ille diu iam non erit, ex hodierno
> lumine qui finem vitai fecit, et ille
> mensibus atque annis qui multis occidit ante.[2]

---

[1] Coleridge, S. T.: *The Rime of the Ancient Mariner.* In XII. ix. 412–13 this image is
applied to the Western Civilization's situation in the twentieth century of the Christian
Era.

[2] Lucretius: *De Rerum Natura*, Book III, ll. 1087–94.

C. UNIVERSAL STATES AS MEANS

(I) THE PRICE OF EUTHANASIA

THE attempt to secure immortality in This World is a vain effort, whether blind or deliberate, to thwart the economy of Nature.

> Cedit enim rerum novitate extrusa vetustas
> semper, et ex aliis aliud reparare necessest . . .
> materies opus est ut crescant postera saecla;
> quae tamen omnia te vitâ perfuncta sequentur;
> nec minus ergo ante haec quam tu cecidere, cadentque.
> sic alid ex alio nunquam desistet oriri,
> vitaque mancipio nulli datur, omnibus usu.[1]

The fate of Tithonus testifies that 'whosoever will save his life shall lose it'; but is it likewise true that 'whosoever will lose his life for My sake, the same shall save it?'[2] In an earlier version of this saying, it is driven home still more pointedly that the sacrifice has to be altruistic in order to be efficacious. 'Whosoever shall lose his life for My sake and the Gospel's, the same shall save it.'[3] On this showing, a universal state that eschews the vain quest for immortality and aspires to euthanasia must emulate the Phoenix. It must not only sacrifice its own life; it must make this sacrifice for the sake of something beyond itself. Such voluntary altruism is unheard-of in any universal state and indeed in any institution, since the besetting sin of all institutions is to become idolized ends in themselves.[4] There had indeed been universal states which, through a fortunate failure to bring upon themselves Tithonus's fate, had won the Phoenix's reward without having risen to the Phoenix's virtue. The Phoenix's reward for the agony of being burnt alive is to conjure up his own double out of his ashes; and there had been universal states which, by dying betimes, had won this reward for the moribund civilizations of which they had been the last political embodiments. For example, the Western and Orthodox Christian civilizations had sprung from the ashes of the Roman Empire,[5] which had been the Hellenic universal state; the Iranic and Arabic civilizations from the ashes of the 'Abbasid Caliphate,[6] which had been the Syriac universal state; the Hellenic and Syriac civilizations themselves from the ashes of Cnossos, the seat of 'the thalassocracy of Minos';[7] the Babylonic and Hittite civilizations, and perhaps the Indic Civilization too, from the ashes of the Empire of the Four Quarters,[8] which had been the Sumeric universal state; the Hindu Civilization from the ashes of the Guptan Empire,[9] which had been the Indic universal state; the Far Eastern Civilization from the ashes of the Han Empire,[10] which had been the Sinic universal state; the Mexic and Yucatec civilizations from the ashes of the 'First Empire' of the Mayas,[11] which had been the Mayan universal state and

---

[1] Lucretius: op. cit., Book III, ll. 964–5 and 967–71, quoted in I. i. 48.
[2] Luke ix. 24; cf. Matt. xvi. 25 and x. 39.   [3] Mark viii. 35.
[4] See IV. iv. 303–423.   [5] See xi, maps 33 and 34.
[6] See xi, map 50.   [7] See xi, maps 15 and 16.   [8] See xi, map 11.
[9] See xi, map 30.   [10] See xi, maps 27A and 28.   [11] See xi, maps 70 and 71.

which, on one interpretation of the fragmentary and cryptic evidence as
to the circumstances of its demise, would have been the only universal
state so far known to history that had gone into voluntary liquidation.[1] It
is indeed something of a miracle that an institution that is a by-product
of social disintegration should play any part at all in a fresh act of
creation. Yet, before we attempt to assess what the Phoenix's reward
amounts to, we must ask ourselves whether the mere reproduction of its
own kind is after all the highest purpose that a broken-down civilization
can hope to serve. We will not beg that question, but will reserve it for
discussion later.[2] What concerns us in our present inquiry is the possibility that a universal state may find euthanasia in spite of itself; and we
can see at once that this unsought and unmerited good fortune can only
be obtained through the tender mercy of God in the guise of stern compulsion.

'Lead me, O Zeus, and thou too, Fate, to that goal, whatsoe'er it be, to
which ye have posted me. I will follow without flinching—though, if I
turn coward and hang back, I shall follow just the same.'[3]

The hard but saving truth thus baldly stated by a Stoic philosopher has
been expressed by a Christian seer in more movingly mysterious words.

'When thou wast young, thou girdedst thyself and walkedst whither thou
wouldest; but, when thou shalt be old, thou shalt stretch forth thy hands
and another shall gird thee and carry thee whither thou wouldest not.'[4]

The grace of God can lead even the reluctant soul or society into sharing
in God's creative work. In the simile of the sowing of the seed[5] the issue
between freedom and compulsion is left dormant.

The destinies of universal states thus prove to be paradoxical. These
imposing polities are, as we have seen,[6] the last works of dominant
minorities in the disintegrating bodies social of moribund civilizations,
and these dominant minorities are far indeed from consciously accepting
the role of self-abnegation that is evidently the only condition on which
their latest handiwork can bear fruit. Their conscious purpose, in every
case, is to preserve themselves by conserving the wasting energies of the
society with whose fortunes their own are bound up, and their intention
in establishing a universal state is to use it as a means to this self-
regarding end. This intention, however, is never fulfilled. A universal
state, however long its life may be drawn out, always proves to have been
the last phase of a society before its extinction, and the pursuit of the
mirage of immortality, into which a dominant minority is misled through
mistaking its ephemeral universal state for the goal of human endeavours,
leads the deluded pursuer towards the unsuspected and uninviting goal
of petrifaction, from which the only means of release is the ignominious

---

[1] For alternative possible explanations of the abandonment of the cities of the First
Empire of the Mayas, see Morley, S. G.: *The Ancient Maya* (Palo Alto, Cal. 1946,
Stanford University Press), pp. 67–72, and the present Study, I. i. 125–6 and II. ii.
413–20.   [2] On pp. 422–3, below.
[3] Cleanthes: *Hymn to Zeus*. The original Greek text has been quoted from von Arnim,
J.: *Stoicorum Veterum Fragmenta*, vol. i (Berlin and Leipzig 1905 Teubner), p. 118, in
III. iii. 47, n. 1, and in V. v. 421.   [4] John xxi. 18.
[5] See III. iii. 256–9 and V. vi. 99.   [6] In V. v. 35–57.

fate of eventually being swallowed up and assimilated by an alien civilization.[1] If a dominant minority takes the contrary path that leads through self-abnegation to a fresh opportunity for sharing in a creative act, it always does so in spite of itself. A dominant minority is incapable either of the resignation with which Moses accepted the sentence that he should see the Promised Land, but should not go over thither, or of the selflessness with which he carried out his instructions to charge, encourage, and strengthen his designated successor Joshua for the enviable mission of reaping the fruits of Moses' own thankless labours.[2] A dominant minority will never show the generosity of David in assembling the materials for a Temple which not he but Solomon is to build,[3] or the humility of John the Baptist in confessing 'I am not the Christ';[4] 'he that cometh after me is preferred before me';[5] 'he must increase, but I must decrease'.[6] The actor who has thus been forced into playing the forerunner's part after having failed in an attempt to pose as the heir of the Kingdom[7] is not a sublime or sympathetic figure; yet even a grudging performance may fulfil the playwright's purpose by carrying out his plot to its designed denouement.

The makers and masters of a universal state have perhaps one excuse for thus kicking against the pricks. However low their handiwork may rank in the general scale of creative achievements, it is at any rate indisputably the highest representative of its kind. Whereas parochial states prey on one another, and for this pernicious purpose cause human beings to shed one another's blood and to regard an anti-social practice as a public virtue, universal states come into existence in order to put a stop to wars and to substitute co-operation for bloodshed. If even universal states prove to be, not permanent ends in themselves, but merely ephemeral creatures whose happiest destiny is to find euthanasia by spending themselves in the service of others, this suggests that, in the hierarchy of human institutions, the place of states in general must be a relatively low one.

If a universal state finds its significance as a means for the performance of services, who are its beneficiaries? They must be one or other of three possible candidates for the part—the internal proletariat or external proletariat of the moribund society itself, or some alien civilization which is its contemporary—and in serving the internal proletariat a universal state will be ministering to one of the higher religions that make their epiphany in the internal proletariat's bosom. In the traditional language of an outgoing Early Modern Age of Western Christian history,

'Tous les grands empires que nous avons vus sur la terre ont concouru par divers moyens au bien de la Religion et à la gloire de Dieu, comme Dieu même l'a déclaré par ses prophètes.'[8]

---

[1] For this fate, which is one of the alternative possible ends of a disintegrating civilization, see IV. iv. 76–114.

[2] Deut. xxxiv. 1–6; cf. Deut. iii. 23–28 and Num. xxvii. 12–14.

[3] I Chron. xxii. [4] John i. 20 and iii. 28.

[5] John i. 15. [6] John iii. 30.

[7] For the relation between heirs of the Kingdom and their forerunners in the series of saviours with the sword, see V. vi. 185–95.

[8] Bossuet, J.-B.: *Discours sur l'Histoire Universelle*, 3rd ed. (Paris 1700), Troisième Partie, chap. i.

(II) SERVICES AND BENEFICIARIES

(a) THE CONDUCTIVITY OF UNIVERSAL STATES

Our next task is to make an empirical survey of the services involuntarily offered by universal states and of the uses made of these facilities by internal proletariats, external proletariats, and alien civilizations; but we have first to find the answer to a preliminary question: How can any services at all be rendered to anyone by an institution that is passive, conservative, archaistic, and in fact negative in every respect?

'The world empire of Rome was a negative phenomenon: the result, not of any surplus of power on the one side (the Romans ceased to enjoy that after [their victory at] Zama), but of an absence of resistance on the other side. It would be quite untrue to say that the Romans conquered the World. They merely took possession of something that was lying about for anyone to pick up. The Roman Empire was brought into existence, not by an extreme exertion of Rome's total military and financial energies, as these had once been exerted against Carthage, but through a renunciation, by the contemporary Oriental World, of the externals of self-determination. . . . The petrified remains of Imperialism are to be seen in empires like the Egyptian, the Chinese and the Roman and in societies like the Indian World and the World of Islam, which remain in existence for hundreds and thousands of years and may pass from one conqueror's hand to another's: dead bodies, shapeless masses of humanity from which the soul has departed, the used-up material of a great historical past.[1] The imperialism that leaves such débris is the typical symptom of social dissolution.'[2]

How—in terms of the expressive Sinic notation for the rhythm of the Universe[3]—can so unpromising a Yin-state give rise to a new burst of Yang-activity? It is easy, of course, to see that, if once a spark of creative energy has been kindled in the shelter of a universal state, it will have a chance of swelling into a steady flame which it might never have had if it had been exposed to the buffeting blast of a Time of Troubles. The establishment of a universal state marks the beginning of the second rally in the succession of bouts of the rhythm of Rout-and-Rally through which the life of a civilization runs out from breakdown to dissolution,[4] and this second rally is usually the most vigorous in the series. But this service, though valuable, is negative. What feature in the social situation arising under a universal state is the positive source of that new capacity to create, which is the supreme benefit that a universal state confers on its beneficiaries, though it is apparently unable to profit by it for its own account? Perhaps one clue is to be found in the tendency shown by

---

[1] This aspect of the psychological condition of the subject populations of universal states has been discussed in the present Study in V. v. 60–95.—A.J.T.

[2] Spengler, Oswald: *Der Untergang des Abendlandes*, vol. i, 11th–14th edition (Munich 1920, Beck), p. 51. Cp. vol. ii, 1st–15th edition (Munich 1922, Beck), p. 529, quoted in V. v. 620, n. 1. The pith of the point that Spengler is making in these two passages is concentrated in Francis Bacon's dictum, quoted on p. 110, below, that 'it was not the Romans that spread upon the World, but it was the World that spread upon the Romans'.

[3] For the Sinic conception of Yin and Yang, see II. i. 201–3.

[4] This rhythm of disintegration has been analysed in V. vi. 278–87.

Archaism to defeat itself by being inveigled into construction in its efforts to justify itself by 'making things work'.[1]

A universal state is pushed into constructive action primarily, no doubt, by the impulse, which is strong in every state, to work for its own self-preservation and do whatever may prove necessary for this purpose. But, though this impulse may be the primary one, it is not the predominant one in this case; for a universal state is not subject to the pressure from other representatives of its kind which is so potent an influence in the life of parochial states—especially at the climax of a Time of Troubles, when the struggle for existence between the warring parochial states of a disintegrating society is apt to attain its highest degree of intensity. The establishment of a universal state brings with it an abrupt transition from internecine warfare to profound peace; and the victims of a change that is a blessing for Society as a whole might appraise the victorious empire-builders' achievement by applying to it the ironic judgement: 'Ubi solitudinem faciunt, pacem appellant.'[2] A universal state is established through a knock-out blow by which some single parochial state wipes all competitors off the map and so emerges from the struggle as the sole survivor. A universal state is *ex hypothesi* unique within its own world; and the prestige of this uniqueness works together with the *vis inertiae* of an exhausted society to keep a universal state in being when once it has come into existence. A universal state on the morrow of its foundation thus has little cause to be concerned over its own security. Instances can, no doubt, be found in which this has been the motive of a universal state's policy. For example, the first founder of the Sinic universal state, Ts'in She Hwang-ti, deliberately obliterated the old inter-state frontiers and remapped his now unified Sinic World into a new pattern of artificial provinces which cut across the old pattern of historic principalities; and the second founder, Han Liu Pang, who began by discarding Ts'in She Hwang-ti's new political map as an unnecessarily revolutionary innovation, was led by his own experience virtually to reimpose it.[3] The Napoleonic Empire,[4] which was the abortive universal state of the medieval Western city-state cosmos,[5] employed the same device in its efforts to wipe out the traces of the states that it had supplanted.[6] Again, the Inca makers and masters of an Andean universal state modified and systematized the institutions of the conquered peoples, though this without destroying them;[7] and the Imperial Roman Government displayed what might seem to be an excessive nervousness in suppressing all manner of private associations, and showing some suspicion even of such humble and apparently harmless varieties of the species as friendly societies and funeral clubs. Such symptoms are, however, rare on the whole, and this is an indication

---

[1] This self-defeat of Archaism has been examined in V. vi. 94–97.
[2] Tacitus: *Agricola*, chap. 30, § 7.
[3] See pp. 169–74, below.
[4] See xi, map 60.   [5] See V. v. 619–42.
[6] This remapping of the medieval Western city-state cosmos by Napoleon and of the Sinic World by Ts'in She Hwang-ti and Han Liu Pang is an instance of the breach in institutions that is one of the manifestations of Futurism (see V. vi. 107–11).
[7] See Markham, Sir C.: *The Incas of Peru* (London 1910, Smith Elder), p. 161. See also the other authorities quoted in the present Study, V. v. 90, n. 2.

that, in the policy of universal states, the motive of self-preservation does not play an important part.

A different motive for action, which is strong in proportion to the weakness of the universal state's concern for self-preservation, is supplied by the need for conserving, not a state that is universal in virtue of having no surviving competitors, but the society itself that has been unified politically in the universal state—or, rather, what remains of this society and its institutions by the time when the tardy and violent imposition of peace by a single surviving Power has put an end at last to the long-drawn-out and ever-mounting agony of a Time of Troubles. In the course of that terrible experience, most of the institutions inherited from the age of growth have either been destroyed outright or else been so badly hurt that, even after the process of attrition has been arrested by the establishment of the universal state, they crumble and collapse, one after another, through the delayed but inescapable effects of fatal injuries previously received. The inclusion of the surviving fabric of the shattered society within the universal state's political framework does not avail either to restore what has already perished or to prevent the progressive collapse of the remainder; and the menace of this immense and constantly extending social vacuum compels the Government of the universal state to act against its own inclinations by constructing stop-gap institutions to fill the void, as the only means open to it of conserving Society itself—the fundamental task that is the universal state's *raison d'être*.

A classic illustration of this necessity of stepping ever farther into an ever-widening breach is afforded by the administrative history of the Roman Empire during the two centuries following its establishment in 31 B.C. as a result of the Battle of Actium. The Roman *arcanum imperii* was the principle of indirect rule. The Hellenic universal state was conceived of by its Roman founders as an association of self-governing city-states[1] with a fringe of autonomous principalities in regions where the Hellenic culture had not yet struck political root. The burden of administration—which, even at the end of an Hellenic Time of Troubles, was still, in the public estimation, an honourable and covetable load—was to be left resting on the shoulders of these responsible self-governing local authorities; the Imperial Government was to confine itself to the twofold task of keeping the local communities in harmony with one another and protecting them against attack on the part of the outer barbarians; and, for these limited Imperial activities, a slender military framework and light political superstructure were all that was required. This fundamental policy was never deliberately revised; yet, if we resurvey the Roman Empire as it emerged from a spell of two centuries of Roman Peace, we shall find that its administrative structure had in fact been transformed as a result of innovations that were reluctant and piecemeal but were far-reaching in their cumulative effect because they were all in the same direction.

By the end of the reign of Marcus Aurelius (*imperabat* A.D. 161-80) the last of the client principalities had been *gleichgeschaltet* with the

---

[1] See IV. iv. 310.

provinces,[1] and, more significant still, the provinces themselves had become organs of direct administration instead of remaining mere frameworks for local groups of self-administering city-states. The cause of these far-going moves towards a centralization of world-government was not any desire on the part of the Imperial authorities to take over the responsibility for details; it was a progressive loss of efficiency on the part of the local authorities that forced the Imperial Government to step in. In the generation of Augustus the government provided by client princes of the stamp of Herod the Great had in general been as effective as it had been ruthless. Among other things, it had been observed that these were more active than the Roman governors of adjoining provinces in defending their territories against the raids of pirates from beyond the pale.[2] The city-states, again, whatever their juridical status, had been mostly successful in still finding sufficient numbers of citizens of sufficient public spirit, integrity, ability, and affluence to administer their affairs without remuneration and to consider themselves richly rewarded by the honour and prestige which local office still carried with it. In the course of the next two centuries the human resources for the conduct of local government gradually ran dry, and the Central Government, faced with this increasing dearth of the local administrative talent on which it had been accustomed to rely, found itself constrained not only to replace client princes by Imperial governors but to put the administration of the city-states in the hands of 'city managers' who were appointed by the Imperial authorities instead of being elected (as the city-state magistrates were) by the local notables, and who were responsible, through the provincial governor, to the Emperor himself.

In the second century of the Empire's existence, at the very opening of a delusive 'Indian Summer',[3] we can follow the progress of this disquieting administrative development in the famous correspondence between the Emperor Trajan (*imperabat* A.D. 98–117) and his friend and subordinate Pliny the Younger during the latter's term of service as governor of the province of Bithynia. Before the end of the story, the whole administration of the Roman Empire, from top to bottom, had passed into the hands of a hierarchically organized bureaucracy, while the self-complacent local magistrates and town councillors of the once self-governing city-states had been degraded into becoming the unwilling

---

[1] See further p. 166, below. The religious consequences of this process of *Gleichschaltung*—which is not a peculiarity of the Roman Empire but is characteristic of universal states as a species—have been touched upon in V. vi. 36.

[2] Strabo, writing on the morrow of the establishment of the Augustan Peace, makes the following observation at the end of his description of the piratical raids into the domain of the Hellenic universal state which were at that time the main source of livelihood for the barbarians (Achaei, Zygi, Heniochi) inhabiting the strip of inhospitable country between the crest of the North-Western Caucasus Range and the north-eastern coast of the Black Sea:

'In places under [the] autocratic rule [of princes of client states of the Roman Empire] the victims [of these piratical raids] are afforded some protection by their rulers; for the princes make frequent counter-attacks and bring the war-canoes down, crews and all. The territory under direct Roman administration receives less effective protection owing to the indifference shown by the non-permanent lieutenant-governors sent out from Rome' (Strabo: *Geographica*, Book XI, chap. ii, § 12 (C 496)).

[3] For these 'Indian Summers' in the lives of universal states, see IV. iv. 58–70.

instruments of the central exchequer for extracting ruinously heavy taxes from the local notables.[1]

The central authorities themselves had been no more eager to impose these changes than the local authorities had been to suffer them. Both alike had been the victims of *force majeure*; and, in yielding to such necessity, the government of a universal state is indeed defeating its own ends, since the new institutions which it reluctantly constructs with a conservative intention inevitably have an innovating effect. The consequences are revolutionary because these new institutions are highly 'conductive'. In a previous context[2] we have seen that two leading motifs in the *Zeitgeist* of an age of social disintegration are a sense of promiscuity and a sense of unity; and, though these two psychological tendencies may be antithetical from the subjective standpoint, they conspire to produce an identical objective result. Receptivity is a distinguishing mark of the empire-builders themselves,[3] notwithstanding their conservative intentions, and this undesired and unvalued characteristic of theirs may have been one of the causes of their victory in their life-and-death struggle, during a Time of Troubles, with their competitors in command of the other parochial states of their world for the prize of surviving to become the founders of the ultimate universal state. This dominant spirit of the age endows the new stop-gap institutions thrown up by a universal state with a 'conductivity' comparable to that which the Ocean and the Steppe derive, not from a human psychological atmosphere, but from their own physical nature.[4]

'As the surface of the Earth bears all Mankind, so Rome receives all the peoples of the Earth into her bosom, as the rivers are received by the sea.'[5]

And the spectacle of the same universal state had suggested the same simile to the writer of this Study, before he had become acquainted with the passage, just quoted, from the pen of a Greek man of letters who knew the Roman Empire at first hand during the last days of its 'Indian Summer'.

'The writer can best express his personal feeling about the Empire in a parable. It was like the sea round whose shores its network of city-states was strung. The Mediterranean seems at first sight a poor substitute for the rivers that have given their waters to make it. Those were living waters, whether they ran muddy or clear; the sea seems just salt and still and dead. But, as soon as we study the sea, we find movement and life there also. There are silent currents circulating perpetually from one part to another, and the surface water that seems to be lost by evaporation is not really lost, but will descend in distant places and seasons, with its bitterness all distilled away, as life-giving rain. And, as these surface-waters are drawn off into the clouds, their place is taken by lower layers continually rising from the depths. The sea itself is in constant and creative motion, but the influence of this great body of water extends far beyond its shores.

---

[1] See III. iii. 99–100.
[2] In V. v. 439–568 and V. vi. 1–49.   [3] See V. v. 439–45.
[4] The conductivity of Nomadism has been noticed in III. iii. 391–4.
[5] Aristeides, P. Aelius: *In Romam*, § 62 in B. Keil's edition (*Aelii Aristidis Quae Supersunt Omnia*, vol. ii (Berlin 1898, Weidmann), p. 108), quoted in V. v. 344.

One finds it softening the extremes of temperature, quickening the vegetation, and prospering the life of animals and men, in the distant heart of continents and among peoples that have never heard its name.'[1]

The social movements that make their way through the conductive medium of a universal state are in fact both horizontal and vertical. Examples of horizontal motion are the circulation of medicinal herbs in the Roman Empire and the spread of the use of paper from the eastern to the western extremity of the Arab Caliphate.

'Different herbs', says Pliny the Elder, 'are brought from different quarters to and fro all over the World for the welfare of the Human Race. The immense majesty of the Roman Peace reveals to one another not merely human beings, in all their diversity of countries and nationalities, but also the mountains and the ranges that tower up into the clouds, with their fauna and flora. God grant that this divine benefaction may be eternal. The gift bestowed by the Romans on Mankind can only be described as a new form of light.'[2]

As for the transit of the Far Eastern invention of paper across the conductive expanse of the Arab Caliphate, this was impressively rapid. Reaching Samarqand from China in A.D. 751, the use of paper had spread to Baghdad by A.D. 793, to Cairo by A.D. 900, to Fez (Fas), almost within sight of the Atlantic, by about A.D. 1100, and to Jativa in the Iberian Peninsula by A.D. 1150.[3]

The vertical movements are sometimes more elusive but often more important in their social effects—as is illustrated by the history of the Tokugawa Shogunate,[4] which was the universal state of the Far Eastern Society in Japan. The Tokugawa régime set itself to insulate Japan from the rest of the World, and was successful for nearly two and a half centuries in maintaining this political *tour de force*; but it found itself powerless to arrest the course of social change within an insulated Japanese Empire, in spite of its efforts to petrify a feudal system, inherited from the preceding 'Time of Troubles', into a permanent dispensation.

'The penetration of money economy in Japan . . . caused a slow but irresistible revolution, culminating in the breakdown of feudal government and the resumption of intercourse with foreign countries after more than two hundred years of seclusion. What opened the doors was not a summons from without but an explosion from within. . . . One of [the] first effects [of the new economic forces] was an increase in the wealth of the townspeople, gained at the expense of the samurai and also of the peasants. . . . The *daimyō* and their retainers spent their money on luxuries produced by the artisans and sold by the tradesmen, so that by about the year [A.D.] 1700, it is said, nearly all their gold and silver had passed into the hands of the townspeople. They then began to buy goods on credit. Before long they were deeply indebted to the merchant class, and were obliged to pledge, or to make forced sales of, their tax-rice. . . . Abuses and disaster followed thick and fast. The merchants took to rice-broking,

---

[1] Toynbee, A. J., in *The Legacy of Greece* (Oxford 1922, Clarendon Press), p. 320.
[2] Plinius Secundus, C.: *Historia Naturalis*, Book XXVII, chap. i (i), § 3.
[3] See Carter, T. F.: *The Invention of Printing in China and its Spread Westward*, revised ed. (New York 1931, Columbia University Press), pp. 97–100; Lévi-Provençal, E.: *L'Espagne Musulmane au Xème Siècle* (Paris 1932, Larose), p. 185.
[4] See xi, map 55c.

and then to speculating. . . . It was the members of one class only, and not all of them, who profited by these conditions. These were the merchants, in particular the brokers and money-lenders, despised *chōnin* or townsmen, who in theory might be killed with impunity by any samurai for mere disrespectful language. Their social status still remained low, but they held the purse and they were in the ascendant. By the year 1700 they were already one of the strongest and most enterprising elements in the state, and the military caste was slowly losing its influence.'[1]

If we regard the year 1590 of the Christian Era, in which Hideyoshi overcame the last resistance to his dictatorship, as the date of the foundation of the Japanese universal state, we perceive that it took little more than a century for the rising of the lower layers of water from the depths to the surface to produce a bloodless social revolution in a society which Hideyoshi's successor Tokugawa Ieyasu and his heirs had sought to freeze into an almost Platonically utopian immobility. This social upheaval was a result of the operation of internal forces within a closed system, without any impulsion from outside the frontiers of the Japanese universal state.

The extent of the resultant change is impressive—and the more so, considering that, for a universal state, the Tokugawa Shogunate was culturally homogeneous to an unusually high degree. Apart from a little pariah community of Dutch business men who were strictly segregated on the islet of Deshima,[2] the only heterogeneous element in the otherwise culturally uniform Japanese life of that age was a barbarian Ainu strain that was socially impotent in so far as it was not already culturally assimilated.[3] In most universal states, such partially assimilated barbarians have been one only—and this the least alien one—of several alien cultural elements. Owing to the tendency of the parochial states of a broken-down civilization in its Time of Troubles to sharpen their weapons in fratricidal conflicts with one another and to take advantage of this dearly bought increase in their military proficiency to conquer neighbouring societies with their left hands while continuing to fight one another with their right hands,[4] most universal states have embraced not only a fringe of conquered barbarians but substantial slices of the domain of one or more alien civilizations as well. Some universal states, again, have been founded by alien empire-builders, and some have been the product of societies within whose bosoms there has already been some degree of cultural variety—even on a reckoning which does not differentiate between march-men and the denizens of the interior of the same social world.[5] Such cultural diversity, which is the rule rather than the exception in the structure of universal states, is apt to heighten the effects of the social 'conductivity' that is characteristic of them all.

[1] Sansom, G. B.: *Japan: A Short Cultural History* (London 1931, Cresset Press), pp. 460–2. See further eundem: *The Western World and Japan* (London 1950, Cresset Press), chaps. ix–xi (pp. 177–289).
[2] See II. ii. 232–3.
[3] For the barbarian frontier of the Far Eastern World in Japan, and for the effect of this frontier on Japanese history, see II. ii. 158–9.
[4] See III. iii. 139–53.
[5] For the distinction between marches and interiors, and its historical importance, see II. ii. 112–207.

No other universal state known to History appears to have been as homogeneous in culture as Japan under the Tokugawa régime. In 'the Middle Empire' of Egypt,[1] in which a fringe of barbarians on the Nubian glacis of its Theban march was one element of variation from the cultural norm of the Egyptiac Society of the age,[2] there was another and more positive feature of cultural diversity in the Empire's culturally Sumeric provinces and client states in Palestine and Coele Syria. As for 'the New Empire',[3] which was a deliberate revival of the original Egyptiac universal state, it accentuated the pattern of its prototype by completing the assimilation of the barbarians of Nubia[4] and by embracing the domain of an abortive First Syriac Civilization in Syria and North-Western Mesopotamia;[5] and this culturally tripartite structure—in which the cultural domain of the civilization through whose disintegration the universal state has been brought into existence is flanked by culturally alien territories annexed at the expense of both barbarians and neighbouring civilizations—appears to be the standard type.

For example, in the Mauryan Empire,[6] which was the original Indic universal state, an Indic cultural core was flanked by an alien province in the Panjab, which had been at least partially Syriacized during a previous period of Achaemenian rule[7] after having been partially barbarized by an antecedent Völkerwanderung of Eurasian Nomads,[8] while in other quarters the Mauryan Empire's Indic core was flanked by ex-barbarian provinces in Southern India and possibly farther afield in both Ceylon and Khotan as well. The Guptan Empire,[9] in which the Mauryan was eventually reintegrated, possessed an ex-barbarian fringe, with an alien Hellenic tincture, in the satrapy that had been founded by Saka war-bands in Gujerat and the North-Western Deccan,[10] and a Hellenized fringe, with a Kushan barbarian dilution, in the territories under its suzerainty in the Panjab. In a Han Empire[11] which was the Sinic universal state, the Sinic World proper was flanked by barbarian annexes in what was eventually to become Southern China, as well as on the Eurasian Steppe, and by an alien province in the Tarim Basin, where the Indic, Syriac, and Hellenic cultures had already met and mingled before this cultural corridor and crucible was annexed to the Han Empire for the first time in the second century B.C. and for the second time in the first century of the Christian Era.[12] In the Roman Empire,[13] which was the Hellenic universal state, a culturally Hellenic core in Western Anatolia, Continental European Greece, Sicily, and Italy, with outlying enclaves in Cilicia, in Syria, at Alexandria, and at Marseilles, was combined with the domain of the submerged Hittite Civilization in Eastern Anatolia, with the homelands of the Syriac and Egyptiac civilizations in Syria and in the Lower Nile Valley, with the colonial domain of the Syriac Civilization in North-West Africa, and with ex-barbarian hinterlands in North-

---

[1] See xi, map 13.
[2] See II. ii. 115.
[3] See xi, map 14.
[4] See II. ii. 115.
[5] For this abortive First Syriac Civilization, see II. ii. 388–91.
[6] See xi, map 23.
[7] One cultural legacy of the Achaemenian régime here was the Kharoshthī script (see V. v. 500).
[8] See pp. 651–2, below.
[9] See xi, map 30.
[10] See V. v. 603–4.
[11] See xi, maps 27A and 28.
[12] See V. v. 144–6.
[13] See xi, map 29.

West Africa and in Western and Central Europe as far as the left bank of the Rhine and the right bank of the Danube.[1]

There are other cases in which this standard cultural pattern has been enriched by some additional element.

In the Muscovite Tsardom[2] a Russian Orthodox Christian core was flanked by a vast ex-barbarian annex extending northwards to the Arctic Ocean and eastwards eventually to the Pacific, and by an Iranic Muslim annex consisting of the sedentary Muslim peoples of the Volga Basin, the Urals, and Western Siberia. This pattern was afterwards complicated by Peter the Great's deliberate substitution of a Westernized for a traditional Orthodox Christian cultural framework for the Russian Orthodox Christian universal state, and by the subsequent annexation of additional alien territories—at the expense of the Islamic World on the Eurasian Steppe and in the Crimea, the Caucasus, and the Oxus–Jaxartes Basin, and at the expense of Western Christendom in the Baltic Provinces, Lithuania, Poland, and Finland.

In the Achaemenian Empire,[3] which was the original Syriac universal state, there was an antecedent cultural diversity, within the Syriac core itself, between the Syrian creators of the Syriac Civilization and their Iranian converts,[4] and a geographical gap between Syria and Iran that was still occupied by the dwindling domain of the gradually disappearing Babylonic culture.[5] The Achaemenian Empire also embraced the domain of the submerged Hittite culture in Eastern Anatolia, the best part of the domain of the Egyptiac Civilization,[6] fringes torn from the Hellenic and Indic worlds, and pockets of partially reclaimed barbarian highlanders and Eurasian Nomads. Moreover, after its life had been prematurely cut short by Alexander the Great, its work was carried on by his political successors, and especially by the Seleucidae, whom it would be more illuminating to describe as alien Hellenic successors of Cyrus and Darius. In the Arab Caliphate,[7] in which the Achaemenian Empire was eventually reintegrated,[8] the Syriac core—in which the earlier diversity between Syrian creators and Iranian converts had been replaced by a cleavage, along approximately the same geographical line, between ex-subjects of the Roman and ex-subjects of the Sasanian Empire—was united politically, by Arab barbarian empire-builders, with barbarian annexes—in North-West Africa, in the fastnesses of Daylam and Tabaristan between the Elburz Mountains and the Caspian Sea,[9] and on the fringes of the Eurasian Steppe adjoining the Oxus–Jaxartes Basin—and with fragments of alien civilizations: a slice of the new-born Hindu World in Sind;[10] the potential domain of an abortive Far Eastern Christian Civilization in the Oxus–Jaxartes Basin;[11] an

---

[1] Leaving out of account the late-acquired and early-lost Transdanubian bridgehead in Dacia.   [2] See xi, map 49.

[3] See xi, maps 20 and 21.   [4] See I. i. 79–82.

[5] For the gradual assimilation of the Babylonic Society by the Syriac, see I. i. 79 and 119; II. ii. 138; IV. iv. 100–3 and 471; V. v. 122–3 and 370.

[6] For the permanent political partition of the Egyptiac World from the middle of the seventh century B.C. onwards, see II. ii. 116.

[7] See xi, map 37.   [8] See I. i. 76–77.

[9] See II. ii. 377–8.   [10] See I. i. 105–6 and II. ii. 130.

[11] See II. ii. 369–85 and 446–52.

Orthodox Christian diasporà in Syria and Egypt; and a fossil of the by then elsewhere extinct Babylonic Society at Harran.[1]

In the Mongol Empire,[2] which was a universal state imposed by alien empire-builders on the main body of the Far Eastern Society in China, the annexes to a Chinese core were unusually extensive—including, as they did, the whole of the Eurasian Nomad World, the whole of Russian Orthodox Christendom, and the ex-Sasanian portion of a Syriac World which by that time was *in extremis*. The Mongols themselves were barbarians with a tincture of Far Eastern Christian culture.[3] In the Manchu empire-builders,[4] who subsequently repeated the Mongols' performance on a less gigantic yet still imposing scale, there was the same tincture in a more diluted form;[5] and the Chinese universal state in its Manchu avatar once again embraced, in addition to its Chinese core, a number of alien annexes: a 'reservoir' of barbarians in the still unfelled backwoods and still virgin steppes of Manchuria, the whole of the Tantric Mahayanian Buddhist World in Tibet, Mongolia, and Zungaria,[6] and the easternmost continental outposts of the Islamic World in the Tarim Basin, the north-western Chinese provinces of Kansu and Shansi, and the south-western Chinese province of Yunnan.[7]

In the Ottoman Empire,[8] which provided, or saddled, the main body of Orthodox Christendom with its universal state, the alien 'Osmanli empire-builders united an Orthodox Christian core with a fringe of Western Christian territory in Hungary, with the whole of the Arabic Muslim World except Morocco, the Sudan, and South-Eastern Arabia, and with pockets of barbarians and semi-barbarians in Serbia, Bosnia, Albania, the Mani, the Caucasus, the Crimea, and on the Arabian Steppe. In the Mughal Empire,[9] which was the Ottoman Empire's counterpart in the Hindu World, the pattern was simpler, since, apart from the Iranic Muslim empire-builders and their co-religionists who had been deposited in the Hindu social environment by earlier waves of invasion from the Middle East and Central Asia,[10] the Mughals' only non-Hindu subjects were the Pathan barbarian highlanders on the north-western fringe of their dominions. When, however, the Mughal Rāj was replaced by a British Rāj,[11] the pattern of the Hindu universal state became more complex; for the advent of a new band of alien empire-builders, which substituted a Western element for an Islamic at the political apex of the Hindu universal state, did not expel the Indian Muslims from the stage of Hindu history, but merely depressed their status to that of a numerically still formidable alien element in the Hindu internal proletariat, so that the Hindu universal state in its second phase combined elements drawn from two alien civilizations with a Pathan barbarian fringe and a Hindu core.

There had been other universal states in which, as in the Mughal

1 See IV. iv. 101, n. 1; V. v. 125, n. 1; and IX. viii. 408, n. 5.
3 See V. v. 348–51.
2 See xi, map 47.
5 See loc. cit.
4 See xi, map 54.
6 See I. i. 35 and 90–2; II. ii. 405, n. 1; IV. iv. 497; and V. v. 309–10.
7 See V. v. 116.
8 See xi, map 51.
9 See xi, map 52.
10 See II. ii. 78; II. ii. 130–1 and 149; IV. iv. 96–99.
11 See xi, map 53.

Empire, the cultural pattern had been less complex than the standard type yet not so simple as that of the Tokugawa Shogunate.

The Empire of Sumer and Akkad,[1] which was the Sumeric universal state, included no representatives of an alien civilization—unless Byblus and other Syrian coast-towns are to be counted as such in virtue of their tincture of Egyptiac culture. On the other hand, the Sumeric Civilization itself was represented in two varieties at least—a Sumero-Akkadian and an Elamite[2]—and in no less than three if the domain of the Indus Culture should prove also to have been included in 'the Empire of the Four Quarters of the World'.[3] Moreover, the Babylonian Amorites, who eventually restored a polity that had been first constructed by the Sumerian Ur-Engur (alias Ur-Nammu) of Ur,[4] were not merely marchmen but marchmen with a barbarian tinge. So, on a broader and a longer view, the cultural pattern of the Sumeric universal state proves to have been less homogeneous than might appear at first sight. 'The thalassocracy of Minos',[5] again, which was the Minoan universal state, probably included representatives of the continental Mycenaean variety of the Minoan culture as well as the creators of that culture in its Cretan homeland, even if it did not embrace any representatives of an alien civilization.

In the Central American World[6] two once distinct sister societies—the Yucatec Civilization and the Mexic—had not yet lost their distinctive characteristics, though they had already been brought together by force of Toltec arms, when the task, and prize, of establishing a Central American universal state was snatched, at the eleventh hour, out of the hands of barbarian Aztec empire-builders by Spanish representatives of an utterly alien Western Christendom.[7] In the Andean World the Empire of the Incas,[8] which was the Andean universal state, already included representatives of the Kara variety of the Andean culture as well as the creators of that culture in the Peruvian coastlands and its propagators on the Peruvian, Bolivian, and Argentinian sections of the Andean Plateau,[9] before the indigenous Incan empire-builders were suddenly and violently replaced by Spanish conquistadores from Western Christendom who turned the Andean World upside-down, with a vigour reminiscent of Alexander the Great's, by proceeding to convert the indigenous population to Christianity and to variegate the social map by studding it with immigrant Spanish landlords[10] and self-governing municipalities.[11]

The Danubian Hapsburg Monarchy,[12] which served as a carapace for Western Christendom against the assaults of the 'Osmanlis, and which,

[1] See xi, maps 10 and 11.
[2] For the distinction between them, see I. i. 117, n. 4.
[3] This possibility has been suggested in I. i. 108.
[4] See I. i. 106 and V. vi. 297–8.
[5] See xi, maps 15 and 16.   [6] See xi, map 71.
[7] See I. i. 123–4.   [8] See xi, map 68.
[9] If we compare the Andean and Sumeric societies in their respective universal state phases, we may see in the coastal communities of Chimu and Nazca the cultural counterparts of Sumer; in the highland communities, south of Ecuador, the counterparts of Akkad; in the Karas of Ecuador the counterparts of Elam; and in the Chibchas of Colombia the counterparts of the makers of 'the Indus Culture'.
[10] See p. 144, below.
[11] See pp. 135 and 145, below.   [12] See xi, map 51.

seen from the south-east, wore the deceptive appearance of being a full-blown Western universal state,[1] set itself, like the Tokugawa Shogunate, to achieve domestic cultural uniformity, but lacked both the ruthlessness and the insularity which, between them, enabled the Japanese isolationists for a time to put their policy into effect. In pursuing its aim of being totally Catholic, the Hapsburg Power did succeed, more or less, in extirpating Protestantism within its frontiers; but the very success of its stand, and eventual counter-attack, against the Ottoman embodiment of an Orthodox Christian universal state broke up the Danubian Monarchy's hardly attained Catholic homogeneity by transferring to Hapsburg from Ottoman rule a stiff-necked minority of Hungarian Protestants and a host of Orthodox Christians of divers nationalities, most of whom proved unwilling to accept the ecclesiastical supremacy of Rome, even when the yoke was proffered in the easy form of Uniatism, while, among those who did accept this relatively light burden, the rank and file remained nearer in heart and mind to their dissident Orthodox ex-co-religionists than they ever came to be to their fellow Catholics who were of the Latin Rite.

The Neo-Babylonian Empire,[2] which was the Babylonic universal state, similarly forfeited its cultural purity—and thereby worked unwittingly for the eventual extinction of the Babylonic Civilization itself—when Nebuchadnezzar conquered and annexed the homeland of the Syriac Civilization west of the Euphrates; and the impress of the indigenous Babylonic culture became progressively fainter as the domain which Nebuchadnezzar had bequeathed to a short line of native successors was incorporated first into the barbaro-Syriac Empire of the Achaemenids and then into the Hellenic Empire of the Seleucids.

Our survey has shown that, in the cultural composition of universal states, a high degree of diversity is the rule; and, in the light of this fact, it is evident that one effect of the 'conductivity' of universal states is to carry farther, by less violent and less brutal means, that process of cultural pammixia that is started, in the antecedent Times of Troubles, by the atrocities that these bring in their train. The refugees, exiles, deportees, transported slaves, and other *déracinés* of the more cruel preceding age are followed up, under the milder régime of a universal state, by merchants, by professional soldiers, and by philosophic and religious missionaries and pilgrims who make their transit with less tribulation in a more genial social climate.

The cumulative cultural effect of these voluntary and involuntary migrations within the ambit of a disintegrating society has been examined at earlier points in this Study[3] and need not be resurveyed here. The Israelites who were deported by the Assyrians to the cities of the Medes and the exiles from Jerusalem whose memories made them weep by the waters of Babylon may serve as typical representatives of the *déracinés* of a Time of Troubles. In the Papal emissary Friar William of Rubruck's poignant account of how he spent Palm Sunday, A.D. 1254, in the Mongol capital, Qāraqorum, in the company of fellow Catholic deportees from

---

[1] See II. ii. 177–88 and V. v. 325–7.   [2] See xi, map 19.
[3] Especially in V. v. 58–194 and 439–80.

far-away Western Christendom,[1] we can catch the anarchy of a Time
of Troubles in the act of turning into the orderly peace of a universal
state. In the secret and silent circulation of the waters of that seemingly
motionless sea, the Orontes discharges into the Tiber and the sands of
the Shāmīyah are deposited on the banks of the Tyne. The missionary
of Christianity, Saint Paul, travels from Antioch to Rome, and, 'as an
inscription from South Shields informs us, a Romano-Oriental from
Palmyra could marry a Romano-British wife and settle down for the
rest of his days in the neighbourhood of Hadrian's Wall'.[2]

Judgements passed on the effects of this pammixia diverge, poles
apart, according to the divers social, political, and historical standpoints
of the observers who make them. A grandchild of those European Greeks
whose heroic resistance against enormous odds had barely saved them
from being incorporated, at the blossoming-season of their own civilization's growth, into the world-empire of the Achaemenidae, can write of
'the appalling present condition of the populations under the Persian
yoke, which have been quite disintegrated by being interlarded and
kneaded up together'.[3] Another Greek, born more than five hundred
years later into the 'Indian Summer' of an Hellenic universal state which
he could readily appreciate because it was so long overdue, could say to
Rome, as the highest praise that he could give her: 'You have made one
single household of the entire Inhabited World';[4] and a Gallic poet,
writing more than two hundred years later again, at a moment when the
Roman Empire in the West had already received its death-blow, could
give the Greek stylist's phrase a Latin echo in the famous epigrammatic
line: 'Urbem fecisti quod prius Orbis erat.'[5] On this controversial
question of the value of the result, points of view may differ completely;
but there is no disputing the facts themselves, however depreciatory or
laudatory may be the literary framework in which they are presented.

'I am not unaware', writes a Roman encyclopaedist towards the end of
the first century of the Roman Peace, 'that it may justly be regarded as the
lapse of an insensitive and lazy mind to have given so brief and cursory a
description of a country that is the nurse of all countries—their nurse and
their parent and the chosen vessel of divine grace for the mission of making
the skies themselves clearer, gathering the scattered realms into one flock,
softening harsh traditional practices, bringing together into mutual con-
verse, through a common medium of linguistic exchange, the discordant
and barbarous tongues of innumerable peoples, conferring humanity on
Man, and, in a word, becoming the single fatherland of all nations throughout the World.'[6]

What Pliny writes of Roman Italy and of the world-empire that she had
built up around herself is true, in some degree, of every universal state.

[1] See the passage quoted from Friar William's narrative in V. v. 113–14.
[2] Toynbee, J. C. M.: 'Catholicism and the Roman Imperial Cult', in *The Month*, vol.
clviii, November 1931, citing *Ephemeris Epigraphica*, vol. iv (Berlin 1881, Reimer),
p. 212, No. 718 a: 'D. M. Regina, liberta et coniuge, Barates Palmyrenus, natione
Catuallauna, an. xxx.'
[3] Plato: *Leges*, 693A, quoted already in V. v. 124, n. 2.
[4] Aristeides, P. Aelius: *In Romam*, § 102 in B. Keil's edition (*Aelii Aristidis Quae
Supersunt Omnia*, vol. ii (Berlin 1898, Weidmann), p. 121), quoted already in V. v. 343.
[5] Rutilius Namatianus, C.: *De Reditu Suo*, Book I, l. 66, quoted already in V. v. 345.
[6] Plinius Secundus, C.: *Historia Naturalis*, Book III, chap. v (vi), § 39.

(b) THE PSYCHOLOGY OF PEACE

A universal state is imposed by its founders, and accepted by its subjects, as a panacea for the ills of a Time of Troubles. In psychological terms it is an institution for establishing and maintaining concord;[1] and this is the true remedy for a correctly diagnosed disease. The malady from which a broken-down civilization is suffering as the penalty for its breakdown is that of being a house divided against itself, and this schism in Society is a double one. There is a horizontal schism between contending social classes as well as a vertical schism between warring states, and a universal state is born of a paroxysm which exacerbates this twofold strife to an unprecedented and intolerable degree of intensity and, in the same act, puts a sudden stop to it for the time being. The immediate and paramount aim of the empire-builders, in making a universal state out of the Power that emerges as the sole survivor from a war of annihilation between the parochial states of the preceding age, is to establish concord among themselves and with their fellow members of the dominant minority of their society who are survivors of the former ruling element in those parochial states that have succumbed in the fratricidal struggle. Non-violence, however, is a state of mind and principle of behaviour that cannot be confined to one compartment of social life; it must apply in some degree to all social relations if it is to apply to any; and therefore the concord which a dominant minority, in urgent need of being at peace within itself, is moved to seek and ensue[2] in its own domestic life has to be extended to the dominant minority's relations with the internal and external proletariats and with any alien civilizations with which the disintegrating civilization is in contact. In these relations, if there cannot be perfect and permanent peace, there must at least be an armistice and a *modus vivendi*.

This universal concord, which is the prevailing psychological climate under the dispensation of a universal state, profits its divers beneficiaries in different degrees. While it enables the dominant minority to recuperate to some extent—and indeed is the condition *sine qua non*, if it is to recuperate at all—it brings a greater relative access of strength to the proletariat. Concord is, in itself, a negative boon. 'A bruised reed shall he not break, and the smoking flax shall he not quench.'[3] The practical effect of such forbearance varies with the quality of the flax and the reed; and, in the case in point, the life has already gone out of the dominant minority and cannot be revived by a belated relief from attrition, whereas the same relief enables the proletariat, which has been stimulated and not crushed by its foregoing tribulations, to 'shoot up and thrive'.[4] Accordingly, during the armistice inaugurated by the establishment of a universal state, the proletariat must increase but the dominant minority must decrease.[5] Under the common régime of concord the dominant minority's conservation of energy freezes into

---

[1] See V. vi. 2–13. [2] 1 Pet. iii. 11.
[3] Isa. xlii. 3, quoted in Matt. xii. 20.
[4] The phrase used by Herodotus (Book I, chap. 66) to describe the progress of Sparta under the impetus that she received from the institution of the Lycurgean *agôgê*.
[5] John iii. 30.

Archaism,[1] and this Archaism rankles into Esotericism—a regressive Esotericism distinguishable from the progressive form of the same social aberration which is one of the perilous stepping-stones of a civilization in its growth-phase. On the other hand the toleration practised by the founders of a universal state for the sake of getting rid of fratricidal strife among themselves incidentally gives the internal proletariat a chance to found a universal church, while the atrophy of the martial spirit among the subjects of a universal state, resulting from the monopoly of the military profession by the Imperial Power, gives the external proletariat or a neighbouring alien civilization a chance of breaking in and seizing for itself the dominion over an internal proletariat that has been conditioned by the peculiar climate of a universal state to be passive on the political plane, however active on the religious.

The relative incapacity of the dominant minority to profit by conditions which it itself has called into existence through the act of establishing a universal state is strikingly illustrated by its almost invariable failure to propagate a philosophy or a 'fancy religion' of its own from above downwards.[2] In this matter the political pressure which the sovereign or the ruling element in a universal state is able to bring to bear upon the mass of the population seems to be a positive obstacle to the attainment of the ruler's desire, and his will here defeats itself in attempting to gain its ends by means that generally prove effective in other spheres. The working of this psycho-social 'law' has been examined in this Study already in an earlier passage[3] which need not be recapitulated.

It is all the more remarkable to observe how effective a use the representatives of the internal proletariat are apt to make of the opportunity offered by the pacific atmosphere of a universal state for propagating, from below upwards, a higher religion and eventually establishing a universal church. We may recall the more striking examples from a fuller survey that we have made in a previous chapter of this Study.[4]

'The Middle Empire' of Egypt, for instance, which was the original Egyptiac universal state, was used to this effect by the Osirian Church.[5] The Neo-Babylonian Empire, which was the Babylonic universal state, and its successive alien successor-states, the Achaemenian Empire and the Seleucid Monarchy, were similarly used by Judaism and by its sister-religion Zoroastrianism[6]—a creation of the Iranian wing of the proletariat of the Babylonic World which made converts of the Achaemenid empire-builders but escaped the blight that might have been the penalty for its having become the religion of the powers that be, thanks to the studied religious tolerance of all the Achaemenidae except, perhaps, Cambyses and to the personal religious laxity of the later rulers of the dynasty from

[1] See V. vi. 49–97.

[2] The most striking apparent exception is the successful establishment of Confucianism as the official philosophy of the Sinic universal state by the Emperor Han Wuti. The success of this imposition of a philosophy of the dominant minority upon the internal proletariat of the Sinic World is at least partly explicable by the fact that the 'Confucianism' which thus became a going concern was an amalgam in which an element of authentic philosophy was heavily alloyed with popular superstitions (see V. v. 418–19, 555–7, 654–5, and 708).

[3] See V. v. 646–712.   [4] In V. v. 58–194.
[5] See V. v. 149–52.   [6] See V. v. 120–4.

Artaxerxes II onwards.[1] The opportunities offered by the Roman Peace were seized by a number of competing proletarian religions—by the worships of Cybele and Isis and by Mithraism and Christianity,[2] as well as by the Babylonic philosophy of astral determinism.[3] The corresponding opportunities offered by a *Pax Hanica* in the Sinic World were competed for by an Indic proletarian religion, the Mahāyāna, which had arisen out of a philosophy of the Indic dominant minority in the crucible of the Kushan Empire,[4] and by the indigenous Sinic proletarian religion of Taoism, which likewise created itself out of a philosophy in emulation of the equally astonishing genesis of its Indic rival.[5] The Arab Caliphate provided a comparable opportunity for Islam—thanks to the êthos of the Umayyad Caliphs, who, with the exception of 'Umar II, were as tolerant and as lax as the Achaemenidae[6]—and the Gupta Rāj in the Indic World for Hinduism.[7] The Mongol Empire, which for a moment extended an effective *Pax Nomadica* over the Continent from the west coast of the Pacific Ocean to the east coast of the Baltic Sea and from the southern fringes of the Siberian tundra to the northern fringes of the Arabian desert and the Burmese jungle, struck the imagination of the missionaries of a host of rival religions by the portentous scale of the opportunity which this almost literally universal state appeared to offer; and, considering how brief this passing moment actually was, it is remarkable to observe how successfully it was turned to account by the Nestorian and the Western Catholic Christian churches and by Islam, as well as by the Lamaist Tantric sect of Mahayanian Buddhism.[8] The successive Ming and Manchu avatars of the universal state which the Mongol Empire had provided for the main body of the Far Eastern World gave Western Catholic Christianity a second opportunity of attempting the conquest of a new world,[9] and the same church made a simultaneous attempt to take advantage of the foundation of a Japanese universal state in the shape of the Tokugawa Shogunate.[10] The Ottoman Empire gave an opening for Bedreddinism, Imāmī Shī'īsm, and Bektāshism,[11] and the Mughal Rāj in the Hindu World for Kabirism and Sikhism.[12]

The exponents of the higher religions that had thus so frequently profited by the favourable social and psychological climate of a universal state had in some cases been conscious of the boon and had ascribed its bestowal upon them in an auspicious hour to the providence of the One True God in whose name they had been going forth converting and to convert their fellow men. In the eyes of the authors of the Books of 'Deutero-Isaiah', Ezra, and Nehemiah,[13] the Achaemenian Empire was the chosen instrument of Yahweh for the propagation of Judaism,[14] and

---

1 See V. v. 704–5.   2 See II. ii. 215–16 and V. v. 80–82.
3 See V. v. 56–57.   4 See V. v. 139–40.   5 See V. v. 146–7.
6 See V. v. 675–7 and 704–5.   7 See V. v. 137–8.
8 See V. v. 112–17.   9 See V. v. 365–7.
10 See V. v. 365.   11 See V. v. 111.   12 See V. v. 106.
13 According to van Hoonacker, A.: *Une Communauté judéo-araméenne à Elephantine aux vie et ve siècles avant J.C.* (London 1915, Milford), pp. 22–23, Nehemiah (whose first mission this scholar dates in 445 B.C.) really preceded Ezra (whose mission he dates in 398 B.C.).
14 See V. vi. 17, 122, n. 3, and 130, n. 3. In inverse form and in non-supernatural terms the same conception of the relations between Judaism and the Achaemenian

this conception of the final cause of a universal state was applied to the Roman Empire by a Father of the Christian Church in a passage so felicitous that it gave birth to a patristic commonplace.

'The incarnation of the Word of God united divine nature with human nature so [completely] that God's nature was able to stoop to the depths and ours to be raised up to the heights. In order that the effects of this ineffable act of grace might be spread throughout the World, God's providence previously brought into existence the Roman Empire. Its territorial acquisitions were carried to the lengths required for enabling all nations everywhere to become neighbours in the intimate contact that is established in a universal state. It was thoroughly consonant with the divine plan of action that many kingdoms should thus be confederated in a single empire and that the evangelization of all Mankind should find itself able to make an unimpeded and rapid progress through the ranks of peoples held together under the rule of a single polity.'[1]

The inspiration, direct or indirect, of this passage in a fifth-century Christian sermon can be discerned in an ode from the pen of a seventeenth-century Christian poet, when he imagines Nature put out of countenance by her Maker's overwhelming act of becoming incarnate.

> But He, her fears to cease,
> Sent down the meek-eyed Peace;
> She, crown'd with olive green, came softly sliding
> Down through the turning sphere,
> His ready harbinger,
> With turtle wing the amorous clouds dividing;
> And, waving wide her myrtle wand,
> She strikes a universal peace through sea and land.
>
> No war or battle's sound
> Was heard the world around:
> The idle spear and shield were high uphung;
> The hookèd chariot stood

Empire is presented by Eduard Meyer: 'Once again [i.e. in the light of the newly discovered Elephantinê papyri] it is made unquestionably manifest that Judaism is a creation of the Persian Empire: the Babylonian Jews actually set in motion [for their own purposes] the engine of the Imperial Government and made use of its authority to impose on the Jews in Palestine and the Diasporà the Law which Ezra had composed' (Meyer, E.: 'Zu den aramäischen Papyri von Elephantinê' in the *Mittheilungen* of the Königliche Preussische Akademie der Wissenschaften, Gesammtsitzung vom 23 November, 1911). According to Van Hoonacker, op. cit., p. 20, Meyer exaggerates the extent of the new departure in the development of Judaism in the fifth century B.C.

[1] '[Verbum] caro factum ita divinam naturam naturae univit humanae ut illius ad infima inclinatio, nostra fieret ad summa provectio. Ut autem huius inenarrabilis gratiae per totum mundum diffunderetur effectus, Romanum regnum divina providentia praeparavit; cuius ad eos limites incrementa perducta sunt quibus cunctarum undique gentium vicina et contigua esset universitas. Disposito namque divinitus operi maxime congruebat ut multa regna uno confoedarentur imperio et cito pervios haberet populos praedicatio generalis quos unius teneret regimen civitatis' (Leo the Great, Pope: Sermo lxxxii, chap. 2, in Migne, J.-P.: *Patrologia Latina*, vol. liv, col. 423). Leo the Great has been cited as an exponent of the gentle response of Christianity to the challenge of social disintegration in V. v. 77. Another passage in the same sermon, on Rome's debt to the Christian Church, is quoted on p. 697, below. The present passage is anticipated in an address to an Antonine emperor by Bishop Melito of Sardis, which is quoted by Eusebius: *Historia Ecclesiastica*, Book IV, chap. xxvi, §§ 7-8.

Unstain'd with hostile blood;
The trumpet spake not to the armèd throng;
And kings sat still with awful eye,[1]
As if they surely knew their sovran Lord was by.[2]

An opportunity so marvellous as to seem truly heaven-sent is indeed presented to a higher religion by the establishment of an imperial peace; yet, in the relation between a successful missionary church and the universal state within whose framework it is carrying out its purpose of converting Mankind, the climate of toleration, which gives the work of conversion so favourable a start, does not always persist till the end of the story and is sometimes actually transformed into its own opposite by the very success of the tolerated religion in taking advantage of it during the first chapter.

There have, no doubt, been cases in which there has been no such sinister termination of the armistice between an internal proletariat and a dominant minority that is inaugurated by the establishment of a universal state.

For example, in the history of the Osirian Church in the Egyptiac World, the apprehensive hostility which the rising proletarian religion evoked in the hearts of the ruling element in the Egyptiac Society at as early a date as the eve of the Time of Troubles[3] does not appear to have led on to any overt trial of strength between this would-be universal church and 'the Middle Empire' that was the Egyptiac universal state; and in the ensuing interregnum the rival religions of the Egyptiac internal proletariat and dominant minority actually made common cause against the religion of an external proletariat with an alien cultural tinge, and entered into an alliance which proved to be the prelude to amalgamation.[4] Peace likewise seems to have been preserved in the Sinic World between the Mahāyāna and the Taoist Church on the one side and the Han Empire on the other until the Sinic universal state went into dissolution towards the end of the second century of the Christian Era.

When we come to Judaism and Zoroastrianism, we cannot tell what their ultimate relations might have been with either the Neo-Babylonian or the Achaemenian Empire, since each of these universal states in turn had its life cut short by an alien conqueror at an early stage of its history. We only know that, when the Achaemenian régime was abruptly replaced by the Seleucid and eventually, west of the Euphrates, by the Roman, the impact of an alien Hellenic culture, of which the Seleucid and the Roman Powers were the successive political instruments,

---

[1] This image is perhaps a reminiscence of a passage of Latin poetry (Lucretius: *De Rerum Natura*, Book V, ll. 1222–5) depicting the psychological effect produced by the descent from heaven, not of Peace, but of a thunderbolt:

Non populi gentesque tremunt, regesque superbi
corripiunt divom percussi membra timore
nequid ob admissum foede dictumve superbe
pœnarum grave sit solvendi tempus adultum?

[2] Milton, John: *Ode on the Morning of Christ's Nativity.*

[3] See I. i. 140–3. This presentation of Osirism, which had been adopted by the writer of this Study from J. H. Breasted: *The Development of Religion and Thought in Ancient Egypt* (London 1912, Hodder & Stoughton), pp. 29 and 140, is contested by Breasted's successor, J. A. Wilson, in his *The Burden of Egypt* (Chicago 1951, University Press), p. 32, n. 12.

[4] See I. i. 143–4.

deflected both Judaism and Zoroastrianism from their original mission of preaching a gospel of salvation to all Mankind, and transformed them into weapons of cultural warfare in the Syriac Society's retort to the Hellenic Society's aggression.[1] If the Achaemenian Empire, like its post-Hellenic avatar, the Arab Caliphate, had run out its full course, we may conjecture that, under the auspices of a tolerant or indifferent Achaemenian Imperial Government, either Zoroastrianism or Judaism or some syncretism of these two higher religions would have anticipated the achievement of Islam, which—profiting by the indifference of the Umayyads and the conscientious observance, by the 'Abbasids, of the tolerance, prescribed by the *Sharī'ah*, towards non-Muslims who were 'People of the Book'[2]—made gradual headway, uncompromised by the frustrating assistance of the civil arm, until the collapse of the 'Abbasid régime brought a landslide of voluntary mass-conversions among ex-subjects of the Caliphate seeking shelter, in the courtyard of the Mosque, from the storm of an approaching political interregnum.[3] Similarly, under a Guptan Empire which was a reintegration of the original Mauryan Hindu universal state, the ousting of the philosophy of Buddhism by the post-Buddhaic higher religion of Hinduism was not only unopposed by a dynasty who were, themselves, adherents of the rising Hindu faith, but was also unimpeded by any left-handed stimulation of the outgoing philosophy through acts of official persecution that would have been alien to the intrinsically tolerant and syncretistic religious êthos of the Indic Civilization.[4]

In contrast to these cases in which a higher religion, profiting by the peace of a universal state, had been tolerated by the Imperial Government from first to last, there were other cases in which its peaceful progress had been interrupted by official persecutions that had either nipped it in the bud or had denatured it by goading it into going into politics and eventually taking up arms or, at the lightest, had compelled it to pay a heavy toll of suffering as the price of spoiling the Egyptians.

Western Catholic Christianity, for example, was almost completely extirpated in Japan by the Tokugawa régime in the seventeenth century of the Christian Era,[5] and was effectively checked in China in the eighteenth century by the less drastic measures then taken against it by the Manchu Power.[6] Shi'ism was crushed in the Ottoman Empire in A.D. 1514 by Sultan Selīm the Grim.[7] Islam was persecuted by the pagan Mongol khāqāns—partly because of the Muslims' steadfastness in refusing to abandon Islamic ritual observances that were offensive to Mongol tribal custom, and partly owing to the influence, in Mongol counsels, of Islam's Nestorian Christian enemies[8]—and, though this persecution was more than counter-balanced in the long run by a temporary political union, under Mongol rule, of China and Dār-al-

---

[1] See I. i. 90–91; II. ii. 203, 234–6, 285–6, and 374; V. v. 125–6 and 657–61.
[2] See V. v. 674–5 and 678.   [3] See V. v. 678.   [4] See V. v. 706.
[5] The faithful remnant was driven underground, like the Jews and Muslims in Catholic Spain and Portugal (see II. ii. 232–3 and 244–8 and IX. viii. 569).
[6] See V. v. 365–7.   [7] See I. i. 365 and 382–3 and V. v. 365.
[8] For the adverse consequences of this influence for Islam, see II. ii. 122, n. 2, 237–8, and 449–52; V. v. 3, n. 3, and 250; in the present volume, pp. 256–7 below; IX. viii. 355; and X. ix. 36.

Islām which led to the permanent introduction of Islam into China,[1] Islam in China under the Mongols, like Western Catholic Christianity in China under the Ming and the Manchus, missed its possible destiny of becoming the universal church of the main body of the Far Eastern Society. Islam gained no substantial foothold in China outside the two far north-western provinces of Kansu and Shensi and the new south-western province of Yunnan which was added to China's patrimony by force of Mongol arms; and, even in these two lodgements, the Islamic community in China never became anything more than an alien minority which was goaded, by the precariousness of its position, into recurrent outbreaks of militancy.

This denaturing effect of official persecution, which thus left its mark in China on Islam, is more signally exemplified in the perversion of Sikhism in India in reaction to the sustained and violent persecution to which this possible embryo of a Hindu universal church was subjected by the Mughal Rāj.[2] In allowing itself to be provoked into militancy, Sikhism renounced its spiritual birthright and opted for the limited and uncreative role of becoming a local political community in a single province of the Hindu World, where, down to the time of writing, the height of its political success had been the dubious achievement of having once carved out one of the ephemeral successor-states of the Mughal Empire.

In contrast to the cases just cited, the untoward after-effects on Christianity of the trial of strength that was the prelude to its triumph over the Roman imperial régime were comparatively slight.[3] During the three centuries ending in the conversion of Constantine, while Christianity was benefiting by the facilities unintentionally offered to it by the Roman Peace, it was never out of danger of falling foul of Roman policy; for, besides the suspicion of private associations of all kinds that haunted the Roman State in the Imperial Age,[4] there was an older and more deeply graven Roman tradition of special hostility to private associations for the practice and propagation of foreign religions; and, though the Roman Government had relaxed this hardset policy in two notable instances—in its official reception of the worship of Cybele at the psychological crisis of the Hannibalic War[5] and in its persistent toleration of Judaism as a religion, even when the Jewish Zealots forced Rome's hand and ultimately compelled her to obliterate the last vestiges of a Jewish state[6]—the suppression of the Bacchanals in the second century B.C. was an augury of what the Christians were to suffer in the third century of their era.[7] Unlike the Sikh community under the Mughal

---

[1] See Broomhall, M.: Islam in China (London 1910, Morgan & Scott); de Thiersant, D.: Le Mahométisme en Chine et dans le Turkestan Oriental (Paris 1878, Leroux, 2 vols.); Devéria, G.: Musulmans et Manichéens Chinois (Paris 1898, Imprimerie Nationale); and the present Study, IV. iv. 496 and V. v. 116. This was an incidental consequence of the Mongols' general policy of intermixing the peoples and cultures of their empire (for an instance of this see V. v. 350–1).

[2] See V. v. 187 and 665–8.

[3] These untoward after-effects are considered again, in a different connexion, on p. 439, below.

[4] See p. 57, above.   [5] See II. ii. 216 and V. v. 685–8.

[6] See IV. iv. 224–5; V. v. 68 and 657–9; and V. vi. 120–3.

[7] See II. ii. 216.

Rāj, the Christian Church under the Roman régime resisted the temptation to retort to official persecution by perverting itself from a religious into a politico-military association; and it was duly rewarded for remaining substantially true to its own nature by becoming a universal church and an heir of the future. Yet the Christian Church did not come through this ordeal unscathed. Instead of reading and taking to heart the manifest lesson of the triumph of Christian gentleness over Roman force, she presented her discomfited persecutors with a gratuitous vindication and a posthumous moral revenge by taking to her bosom the sin which had consummated their failure. The habit of resorting to persecution as a would-be short cut to overcoming opposition to her practice and beliefs was adopted by the Christian Church before the close of the fourth century of the Christian Era[1] and clung to her thereafter. Even the desperate remedy of clutching at tolerance at the cost of losing hold of faith—an expedient in which Western Christendom had been experimenting since the latter part of the seventeenth century[2]—had not proved a lasting cure for this wantonly contracted spiritual disease.

Such sinister legacies, bequeathed to higher religions by universal states, are not, however, of the same order of significance as the benefits which are offered to a higher religion by the facilities that a universal state provides. It was within, and with the aid of, this political and social framework that Christianity, Islam, Hinduism, and the Mahāyāna won their way to becoming universal churches.

While the internal proletariat, as the creator of the higher religions, is thus the principal beneficiary on the spiritual plane from the dominant minority's impermanent yet momentous achievement of establishing a universal state, the benefits on the political plane are harvested by other hands; and this distribution of advantages arises from the very nature of the situation. The enforced peace of a universal state gives the internal proletariat its opportunity for spiritual prowess in so far as it debars it from the privilege of exercising political power and relieves it of the necessity of bearing arms; and even the empire-builders, bled white by the supreme effort of imposing peace through a knock-out blow that has been the climax of a crescendo of fratricidal warfare, lose the zest that has carried their forefathers to victory in their struggle for existence in the foregoing Time of Troubles. The military service once readily accepted as an honour and as an opportunity for ambition now comes to be shunned as an unwelcome burden; and, in looking about for stalwart and willing shoulders to which this load might be transferred, the imperial authorities are apt to draw an ever larger quota of their military recruits from the ranks of an untamed external proletariat.[3] The psychology of peace under the auspices of a universal state thus unfits the rulers themselves for the task of retaining their own political heritage; and accordingly the political beneficiaries of this process of psychological disarmament that is induced by the moral climate of a universal state are neither the rulers nor the ruled; they are intruders from beyond the

---

[1] See IV. iv. 226-7.   [2] See IV. iv. 227-8 and V. v. 669-71.
[3] See VIII. viii. 43-44. The consequent barbarization of the dominant minority has been discussed in V. v. 459-80.

imperial frontiers who may be either members of the disintegrating society's external proletariat or representatives of some alien civilization.

At an earlier point in this Study[1] we have, in fact, observed that the event which registers the extinction of a civilization—as distinct from the event which precipitates its antecedent breakdown and disintegration—is usually the occupation of the domain of the defunct society's universal state either by barbarian war-lords from beyond the pale or by conquerors coming from another society with a different culture, or in some cases by both kinds of invader, one following at the heels of the other. Barbarians overran the Empire of Sumer and Akkad, the Guptan Empire, the Empire of Ts'in and Han, the Roman Empire, the Arab Caliphate, 'the thalassocracy of Minos', and both 'the Middle Empire' and 'the New Empire' of Egypt.[2] The Neo-Babylonian Empire, which was the Babylonic universal state, was cut short by Iranian barbarians who were in the act of becoming converts to the Syriac Civilization and architects of the original Syriac universal state; and this Achaemenian Empire, in its turn, was cut short by Macedonian barbarians who had already become disciples and missionaries of Hellenism before the whirlwind campaign in which Alexander the Great overthrew the Achaemenian Power. The Mauryan Empire, which was the Indic universal state, suffered the Achaemenian Empire's fate, 150 years later, at the hands of an Hellenic successor of the Achaemenian Empire in Bactria; and the Empire of the Incas, which was the Andean universal state, was similarly cut short by militant apostles of Western Christendom whose leader emulated the demonic energy, but not the chivalrous generosity, of the Macedonian Alexander. At the break-up of the Ottoman Empire, which had provided an alien universal state for the main body of Orthodox Christendom, incipient barbarian invasions were overtaken, and were then either brought to a halt or changed in character, by the mightier march of Westernization: partly in the form of conquests by Western or Westernizing Powers, and partly through the cultural conversion of the subject peoples of the Empire and of the invading barbarians themselves.[3] At the break-up of the Mughal Empire, which had provided an alien universal state for the Hindu World, incipient barbarian invasions were stopped dead by the restoration of the universal state in the form of a British Rāj.[4]

The benefits secured by barbarian or alien aggressors who have succeeded in taking advantage, for their predatory purposes, of the psychological climate induced by a universal state are palpable and, on a short view, imposing. Yet we have observed already,[5] and shall be verifying in a later part of this Study, that the barbarian invaders of the

---

[1] In IV. iv. 56–119.
[2] The Hyksos barbarians who came in at the death of 'the Middle Empire' of Egypt had acquired *en route*, as we have seen, a tincture of the alien Sumeric culture, and this is one possible explanation of the fanatical fury with which the Egyptiac Society rose against them, drove them out, and restored a universal state that had already run its full course before the Hyksos had appeared on the scene (see VI A, Annex, pp. 574–6, below, and the references there given to previous passages in this Study that bear upon this point).
[3] See IV. iv. 68–70 and 76–78.   [4] See V. v. 304 and 305, n. 2.
[5] In I. i. 58–62 and V. v. 194–337, *passim*.

derelect domain of a crumbling universal state are heroes without a future;[1] and Posterity would assuredly have recognized them as being the disreputable adventurers that they are, but for the retrospective glamour of romance and tragedy that is cast over their sordid escapades by their redeeming intuition of their fate and their marvellous capacity for writing their own epitaphs on their own terms in the language of high poetry.[2] As for the achievements of the militant missionaries of an alien civilization, these too, though seldom so short-lived as the triumphs of the barbarians, are, like them, delusive and disappointing by comparison with the historic achievement of an internal proletariat that has taken advantage of a *pax oecumenica* by founding, under its aegis, a universal church.

In two instances in which we know the whole story, we have seen that a civilization whose universal state has been prematurely cut short by alien conquerors is capable of going to earth, hibernating for centuries, biding its time, and eventually finding its opportunity to expel the intrusive civilization and resume the universal state phase of its history at the point where this has been interrupted. The Indic Civilization achieved this *tour de force* after nearly six hundred years, and the Syriac after nearly a thousand years, of submergence beneath an Hellenic flood; the monuments of their achievement were the Guptan Empire and the Arab Caliphate, in which they respectively resumed the universal states originally embodied in the Mauryan Empire and in the Achaemenian Empire.[3] On the other hand the Babylonic and Egyptiac societies were eventually absorbed into the body social of the Syriac, though the Babylonic Society succeeded in preserving its cultural identity for about six hundred years after the overthrow of the Neo-Babylonian Empire of Nabopolassar and Nebuchadnezzar by Cyrus the Achaemenid, while the Egyptiac Society[4] maintained itself for no less than two thousand years after the termination of its natural expectation of life had been signalled by the collapse of 'the Middle Kingdom' in which we have seen its original universal state.[5]

On the evidence of past history there are thus two alternative denouements to attempts on the part of one civilization to devour and digest another civilization by force. The evidence shows, however, that, even when such an attempt is ultimately successful, there may be a period of probation, lasting for centuries or even millennia, before the result is assured; and the Time-scale here revealed might incline twentieth-century historians to be chary about forecasting the outcome of the Western Civilization's latter-day attempts to swallow its contemporaries, considering how relatively short the time had been since even the oldest of these attempts had been inaugurated, and how little had yet been seen of the gradually unfolding story.

In the case of the Spanish conquest of the Central American World, for example, in which the alien conquerors had actually anticipated the

---

[1] See VIII. viii. 45–72.   [2] See VIII. viii. 73–81.
[3] See I. i. 75–77 and 85–86 and pp. 569–76, below.
[4] See p. 575, below, with the references there given to previous passages in this Study.
[5] See pp. 49–50, above, and pp. 569–76, below.

establishment of a universal state by indigenous empire-builders, it might well have been supposed that, when the alien substitute, in the shape of the Spanish Viceroyalty of New Spain,[1] had in due course been supplanted by a Republic of Mexico which had sought, and gained, admission into the comity of Western states, the assimilation of the Central American Society into the body social of the Western Society had become an irreversibly accomplished fact. Yet the Mexican Revolution of A.D. 1821, which might thus have appeared to have completed the incorporation of the Central American into the Western World, had been followed by the Revolution of A.D. 1910, in which the buried but hibernating indigenous society had suddenly bestirred itself, raised its head, and broken through the crust of culture deposited by officious Castilian hands on the grave into which the *conquistadores* had thrust a body that they believed themselves to have slain. This portent from Central America raised the question whether the apparent cultural conquests of Western Christendom in the Andean World and elsewhere might not likewise prove, sooner or later, to have been no more than superficial and temporary.

The Far Eastern Civilization in China, Korea, and Japan, which had succumbed to the influence of the West within the last century before the time of writing, was manifestly far more potent than the Central American Civilization had ever been; and, if the indigenous culture of Mexico was reasserting itself after a four hundred years' eclipse, it would be rash to reckon that the Far Eastern Society was destined to be assimilated by the West or by Russia. As for the Hindu World, the inauguration of two 'successor-states' of the British Rāj in A.D. 1947 might be interpreted as a peacefully accomplished counterpart to the establishment of a Republic of Mexico by revolution in A.D. 1821, and at the time of writing it seemed possible that in this case, as in that, an act of political emancipation which had superficially set the seal upon the process of Westernization by bringing the emancipated state into the comity of Western nations, might prove in retrospect to have been the first step towards the cultural emancipation of a civilization that had been temporarily submerged by a Western tide.

The Arab countries, again, which had recently been gaining admission to the Western comity of nations as sovereign independent states,[2] had been able to achieve this ambition in virtue of their success in shaking off an Ottoman political ascendancy and an Iranic cultural veneer by which they had been overlaid for four centuries.[3] Was there any reason to expect that the latent survival power of the Arabic culture, which had enabled the Arabs to resist assimilation to the kindred culture of a sister society, would not assert itself, sooner or later, against the influence of the far more alien culture of the West? And, if the permanent Westernization of the Arabic World was not assured, there was also no assurance that the Ottoman Turkish converts from the Iranic culture, or even the Greek, Serb, Ruman, Bulgar, Georgian, and Russian converts from the Western Society's sister civilization, Orthodox Christendom, would abide in their new cultural allegiance. We can merely speculate on the

[1] See xi, map 72.   [2] See IV. iv. 82 and 107.   [3] See IV. iv. 113-14.

possibility that cultural conversions which, like those of the Aztecs, the Incas, and the Hindus, have been initiated by force of alien arms may prove less stable than conversions which have been entered into on the converts' own initiative, like those of the Irish,[1] the Scandinavians,[2] the Orthodox Christians,[3] the Japanese,[4] and the Jews[5] to the culture of the West, or the assimilation of the Manchus to the Far Eastern Civilization in China.[6]

The general effect of this survey of the ultimate consequences of 'cultural conversions' is to confirm our conclusion that the sole sure beneficiary from the services afforded by a universal state is the internal proletariat. The benefits obtained by the external proletariat are always illusory, while those obtained by an alien civilization are apt to be impermanent.

(c) THE SERVICEABILITY OF IMPERIAL INSTALLATIONS

1. *Communications*

An Analysis of Imperial Institutions

Having now examined the effects of two general characteristics of universal states—their conductivity and their peace—we may go on to survey the services afforded to their beneficiaries by particular concrete institutions which they themselves deliberately create and maintain, but which are apt to find their historic mission in roles for which they had never been cast by their makers. These imperial institutions may be grouped under the three heads of installations, currencies, and corporations, and each of these heads may be subdivided. The principal installations set up by a universal state are its communications, its garrisons and colonies, its provinces, and its capital city. Its most important currencies are its official language and script, its legal system, and its money, weights and measures, and calendar. Its major corporations are its army, its civil service, and its citizen body. If we consider each of these institutions in turn, we shall find it serving some unintended beneficiary in some measure.

The Spider's Web

Communications head the list, because they are the master-institution on which a universal state depends for its very existence. They are the instrument not only of its military command over its dominions but

---

[1] The first act in the assimilation of the Irish was their voluntary decision, at the time of the Reformation, when their English rulers turned Protestant, to maintain their allegiance to a Catholicism which had been thrust upon them in the Early Medieval Age of Western history (see II. ii. 421–3). The second act was the captivation of the Irish, in the nineteenth century of the Christian Era, by the contemporary Western movement of Nationalism. (For recent Irish Linguistic Archaism as a symptom of Nationalism, see V. vi. 65–67 and 71).

[2] See II. ii. 347–60 and V. vi. 64–65 and 71.

[3] For the Westernization of the Modern Greeks, see II. ii. 226–7; V. vi. 68–70 and 71; and IX. viii. 161–84. For the deliberate attempt to transform the Russian Orthodox Christian universal state into a member of the comity of Western states, see IV. iv. 88–91.   [4] See IV. iv. 88–91.

[5] See II. ii. 252–4; V. vi. 70–71; and IX. viii. 286–8.   [6] See V. v. 348–9 and 352.

also of its political control through overt imperial inspectors and unavowed secret service agents. For this imperial life-line does not consist
merely of the physical media of travel. The highways offered ready-
made by Physical Nature, in the shape of rivers,[1] seas,[2] and steppes,[3] do
not provide practicable means of communication except in so far as they
are effectively policed;[4] and the same political condition governs, *a
fortiori*, the use of artificial or regulated inland waterways and man-made
roads. Nor is the maintenance of public security enough in itself to make
the potentialities of communication practically operative. In a geographical area so large as is the domain of even the least extensive universal
state if measured by the standard of an individual human being's mobility
even in a technologically efficient society, the traveller may be hard put
to it to reach his destination unless he is given the privilege of using
public means of transportation. In most of the universal states so far
known to History, these means had taken the form of an imperial postal
service; and the imperial postmaster-general at the seat of the central
government, with his host of subordinates strung out along the roads
radiating from the capital to the frontiers, had been apt to acquire the
additional function of a chief of secret police whose most important
duty, in the eyes of his masters, had been to turn his opportunities of
intelligence to the central government's account by reporting on the
conduct and ambitions of provincial governors and frontier commanders,
and on the public opinion and temper of imperial troops and subject
populations.

A public postal service seems to have been part of the machinery of
government of the Empire of Sumer and Akkad. In its metropolitan
territory of Shinar, the embankments of the irrigation canals appear to
have served as highways for land-traffic.[5] 'The New Empire' of Egypt,
which established its authority over the derelict Syrian and Mesopotamian provinces of the Empire of Sumer and Akkad after an interlude of
barbarian Hyksos rule, used the roads which it inherited here from its
predecessors for keeping control over the native princelings by a service
of diplomatic couriers and travelling inspectors. In the Achaemenian
Empire we find the same installations apparently raised to a higher level
of organization and efficiency—though this apparent superiority in

---

[1] In the geographical structure of an Egyptical universal state the natural waterway
provided by the River Nile served as a spinal cord, and a corresponding service was
performed by the rivers Euphrates and Tigris for the Empire of Sumer and Akkad.

[2] 'The [Mediterranean] Sea stretches in a belt across the middle of the Inhabited
World and across the middle of your [Roman] empire; and round the sea the continents
extend "grand and grandly" (μεγάλαι μεγαλωστὶ κέκλινται)—continually supplying your
needs with consignments of their products' (Aristeides, P. Aelius: *In Romam*, §§ 10–11
in B. Keil's edition (*Aelii Aristidis Quae Supersunt Omnia*, vol. ii (Berlin 1898, Weidmann), p. 94)). For the role of the Mediterranean Sea in the life of the Roman Empire,
see further pp. 216–20, below.

[3] For the conductivity of the Steppe, see III. iii. 391–4. The centrally situated medium
of communication which was provided for the Roman Empire by the Mediterranean
Sea—as depicted by Aelius Aristeides in the passage quoted in the preceding footnote—
was provided by the Great Western Bay of the Eurasian Steppe (see III. iii. 401) for the
Nomad empires of the Royal Scythians, the Khazars, and the Golden Horde (see
V. v. 281–9), and by the entire Eurasian Steppe for the short-lived Nomad Empire of
the Mongol khāqāns who ruled from Qāraqorum (see p. 198, below).

[4] See the passage quoted from Epictetus in V. vi. 3 and 142, and on p. 92, below.

[5] See Woolley, L.: *Abraham* (London 1936, Faber), p. 122.

standard may be an illusion reflecting a mere difference in the amount of our information.

'The farther the bounds of the Empire were extended, the more powerful became the position of the provincial governors; and this made it the more necessary to create institutions for preserving the Empire's unity and for ensuring a prompt and unhesitating execution of Imperial commands. Instruments for holding the Empire together were the great roads converging on Susa and traversing the Empire in all directions in the track of the previously existing trade-routes. . . . These roads were measured in parasangs and were permanently maintained in good condition. The Imperial Highway[1] was provided, at intervals of about four parasangs on the average, with "imperial post-stations and excellent inns".[2] The provincial boundaries and the river crossings were guarded by strongly garrisoned fortresses ($\pi \acute{\nu} \lambda a \iota$)[3] (the desert frontier of Babylonia, among others, was provided with defences of the same kind).[4] At these points the traffic was subjected to searching supervision. All post-stations were manned by mounted couriers whose duty it was to convey imperial commands and official dispatches post-haste, travelling day and night without a break—"swifter than cranes", as the Greeks put it.[5] There is also said to have been a system of telegraphic communications by beacon-signals. To keep the satraps under control, the Emperor would take every opportunity of sending out into the provinces high officials, like the Emperor's "eye" or his brother or son, with troops at their back. These would arrive, without warning, to inspect the administration and report abuses. Further safeguards against misconduct on the satraps' part were provided by the presence of the imperial secretary who was attached to the provincial governor,[6] and of the commandants of fortresses and other military officers in his province, who all served as instruments of supervision. These checks were supplemented by a highly developed espionage system. The Emperor had a ready ear for denunciations.'[7]

This Achaemenian policy of utilizing the imperial communications system as an instrument for maintaining the central government's control over the provinces reappears in the administration of the Roman Empire, which eventually fell heir to the former Achaemenian dominions west of the Euphrates, and of the Arab Caliphate—a reincarnation of the Achaemenian Empire in which the Syriac universal state found its

---

[1] i.e. the Great North-West Road connecting Susa with Sardis and Ephesus (see xi, map 20). The central section of this Achaemenian Imperial Highway, between Assyria and Cappadocia, had originally been opened up, as early as the third millennium B.C., by Assyrian pioneer traders whose settlements in Cappadocia had subsequently been embraced in the Empire of Sumer and Akkad (see I. i. 110–11).—A.J.T.

[2] $\Sigma \tau a \theta \mu o \acute{\iota} \ \tau \epsilon \ \pi a \nu \tau a \chi \hat{\eta} \ \epsilon \emph{i} \sigma \iota \ \beta a \sigma \iota \lambda \acute{\eta} \emph{i} o \iota \ \kappa a \emph{i} \ \kappa a \tau a \lambda \acute{\upsilon} \sigma \iota \epsilon \varsigma \ \kappa \acute{a} \lambda \lambda \iota \sigma \tau a \iota$ (Herodotus, Book V, chap. 52).

[3] The corresponding installations were called $\kappa \lambda \epsilon \acute{\iota} \sigma o \upsilon \rho a \iota$ (i.e. 'clausurae') in the East Roman Empire and 'derbends' in the Ottoman Empire.—A.J.T.

[4] See Xenophon: *Expeditio Cyri*, Book I, chap. 5, § 5.—A.J.T.

[5] Reminiscences of Herodotus's account of the Achaemenian system of communications, blending with the tenth verse of the seventh chapter of the Book of Daniel (quoted in the present Study, V. vi. 34), may have inspired Milton to write:

> His state
> Is kingly. Thousands at His bidding speed
> And post o'er land and ocean without rest.
> They also serve who only stand and wait.

The poet's application of this Achaemenian imagery is, of course, all his own.—A.J.T.

[6] See Herodotus, Book III, chap. 128.—A.J.T.

[7] Meyer, E.: *Geschichte des Altertums*, vol. iii (Stuttgart 1901, Cotta), pp. 66–68.

second avatar after the long interruption caused by the intrusion of the Hellenic Civilization upon the Syriac World between the Macedonian conqueror Alexander's crossing of the Hellespont in 334 B.C. and the Roman Emperor Heraclius's withdrawal behind the Amanus in A.D. 636.[1] In the case of the Caliphate a twentieth-century historian had at his disposal a wealth of information; for a full and accurate account of the 'Abbasid road network and postal system had been extracted from the official records and preserved for Posterity in a corpus of treatises which was a notable monument of the classical Arabic literature,[2] while a picture of the Roman road network and postal system had been pieced together from archaeological and epigraphical evidence by Modern Western classical scholars.[3]

The Roman Imperial Cursus Publicus was instituted by Augustus himself—perhaps consciously on the Achaemenian pattern[4]—and the burden of providing the service, which was originally imposed on the local public authorities, appears to have been progressively taken over by the Imperial Treasury in the reigns of Hadrian and Septimius Severus, though this without ever ceasing to bear heavily on the populations of the territories through which the imperial highways ran.[5] Official dispatches were carried overland by corps of *tabellarii* and *cursores*, and oversea by *naves tabellariae*.[6] The Achaemenian inspiration of this Roman institution is betrayed in a characteristic use of couriers as spies. The emissaries of the Roman Imperial Government who went under the euphemistic names of *frumentarii* ('foragers') in the Age of the Principate and of *agentes in rebus* in the post-Diocletianic Age were counterparts, in Roman dress, of an Achaemenian emperor's 'eye'. Their administrative duty of superintending the conduct of the imperial postal service was coupled with the political duty of espionage.[7]

In the Caliphate under the 'Abbasid régime the administration of the public postal service was turned to account for purposes of intelligence and police.

'At the capital of each of the large provinces into which the mighty empire was articulated there was a postmaster (*Sāhib al-Barīd*)[8] whose

---

[1] See I. i. 75–77.
[2] The Arabic texts of this corpus had been published by de Goeje, M. J., in his *Bibliotheca Geographorum Arabicorum* (Leyden 1870–94, Brill, 8 vols.). A masterly summary and appreciation of the facts was to be found in Le Strange, Guy: *The Lands of the Eastern Caliphate* (Cambridge 1905, University Press).
[3] See Hirschfeld, O.: *Die kaiserlichen Verwaltungsbeamten bis auf Diocletian* (Berlin 1905, Weidmann), pp. 190–204, 'Die Reichspost', and pp. 205–11, 'Die Italischen Strassen'. [4] See ibid., p. 190.
[5] See ibid., pp. 192–3. [6] See ibid., pp. 200–4.
[7] See Grosse, R.: *Römische Militärgeschichte von Gallienus bis zum Beginn der byzantinischen Themenverfassung* (Berlin 1920, Weidmann), pp. 105–6. The postal service itself must, all the same, have been efficient—at any rate during the halcyon days of an Antonine Indian Summer. Otherwise Aelius Aristeides would hardly have ventured to write:
'An administrator sitting [in Rome] can govern the whole Inhabited World with the greatest facility by correspondence. The despatches are no sooner written than they are delivered, just as if they had travelled by air' (*In Romam*, edited by Keil, B., in *Aelii Aristidis Quae Supersunt Omnia*, vol. ii (Berlin 1898, Weidmann), p. 101 (Or. XXVI, § 33)).
[8] This word *barīd*, which is used in Arabic to mean 'postal system', is derived from the Latin *verēda* meaning 'mail-cart'.—A.J.T.

duty it was to keep the Caliph continually informed of all affairs of any importance. The postmaster had even to keep an eye on the conduct of the governor and was thus a confidential agent of the Central Government's, appointed direct by them. The report of a Chief Postmaster of Baghdad, addressed to the Caliph Mutawakkil, has come down to us. . . . We even know the form of appointment of a postmaster. The Caliph commissions him therein to report from time to time on the conduct of the financial officials and of the administrators of the crownlands, on the state of agriculture, on the situation of the peasants, on the behaviour of the officials, and on statistics of the minting of gold and silver coin. He was also to be present when the troops were being reviewed and paid. It is clear that the postal service, as we understand it, was quite a secondary consideration.'[1]

The primary consideration was what it had been under the Achaemenian Government.

'The postmasters . . , were the sensitive octopus-arms which the Court of Baghdad extended into the provinces. . . . The postal system was made to serve the purposes of espionage: in this far-flung empire the intelligence service was most efficiently organized. In the later parts of his work, Tabarī gives the dates, not merely of the events themselves, but of the arrival at Court of the news of them.'[2]

The same institutions reappear in two empires built by representatives of an Iranic Muslim Civilization that was affiliated to the Syriac and had retained a memory of the parent society's achievements. Seventeenth-century Western observers of the Ottoman Empire avowed their admiration for the imperial highways—the like of which were not to be found in the Western Europe of that day—and for the courier service, staffed with mounted Tatars, who emulated the hard riding of Darius's Persian equerries. The contemporary empire of the Timurid Mughals in India never attained the Ottoman standard either in the material quality of its roads or in the effectiveness of its public police, but these shortcomings did not prevent it from operating an espionage and intelligence system in the Achaemenian and 'Abbasid tradition. Confidential news bulletins were systematically sent in from each province by an official reporter (wāqiʿah nawī) and were submitted to the Emperor by his mīr bakhshī.[3] When the Mughal Power went to pieces in the eighteenth century of the Christian Era, this intelligence organization continued to function longer than most other parts of the dilapidated imperial administrative machine.

Napoleon, who was an active and ubiquitous builder of roads during the short life of the transitory universal state[4] which he provided for an abortive Medieval Western city-state cosmos,[5] was in this, as in so much of the rest of his work, making a conscious attempt to evoke a ghost of the Roman Empire; and the Petrine Russian Empire had deliberately set itself to acquire the Western technique which it used in its latter days for establishing and consolidating its hold over Transcaucasia, Trans-

[1] von Kremer, A. *Culturgeschichte des Orients unter den Chalifen* (Vienna 1875–7, Braumüller, 2 vols.), vol. i, pp. 193 and 195; English translation by S. Khuda Bukhsh: *The Orient under the Caliphs* (Calcutta 1920, University Press), pp. 230 and 232.
[2] Wellhausen, J.: *Das Arabische Reich und sein Sturz* (Berlin 1902, Reimer), p. 350.
[3] See Ibn Hasan: *The Central Structure of the Mughal Empire* (Oxford 1936, University Press), pp. 220–1.   [4] See xi, map 60.
[5] This aspect of the Napoleonic Empire has been examined in V. v. 619–42.

caspia, the Oxus–Jaxartes Basin, and a Maritime Province on the Pacific coast of the Continent by railway-building on a scale that outstripped all contemporary achievements in the United States and Canada. But similar circumstances and requirements likewise called similar administrative machinery into existence in other universal states which could not have drawn their inspiration, even at second or third hand, from the practice and experience of imperial chanceries at Ur or Susa or Rome or Baghdad.

Ts'in She Hwang-ti, the revolutionary founder of a Sinic universal state, was a builder of roads radiating from his capital, which he used for making political inspections and carrying out statistical surveys.[1] The inspectorate was elaborately organized. An Inspector-General, with two deputies, in the capital was served by a numerous staff of subordinates both in the capital and in the provinces, and there were special inspectorates, besides, for 'subject barbarians' and 'subject states'.[2] The Incas, likewise, were builders of roads and fortresses.[3] Like the Roman conquerors of Italy, the Incas, in their systematic northward conquests, used these instruments to consolidate each gain of ground, in preparation for the next advance.[4] The completed system consisted of two main roads running parallel, south and north, one along the Andean Plateau and the other along the Pacific Coast, with transverse connecting roads at intervals. These roads were carried across the rivers by bridges of stone and wood, by suspension bridges of rope, or by cable and basket.[5] There were store-houses strung along the route, and relays of post-runners[6] were stationed at intervals of one and a half leagues. A message could travel from Cuzco to Quito—a distance of more than a thousand miles as the crow flies and perhaps half as much again by road—in as short a time as ten days.[7] The organization of this service was attributed to the eighth Inca, Pachacutec (*imperabat circa* A.D. 1400–48).[8] The travelling facilities were used by the Inca himself and by itinerant imperial inspectors, intendants, and judges.[9]

'The surveillance [of the Central Government over the provinces] was provided for by inspectors, drawn from the ranks of the *orejones*,[10] who

[1] See Hackmann, H.: *Chinesische Philosophie* (Munich 1927, Reinhardt), p. 168; Fitzgerald, C. P.: *China, A Short Cultural History* (London 1935, Cresset Press), p. 138; Franke, O.: *Geschichte des Chinesischen Reiches*, vol. i (Berlin and Leipzig 1930, de Gruyter), p. 233. Ts'in She Hwang-ti imposed a standard measure for the axle-length of carts, in order that any cart might be able to travel over any of the deeply rutted roads in the loess country in the North and North-West. In the foregoing period of the Contending States, when each locality had had a customary axle-length of its own, through-traffic had been hampered by the necessity, at frequent intervals, of either changing the axles of the cart or else trans-shipping the freight to another cart of the right axle-gauge for the next stage of the journey (Fitzgerald, op. cit., p. 138; Franke, op. cit., vol. cit., p. 233).
[2] See Franke, op. cit., vol. cit., pp. 230 and 231.
[3] See Joyce, T. A.: *South American Archaeology* (London 1912, Lee Warner), p. 56.
[4] See ibid., p. 94.
[5] See ibid., pp. 106–7; Baudin, L.: *L'Empire Socialiste des Inka* (Paris 1928, Institut d'Ethnologie), pp. 189–96. [6] See ibid., pp. 196–8.
[7] See ibid., p. 197. [8] See Joyce, op. cit., p. 108.
[9] See ibid., p. 109; Markham, Sir Clements: *The Incas of Peru* (London 1910, Smith Elder), pp. 162–3; Baudin, op. cit., pp. 198–9.
[10] The nickname given to the ruling minority in the Inca Empire by their Spanish conquerors (see V. v. 50–51).—A.J.T.

made general tours of the Empire every three years, and by secret agents of the Inca . . . who paid visits, incognito, to all districts. These agents' instructions were to observe, to listen to complaints, and to report, but it was not within their competence to take measures for the suppression of abuses. Under this system, several brothers of the Inca Tupac Yupanqui were successively appointed inspectors. . . . The duties of inspector-in-chief were performed by the Inca himself; he travelled over the Empire in his golden litter, and during the whole period of his visits—which were very long, considering that he sometimes remained absent [from the capital] for as much as three or four years—he would be hearing petitions and dispensing justice.'[1]

While the means of communication with which the Inca Empire equipped itself were thus assiduously used by the public authorities, including the Emperor in person, they were not at the disposal of private travellers—in contrast to contemporary practice in Central America, where travelling companies of merchants, organized in a guild, were continually extending the field of their private economic enterprise[2] in advance of the expansion of the Aztec Empire,[3] like the Roman *negotiatores* who, in their irrepressible eagerness for profits, used to push their way in advance of the legions into perilous no-man's-lands,[4] and linger there after the legions had retreated.[5] This active international trade in private hands seems to have been part of the heritage of the Mexic Civilization from its Mayan predecessor.[6] On the other hand no evidence had survived to show that the Aztec Empire had been prompted by memories of 'the First Empire' of the Mayas when it had turned its commercial travellers to account as sources of military and political intelligence[7] or when it had constructed the installations with which it had confirmed its hold on its conquests in the manner of the contem-

[1] Baudin, op. cit., pp. 120-1. This particular duty afterwards devolved upon the Inca's alien successor the Spanish viceroy. 'The welfare of the Indians was presumed to be his special care, and he was expected to devote a part of two or three days each week to the consideration of Indian petitions' (Haring, C. H.: *The Spanish Empire in America* (New York 1947, Oxford University Press), p. 119).
[2] On this point see Joyce, T. A.: *Mexican Archaeology* (London 1914, Lee Warner), pp. 126-7; Gann, T.: *Mexico from the Earliest Times to the Conquest* (London 1936, Lovat Dickson), pp. 172-4; Vaillant, G. C.: *The Aztecs of Mexico* (London 1950, Penguin), pp. 122-3 and 208.   [3] See xi, map 71.
[4] As, for example, those who were massacred in Anatolia in 88 B.C. by Mithradates Eupator—to the number, it was said, of eighty thousand (see V. v. 69).
[5] As, for example, those whom, in A.D. 448, the Constantinopolitan envoy Priscus found doing their business in Attila's ordu in the former Roman province of Pannonia (for Priscus's mission see V. v. 473-4).
[6] See Gann, T., and Thompson, J. E.: *The History of the Maya* (London 1931, Scribner), pp. 200-1.
[7] 'In the Aztec period the travelling merchants became a special class, and their security of body and property, preserved at first for the advantages which each town could derive from their wares, was guaranteed by the force of Aztec arms. . . . Having to move step by step, and to intimidate or win over town after town, [the Aztecs] needed patience and knowledge of geographical and political conditions. One reason for the honour in which merchants were held was the information of this character which they could furnish from their travels. . . . In time they performed an important political function, spying out towns to conquer and reporting on the tribute which could be exacted. There is a very modern touch about the economic and political functions of these merchants who so often brought military conquest in their train' (Vaillant, op. cit., pp. 122-3, 208, and 213).
It will be seen that these merchants played in the acquisition of the Aztec Empir the role that in the maintenance of the Achaemenian Empire was played by 'the King ye', and in the maintenance of the 'Abbasid Empire by the postmasters.

porary Inca Power. The Aztec Imperial Government built and maintained highroads, threw bridges of stone, wood, or rafts across the rivers, and operated on these thoroughfares an imperial postal service manned by relays of couriers at intervals of five or six miles.[1]

In Japan the Great North-East Road,[2] running up the south-eastern side of the Main Island from the civil capital at Kyoto in the interior to the successive military capitals at Kamakura and Yedo, served first to secure the conquests made by the Far Eastern Civilization in Japan at the expense of the Ainu barbarians and afterwards to bring and keep Yamato under the domination of the Kwanto—as the new northern marches came to be called, after the name of the road by which they had been opened up.[3] Under the Tokugawa régime, which provided the Far Eastern Society in Japan with its universal state, this trunk road and its branches ministered to the policy of the Shogun's government at Yedo as an instrument not only for keeping an eye on the impotent Imperial Court at Kyoto, but also for the more formidable task of keeping to heel the feudal lords all over the Empire—especially those 'Outside Lords' (*Tozama*) whose houses had once been rivals of the Tokugawa in the grim struggle for power at the climax of a Japanese Time of Troubles.

These *daimyō* were required by the Shogun to reside in Yedo, with their principal retainers, for so many months in the year, and to leave their wives and families there as hostages when they themselves were in residence in their fiefs, with the triple object of keeping them under supervision, loosening their personal hold on the fiefs from which they drew their political and military strength, and weakening them financially by putting them under social pressure to live, while in the capital, in a style beyond their means.[4] The migration, twice a year, of these feudal lords, with their retinues, between their fiefs in the provinces and their residences in the capital was one of the distinctive features of Japanese life in the Tokugawa Age; and the grand trunk road and its ramifications were the media of communication for their perpetual coming and going. While the Government were interested in seeing the means of communication kept up sufficiently well to serve this police purpose, they were equally interested in seeing to it that they should not be kept up well enough to tempt disaffected feudal forces into planning a convergent march on the capital; and they 'deliberately refrained from building bridges and otherwise facilitating communications on the main lines of approach to Yedo'.[5]

The Grand Canal

In the main body of the Far Eastern World in China the long-distance transportation of foodstuffs in bulk came to be one of the besetting

[1] See Gann, op. cit., p. 174.
[2] See xi, map 55A.　　　　　　　　　　　　　　　[3] See II. ii. 158–9.
[4] See Sansom, G. B.: *Japan, a Short Cultural History* (London 1932, Cresset Press), p. 436; Sadler, A. L.: *A Short History of Japan* (Sydney 1946, Angus & Robertson), p. 217.
[5] Sansom, op. cit., p. 437. Perhaps their scholars had reminded them of the unintended and untoward service that the roads built by Ts'in She Hwang-ti had once rendered to the rebels who had overthrown his régime a few years after his death (see pp. 99–100, below).

problems of public administration, owing to a tendency towards political unification under an oecumenical government seated in the North which persisted after the economic centre of gravity had shifted conclusively from the North to the Yangtse Valley.

'Commercial growth in China never reached a level which would enable it to overcome the localism and narrow exclusiveness of an agricultural economy. [The] regional groupings were highly self-sustaining and independent of each other; and—in the absence of machine industry, modern facilities of transport and communication and an advanced economic organisation—state centralisation in the modern sense was impossible. In the circumstances, the unity or centralisation of state power in China could only mean the control of an economic area where agricultural productivity and facilities of transport would make possible the supply of a grain tribute so predominantly superior to that of other areas that any group which controlled this area had the key to the conquest and unity of all China. It is areas of this kind which must be designated as the Key Economic Areas. . . .[1]

'The Yangtse Valley grew in importance as a productive centre during the Eastern Tsin (A.D. 317–420) and the other Southern dynasties (A.D. 420–589), definitely assuming the position of the Key Economic Area from the time of the T'ang Dynasty (A.D. 618–907).[2] Politically, the centre of gravity still lay in the North. . . . This anomalous situation rendered the development and maintenance of a transport system linking the productive South with the political North a vital necessity. The link was provided by the Grand Canal,[3] which engaged the attention of the best minds of China for more than ten centuries and demanded countless millions of lives and a large portion of the wealth of the country for its improvement and maintenance. . . .[4]

'Although traditionally the canal is ascribed to the genius and extravagance of Yang-ti [*imperabat* A.D. 605–18] of the Sui, it was not built in one period or by one emperor. Like the Great Wall, it was constructed in disconnected sections at different periods.[5] Yang-ti of the Sui completed

[1] Chi, Ch'ao-ting: *Key Economic Areas in Chinese History as Revealed in the Development of Public Works for Water-Control* (London 1936, Allen & Unwin), pp. 4–5. The quotations from this book have been made with the permission of the publishers.

[2] In the time of Han Yü, a writer on the subject of water control who lived from A.D. 768 to A.D. 824, 'Kiangnan' (i.e. the combined areas of the latter-day provinces of Kiangsu, Chekiang, Kiangsi, and Nganhwei) yielded nine-tenths of the total land-tax of the T'ang Empire (Chi, Ch'ao-ting, op. cit., p. 125).

[3] See xi, maps 46, 47, 54.—A.J.T.

[4] Chi, Ch'ao-ting, op. cit., p. 113.

[5] Waterways for the transportation of troops, tribute, grain, and merchandise were already being constructed in the Sinic World before the close of the period of Chan Kuo, 'the Contending States', which was the second and climacteric bout of the Sinic Time of Troubles (see ibid., p. 65).

Han Kou, the earliest canal linking the Yangtse River with the Hwai River, was dug in the second decade of the fifth century B.C. by King Fu Ch'ai of Wu (see ibid., pp. 65 and 117). This Yangtse–Hwai canal was straightened out, after the collapse of 'the United Tsin régime', by the Emperor Moti of the refugee Tsin Dynasty in the South (*imperabat* A.D. 345–61) (see ibid., pp. 112 and 117); and it was restored in A.D. 587, to facilitate the transportation of tax-grain, by Sui Yang Kien (Wên-ti), who, in the ninth decade of the sixth century of the Christian Era, united the North and South of the main body of the Far Eastern World in a single oecumenical empire (see ibid., p. 117). This section was improved by Sui Yang-ti in A.D. 605 (see ibid., p. 117).

The Pien Canal, linking the Hwai River with the Yellow River, is likewise recorded to have been in existence already during the Chan Kuo period of Sinic history (see ibid., pp. 114–15); it appears to have been completed in A.D. 204 (see ibid., pp. 100–1); and under the refugee Tsin it was used by Wang Chün for the conquest of Wu (see ibid., p. 115). The Sui alinement of the Pien Canal was more direct than the preceding

it by linking the various waterways running in a north and south direction into a connected system[1] and adding long sectors both in the North and South.'[2]

While the completion of the Grand Canal, in its original alinement from Hangchow via Loyang to Si-Ngan, was thus the work of Sui Yang-ti, the solution of the problem of provisioning Si-Ngan from Kiangnan was worked out, after the fall of Yang-ti and his house, by the public servants of the succeeding T'ang régime. Granaries were built *en route*— particularly at either end of the Yellow River gorge ('the San Men Gates'), where storage facilities were required in order to allow of a six-mile portage overland.[3] This T'ang system of inland water communications was perfected between A.D. 764 and 780 by a public servant named Liu Yen, who, among other improvements, built five different types of boats for use on different sections;[4] but seven-tenths of the works accomplished under the T'ang Dynasty had been carried out before the outbreak of the devastating rebellion of An Lu-shan (*saeviebat* A.D. 755-66).[5]

This disaster was a premonition of a Time of Troubles that overtook the main body of the Far Eastern Society when the T'ang Dynasty finally went to pieces at the turn of the ninth and tenth centuries of the Christian Era.[6] After this Time of Troubles had entered on its second and more violent bout in the reign of the Sung Emperor Huitsung (*imperabat* A.D. 1101-25),[7] China relapsed into political disunity and,

one; it took off from the Yellow River at a point in the neighbourhood of Loyang, instead of at Kaifêng, and from this point it ran direct to the Hwai (see ibid., p. 115); but in this Hwai-Yellow River section of the Grand Canal, as in the Hwai-Yangtse section, Sui Yang-ti still had the advantage of having had predecessors.

The Yangtse-Hangchow section was dug by Yang-ti in A.D. 610, and thereby a continuous waterway was established between Yangchow and Loyang, the former capital of the Eastern Chóu and the Posterior Han (see pp. 212-13, below), which was erected by Yang-ti into a subsidiary imperial capital. The main capital of the Sui Empire was Si-Ngan, on the site of the Prior Han Dynasty's capital Ch'ang Ngan (see pp. 212 and 213, below); and Yang-ti carried his through-waterway to Si-Ngan from the new 'key economic area' in the South by restoring a canal, cut by Han Wuti in the seventh decade of the second century B.C., which had connected Ch'ang Ngan directly with the Yellow River—by-passing the Wei River, which was difficult to navigate in the gorge through which it made its way out of 'the Country within the Passes' into the Lower Yellow River Plain (see Chi, Ch'ao-ting, op. cit., pp. 81-82 and 119-20).

[1] These vast public works were carried out by correspondingly onerous corvées. One hundred thousand men and women are said to have been conscripted by Sui Yang-ti to dig his Yangtse-Hwai canal; one million to dig his Yellow River-Hwai canal (see Chi, Ch'ao-ting, op. cit., pp. 117 and 116); and another million—again including women, to make good a shortage of men—to dig a branch taking off from the Yellow River in the Great Eastern Plain and linking up the main line of the Grand Canal with the Hai Ho Basin (see ibid., p. 120). The terrible harshness and brutality with which the workers on the Yellow River-Hwai (Pien) canal were treated are described in an anonymous contemporary monograph (see ibid., pp. 123-4). The means of communication created at this cost in human suffering served, when in existence, as instruments for enabling a ruling minority to intensify its exploitation of the masses. Hence the unpopularity of Han Wuti and Sui Yang-ti (see ibid., p. 122). The first of the revolts that ended in the overthrow of the Sui Dynasty was provoked by Yang-ti's enterprise of digging his Yellow River-Hai Ho branch of the Grand Canal to bring supplies to Sui armies engaged in a war with the Sui Empire's neighbour the North-West Korean state of Koguryŏ (see Bingham, W.: *The Founding of the T'ang Dynasty: The Fall of Sui and the Rise of T'ang: A Preliminary Survey* (Baltimore 1941, Waverley Press), pp. 37-46).

[2] Chi, Ch'ao-ting, op. cit., pp. 113-14.
[3] See ibid., pp. 125-7.
[4] See ibid., p. 127.
[5] See ibid., p. 128.
[6] See IV. iv. 86 and 87-88 and V. vi. 306.
[7] See V. vi. 307.

therewith, the problem of long-distance grain transport automatically fell into abeyance; but, when unity was restored, and the Time of Troubles brought to an end, by Mongol empire-builders who established a Far Eastern universal state with its capital at Peking, this problem of grain transport presented itself again, and this time in geographical circumstances that made it more difficult to solve than it had been in the days of an oecumenical government seated 'beyond the passes' at Si-Ngan—which the T'ang, like the Sui, had chosen for their capital —and still more difficult than in the days, between A.D. 960 and the disastrous year A.D. 1124, when the Sung had ruled virtually the whole of China from Kaifêng[1]—the most convenient of all possible sites in the Yellow River Basin for water communications with the South, lying, as it did, in the very middle of the Great Eastern Plain.

The Mongols had followed the lead of their forerunners the Kin in choosing Peking for their capital because this site lay just inside the northernmost limits of the cultivated land of China, within convenient proximity to the steppes on which the Nomad conquerors of China were at home. Unlike the Kin, however, who had never succeeded in pushing southward beyond the basin of the Yellow River into the basin of the Yangtse, the Mongols had proceeded to conquer the whole of China right down to Canton inclusive; and this achievement raised for them the questions how they were to administer this vast, populous, and wealthy domain from a capital located on its extreme northern verge and how they were to keep this capital supplied from a southern 'key economic area' which was more remote from Peking than it was from Kaifêng, Loyang, or even Si-Ngan. This problem was inherited from the Mongols by their indigenous Chinese supplanters the Ming, who soon found by experience that the military and political considerations telling in favour of Peking outweighed those considerations of cultural sentiment and economic convenience that had led the founder of the new dynasty to try the experiment of transferring the capital to the historic site of Nanking.[2] But a reunited China could not be governed from Peking without some effective medium of communication for maintaining the Imperial Government's political control over the distant Yangtse Basin and still more distant southern seaboard, and for bringing rice northward in bulk for the two purposes of paying in kind the taxes due to the Imperial Government from the rice-growing provinces and at the same time feeding the vast and increasing population of an economically eccentric capital. This problem was solved by a re-alinement of the Grand Canal which made Peking instead of Kaifêng its northern terminus.

From Peking southwards as far as the River Hwai, the Yüan (Mongol) Grand Canal was an entirely new enterprise, for Sui Yang-ti's branch, linking the Hai Ho with the Yellow River, had not been alined with the direct route between the Hai Ho Basin and the southern sections of the main line, and in any case the whole of the northern part of the Sui canal system had been wrecked by the retreating Sung in A.D. 1128, when they had breached the embankments of the Yellow River in order

---

[1] See p. 213, below.   [2] See II. ii. 121–2.

to check the advance of the pursuing Kin invaders.[1] The cutting of the new northern section was started, from Peking southwards, in A.D. 1292, and the completed Yüan Grand Canal continued to be used, after the expulsion of the Mongols, by their successors the Ming and the Manchus,[2] as the Sui Grand Canal had continued to be used by the Sui's successors the T'ang and the Sung. The Grand Canal served, in fact, as the spinal cord of the Chinese body politic and body economic[3] until the dissolution of the traditional structure of Chinese social life in the course of the nineteenth century of the Christian Era under the economic impact of the West.[4]

In all chapters of its history the Grand Canal was, of course, mainly a medium for the slow transport of commodities in bulk, and it could not take the place of roads as media for a postal service. Accordingly, when the main body of the Far Eastern World was politically united, an oecumenical network of roads, to carry an imperial postal service, had to be maintained side by side with an oecumenical system of inland water transport. The Manchus revived a postal system, once maintained by the Ming,[5] which was perhaps ultimately derived from the system with which a Sinic universal state had been endowed by Ts'in She Hwang-ti.[6]

'All Roads Lead to Rome'

It will be seen that, in constructing and maintaining their impressive systems of communications, the makers and masters of universal states usually had a clear and precise idea of the purposes for which they were burdening their subjects with these costly public works. Yet the sequel shows that the most sagaciously organized system of imperial communications may be utilized by other parties than the Imperial Government— and this for purposes to which the official owners and operators of the system would have been either indifferent or hostile if they could have foreseen this unintended use to which their carefully designed installations were to be put.

This variation on the motif of the victory of the dark horse[7] is piquantly illustrated in the history of the magnificent communications system of the Roman Empire.

The splendour of this achievement on the social and political plane is ungrudgingly admitted in a passage already quoted[8] from the pen of a Greek Stoic philosopher, living and teaching near the beginning of the second century of the Roman Peace, who is at the same time sharply

---

[1] See Chi, Ch'ao-ting, op. cit., p. 140. [2] See ibid., p. 140.

[3] In the last days of the Yüan régime, when the Mongols were losing their grip on the 'key economic area' in the Yangtse Basin which they had linked with Peking by their new alinement of the Grand Canal, they attempted, from A.D. 1352 onwards, to develop a subsidiary source of supply in the immediate neighbourhood of Peking in the Hai Ho Basin; but this policy never had much success (ibid., pp. 144–6).

[4] Chi, Ch'ao-ting, op. cit., p. 149. An interesting account of an excursion on the Yüan Grand Canal that was made in A.D. 1853 by an acute Western student of the Far Eastern Civilization in China will be found in Meadowes, T. T.: The Chinese and Their Rebellions (London 1856, Smith Elder), pp. 213–50.

[5] See Michael, F.: The Origin of Manchu Rule in China (Baltimore 1942, Johns Hopkins Press), p. 118, n. 16. [6] See p. 85, above.

[7] For other variations on the same elemental theme see IV. iv. 245–584, passim.

[8] Epictetus: Dissertations, Book III, chap. xiii, §§ 9–13, quoted in V. vi. 3 and 142 (in the latter place, including the moral).

aware of the psychological and spiritual limitations of Caesar's power and, indeed, cites his potency in policing the Hellenic World only in order to bring out this contrast.

'You see that Caesar appears to provide us with a great peace, because there are no longer any wars or battles or any serious crimes of brigandage or piracy, so that one can travel at any season and can sail from the Levant to the Ponent.'

Towards the close of the same century the eulogy was repeated, without the philosopher's reservation, by a Greek man of letters of a school which had recognized the Roman Empire as the Hellenic universal state.

'The common saying that Earth is the all-mother and the universal home has been demonstrated by you Romans to perfection; for to-day Greek or barbarian, travelling heavy or travelling light, is at liberty to go where he pleases, at his ease; and, wherever he goes, he will never be leaving home behind him. The Cilician Gates and the narrow sandy passage through the Arab country to Egypt[1] have both alike lost their terrors. The mountains are no longer trackless, the rivers no longer impassable, the tribesmen no longer ferocious; it is a sufficient passport to be a Roman citizen or indeed a Roman subject; and Homer's saying that "the Earth is common to all men" has been translated into fact by you, who have surveyed the whole Inhabited World and have thrown all manner of bridges over the rivers and have hewn cuttings through the mountains until you have made the Earth *carrossable*—with your post-houses planted in the wilderness and your system and order spreading civilisation far and wide.'[2]

If the makers and the panegyrists of the Roman imperial system of communications could have foreseen the future, they would have found it intolerable no doubt, but not unintelligible in a world in which 'all roads' led 'to Rome', that the thoroughfares which in their time were bringing prisoners, petitioners, and sightseers to the Imperial City should one day bring barbarian war-bands or the armies of rival empires. They might even have taken a rueful pride in the thought that, in their impartial service to foes and friends alike, the Roman roads would still be bearing witness to the Empire's former greatness in those latter days of her adversity. These imperial highways certainly enabled, and possibly inspired, the barbarians to make straight for the heart of the Hellenic World.[3]

The Vandals, for instance, entered Spain within three years, and appeared before the walls of Carthage within twenty-four years, of their passage of the Rhine on the 31st December, A.D. 406. The Arabs arrived in Egypt within six years, at Carthage within sixty-four years, and all but in sight of the River Loire within ninety-nine years of their first raid across the Syrian *limes* of the Roman Empire in A.D. 633. And the Romans' Persian rivals for world dominion reached Calchedon, the

---

[1] See Herodotus, Book III, chaps. 4–7 and 88.—A.J.T.
[2] Aristeides, P. Aelius: *In Romam*, §§ 100–1 in B. Keil's edition (*Aelii Aristidis Quae Supersunt Omnia*, vol. ii (Berlin 1898, Weidmann), pp. 120–1).
[3] This strategy of the barbarian invaders of the Roman Empire is pointed out by Nilsson, M. P.: *The Minoan-Mycenaean Religion and its Survival in Greek Religion* (London 1927, Milford), p. 33.

Asiatic suburb of Constantinople, within twelve years, and Alexandria within sixteen years, of their crossing of the Mesopotamian frontier of the Roman Empire in A.D. 603.

The inland sea which the Romans had confidently styled *mare nostrum*[1] proved even more serviceable to barbarian raiders than the Empire's overland media of communication. Goths who had won a frontage on the north coast of the Black Sea by descending from the interior of the Continent and seizing the Roman Empire's local client state, the Bosporan principality, took to the water in A.D. 254 and, forcing their way out through the Straits into the Aegean, sacked Athens in A.D. 268. A band of Franks, who had been planted by the Emperor Probus (*imperabat* A.D. 276–82) on the sea-coast of Pontus, to hold for the Empire against the Alans a frontier at the opposite extremity to the sector that was threatened by the Franks themselves from their native lair, seized ships and succeeded in exploring their way 'from the mouth of the Phasis to that of the Rhine'.[2] This Frankish exploit was subsequently surpassed by the Vandals, who, after establishing themselves in Carthage, likewise took to the sea and put Epictetus's limited homage to Caesar out of date by turning a Mediterranean that had been 'a Roman lake' since the morrow of the Battle of Actium into the naval arena that it had been at the climax of the foregoing Time of Troubles, when Sextus Pompeius was defying Augustus, or when the Cilician pirates were challenging the might of a Roman Republic that had overthrown all its peers, or when Carthage was contending with Rome for the dominion of the Hellenic World. Indeed the Vandals achieved what the Pompeians and Cilicians and Carthaginians had hardly dreamed of accomplishing. In A.D. 455 they captured Rome from the sea. Such a sensational reversal of maritime fortunes had not been witnessed in Mediterranean waters since, more than eighteen hundred years before, 'the thalassocracy of Minos' had been overthrown by Vandal-like Mycenaean and Goth-like Achaean sea-rovers.

If Romans of the generation of Domitian or of the seemingly halcyon Age of the Antonines could have foreknown these coming events, they might have been overcome by horror and indignation, yet they would hardly have been bewildered as they certainly would have been if they had been told that, by their time, the superb imperial system of communications had already fulfilled its historic mission by facilitating the journeys of a private Roman citizen of whom they had never heard. When Augustus imposed the Roman Peace on a Pisidia that had not been effectively subdued by either the Achaemenids on the Seleucids, he was unconsciously paving the way for Saint Paul, on his first missionary journey from Antioch-on-Orontes, to land in Pamphylia and travel inland, unmolested, to Antioch-in-Pisidia, Iconium, Lystra, and Derbe. And Pompey had swept the Cilician pirates off the seas in order that Paul might make his momentous last voyage from a Palestinian Caesarea

---

[1] See p. 81 with n. 2, above, and pp. 216–17, below.

[2] Gibbon, Edward: *The History of the Decline and Fall of the Roman Empire*, chap. xii, following Panegyrici Veteres (the passage will be found on p. 145 of Bährens' edition) and Zosimus, *Historiae*, Book I, chap. lxxi, §§ 3–5. The audacious adventurers sacked Syracuse *en route*.

to an Italian Puteoli without having to brave man-made perils in addition to the ordeals of tempest and shipwreck.

If we think of Antioch-on-Orontes as the base of operations from which Saint Paul achieved his spiritual conquests, we shall realize how successful and enduring Paul's achievements were by comparison with the military and political enterprises of the House of Seleucus, which had operated from the same headquarters from the day when Seleucus Nîcâtôr had ousted his rival war-lord Antigonus Monophthalmus from this key position and had removed the rising city of Antigoneia to a more commanding adjacent site to which he had given the new name of Antioch.[1] The appeal 'Come over into Macedonia and help us',[2] which moved Saint Paul to deliver his triumphantly audacious assault upon the European shore of the Hellenic World's Aegean heart, had been heard, and responded to, by Seleucus Nîcâtôr at the height of his fortunes, in an hour when the overthrow of Lysimachus in succession to the over-throw of Antigonus had made him master of the lion's share of the Achaemenian heritage in Asia; and it had sounded again in the ears of Nîcâtôr's descendant Antiochus the Great, when, after emulating his ancestor's exploits by driving to the wall Lysimachus's Pergamene heirs, he was hovering, like Paul in a later age, in the Asiatic hinterland of the Hellespont. Yet the enterprise which Paul was to carry to so brilliant a conclusion on the spiritual plane had ended in both political and personal disaster for Seleucus I and Antiochus III.

Seleucus—impelled by homesickness to revisit at last the native land which he had not seen since he had crossed the Hellespont with Alexander fifty-three years before—had hardly recrossed the Straits and set foot again in Europe when he was treacherously assassinated by an unscrupulous adventurer; Antiochus, ambitiously aspiring to snatch the championship of the Macedonian cause against Rome out of the hands of Antigonus's descendant King Philip V of Macedon and to avenge, in his rival's stead, the honourable defeat which Macedonian arms had suffered at Cynoscephalae, only brought upon himself his ignominious military fiascos at Thermopylae and Magnesia, and had to pay the political penalty of surrendering all Seleucid possessions in Europe and Asia north-west of Taurus. Following in these inauspicious footsteps, Saint Paul, in his spiritual campaigns, succeeded where the Seleucidae had failed. In the Hellespontine city of Alexandria Troas, which had closed its gates against Antiochus,[3] Paul succeeded in found-ing a Christian congregation.[4] And the fatuous boast of Antiochus's swashbuckler Aetolian allies that they would pitch their camp on the banks of the Tiber[5] sets a standard by which we may measure Paul's successful fulfilment of his prediction that he was to see Rome as well as

---

[1] For the relation between Antioch and its forerunner Antigoneia, see Tscherikower, V.: *Die Hellenistischen Städtegründungen von Alexander dem Grossen bis auf die Römer-zeit* (Leipzig 1927, Dieterich), p. 61; Bouché-Leclercq, A.: *Histoire des Séleucides* (Paris 1913-14, Leroux, 2 vols.), vol. i, pp. 32-33, and vol. ii, p. 522; Bevan, E. R.: *The House of Seleucus* (London 1902, Edward Arnold, 2 vols.), vol. i, pp. 211-12. See also the present Study, pp. 201-3, below.
[2] Acts xvi. 9.
[3] See Livy, Book XXXV, chap. 42.
[4] See Acts xx. 6-12.
[5] See Livy, Book XXXV, chap. 33.

her Oriental and Greek dominions.[1] He reached Rome as a political prisoner, but, whatever the length of his sojourn there and in whatever way he may have met his end in This Life, it is certain that his presence and action in the Imperial City ensured the survival there of an infant Christian congregation that was to have a greater destiny than any other in the Hellenic World.[2]

The Roman Roads' Service to the Christian Church

If this contrast between Paul's success and the Seleucids' failure is mainly to be explained by the difference of the planes on which the Apostles of Jesus and the Successors of Alexander were operating, the no less striking contrast between Paul's success and the Mauryan Emperor Açoka's failure in a philosophic missionary enterprise in the same Mediterranean area may be ascribed in a large measure[3] to the establishment of the Roman Peace in the Hellenic World between the Buddhist philosopher-king's and the Christian Apostle's day. Açoka has left us a notice of the philosophic missions which he sent to the realms of five of Alexander's successors in the second generation,[4] but no record of his emissaries' activities has come to us from their mission field, and, whatever their fortunes may have been, they made no discernible effect upon the history of Mankind. In seeking to propagate the philosophy of Siddhārtha Gautama beyond the western limits of his own Mauryan Peace, Açoka was unlucky in his generation, for the Achaemenian Peace, which had proved so conductive a medium for Judaism and Zoroastrianism,[5] and had perhaps conveyed to the Hellenic World the Zoroastrian and Indic elements that are to be found in Orphism,[6] had been broken up by force of Macedonian arms two generations before Açoka's time, and the anarchy that racked the Syriac and Hellenic worlds, with little intermission, from this break-up of the Achaemenian Peace to the establishment of the Roman Peace was particularly unpropitious for missionary work.

On the other hand the Roman Peace proved as propitious a social environment for Paul's successors as it had been for Paul himself. In the latter part of the second century of the Roman Empire's existence, Saint

[1] See Acts xix. 21.

[2] Though Rome had been the queen of Christian cities in the history of Christianity so far, it would have been unwarrantable in A.D. 1952 to assume that she was destined to retain her historic primacy in perpetuity. The advent of Christianity was then still a recent event, even on that time-scale of the histories of civilizations which was so infinitesimally short by comparison with the age of the Human Race or with the aeons of geological and astronomical reckonings (on this point see I. i. 173, n. 2). At the time when these lines were being written, Christianity had hardly yet begun to retrieve the loss of its former Nestorian and Monophysite provinces by winning converts beyond the bounds of the two societies—those of Western and Orthodox Christendom—which were the daughter civilizations of the Hellenic Society. By the same date, however, the Western Civilization had already thrown the tentacles of its communications system and its technology round the whole habitable and traversable surface of the planet. If Christianity were to make as good a use of this opportunity as it had once made of the similar opportunity presented by the Roman Empire, there was no knowing where in the World its eventual centre of gravity would be found.

[3] In large measure, yet only in part, for Açoka was handicapped in his spiritual enterprise by his political power. The ineffectiveness of political power as an instrument for propagating philosophies or religions from above downwards has been discussed in V. v. 646–712.

[4] See V. v. 131–2.   [5] See V. v. 124–5.   [6] See V. v. 85–87.

Irenaeus of Lyon—a Christian Father who was an approximate contemporary of the pagan Greek man of letters Publius Aelius Aristeides—
was paying an implicit tribute to the Empire in extolling the unity of the
Catholic Church throughout the Hellenic World.

'Having received this gospel and this faith, . . . the Church, in spite of
her dispersal throughout the World, preserves these treasures as meticu-
lously as if she were living under one single roof. She believes in these
truths as unanimously as if she had only one soul and a single heart, and
she preaches them and expounds them and hands them down as concord-
antly as if she had only one mouth. While the languages current in the
World are diverse, the force of the [Church's] tradition is one and the same
everywhere. There is no variety in the faith or in the tradition of the
churches that have established themselves in the Germanies or in the
Spains or among the Celts or in the East or in Egypt or in North-West
Africa, or, again, of the churches that have established themselves at the
World's centre. Just as God's creature the Sun is one and the same
throughout the World, so likewise the Gospel of the Truth shows its light
everywhere.'[1]

This successor of Paul's failed to recognize—or at any rate forbore to
acknowledge—how much the Christian Church was indebted for her
marvellous unanimity-in-ubiquity to the communications system of the
Roman Empire. But the connexion was disagreeably evident two hundred
years later, in an age when the Church had become the official partner
of the Roman State, to a pagan historian bred in the city that had been
the spiritual headquarters of Saint Paul and the political headquarters
of the Seleucidae.

'[The Emperor] Constantius [II]',[2] writes Ammianus Marcellinus of
Antioch, 'found the Christian religion uninvolved and straightforward and
proceeded to muddle it up with old wives' superstitions. As his delight in
complicated theological hair-splitting was greater than his sense of
responsibility for maintaining harmony, he provoked innumerable dissen-
sions, and he added fuel to the galloping flames by organizing acrimonious
debates. One consequence was that crowds of prelates made use of the
public post-horses (*iumentis publicis*) for rushing to and fro on the business
of these "synods", as they call them. The prelates' object was to wrench
the whole practice of their religion into conformity with their own
caprice; Constantius's achievement was to ham-string the postal service
(*rei vehiculariae succideret nervos*).'[3]

The sentiments of Ammianus, a Roman soldier of Greek birth writing
history in the Latin tongue, would have been applauded by the Roman
administrators who had called the imperial system of communications
into existence and by the Greek men of letters who had eulogized it as
its apogee. Though the waters of the Mediterranean Sea and the pavement of the chaussées leading inland from its shores were free for all
comers to traverse at their own risk, exertion, and expense, the imperial
postal service was not a facility provided by the Government for the

---

[1] Irenaeus: *Contra Haereses*, Book II, chap. x, § 2 (Migne, J.-P.: *Patrologia Graeca*,
vol. vii, cols. 552–3), quoted already in V. v. 407, n. 4.
[2] Constantius II *imperabat* A.D. 337–61.—A.J.T.
[3] Ammianus Marcellinus: *Res Gestae*, Book XXI, chap. xvi, § 18.

convenience of the public, but a burden imposed on the public by the Government for strictly official purposes;[1] and, before the bishops took the mail-carts by storm, the passes (*diplomata*) entitling private persons to travel by public post were issued very sparingly, and this only on warrants from the very highest authorities.[2] Itinerant second-century Greek lecturers who would have been happy to receive passes for themselves would have grudged them to itinerant fourth-century prelates if they could have foreseen the appearance of such strange personages above the historical horizon of their conventional-minded age. But the Roman system of imperial communications is not the only one that illustrates the irony of history.

The Beneficiaries of Means of Communication created by Other Universal States

The Empire of Sumer and Akkad was as hard hit by its own efficiency in this department of imperial administration as the Roman Empire was in the last chapter of the story. Its north-eastern highways[3] eventually conveyed both the flood of Mitanni Nomad invasion which swept across Mesopotamia and over Syria into the Nile Delta[4] and the contemporary infiltration of Kassite mountaineers into Shinar—a sluggish flow whose waters, eventually submerging Babylon, turned the latter-day capital of a Sumeric universal state into a cultural morass that it was to take the best part of a thousand years to reclaim.[5] The corresponding north-western highway[6] conveyed Hittite marauders from the Anatolian Plateau on the lightning raid in which they sacked Babylon *circa* 1595 or 1531 B.C.[7] The success with which the barbarians thus used the imperial thoroughfares of the Empire of Sumer and Akkad to break the Empire's power and to plunder its wealth was sensational, yet at the same time it was a performance which was to have little lasting effect on the fortunes of Mankind, as was evident in the perspective of some three and a half millennia of subsequent history. There was, however, another unintended beneficiary from these roads whose influence, under many masks, was still at work in the World in A.D. 1952; for it was the forerunners of this Sumeric

---

[1] See Hirschfeld, op. cit., pp. 190–1 and 204.   [2] See ibid., pp. 198–200.
[3] See xi, map 11.   [4] See I. i. 104–7.
[5] The Babylonic Civilization which eventually arose on the derelict site of the Sumeric World must have been in full cultural health in the eighth century B.C., when it began to make major discoveries in the field of astronomy (see IV. iv. 23–24).

'Astronomy was not a science at a fabulously early time; its beginnings as a science date back only to the late Assyrian period, its best-known devotees lived under the Achaemenid Persians, its greatest triumphs were under Seleucid or even Parthian rule. . . . The first advance is attributed to the Babylonian King Nabu-naṣir, whose era, beginning 747 and remembered to late classical times, introduced a nineteen-year cycle of intercalation which was later modified but never abandoned in principle. Significant is the fact that the first eclipses quoted by Ptolemy date from exactly this time. Evidently there was a new emphasis on observation. . . . Scientific astronomy was primarily developed from practical considerations, and, in particular, from the need of adjusting the calendar' (Olmstead, A. T.: 'Babylonian Astronomy—Historical Sketch', in the *American Journal of Semitic Languages and Literatures*, vol. lv, April 1938, No. 2, pp. 114 and 117).   [6] See xi, map 11.
[7] The historical context, as well as the dating, suggested for the Hittite sack of Babylon in I. i. 111 and V. v. 263–4, had to be reconsidered in the light of archaeological discoveries made since the writing of the first six volumes of this Study (see the Note on Chronology in vol. x, on pp. 167–212, below).

imperial communications system that had conveyed the worship of Ishtar and Tammuz, the Mother and her Son, on the first stages of that long journey which—in diverging directions and through continual metamorphoses—was to carry this rudiment of a Sumeric higher religion over Syria to the shrine at Abydos on the banks of the Nile, and over Asia Minor to the Island of Heligoland among the waters of the North Sea.[1]

When the Achaemenidae, establishing a wider empire on the site of Ur-Nammu's and Šulgi's, reconditioned the same north-western highway and extended it to the shores of the Aegean and the Hellespont, they, in their turn, were leading a lightning conductor into the heart of their dominions. Their magnificent installations opened the way for the Pretender Cyrus the Younger to march his invincible ten thousand Greek mercenaries from Sardis to Cunaxa,[2] and for Alexander to follow, from the Granicus to Arbela, the trail which the Ten Thousand had blazed for an Hellenic conquest of South-Western Asia. The lightning speed of Alexander's marches in the western and central provinces of the Empire bears witness to the excellence of the Achaemenian roads as well as to the endurance of the Macedonian troops and to their leader's own demonic energy.[3] The political achievements of Alexander and his successors were, however, as negative and ephemeral as they were astonishing. While it took them no more than five years to break the Achaemenian Empire up, they never succeeded in putting the fragments together again. The true beneficiaries of the Achaemenian empire-builders' constructive work were two higher religions, Judaism and Zoroastrianism, and the tragically efficient destructive ability of the Macedonian *conquistadores* cleared the field, not for a Macedonian reproduction of the Achaemenian Empire, but for an influx of Hellenic culture.

When, after an interval of nearly a thousand years of Hellenic intrusion, the Syriac universal state, originally embodied in the Achaemenian Empire, was reconstituted at last in the shape of the Arab Caliphate,[4] it was the turn of the north-eastern highway—now pushed forward again by Arab empire-builders up to the Transoxanian shore of the Eurasian Steppe[5]—to serve as the suicidally directed lightning conductor for a *Blitzkrieg* in the Nomadic style of warfare. The *coup de grâce* which the Empire of Sumer and Akkad had received from the Hittites, and the Achaemenian Empire from the Macedonians, pouring down the north-west highway from a barbarian reservoir in Europe, was administered to the Caliphate by Turks and Mongols breaking in from the Eurasian Steppe in the track of the Mitanni.[6] Contemporaneously, other barbarian

---

[1] See V. v. 148–52 and IX. viii. 453.

[2] The efficiency of the Achaemenian system of communications is attested, not only by the ease and rapidity of Cyrus the Younger's south-eastward march, but by the necessity in which the Ten Thousand found themselves, on their subsequent retreat, of abandoning the Imperial Highway, and taking to the trackless mountains of Kurdistan, in order to shake off their pursuers (see Xenophon: *Expeditio Cyri*, Book III, chap. v, §§ 7–18).

[3] North-east of the Caspian Gates, Alexander had a very much rougher and slower passage. An explanation of this contrast has been offered in II. ii. 139–40.

[4] See I. i. 73–77.   [5] See II. ii. 141–2 and 378–84.

[6] On this point see I. i. 104–6.

invaders of the Caliphate were sped on their way by other imperial thoroughfares. The North African coast-road from Alexandria to the Straits of Gibraltar,[1] which the Primitive Muslim empire-builders had opened up, and the road from the Straits of Gibraltar to the Rhône,[2] which they had taken over from the Roman Empire's Visigothic successor-state, served to carry the barbarian Arab Banu Hilāl and Sulaym from east to west, the Western Christian invaders of the Peninsular domain of Dār-al-Islām from north to south, and Berber war-bands—unsuccessfully disguised by the high-sounding names of 'Fāṭimids', Murābits, and Muwaḥḥids—both eastward to the Nile and northward to the Ebro. Here too, however, the lasting beneficiary from the imperial system of communications was not any barbarian invader. The historic mission of the wonderful organization described in the Corpus of Arab Geographers[3] was to facilitate the propagation of Islam.

A few more illustrations of our theme may be cited to complete the tale. The thoroughfares traversing the Eurasian Steppe in all directions —from the Carpathians, Pamirs, and Kwenlung to Qāraqorum and Peking—that were opened up for the short span of about ninety years[4] by the Mongol Empire, were to serve, not the Mongol empire-builders, but alien religious missionaries. These Mongol-made thoroughfares gave Western Catholic Christianity its first opportunity to attempt the conversion of China;[5] they gave Islam two footholds within China's western borders;[6] and they prepared the way for the eventual conversion of the Mongols themselves and their Calmuck kinsmen to the Tibetan Tantric form of Mahayanian Buddhism.[7] The Grand Trunk Canal which was the *chef d'œuvre* among the public works of the Far Eastern universal state in China served to convey a second wave of Western Catholic Christian missionaries from the southern ports to Peking. The communications system of the Timurid Mughal Empire in India, which was too ramshackle to hold the Empire together, sufficed to carry contemporary Catholic missionaries on successive expeditions from Goa to Agra and made it possible for the Emperor Akbar to assemble at his court a mixed company of exponents of rival faiths whose seances in his presence inspired him to promulgate his own abortive *Din Ilāhī*.[8] The roads efficiently provided by the Aztecs and the Incas enabled Cortés and Pizarro to overrun two new worlds with the lightning speed of a Macedonian Alexander, and thereby opened the way for Catholicism to make lasting spiritual conquests in these evanescent military *conquistadores*' wake. In the Sinic World, Ts'in She Hwang-ti's work was overtaken by the same nemesis.

'The construction of roads was a benefit to the Empire, but it proved a danger to the Ts'in Dynasty. When the great revolt occurred, the armies of the rebels found that the new roads served their purposes as well [as], or better than, those of the soldiers of Ts'in. For all the roads centred on the capital. The rebel armies were thus able to move swiftly and easily into the western hill country, hitherto so difficult of access, while the Ts'in

---

[1] See xi, maps 33 and 37.   [2] See ibid.
[3] See p. 83, above.   [4] *Circa* A.D. 1241–1328 (see V. v. 112 and XIII. x. 76, n. 3).
[5] See V. v. 113–15.   [6] See pp. 74–75, above, and p. 160, below.
[7] See III. iii. 451; IV. iv. 497; and V. v. 309–10.   [8] See V. v. 699–704.

generals, endeavouring to cope with rebellion in all parts of China, were hampered by the lack of lateral communications.'[1]

During a Napoleonic occupation of Dalmatia that lasted less than ten years, the French empire-builders did their road-building so well for the benefit of a Hapsburg Monarchy which was to enter into the fruits of their labours that the subsequent spectacle of these fine public works which the French had left behind them startled the astonished Emperor Francis into exclaiming that it was a pity that the French had not stayed in Dalmatia a bit longer.[2]

An Islamic Pilgrims' Way[3]

There was one famous road, 'the King's Highway',[4] which had played an historic part in the life of one empire after another. This thoroughfare ran north and south, along the border between Syria and the Syrian Desert, from the crossings of the Euphrates, at the point where the river bends nearest to the Mediterranean, through Damascus and Transjordan to the head of the Gulf of 'Aqabah, where the road branched westwards across the Desert of Sinai towards Egypt and south-eastwards into Arabia. This King's Highway had served successively the Empire of Sumer and Akkad, 'the New Empire' of Egypt, the Neo-Babylonian Empire, and the Achaemenian Empire. After the shattering of the Achaemenian Peace by Alexander, the Ptolemies and the Seleucids, holding opposite ends of the thoroughfare, had contended with one another for possession of the whole of it, and the Seleucids had won the contest only to give place to Rome—till the King's Highway had changed hands again from the Roman Empire to the Arab Caliphate and thereafter, in its southern sector, from the 'Abbasids' Fātimid successor-state to the Crusader Kingdom of Jerusalem.

In the course of its long and chequered history the King's Highway has been used, not only by its official masters of the moment, but by rebels, raiders, and rival Powers. The Elamite and Babylonian warlords who had twice taken this road in the eighteenth century B.C. in order to reimpose the long dormant authority of an Empire of Sumer and Akkad on the princelings of Syria had been pursued along their own highway on their return march, and been relieved of their booty, by an untamed band of Hebrew Nomads.[5] In the eighteenth or seventeenth

---

[1] Fitzgerald, C. P.: *China, A Short Cultural History* (London 1935, Cresset Press), p. 138. This mistake of Ts'in She Hwang-ti's was avoided by the Tokugawa (see p. 87, above).

[2] See V. v. 636, n. 3.   [3] See xi, maps 11, 14, 20, and 21A.

[4] Num. xx. 17 and xxi. 22. See Wright, V. E., and Filson, F. V.: *The Westminster Historical Atlas of the Bible* (London 1946, Student Christian Movement Press), p. 40, fig. 25, for an aerial photograph of a section of this road in Transjordan.

[5] See Gen. xiv. The historical events which here loom through a mist of tradition may perhaps be dated some time between the annexation of the Sumerian Empire of Isin by the Elamite State of Larsa *circa* 1799–1793 or 1735–1729 B.C. and the annexation of Larsa by the Amorite State of Babylon in 1762 or 1698 B.C. (see V. vi. 297). The account in Gen. xiv. 13–24 of Abraham's audacious but successful surprise attack on the plunder-laden army of the retreating imperialists is reminiscent of the attack by the Brygi on an Achaemenian army marching along the coast road from the Hellespont to European Greece *circa* 492 B.C. (Herodotus, Book VI, chap. 45) and of the similar attack by Thracians on a Roman army following the same route in 188 B.C. (Livy, Book XXXVIII, chap. 40).

century B.C. the King's Highway had carried a Palestinian barbarian Hyksos war-band to the north-eastern corner of Egypt, and perhaps also an advance guard of the Eurasian Nomad Mitanni to the north-western corner of Arabia, on the last stage of their long trek from the south-western shore of the great Eurasian Steppe.[1] In the fourteenth or thirteenth century B.C. the Children of Israel had been refused a passage along the southernmost section of the King's Highway by the Edomite successor-state of 'the New Empire' of Egypt,[2] and had forced a passage along another section in the teeth of opposition from an Amorite successor-state in the Peraea,[3] on their way to carve out a domain for themselves on the western side of Jordan. In the ninth, eighth, and seventh centuries B.C. the independent principalities of Syria that had emerged from a dark age following the collapse of 'the New Empire' of Egypt and the overthrow of 'the thalassocracy of Minos' had fallen victims to Assyrian aggressors following on Chedorlaomer's track; and when the downfall of Assyria had seemed to promise them relief they had been cheated of it by the immediate substitution of Babylonian for Assyrian rule. On the eve of the overthrow of the Neo-Babylonian Empire by Cyrus the Achaemenid, the King's Highway had once again come to the fore in the play of international politics, and a would-be leader of an anti-Babylonian movement among the remnant of Judah had exhorted his countrymen to recondition this historic route in order to expedite the passage of Cyrus's liberating armies.

'The voice of him that crieth in the wilderness: Prepare ye the way of the Lord; make straight in the desert a highway for our God. Every valley shall be exalted, and every mountain and hill shall be made low; and the crooked shall be made straight, and the rough places plain.'[4]

'The road was to follow much the same route that Nabonidus', the last emperor of the short-lived Neo-Babylonian Empire,[5] 'had taken east of Jordan and through Ammonitis, Northern and Eastern Edom.'[6]

At the break-up of the Achaemenian Empire's Seleucid successor-state, Nabataean intruders from Arabia, treading in the footsteps of the Children of Israel, had followed the King's Highway, without turning off it to pass over Jordan, till they had reached and occupied Damascus; and at the break-up of the Roman Empire the Primitive Muslim Arabs —taking the same war-path, and avenging, in a decisive victory at the passage of the Yarmuk, their discomfiture at Mu'tah in their first encounter with the Roman veterans of the last and greatest Romano-Persian War—had not only captured Damascus but had established

---

[1] See the Note on Chronology in vol. x, and p. 201, n. 3, below.

[2] Num. xx. 14–22 and xxi. 4.   [3] Num. xxi. 21–32.

[4] Isa. xl. 3–4. The technique of making military thoroughfares seems to have been borrowed by successive empire-builders from their predecessors, to judge by the remarkable correspondence between the Pentateuch Greek version of this passage of Deutero-Isaiah, quoted in the Gospels, and a passage in Plutarch's *Lives of the Gracchi* (chap. 28). These two passages have been compared in V. vi. 418–19, and it has, there been pointed out that the correspondence cannot be due to any literary influence of either passage on the other.

[5] Nabonidus *imperabat* 556–539 B.C.—A.J.T.

[6] Smith, Sidney: *Isaiah, Chapters XL–LV: Literary Criticism and History* (London 1944, Milford), pp. 65–66.

there the capital of an empire whose boundaries they had pushed out, within the next hundred years, to Farghānah on the one side and to the Atlantic coasts of Morocco and the Iberian Peninsula on the other. At the break-up of the Arab Caliphate the Crusaders, bursting into Syria through the Cilician Gates and by sea, had forced the passage of the Jordan in the reverse direction to that of the Israelites' trek, and had pushed their way southwards, down the southernmost stretch of the King's Highway, till they had reached the head of the Gulf of 'Aqabah and had thereby momentarily cut the land communications between the African and Asiatic domains of Dār-al-Islām.[1]

This history of the King's Highway over a period of some three thousand years might look like a monotonous repetition of contests between successive universal states claiming legitimate sovereignty over the thoroughfare and outsiders disputing their title by force of arms. Yet the historic importance of the King's Highway lay in none of these episodes. This long-fought-over thoroughfare was to find its destiny at last as an Islamic Pilgrims' Way on which, year by year, a peaceful multitude of Muslims—converging from the far-flung outposts of Dār-al-Islām in Fez and Sarayevo and Vilna and Qāzān and Kāshghar—would make the Hajj, at first on foot or camel-back and latterly by train,[2] to the Holy Cities of the Hijāz.

The Mahāyāna's Transcontinental Royal Road

This pacific exploit of Islam was surpassed by the Mahāyāna, which laid one empire after another under contribution to prepare the way for its astonishing journey from the Ganges to the Yellow River round three sides of the Tibetan Plateau.[3] When Cyrus II had opened a road from Oxus to Indus over the Hindu Kush in order to annex the Panjab to the Achaemenian Empire; when Chandragupta had carried Cyrus's high-land highway on south-eastwards, across the whole expanse of the plains of Hindustan, from Taxila to Magadha, in order to clinch his hold on

---

[1] This curiosity of historical geography had an effective precedent in the Völker-wanderung that followed the collapse of 'the Middle Empire' of Egypt and an Empire of Sumer and Akkad that had been momentarily re-established by Hammurabi, and it also had an abortive parallel in the Völkerwanderung that had followed the collapse of 'the New Empire' of Egypt and 'the thalassocracy of Minos'. In the eighteenth or seventeenth century B.C. an advance guard of the Hurrian highlanders, who had been set on the move by the impact of the Eurasian Nomad Mitanni, had established them-selves in the highlands overhanging the Wādi 'Arābah (see Gen. xiv. 6). In the twelfth century B.C., when the main body of the Philistine refugees from the Aegean Basin and invaders of the Egyptiac World had ensconced themselves in the coastal cities of the Shephelah, one war-band of Cherethite intruders from overseas had penetrated into the arid Negeb, south-east of Gaza, and had established themselves there at Ziklag (see 1 Sam. xxvii. 6 and xxx. 14). Possibly they had been attempting the feat, which the Crusader Kingdom of Jerusalem was momentarily to achieve in its day, of gaining possession of a land-bridge between the Mediterranean and the Red Sea. If that had been their objective, they had been foiled by the successful establishment of an Edomite successor-state of 'the New Empire' of Egypt in the Wādi 'Arābah and on the plateau to the east of it, whose Hurrite occupants the Edomite invaders had exterminated (see Deut. ii. 4–5, 12, and 22). See further IX. viii. 358, n. 1.

[2] The building of the Hijāz railway southwards from Damascus along the route of the King's Highway was begun in A.D. 1900 and was completed as far as Medina in A.D. 1908. Put out of action in the war of 1914–18, the Hijāz Railway remained derelict thereafter from Ma'ān southwards.

[3] For this adventurous route see II. ii. 405, n. 1.

an Indic universal state which he had founded by expelling Alexander's feeble garrisons from Cyrus's and Darius's derelict Indian provinces; when the Greek princes of Bactria and their Kushan successors had taken an unintended advantage of Cyrus's and Darius's and Chandra-gupta's work in order to 'abolish the Hindu Kush' by establishing their rule from Farghānah to Bihar;[1] when the Prior Han, feeling their way westward beyond the north-western extremity of Ts'in She Hwang-ti's Wall and crossing the sand-sea in the Tarim Basin from oasis to oasis, had 'abolished the Tien Shan' by descending on Farghānah;[2] when the Posterior Han had contended for the possession of this coveted route with the Kushan Emperor Kanishka:[3] not one of these empire-builders can have suspected that the mighty public works which each had believed himself to be carrying out for his own carefully calculated purposes were mere fragments of a grand design in which he and his rivals and adver-saries, and his and their predecessors and successors, were each un-consciously performing their allotted task in the *corvée*. He would have been still more astonished to learn that this gigantic network of com-munications was being constructed by a press-gang of empire-builders for the benefit, not of some superlative secular empire of Pan-Asian dimensions, but of an Indic philosophy which was being transfigured into a religion[4] as it travelled—along the road that captains and kings had prepared for it—towards its mighty mission field among the peoples of the Far East.[5] This truth was, nevertheless, to be revealed by the course of history; and, where the Mahāyāna had shown the way, a procession of other religions—Manichaeism, Nestorianism, Islam, and Western Christianity[6]—was to follow as soon as facilities were unin-tentionally provided for them by other empire-builders: the T'ang whose political necromancy succeeded in evoking a ghost of the Sinic universal state to haunt a nascent Far Eastern World,[7] and the Mongols who, after China had been crushed by the incubus of the T'ang's success, imposed on her an alien universal state[8] which momentarily embraced, besides, all the other shores of the vast Eurasian Steppe.

The Challenge to Christianity in a Western Technology's 'Annihilation of Distance'

Our survey has brought to light so many cases in which a brilliantly planned and magnificently executed system of public communications has ultimately been turned to account by unexpected and unintended beneficiaries that we may tentatively regard this tendency as illustrating an historical 'law', and in A.D. 1952 this conclusion raised a momentous question about the future of the Westernizing World in which the writer of this Study and his contemporaries were living.

By the year A.D. 1952 the initiative and skill of Western Man had been engaged for some four and a half centuries in knitting together the whole habitable and traversable surface of the planet by a system of

[1] See II. ii. 141, n. 2, and 370–3.   [2] See V. v. 143.
[3] See II. ii. 373 and V. v. 144–5.   [4] See V. v. 136 and 362.
[5] See V. v. 139–40, 144–6, and 356.   [6] See V. v. 112–17.
[7] See pp. 20–21, above, and X. ix. 16 and 20.   [8] See V. v. 105 and 116.

communications that was unprecedented in the two features of being literally world-wide and being operated by a technique which was constantly surpassing itself at a perpetually accelerating pace. The wooden caravels and galleons, rigged for sailing in the eye of the wind, which had sufficed to enable the pioneer mariners of Modern Western Europe to make themselves masters of all the oceans, had given way to mechanically propelled iron-built ships of relatively gigantic size;[1] 'dirt-tracks' travelled by six-horse coaches had been replaced by macadamized and concrete-floored roads travelled by automobiles; railways had been invented to compete with roads, and aircraft to compete with all land-borne or water-borne conveyances. Concurrently, means of communication which did not require the physical transportation of human bodies had been conjured up, and put into operation on a world-wide scale, in the shape of telegraphs, telephones, and wireless transmission—visual as well as auditory—by radio. The movement of sea-borne and air-borne traffic had been made detectable at long range by radar. There had been no period in the history of any other civilization in which so large an area had been made so highly conductive for every form of human intercourse.

In the light of the histories of all other known civilizations, the development of this system of communications foreshadowed the eventual political unification of the society in which these technological portents had appeared. At the time of writing, however, the political prospects of the Western World were still obscure;[2] for, even though an observer might feel certain, in his own mind, that political unity would come about in some form sooner or later, neither the date nor the manner of this apparently inevitable unification was yet possible to divine. In a world which was still partitioned politically among sixty or seventy self-assertively sovereign parochial states, but which had already discovered the technique of flying and the 'know-how' of manufacturing the atom bomb, it was manifest that political unity might be imposed by the familiar method of the 'knock-out blow'; and it was also probable that, if peace was thus to be imposed in this case, as it had been in so many others, by the arbitrary fiat of a single surviving Great Power, the price of unification by force, in terms of moral, psychological, social, and political, as well as material, devastation, would be relatively still higher than it had been in other performances of this tragedy. At the same time it was possible that—even if political unification were inevitable and indeed indispensable—it might be achieved by the novel alternative method of voluntary co-operation, without coercion or catastrophe, which had been tried after the war of 1914–18 in the League of Nations and was being tried again after the war of 1939–45 in the United Nations Organization. The prospects of this great political experiment, as they appeared at a date rather more than half-way through the twentieth century of the Christian Era, are discussed in a later part of this Study.[3] But, whether the political future of the Westernizing World of the day was to be rough or smooth, and whatever form of political

[1] See XI. ix. 364–74.   [2] See XII, *passim*, ix. 406–644.
[3] In XII, *passim*, ix. 406–644.

unity was to be attained in this world by whatever road, it could be predicted with some confidence that the world-wide network of unprecedentedly efficient communications which the Western Civilization had already installed for its own purposes would find its historic mission in the familiar ironic role of being turned to account by unintended beneficiaries.

Who would draw the largest benefits in this case? In another context we have seen reason for expecting that, in this Western World that had come to embrace the whole surface of the planet, the barbarians of the external proletariat would play an even less significant part than they had played in the histories of other civilizations.[1] On the other hand the extant higher religions, whose domains had been linked up with one another, and with the dwindling tenements of pagan Primitive Man, by the West European technologist's ever closer-meshed spider's web, had already begun to take advantage of the fresh opportunities thus opened to them, without waiting for the establishment of a universal peace. Saint Paul, who had once travelled from the Orontes to the Tiber under the aegis of a *Pax Romana*, had been eagerly venturing forth on other seas still broader and stormier than the Mediterranean. On board a Portuguese caravel he had travelled on from Rome round the Cape of Good Hope on his second journey to India,[2] and farther afield again, through the Straits of Malacca, on his third journey to China.[3] Trans-shipping to a Spanish galleon, the indefatigable Apostle had crossed the Atlantic from Cadiz to Vera Cruz, and the Pacific from Acapulco to the Philippines. Nor had Western Christianity been the only living religion to take this advantage of Western technique. While Western Catholic Christianity was reaching the Pacific coasts of China and Japan by sea, Eastern Orthodox Christianity, in the train of Cossack pioneers equipped with Western fire-arms, had been making the long trek from the River Kama to the Sea of Okhotsk;[4] and these sixteenth-century and seventeenth-century missionary enterprises of Christianity in Asia had been emulated in Tropical Africa in the nineteenth century by Christianity and Islam in competition. It was not inconceivable that the Mahāyāna might one day recollect its marvellous journey over a succession of royal roads from Magadha to Loyang, and, in the strength of this buoyant memory, might turn such Western inventions as the aeroplane and the radio to as good account for its own work of preaching salvation as it had once turned the Chinese invention of the printing-press.[5]

The issues raised by this stimulation of missionary activities on a world-wide range were not just those of ecclesiastical 'geo-politics'. The

[1] See V. v. 332–4.
[2] Reckoning the Nestorian lodgement in Travancore as the first attempt of Christianity to convert India, and the Jesuit mission to the court of Akbar as the second.
[3] Reckoning the seventh-century Nestorian lodgement at Si-Ngan as the first attempt of Christianity to convert China, the thirteenth-century and fourteenth-century Western Christian missions overland as the second, and the sixteenth-century and seventeenth-century Western Christian missions by sea as the third.
[4] See II. ii. 157 and IV. iv. 497.
[5] For the use of printing in China, from the ninth century of the Christian Era onwards, in the propagation of the Mahāyāna among the masses, see Carter, T. F.: *The Invention of Printing in China and its Spread Westward*, revised edition (New York 1931, Columbia University Press), pp. 17–19 and 39–46.

entry of established higher religions into new missionary fields brought
up the question whether the eternal essence of a religion could be
distinguished from its ephemeral accidents; the encounters of the
religions with one another brought up the question whether they could
live and let live side by side or whether one of them would supersede
the rest.

The ideal of religious eclecticism had appealed to certain rulers of
universal states—an Alexander Severus[1] and an Akbar[2]—who had
happened to combine a sophisticated mind with a tender heart; and
Akbar's decorous séances had been crudely and clownishly anticipated
at the Court of the Mongol Khāqān Mangū.[3] But in each of these
instances the attempt to attain religious unity by the political device of
confederation had been abortive, and a different ideal had inspired the
pioneer Jesuit missionaries—a Francis Xavier and a Matteo Ricci—who
were the earliest Apostles of any religion to grasp the opportunities
opened for missionary enterprise by the Modern Western technician's
titanic conquest of the oceans. These audacious spiritual pathfinders
aspired to captivate for Christianity, in their own day, the Hindu and
Far Eastern worlds, as Saint Paul and his successors had captivated the
Hellenic World in theirs; but—endowed, as they were, with an intellectual genius that matched their heroic faith—they did not fail to
recognize that their audacious enterprise could not succeed without fulfilling one exacting condition, and they did not shrink from accepting the
consequences in their own missionary strategy and tactics.[4] They perceived that a missionary, if he was to give himself a chance of success,
must convey his message in terms—intellectual, aesthetic, and emotional
—that would appeal to his prospective converts. The more revolutionary
the message in its essence, the more important it would be to clothe it in
a familiar and congenial presentation. But this would require that the
message should be stripped of the incompatible clothing in which the
missionaries themselves happened to have inherited it from their own
cultural tradition; and that, in turn, would demand of the missionaries
that they should assume the responsibility, and take the risk, of attempting to determine what the essence of their religion might be.

The crux of this policy was that, in removing a stumbling-block from

---

[1] See V. v. 549.   [2] See V. v. 700–1.

[3] See V. v. 115. Mangū was not the only Eurasian Nomad ruler to anticipate Akbar
in taking a comparative survey of living higher religions by listening to disputations in
his presence between their rival spokesmen. The Khan of the Khazars, who ruled over
a parochial steppe empire in the Eurasian Steppe's Great Western Bay (see III. iii.
428–30) is said (see Dvornik, F.: *The Making of Central and Eastern Europe* (London
1949, Polish Research Centre), p. 169, n. 92) to have listened to a disputation of the
kind before opting for Judaism in the eighth century of the Christian Era (see II. ii.
410 and V. v. 285); and in the following century a successor of this royal Khazar convert's is said to have given the East Roman Orthodox Christian missionary Constantine-
Cyril an opportunity of disputing in his presence with representatives of Judaism,
Islam, and paganism. The familiarity of this practice is attested by the two celebrated
stories of the disputation between Khazar advocates of Judaism, White Bulgarian
advocates of Islam, and East Roman advocates of Orthodox Christianity at the court of
the Russian war-lord Vladímir before he opted for the East Roman faith, and of the
disputation between Wilfrid and Colman in King Oswiu's presence at Whitby in A.D. 664
(see II. ii. 335).

[4] The policy of the Jesuits in China has been touched upon, by anticipation, in
V. v. 366–7.

the path of the non-Christian societies which he was setting out to convert, a missionary would be placing another stumbling-block before the feet of his own co-religionists. On this rock the Early Modern Jesuit missions in India and China suffered an undeserved and tragic shipwreck. They were the victims of an unscrupulous jealousy on the part of rival missionaries of other orders and of a timid conservatism in high places in the Vatican. Yet the frustration of their noble and imaginative enterprise at the dawn of the unification of the Inhabited World (*Oikoumenê*) by Modern Western technique seemed unlikely to be the end of the story; for the underlying issue which they had raised was a crucial one for the destinies of all the higher religions.

If the local swaddling clothes in which Christianity had been wrapped when it came into the World in Palestine had not been masterfully removed by Paul of Tarsus, the Christian artists of the Catacombs at Rome and the Christian philosophers of the divinity school at Alexandria[1] would never have had their chance of presenting the essence of Christianity in terms of Greek vision and thought and thereby paving the way for the conversion of the Hellenic World. And, if, in the twentieth century of the Christian Era, Origen's and Augustine's Christianity could not divest itself of trappings acquired in those successive Syriac, Hellenic, and Western posting-stations at which it had once paused to rest on its historic journey, it would not be able to take advantage of the world-wide opportunity that had now been opened up for every living higher religion by the technical achievements of a Modern Western secular civilization. A higher religion that allows itself to become 'dyed in the wool' with the imprint of a temporary cultural environment is condemning itself to become stationary and earth-bound—to be the slave, and not the master, of the secular civilizations and their works. On the other hand any living higher religion that might save itself from this fate by taking Ricci's lesson to heart and putting his policy into practice would be opening for itself thereby a boundless field for new spiritual action. And, if Christianity itself were, after all, to embrace this manifest destiny, it might repeat in a latter-day *Oikoumenê* what it had once achieved in the Roman Empire.

In the spiritual commerce that had been served by Roman means of communication, Christianity had drawn out of, and inherited from, the other higher religions and philosophies, which it had thus encountered, the heart of what had been best in them. In a world materially linked together by the many inventions of Western technique, Hinduism and the Mahāyāna might make no less fruitful contributions than Isis-worship and Neoplatonism had once made to Christian insight and practice. And if, in a Western World too, Caesar's empire were to rise and fall—as his empire always had collapsed or decayed after a run of a few hundred years—an historian peering into the future in A.D. 1952 could imagine Christianity then being left as the heir of all the philosophies from Ikhnaton's to Hegel's and of all the higher religions as far back as the ever latent worship of a Mother and her Son who had started on

[1] For the significance of the interpretative work of Clement of Alexandria and Origen, see V. v. 366–7.

their travels along the King's Highway under the names of Ishtar and Tammuz.

2. Garrisons and Colonies

The Mixture of Motives in the Minds of Imperial Authorities

Whereas Imperial systems of communications are installed by their makers with the single-minded self-regarding aim of maintaining the imperial government's authority, imperial garrisons and colonies have a dual function. Like the public highways along which they are strung, they are, of course, designed primarily to preserve the universal state by whose rulers they have been planted; but in some cases they are also intended to serve the distinct purpose of preserving the civilization whose domain has been embraced within the universal state's frontiers.

Plantations of loyal supporters of the imperial régime—who may be soldiers on active service, militiamen, discharged veterans, or civilians—are an integral part of any imperial system of communications linking the capital of a universal state with its frontiers across intervening tracts of subject territory. The presence, prowess, and vigilance of these human watch-dogs provide the indispensable security without which the most efficient physical installations—roads, bridges, posting-stations, and the rest—would be of no practical use to the imperial authorities (as in fact they eventually fall out of use when the imperial system of security and defence breaks down). This imperial network of practicable communications in the shape of garrisoned roads does not consist merely of the thoroughfares radiating from the capital to the frontiers; the frontiers themselves are part and parcel of the same system; for even the most elaborately fortified frontier lines—such systems as the Military Frontiers of the Hapsburg Empire over against the Ottoman Empire during the century beginning in A.D. 1777[1] or the Roman *limites* in Germany and Britain or 'the Great Wall of China' itself—prove, on analysis, to be lateral highways, skirting the outermost verge of an empire's domain, along which the fortresses have been strung so close together that they have coalesced into a continuous chain.[2]

Some of these frontier garrisons—or lines of garrisons dressed in close order to hold a *limes* or a wall—are new installations, established by the universal state *in partibus barbarorum* where it has had no predecessors. Others, on the other hand, are replacements of garrisons formerly posted along the same line, for defence against the same barbarian or alien adversary, by parochial Powers that have perished in the fratricidal struggle that has ended in the imposition of a universal peace by a single survivor among the competitors. Thus Rome, in the acts of imposing her hegemony on the city-states of Etruria and extinguishing the Carthaginian and Macedonian Powers, was taking upon her own shoulders a

---

[1] See V. v. 463.

[2] 'The Great Wall' of China and 'the Roman Wall' in Britain between Tyne and Solway were each originally laid out as a chain of garrisoned fortresses strung along a road and connected by an embankment of earthwork which served as a demarcation line rather than as a military barrier. In both cases the construction of an actual wall of masonry, along the line of the embankment, was the last phase. (For the structural evolution of the Chinese Wall, see Franke, O.: *Geschichte des Chinesischen Reiches*, vol. i (Berlin and Leipzig 1930, de Gruyter), pp. 240–2.)

responsibility for holding the former Etruscan frontiers against the barbarians of Northern Italy, the former Carthaginian frontiers against the barbarians of the Iberian Peninsula and North-West Africa, and the former Macedonian frontiers against the barbarians of South-Eastern Europe.[1] In the Sinic World the march state of Ts'in, which won the last round in the long strife of the Contending States, had to pay for its victory by taking over the frontiers previously held by the other two march states, Chao and Yen, against the Nomads of the Eurasian Steppe. The overthrow of these two frontier Powers left a gap in the defences of the Sinic World between the eastern terminus of the sectional anti-barbarian frontier of Ts'in and the Pacific coast of the Sinic World; and, in filling this gap, Ts'in She Hwang-ti, the founder of the Sinic universal state, had at least to double the length of the frontier against the Eurasian barbarians that had been held by his own predecessors.[2] In the Hindu World, likewise, the British Rāj had to take over the north-west frontier of the Sikh principalities against the highlander barbarians of North-Eastern Iran;[3] and in the Egyptiac World, when the alien empire of the Achaemenidae had conquered the Saïte Kingdom, the conquerors found themselves saddled with the defence of their Saïte victims' southern frontier at Elephantinê[4] against the still independent Napatan Power in the southern portion of the Egyptiac Society's domain.

In taking over the defence of derelict frontiers from extinguished parochial Powers, a universal state is, of course, acting in self-preservation as well as in the interests of the society over whose domain it has established its rule. But, besides planting garrisons along frontiers of which it finds itself the residuary legatee, a universal state may be moved to plant colonies in the interior, not for purposes of defence or police, but in order to repair ravages inflicted by the devastating struggle for power during a Time of Troubles before the imposition of the imperial peace.

It was this that was in Caesar's mind when he planted self-governing colonies of Roman citizens on the desolate sites of Capua, Carthage, and Corinth. In the course of the foregoing struggle for survival between the parochial states of the Hellenic World, the Roman Government of the day had deliberately made an example of Capua for her treacherous secession to Hannibal at a moment when Rome had been at the nadir of her fortunes,[5] and of Carthage for the crime of having almost got the better of Rome in the struggle between them for world power, while Corinth had been arbitrarily singled out for the same treatment among the states members of an Achaean League whose declaration of war on Rome had endangered the existence of no state except the puny commonwealth that had so frivolously put itself in the wrong by assuming the role of the aggressor. Under the pre-Caesarean republican régime at

---

[1] See II. ii. 161–4 and V. v. 212–22.
[2] See Franke, op. cit., vol. cit., loc. cit. Fitzgerald, C. P.: *China, A Short Cultural History* (London 1935, Cresset Press), p. 137; and the present Study, II. ii. 119 and V. v. 270. [3] See V. v. 304–8.
[4] For the crystallization of this frontier *circa* 661–655 B.C., see II. ii. 116.
[5] See II. ii. 19.

Rome, the conservative party had been stubbornly and bitterly opposed to the restoration of these three famous cities. They had succeeded in frustrating or undoing or arresting three attempts to recolonize Capua,[1] and one attempt to recolonize Carthage,[2] before Caesar succeeded in forcing through what amounted to a re-establishment of Capua in his agrarian law of 59 B.C., and thereafter re-established Carthage and Corinth in 45 B.C. over the dead body of the Roman Senatorial régime.

By the time that Capua had lain desolate for 153 years (211–58 B.C.) and Carthage and Corinth for a hundred, while Rome had been confirming her already unchallengeable supremacy, the ground of the opposition to rescinding the three penal sentences had, of course, long ceased to be the original motive of fear. The long-drawn-out controversy in Roman domestic politics over the treatment of the three cities had by that time become the symbol of a wider issue. Was the *raison d'être* of the Roman Empire the selfish interest of the particular Power that had succeeded in establishing it by conquest? Or did the Empire exist to serve the common weal of the Hellenic World of which it was a political embodiment? Caesar's defeat of the Senate was a victory for the more liberal, humane, and imaginative of these two views; and the praise which an English philosopher-statesman has given to the Romans *sans phrase* should be reserved—as it was by Greek men of letters in the Antonine Age—for the Roman Imperial régime which Caesar inaugurated.

'Never any state was . . . so open to receive strangers into their body as were the Romans; therefore it sorted with them accordingly, for they grew to the greatest monarchy. Their manner was to grant naturalisation (which they called "ius civitatis"), and to grant it in the highest degree— that is, not only "ius commercii, ius connubii, ius hereditatis", but also "ius suffragii" and "ius honorum"; and this not to singular persons alone, but likewise to whole families—yea, to cities, and sometimes to nations. Add to this their custom of plantation of colonies, whereby the Roman plant was removed into the soil of other nations, and, putting both constitutions together, you will say that it was not the Romans that spread upon the World, but it was the World that spread upon the Romans.'[3]

This striking difference in moral character between the régime which Caesar inaugurated and the régime which he superseded was not a peculiar feature of Roman and Hellenic history. A similar change of attitude towards the use and abuse of power had accompanied the transition from a Time of Troubles to a universal state in the histories of other civilizations and other empire-builders, and in a general way it would appear that the devastation of cities, destruction of communities, and uprooting of populations are characteristic crimes of the rulers of

---

[1] Gaius Gracchus's abortive colony projected in 123 B.C. and cancelled after his tragic death in 121 B.C.; Marcus Iunius Brutus's colony planted in 83 B.C. and uprooted in 82 B.C. by Sulla; and the abortive project embodied in an agrarian law introduced by Publius Servilius Rullus in 64 B.C. and withdrawn by its author next year (see Cicero's speech *In Rullum*, which helped to kill the bill).

[2] Gaius Gracchus's colony planted in 123 B.C.

[3] Bacon, Francis: *The Essays, or Counsels Civil and Moral*, xxix: 'Of the True Greatness of Kingdoms and Estates'. Compare the dicta of Oswald Spengler's that have been quoted in the present Study, V. v. 620, n. 1, and p. 56, above.

contending parochial states, while it is a characteristic virtue of the governments of universal states that they attempt to repair the moral and material ravages perpetrated by their predecessors. But, though this historical 'law' may be discernible, it is far from being absolute or exact.

On the one hand we find Times of Troubles generating not only uprooted and embittered proletariats[1] but constructive and successful colonization enterprises on the grand scale—as exemplified by the host of Greek city-states that were planted far and wide over the former domain of the conquered Achaemenian Empire by Alexander the Great and his successors, and by the contemporary colonies of Latins and Roman citizens that were founded by Republican Rome to secure her conquests in Italy.[2] This constructive work of the Hellenic Time of Troubles was the foundation on which Caesar and his successors built in the subsequent Imperial Age—just as Caesar's liberality in conferring Roman citizenship, which was a revolutionary departure from the narrow-hearted policy of the Roman republican régime of the Post-Hannibalic Age, was a reversion to the more generous-hearted policy of the Republic in the age before that,[3] at a time when the Roman governing class of the day had been inspired with confidence by its success in conquering Italy, and had not yet had its heart seared by having to face the formidable issue of world-power or downfall with which Rome was to be confronted in the next chapter of her history by her encounter with Carthage.

Conversely the change of heart on the part of a dominant minority, which is the moral and psychological counterpart of the institutional reform accomplished in the establishment of a universal state,[4] is seldom so thorough or so steadfast that it does not occasionally relapse into the brutal practice of a foregoing Time of Troubles. The Neo-Babylonian Empire, which stood on the whole for a moral revolt of the interior of the Babylonic World against the brutality of its Assyrian marchmen,[5] lapsed into uprooting Judah as Assyria had uprooted Israel, Damascus, and Babylon itself. The Achaemenidae, who permitted and assisted the Jews to return home to Judea from their Babylonish captivity, and who were welcomed as liberators by the Phoenicians,[6]

---

[1] See V. v. 58–194, passim.

[2] A conspectus of the Macedonian and Roman plantations of colonies will be found in Tscherikower, V.: Die Hellenistischen Städtegrundungen von Alexander dem Grossen bis auf die Römerzeit (Leipzig 1927, Dieterich); Jones, A. H. M.: The Cities of the Eastern Roman Provinces (Oxford 1937, Clarendon Press); eodem: The Greek City from Alexander to Justinian (Oxford 1940, Clarendon Press); Beloch, K. J.: Der Italische Bund unter Roms Hegemonie (Leipzig 1880, Teubner); eodem: Römische Geschichte bis zum Beginn der Punischen Kriege (Berlin and Leipzig 1926, de Gruyter).

[3] Salient examples of this policy are to be seen in the treatment of the Sabines and the Picentes. The Sabines were granted passive Roman citizenship immediately after their conquest by Rome in 290 B.C.; this was converted into active citizenship as early as 268 B.C., and a new Roman tribal constituency was created in 241 B.C. for Sabine voters. The Picentes, who were conquered after 290 B.C., were given passive Roman citizenship in 268 B.C., and this had been converted into active citizenship by 241 B.C., when a new Roman tribal constituency was created for Picentine voters (see Beloch, Der Italische Bund, pp. 32, 54–55, and 76).

[4] For this change of heart, which gives the public servant and the philosopher a chance of repairing the ravages of the conqueror, the wastrel, and the hangman, see V. v, especially pp. 38–40 and 47–52.

[5] See II. ii. 135–6 and IV. iv. 468–84.

[6] See V. v. 123, n. 2.

uprooted the Greek city-states Samos, Barca, Miletus, and Eretria,[1] and colonized the inhospitable islands of the Persian Gulf with *déracinés* who appear to have been themselves of Iranian origin.[2] The Jews whom the Persians had repatriated encountered a new Nebuchadnezzar in the Seleucid King Antiochus Epiphanes, whose house was as well liked by the Babylonians as the Achaemenidae had been by the Jews,[3] and they were uprooted for the second time—and this far more drastically than in their first experience at Nebuchadnezzar's hands— by a Roman Imperial Government which had manifested its intention of breaking with the inhuman policy of its republican predecessors when it had re-peopled the desolate sites of Capua, Carthage, and Corinth.

It is true that Nebuchadnezzar's prisoner of state, the ex-King of Judah, Jehoiachin, was released from prison (after he had languished there for thirty-seven years) by Nebuchadnezzar's successor Amel-Marduk;[4] that the Achaemenidae showed concern for the welfare of the Greek communities which they had carried away captive;[5] and that the Romans, in their dealings with the Jews, exercised almost super-human self-restraint before the Zealots forced their hand in A.D. 66 and finally in A.D. 132[6]. It must be noted, however, on the other side of the account, that the constructive colonization that is characteristic of a universal state is not easy to distinguish sharply from the destructive tearing up of social roots that is characteristic of a Time of Troubles; for, if the hallmark of a Time of Troubles is violence and coercion, it is also true that redistributions of population under the auspices of a universal state are not always, or altogether, voluntary. The selected colonists may be reluctant to make a change of domicile which may be judged by their rulers to be desirable in the public interest without being, on that account, acceptable to the men, women, and children who are required to undergo this ordeal. It is known that the Incas—in spite of the immensity of their prestige and the general benignity and efficiency of their administration—met with resistance, now and again, among loyal populations whom they were proposing to transplant.[7] The Greek veterans whom Alexander the Great had planted in the recalcitrant Eurasian marches of the Achaemenian Empire, north-east of the Caspian Gates, four or five months' journey up country from the Greeks' beloved Mediterranean Sea, left their posts and drifted westwards again *en masse* as soon as they heard the news of Alexander's death; and we may guess that, if we knew the full story of the colonies planted by Rome, we should come across similar cases here.[8] Moreover, a willing or even

---

[1] See V. v. 124, n. 2.   [2] See V. v. 124, n. 2, and p. 602, below.
[3] See V. v. 94, 123, and 347, and V. vi. 442.
[4] See Jer. lii. 31–34; 2 Kings xxv. 27–30.
[5] See Herodotus, Book IV, chap. 204; Book VI, chaps. 20 and 119.
[6] See V. v. 68.
[7] See Baudin, L.: *L'Empire Socialiste des Inka* (Paris 1928, Institut d'Ethnologie), pp. 134–5. In general, the Spaniards found the transplanted elements in the population of the Inca Empire more ready than the un-uprooted elements to leave their domiciles in the service of their new masters (op. cit., p. 135).
[8] Though the Roman peasantry in the Ager Romanus in Italy south of the Appennines had been ruined and uprooted by the Hannibalic War and, after Carthage had

eager candidate for resettlement may have been the victim of social or political upheavals that have uprooted him from a home which he would never have left except under *force majeure*.[1] And in the third place a demand for new homes on the part of one element in the population of a universal state may require for its satisfaction the forcible uprooting of another element. Augustus found farms in Italy for his demobilized veteran soldiers by evicting a civilian peasantry;[2] and in resorting to this ruthless expedient he was following a precedent set by the reactionary war-lord Sulla in an age that had not yet been graced by a Caesarean clemency or an Augustan Peace.

capitulated, by a continuing drain of manpower to maintain the Roman armies of occupation in the former Carthaginian dominions in the Iberian Peninsula, the Roman settlers in the new Latin colony Bononia (Bologna)—founded in 189 B.C., twelve years after the conclusion of peace between Rome and Carthage—had to be bribed with allotments of land of 50 acres each for infantrymen (i.e. more than seven times the pre-war standard allotment of 7 acres) and 70 each for cavalry troopers (see Livy, Book XXXVII, chap. 57). Alarmed at having thus set a precedent that would rapidly use up even the vast tracts of public land available for colonization north of the Appennines, the Roman Government next tried the experiment of converting the bribe to colonists from an economic into a political currency. In founding the colonies Parma and Mutina (Modena) in 183 B.C., they reduced the size of the standard allotments to 8 acres and 5 acres respectively, but, in compensation, they allowed the colonists not only to retain their Roman citizenship but to incorporate themselves in local city-states with substantially the same powers of self-government as they would have enjoyed if they had been constituted as Latin communities instead of being allowed, as they were, to remain within the Roman body politic (see Livy, Book XXXIX, chap. 55). The new political precedent thus set at Parma and Mutina appears, however, to have alarmed the Roman authorities as much as the new economic precedent set at Bononia, and, in founding Aquileia in 181 B.C., they reverted to customary constitutional practice and gave the new colony the Latin status. They found, however, that, in order to induce even ruined Roman peasants to settle in the extreme north-eastern corner of the Po Basin and to pay for this drastic transplantation by forfeiting their Roman citizenship, they must again allot 50 acres to the private infantry soldier and, this time, 70 to the centurion and no less than 140—a veritable estate—to the cavalry trooper (see Livy, Book XL, chap. 34).

   1 For example, the colonists from Italy south of the Appennines who were planted in the Po Basin by the Roman Government between 190 and 173 B.C. had been uprooted by the Hannibalic War and its aftermath. The host of landless agricultural labourers whom the Gracchi planted on public land, of which the state had resumed possession for the purpose, was a product of the continuing consequences of the same great social catastrophe—and so were the veterans of the semi-private armies raised by Marius, Sulla, Caesar, the Second Triumvirate, and finally Augustus after the elimination of his two colleagues. An economic interpretation of History would account for the Roman civil wars of the century preceding the establishment of the Augustan Peace as being a desperate device for endowing by force a landless rural proletariat which had failed to obtain satisfaction for their needs by the peaceful methods of Tiberius Gracchus. In effect the armies that fought the civil wars were trade unions of unemployed agricultural workers, and the war-lord politician who raised an army to back him was a labour boss. The understanding between the war-lord and his soldiers was that, if they were to succeed in bringing him into political power by winning a civil war for him, he on his part would use his power to reward their services by planting them on the land in Italy—no matter by what methods or at whose expense. This incentive explains the relative ease with which armies were raised by a succession of Roman war-lords from Marius to Augustus inclusive, in contrast to the difficulty of recruitment during the hundred years between the end of the Hannibalic War and the beginning of Marius's career. (This point has been touched upon, by anticipation, in V. v. 62–3.)

   2 The individual exemption of the poet Virgil from this grievous injustice that was being inflicted on his neighbours is the celebrated theme of his First Eclogue. If we can shake off the spell that the poetry casts over us and see the picture through Meliboeus's instead of Tityrus's eyes, we shall be less impressed with the young Octavian's capricious act of generosity towards one man of genius than with the harsh rule that was broken by this facile exception. Meliboeus's fellow sufferers were legion; Tityrus's companions in good fortune were an insignificant minority. The *beau rôle* conferred on Augustus by Virgil's magic words was cheaply bought and ill deserved.

Incaic Examples of Divers Types of Resettlement

Notwithstanding these overlaps and inconsistencies, it is still broadly true that a relatively constructive and humane colonization policy is one of the distinguishing marks of a universal state.

The most extensive, scientific, and beneficent application of such a policy among the instances on record is the system worked out by the Incas.[1] During the relatively short period of little more than a century which intervened between the foundation of the Andean universal state and its overthrow by the Spaniards, if we date its foundation from the accession of the Inca Pachacutec (*imperabat circa* A.D. 1400–48),[2] the Incas redistributed the population of their dominions on so large a scale that, according to the testimony of subsequent Spanish observers, there remained hardly a valley or a village in all Peru where there was not a settlement of *mitimaes*, as these deportees were called. This high-handedly systematic manipulation of human communities as though they were pawns on a chessboard is said to have been initiated by Pachacutec himself.[3]

The resettlements fell into four classes,[4] of which only one was penal, while one was for military and two were for economic purposes.

Rebellious populations were compulsorily exchanged with loyal populations,[5] who received as their reward what was meted out to the rebels as their punishment.[6] But these penal and precautionary deportations in the Assyrian style seem to have been much less characteristic of the Inca régime than those falling within the other three categories. Military colonies, recruited from populations that were both loyal and martial, were settled along the frontiers,[7] where they were employed in agriculture and on public works as well as on their military duties. The honourableness of their status was advertised by the gift of wives, garments, and valuables which they received from the Inca. These military colonies in the marches had their counterpart, in the interior, in civilian settlements of small groups of families which corporately performed the function of permanently domiciled inspectors or spies.[8]

Of the two types of resettlement for economic purposes, one began with transfers of surplus population from overpopulated to underpopulated districts, and developed—through a practice of requiring the settlers to contribute to the food-supply of their original homes—into a systematic linking together of economically complementary districts (e.g. a highland district with a lowland one) with a view to an interchange of products.[9] Settlers of this class were treated by the Govern-

---

[1] This has been touched upon by anticipation in V. v. 90, n. 2.
[2] See IV. iv. 103.   [3] See Baudin, op. cit., p. 135, n. 2.
[4] Described in Baudin, op. cit., pp. 132–4.
[5] After the conquest of the warlike and recalcitrant Karas of Ecuador, loyal elements were drafted into their country to hold them in check (Baudin, op. cit., p. 135).
[6] 'As has been well said, what the Magyars received as punishment was bestowed upon the non-Magyars as reward' [after the *émeute* of A.D. 1848–9 in the Danubian Hapsburg Monarchy] (Seton-Watson, R. W.: *The Southern Slav Question* (London 1911, Constable), p. 35, quoted in V. v. 293, n. 2).
[7] For example, a military march was organized in Chile over against the unconquered Araucanians (Joyce, T. A.: *South American Archaeology* (London 1912, Lee Warner), p. 224).   [8] See Baudin, op. cit., p. 135.
[9] This type of resettlement and interchange seems to have been an officially organized

ment with studied consideration. They were granted long terms of exemption from all taxation. They were also exempted from the jurisdiction of the local authorities in the districts in which they were planted, and were allowed to form autonomous communities administered by headmen of their own. In addition it was arranged that their kinsmen who had been left at home should come periodically to help them in their agricultural labours at the busy seasons of the year.[1] The second type of resettlement for economic purposes was designed to raise, not the quantity of production, but its quality, and in this case the re-settlement was not by whole communities but by single families. Selected families of specially skilful cultivators were settled in districts where the standard of agricultural technique was low, and, conversely, skilled families of artisans were drafted away from centres where there was a surplus of skilled workmanship.

'To sum up, the Inca regulated all displacements of population; he installed good husbandmen where there was a dearth of them, he provided instructors for populations that lacked them, he planted restless and stiff-necked communities in the neighbourhood of submissive ones; he distributed his subjects over the different regions under his rule with a sovereign hand, as though they had been pawns on a chessboard, and brewed together the peoples under his rule in order to unify his empire.'[2]

These different types of resettlement for divers purposes, which were combined and co-ordinated in the Empire of the Incas, have partial counterparts in the institutions of other universal states.

Penal Deportations

A classical case of penal deportation is the treatment of Judah by Nebuchadnezzar (*imperabat* 605–562 B.C.) when this little but never negligible highland principality overlooking the southernmost sector of the coast road between Damascus and Pelusium[3] persistently refused to acknowledge that, in forcing the Saïte Power to withdraw from Asia once for all in 605 B.C.,[4] the Neo-Babylonian Empire had become the legitimate heir to all its Assyrian predecessor's rights and titles in the

and systematically applied version of practices that had grown up piecemeal and haphazard before the establishment of the Inca Empire. For example, Aymará settlers from the highlands had already migrated to the coastal lowlands, not under governmental auspices, but under the spur of economic need, and in their new settlements they had maintained commercial relations with their former fellow countrymen. Conversely, the Chincha and Chimu lowlanders had already acquired landed property in the highlands, which they used for pasturing llamas in order to obtain a wool-supply for their clothing industry (Baudin, op. cit., p. 133). There was also an interchange of products between the highlands and the tropical forest-clad lowlands to the east of them, on the western fringe of the Amazon Basin (see Markham, Sir C.: *The Incas of Peru* (London 1910, Smith Elder), p. 199).

[1] This practice of mutual aid survived the overthrow of the Inca imperial régime by which it had been fostered. An instance in which it operated for the benefit of a community that had been the victim of Spanish atrocities is recorded by the Spanish historian Cieza de Leon (see Markham, op. cit., p. 166).

[2] Baudin, op. cit., pp. 135–6.

[3] This road—which followed the present track of the Hijāz Railway from Damascus to Haifa, running down the gorge of the Yarmuk and along the Vale of Esdraelon to Megiddo, where it found its way between Mount Carmel and the Hill Country of Ephraim and so descended into the Shephelah—was a variant of the southernmost section of 'the King's Highway' (see pp. 100–2, above), from which it branched off in the Hawrān.   [4] See 2 Kings xxiv. 7.

former Assyrian dominions and dependencies between the Middle Euphrates and the Desert of Sinai. King Jehoiachin's recalcitrance was punished in 597 B.C. by the deportation to Babylon of the contumacious king himself, the royal family, the members of the court and administrative service, 7,000 fighting-men, and 1,000 metal workers and other artisans, the total number of deportees amounting to about 10,000 souls in all.[1] The subsequent rebellion of Zedekiah, whom Nebuchadnezzar had set on the throne of Judah, in Jehoiachin's stead, to play the part of a quisling, was punished in 586 B.C. by the execution of Zedekiah's sons before their father's eyes, the blinding and relegation to Babylon of the rebel king himself, the burning of Jerusalem—including private houses as well as public buildings—and a second deportation which was perhaps larger and less discriminating than that of 597 B.C.[2]

Ts'in She Hwang-ti's penal deportations seem to have been more sweeping than Nebuchadnezzar's—even allowing for the difference in scale between the Sinic World of the third century B.C. and the Babylonic of the sixth. The founder of the Sinic universal state deported no fewer than 120,000 families of feudal notables from the conquered and extinguished parochial states that had once been rivals and adversaries of Ts'in, and planted them in the citadel of Ts'in, 'the Country within the Passes' (the latter-day Province of Shensi).[3] This tide of compulsory migration from the East and South to the North-West was crossed by another flowing in the opposite direction, if we are to credit the statement that Ts'in She Hwang-ti clinched his hold on the ex-barbarian territories that he was annexing in the South-East and South by coloniz-ing them with deported criminals.[4] There are parallels in the Achae-

---

[1] See 2 Kings xxiv. 14–16.

[2] Eduard Meyer estimates the numbers deported in 586 B.C. at something between 30,000 and 50,000 (*Geschichte des Altertums*, vol. iii (Stuttgart 1901, Cotta), p. 175). This estimate appears to be based on the record, preserved in the Book of Nehemiah, chap. vii, of the numbers that returned from Babylonia to Judaea in 538 B.C. after Nebuchadnezzar's sentence of deportation had been rescinded by Cyrus. The total given in this document amounts to no less than 42,360 free persons and 7,337 slaves, and the figures are convincing, since they are the sum total of thirty-nine precise items, while there is also a note of one group that was of doubtful legitimacy and of another that was definitely rejected. All the same, Eduard Meyer's estimate for the deportation of 586 B.C. seems hazardously high in the light of the information (fragmentary and ambiguous though it is) in the second Book of Kings and in the Book of the Prophet Jeremiah. Even in 586 B.C. Nebuzar-adan, Nebuchadnezzar's captain of the guard, 'left of the poor of the people, which had nothing, in the land of Judah, and gave them vine-yards and fields at the same time' (Jer. xxxix. 10; cf. 2 Kings xxv. 12); and this statement means, on the face of it, that the agricultural population of Judah was not only left undisturbed, even in 586 B.C., but was given possession of the former property of the executed or deported notables. Even the deportation of 586 B.C. may have been confined to the inhabitants of Jerusalem, and we cannot be certain that the urban population was deported *en masse* even on this second occasion. 'Now the rest of the people that were left in the city, and the fugitives that fell away to the King of Babylon, with the remnant of the multitude, did Nebuzar-adan . . . carry away' (2 Kings xxv. 11; cf. Jer. xxxix. 9) has to be taken with a grain of salt considering that the same authority declares that Nebuchadnezzar had 'carried away all Jerusalem' in 597 B.C. (2 Kings xxiv. 14). More-over, a quite incompatible set of figures, on a far smaller scale, is given from some different source in Jer. lii. 28–30: 3,023 persons deported by Nebuchadnezzar in 597 B.C.; 832 deported by Nebuchadnezzar in 586 B.C.; 745 deported by Nebuzar-adan in 581 B.C.; making only 4,600 souls in all.

[3] See Fitzgerald, C. P.: China, *A Short Cultural History* (London 1935, Cresset Press), p. 139.

[4] See Franke, O.: *Geschichte des chinesischen Reiches*, vol. i (Berlin and Leipzig 1930, de Gruyter), pp. 244–6, cited in the present Study, V. v. 141.

menian Government's policy of marooning *déracinés* on the islands of the Persian Gulf[1] and in the Muscovite Government's policy of granting toleration to religious dissenters from the Orthodox Faith when these consented to serve the interests of the Muscovite empire-builders by going out as pioneers into the wilderness to prepare the way for future advances of the Muscovite Empire's frontiers.[2]

Garrisons along the Frontiers

A classical example of a chain of military garrisons strung along a frontier is afforded by the Roman Empire, which held by this means its two cross-country *limites* in Germany and Britain, its three river lines along the Rhine, the Danube, and the Euphrates, and its two desert frontiers over against the Syrian Desert and the Sahara. This Roman institution was reproduced, whether consciously or not, with remarkable similarity in the Military Frontier over against the Ottoman Empire[3] that was the *raison d'être* of the Danubian Hapsburg Monarchy.[4]

The Hapsburg frontiersman[5] was liable to military service from the age of eighteen onwards,[6] but, like the Roman legionary cantoned on the military frontiers organized by Augustus, he was also a cultivator of the soil on regimental lands corresponding to the Roman *prata legionum*. During the static last phase of the Hapsburg-Ottoman frontier, after the 'Osmanlis had been expelled from their conquests in Hungary and Croatia-Slavonia, but before they had ceased to be a formidable military power, a continuous strip of Hapsburg territory, extending from the Adriatic coast of Croatia, between Fiume and Dalmatia, to the south-western extremity of the Carpathian Mountains, where these overhang the north bank of the Danube at the Iron Gates,[7] was kept administratively separate from the Crownlands through which it ran, and was articulated into a number of local regimental districts under the direct control of the military authorities at Vienna.[8] The Hapsburg Military Frontier was organized along this line in A.D. 1777[9] and was reabsorbed into Croatia-Slavonia between the years 1871 and 1881,[10] when both the military and the political situation had been transformed by the cumulative effect of the departure of the Turkish military garrisons from Belgrade and the other Ottoman fortresses in Serbia in A.D. 1867, the

---

[1] See V. v. 124, n. 2, and p. 602, below.   [2] See II. ii. 222.

[3] *Vojna Krajina* in the Serbo-Croat language that was the mother tongue of a majority of the troops composing the garrisons in the last phase of this Hapsburg military installation.

[4] The Danubian Hapsburg Monarchy took shape after the overthrow of the Kingdom of Hungary at the Battle of Mohacz in A.D. 1526 in order to provide Western Christendom with a new and more effective anti-Ottoman carapace (see II. ii. 177–90 and V. v. 325–8).   [5] In Serbo-Croat, *granichar* (see V. v. 462–3).

[6] See Seton-Watson, R. W.: *The Southern Slav Question* (London 1911, Constable), pp. 22–23.

[7] The Hapsburg-Ottoman frontier came to rest along this line in the peace settlement concluded at Belgrade in A.D. 1739.

[8] A list of eleven such districts will be found in Seton-Watson, op. cit., p. 373. The territories of the six most easterly Grenzregimenten, and the Czaikistenbataillon cantoned in the angle between the Danube and the Tisza, are shown in the map inset in the bottom right-hand corner of Plate 75 of Spruner, K. von, and Menke, T.: *Hand-Atlas für die Geschichte des Mittelalters und der Neueren Zeit*, 3rd edit. (Gotha 1880, Perthes). The name 'Czaikisten' ('boatmen') is derived from the Turkish word *qayyq*   [9] See Seton-Watson, op. cit., p. 44.   [10] See ibid., p. 93.

Austro-Hungarian *Ausgleich* of 1867 and Hungaro-Croatian *Ausgleich* of A.D. 1868, and the evaporation of the last vestiges of Ottoman power from the regions adjoining the Hapsburg frontier as a result of the Russo-Turkish War of 1877–8 and the consequent grant, at the Berlin Conference of 1878, of independence to Serbia and Rumania, autonomy to Bulgaria and Eastern Rumelia, and a mandate to Austria-Hungary to occupy Bosnia-Herzegovina.[1] It is one of the more interesting curiosities of history that, for some 350 years from first to last—reckoning to the morrow of the Berlin Conference from the morrow of the Battle of Mohacz—so close a replica of the Roman system of frontier defence should have been installed by Hapsburg Emperors who laid claim to *Caesarea Majestas* over against Ottoman Pādishāhs styling themselves *Qaysar-i-Rūm*.

By comparison with either the Danubian Hapsburg Monarchy's or the Roman Empire's problems of frontier defence,[2] 'the New Empire' of Egypt had a simple task when once it had tacitly abandoned the attempt to retain an effective hold over its Asiatic dominions.[3] Thereafter, it was in a position to seal its frontiers against attack from any quarter by maintaining one fortress at the north-eastern corner of the Delta barring the coast road from Asia, a second fortress at the north-west corner of the Delta barring the coast road from North-West Africa, and a third at some point on the Upper Nile to block invasions from farther upstream. In a different context[4] we have noticed that the north-eastern frontier fortress, Ramses, actually became the capital of the Empire in the thirteenth century B.C., when this frontier was being subjected to cumulative pressure from the Nomads of the North Arabian Steppe, the Hittite Power from beyond the Taurus, and 'the Sea Peoples' pouring out of the Aegean Basin in a Völkerwanderung precipitated by the collapse of 'the thalassocracy of Minos'.

After the Libyan barbarians had succeeded in gaining by 'peaceful penetration' the entry into Egypt which had been denied them when they had sought to break in by force of arms,[5] and had subsequently demonstrated their incapacity to serve the Egyptiac Society as a military caste by their utter ineffectiveness when, at the turn of the eighth and seventh centuries B.C., the Assyrians and the Ethiopians had borne down, from opposite quarters, upon the heart of the Egyptiac World,[6] the founder of the Saïte Power, Psammetichus I (*regnabat* 663–609 B.C.), who eventually succeeded in getting rid of both invaders, perceived that he must find more mettlesome troops than the official defenders of

---

[1] See p. 17, above.

[2] The Roman Empire's problem was aggravated by the Empire's failure to carry its European land-frontier forward to the short line across the waist of Eastern Europe, between the north-west corner of the Black Sea and the south-east corner of the Baltic, and its further failure to maintain its Asiatic land-frontier along the short line across the waist of South-Western Asia, between the head of the Persian Gulf and the south-west corner of the Caspian Sea (for the European frontier see V. v. 591–5; for the Asiatic frontier see I. i. 390).

[3] Egyptian rule in Syria seems to have ceased to be more than nominal by the time of the infiltration of the Israelites, which appears to have taken place in the thirteenth century B.C. The existence of the Egyptian régime is ignored in the Hebrew tradition (see V. v. 611, n. 3).

[4] In II. ii. 113.

[5] See IV. iv. 422, n. 3; V. v. 269–70 and 353.

[6] See II. ii. 116.

the country to garrison the frontiers, if Egypt was to be preserved from the fate of again becoming a battlefield for neighbouring Powers. At the cost of alienating the established Libyan military caste, and perhaps even provoking some of their number to emigrate from the Saïte dominions to new cantonments offered them by the rival Ethiopian Power on its own southern frontier between the White and Blue Niles,[1] Psammetichus recruited Greek and Jewish mercenaries[2] to man his three frontier-fortress Daphnê-by-Pelusium, Marea barring the approaches from the Western Desert, and Elephantinê at the First Cataract,[3] where the frontier between the Saïte and Napatan Powers, between whom the Egyptiac World was now partitioned, settled down about 655 B.C.[4]

When the Saïte Power was extinguished by Cambyses, the Achaemenian Government continued to maintain the two fortresses of Daphnê and Elephantinê.[5] Persian garrisons were posted at both places,[6] but at Elephantinê an economy was made in the employment of Persian manpower by taking over and retaining the Jewish military colony which the Saïtes had planted there.[7]

---

[1] For the expansion of Ethiopia up-river, see II. ii. 117. For the story of 'the Deserters', see Herodotus, Book II, chap. 30.

[2] The Ionian Greeks' exploits in the Saïte Government's service in the seventh and sixth centuries B.C. have been touched upon, in another context, in IV. iv. 21. The Greek inscriptions carved upon the two southern colossi of the Great Temple at Abu Simbel prove that Greek troops in Saïte service were at least once employed in an expedition against Ethiopia in the reign of Psammetichus II (*regnabat* 593–588 B.C.), but there seems to be no evidence of their having shared with the Jewish military colony at Elephantinê the duty of permanently garrisoning the southern frontier of the Saïte dominions. The reception of Jewish settlers on Egyptiac ground had precedents of very long standing in Egyptiac history. Whatever may be the truth about the Israelite tradition of a sojourn of Israel in the north-eastern marches of 'the New Empire' of Egypt, there is documentary evidence that under 'the Middle Empire', in the sixth year of the reign of the Emperor Senwosret II (i.e. in the year 1892 B.C.), a 'barbarian chief' called Ebsha, with thirty-seven 'Amu followers from the desert, made application to the Imperial Warden of the Eastern Desert for permission to settle on Egyptiac territory (Meyer, E.: *Geschichte des Altertums*, vol. i, Part II, 3rd ed. (Stuttgart and Berlin 1913, Cotta), pp. 283–4).

[3] See Herodotus, Book II, chap. 30.   [4] See II. ii. 116.

[5] See Herodotus, Book II, chap. 30.   [6] See Herodotus, loc. cit.

[7] Modern Western archaeological enterprise had unearthed a cache of documents, written on papyrus in Aramaic, which threw a flood of light on the life and fortunes of this community under the Achaemenian régime during the fifth century B.C. This information had been sifted and interpreted by Eduard Meyer in *Der Papyrusfund von Elephantinê* (2nd ed.: Leipzig 1912, Hinrichs) and by A. van Hoonacker in *Une Communauté Judéo-Araméenne à Éléphantine en Égypte aux vie et ve siècles avant J.-C.* (London 1915, Milford). This Jewish community was treated by the Achaemenian Government with studied consideration. For instance, Cambyses spared their temple at Elephantinê when he destroyed the temples of the Egyptians (Meyer, p. 36; van Hoonacker, p. 42). In 410 B.C. the Egyptian priests of the local temple of Khnum took advantage of the absence of the Governor-General of Egypt, Arsham, on a visit to Susa to induce the local Persian commandant Widarnag (*Graecè* Hydarnes) to destroy the Jewish temple. The Jewish community's protest at this outrage appears to have moved the Achaemenian Government to put Widarnag and his son to death (Meyer, op. cit., pp. 78–79; van Hoonacker, op. cit., pp. 40–42 and 45–46). The Achaemenian Government had as good reasons for retaining and conciliating the Jewish military colony at Elephantinê as it had for mistrusting and disbanding the Greek garrison at Daphnê. The Greeks were the Persians' rivals for the immense prize of domination over the Egyptiac, Syriac, and Babylonic worlds, which had been left exhausted, and incapable of defending themselves against any vigorous aggressor, by the appalling after-effects of the last and most ferocious bout of Assyrian militarism (see IV. iv. 475–6). The Jews were the Achaemenids' protégés, whom they had liberated from the yoke of the Neo-Babylonian Empire and allowed to return home from their Babylonish

A Persian frontier garrison of which the Achaemenidae were justly proud was the isolated outpost at Doriscus, on the Thracian coastal road from the Hellespont to Continental European Greece, which, after the disastrous outcome of Xerxes' attempt in 480–479 B.C. to unite the Hellenic World under Achaemenian rule by force of arms, was the sole surviving fragment of the pre-war Achaemenian province between the Hellespont and the Strymon styled 'Those beyond the Sea' in the official lists.[1] This vestige of a lost dominion was preserved for the Empire, in the teeth of Athenian sea-power and in defiance of repeated assaults, for perhaps not less than half a century after the disasters of 480–479 B.C., by the valour of its commandant Mascames and his descendants.[2]

While we are thus informed about the Achaemenian garrisons at Doriscus and Elephantinê, we have no record of any corresponding installations for the defence of the north-east frontier of the Empire over against the Eurasian Steppe, though this frontier, on which Cyrus himself had met his death, must always have been the most critical and most important of all in the estimation of the Government at Susa.[3] This silence may be due to an accidental gap in our knowledge; but it is also possible that the north-eastern frontier was not in fact guarded by imperial frontier garrisons of the kind familiar on the west because its defence was provided for otherwise. On its Sogdian sector this frontier was screened by a military alliance with a Nomad horde in Farghānah described in the official lists as 'the Hauma-(?)drinking Saka' (Saka Haumavarga, *Graecè* Amyrgioi);[4] and, behind this screen of barbarian *foederati*, a defence in depth that would undoubtedly be more effective than any fixed garrisons could be for foiling Nomad raids was afforded by the presence of a warlike feudal nobility throughout the broad territories, running back from the north-east frontier to the Caspian Gates, that constituted the imperial marches in this quarter. This mobile feudal cavalry based on almost impregnable castles was master, like its counterpart in a Medieval Western Christendom,[5] of the local military situation.

---

captivity to Judaea. Moreover, in Egypt the Jews, though they had originally been planted at Elephantinê by a native Egyptian régime, were as odious as the Persian conquerors themselves in the sight of the native Egyptian population in the fanatical temper that was invariably aroused in Egyptian hearts by alien domination (see V. v. 351–3; pp. 5–6 and 49–50, above; and Meyer, op. cit., p. 75). The Jewish colony at Elephantinê fell a victim to this temper in the end, if there is truth in the conjecture that it was finally wiped out by massacre during the Egyptian nationalist revolt against Achaemenian rule that was led by Amyrtaeus II in 404 B.C. (see van Hoonacker, op. cit., pp. 51–52). This Jewish garrison at Elephantinê under the Achaemenian régime has a counterpart in the cluster of Bosniak garrisons, planted in A.D. 1520 by the 'Osmanli conqueror of Egypt, Selīm I, who held for the Ottoman Empire the Nubian march, between the First and the Third Cataract, which it had taken over from the extinguished Mamlūk régime (see Budge, E. A. Wallis: *The Egyptian Sudan, Its History and Monuments* (London 1907, Kegan Paul, 2 vols.), vol. ii, pp. 207–8; Toynbee, A. J.: *Survey of International Affairs, 1925*, vol. i (London 1927, Milford), p. 236).
   [1] See pp. 682–4, below.
   [2] See Herodotus, Book VII, chaps. 105–6. It is to Xerxes' credit that he singled Mascames out for appointment to this post in place of the previous commandant installed by Darius.
   [3] On this point see II. ii. 138–9.   [4] See pp. 644–5, below.
   [5] The trouble which this feudal nobility in the north-eastern marches of the Achaemenian Empire gave to Alexander the Great has been noticed above in II. ii. 139–40.

When the Arab Caliphate re-established the Syriac universal state of which the Achaemenian Empire had been the first embodiment, and took over from its own immediate predecessors, the Sasanidae, the responsibility for defending the north-eastern borders of the Syriac World, the Arab empire-builders garrisoned Khurāsān—which had been the frontier province since the submergence of the Oxus–Jaxartes Basin under a flood of Eurasian Nomad invasion in the second century B.C.[1]—with Arab tribal cantonments of the kind that they had already established in the interior of their dominions;[2] and, when, in the eighth century of the Christian Era, the north-eastern frontier of the Caliphate was carried forward from Khurāsān to Farghānah, the political reunion of the Oxus–Jaxartes Basin with the rest of the Syriac World was confirmed by the establishment of similar Arab cantonments in the newly conquered territories.[3] The north-western frontier of the Caliphate was not stabilized until the Umayyads' ambition to complete their conquest of the Roman Empire had been quenched by the disastrous ending, in A.D. 718, of their second attempt to capture Constantinople and by the overthrow of the Umayyad Dynasty itself twenty-two years later. After the 'Abbasids had transferred the capital of the Caliphate from Damascus, within short range of the East Roman frontier, to the more distant site of Baghdad, the north-western marches were stabilized and organized by Hārūn-ar-Rashīd (*imperabat* A.D. 786–809). The forward zone, in which the two principal military centres were Tarsus[4] and Malatīyah,[5] became known as the Thughūr ('the barrier fortresses'),[6] the rearward zone as the 'Awāsim ('the [places] that give protection').[7]

The Ottoman Empire practised on the grand scale the policy, followed by the Achaemenian Empire at Elephantinê, of drawing on loyal peoples who were not themselves members of the ruling nationality for the purpose of frontier defence, and thereby kept down to a minimum the proportion of their own admirable professional army[8] that had to be locked up in garrisons and so withdrawn from active service in the field. On their critical eastern frontier over against the Safawī Power, the 'Osmanlis induced the local Kurdish tribal chiefs to serve as wardens of the Ottoman marches by investing them with the insignia of Ottoman feudatories without requiring them to give up their own ancestral

Our records do not tell us whether these barons were the native aristocracy of the North-East Iranian peoples, or whether they were incomers of Persian origin who had been endowed with fiefs in these territories at the time when the Achaemenian Power had salvaged them from Nomad occupation (see II. ii. 138).

1 The consequent segregation of the Oxus–Jaxartes Basin from the main body of the Syriac World between the Saka conquest in the second century B.C. and the Arab conquest in the eighth century of the Christian Era has been noticed in II. ii. 141, with n. 2.

2 For the cantonments in Khurāsān, see Wellhausen, J.: *Das Arabische Reich und sein Sturz* (Berlin 1902, Reimer), pp. 256–9, and the present Study, II. ii. 141, n. 3. The cantonments in the interior are dealt with on pp. 130–1, below.

3 See Wellhausen, op. cit., pp. 272–3.

4 See II.ii. 368, n. 1.   5 See V. v. 254.

6 See Ahmad al-Balādhurī: *Kitāb Futūh-al-Buldān*, English translation by Khitti, P. Kh., vol. i (New York 1916, Columbia University Press), pp. 253–65.

7 See op. cit., pp. 202–3; and the present Study, II. ii. 368, with n. 1, and p. 150, n. 3, below.

8 For the recruitment, training, and êthos of the Ottoman professional army, see III. iii. 22–50.

hereditary tenures.[1] And, with the same audacious disregard for Human Nature's sensitiveness to climate which the Incas showed in interchanging the populations of the Andean Plateau and the Pacific coastal plain, the 'Osmanlis planted Bosniaks in Nubia in the sixteenth century of the Christian Era to hold a new frontier there,[2] and Circassians in Transjordan in the nineteenth century to guard an old Ottoman frontier against the Arab Nomads of the Hamād.

The policy by which the 'Osmanlis enlisted the services of the Kurds for the defence of their frontier against the Safawīs has an almost exact counterpart in the Manchus' policy towards the Mongols. The Manchus roped these elusive Nomads into their system of frontier defence against the Zungar Calmucks and the Russians by giving the Mongol tribes the nominal status of 'banners' (i.e. units of the Manchu Government's regular standing army), without attempting in practice to interfere with the traditional Mongol tribal organization.[3] In this light-handed treatment of the Mongol tribesmen the Manchu Imperial Government was applying to them a policy which its predecessor the Ming Imperial Government had previously applied to the Imperial Manchus' own tribal ancestors; for the original nucleus of the Manchu state had been a Manchu war-band which the Ming had organized into a feudatory statelet in order to use it as a frontier garrison of barbarian *foederati*.[4]

Garrisons in the Interior

In turning our attention from garrisons on the frontiers to garrisons in the interior of a universal state, we shall find, as might be expected, that, the more efficient the defence of the frontiers and the more successful the pacification of the subject peoples inside them, the smaller, in general, are the forces that an imperial government finds it necessary to maintain for the preservation of internal law and order.

In the Roman Empire Augustus was so successful in dealing with pockets of recalcitrant barbarism within the vast area embraced by his new frontiers along the Rhine, the Danube, and the Euphrates that by the end of his reign three legions sufficed to keep in order the highlanders of North-Western Spain,[5] and nine colonies of time-expired soldiers to overawe Pisidian highlanders who had defied successive attempts of Achaemenids, Seleucids, Attalids, and Galatians to subdue them.[6] The newly subjected Alpine peoples seem to have required no

[1] See I. i. 389–90. In the Mughal Empire the Rājput chiefs were given a similar status *de facto*.   [2] See p. 119, n. 7, above.
[3] See Lattimore, O.: *The Mongols of Manchuria* (London 1935, Allen & Unwin), pp. 145–6 and 148–51, quoted in the present Study, V. v. 315, n. 3.
[4] See Michael, F.: *The Origin of Manchu Rule in China* (Baltimore 1942, Johns Hopkins University Press), p. 39.
[5] See Sutherland, C. H. V.: *The Romans in Spain, 217 B.C.–A.D. 117* (London 1939, Methuen), p. 150. One of these three legions was withdrawn with impunity by Claudius soon after A.D. 43 (op. cit., p. 177), and another by Vespasian in A.D. 71 (op. cit., pp. 190 and 191–2). The single remaining legion sufficed to keep the Roman peace in Spain thenceforward.
[6] Augustus's Roman military colonies in and round Pisidia were Pisidian Antioch (an originally Seleucid foundation which was reinforced with a Roman military colony in or before 27 B.C.); Olbasa, Comama, Cremna, Parlais, Lystra, Germe, and Ninica, all founded in 6 B.C.; and Isaura of uncertain date (see Hahn, L.: *Rom und Romanismus im Griechisch-Römischen Osten* (Leipzig 1900, Dieterich), pp. 93–94). Claudius found it necessary to add Claudiopolis, Seleucia Sidera, and Iconium (Hahn, op. cit., p. 148).

garrisons at all. In the heyday of the Roman Peace the only garrison on the road between Rome and the Upper Rhine via the Riviera and the Rhône Valley was a battalion, perhaps 1,200 men strong, at Lyon; and this was merely one of the *Cohortes Urbanae* ('Metropolitan Battalions')— an armed police force that could hardly be counted as part of the Roman combatant army.[1] A sister-battalion at Carthage was the only garrison, in the opposite direction, between Rome and the frontier of the Empire in the desert hinterland of North-West Africa. In the latter days of an Antonine 'Indian Summer', it could be declared that

'The cities are free from garrisons, and mere battalions ($\mu \acute{o} \rho a \iota$) and squadrons ($\emph{ἴλαι}$) are sufficient to provide for the security of whole nations. Even these units are not posted in large numbers in every city in each national territory. They are scattered so thinly over the countryside in such small numbers that there are many nations that do not know where their garrison is posted. . . .

'Yet [, in spite of your devotion to the arts of peace,] you have not made the mistake of depreciating the god of War. . . . Nowadays, however, Arês dances his unceasing dance on the banks of the frontier rivers, and he keeps his arms unsullied by the stain of blood.'[2]

Less secure or less well-ordered régimes have to devote a higher proportion of their military resources to the preservation of internal peace. When Hammurabi (*imperabat circa* 1792–1750 or 1728–1686 B.C.) had succeeded in restoring the Empire of Sumer and Akkad after a 260-years-long eclipse,[3] he sought to safeguard the results of his efforts by building fortresses[4] and by endowing his army with fiefs of land in order to keep it in being.[5] Similar measures were taken for the same purpose by the Achaemenidae.

In addition to the detachments of troops which they posted at river-crossings, mountain-passes, and other strategic points on the roads connecting the capital with the frontiers,[6] the Achaemenian Government maintained standing garrisons in fortresses in the interior.[7] All these units were under the command of the Central Government and not of the Governor of the province within whose boundaries their posts happened to lie.[8] The Achaemenian Crown was also generous in rewarding distinguished services by the grant of appanages in conquered territories,[9] and, whether as a fortuitous or as a designed result of this policy, an Iranian feudal nobility like that in the north-eastern marches[10] struck root in other parts of the Empire where the mass of the population

---

[1] See Arnold, W. T.: *Studies of Roman Imperialism* (Manchester 1906, University Press), p. 110.

[2] Aristeides, P. Aelius: *In Romam*, in *Aelii Aristidis Quae Supersunt Omnia*, edited by Keil, B., vol. ii (Berlin 1898, Weidmann), p. 110 (Or. XXVI, § 67) and pp. 122–3 (Or. XXVI, § 105).

[3] This eclipse had lasted from the overthrow of Ibbi-Sin of Ur by Elamite insurgents *circa* 2025 or 1961 B.C. to the overthrow of the Elamite war-lord Rimsin of Larsa by Hammurabi in 1762 or 1698 B.C. (V. vi. 297).

[4] See Meyer, Eduard: *Geschichte des Altertums*, vol. i, 3rd ed. (Stuttgart and Berlin 1913, Cotta), Part II, Book 2, p. 630.

[5] See Meyer, op. cit., vol. cit., p. 627.

[6] See the passage quoted from Eduard Meyer on p. 82, above.

[7] See Meyer, E.: op. cit., vol. iii (Stuttgart 1901, Cotta), p. 68.

[8] See ibid., p. 70.

[9] See ibid., pp. 36 and 60–61.   [10] See p. 120, above.

was non-Iranian.[1] Cappadocia, from the north-western slopes of Taurus
to the coast of the Black Sea, became in this way a New Iran on a small
scale;[2] and the top dressing of Iranian population and culture that was
deposited under the Achaemenian régime continued to make its presence
felt after the Achaemenian Empire's downfall. The Iranian barons in
Cappadocia managed to avoid being conquered by either Alexander or
any of his Macedonian successors; and two of the leading local Iranian
feudal houses succeeded, with the support of their peers, in founding
here, on this distant Hittite ground, two of the three earliest of the
Achaemenian Empire's Iranian successor-states.[3] The greatest statesman
whom these dynasties produced, Mithradates Eupator, King of Pontic
Cappadocia (*regnabat* 115–63 B.C.), almost succeeded in undoing all that
Alexander the Great had done[4] and achieving all that Xerxes had failed
to achieve. And, though both the Iranian dynasties of Cappadocia sought
and obtained admission, at an early date, into the comity of Hellenic
states, the Cappadocian kingdoms were slower than Transjordan or
Bactria in accepting anything more than a tincture of Hellenic culture.
It was not till the fourth century of the Christian Era that Cappadocians,
educated at Athens, won a tardy distinction as Greek men of letters who
found their field of action in the Christian Church.

The policy of planting the interior of a universal state with feudal
barons of the ruling nationality was applied, with a thoroughness unknown to the Achaemenidae, by the architects of the Ottoman Empire.[5]

The Ottoman network of military fiefs extended over all the European
provinces of the Empire, the provinces in Asia Minor in which the predominant element in the population was Muslim and Turkish-speaking,
and some of the provinces beyond the Taurus in which the population
was Muslim and Arabic-speaking.[6] It was in fact almost ubiquitous
except for Ottoman Kurdistan, where the native hereditary chiefs were
incorporated into the Ottoman feudal system only nominally,[7] and
Egypt, where the Ottoman conquerors tolerantly—but, as it turned out,
unwisely—allowed the Mamlūks to perpetuate themselves under

---

[1] See Meyer, op. cit., vol. cit., p. 37.
[2] The success with which an Iranian feudal nobility struck root here may perhaps be
accounted for partly by the presence in Cappadocia of an earlier stratum of Iranian
population—the sediment left by the invasion of the Cimmerian Nomads (see III. iii.
404 and 431, n. 1, and the present volume, pp. 606–10, below)—and partly by the
physical similarity between the Anatolian and the Iranian Plateau, which would make
a settler from Media or Persis feel at home in Cappadocia.
[3] The third was the principality of Media Atropatênê (Azerbaijan).
[4] See V. v. 69.
[5] Convenient summaries of our information about the Ottoman feudal system will
be found in Bélin, F. A.: 'Du Régime des Fiefs Militaires dans l'Islamisme et parti-
culièrement en Turquie' (*Journal Asiatique*, vie série, tome xv, Paris 1870) and in
Tischendorf, P. A.: *Das Lehnswesen in den Moslemischen Staaten, insbesondere im
Osmanischen Reiche* (Leipzig 1872, Giesecke & Devrient). The principal Ottoman
sources on which these Western scholars draw are the treatise of 'Aynī 'Alī (written
circa A.D. 1606, when an attempt was being made to retrieve the Ottoman feudal system
from the decay into which it had fallen by that date) in Ahmed Vefik Efendi's edition,
and a *Mémoire sur les Causes de Décadence de l'Empire* written in A.D. 1630 by Khoja
Beg (*alias* Kuchi Bey) and translated by Behrnauer in the *Zeitschrift der Deutschen
Morgenländischen Gesellschaft* for 1861, pp. 272–332 (see Bélin, op. cit., pp. 237–8).
[6] While effective in Syria and the Jazīrah, the Ottoman feudal system was very
imperfectly established in the province of Baghdad (see Bélin, op. cit., pp. 259–89).
[7] See p. 121, above.

Ottoman rule.[1] The military obligation incumbent on a fief-holder was to reside on his fief,[2] to serve personally in the field, and to bring with him a retinue of men-at-arms (*jebeli-ler*), whose number was determined by the officially registered annual value of his fief in terms of money,[3] whenever the feudal force of his province was called up for active service by the Central Government. In all provinces the fiefs were on two standard scales;[4] but any fief-holder who distinguished himself might be rewarded by the grant of an additional 'portion', the tenure of which was personal to the recipient and automatically terminated at his death.[5] Though in both Rumili and Anadolu there were fiefs that were hereditary freeholds,[6] this was exceptional. In general the indispensable condition for legal investiture with even the smallest fief was the receipt, from the Pādishāh himself, first of a waiting-ticket of candidature[7] and then of a warrant of appointment—and this whether the fief in question was officially registered in the 'ticket' or the 'non-ticket' category (*teskereli* or *teskeresiz*).[8]

When the Ottoman feudal system was in its heyday, the fief-holders were recruited from two sources only: from the sons of deceased fief-holders and from the issue of members of the Pādishāh's slave-household, who were invested with fiefs as a consolation prize to compensate them for the personal hardship inflicted on them by the rigid rule debarring the grandsons of administrative officials and of troopers in the household cavalry ('Sipāhīs of the Porte'),[9] and the sons of all public slaves of lower categories, from being admitted into the slave-household themselves.[10] No allowances were paid to the sons of a fief-holder in their father's lifetime, but the father might retire in favour of one of his sons, and, if the father died in battle, a 'portion' might be given to his son as a retaining fee while he was a candidate for a vacant fief.[11] The rules governing the assignment of 'portions' and the award of fiefs to sons of fief-holders were worked out by Sultan Suleymān the Magnificent[12] (*imperabat* A.D. 1520–66). He ruled that more than one son of a deceased fief-holder might be enfeofed.[13] Sons of fief-holders offering themselves as candidates were, however, required to substantiate their claim to be their fathers' sons.[14] Suleymān rather grudgingly admitted, under strict

---

[1] See III. iii. 30–31.   [2] See Tischendorf, op. cit., p. 95.
[3] See ibid., p. 87. In the province of Anadolu the fief-holders themselves were exempt from personal service and were required merely to send men-at-arms (see Bélin, op. cit., p. 254).
[4] The holders of the larger fiefs (*timars*) were known as *timarjy-lar*, those of the smaller fiefs (*zi'āmets*) as *zā'im-ler*.
[5] See Bélin, op. cit., p. 240; Tischendorf, op. cit., pp. 37–38. Conversely, any excess of the actual income of a fief over its registered value had to be surrendered by the fief-holder to the Treasury, which applied it to the creation of a separately bestowable 'portion' (see Tischendorf, op. cit., p. 87).
[6] See Bélin, op. cit., pp. 253–4; Tischendorf, op. cit., pp. 98–99.
[7] See Tischendorf, op. cit., p. 95. During the period of probation the candidate had to serve in the field as a volunteer who had 'staked his head' (*serden gechdi*) on a forlorn hope (see Bélin, op. cit., pp. 232–3).   [8] See Bélin, op. cit., p. 251.
[9] These privileged members of the Pādishāh's slave-household must not be confused with the provincial feudal cavalry, who were also known as sipāhīs.
[10] On this point see the present Study, III. iii. 34, n. 2.
[11] See Tischendorf, op. cit., pp. 37–38 and 95; Bélin, op. cit., p. 250.
[12] See Tischendorf, op. cit., p. 44.
[13] See ibid., p. 47.   [14] See ibid., p. 40.

control and limitations, a father's right to bequeath to his son a fief of the *yurd* or *ojāq* category of tenure.[1] He did not show the same hesitation about giving protection to the peasantry (*ra'īyeh*) by whom the fiefs were cultivated and the rents paid. He affirmed their right to bequeath their holdings to their children, and he made it illegal for fief-holders to bestow vacant peasant holdings upon their own relatives.[2] The peasant was thus deliberately given a security of tenure which was no less deliberately withheld from the holder of the fief on which the peasant lived and worked.[3] All these regulations were enforced by a strict system of official control. The records of the fiefs were kept in provincial registers, and these were called in and examined at the Porte by Suleymān when he made his general review of the Ottoman feudal system.[4]

As a basis of Ottoman military and political power, this feudal system was second in importance only to the Pādishāh's slave-household itself; and, though, after the death of Suleymān, the feudal system was affected by the general decay of the Ottoman body politic which then set in, determined efforts were made, some seventy years later, to bring the system back to its former level of efficiency. During the years A.D. 1632–7, in the reign of Sultan Murād IV (*imperabat* A.D. 1623–40),[5] musters of fief-holders were held, and fiefs found vacant were given to members of the Pādishāh's slave-household in lieu of pay.[6] The two fundamental institutions of the Ottoman Empire were finally abolished by the same reforming hand. After destroying the Janissaries in A.D. 1826,[7] Sultan Mahmūd II (*imperabat* A.D. 1808–39) liquidated the feudal system as well. The fiefs were reabsorbed into the public domain, and the living fief-holders were pensioned off, under the terms of the *Khatt-i-Sherīf-i-Gülkhāneh* of A.D. 1839.[8]

While the Ottoman feudal system was more highly organized than the Achaemenian, both institutions alike were of secondary importance— both for the defence of the imperial frontiers and for the maintenance of the Imperial Government's authority in the interior of the Empire— by comparison with the garrisons and mobile formations of professional troops in the Imperial Government's service. By contrast, the Mughal Imperial Government, which made similar efforts to maintain a professional force drawing its pay from the Imperial Treasury and therefore directly subject to the Emperor's control, found itself unable to prevent this Imperial Army from disintegrating into a host of feudal contingents, each virtually at the disposal of its own commander in consequence of their coming to be paid out of provincial land-revenue assigned to their commanders for collection by them without this revenue any longer passing into and out of the Imperial Treasury on the way.

While even the later Mughal emperors did succeed in keeping up a

---

[1] See Tischendorf, op. cit., p. 47.   [2] See ibid., p. 49.

[3] Ottoman fief-holders had no political authority over their peasants, and a peasant had the right to prosecute his feudal lord in the qādi's court (see Bélin, op. cit., p. 189).

[4] On this occasion Suleymān confirmed in their holdings any *ra'īyeh* whom he found in actual occupation of fiefs.

[5] For Murād IV's herculean efforts to put the Ottoman Empire on its feet again, see V. vi. 207.

[6] See Tischendorf, op. cit., p. 105.   [7] See III. iii. 49–50 and IX. viii. 239.

[8] See Bélin, op. cit., p. 294; Tischendorf, op. cit., p. 110.

small body of artillerymen, matchlockmen, and cavalry organized and commanded, as well as paid, by the imperial authorities themselves,[1] the Imperial Government, as early as Akbar's day, depended for the recruitment and maintenance of the greater part of its cavalry on *bloc* grants of divers grades of salary to office-holders (*mansabdārs*) who, in return, were required to produce proportionate numbers of troops. Even when these *mansabdārs* were paid their salaries—as Akbar made a point of paying them—out of the Imperial Treasury, the Imperial Government seems to have failed to secure from them the upkeep of their full stipulated quotas of men-at-arms; and, after Akbar's death, his successors lapsed into the slovenly and perilous practice—traditional among pre-Mughal Central Asian Muslim *conquistadores* in India—of compounding for the payment of the *mansabdārs*' salaries by assigning to them the right to collect particular local allotments (*jāgīrs*) of provincial revenue up to an equivalent value. In thus signing away its own right to collect the local revenue, the Imperial Government was in effect relinquishing its hold on the local administration as well; and the effect of a widespread grant of *jāgīrs* was thus no less pernicious for the political integrity of the Mughal Empire than it was for the military efficiency of the Mughal Imperial Army.[2]

The deadliness of Feudalism in the history of the Mughal Empire in India throws into relief, against a foil of Mughal inefficiency, the masterliness of the Tokugawa Shogunate in Japan. A traditional institution that was the death of the Mughal Empire was deliberately adopted by the Tokugawa as the basis for the establishment of an oecumenical peace after a Time of Troubles; yet the Tokugawa régime's experience in Japan was just the opposite of the Mughal régime's in India. In Japan, down to the moment when the internal play of forces was suddenly upset by the impact of the Western Civilization in the nineteenth century of the Christian Era, the local feudal lords, so far from progressively shaking off the Central Government's control, found themselves caught more and more tightly in its toils as time went on.

Immediately after the inauguration of their rule the Tokugawa were so successful in insulating the Japanese Archipelago from contact with the outside world that, for some two and a half centuries ending at the appearance of Commodore Perry's squadron in Yedo Bay in A.D. 1853, they were not called upon to provide for frontier defence. But their very success in relieving Japan from foreign pressure must have reduced almost to vanishing-point, in Japanese minds, one powerful motive for loyalty to the Tokugawa régime, and this must have added to the intrinsic difficulty of the Tokugawas' crucial political problem of maintaining their domination over the great feudal lords who had submitted to their suzerainty only under *force majeure*, and then only at the

---

[1] See p. 319, below.
[2] See H. Blochmann's note on the Mughal *mansabdārs* on pp. 236–47 of vol. i of his translation of the *'Ayn-i-Akbarī* (Calcutta 1873, Baptist Mission Press); Irvine, W.: *The Army of the Indian Moghuls* (London 1903, Luzac), chaps. 1, 2, and 6; Smith, V. A.: *Akbar the Great Mogul, 1542–1605*, 2nd ed., revised (Oxford 1919, Clarendon Press), pp. 360–7; Moreland, W. H.: *India at the Death of Akbar* (London 1920, Macmillan), pp. 65–68.

eleventh hour. Some of these lords had been more powerful than the Tokugawa themselves had been until the eve of the establishment of their ascendancy; many of them could boast of a much more illustrious past; and even under Tokugawa overlordship they still retained much of their former wealth and prestige.[1] To hold them in check and gradually reduce their power was a delicate and difficult task. In another context[2] we have noticed the device of requiring the periodic residence of the *daimyō* and their families at the Shogun's capital at Yedo. Another method of 'belling the cat' was to make Feudalism itself serve as an instrument for keeping Feudalism in order.

'The Shogunate . . . depended for its supremacy on the balance of power of its possible opponents. The *daimyōs* were by this time divided into three classes: first, the Related Houses (*Shimban* or *Kamon*), sons of Ieyasu [the first Tokugawa Shogun] and their descendants; second the Vassal Clans (*Fudai*), hereditary vassals of his house and their descendants; the third, Outside Feudatories (*Tozama*), or lords who did not come under this head. The *Bakufu* [i.e. the Shogunal Government] arranged that all the strategic positions should be held by the first two classes,[3] and that the "Outside Lords" should be so placed that they were separated by these, and adjacent to unfriendly neighbours. Thus these "Outside Lords" mutually checked each other and were in turn restrained by the hereditary vassals. The Related Houses also might in an emergency be controlled by the hereditary vassals, and both these classes were finally overawed by the Shogun's personal bodyguard, the *Hatamoto*, whose interests were entirely bound up with those of the *Bakufu*. How successful was this system that Ieyasu put together with such shrewdness can be seen from the fact that from this day till the latest period of the Shogunate in 1850 there was not a single rebellion of any of these feudatories.'[4]

While the Achaemenian institution of a feudal system thus found its classic application in Japan under the Tokugawa Shogunate, the Achaemenian institution of imperial garrisons posted at key-points in the interior of the Empire was likewise unconsciously reproduced, in a more thoroughgoing form, in a Far Eastern universal state in China under the Ming régime and its Manchu successor. The Ming planted garrisons of hereditary professional troops throughout their empire—not only along the frontiers over against the Eurasian Steppe and the Manchurian forests, but also along the coasts (which were harried by Japanese pirates) and along the vital inland waterway of the Grand Canal.[5] In the interior of the Empire the military districts occupied by such garrisons were thinly scattered enclaves in the territory under ordinary civil administration;[6] but the south-western corner of Manchuria, outside the Great

---

[1] See Sansom, G.: *Japan, A Short Cultural History* (London 1932, Cresset Press), p. 436.   [2] See p. 87, above.
[3] 'The hereditary vassals, though not so rich in estates as the great *Tozama*, were assigned lands at points of strategic importance, commanding the main highways and towns, or so situated with relation to the domains of possible enemies of the Shogun as to threaten their flank or rear should they ever venture to march upon Yedo' (Sansom: op. cit., p. 436).
[4] Sadler, A. L.: *A Short History of Japan* (Sydney 1946, Angus & Robertson), pp. 209–10.
[5] See Michael, F.: *The Origin of Manchu Rule in China* (Baltimore 1942, Johns Hopkins University Press), pp. 29–30.   [6] See ibid., loc. cit.

Wall but inside the Willow Palisade, which had been a Chinese-inhabited country since the Age of the Contending States, was mapped out into military districts exclusively.[1] The original nucleus of the Manchu state that was to be the Ming's successor had, as we have observed,[2] been a local Manchu tribe whom the Ming had fitted into their military system; and this system was the model followed by the architect of the Manchu Power, Nurhachi.[3]

The organization of the Manchu military establishment in 'banners' on the Ming pattern preceded the beginning of the Manchu conquest of the Chinese-inhabited country between the Willow Palisade and the Great Wall.[4] A social and administrative, as well as a military, revolution was carried out in A.D. 1601 when the Central Government of the nascent Manchu Power registered its subjects, organized them in 'banners' for civil as well as military purposes, and decreed that this new order was to override all traditional feudal claims and ties.[5] After the subsequent Manchu conquest of China, these 'banners' were the units out of which a Manchu Imperial Government reigning in the former Ming Imperial Government's stead constituted the garrisons that it stationed in Peking, the imperial capital, and in the Chinese provinces inside the Great Wall, as well as outside the Great Wall in both the Chinese-inhabited and the Manchu-inhabited zone of the Dynasty's previous domain. In the standard 'banner' of the Manchu Imperial Government's professional army after the Conquest, one battalion of Manchu troops was brigaded with one of Chinese and one of Mongols;[6] but there were some 'banners' in which the Manchu component had no Chinese or Mongol complement. The standard garrison consisted of detachments[7]—corresponding to the *vexillationes* of the Roman Imperial military organization—drawn from four 'banners' in each case originally and afterwards from eight; but there continued to be some garrisons of less than eight units, while some were raised to a still higher number, though the maximum was always less than sixteen.[8]

Sedentary barbarians, like the Manchus,[9] find less difficulty than Nomads, like the Mongols, in assuming the role of an imperial people. The antecedent attempt of the Mongols to impose an alien peace on China on their own account had been markedly less successful than the Manchus' repetition of the enterprise, in which the Mongols had to be content to serve as the Manchus' junior partners. It is true that the Mongols were handicapped not only by their Nomad background but

---

[1] See ibid., pp. 30–31.   [2] On p. 122, above.

[3] See Michael, op. cit., pp. 33, 62, and 75.

[4] See ibid., p. 63.   [5] See ibid., p. 64.

[6] These Mongol battalions of hereditary professional soldiers, individually recruited, in the 'banners' of the Manchu imperial army must be distinguished from the so-called Mongol 'banners', which were the war-bands of the Mongol tribes under Manchu suzerainty (see p. 122, above).

[7] See Michael, op. cit., pp. 65–66.

[8] See Lattimore, O.: *The Mongols of Manchuria* (London 1935, Allen & Unwin), pp. 146–8, and eundem: *Manchuria Cradle of Conflict* (New York 1932, Macmillan), p. 32. The military organization of the Manchus has been touched upon, by anticipation, in V. v. 315, n. 3, and 447.

[9] For the social and economic background of the Manchu restorers of a Far Eastern universal state in China, see II. ii. 122, n. 2; III. iii. 16, 19, and 423, n. 1; and V. v. 315.

by a taint of Far Eastern Christian culture which provoked the demonic
uprising of the Chinese against them,[1] and we have seen that the Libyan
Nomads, who were undefiled—or unredeemed—by any such alien cultural tincture, were suffered by a hyper-sensitively anti-alien Egyptiac
Society not only to drift into the Egyptiac World but to remain there
without bringing down upon their heads any counter-stroke from the
hands of the population on whose labours they had settled down to live
as parasites.[2] The Libyans, however, made the fatal mistake of severing
their connexion with an ancestral Nomadic way of life in which their
martial qualities had been bred. They spread themselves over the
Egyptian countryside[3] and, in so doing, forfeited their strength, like
Sampson when he allowed Delilah to shear his locks.[4] This Libyan
mistake was not repeated by the Primitive Muslim Arab Nomad warriors
when they burst into the Roman and Sasanian empires, broke down the
seven-centuries-old political partition between them,[5] and thereby re-
established a Syriac universal state that had been originally embodied
in the empire of the Achaemenidae.[6]

The Arab empire-builders realized that, if they were to retain a lasting
hold over the vast dominions which they had so swiftly won, they must
preserve the martial qualities of their badawī soldiery and must also keep
their garrisons *in partibus agricolarum* in close and constant touch with
the reservoir of badawī man-power on the Arabian steppes. Their
device for meeting both these requirements was to plant permanent
cantonments (*junds*) of badawī professional troops (*muqātilah*)[7] along
the borderline between the Desert and the Sown, as the sea-faring
empire-builders of a thalassocracy control their overseas dominions
from the sea-ports linking them with the metropolitan territory across
the water.[8]

The first four Arab Muslim cantonments of this type were planted,
along the borderline between the Syrian Steppe and Syria, in Transjordan, at Damascus, at Homs (*alias* Hims, *alias* Emesa), and at
Qinnasrīn.[9] These four garrisons were located in existing centres of

---

[1] See V. v. 348–51.

[2] See IV. iv. 422, n. 3; V. v. 269–70 and 352–3.

[3] The only districts in which the Libyan intruders did not plant themselves were
those reserved for the temple-states which were established by their confederates the
Egyptiac priesthood.

[4] An elaborately dressed side-lock was part of the insignia of a Libyan warrior.

[5] See I. i. 75–76.   [6] See I. i. 76–77.

[7] Also called 'migrants' (*muhājirah*), because they had left their ancestral tribes or
oases in order to become members of one of these newly constituted military communities
(see Wellhausen, J.: *Das Arabische Reich und sein Sturz* (Berlin 1902, Reimer), p. 16).

[8] The typical structure of a thalassocracy is illustrated on the Aegean scale by 'the
thalassocracy of Minos' and by the Athenian Empire that grew out of the Delian League,
and on the Oceanic scale by the British Empire. The British conquered India from
three maritime bases: the river-port of Calcutta, the sea-port of Madras, and the inshore
island of Bombay. The transfer of the political capital of the British Indian Empire
from Calcutta to New Delhi in A.D. 1912 was a step towards the renunciation of British
rule over India (on this point see pp. 194–5, below).

[9] See Ahmad Al-Balādhurī: *Kitāb Futūh-al-Buldān*, English translation by Hitti,
P. Kh., vol. i (New York 1916, Columbia University Press), p. 202. Quinnasrin was
constituted into a separate *jund* by the Caliph Yazīd (*imperabat* A.D. 680–3). It had
previously been included in the Jund of Homs. Balādhurī, in this passage, leaves it
uncertain whether there was or was not also a Jund of Filastīn (i.e. Cis-Jordanian
Palestine).

population, but their counterparts on other coasts of the desert were all laid out on previously unoccupied sites.[1] 'Irāq was overawed from cantonments at Basrah (*conditum* A.D. 635) and Kūfah (*conditum* A.D. 636) on the right bank of the Euphrates, where the Arab garrisons were not insulated by any water-barrier from their Arabian source of reinforcement.[2] A corresponding site on the right bank of the Nile, just above the head of the Delta, was chosen for Fustāt (*conditum* A.D. 641), 'the camp' from which the Arabs dominated Egypt. North-West Africa was dominated from Qayrawān (*conditum* A.D. 670) on a site, at the meeting-point between the low-lying arid south-eastern zone and the mountain-ribbed fertile north-western zone of Ifrīqīyah, which corresponded topographically to the sites of the cantonments dominating Syria.

Owing to the acquisition of the Caliphate and foundation of a dynasty by an Arab war-lord—the Umayyad Mu'āwīyah—who had started his career, and made his fortune, as governor of Syria, the Arab cantonments, not only on the desert coasts of Syria, but on those of 'Irāq, Egypt, and North-West Africa as well, were garrisoned by Syrian Arab troops.[3] The basis of military organization was tribal. Ziyād, whom Mu'āwīyah appointed as his governor, first of Basrah and then of Kūfah as well, tried to reorganize the military colony at Kūfah on non-tribal lines, but he seems to have achieved no permanent success in this, and in his parallel reorganization at Basrah he did not even make the attempt.[4] Tribal loyalties and rivalries were the governing factors in the life of the Arab cantonments throughout the Umayyad Age; and the resulting disunity and disorder, which was chronic and irrepressible, was no doubt one of the causes of the downfall of the Umayyad dynasty and of the eventual decay and disappearance of the cantonments themselves.

[1] See Wellhausen, op. cit., p. 17.

[2] Wāsit ('the centre') was planted by Al-Hajjāj on the far side of the Euphrates, on an island between two arms of the Shatt-al-Hayy; but this aptly named military centre for the Syrian garrison of 'Irāq was not laid out till A.D. 702, and by that time Arab rule over 'Irāq had long since been securely established.

[3] See Wellhausen, op. cit., pp. 155–6. These troops were 'Syrian' for the most part in the sense of being drawn from those badawī Arab armies, recruited in Arabia, that happened to have been directed to the Syrian theatre of the Primitive Muslim Arab wars of conquest and to have remained in Syria, after its subjugation, under the command of Mu'āwīyah. There were also, however, Syrian Arab troops whose connexion with Syria was less casual. Before the Muslim Arabs had invaded Syria, there had been two Arab infiltrations—one in the last century B.C. and the second since the latter part of the fourth century of the Christian Era—and, since the sixth century, the wardenship of the Arabian marches of Syria had been entrusted by the Roman Government to the Christian Arab dynasty of the Banu Ghassān (see I. i. 73, n. 1, and VIII. viii. 50–51) Alone among the peoples conquered by the Primitive Muslim Arabs, the Christian Arabs already established in the conquered territories were compelled (except for the Banu Taghlib in 'Irāq) to embrace Islam (see Wellhausen, op. cit., pp. 14–15) and were thereby compulsorily included in the ruling element in the Arab Empire. The Umayyad Caliphate might be described as an aggrandisement of the Ghassānid principality, and we may guess that the Syrian garrisons of the Umayyad cantonments were, to quite a large extent, of Ghassānid origin (see Wellhausen, op. cit., p. 83). Analogously the abortive Caliphate of 'Alī b. Abī Tālib, who established his seat of government at the Arab cantonment of Kūfah, on the desert border of 'Irāq, might be described as an aggrandisement of the rival pre-Muslim Arab principality of the Lakhmids who had served as wardens of the Arabian marches of the Sasanian Empire, considering that Kūfah had been planted in the immediate vicinity of Hīrah, the Lakhmids' former capital (see VIII. viii. 51, n. 1).

[4] See Wellhausen, op. cit., p. 79.

Civilian Settlements

The installation of standing military garrisons along the frontiers and in the interior of a universal state by the empire-builders can hardly fail to bring civilian settlement in its train. The Arab military *muhājirah* were allowed to bring their wives and children with them to the cantonments in which they settled.[1] The Roman legionaries, though debarred from contracting legal marriages during their term of active service, were permitted in practice by the military authorities to enter into permanent marital relations with concubines and to bring up families; and, after their discharge, they were able, by an easy process of law, to convert a concubinate into a legal marriage and to obtain retrospective legitimization for their children born out of wedlock. Moreover, the auxiliaries, who, unlike the legionaries, were recruited from among the Roman Empire's subjects, and not from among its citizens, seem to have been given the franchise upon their discharge at the end of the full statutory term of service, and sometimes earlier.[2] Thus the Roman *canabae*[3] and Arab cantonments became nuclei of civilian settlements which, in turn, became sources of recruitment for the garrisons round which they had gathered. The growth of the civilian element in the Arab cantonments was given a further impetus when the Caliph 'Umar II (*imperabat* A.D. 717–20) granted to members of the non-Arab subject population who became converts to Islam the option of migrating to an Arab cantonment from their home town or village.[4] On these analogies we may infer that the Turkish Muslim civilian population, which amounted, at the beginning of the nineteenth century, to a considerable proportion of the total population of the Ottoman provinces in Europe, and this not only in the towns but also on the land, was a by-product of the Ottoman military fiefs which, by that date, had been in existence in these provinces for about four hundred years on the average. And we may guess that a Persian civilian population had been generated in Cappadocia by the Persian feudal baronies there before the Achaemenian régime was brought to its premature close.

Besides arising as undesigned by-products of military establishments, civilian colonies are also planted by empire-builders as an end in themselves. For example, the North-East Anatolian districts in which the Achaemenidae had granted appanages to Persian barons were colonized by the 'Osmanlis with Albanian converts to Islam, on whose loyalty they

[1] See Wellhausen, op. cit., p. 16.

[2] See Last, H., in *The Cambridge Ancient History*, vol. xi (Cambridge 1936, University Press), p. 443, and pp. 140 and 155, below.

[3] See Rostovtzeff, M.: *The Social and Economic History of the Roman Empire* (Oxford 1926, Clarendon Press), p. 51.

[4] In this ruling, 'Umar was deliberately rescinding the practice of the celebrated governor of 'Irāq, Hajjāj (*proconsulari munere fungebatur* A.D. 691–713), who had forbidden converts to migrate and had even forcibly repatriated those who had done so. Under 'Umar's ruling, migration presumably became the rule, as the theoretical alternative of remaining on the land and continuing to pay, under the less offensive name of 'rent', the tribute (*kharāj*) due from non-Muslims was hardly likely to be attractive to many converts (see Wellhausen, op. cit., p. 175). The fiscal considerations that inclined the earlier Umayyad Caliphs, first and foremost Mu'āwiyah I, to refrain from encouraging the conversion of the Arab Empire's non-Muslim subjects are discussed by Lammens, S.J., le Père H.: *Études sur le Règne du Calife Omaiyade Mo'âwia Ier* (Paris 1908, Geuthner), pp. 424–6.

could count for helping them to hold these anti-Safawī marches.[1] In the commercial centres in the heart of their dominions—Constantinople, Smyrna, Salonica, Sarayevo—the 'Osmanlis settled civilian communities of refugee Sephardī Jews from Spain and Portugal.[2] In the Roman Empire, not only military cantonments but civilian settlements—of which Caesar's colonies of Roman citizens at Capua, Carthage, and Corinth may be regarded as the exemplars[3]—were planted by Caesar, Augustus, and their successors.

Caesar himself may have been the founder of the Roman colonies in three ports of entry—Dyrrhachium (Durazzo), Buthrotum (Butrinto), and Dyme—from Italy to Continental European Greece; in two other Greek cities—Dium and Philippi—which commanded respectively the southern and the eastern exit from the province of Macedonia;[4] and in four Anatolian ports—Lampsacus, the Bithynian Apamea, Heraclea Pontica, and Sinope—on the coastal shipping route through the Hellespont to the mouth of the Phasis.[5] Augustus reinforced these three groups of Roman civilian colonies by adding Byllis and Patrae to the first, Pella and Cassandrea to the second, and Alexandria Troas and Parium to the third. He did something to repair the ravages of his civil war with Sextus Pompeius[6] by founding other Roman civilian colonies in Sicily, and he made a momentous new departure in policy when in 15 B.C. he planted two Roman civilian colonies in Syria:[7] one at Berytus (Bayrūt)[8] and the other at Heliopolis (Ba'lbak). Claudius added a Roman colony at Ptolemais in Palestine to Augustus's Syrian foundations, and broke new ground in two regions—Cappadocia and Thrace—which had both hitherto shown an exceptional imperviousness to Hellenism. After suppressing the native client kingdom in Thrace which had been ruled for Rome by the princes of the Odrysae, Claudius founded a colony of Roman citizens at Apri, where the Great East Road running from Dyrrhachium and Apollonia through Thessalonica and Philippi forked

---

[1] One of these Albanian settlements in North-Eastern Anatolia, Vezīr Köprü, gave birth to the Köprülü family whose eventual flowering, in a crop of distinguished statesmen, was one of the causes of the rally of the Ottoman Empire in the latter part of the seventeenth century of the Christian Era (see V. vi. 208, with n. 3, and 299).

[2] For the motives of this deed of humanity and stroke of statesmanship, see II. ii. 244–6.

[3] For the long-drawn-out conflict between opposing policies and political ideals which was the historical background of these three foundations, see pp. 109–10, above.

[4] For the plantation of Macedonia with Roman colonies and municipia under the early Principate, see The Cambridge Ancient History, vol. xi (Cambridge 1936, University Press), pp. 567–8.

[5] See Hahn, L.: Rom und Romanismus im Griechisch-Römischen Osten (Leipzig 1906, Dieterich), pp. 60–61.   [6] See V. v. 71 and V. vi. 239.

[7] See Hahn, op. cit., pp. 92–94. Another civilian settlement of Roman citizens planted by Augustus on Asiatic ground was his Roman colony at Tralles, founded in 26 B.C. (ibid.).

[8] This Syrian outpost of the Latin-speaking world was so successful in preserving its Latin character that it became a centre for the study of Roman Law. Justinian treated the academy of law at Berytus as the peer of those at Constantinople and Rome (see Cumont, F., in The Cambridge Ancient History, vol. xi, pp. 626–7, and Collinet, P.: Études Historiques sur le Droit de Justinien, vol. ii: 'Histoire de l'École de Droit de Beyrouth' (Paris 1925, Recueil Sirey)). According to Collinet, op. cit., vol. cit., pp. 20–22, the law school at Berytus owed its rise to the Imperial Government's practice—established at some date before A.D. 196—of using Berytus, in virtue of its being the easternmost Latin-speaking community in the Empire, as its depot for the distribution, in the Oriental provinces, of the texts of new laws.

on its divergent ways to the Hellespont and the Bosphorus. In Cappadocia, which Tiberius had brought under direct Roman administration, Claudius founded a Roman colony at Archelais, just within the western borders of the province. Vespasian followed up Claudius's initiative in Thrace by founding a Roman colony at Deultum under the name of Flaviopolis, and Claudius's initiative in Palestine—where Vespasian blasted away the Jewish obstruction to Hellenization which Antiochus Epiphanes had failed to overcome—by reinforcing Ptolemais on the coast with two new Roman colonies in the interior: one at Emmaus and the other at Samaria, which Vespasian renamed Flavia Neapolis.[1]

The Roman Imperial Government did not, however, confine its programme of civilian colonization to the establishment of colonies of the ruling Latin nationality. While it did set itself systematically to Latinize—and thereby indirectly Hellenize in Latin dress—the barbarians on whom it had imposed its peace in the Danubian territories beyond the former northern frontiers of Macedonia[2] and in the West European and North-West African territories whose political destinies had been decided by Rome's victory in her struggle with Carthage,[3] the foundation of Roman colonies on Greek or Oriental ground was in this quarter only a side-line of Roman Imperial policy. In European Greece and in all parts of the Empire lying to the east of it the predominant aim of Roman Imperial statesmanship was to preserve and complete the Hellenizing work of Alexander the Great and his successors; and this aim was pursued with a steadiness and effectiveness which were tardily recognized and rewarded when, in the second century of the Imperial Peace, the Empire was at last acclaimed by Greek men of letters as an embodiment, on an oecumenical scale, of the Platonic ideal of the rule of the philosopher-king.[4]

The exemplar of this Hellenizing aspect of the Roman Imperial Government's policy of internal colonization was the synoecism by Augustus, *more Alexandrino*, of a new Greek city on the grand scale under the name of Nicopolis to adorn the scene of his crowning victory at Actium and to keep its memory alive by periodical celebrations in honour of the event. Trajan's foundation of a Greek city of the same name in the Trans-Haeman fringes of the province of Thrace[5] was evidence of the sincerity of the Roman Government's intention to make Thrace a replica of Greek-speaking Macedonia and not of Latin-speaking Moesia.[6] This Hellenization of Thrace in Greek dress at Roman

---

[1] See Hahn, op. cit., pp. 148–9.   [2] See II. ii. 163–4.   [3] See I. i. 40.
[4] See V. v. 343–4, and pp. 41–44, above. Aelius Aristeides goes so far as to suggest that Alexander's enduring achievement lay in his having served as Rome's forerunner:
'The only achievement and memorial, worthy of his genius, that Alexander left behind him was the city on the coast of Egypt that bears his name; and it is his merit that he founded Alexandria for you Romans, in order that she might be yours, and that you might be masters of the city which is the greatest in the World, next to your own'— (Aristeides, P. Aelius: *In Romam*, edited by Keil, B., in *Aelii Aristidis Quae Supersunt Omnia*, vol. ii (Berlin 1898, Weidmann), p. 99 (Or. XXVI, § 26). Cp. p. 119 (§ 95)).
[5] The grounds for believing that Nicopolis-ad-Istrum was originally included in the province of Thrace, and not in that of Lower Moesia, are given by Mommsen, Th.: *The Provinces of the Roman Empire*, English translation, vol. i (London 1886, Bentley), p. 307, n. 2.
[6] For the spread of the Latin language all the way down the right bank of the Danube, see IV. iv. 326, n. 2.

hands was consummated by Hadrian when he gave his own name to the Greek city that he founded on a site which, under a Nomad-minded Odrysian régime, had been crying out, unheeded, for synoecism ever since the time, five hundred years back, when the sister-city of Philippopolis had been duly founded by the father of Alexander the Great. Planted, as it was, at the junction of the River Hebrus with its principal tributary, on the military road to the Bosphorus from Aquileia and Sirmium, Adrianople provided Thrace with the convenient urban centre that it had lacked hitherto.[1]

This practice of diffusing Hellenism in the Roman Empire by means of the foundation of city-states was reproduced in the Spanish Empire of the Indies; and the Medieval Spanish institution which was thus propagated in the Americas in an Early Modern Age of Western history was in truth a renaissance of the Hellenic institution that had originally been propagated in Spain by Roman *conquistadores* from Italy.[2] Like the Hellenic cities planted in the post-Alexandrine Age by Macedonian empire-builders in South-West Asia and Egypt and by Roman empire-builders round all the shores of the Mediterranean, these Spanish cities in the Americas had individual founders;[3] they were laid out on the rectangular plan that, in the history of Hellenic town-planning, had been inaugurated in the fifth century B.C.[4] by Hippodamus's layout of the Peiraeus; and each *civitas* had a rural *territorium* 'attributed to' it, to use the Roman technical term.[5] In the more settled regions of the Spanish Empire these municipal *territoria* were conterminous; and, in the undeveloped regions on the fringes, some of them were of vast extent.[6] By A.D. 1574 about a hundred Spanish city-states had already been founded within the area of the Incaic Empire's former domain.[7] 'The Spanish American provinces, therefore, were in many instances a collection of municipalities, the latter . . . being the bricks of which the whole political structure was compacted.'[8]

If these Spanish colonial city-states thus resembled the post-Alexandrine Hellenic colonial city-states in serving as the cells of an intrusive alien régime's administrative and judicial organization, they likewise resembled them in enjoying little more than a simulacrum of local self-government; for they had no sooner been founded than the Crown took into its own hands the appointment of the municipal officers.[9] Above all, they resembled their Hellenic prototypes in being parasitic.

'In the Anglo-American colonies the towns grew up to meet the needs

---

[1] Though Adrianople was thus marked out by its geographical position for playing the part of a capital city, it had not so far achieved its manifest destiny except during the century ending in A.D. 1453, when it had been the seat of government of the Ottoman Empire. There had, on the other hand, been two periods in which Adrianople had had the misfortune to find itself serving as a frontier fortress: first during the three centuries ending in the annexation of Eastern Bulgaria by the East Roman Empire in A.D. 972 (see IV. iv. 389) and again since the carving of the autonomous principalities of Eastern Rumelia and Bulgaria out of the body of the Ottoman Empire in A.D. 1878 (see p. 17, above).

[2] See Haring, C. H.: *The Spanish Empire in America* (New York 1947, Oxford University Press), p. 159. [3] See ibid., p. 160.
[4] See ibid., p. 161. [5] See the present Study, III. iii. 98, with n. 2.
[6] See Haring, op. cit., pp. 161–2. [7] See ibid., p. 160, n. 4.
[8] Ibid., p. 162. [9] See ibid., pp. 164–5.

of the inhabitants of the country: in the Spanish colonies the population of the country grew to meet the needs of the towns. The primary
object of the English colonist was generally to live on the land and derive his support from its cultivation; the primary plan of the Spaniard was
to live in town and derive his support from the Indians or Negroes at
work on plantations or in the mines. . . . Owing to the presence of aboriginal
labour to exploit in fields and mines, the rural population remained
almost entirely Indian.'[1]

The Spanish empire-builders' Inca predecessors' practice of linking
together districts that were geographically far apart and at the same time
economically complementary[2] has counterparts in the economy of both
the Roman Empire and the Arab Caliphate.

The vacant public land which the Roman Government acquired in the
Po Basin through the conquest of the country between the years 197 and
173 B.C. and the concomitant eviction of the more recalcitrant of its
native Gallic and Ligurian inhabitants[3] was not all transferred to individual ownership through the foundation of Latin and Roman colonial
communities of freeholders and the grant of freeholds to other settlers
individually (viritim). Tracts were also granted to corporations domiciled
in Italy south of the Appennines—both ecclesiastical corporations, such
as the sorority of the Vestal Virgins and other colleges of priests belonging to the established public service of the Roman State,[4] and political
corporations in the shape of self-governing city-states that were incorporated in, or externally associated with, the Roman body politic.[5]

[1] Haring, op cit., pp. 160 and 159.   [2] See pp. 114–15, above.   [3] See V. v. 569–74.
[4] See Hyginus: De Condicionibus Agrorum (in Die Schriften der Römischen Feldmesser,
ed. by Blume, F., Lachmann, K., and Rudorff, A., vol. i (Berlin 1848, Reimer), p. 117)
and Siculus Flaccus: De Condicionibus Agrorum (in op. cit., pp. 162–3).
[5] The self-governing communities incorporated in the Roman body politic were
colonies and municipia of Roman citizens; those externally associated with it were Latin
city-states, whose relations with the Roman State were governed by custom, and
civitates foederatae which were bound to Rome by written treaties, the terms of which
varied in accordance with the particular circumstances in which each community had
entered into permanent political association with Rome. Cis-Appennine city-states of
both classes received corporate grants of land in the Po Basin from the Roman Government—presumably as a recompense for services rendered by the military contingents
from these states in the Roman armies by which the Po Basin had been conquered from
its native inhabitants. The aggregate extent of their holdings must have been considerable,
to judge by the part that they played in the opposition of the various vested interests to
the Gracchan policy of reasserting the Roman State's right of eminent domain over all
Roman public land that had not been assigned in freehold to individual proprietors (see
Appian of Alexandria: Studies in Roman History, 'The Civil Wars', Book I, chap. x, § 6,
and chap. xix, § 1, where πόλεις ἰσοπολίτιδες signifies municipia civium Romanorum,
πόλεις ἄποικοι the coloniae Latinae, and 'Ιταλιῶται the citizens of civitates foederatae).
Both the ecclesiastical and the municipal corporations that possessed these endow-
ments of land in the Po Basin appear to have turned them to account by letting them to
tenants. The ecclesiastical tenancies ran for either one-year or five-year periods (Hyginus:
De Condicionibus Agrorum, in Die Schriften der Römischen Feldmesser, ed. cit., vol. i, p. 117).
We have two glimpses of the management of the municipal estates in the collected
correspondence of Cicero. In a letter written in 46 B.C. (Ad Familiares, Book XIII, Letter
11), Cicero introduces to his correspondent, Decimus Iunius Brutus, governor of
Cisalpine Gaul, the three commissioners whom the municipal authorities of Arpinum
(Cicero's own home town) are sending out with instructions 'to inspect the properties let
out on lease (vectigalia) which they possess in the Province of Gaul, to collect the rents
due from the tenants (colonis), and generally tò examine and deal with the situation there'.
In a letter written in 45 B.C. (Ad Familiares, Book XIII, Letter 7), Cicero asks his correspondent Cluvius to intercede with Caesar on behalf of the municipality of Atella in the
matter of that community's agricultural property let out on lease (de agro vectigali
municipii), which was threatened with confiscation. According to Cicero these rents were

In the Arab Caliphate under the Umayyad régime we find a parallel
to the Inca practice which is almost exact from the geographer's standpoint though perhaps not so close from the sociologist's. Just as the
Incas established economic partnerships between lowland districts and
highland districts, so the Umayyads endowed the two cantonments of
Basrah and Kūfah not only with arable land on the adjoining plains of
'Irāq (the fabulously productive 'Black Earth': *As-Sawād*), but also
with meadow-land, pasture, and forest in 'the Highlands' (*Al-Jibāl*)
through which the Great North-East Road wound its way up towards the
frontier of the Syriac World over against the Eurasian Steppe.[1] The
difference between the Umayyad and the Inca application of the same
device lies in the motive, which in the Umayyads' case seems to have
been primarily military and only incidentally economic. The frontier
garrisons which the Arab empire-builders pushed forward up the Great
North-East Road,[2] first into Khurāsān and eventually into Transoxania,[3] were originally recruited, and subsequently reinforced, by
drafts from the cantonments at Basrah and Kūfah;[4] and the grant to these

an important item in the budgets of the municipalities to which they were payable. In
the first of the two letters here cited, he writes that the people of Arpinum depend on this
source of income for 'all their ways and means of providing for public worship and keeping public buildings, both religious and secular, in a sound state of repair'. In the second
letter he goes so far as to write that 'the municipal finances of Atella are entirely dependent on this source of income'.

Evidence of a grant of forest and pasture land in the Po Basin to the *civitas foederata*
Aquinum, situated in the distant basin of the Liris (Garigliano), is preserved in the
name 'Saltus Galliani qui cognominantur Aquinates' (meaning 'Estates, situate in
Cisalpine Gaul, of the city-state of Aquinum') which was borne by one of the self-
governing municipalities of Roman citizens in the eighth of the eleven regions into which
Augustus grouped the city-states of Italy (see the list in Plinius Secundus, C.: *Historia
Naturalis*, Book III, chap. xv (xx), § 116). At some date between the end of the first
quarter of the second century B.C. and Augustus's day, the tenants and squatters on this
estate must have been incorporated as an autonomous community.

[1] For example, the revenues of the city and district of Dīnawar were payable to the
cantonment of Kūfah, and those of Nihāwand to the cantonment of Basrah (Le Strange,
Guy: *The Lands of the Eastern Caliphate* (Cambridge 1905, University Press), pp. 189
and 197).

[2] See xi, map 37.　　　　　　　　　　　　　　　[3] See p. 121, above.

[4] In the Arab military occupation of Khurāsān, it was Basrah, not Kūfah, that played
the predominant part, and this fact was unhappily reflected in the transplantation to
Khurāsān not only of the Basran soldiery but of the inter-tribal feuds that were Basrah's
heritage from a pre-Islamic Arabia (see Wellhausen, J.: *Das Arabische Reich und sein
Sturz* (Berlin 1902, Reimer), pp. 247, 256, and 131). The Basran Arab garrisons in
Khurāsān were not deterred from pursuing these inter-tribal feuds either by the
numerical preponderance of the native Iranian population or by the proximity of the
Eurasian Nomad adversary on the farther side of the frontier. Ziyād—whom the Caliph
Mu'āwiyah appointed governor not only of Basrah and Kūfah but of all Arab dominions
beyond them, as far as Khurāsān inclusive, which were dominated from the cantonments
on the Euphrates by way of the Great North-East Road—sent large numbers of Basran
and Kufan Arab families to Khurāsān (see ibid., p. 79). Further drafts of 25,000 men
each from the two cantonments were sent to Khurāsān by Ziyād's son Rabī', on whom
his father's governor-generalship was conferred by Mu'āwiyah after Ziyād's death. By
the end of the seventh century of the Christian Era there was in Khurāsān an Arab
population of about 200,000, including about 40,000 fighting-men (see ibid., p. 266). The
military and political dependence of the greater part of the Iranian Plateau on a Power
installed on the plains of 'Irāq, which was a salient feature in the administrative organization of the Umayyad Empire, has its counterpart in the similar situation after the overthrow of the Achaemenian Empire, when the successors of Alexander were contending
for the fragments of the carcass. In that struggle, Seleucus Nicator emerged as one of the
victors largely owing to his ability to dominate, from his base at Babylon, all the former
Achaemenian dominions lying to the north-east and east of Babylonia, save for an
easternmost fringe which he was constrained to cede to Chandragupta in exchange for a
park of war-elephants.

two Arab military corporations in 'Irāq of estates on the Iranian Plateau
—whose productive resources were thus laid under contribution for the
benefit of Basrah's and Kūfah's war-chests—was an economic reflection
of the military fact that the outlying garrisons protecting the Iranian
provinces of the Caliphate were detachments from the two great nurseries
of soldiers cantoned on the distant borderland between the Euphrates
and the Arabian Steppe.

The Inca practice of transporting individually selected skilled workers
and their families, in order to improve the quality of production
in economically backward districts, has counterparts—economically
comparable, though incomparably brutal and indiscriminate from the
human standpoint—in both Hellenic and Syriac history. The scientific
agricultural exploitation, with imported slave labour, of the coastlands
of the Western Mediterranean from the fifth century B.C. onwards and
of the seaboard of Lower 'Irāq in the ninth century of the Christian Era
has already been noticed in this Study in another context.[1] There are
indications that the Incas may have brought artificers from the culturally
maturer lowland region of Chimu to raise the standard of workmanship
in their own highland capital at Cuzco.[2] This was certainly the purpose
of the Mongols in carrying Chinese, Russian, and Western Christian
craftsmen away captive from the extremities of the Old World to its
heartland when they were trying to transform Qāraqorum from an en-
campment of Nomads into a city fit to be the capital of a world empire.[3]
Ts'in She Hwang-ti may have had the same end in view in bringing
selected settlers from other parts of his empire to recruit the population
of Hien-yang,[4] when he was making an imperial capital out of a city
that had hitherto only had to serve as a capital for the parochial state
of Ts'in.[5] On the other hand Nebuchadnezzar, in deporting to Babylon
from Jerusalem 'all the craftsmen and smiths',[6] was probably more concerned to deprive Judah of her armaments industry—and thereby render
it impossible for her to make any further attempt at armed insurrection
against the Neo-Babylonian régime[7]—than he was to improve the age-
old craftsmanship of Babylon, whose practitioners would have felt that
they had little to learn from a handful of artisans picked up from a rustic
highland principality in a remote corner of the empire.

A type of internal colonization which is apt to become prominent
in the last phase of the history of a universal state is the plantation of
barbarian husbandmen on lands that have come to be depopulated
either as a result of raids perpetrated by these barbarians themselves (or
by neighbours of theirs in their former homes in the no-man's-land
beyond the *limes*) or as a result of some social sickness, native to the

[1] In V. v. 66 and 129.
[2] Baudin, L.: *L'Empire Socialiste des Inka* (Paris 1928, Institut d'Ethnologie), p. 134.
[3] See the passage quoted from Friar William of Rubruck's narrative in V. v. 113–14,
and Olschki, L.: *Guillaume Boucher, A French Artist at the Court of the Khans* (Baltimore
1946, Johns Hopkins University Press).   [4] See V. v. 141.
[5] The successive changes in the location of the capital of the Sinic universal state are
dealt with below on pp. 210–13.
[6] 2 Kings xxiv. 14 and 16, cited already on p. 116, above.
[7] This had unquestionably been the motive of the Philistines when, in the eleventh
century B.C., they had placed a ban upon the practice of the metallurgical industry in the
subjugated territory of Israel (see I Sam. xiii. 19–22).

depopulated empire itself, which has laid it open to barbarian attack by sapping its powers of resistence.

A classic example is presented in the picture of a post-Diocletianic Roman Empire in the *Notitia Dignitatum*, which records the presence of a number of German and Sarmatian barbarian corporate settlements on Roman soil in Gaul, Italy, and the Danubian provinces. The technical term *laeti*, by which these barbarian settlers were known, is derived from a West German word[1] denoting semi-servile resident aliens; and we may infer that the Romans' *laeti* were the descendants of defeated barbarian adversaries of the Roman Imperial Government who had been punished or rewarded for past acts of aggression by being coerced or coaxed into migrating permanently to become peaceful cultivators of the Promised Land on the inner side of the *limes* which they had formerly devastated as raiders. From the Roman Government's standpoint this arrangement would serve the dual purpose of employing the barbarians to repair the damage that they themselves had inflicted and of giving them at the same time an interest in keeping the peace for the future instead of continuing to break it. The *laeti* were cautiously planted in the interior of the Empire, not in the immediate neighbourhood of the *limites*,[2] and in Gaul, at any rate, each settlement of *laeti* was attached to a particular Gallic canton and was required to pay its land-tax to the municipal authorities, not to the Imperial Treasury.[3] In its gazetteer of the western portion of the Empire the *Notitia Dignitatum* mentions twelve *praefecturae* of German *laeti* attached to divers Gallic cantons[4] and twenty-two *praefecturae* of Sarmatian *laeti* in Gaul and Italy,[5] as well as a settlement of Sarmatae and Taifali Gentiles in the Gallic canton Pictavi[6] and a Gens Marcomannorum, administered by a tribune, in the Middle Danube province of Pannonia Prima.[7]

'The Melting-pot'

Our survey of garrisons and colonies installed by builders of universal states has perhaps borne out our contention that these systematic transfers of population—which are characteristic of the universal state phase in the decline of a civilization—are on the whole much more humane, in execution as well as in design, than the capricious and vindictive uprooting of individuals and communities which is characteristic of the antecedent Time of Troubles. At the same time our survey has brought to light the truth that these two morally diverse processes produce similar social results. And the cumulative effect of the empire-builders' statesmanship, following upon the war-lords' atrocities,[8] is to

---

[1] *Leto, litu, let, laet, lat* (see Grosse, R.: *Römische Militärgeschichte von Gallienus bis zum Beginn der Byzantinischen Themenverfassung* (Berlin 1920, Weidmann), p. 208).

[2] See ibid., p. 209.

[3] See ibid.

[4] *In Partibus Occidentis*, chap. xlii, §§ 33–44.

[5] Ibid., §§ 46–63 and 66–70; cp. Codex Theodosianus VII. 20, 12, of A.D. 400: 'Laetus (MS. luctus) Alamannus, Sarmata'.

[6] *In Partibus Occidentis*, chap. xlii, § 65.

[7] Ibid., chap. xxxiv, § 24.

[8] The successive types of 'saviours with the sword' whose sequence punctuates the stages of the decline and fall of a civilization have been reviewed in V. vi. 178–213.

intensify and accelerate a process of pammixia and proletarianization[1] that is characteristic of Times of Troubles and universal states alike.

Permanent military garrisons installed on the frontiers of universal states become 'melting-pots' in which the dominant minority of a disintegrating society fuses itself with both the external and the internal proletariat. In an earlier part of this Study[2] we have observed that, on the organized military frontier of a civilization over against outer barbarians, the wardens of the marches and the opposing barbarian warbands tend, with the passage of time, to become assimilated to one another first in military technique and equipment and eventually also in culture and êthos. But, long before the dominant minority of a disintegrating society has been barbarized by hostile contact, across the frontier, with the external proletariat, it will have been vulgarized by fraternization, within the frontier, with the internal proletariat.[3] For empire-builders who have gained their position by emerging as sole survivors from a struggle for existence between the parochial states of their world do not often preserve either sufficient manpower or sufficient zest for the profession of arms to be able to contemplate holding and defending their hardly won empire unaided.

In this quandary their first recourse is to reinforce their own military strength by enlisting, not barbarians from beyond the pale, but subjects of the empire who have not lost their martial virtues. While they seldom push this policy to the extreme to which the Achaemenidae went when they took over into their own service the Jewish military colony that had been installed in the Egyptian frontier fortress of Elephantinê by their Saïte predecessors,[4] they frequently raise new military formations from among their subjects and brigade these with the troops of their own ruling nationality. Thus Augustus and his successors manned the immensely long frontiers of the Roman Empire, which Augustus had staked out, by brigading with the Roman legions *auxilia* recruited from Roman subjects who were not Roman citizens.[5] The detachments of Arab professional soldiery from Basrah and Kūfah, which were posted in Khurāsān to hold the north-east frontier of the Umayyad Empire, enlisted the help of the warlike native Iranian inhabitants of the province and fraternized with their new comrades-in-arms, in contrast to the aloofness of the parent cantonments on the Euphrates from the subject civilian population of 'Irāq.[6] Khurāsānī Arab officers adopted the Iranian custom of surrounding themselves with a *comitatus* of picked Iranian fighting-men, and they also raised separate Iranian military formations under Iranian officers.[7] The local Iranians, on their side, had good reasons for responding favourably to these bids for their co-operation that were made to them by their Arab conquerors.

'As a result of the conquest, their position, on the whole, changed only slightly, and this hardly for the worse. The defence of Khurāsān against enemies from outside—that is, against the Turks—was conducted by the

---

[1] For this process, see V. v. 439–80, *passim*.　　[2] In V. v. 459–80.

[3] See V. v. 439–59.

[4] See pp. 118–19, above.

[5] See V. v. 446, and p. 132, above.

[6] See V. v. 447, and Wellhausen, op. cit., p. 307, quoted in the present Study in V. v. 450.

[7] See Wellhausen, op. cit., p. 309.

Arabs more successfully than it had been managed under the Sasanian régime. . . . The *Mawāli* (as non-Arabs who had become converts to Islam and become adopted members of the Arab tribes were called in Khurāsān, as elsewhere) fought shoulder to shoulder with the Arabs against their traditional national enemy, the Turks. They also fought for Islam against their own Sogdian kinsmen, in so far as the latter were Islam's enemies and the Turks' confederates. . . . The domestic life of Khurāsān was not interfered with by the Arabs very much. They left the administration to the *marzbans* and *dihqans* and did not impinge upon the subject population except through these native intermediaries. Even in the garrison towns and in the seats of administration the native authorities continued to play their part side by side with their Arab colleagues. For one thing, they had to collect the taxes, for the due payment of which, on the agreed scale, they were responsible to their conquerors. However, the burden of taxation had doubtless weighed as heavily on the *misera contribuens plebs* under the Sasanian régime.[1] The Iranians were also left undisturbed in the practice of their religion; in the agreements providing for payment of tribute it is always assumed that they are going to retain their ancestral faith. . . . They appear, all the same, to have had no very serious attachment to Zoroastrianism. . . . The attraction of Islam for the Iranians was in the first instance not so much on account of its intrinsic merits as for the sake of the material advantages which it had to offer. They used it as a means of diminishing the gulf between themselves and the ruling class and of obtaining a share in their privileges by "going Arab". They adopted Arabic names and secured admission into an Arab tribe.'[2]

Even the Manchus—who, as mere restorers of their Mongol predecessors' empire-building work in China, had not to pass through the ordeal that is the usual price of founding a universal state—did not attempt to hold, with their own unaided strength, the vast and populous domain of which they had made so easy a conquest. In the 'banners' of which their garrisons were composed, their general practice was, as we have seen,[3] to brigade a Chinese and a Mongol with each Manchu battalion.

Our records, fragmentary though they are, give us vivid glimpses, here and there, of 'the melting-pot' at work. A piece of first-hand evidence for the mutual assimilation of the Chinese 'bannermen' in Manchu service and their Manchu fellow soldiers has been quoted in this Study at an earlier point.[4] At Elephantinê under the Achaemenian régime—which was particularly liberal[5] in giving openings to non-Persians—the Jewish military unit constituting the garrison had on its strength not only some soldiers of Babylonian origin but also at least one

1 According to Wellhausen, op. cit., p. 310, Khurāsān was not exempt from the general rule that land-tax continued to be payable, both by native converts to Islam and by Muslim Arabs who had become local landowners, on land originally belonging to the native non-Muslim population. On the other hand, according to the same authority, op. cit., p. 19, non-Muslim subjects of the Caliphate who performed military service for frontier defence were exempted from taxation.—A.J.T.

2 Wellhausen, op. cit., pp. 308–9.

3 See pp. 128–9, above, with the references there given.

4 In V. v. 457–8; cp. p. 449.

5 On this point see Meyer, E.: *Der Papyrusfund von Elephantinê*, 2nd ed. (Leipzig 1912, Hinrichs), p. 26.

Chorasmian.[1] It is remarkable that this soldier should have found his
way to the First Cataract of the Nile from his native land in the delta of
the Oxus, at the opposite extremity of the Achaemenian Empire. It is
still more remarkable that this representative of the high-spirited
Iranian peoples of the north-eastern marches, who were to offer such a
stubborn resistance to Alexander the Great,[2] should not have felt it
beneath his dignity to serve shoulder to shoulder with Syrians in a
regiment of mercenaries.

In the civil life of this Jewish military colony, Babylonic influence was
strong, though the colony had originally been founded by the Neo-
Babylonian Empire's Saïte rivals and adversaries, and though it is
probable that the Saïtes had recruited at least the first nucleus of the
force from among those 'die-hards' in Judah who had preferred to be
refugees in Egypt rather than deportees in Babylonia.[3] The marriage
contracts, for example, that had survived from the community's archives
were Babylonian rather than Israelite in form, and this Babylonicizing
tendency in Elephantinian Jewish personal law had been strong enough
to raise the general status of women above the customary Jewish level of
that age.[4] One medium through which this Babylonic influence had
seeped in was the Aramaic language and alphabet of the Jewish community at Elephantinê, which were identical with those in use in contemporary Babylonia and Assyria.[5] The tincture of Babylonic polytheism
in the Yahweh-worship of the Elephantinê community[6] suggests that
there may have been Babylonian elements in the community itself; and
this, in turn, suggests that the original nucleus may have been a mixed
band including refugees from Samaria as well as from Judah,[7] since the
Samaritans were a hybrid community in which a remnant of Israel
was mingled with deportees from Babylonia whom the Assyrian war-
lord Sargon had planted in place of the Israelites whom he had deported
to 'the cities of the Medes'.[8] These facts and probabilities indicate that
Achaemenian Elephantinê was a 'melting-pot' indeed; and, on this
analogy, we may picture the corresponding role of the Arab military
cantonments in the Umayyad Empire.

'[The non-Arabs] went over to Islam in large numbers, and such conversions were particularly numerous among the masses of Iranian
prisoners-of-war in Kūfah and Basrah.'[9]

This non-Arab element in the cantonments was continually reinforced
by the effect of 'Umar II's ruling that non-Arab converts in the provinces

---

[1] See Meyer, op. cit., p. 28, and van Hoonacker, A.: *Une Communauté Judéo-
Araméenne à Elephantinè en Égypte aux vie et ve siècles avant J.-C.* (London 1915,
Milford), p. 5.

[2] See II. ii. 140.   [3] See 2 Kings xxv. 26 and Jer. xl-xliii.

[4] See van Hoonacker, op. cit., pp. 25-29.

[5] See ibid., pp. 29-30. For the process of peaceful penetration by which the Aramaic
language and alphabet replaced the Akkadian language and cuneiform characters in the
homelands of the Babylonic Civilization, see I. i. 79-80, and V. v. 486-91 and 499-501.

[6] See V. v. 125, n. 1.

[7] This is van Hoonacker's conjecture, in op cit., pp. 84-85.

[8] See 2 Kings xvii.

[9] Wellhausen, op. cit., p. 45. For instances, see Ahmad Al-Balādhurī: *Kitāb
Futūh al-Buldān*, English translation by Hitti and Murgotten, Part (ii) (New York 1924,
Columbia University Press), pp. 105-11.

must migrate to a cantonment if they wanted to avoid the alternative of continuing, after their conversion, to pay the tax imposed on non-Muslim subjects of the Empire.[1] All non-Arab converts had to obtain affiliation to some Arab tribe or clan,[2] and this institution of clientship

---

[1] For this ruling, see p. 132, above.
[2] See Wellhausen, op. cit., p. 45. For example, the soldiers of a Persian cavalry force in Ahwāz which deserted to the Arabs and turned Muslim en masse appear to have settled first in Basrah as clients of the Banu Tamīm and afterwards to have transferred their allegiance to the Banu S'ad. Besides these Persian Asāwirah, there were Sindi deserters from the Persian army known as Zutt (i.e. Jāts), and others known as Sayābijah and Andaghār. Under the Sasanian régime these Zutt had had their pastures on the borders (tufūf) of 'Irāq over against the North Arabian Steppe, while the Sayābijah had been settled on the coast of the Persian Gulf, and the Andaghār in the desert borderland between Kirmān and Seistan. These three peoples were all now settled at Basrah as clients of the Banu Tamīm, and they afterwards transferred their allegiance to the Banu Hanthalah (see Balādhurī, op. cit., Part (ii), pp. 105-107, 109, and 111). We also hear of a Persian family from Umān migrating to Basrah via Yamāmah (see ibid., p. 100), and of the inhabitants of the Persian city of Qazwīn surrendering to the Arabs on terms, accepting Islam, and settling in Kūfah, under the name of Hamrā' ad-Daylam, as clients of Zuhrah b. Hawiyah (see ibid., p. 10). Prisoner-converts from Bukhārā were settled by 'Ubaydallah b. Ziyād at Basrah (see ibid., p. 111).

Some of the Zutt and Sayābijah deserters from the Persian army were transplanted in A.D. 669 or 670 by the Caliph Mu'āwiyah I from Basrah to Antioch (see ibid., pp. 110-11, and vol. i (New York 1916, Columbia University Press), p. 250). When the Arabs conquered Sind, another batch of Zutt, whom the conquerors had uprooted from their native pastures, seem to have been sent to Syria by Hajjāj (proconsulari munere fungebatur A.D. 691-713) and eventually to have been sent on by the Caliph Walīd I (imperabat A.D. 705-15) to join the previous batch of Zutt deportees at Antioch (see Balādhurī, op. cit., Part (ii), p. 111, and vol. i, p. 250)—whence some, again, were sent on by the Caliph Yazīd II (imperabat A.D. 720-4) to Massīsah (Mopsuestia) in Cilicia (see Balādhurī, op. cit., vol. i, p. 259). But the bulk of Hajjāj's deportees from Sind—who included representatives of other Sindī tribes besides the Zutt, and who were 'accompanied by their wives, their children and their buffaloes' (Balādhurī, op. cit., Part (ii), p. 109)—seem to have been settled by Hajjāj in 'Irāq, in the Kaskar district. Here their numbers were subsequently recruited, according to Balādhurī (ibid., p. 109), by runaway black slaves and by contumacious clients of an Arab tribe and an Arab grandee; and in the reign of the 'Abbasid Caliph Ma'mūn (imperabat A.D. 813-33) they broke out into a rebellion which it took him and his successor Mu'tasim (imperabat A.D. 833-42) the best part of twenty years to quell. According to Mas'ūdī (in his Tanbih, Baron Carra de Vaux's translation, p. 455) these ninth-century Zutt insurgents in the marches of South-Western 'Irāq were the descendants of immigrants from Sind who had migrated to 'Irāq in large numbers across Kirmān, Fars, and Khūzistān. Whether there had or had not been a voluntary immigration as well as a compulsory deportation of Zutt to 'Irāq from Sind, we may take it that, in the course of the first two centuries of Arab rule, man-power from Western India had, in one way or another, been flowing into a South-Western Asia that, on the eve of the Arab conquest, had been depopulated by the two last and most devastating of the Romano-Persian wars.

After the capitulation of the 'Irāqī Zutt insurgents in A.D. 834, Mu'tasim deported some of them to Jalūlah and Khāniqīn, astride the Great North-East Road, and the rest to 'Ayn Zarbah (Graecè Anazarbus) in Cilicia, in the valley of the River Jayhān (Graecè Pyramus) to the north-east of Massīsah (see Balādhurī, op. cit., Part (ii), p. 110, and vol. i, p. 264, and the other authorities cited by M. J. de Goeje in Mémoires d'Histoire et de Géographie Orientales, No. 3: 'Mémoire sur les Migrations des Tsiganes à travers l'Asie' (Leyden 1903, Brill), pp. 30-31). These were not the first Zutt to be settled at 'Ayn Zarbah; for Zutt from 'Ayn Zarbah had already been drafted by Hārūn-ar-Rashīd (imperabat A.D. 786-809) to reinforce the garrison of the neighbouring Cilician fortress Kanīsat as-Sawdā' (see Balādhurī, op. cit., vol. i, p. 264). Thereafter, in A.D. 855, the East Romans descended on 'Ayn Zarbah and carried off into East Roman territory, to the north-west of the Taurus Range, the Zutt deportees there, together with their women and children and buffaloes (Tabari III, 1426, cited by de Goeje in op. cit., p. 31). This thrice deported detachment of the Zutt were the advance guard of the Gypsies of Orthodox and Western Christendom. We may guess that they were reinforced by their kinsmen at Massīsah and Antioch after the reconquest of Cilicia and Northern Syria by the East Roman Empire in the tenth century of the Christian Era.

It will be seen that the Arab Caliphate played a part in the dissemination of the Gypsies that corresponded to the part played by the East Roman Empire in the dissemination of the Paulicians (see IV. iv. 624-34).

made the relation between non-Arab and Arab Muslims intimate, even though it did not place the two categories of Muslims on a footing of equality with each other. The resulting social fusion went far. Even at Basrah and Kūfah, at least as much Persian as Arabic was spoken in the markets,[1] and in Khurāsān the process naturally went farther still. In the Khurāsānī army which, under Abu Muslim's leadership, overthrew the Umayyad régime in the great insurrection of A.D. 747–50, even the Arabs were predominantly Persian-speaking.[2] The Khurāsānī Arab officer who caught and killed the fugitive Umayyad Caliph Marwān in Upper Egypt in the summer of A.D. 750 gave the word of command in Persian when he ordered his troops to attack.[3]

In the Roman Empire, likewise, the military cantonments and civilian colonies acted as social 'melting-pots'.[4] The ferment must have been particularly active in the Roman colony planted in 45 B.C. by Caesar at Corinth,[5] since the Roman citizens whom Caesar settled here were freed-men;[6] and these 'stepsons of Italy'[7]—as Publius Scipio Aemilianus had once called the free populace of the city of Rome to their face, in con-temptuous allusion to the servile source to which so many of them owed their origin, even as early as Aemilianus's day—were drawn from all quarters of the Hellenic World and its hinterlands. In their settlement at Corinth, Caesar's freedman-colonists were merely consummating a process of pammixia of which they themselves were earlier products.

Who are the Beneficiaries?

In promoting this process of pammixia and proletarianization in the body social of a universal state, for whose benefit do civilian colonies and military garrisons chiefly operate?

There have been cases in which the beneficiary has been an alien civilization. For example, the transfers of population on the grand scale, to which the Incas' subjects had been broken in by their rulers' benevo-lently high-handed policy, prepared the ground for the more revolu-tionary acts of the Incas' Spanish supplanters and successors. The Spanish authorities were adopting Incaic practice in attempting to re-group the subject 'Indian' population into new local communities[8] and in retaining and protecting the village headmen[9] whom the foregoing Incaic régime had installed.[10] The Spanish Viceroy of Peru, Francisco de Toledo (*proconsulari munere fungebatur* A.D. 1569–81) was said also to have been consciously and deliberately following Incaic precedent when he organized a system of universal compulsory conscription for

---

[1] See Wellhausen, op. cit., p. 307.
[2] According to Tabarī, cited by Wellhausen in op. cit., p. 308.
[3] See ibid., p. 342.
[4] The Roman Army's role in propagating the Latin version of the Hellenic culture in the Greek-speaking and Oriental provinces of the Roman Empire and at the same time introducing Greek and Oriental influences into the Latin western provinces is described in Hahn, L.: *Rom und Romanismus* (Leipzig 1906, Dieterich), pp. 160–6.
[5] See pp. 109–10, above.   [6] See IV. iv. 270, with n. 4.
[7] 'Quorum noverca est Italia' (Velleius Paterculus, C.: *Historia Romana*, Book II, chap. iv, § 4).
[8] See Haring, C. H.: *The Spanish Empire in America* (New York 1947, Oxford University Press), pp. 70–71, 142, and 174–5.
[9] See ibid., p. 63, n. 44, and p. 215.   [10] See p. 115, above.

civilian labour, under which 'the Indians' were called up in rotation for periods of three or four months' service at a time in numbers that kept one-seventh of the total labour force perpetually mobilized;[1] and the long-suffering native peasantry that was thus periodically rounded up[2] like Ottoman *ra'īyeh* to meet the Spanish colonists' seasonal demands for labour were also placed, when at home, at the disposal of Spanish *encomienderos*.[3] These Spanish counterparts, in the Andean countryside, of the Persian barons whom the Achaemenidae planted in Cappadocia were not the only agents of a Western Christian cultural penetration of the Andean Society under the newly imposed alien régime. The Spanish self-governing municipalities founded at key-points in the Andean World had as potent an effect as the Greek self-governing city-states that were founded in Egypt and South-Western Asia by Alexander and his successors;[4] and these municipalities, like the *encomienderos*, were beneficiaries of an antecedent Incaic Imperial régime which had schooled an uprooted and regimented Andean population to become docile 'Indians' for *conquistadores* from the Old World.

In the European interior of the Western World a quarter of a millennium later, the main body of the Western Society was the beneficiary of the short-lived universal state which was provided for the mouldering remains of a Medieval Western city-state cosmos by the Napoleonic Empire. The stagnation into which the life of Flanders, Western Germany, and Northern Italy had sunk since the Medieval Western city-state cosmos's decay[5] was stirred into fresh and vigorous movement by the intrusion of semi-alien French garrisons; and, brief though this disturbing French visitation was, it had the decisive and historic effect of drawing back into the main stream of Western life the waters of a branch that had become a backwater.[6] The impact of the Napoleonic soldiery, and of their more polished forerunners under the *ancien régime*, on the mustily vegetating society of eighteenth-century Frankfurt and Düsseldorf has been vividly depicted in two masterpieces of German literature.[7]

Such cases, however, as these are as rare as they are interesting, and it is evident that an alien civilization is not the normal beneficiary from the colonies and garrisons that have been installed by a universal state. On the other hand, the barbarians beyond the pale of a civilization derive conspicuous benefits from cantonments screening a universal state's

---

[1] See Haring, op. cit., p. 64.   [2] See p. 112, n. 7, above.

[3] An exact account of the *encomienda* will be found in Haring, op. cit., pp. 44–45 and 62. The strictness with which, at least in juridical theory, the rights of the Crown on the one hand and of the peasants on the other hand were safeguarded in the terms on which an *encomienda* was granted to a Spanish *conquistador* is reminiscent of the limitations on the rights of Ottoman fief-holders (see pp. 124–6, above).

[4] See p. 135, above.

[5] See III. iii. 344–50.   [6] See V. v. 619–42.

[7] In Goethe's *Dichtung und Wahrheit*, Book III, there is an account of the impression made on Goethe in his childhood by the French 'town major', Count Thorane of Grasse, who was billeted in Goethe's father's house after the occupation of Frankfurt by the French Army on the 2nd January, 1759. In Heine's *Reisebilder*, in 'Das Buch Le Grand', there is an analogous picture of the impression made on Heine in his childhood by the French drummer who was billeted in Heine's father's house in Düsseldorf. The Jewish child was captivated by the French plebeian, as the Frankfurter patrician child had been by the French aristocrat.

outer frontiers; for the education which the barbarians gradually acquire from these military outposts of a civilization—first as adversaries and later as mercenaries of the imperial power—makes them capable, at the moment when the empire collapses, of swooping across the fallen barrier and carving barbarian successor-states out of derelict imperial provinces. This adventure and its sequel have been discussed in previous parts of this Study[1] and are dealt with further below.[2] At this point it is only necessary to remind ourselves that the barbarians' triumphs are as short-lived as they are sensational.[3] The transfers and mixtures of population in a universal state produce deeper effects, with more important historical consequences, on the relations between the dominant minority and the internal proletariat.

In both the Roman Empire and the Arab Caliphate, for example, the relative positions of these two social factions had undergone a revolutionary change to the dominant minority's disadvantage—though this without any commensurate gain for the internal proletariat—long before the barbarians succeeded in founding their ephemeral successor-states. In the Arab Caliphate this internal social revolution expressed itself politically in the substitution of the 'Abbasid for the Umayyad régime after the short and sharp civil war of A.D. 747–50. In the Roman Empire the political expression of the corresponding social revolution was the replacement of an Augustan 'principate' by a Diocletianic despotism after a long-protracted bout of disorder which, in its most acute phase, rankled into outright anarchy.[4] In both cases the revolution was provoked by the disillusionment of the internal proletariat with a formal enfranchisement which had not made them genuine equals of the dominant minority; in both cases the insurgent internal proletariat succeeded in depriving the dominant minority of the power and privileges which they had retained till then *de facto*; and in both cases, again, the ruin of the dominant minority did not achieve the revolutionists' aim of setting the victorious internal proletariat in their former masters' seat. Equality, indeed, was attained, but on the level of a common servitude to a new master in the shape of a totalitarian régime.

This ironical turn of events through which History cheated the proletarian insurgents of the fruits of their victory was a consequence of the violence with which the revolution had been carried out. This recurrence of disorders characteristic of a Time of Troubles put to rout the social rally that had been achieved through the foundation of a universal state. Therewith, the temporarily arrested disintegration of a declining civilization was set in motion again, and the social effort thenceforth fruitlessly expended on the forlorn hope of saving the life of a civilization that was by that time *in extremis* took such a tremendous toll from the society's fast-dwindling energies that no margin remained for allocation to individual liberties—not even on the restricted scale of inordinate privileges for a small minority. The totalitarian régime, which was a last

---

[1] In V. v. 194–337 and 459–480.   [2] In VIII. viii, *passim*.
[3] On this point, see I. i. 58–62 and VIII. viii. 45–87.
[4] The period of disorder lasted from the death of the Emperor Marcus Aurelius in A.D. 180 to the accession of Diocletian in A.D. 284. The chapter of anarchy ran from the murder of Alexander Severus in A.D. 235 to the official triumph of Aurelian in A.D. 274.

desperate and swiftly bankrupt expedient for staving off social dissolution, demanded, and exacted to the uttermost farthing, the surrender of the individual's residual treasure of personal freedom.

The Triumph of Equality and Despotism in the Arab Caliphate

The dissatisfaction of the non-Arab converts to Islam[1] with their treatment under the Umayyad régime had substantial grounds. For example, non-Arab prisoners-of-war

'secured by conversion their personal freedom,[2] but not the full status of citizens and members of the army, and therefore not the privileges which this status carried with it: they became *Mawāli*, i.e. clients of an Arab clan. It was only on these terms, as subordinate hangers-on of Arab clans, that converts obtained admission to the ranks of the theocracy; for Islam by itself did not suffice to produce this result. The theocracy was in reality a specifically Arab state, an imperium exercised by the Arabs over the conquered peoples.'[3]

Even the Khurāsānī Iranians whom the local Arab military colonists had accepted as their comrades-in-arms[4]

'were not looked upon by the Arabs as being fully their peers. If they served in the army they had to fight on foot and not on horseback, and if they distinguished themselves they were regarded with mistrust. They did receive pay and a share in prize-of-war, but no regular salary. Their names did not appear on the military salary-roll (*dīwān*). Though they were adopted into the Arab tribes, they were still distinguished, as "peasants", from the "tribesmen". And, though they were Muslims, they were not exempted from the tax payable by subjects.'[5]

In their natural dissatisfaction with an Umayyad régime under which they were kept in this ambiguous, uncomfortable, and irritating position, the Iranian converts to Islam found allies in members of the Arab ruling race who were hostile to the Umayyads on religious grounds; and a series of attempts on the part of these two different dissident elements to make common cause, against a régime that was obnoxious to both, resulted eventually in the Umayyads' overthrow.

The first attempt—an unsuccessful one—was made under the auspices of Sabaism, an extreme form of the Shī'ah which glorified the Caliph 'Alī at the cost of tampering with a fundamental tenet of Islam.[6] This sect struck root in some of the Arab clans in the cantonment of Kūfah, which 'Alī had made the seat of his government; it gained adherents among the numerous Persian freedmen there; and in the anarchy let loose by the civil war between the adherents of 'Alī and those of Mu'āwīyah the Sabaïtes momentarily succeeded in overthrowing the ruling Arab aristocracy of Kūfah and substituting a Sabaïte régime

---

[1] See V. v. 449–50 and 501, n. 2.
[2] 'It was, however, only customary, and not obligatory, to grant their freedom to prisoners-of-war if they accepted Islam.'   [3] Wellhausen, op cit., p. 45.
[4] See the passage quoted from Wellhausen, op. cit., on pp. 140–1, above.
[5] Wellhausen, op. cit., pp. 309–10.
[6] See ibid., pp. 42 and 312–13. The Sabaïtes perverted the Islamic belief in the singleness and transcendence of God by introducing the doctrine that the prophets were successive vehicles of the spirit of God, and that 'Alī was the next of these avatars in succession to Muhammad.

under which the invidious distinction of status between Arab Muslims and non-Arab converts was abolished.[1] After the collapse of a movement that was too heretical to succeed, the Iranian converts found more effective allies in less extreme representatives of the Shī'ah and in the hyper-orthodox and militantly anti-Umayyad Kharijites (Khawārij), who condemned 'Alī himself for his half-heartedness in the cause of God.[2] Seeds of both Kharijism and Shi'ism were carried from Kūfah to Khurāsān by the drafts of Kufan fighting men that were sent to reinforce the garrisons on the North-East Frontier;[3] and, after the Umayyads and their Syrian Arab war-bands had enjoyed nearly a century of ascendancy over all other elements in the Empire, they were overthrown at last by Khurāsānī Iranian converts to Islam with Arab co-operation and largely under Arab leadership.[4]

The anti-Umayyad movement in Khurāsān which came to a head in A.D. 747 in the armed insurrection of Abu Muslim at Merv, and which ended in the replacement of the Umayyads by the 'Abbasids, had been set on foot, about A.D. 720, by agitators from Kūfah who had been Iranian converts by descent and shopkeepers and artisans by profession.[5] Abu Muslim himself appears to have been of the same origin,[6] while the nucleus of his rebel army was mainly recruited from peasant Iranian converts in the Merv oasis.[7] But, though the targets of the insurgents' attack were the Arab representatives of the Umayyad régime, Khurāsānī Arabs were in a majority among Abu Muslim's lieutenants and the insurgents were not consciously working for the cause of Iranian nationalism; the insurrection was an *union sacrée* of Iranian and Arab Khurāsānī Muslims in the cause of Islam;[8] yet its very success inevitably transformed it into an Iranian *revanche* for the Arab conquest of the Sasanian Empire a hundred years back.

The Khurāsānī conquerors took full advantage of the admirable network of roads which the Umayyads had inherited from the Sasanidae and from the Romans and from those Powers' Achaemenian predecessors. While it had taken the Primitive Muslim Arabs nineteen years (A.D. 634–51/2) to conquer the Sasanian dominions from the Euphrates to Merv, and the Macedonians five years (334–330 B.C.) to conquer the Achaemenian dominions from the Hellespont to the scene of Darius's death beyond the Caspian Gates,[9] it took the Khurāsānīs

---

[1] See Wellhausen, op. cit., p. 43.
[2] For the *Khawārij* see Wellhausen, op. cit., pp. 40–41. In the Primitive Islamic community this faction—whose name means 'the Withdrawers'—took the same line towards the political-minded supporters of both 'Alī and Mu'āwiyah as the synonymous 'Pharisees' took towards the Maccabees in the second century B.C. They differed, however in their consequent tactics, for the *Khawārij* took to militancy while the Pharisees persevered in non-violence (see V. v. 73).   [3] See pp. 137–8, above.
[4] See Wellhausen, op. cit., p. 310.   [5] See ibid., pp. 315 and 320.
[6] See ibid., p. 323.   [7] See ibid., p. 331.
[8] See ibid., pp. 320 and 333–4. In the recently conquered province of Tukhāristān, adjoining Khurāsān on the north-east, Arab conquerors and native Iranians likewise made common cause in this crisis, and likewise accepted a non-Arab as their leader because the Arab aspirants to leadership could not agree among themselves. But this *union sacrée* in Tukhāristān was directed not against the Umayyads but against the Khurāsānī rebels (see ibid., p. 334). This loyalty of the recently conquered Iranians of Tukhāristān to the Umayyad régime is reminiscent of the loyalty of the recently conquered Sikhs in the Panjab to the British Rāj in the crisis of the Indian Mutiny.
[9] See II. ii. 140.

less than three years to sweep over the Umayyad dominions from Merv to the point in Upper Egypt where they caught and killed their quarry the Umayyad Caliph Marwān. The capitulation, in the summer of A.D. 749, of the Syrian Arab garrison of Nihāwand—the fortress commanding the Great North-East Road at an easily defensible point on the western brow of the Iranian Plateau—retrieved the disgrace of the catastrophic defeat of the Persians by the Arabs on the same spot in A.D. 641 or 642. The crushing defeat of Marwān himself by a mere detachment of the Khurāsānī forces in a ten days' battle (*commissum* 16th–25th January, A.D. 750) on the banks of the Greater Zāb wiped out the older score of the equally crushing defeat that had been inflicted in this neighbourhood in 331 B.C. on the last Darius's last army by Alexander's expeditionary force. In bursting out of Asia into Egypt, and obtaining the allegiance of all the former Umayyad dominions in Africa up to the Atlantic coast of Morocco, the Khurāsānī adherents of the 'Abbasids surpassed the feat of the Sasanian army which had occupied Alexandria in A.D. 619, but had exhausted its impetus some distance short of Carthage,[1] in the course of the last and worst of the Romano-Persian wars. Indeed, they achieved the ambition of the Achaemenid conqueror Cambyses, whose intention of following up his conquest of Egypt by a naval expedition against Carthage had been frustrated by the refusal of the indispensable Phoenician contingent in his fleet to carry out an order to subjugate their colonial kinsmen.[2]

The brilliant victory of the Khurāsānīs in the civil war that swept across the dominions of the Caliphate in A.D. 747–50 was decisive in its negative results. The Umayyad régime and the hegemony of the Syrian Arab military cantonments, of which the régime had been an expression, were overthrown once for all,[3] and the Khurāsānīs ostensibly reigned in their stead under the banner of the 'Abbasids.

'The Khurāsānīs had won for the 'Abbasids their victory and they took their own share of the spoils. In a certain sense they became the heirs of the Syrians, though their relation to the Government was not the same.

---

[1] See p. 93, above.

[2] 'Cambyses gave orders to his fleet to sail against Carthage, but the Phoenicians refused to obey. They submitted that they were bound by solemn engagements and that they would be guilty of a crime if they made war on a daughter-community. This unwillingness of the Phoenicians [to lend themselves to Cambyses' designs against Carthage killed the project, since] the remainder of the fleet was inadequate for the task. So, thanks to their Phoenician kinsmen, the Carthaginians escaped subjugation at Persian hands; for Cambyses felt it impolitic to try to coerce the Phoenicians, considering that they had come under Persian sovereignty voluntarily and that the naval power of the Persian Empire depended entirely on them' (Herodotus, Book III, chap. 19). For the relations of the Phoenician city-states to the Achaemenian Imperial Government, see V. v. 123, n. 2.

[3] See Wellhausen, op. cit., p. 347. As this authority here points out, the success of the subjects of the Caliphate in throwing off the yoke of the Arab cantonments on the borders of the Desert and the Sown had the effect of breaking those links between the subject territories of the Caliphate and the reservoir of badawi Arab military man-power on the Arabian Steppe which had been forged with such care and skill by the original Arab empire-builders. 'The ancient home of the Arabs now "went native" (*verwilderte*) again so completely that it actually became a dangerous business to make the pilgrimage.' Cp. Caetani, L.: *Studi di Storia Orientale*, vol. iii (Milan 1914, Hoepli), p. 50. In the post-Syriac interregnum *circa* A.D. 975–1275, in which the 'Abbasid Caliphate foundered, the Nomads of Arabia played the role, not of upholders of the tottering empire, but of invading barbarians on all fours with the Berbers and the Turks (see III. iii. 445–6).

They were called the *Shī'ah* ('the Party'), the *Ansār* ('the Helpers')[1] or the *Abnā'-ad-Dawlah* ('the Sons of the New Era').[2] They held in their hands the external power; they had a military organization. . . . They constituted the Caliph's standing army, and the Caliph lived in the midst of these guards of his. Baghdad was in fact laid out, not as an oecumenical capital, but as a cantonment for the Khurāsānīs in which the Caliph could reside at a safe distance from Kūfah. In this cantonment they still maintained their links with their home,[3] and the predominance which they had won in the service of the 'Abbasids, both as a party and as a military force, became a predominance of their nation and their country—Eastern Iran—over the rest of the Empire.'[4]

This ostensible hegemony was retained by the Khurāsānī garrison of Baghdad for rather more than a century before the military control over the central government of the 'Abbasid Caliphate passed into the hands of a Turkish slave-bodyguard recruited from the Eurasian Steppe beyond the pale of both Khurāsān and Transoxania; and, in terms of the nationality of the founders of successor-states, the general Iranian political ascendancy in the 'Abbasid dominions may be reckoned to have lasted for more than three centuries, if we place to its credit the Transoxanian Iranian successor-state established by the Sāmānids,[5] and if we take as the terminal date the overthrow of the Daylamī Iranian Buwayhids by the Turkish Saljūqs in A.D. 1055–6.[6] Compared with the ephemeral subsequent triumphs of the barbarian war-bands that came in at the death of the Caliphate—an ill-assorted mob of Turks and Mongols, Arabs and Berbers, Normans and Franks—the Iranian ascendancy in

---

[1] The original *Ansār* had, of course, been the people of Medina who had invited the Prophet Muhammad to come and rule over them. Under this name they had been distinguished from the *Muhājirīn* who were the Prophet's Meccan fellow refugees. Now that the name *Muhājirīn* had come to signify the Arab military settlers in the cantonments, the adoption of the name *Ansār* by the Khurāsānīs had an obvious political connotation.—A.J.T.

[2] Wellhausen notes (op. cit., p. 347) that the original meaning of *dawlah* was 'new era' and that it was the choice of this term by the 'Abbasids to describe their régime that led to its acquiring the general meaning of 'government' or 'dynasty'. Wellhausen also draws attention to the affinity between the title 'Sons of the Kingdom' and the language of Matt. xvii. 25; 'Of whom do the kings of the Earth take custom or tribute? Of their own children, or of strangers?'—A.J.T.

[3] The geographical situation of Baghdad in relation to the Iranian Plateau corresponded exactly to that of Basrah and Kūfah in relation to the Arabian Steppe. Baghdad was laid out on a site as near to the heart of 'Iraq as a Khurāsānī garrison could post itself without placing a river barrier between itself and its sources of reinforcement in North-Eastern Iran. The 'geopolitical' significance of the sites of Basrah and Kūfah has been noticed on p. 131, above. When Hārūn-ar-Rashīd (*imperabat* A.D. 786–809) organized the North-Western March of the Caliphate over against the East Roman Empire (see p. 121, above), he planted Khurāsānī garrisons at Adana, Tarsus, and 'Ayn Zarbah, *alias* Anazarbus (Ahmad Al-Balādhurī: *Kitab Futūh-al Buldān*, English translation by Khitti, P. K., vol. i (New York 1916, Columbia University Press), pp. 260, 262, and 264).

[4] Wellhausen, op. cit., p. 348.

[5] See II. ii. 142, above. Iranian successor-states of the 'Abbasid Caliphate arose to the west as well as to the east of the 'Abbasid metropolitan province of 'Iraq. The Zanāta Berber Kharijite principality which held the hinterland of Ifrīqīyah from A.D. 761 to A.D. 908 was founded by a Persian adventurer named Rustem, and the ancestor of the so-called 'Fātimids' was said to have come from Ahwāz in the Iranian province of Khūzistān (see I. i. 355). The Ikhshīd, who in A.D. 935 founded for himself and his heirs a successor-state in Egypt and Syria by carrying out the 'Abbasid Government's mandate to suppress the previous local successor-state ruled by the Tulunids, was a Transoxanian Iranian princeling. His ancestral principality was Farghānah (see Lane-Poole, S.: *A History of Egypt in the Middle Ages*, 2nd ed. (London 1914, Methuen), pp. 81–82).

[6] See I. i. 356.

the more palmy days of the 'Abbasid Era was long-lived and historically important. On the other hand it was unsubstantial by comparison with the antecedent Arab hegemony which had been brought to an end by the Khurāsānī insurrection of A.D. 747–50. The effective immediate heir of the Syrian Arab cantonments in Syria and 'Irāq was not the Khurāsānī cantonment at Baghdad but the 'Abbasid totalitarian régime—which did indeed inaugurate a 'new era' when it supplanted its comparatively easy-going Umayyad predecessor.

'The change of dynasty brought with it a transformation of the inward nature of the régime. . . . The Arabs had imposed themselves, by right of conquest, as a ruling nobility over against the populations which they had subjugated. . . . Under the Umayyads this primitive system persisted in essentials. . . . Under the 'Abbasids it vanished—along with the distinction of classes which was its pre-supposition. The 'Abbasids did not, like the Umayyads, stand on the shoulders of a strong aristocracy of which they themselves were members; the Khurāsānīs, on whom their power was based, were not their kinsmen; they were merely their tools. The whole Muslim community stood in a uniform relation to the 'Abbasids, without any gradations of a natural order in the political standing of different elements; the dynasty alone possessed the divine right to rule as heirs of the Prophet. There were no impediments to prevent them from shaping the régime in accordance with technical considerations, as might seem best for efficiency and also for the interests of the dynasty itself. They succeeded in bringing greater order into the administration, especially in the departments of taxation and justice; they were zealous in giving a hearing to, and taking action on, the complaints of subjects who appealed to them as a court of supreme instance.[1] But they suppressed the general living interest in politics—which had formerly been part and parcel of religion—far more thoroughly than had proved practicable for the Umayyads. . . . The State shrank to the dimensions of the Court. . . . And the Court comprised a

---

[1] This 'Abbasid and likewise Caesarean *arcanum imperii* was also taken to heart by the 'Abbasids' Sāmānid successors in the North-East. It was remembered of the Sāmānid prince Ismā'īl b. Ahmad, surnamed 'Al-'Ādil' ('the Just') (*dominabatur* A.D. 892–907) that, even in the depth of winter, when the ground was under snow, he would sit motionless on horse-back, armed cap-à-pie, in open court, in order to render himself continually accessible to petitioners.

'I have read, in the works of our forefathers, that it was the usual practice for the Kings of Persia to have a lofty scaffold erected and to station themselves there on horseback, to enable them to distinguish, among the multitude assembled on the plain, all petitioners complaining of oppression, and so to give themselves the opportunity of doing justice. The reason for this custom was that, when a prince remains inside a palace with doors, barriers, vestibules, corridors and curtains, perverse and ill-intentioned persons can obstruct the entry of petitioners and prevent them from reaching the royal presence. . . .

'Ismā'īl b. Ahmad had a practice, when the cold was most severe and when the snow was falling most heavily, of repairing, unattended, to the Great Square [at Bukhārā] and remaining there on horseback till the moment of the dawn prayer. It might happen, he used to say, that some victim of injustice might come to my Court to inform us of his needs, and he might have neither money to cover his expenses nor a roof to shelter him. Because of the rain and the snow, they would not allow him to reach my presence; but, when he knew that I was here, he would come to find me, would obtain satisfaction, and would return home re-assured and rejoicing in complete security.'

This Sāmānid royal practice, thus described by Hasan Abu 'Ali Nizām-al-Mulk in his *Siyāsat-Nāma*, chap. 3, *ad initium* and *ad finem* (on pp. 12 and 26 of the French translation by Schefer, Ch.: *Siasset Nameh* (Paris 1893, Leroux)), was still being followed, some nine hundred years later than Ismā'īl b. Ahmad's day, in the Transcaucasian Kingdom of Georgia on the eve of its annexation by Russia, according to a self-complacently contemptuous allusion in the work of a Modern Western publicist (see de Maistre, J.: *Lettres et Opuscules Inédits*, vol. i (Paris 1851, Vaton), p. 215).—A.J.T.

throng of civil servants who were no longer identical with the officers [of the military establishment].[1] Most of these civil servants were creatures and favourites of the sovereign. Freedmen were preponderant among them. Under the previous régime freedmen may have enjoyed the ruler's confidence and exercised a corresponding influence; they now attained to the highest positions in the public service.[2] They were raised from the dust, to be hurled down into the dust again. . . . It was not birth, but the Caliph, that made people's fortunes. . . . The aristocracy was replaced by a Court hierarchy of officials, distributed between recognized grades and kept under one another's surveillance. At the top stood the Wazīr, who was the head of the Caliphial Chancery and eventually became the visible *alter ego* of a Caliph who no longer appeared in public.'[3]

The Triumph of Equality and Despotism in the Roman Empire

This masterly portrayal of the features of the 'Abbasid régime in which it presented so striking a contrast to its Umayyad background could be adapted with little change to portray the corresponding revolution in the Roman Empire which substituted the Diocletianic despotism for the Augustan 'Principate'. The Augustan régime, like the Umayyad Caliphate, had respected in large measure the liberties of an 'ascendancy'[4] as against the Imperial Government at the price of tolerating the maintenance of this 'ascendancy's' privileged position as against the subject population of the Empire. In the Roman Empire under the Principate, as in the Arab Caliphate in the Umayyad Age, these privileges were partly positive and partly negative.

An inner circle of Roman families whose members enjoyed a customary right of entry into the Senate actually shared with the Emperor—who tactfully described himself as 'Leader of the House' (*Princeps Senatus*) in the administration of the Roman dominions. A number of pacific provinces in the interior had been handed back to the Senate by Augustus; and, in the provinces which the Emperor continued to keep in his own hands, with the important and significant exception of Egypt, the governorships were reserved in practice for senators, who were reconciled by the splendour of these posts to the indignity of having to hold them as the Emperor's servants. The senatorial class also staffed the senior posts in the Imperial Army. And, though the administration of Egypt was not the only sphere in which the Emperor delegated the realities of power to non-senatorial agents, the authority still left to the senatorial class was considerable in reality and even more imposing in its carefully-kept-up appearances.

A wider circle of Roman citizens who were not of the senatorial class but who were domiciled in Italy enjoyed a monopoly of the right to serve in the Imperial Guard—the nine 'praetorian' ('headquarters') battalions

---

[1] Compare the segregation of the civil and military services under the Diocletianic régime in the Roman Empire.—A.J.T.

[2] Compare the corresponding transformation of the freedmen-stewards of Caesar's private household into virtual ministers of state (see V. v. 452–3). In the Roman Empire this political consequence of social *Gleichschaltung* occurred at an early stage of 'the Principate'.—A.J.T.   [3] Wellhausen, op. cit., pp. 348–50.

[4] In the sense in which the term came to be used of the Protestant dominant minority in Ireland under the British Crown from the Tudor Era down to the establishment of the Irish Free State.

that were permanently quartered in the City of Rome itself—and further possessed the valuable negative privilege of being exempt from direct taxation. Under the Principate this 'ascendancy' of an inner circle within the Roman citizen body occupied a position not unlike that of the Syrian Arab soldiery on the salary-rolls of the Arab cantonments in the Caliphate under the Umayyad régime. Like the Syrian Arabs, these specially privileged Roman citizens were a small minority of the total population of the Empire; and, just as, in the Caliphate, there came, as time passed, to be an ever larger body of converts to Islam whose conversion proved not, after all, to have made them the peers of their Arab masters, so likewise in the Roman Empire there was an ever larger body of legally naturalized citizens who found themselves still outside the privileged circle.

In the Roman Empire, as in the Caliphate, and indeed for the same reasons, the formal status of membership in the ruling community was easier for members of the subject population to obtain than were the substantial advantages that had originally been associated with that status automatically. The ring of senatorial families was reluctant to see the value of their privileges depreciated by a widening of their circle. Caesar's revolutionary act of making Roman senators out of the uncouth notables of recently conquered Gallic cantons raised so fierce a storm that Augustus beat a retreat in the interests of his policy of reconciling the Senate to the Principate, and it was not till A.D. 48 that it became practical politics for the Emperor Claudius to enrol senators from among the notables of the Aedui, a Gallic canton that had already been Rome's ally before Caesar's conquest.[1] The Roman Imperial Treasury, for its part, was as reluctant to see its sources of revenue diminished as a result of progressive extensions of the Roman franchise to non-citizen subjects of the Empire as the Umayyad Treasury was to suffer a similar loss through the progressive conversion of non-Muslim subjects of the Caliphate to Islam.[2]

The immunity from direct taxation which was enjoyed under the Principate by Roman citizens domiciled in Italy dated from the morrow of the Third Romano-Macedonian War (gerebatur 171–168 B.C.);[3] and at that date the entire Roman citizen body had occupied a territory embracing less than half of Italy south of the Appennines.[4] When the

[1] See The Cambridge Ancient History, vol. x (Cambridge 1934, University Press), p. 377.

[2] All treasuries are apt to think alike, but the Umayyad Treasury was actually the historical heir to the Roman Treasury's tradition. At the time of the conquest the Primitive Arab Muslim Government had taken on the existing inland revenue organization as a going concern—including the official personnel as well as the records and the practice—in both their ex-Roman and their ex-Sasanian dominions. Ruling, as they did, from Damascus, the Umayyads were influenced by the Roman fiscal tradition predominantly.

[3] Having destroyed in that war the last surviving Great Power in the Hellenic World apart from the Roman Commonwealth itself, the Romans felt that the consequent decrease in their own military and political liabilities, and increase in the external sources of their public revenue, made a combination of new circumstances that justified them in ceasing to impose direct taxation on themselves. They did not, however, abolish the tax of 5 per cent. on the manumission of slaves, which had been introduced as early as 357 B.C. and which had a social as well as a fiscal purpose. This tax remained in force under the Empire (see Hirschfeld, O.: Die Kaiserlichen Verwaltungsbeamten bis auf Diocletian, 2nd ed. (Berlin 1905, Weidmann), pp. 106–9).

[4] A map displaying the areas in Italy that were included in the territory of the Roman

Roman citizenship had been subsequently conferred, first on all previously alien Italian communities south of the River Po,[1] and then on all
communities between the Po and the Alps,[2] the exemption from direct
taxation had accompanied the conferment of the franchise as a matter of
course. When, however, under the Principate, the still expanding body of
Roman citizens burst even the generous bounds that had been assigned to
Italy by Augustus and came to constitute an appreciable and increasing
element in the population of the provinces as well, the Imperial Treasury
took alarm, and laid down the new doctrine that the immunity from
direct taxation which had been one of the attributes of Roman citizenship since 167 B.C. was applicable only to citizens domiciled in Italy; all
persons domiciled in provincial Roman territory were now deemed to be
liable to direct taxation even if they happened to be Roman citizens;[3]
the only exception to this ruling was in favour of Roman citizens domiciled in the territory of a Roman municipality, outside Italy, on which
'Italian status' (*ius Italicum*)[4] had been expressly conferred; and the
Imperial Government was very sparing in its grant of this boon: it was
obtained by few non-Italian communities of Roman citizens beyond
those which were at least partially of Italian origin.[5]

The Roman Treasury could, and did, thus create a class of non-
privileged provincial Roman citizens, but it could not prevent this class
either from harbouring resentment or from steadily growing in numbers
until it found itself strong enough to sweep away by main force the
privileges which a favoured minority of the citizen body had so long
retained for itself.

The non-privileged element in the Roman citizen body in the Age of
the Principate was recruited from various sources. The military policy,
inaugurated by Augustus, of insisting that the Roman legionary infantry
of the line should continue to be composed exclusively of Roman citizens
but should be stationed henceforward mainly on the frontiers and wholly
outside Italy[6] ensured, when combined with legal facilities for legitimizing

State between the end of the Hannibalic War and the secession, in 90 B.C., of a confederacy of Italian states hitherto externally associated with the Roman Commonwealth
will be found in Beloch, J.: *Der Italische Bund unter Roms Hegemonie* (Leipzig 1880,
Teubner), *ad finem*.

[1] By the *Lex Plautia Papiria* of 89 B.C.   [2] By Caesar in 49 B.C.

[3] It will be seen that this Roman Treasury ruling was identical with the Umayyad
Caliph 'Umar II's ruling, noticed on p. 132, above, that a non-Arab convert to Islam
must migrate to one of the Arab military cantonments in order to qualify for obtaining
the comparatively favourable fiscal treatment that Arab Muslims enjoyed.

[4] See *The Cambridge Ancient History*, vol. xi (Cambridge 1936, University Press), pp.
455–6. This *ius Italicum* had a juridical as well as a fiscal aspect. Roman citizens not
domiciled in territory possessing this status were thereby debarred, not only from the
right of exemption from direct taxation, but also from the right of owning land in freehold as *ager privatus ex iure Quiritium*.

[5] 'Italian status' was, for example, possessed by the Roman 'colony' of Vienna
Allobrogum (Vienne) in the province of Gallia Narbonensis, in spite of the fact that the
Roman citizens inhabiting this titular Roman colony were Latinized natives and not
settlers from Italy. Yet Vienna was the only municipality in the province that did possess
this *ius Italicum*, though, at an early stage in the history of the Principate, Narbonensis
as a whole had become almost as thoroughly Latinized in language and culture as the
Transpadane fringe of Italy itself. The less exceptional phenomenon of the possession of
the *ius Italicum* by a Roman community situated outside Italy but composed of settlers
of Italian origin is illustrated by the case of Lugdunum (see Arnold, W. T.: *Studies
of Roman Imperialism* (Manchester 1906, University Press), pp. 99 and 107–8).

[6] See II. ii. 20 and p. 117, above.

the legionaries' children retrospectively,[1] that a warlike population of
Roman citizens, who could have the last word in Imperial politics if
ever they awoke to a realization of their power, should establish itself
on the Empire's fringes. Where militarily suitable citizen recruits for
the legions were not forthcoming in sufficient numbers (as, for example,
in the Anatolian areas of recruitment for the eastern legions), it is probable that militarily suitable non-citizens were naturalized *ad hoc* in
order to make them eligible for enrolment,[2] and it is also probable that
soldiers enrolled in the non-citizen formations called *auxilia* could obtain
naturalization as Roman citizens upon their discharge from the service,
if not before.[3]

Moreover, as the civilian population of one ex-barbarian province
after another became Latinized in language and culture, naturalization
was granted wholesale by a regular series of stages. The first stage was to
confer on a subject community the political status of a city-state externally
associated with the Roman Commonwealth on the customary terms
traditionally called the *ius Latinum*. A citizen of a Latin community who
was elected by his fellow citizens to a local magistracy thereby acquired
Roman citizenship automatically, and this door of entry into the Roman
citizen body came to be known as the *Latium Minus* after the institution
(perhaps in Hadrian's reign)[4] of a *Latium Maius* which automatically
conferred the Roman citizenship on a citizen of a Latin community who
was elected to his local town council.[5] There were even non-Latin
communities—for example, the Gallic canton of the Aedui—whose
elected local magistrates became Roman citizens *ipso facto*.[6] Through
all these avenues the body of non-privileged Roman citizens was steadily
recruited under the Principate for nearly a quarter of a millennium[7] till,

[1] See p. 132, above.

[2] See Parker, H. M. D.: *The Roman Legions* (Oxford 1928, Clarendon Press), p. 170.
Aelius Aristeides seems, in a passage in his *In Romam* (Keil's edition, vol. ii. pp. 112–13
(§§ 75–78)), to imply that, in his day, *all* recruits for the Imperial Army were non-
citizens who were enfranchised when they were enrolled.

[3] See *The Cambridge Ancient History*, vol. xi (Cambridge 1936, University Press),
p. 443, cited on p. 132, above.

[4] 'Between A.D. 100 and the death of Pius' (*The Cambridge Ancient History*, vol. xi
(Cambridge 1936, University Press), pp. 452–3).

[5] See Arnold, op. cit., p. 99, n. 2.   [6] See ibid., p. 111.

[7] It will be seen that the ascendancy of a privileged minority lasted nearly twice as long
in the Roman Empire under the Principate as in the Arab Caliphate under the Umayyad
régime. This notably greater longevity is perhaps to be explained by the fact that in the
Roman case the ascendancy was exercised less crudely and was monopolized less
exclusively. The Augustan settlement was a compromise between the monstrously harsh
and predatory tyranny which the masters of the Roman State had exercised over the
Hellenic World during the last century and a half of the Roman Republican régime and
the drastic dictatorship on behalf of the 'under-dog' that had been the ideal, and the death,
of Caesar; and the Caesarean element in the genius of the Principate tended to gain ground
at the expense of the oligarchic element. For example, the area of recruitment for the
Praetorian Guard, which appears to have been confined to Central Italy when Augustus
founded the corps (see Tacitus: *Annals*, Book IV, chap. 5), was progressively extended,
first up to the limits of Italy within Augustus's boundaries, and later to communities of
Roman citizens in adjacent provinces (e.g. Macedonia and Noricum) and in Baetica.
There was a corresponding tendency to extend the area of recruitment for the Senate;
and, though Senators of non-Italian origin were required by the Emperor Trajan to re-
invest one-third of their property in Italian real estate, the proportion was reduced to
one-fourth by Marcus Aurelius (see *The Cambridge Ancient History*, vol. xi (Cambridge
1936, University Press), pp. 212, 370, and 419). This policy of gradually widening the
privileged circle was eventually applied to the Principate itself. Of the five emperors,
from Nerva to Marcus inclusive, whose successive reigns covered the 'Indian Summer'

in the year A.D. 212, the Emperor Caracalla took the logical concluding step of conferring Roman citizenship on all—or, at any rate, all but an insignificant residue—of the still unenfranchised subjects of the Empire by his celebrated *Constitutio Antoniniana*.[1]

This superficially liberal measure might perhaps have been expected to exorcise the danger of a social revolution; for, after all, the inferior form of Roman citizenship that did not carry the *ius Italicum* with it was nevertheless something well worth having. Whatever its fiscal and juridical shortcomings may have been, it was undoubtedly a palladium of civil liberties—as was found by Saint Paul when he put its efficacy to the test on three critical occasions in his missionary career.[2] Yet the *Constitutio Antoniniana* did not avert the upheaval of A.D. 235–74, and may actually have played some part in bringing it to pass. For on the one hand it did not diminish, and possibly increased, the financial burdens of its beneficiaries;[3] and on the other hand it made the inequity of privileges still enjoyed by a minority *de facto* more glaring now that all inhabitants of the Empire had become Roman citizens *de jure*.

The first stroke in the battle against privilege had indeed been struck already by Caracalla's father and predecessor Septimius Severus. This professional soldier of colonial Phoenician origin[4] had been able to seize a vacant imperial throne thanks to finding himself in command of the frontier defence force nearest to Rome at a moment when the Praetorian Guards had unpardonably abused their trust by assassinating an excellent emperor and proceeding to sell the purple by auction to a worthless bidder. When Severus marched on Rome at the head of his Pannonian legions, the Praetorians proved to be as unwarlike as they were murderous and corrupt. They submitted tamely to a sentence of disbandment and banishment, and the provincial war-lord who had thus given these privileged Italian guardsmen their deserts not only cashiered the men but made a complete break in the basis of recruitment of the corps. It was recruited thenceforth from the *élite* of the legions (in practice, from soldiers of the Danubian legions and of one eastern legion, the Sixth

---

of Hellenic history, two (Trajan and Hadrian) came from Baetica, one (Antoninus Pius) from Narbonensis, while the family of a fourth (Marcus) was of Baetican origin. The only Italian among the five was Nerva, the first—and the least estimable—in the series. No doubt this progressive widening of the privileged inner circle of the Roman citizen body delayed the revolt of the ever-growing mass of Roman citizens of inferior status. Conversely, in the Sinic universal state the ascendency of the victorious empire-building principality of Ts'in was overthrown only twelve years after the establishment of the *Pax Sinica* because it had immediately been made intolerable by the inhumanly revolutionary policy of Ts'in She Hwang-ti.

[1] See V. vi. 7, with n. 4.

[2] In dealing with the magistrates of the Roman colony of Philippi (see Acts xvi. 37–39); in dealing with Claudius Lysias, the Roman military tribune in command of the castle at Jerusalem (see Acts xxii. 23—xxiii. 31); and in dealing with two successive Roman procurators of Judaea: Antonius Felix and Porcius Festus (see Acts xxiii. 31—xxvi. 32).

[3] It is possible that one of the motives and effects of the *Constitutio Antoniniana* was to extend to all inhabitants of the Empire the special taxes—death duties (at the merciful rate of a mere 5 per cent.), a general sales tax (at the rate of 1 per cent.), a special tax on sales of slaves (at the rate of 4 per cent.)—which Augustus had imposed on Roman citizens domiciled in Italy as a device for diminishing the inequality in the distribution of the burden of taxation between this minority and the rest of the inhabitants of the Empire (for details see Hirschfeld, O.: *Die Kaiserlichen Verwaltungsbeamten bis auf Diocletian*, 2nd ed. (Berlin 1905, Weidmann), pp. 93–105).

[4] Severus's home town was the Punic city of Leptis in Tripolitania.

Ferrata). Severus also stationed at Albano, within one short march of Rome, the second of his three new *Legiones Parthicae*. The commanders of these new legions were not of senatorial rank, and the soldiers were probably for the most part Roman citizens from Illyricum and Thrace.[1]

After this decisive demonstration of the military impotence of a still privileged minority, the sequel was almost a foregone conclusion. The upheaval of A.D. 235–74 was a revolt of the provinces against Italy, of the non-senatorial classes against the Senate, and of the uncultivated masses against the heirs of the Hellenic culture; and on all three battlefields the former 'ascendancy' was decisively defeated.[2] The 'ascendancy' did not, indeed, allow itself to be deposed without a struggle. The successful organization of armed resistance to the intolerable Thracian soldier Maximinus was a last triumph of the *concordia ordinum* and *consensus Italiae* that had been the political ideals of Cicero. But the discomfiture of the Senate was made manifest by the exclusion of senators from all military command, direct or indirect, by act of the Emperor Gallienus (*imperabat* A.D. 253–68);[3] and it was sealed when Florianus, the brother of the last senatorial occupant of the imperial throne,[4] was rejected by the Senate itself as a candidate for the succession in favour of the capable Illyrian soldier Probus. This liquidation of the long-respected partnership of the Senate in the government of the Empire was accompanied by a violation of the equally long-respected immunity of Italy from direct taxation. After the devaluation of the currency during the anarchy, the primitive practice of raising a levy in kind (*annona*) for the support of the army and the civil service was applied to Northern Italy as well as to the provinces. After this progressive *Gleichschaltung* of Italy with the provinces and of the Senate with the rest of the inhabitants of the Empire, the inauguration of a totalitarian régime by the Illyrian soldier-statesman Diocletian was inevitable and indispensable.[5] This was the political price that had to be paid for long overdue

---

[1] See Parker, H. M. D.: *A History of the Roman World from A.D. 138 to 337* (London 1935, Methuen), pp. 60 and 80–84. There is, of course, an almost exact analogy between this measure of Severus's and the substitution, by the 'Abbasids, of a Khurāsānī garrison at Baghdad for the Syrian Arab garrisons at Basrah, Kūfah, and the four cantonments on the desert border of Syria itself.

[2] The social and cultural aspects of this great revolution in the Roman Empire have been imaginatively apprehended and brilliantly portrayed by M. Rostovtzeff in *The Social and Economic History of the Roman Empire* (Oxford 1926, Clarendon Press). The scholarly author of this magnificent piece of historical work has incurred some criticism on the ground that he has read into the history of the Roman Empire in the third century of the Christian Era his own experience of the Russian revolution of A.D. 1917. It is possible, perhaps, that here and there Rostovtzeff may have been carried by this analogy beyond the limits of the evidence; but it is certain that his illuminating and instructive interpretation of a momentous passage of history would not have enriched our whole understanding of History, as it has done, if Rostovtzeff had not lived through that experience as a human being and had not possessed the imaginative power to turn it to account as an historian.

[3] This was a portent, considering that the Emperor who pronounced these aristocrats no longer fit for military command was himself a man of culture. Yet the process of pushing the Senate out of public life, which was thus carried a long step farther by Gallienus, had been covertly set in train by his far more cultivated predecessor Augustus (for Gallienus's measures, see Parker, op. cit., pp. 178–80).

[4] For the significance of the reign of Florianus's brother and predecessor Tacitus (*imperabat* A.D. 275–6), see V. vi. 55.

[5] The complete exclusion of senators from the civil service as well as from military command, and the extension of liability to imperial taxation to Cis-Appennine as well as

acts of social justice by which, in reaction against an invidious former discrimination between classes, every Roman citizen in a Roman World in which virtually the whole population had now been enfranchised was made eligible henceforward for appointment to any post, up to the highest, in the Roman Imperial Army[1] and Civil Service.

The Utilization of Imperial Garrisons and Colonies by Higher Religions

In the sequel to this genuine social but illusory political triumph of an internal proletariat over an 'ascendancy', we have still to discover who were the beneficiaries in the long run; for we have already ascertained that the immediately resulting totalitarian régime was transitory and that the subsequent 'heroic age' of the barbarians was ephemeral. The truth would appear to be that while the internal proletariat was not appreciably more successful than any of the other competitors for the spoils of a disintegrating civilization in so far as it was competing with them in their own currency of material power—economic, political, and military—it did achieve an enduring and momentous success in so far as it placed its treasure in the spiritual enterprise of propagating a higher religion. The ultimate beneficiaries from the organized redistribution and intermixture of population that precipitated a social revolution in both the Roman and the Arab Empire were Christianity in the one case and Islam in the other.

The military cantonments and frontier garrisons of the Umayyad Caliphate manifestly served Islam as invaluable *points d'appui* in that extraordinary deployment of latent spiritual forces by which Islam transfigured itself, and thereby transformed its mission, in the course of six centuries. In the seventh century of the Christian Era, Islam had burst out of Arabia as the distinctive sectarian creed of one of the barbarian war-bands that were carving out successor-states for themselves in provinces of the Roman Empire; by the thirteenth century of the Christian Era, Islam had become a universal church providing shelter for sheep left without their familiar shepherds through the collapse of the 'Abbasid Caliphate at the dissolution of the Syriac Civilization.[2]

Time and again it looked, on the surface, as if Islam had been cheated of this spiritual destiny by being successfully exploited for political and social ends.

'The original driving-force behind the insurrection of the Khurāsānīs was Islam and not [Iranian] nationalism . . . [but] the nationality of the victors asserted its preponderance over [the cause of] Islam. . . . The international [fraternity of] Islam was a mask for the triumph of the Iranian cause over the Arabs. . . . This was inherent in the situation, though not in the original design.'[3]

Trans-Appennine Italy, do not appear to have taken place before the Diocletianic reorganization. This was the logical fulfilment of the piecemeal reforms of Septimius Severus and Gallienus.

[1] In the post-Diocletianic Roman Army there were no distinctions of class (see Grosse, R.: *Römische Militärgeschichte von Gallienus bis zum Beginn der Byzantinischen Themenverfassung* (Berlin 1920, Weidmann), p. 196). The classless military hierarchy established by Diocletian and Constantine at the turn of the third and fourth centuries of the Christian era lasted, substantially unchanged, until the seventh century (see ibid., p. 107).

[2] This transfiguration of Islam has been touched upon already in V. v. 127-8, 230, and 673-8.   [3] Wellhausen, op. cit., pp. 334 and 348.

In the next chapter of the story it looked, again on the surface, as if the 'Abbāsids had been still more adroit than the Khurāsānīs in making Islam serve their purpose.

'The 'Abbāsids took credit for having brought Islam—which they accused the Umayyads of having repressed—into its due position of dominance. They professed a desire to bring to life again the extinct tradition of the Prophet. They gathered round themselves in Baghdad the doctors of the Islamic Law from Medina, which had been their head-quarters hitherto, and they constantly took legal opinions from them; for the 'Abbāsids made a point of handling political questions in juristic form and of seeing that decisions were taken on the basis of the Qur'ān and the Sunnah. In reality, though, they made Islam subservient solely to their own ends. They domesticated the doctors of the Law at their court and secured the stamp of their approval for even the most discreditable of their own measures. [In fact,] they made the pious opposition innocuous by the very act of leading it to victory.'[1]

Yet this 'Abbāsid statecraft, in spite of all its cunning, was no more successful in the long run than Iranian nationalism in harnessing Islam to the service of a political purpose. The 'Abbāsid Caliphate itself was merely the last phase of a universal state, and, as such, it was *ex officio* condemned to death before it was born, notwithstanding the mirage of immortality with which it managed to delude its audacious assailants as well as its loyal supporters.[2] When the Mongol war-lord Hūlāgū took and sacked Baghdad in A.D. 1258, 'the Caliphate that had created Baghdad, and for five hundred years had made it a magnificent centre of art, science and letters, was forever extinguished; but Islam did not die'.[3] It not only retained the allegiance of the ex-subjects of the defunct 'Abbāsid Empire; it also took their savage conquerors captive. In spite of the tincture of Nestorian Christianity with which Hūlāgū, like other Chingisids of his generation, was imbued,[4] his descendants who governed, after him, the appanage of the Mongol Empire which Hūlāgū had established in the derelict domain of the Caliphate, from Merv to the east bank of the Euphrates, did not remain pagans or become out-right Nestorians or succumb to the Lamaistic form of the Tantric Mahāyāna which proved so attractive to the main line of the House of Chingis in China and which eventually won the allegiance of those Mongols and Calmucks who had stayed at home on their native steppes;[5] the Mongol Il-Khans of Hūlāgū's line became converts to Islam, and they did not even follow the frequent practice of barbarian converts by adopting the religion of a conquered population in a distinctively hereti-cal version.[6] After playing with the Shī'ah as they had previously played with Nestorianism, the Il-Khans finally embraced Islam in its Orthodox Sunnī form, though this was the form in which it was followed by the Il-Khans' arch-enemies the Mamlūks and by the Mamlūks' puppet 'Abbāsid Caliphs at Cairo.[7]

[1] Ibid., p. 350. [2] See pp. 7–16, above.
[3] Gilman, A.: *The Saracens* (London 1887, Fisher Unwin, in 'The Story of the Nations' series), p. 441.
[4] Hūlāgū himself had a Nestorian Christian wife (see II. ii. 238 and 451).
[5] See IV. iv. 497; V. v. 137 and 309–10.
[6] For this practice see V. v. 229–30 and 235. [7] See I. i. 363–4.

Within little more than a hundred years of the sack of Baghdad by Hūlāgū the example thus set by his house had been followed by the eastern as well as the western branch of the House of Chaghatāy, which dominated the sedentary Muslim population of the Upper Oxus-Jaxartes Basin from the Central Asian Steppe between the Zungarian Gap and the Sea of Aral.[1] The House of Jūjī ('the Golden Horde'),[2] which dominated the sedentary Muslim populations on the Lower Oxus and the Middle Volga from the Great Western Bay of the Eurasian Steppe between the Sea of Aral and the Carpathians, was finally converted within the same period under the influence of its allies the Mamlūks.[3] Even the dissident 'qāzāq' Nomads who hovered out of range of the Golden Horde's long whip-lash on the steppes of Western Siberia[4] followed the Golden Horde's lead in embracing Islam; and the Mongol Khāqāns in the Far East, who had no penchant towards Islam themselves,[5] helped Islam to win new outposts on the north-western and south-western fringes of China.[6] Meanwhile, Islam continued to make spiritual conquests of comparable magnitude in other quarters: in India, in Indonesia, in Tropical Africa.[7] And thus, so far from dying at the death of the Baghdādī 'Abbasid Caliphate, Islam lived on to become, by the fourteenth century of its own era, one of the four principal higher religions of a World that in that age was being unified on a literally oecumenical scale by the world-wide expansion of the Western Civilization.

What was the secret of Islam's power to survive the death of its founder, the downfall of the Primitive Arab empire-builders, the decline of the Arabs' Iranian supplanters, the overthrow of the 'Abbasid Caliphate, and the collapse of the barbarian successor-states that established themselves, for their brief day, on the Caliphate's ruins? The explanation was to be found in the spiritual experience of the converts to Islam among the non-Arab subjects of the Caliphate in the Umayyad Age. 'Islam, which they had originally adopted mainly for external reasons [of social self-interest], struck root in their hearts as well, and was taken by them more seriously than by the Arabs themselves.'[8] A religion which thus succeeded in winning loyalty in virtue of its intrinsic religious merits was not doomed to stand or fall with the political régimes which had successively sought to exploit it for non-religious purposes; and this spiritual triumph of Islam was the more remarkable considering that such exploitation for political ends had proved fatal to other higher religions and that Islam had thus been placed in jeopardy not only by its founder's successors but by Muhammad himself, when he had migrated

[1] For the successive conversions of the Western and the Eastern Chaghatāy to the Sunni form of Islam, see II. ii. 145.   [2] See III. iii. 429.
[3] The bond of this friendship was a commercial one. The most lucrative export from the domain of the Golden Horde was the supply of slaves, drawn from the martial races inside and beyond the Golden Horde's borders, through which the Mamlūks of Egypt recruited their own ranks. The Golden Horde was finally converted to Islam in the reign of Uzbeg Khan (regnabat A.D. 1312–40). The individual conversion of Uzbeg's predecessor Baraqa Khan (regnabat A.D. 1256–66), like that of the Il-Khan Ghazan in 1295, had been a premature flash in the pan.   [4] See V. v. 282.
[5] See pp. 256–7, below.   [6] See pp. 74–75 and 99, above.
[7] See Arnold, T. W.: The Preaching of Islam, 2nd ed. (London 1913, Constable), especially chaps. 8–12.   [8] Wellhausen, op. cit., p. 309.

from Mecca to Medina and had become a brilliantly successful statesman instead of remaining a conspicuously unsuccessful prophet.[1] In
this *tour de force* of surviving its betrayal by its own founder, Islam had
borne witness, through the ages, to the spiritual value of the religious
message which Muhammad had brought to Mankind, and to the dis-
interestedness and sincerity of the messenger himself during the heart-
breaking and hazardous thirteen years of his thankless mission to his
own countrymen at Mecca.

Thus, in the history of the Caliphate, the carefully considered policy
of the empire-builders in planting garrisons and colonies and regulating
the transfer and intermingling of populations had the unintended and
unexpected effect of expediting the career of a higher religion: and
corresponding effects were produced by the same causes in the history
of the Roman Empire.[2]

In the Age of the Principate the most conspicuously active conductors
of religious influences were the military garrisons along the frontiers,
and the religions that were propagated the most rapidly along these
channels were the Hellenized Hittite worship of the 'Iuppiter' of Dolichê
and the Hellenized Syriac worship of the originally Iranian divinity
Mithras. We can follow the transmission of these two religions from the
Roman garrisons on the Euphrates to those on the Danube, on the
German *limes*, on the Rhine, and on the Wall in Britain, and the spectacle recalls the contemporary journey which the Mahāyāna, in the last
stage of its long trek from Hindustan round the western flank of the
Tibetan Plateau,[3] was making from the Tarim Basin to the shores of the
Pacific along the chain of garrisons guarding the frontier of a Sinic
universal state over against the Nomads of the Eurasian Steppe. In the
next chapter of the story the Mahāyāna succeeded in penetrating from
the north-western marches of the Sinic World into the interior and
thereby becoming the universal church of the Sinic internal proletariat[4]
and eventually one of the four principal higher religions of a latter-day
Westernizing World. The destinies of Mithraism and of the worship of
Iuppiter Dolichênus were more modest. Bound up, as they had come
to be, with the fortunes of the Roman Imperial Army, these two military
religions never recovered from the blow dealt to them by the Army's
temporary collapse during the turbulent transition from the Augustan
Principate to the Diocletianic Autocracy; and, as far as they had any
permanent historical significance, it was as forerunners of Christianity
and tributaries to the ever-growing stream of religious tradition fed by
the confluence of many waters in the bed which Christianity dug for
itself as it poured over the Roman Empire along a different channel.

While Iuppiter Dolichênus and Mithras used the frontier garrisons
of the Roman Empire as their stepping-stones in a north-westward
march which brought them in the end from the banks of the Euphrates
to the Empire's opposite extremity on Tyneside, Saint Paul made a
corresponding use of colonies planted by Caesar and Augustus in the

---

[1] See III. iii. 466–72.   [2] See xi, map 29.
[3] See II. ii. 373 and 405, n. 1; III. iii. 131; and V. v. 140.
[4] See V. v. 145.

interior of the Empire as stations on the successive missionary journeys which culminated in his last voyage to Rome itself. On this first journey he sowed seeds of Christianity in the Roman colonies Antioch-in-Pisidia and Lystra;[1] and on his second in the Roman colonies Troas, Philippi, and Corinth as well, while on his third journey he revisited these and other scenes of his previous labours. Paul was, of course, far from confining his activities to places in which Roman colonies had been planted. In the course of his third missionary journey, for instance, he established his headquarters for two years at Ephesus and from that centre systematically evangelized the province of Asia.[2] Nor did all the Christian congregations founded by him in Roman colonies distinguish themselves particularly in the subsequent history of Christianity. Corinth, however, where Paul stayed for eighteen months[3] when he revisited it on his second journey, continued to play an important part in the life of the Church in the post-Apostolic Age, and we may conjecture that the prominence of the Christian community here was due, not only to the unique geographical situation of Corinth at the cross-roads of overland and maritime lines of communication, but also to the cosmopolitan character of the settlement of Roman freedmen that had been planted here by Caesar.[4] While the social origin of the population among which Paul had made his Corinthian converts goes far to explain the moral laxity with which the Apostle had to contend, we may also conjecture that the business ability and the world-wide connexions of this brood of twice-uprooted *déracinés* had something to do with the energy which the Church of Corinth displayed in the next chapter of its history.

The most signal example, however, of a Roman colony being turned to Christian account is not Corinth but Lyons, for the advance of Christianity from colony to colony did not come to a stop when it had reached the metropolis and did not cease with the death of Saint Paul. 'Never was the rise of a great city less accidental and less arbitrary than in the case of Roman Lyons.'[5] Planted in 43 B.C. on a carefully chosen site, in the angle formed by the confluence of Rhône and Saône—a node of land and water communications that rivalled the situation of Corinth itself—Lugdunum was a Roman colony not only in name but in fact; and this settlement of Roman citizens of genuinely Italian origin on the threshold of the vast tracts of Gallic territory that had been added to the Roman Empire by Caesar's conquests had been designed to radiate Roman culture through this Gallia Comata as it had already been radiated through a Gallia Togata by the older Roman colony of Narbonne. Lugdunum, as we have seen, possessed the coveted *ius Italicum*[6] and was the seat of the only Roman garrison between Rome itself and the Rhine.[7] Moreover, it was not only the administrative centre of one of the

---

[1] It is uncertain whether the Roman colony planted at Iconium by the Emperor Claudius (*imperabat* A.D. 41–54) was in existence at the time of Paul's first or second passage through the place, but it must have been established by the date of his third missionary journey.

[2] See Acts xix. 10.   [3] See Acts xviii. 11.

[4] See IV. iv. 270, with n. 4, and pp. 109–10 and 133, above.

[5] Arnold, W. T.: *Studies of Roman Imperialism* (Manchester 1906, University Press), p. 108.

[6] See p. 154, with n. 4, above.   [7] See p. 123, above.

three gigantic provinces into which Gallia Comata had been divided; it was also the official meeting place of 'the Council of the Three Gauls', where the representatives of the sixty or more cantons comprised in these three provinces assembled periodically round an Altar of Augustus erected here by Drusus in 12 B.C.[1] In fact, Lugdunum had been deliberately called into existence to serve particularly important Roman imperial purposes. Yet by A.D. 177 this Roman colony had come to harbour a Christian community of sufficient vitality to provoke a massacre; and here, as elsewhere, the blood of the martyrs was the seed of the Church;[2] for it was as bishop of Lugdunum during the immediately following quarter of a century that Irenaeus—a Greek man of letters of possibly Syrian origin—worked out the earliest systematic presentation of Catholic Christian theology.

Thus, when the Principate, and the 'ascendancy' of which it was the instrument, collapsed in the third century of the Christian Era, the ultimate beneficiary of this political and social revolution was neither the insurgent mass of previously unprivileged Roman citizens nor the Diocletianic autocracy nor Iuppiter Dolichênus nor Mithras but the Christian Church.

Christianity in the Roman Empire, Islam in the Caliphate, and the Mahāyāna in the Sinic universal state each took advantage of the garrisons and colonies installed by secular empire-builders for their own purposes; yet these unintended religious consequences of orderly redistributions of population were not so signal as those of Nebuchadnezzar's relapse into Assyrian methods of barbarism; for, in carrying Judah away captive, the Neo-Babylonian war-lord did not merely foster the progress of an existing higher religion but virtually called a new one into existence.

> Ἄνδρες ἀνάσπαστοι, φῦλον τάλαν, αἰνὰ παθόντες,
> οὓς πάρος ἐκ ῥιζῶν Μῆδος ὑπερφίαλος
> Ἀσσύριός τ' ἀγέρωχος ἀνέσπασε νηλέϊ θυμῷ,
> χαίρετ'· ἐγὼ δ' ὑμῖν ὀψιγενὴς ἕταρος.
> κἀμὲ κατέπληξεν τοῖος μόρος· ἀλλὰ χαρῶμεν,
> ἡμεῖς γὰρ Μεγαλοῦ φίλτατα τέκνα Θεοῦ.
> ἡμεῖς τοῖο προφῆται· ἀπήμονας οὐκ ἐμύησεν·
> μάρτυρας ἀνθρώποις εἵλετο τούς τάλανας.

3. Provinces

The Mixture of Motives in the Minds of Imperial Authorities

Like the garrisons and colonies which the builders of universal states distribute over their dominions, the provinces into which they carve these dominions up have two distinct functions: the preservation of the universal state itself and the preservation of the society for whose body social a universal state provides the political framework. But, whereas in the installation of garrisons and colonies the function of maintaining

---

[1] See Arnold, op. cit., p. 86.
[2] The passage in which this famous phrase of Tertullian's occurs has been quoted in V. vi. 202, n. 3.

the political supremacy of the empire-builders is, as we have seen, the predominant one, we shall find that, in the organization of provinces, the two functions play less unequal parts—though of course their relative weight will vary, *ad hoc*, according to the particular train of historical events through which a universal state has been brought into existence.

The alternative possible functions of an imperial province can be aptly illustrated from the histories of the Roman Empire and the British Rāj in India.

For example, the Roman provinces of Africa, Macedonia, and Bithynia-et-Pontus owed their origin wholly to the Roman State's concern for its own self-preservation. The Romans installed their own administration there not at all for the benefit of their new subjects, but in order to prevent the resurrection of three rival Powers—the Carthaginian Empire and the Kingdoms of Macedon and Pontic Cappadocia—which had proved such formidable and persistent antagonists of Rome that she did not feel her hard-won victory secure till she had erased them once and for all from the political map. On a similar reckoning, the ex-Carthaginian dominions in the Iberian Peninsula were organized into the two Roman provinces of Nearer and Farther Spain,[1] and the ephemeral conquests of King Tigranes of Armenia at the expense of the last of the Seleucidae into the Roman province of Syria, in order to make sure that these strategically important but politically derelict territories should not again fall into hostile hands. On the other hand, when the Romans accepted invitations to undertake the direct administration of the dominions of the client kingdom of Pergamum, and afterwards to take over Cyrenaica and Cyprus, which had been dependencies of the client kingdom of Egypt, they were tempted, no doubt, by the bait of immediate windfalls for the Roman Treasury and of future profits for Roman tax-farmers, investors, and traders; but, though their motives may have been self-seeking, they were in fact undertaking here a public service from which the previous local rulers were seeking relief because they no longer felt equal to continuing to discharge it themselves.

An element of public spirit in a larger cause than the direct political self-interest of Rome herself is less ambiguously apparent in the creation of the Roman province of Cilicia, which in its original extension embraced the fastnesses of all the wild highlanders of South-Eastern Anatolia. When the Romans had taken over the heritage which the last of the Attalids had bequeathed to them some thirty years before,[2] they had deliberately excluded these unremunerative and burdensome territories from their new province of Asia, and they had thereby created in the expanding no-man's-land between the south-eastern boundary of Roman Asia and the north-western boundary of the fast dwindling dominions of the expiring Seleucidae a breeding-ground for pirates who

[1] 'Why did the Roman Government, whose policy at that time evidently did not contemplate the acquisition of countries beyond the sea, not rid itself of so troublesome a possession? . . . They could not abandon Spain without putting it into the power of any adventurer to revive the Spanish empire of the Barcides' (Mommsen, Th.: *The History of Rome*, English translation, vol. ii (London 1888, Bentley), p. 213).

[2] King Attalus III of Pergamum had died in 133 B.C.; the original Roman province of Cilicia was created in 102–101 B.C.

rapidly extended their activities all over the Mediterranean. The Roman Government's assumption of administrative responsibility for this un-inviting no-man's-land that had become a pirates' lair was followed up by the Roman People's successive commissions to Publius Servilius, to Marcus Antonius, and to Pompey to sweep the pirates off the seas,[1] and this series of measures signified Rome's recognition and acceptance of imperial responsibilities. The same motive inspired the restoration of order in Cilicia and the subsidiary operations by which the Romans deprived the pirates of their insular stronghold in Crete and brigaded the island with Cyrene to form a single Roman province.[2] In the mind of Augustus a broad concern for the welfare of the Hellenic World as a whole was evidently combined with the narrower motive of providing for the military security of the Roman State when he extended the area of the province of Hispania Tarraconensis by subduing the wild high-landers of North-Western Spain, and when he carried the frontiers of the Empire up to the line of the Danube at the cost of saddling Rome with the responsibility for administering the vast ex-barbarian territories included in his new provinces of Rhaetia, Noricum, Pannonia, and Moesia.

Similar illustrations of the diversity of the functions that the provincial organization of a universal state may perform are afforded by the history of the British Rāj in India. While the annexations of territory at the expense of the Muslim war-lord Tippu Sahib of Mysore, the Marāthā states in the Deccan and Central India, and the Sikh principalities in the Panjab were mainly dictated by considerations of military and politi-cal security for the British Rāj itself, the annexations in the Ganges Basin, from Bengal to Delhi inclusive, were to some extent forced upon the British East India Company by the decay of the Mughal Empire; and, though no doubt the momentous British decision to take over the administration of Bengal was prompted, like the Roman acceptance of the bequest of the last Attalus, by the prospect of lucrative profits for British empire-builders, one of the effects of this self-seeking British act was to meet the Hindu World's need to be delivered from the anarchy that had arisen through the creation of a political vacuum in the place that the Mughal Empire had formerly occupied. Augustus's annexations of barbarian territory in the joint interests of the Roman Empire and the Hellenic World likewise find their counterpart in British annexations of tribal territory on the North-West frontier of India; and the risk of mili-tary disaster to which empire-builders expose themselves in their search for 'natural frontiers' is exemplified in the outcome of the First Anglo-Afghan War as well as in the results of Crassus's attempt to subdue the

---

[1] A Roman 'province' in the original meaning of a frontier command had been created in the western and northern fringes of this no-man's-land *circa* 102–101 B.C. (see Mommsen, Th.: *The History of Rome*, English translation, vol. iii (London 1888, Bentley), p. 140, n. *; *The Cambridge Ancient History*, vol. ix (Cambridge 1932, University Press), p. 442; Jones, A. H. M.: *The Cities of the Eastern Roman Provinces* (Oxford 1937, Clarendon Press), p. 202) and was called 'Cilicia' though it appears to have included neither Cilicia Tracheia nor Cilicia Pedias. Servilius received his com-mission in 79 B.C., Antonius his in 74 B.C., and Pompey his in 67 B.C.

[2] Cyrenaica was bequeathed to Rome by Ptolemy Apion in 96 B.C. and was definitively organized as a Roman province in 74 B.C. Crete was annexed in 67 B.C.

Parthians and Augustus's attempt to move the North-West European frontier of the Roman Empire forward from the Rhine to the Elbe.

While the histories of the Roman Empire and of the British Rāj in India thus indicate that the two main alternative functions of the provincial organization of a universal state are to maintain the supremacy of the empire-building Power and to fill a political vacuum arising in the body social of the disintegrating society through the destruction or collapse of its former parochial states, the relative importance and the reciprocal relations of the two functions vary widely from case to case.

There is, no doubt, a general tendency for the function of filling a vacuum to become increasingly important with the passage of time, as the memory—and the loyalty evoked by the memory—of the extinguished parochial states grows fainter, while those that have been allowed to survive as clients of the victorious empire-building Power are progressively rotted by the general process of social disintegration that is still creeping on under the veneer of an oecumenical peace. In the Roman Empire, for example, this tendency had resulted,[1] within a century of the establishment of the Augustan Peace at the Battle of Actium, in the conversion into provinces of all client states except three on the eastern frontier,[2] though it was a seldom broken tradition of Roman statesmanship[3] to shrink from the burden of administering alien subject territories and to confine even unavoidable annexations to a minimum area.[4] *Pari passu*, and this likewise against the grain of traditional Roman policy, the Roman Government found itself constrained, in the administration of its provinces, to leave less and less of the responsibility in the hands of local organs of self-government, and to take more and more of it upon the shoulders of the imperial civil service.[5]

This latter process likewise occurred in the administrative history of the British Rāj in India; on the other hand, the process of annexation did not take the same course here as in the history of the Roman Empire. While they were in the act of empire-building, the British conquerors of India showed less hesitation than the Roman conquerors of the Hellenic World in making sweeping annexations of territory and undertaking wide responsibilities for direct administration. The British-administered

---

[1] This point has been touched upon already on p. 58, above.

[2] The Nabataean Principality, Commagêne, and Armenia Minor.

[3] The most flagrant breaches—in the shape of unprovoked annexations—were made by the radical imperialists who annexed Gallia Narbonensis in 120 B.C., by Caesar when he invaded and conquered the rest of Gaul, and by Trajan when he extinguished the Nabataean Principality, not, apparently, on account of any incompetence in the native administration, but because he wished to bring this territory under his own direct control as an overture to his ambitiously aggressive attack on the Parthian Empire. On the other hand, Trajan's creation of the new province of Dacia out of the conquered dominions of a dangerous enemy of Rome was in the same category as Pompey's creation of the province of Bithynia-et-Pontus.

[4] For instance, the Roman province of Africa, within its original boundaries, did not include the whole of the former dominions of Carthage in North-West Africa; the western districts were given to Rome's client state Numidia. Similarly, when the Romans created their province of Asia out of the former dominions of the Attalids, they gave some districts to their surviving client states in Anatolia and left others derelict (see p. 164, above). Again, Pompey's new province of Bithynia-et-Pontus embraced only the semi-Hellenized western parts of the former dominions of Mithradates Eupator.

[5] See pp. 58–60, above.

territories in India were expanded in three successive waves. The first wave (A.D. 1757–66) brought under British rule Bengal, Bihar, and the Northern Circars along the north-west shore of the Bay of Bengal; the second (A.D. 1790–1818) brought the Carnatic, the Upper Ganges Basin, and the Western Deccan; the third (A.D. 1843–9) brought the Indus Basin. In the course of this expansion, all other parts of India were lassoed in an encircling belt of British-administered territories and were reduced to the status of client states; and, under Lord Dalhousie's régime, the annexations of the client states of Satára in A.D. 1848, Jhansi in 1853, Nagpur in 1854, and Oudh in 1856 seemed to portend a rapid extension of direct British rule over the whole of the rest of the peninsula. On the other hand, after the mutiny of the Indian units in the British East India Company's Army in A.D. 1857–8, it became the general policy of the British Government of India to keep the surviving client states intact; and, though this new rule was not invariably observed, nevertheless the annexation of the Kingdom of Oudh, which had been reminiscent of the Roman Emperor Tiberius's annexation of the Kingdom of Cappadocia, was, after all, not followed up by the progressive extinction, *more Romano*, of the remaining Indian client states.

The extent to which the founders of a universal state are tempted to resort to the devices of annexation and direct administration as measures of insurance against the danger of a resurgence of the victorious empire-builders' defeated rivals depends, no doubt, on the degree of the loyalty and regret that the abolished parochial states continue to evoke in the minds of their own former masters and subjects after their overthrow by the empire-building Power; and this, in turn, depends on the pace of the conquest and on the antecedent history of the society in whose domain the universal state has established itself. Victorious empire-builders have most reason to fear a violent undoing of their work when they have established their rule at one stroke and when they have imposed it on a world of parochial states long accustomed to enjoy and abuse a status of sovereign independence.

In the Sinic World, for example, effective political unity was imposed for the first time (at any rate, in recorded history) by the empire-building state of Ts'in within a period of no more than ten years (230–221 B.C.). Within that brief span of time, King Chêng of Ts'in overthrew the six other till then surviving parochial states Han, Chao, Wei, Ch'u, Yen, and Ts'i,[1] and thereby became the founder of a Sinic universal state under the title of Ts'in She Hwang-ti. But, in bringing to this sudden end the long-drawn-out struggle for existence in which the contending states of the Sinic World had been engaged since the beginning of the Sinic Time of Troubles, Ts'in She Hwang-ti could not extinguish with equal rapidity the political selfconsciousness and *esprit de corps* of the former ruling elements in the six states that had survived, side by side with Ts'in, until this last swift round in the contest. The political re-unification of the Egyptiac World by Mentuhotep, the ruler of the

---

[1] See Fitzgerald, C. P.: *China, A Short Cultural History* (London 1935, Cresset Press), p. 70, and Franke, O.: *Geschichte des Chinesischen Reiches*, vol. i (Berlin and Leipzig 1930, de Gruyter), pp. 198–9.

march-state of Thebes who became the founder of 'the Middle Empire',[1] seems likewise to have been achieved by a sudden stroke;[2] and, here too, the victorious empire-builder and his successors had still to reckon with disaffection on the part of nomarchs who had been resubjected by force to an oecumenical authority without having ceased to regret the parochial independence which they had enjoyed in the anarchic sequel to, and reaction against, the inordinately centralized régime of 'the Old Kingdom'.[3]

The political unification, under the Napoleonic Empire, of the relics of an abortive Medieval Western city-state cosmos in Northern Italy, Western Germany, and the Low Countries[4] was also rapidly accomplished, if we reckon that it was begun by the French Revolutionary armies that invaded the Southern Netherlands and the Rhineland in the autumn of A.D. 1792 and was completed on a raft in the River Niemen on the 25th June, 1807, at the personal encounter between Napoleon and the Russian Emperor Alexander I in which the two emperors partitioned between them the European end of the Old World; and, though the French empire-builders had little recalcitrance to contend with among the subjects of the statelets which they had suddenly and unceremoniously swept out of existence, since the once exuberant political vitality of the city-states of Western Christendom had long since sunk into a coma, Napoleon felt his hold on these easily subjugated territories insecure so long as he had not finally disposed of the surrounding Great Powers that had been the peers and competitors of France in the pre-Napoleonic Balance of Power.

The Persian empire-builders who founded the Achaemenian Empire had to cope, like Ts'in She Hwang-ti, with persisting prior parochial loyalties, which flared up into energetic and widespread rebellion upon the assassination of Gaumata in 522 B.C.,[5] when it might have been expected that an established oecumenical peace would have been accepted passively, if not actively welcomed, by populations who, for three hundred years, had had their parochial patriotism pounded out of them by unflagging blows from an Assyrian flail.

This identical problem of having to guard against a resurgence of parochial political feeling was handled by the empire-builders on similar lines in all four cases. They sought to break these traditional parochial loyalties by erasing the traditional parochial frontiers from the political map and replacing the overthrown parochial states by artificially created imperial provinces with new boundaries and a new administrative régime which would ensure the due subordination of the provincial governors to the central government of the parvenu universal state.[6]

---

[1] See I. i. 137 and 140, n. 2; II. ii. 112; IV. iv. 85; V. v. 267 and 530; and V. vi. 190.

[2] Possible evidences of the rapidity of Mentuhotep's rise to fortune are the indications (if these are the correct interpretations of the archaeological data) that, in the course of his reign, he changed his style and title and remodelled his mortuary temple on more sumptuous lines than those of the original plan (see Meyer, E.: *Geschichte des Altertums*, vol. i, Part II, 3rd ed. (Stuttgart and Berlin 1913, Cotta), pp. 257–8; see further Winlock, H. E.: *The Rise and Fall of the Middle Kingdom in Thebes* (New York 1947, Macmillan), pp. 28–32).   [3] See Meyer, op. cit., vol. cit., pp. 226–30 and 262–4.

[4] See II. ii. 104; III. iii. 344–7; and V. v. 619–42.   [5] See pp. 599–604, below.

[6] These deliberately revolutionary redrawings of the political map are instances of

Administrative Policy in the Sinic Universal State

The issue was sharply formulated in the entourage of the Emperor Ts'in She Hwang-ti, and the radical solution was advisedly adopted by a personal decision of the Emperor, as the result of a clash between opposing schools of policy that has been dramatized by the historian Sse-ma Ts'ien in the form of a tournament of set speeches in the Imperial Council.[1] By whatever processes the issue may have been fought out, it is certain that the radical policy prevailed and that in 221 B.C. Ts'in She Hwang-ti ratified the redistribution of the whole territory of his newly established universal state, including not only the dominions of Ts'in's six former rivals and recent victims but also those of the victorious empire-building state as well, into thirty-six military commands (*chün*), which were each sub-divided into a number of prefectures (*hsien*).[2] Each military command had a civilian administrator as well as a military governor, and the prefectures were administered by civilian prefects.[3]

In applying this non-feudal provincial system to the whole of his empire, Ts'in She Hwang-ti was extending to the territories of the six states which he had just subjugated a régime that had been in force in his own ancestral state of Ts'in for more than a hundred years past. As far back as the year 350 B.C. the entire territory of Ts'in, within its frontiers at that date, had been redistributed into thirty-one *hsien* by the radical reformer Shang Yang.[4] This recasting of the internal administrative map had been one of a number of interrelated political and social innovations which had transformed Ts'in from a feudal state of the same type as its contemporaries and rivals in the Sinic World into a centralized bureaucratic and almost 'totalitarian' state of a new pattern; and it had been this political reformation that had enabled Ts'in, from that time onwards, to gain the upper hand over its antagonists in the Sinic arena in a progressive series of successes which had culminated in Ts'in She Hwang-ti's own sensational and conclusive achievement of overthrowing

the psychological phenomenon of Futurism, which has been illustrated already in the political field in V. vi. 107–11.

[1] Renderings of this debate, as presented by Sse-ma Ts'ien, will be found in Fitzgerald, C. P.: *China, A Short Cultural History* (London 1935, Cresset Press), pp. 139–40; Franke, O: *Geschichte des Chinesischen Reiches*, vol. i (Berlin and Leipzig 1930, de Gruyter), pp. 229–30; Bodde, D.: *China's First Unifier: A Study of the Ch'in Dynasty as seen in the Life of Li Ssü* (Leiden 1938, Brill), pp. 78–79.

[2] These two units of non-feudal local administration under the direct authority and control of a central government were not new inventions of Ts'in She Hwang-ti's radical-minded minister Li Sse. They had been made use of in the administration of the former parochial states of the Sinic World from an early stage in the Sinic Time of Troubles. *Hsien* are first heard of in the State of Ts'in itself in 688 B.C., *chün* in the State of Wei (the successor-state of Tsin) *circa* 400 B.C. *Hsien* may have originated as a form of administration for territories conquered by one of the Contending States from another, *chün* as military marches of Sinic states against their Eurasian Nomad neighbours. The radical innovation that was confirmed in 221 B.C. was not the invention of these two units of non-feudal administration but the sudden application to the whole of the Sinic World of a system of non-feudal administration, which had previously been exceptional, in place of a feudal system which had been the general rule (for these points see Bodde, op. cit., pp. 134–43 and 238–46).

[3] See Bodde, op. cit., p. 135; Franke, op. cit., vol. cit., p. 230.

[4] See Bodde, op. cit., p. 143. For this important statesman's life and work, see Duyvendak, J. J. L.: *The Book of Lord Shang* (London 1928, Probsthain).

six rival states in ten years and thereby unifying the Sinic World politically.

In assuming, however, that he could impose abruptly on the rest of the Sinic World a régime that was commended by its proven success in his ancestral state of Ts'in, Ts'in She Hwang-ti was leaving out of his reckoning certain significant differences between Ts'in and her defunct competitors. The statesmen who had carried out these sweeping local reforms in Ts'in with such successful results had been working on an exceptionally malleable human material. In the first place Ts'in was a march-state of the Sinic World,[1] and in the hard school of their perpetual struggle for existence against the outer barbarians the people of Ts'in had been broken in to adapting themselves to any social or technical innovations that might be necessary for securing their own survival. In the second place Ts'in, in virtue of being 'the Country within the Passes', was secluded by physiographical barriers from the rest of the Sinic World, and was culturally backward by comparison with the heart of the Sinic Society on the plains of the lower basin of the Yellow River.[2] Her relation to her western neighbours was like that of Macedon in the fifth and fourth centuries B.C. to the Hellenic city-states beyond the passes of Tempe and Volustana, or like that of Piedmont,[3] in the medieval and early modern ages of Western history, to Lombardy, Venetia, the Romagna, and Tuscany. Like Macedon, Ts'in was culturally plastic, and she thus escaped the cultural ossification which overtook her more cultivated neighbours.

The peoples at the cultural centre of the Sinic World were naturally predisposed to idolize a culture of which they themselves were the principal originators and exponents, and they had latterly been encouraged in this foible by the philosophers of the Confucian school, whose founder had diagnosed the social sickness from which the Sinic Society was suffering in its Time of Troubles as being due to a neglect of traditional rites and practices, and had prescribed as the sovereign remedy a return to the supposed social and moral order of the early Sinic Feudal Age as idealized in retrospect by Confucius himself.[4] This sentimental Confucian canonization of a half-imaginary past had made little impression on the people of Ts'in. The only one of the Sinic philosophical schools of the Confucian and post-Confucian Age that had made its influence felt effectively 'within the passes' was the irreverent ruthless school of the Legists, and it was this radical spirit that had inspired the work of the series of great statesmen from other parts of the Sinic World who had found their field for action in Ts'in, beginning with Shang Yang from Wei[5] (*decessit* 338 B.C.), who had laid the foundations of Ts'in's greatness,[6] and ending with Li Sse of Ch'u (*vivebat*

---

[1] See II. ii. 118.

[2] For this heart and cradle of the Sinic World, see I. i. 318–21.

[3] See IV. iv. 285–9.

[4] See Fitzgerald, op. cit., pp. 140–1.

[5] i.e. the Wei which was one of the three successor-states of the former state of Tsin, though Shang Yang traced his ancestry back to the princely house of the older state of Wei, still nearer to the heart of the Sinic World (see Fitzgerald, op. cit., p. 99).

[6] See Franke, O.: *Geschichte des Chinesischen Reiches*, vol. i (Berlin and Leipzig 1930, de Gruyter), pp. 183–4.

280–208 B.C.), Ts'in She Hwang-ti's minister, who had raised Ts'in to the pinnacle of power.

The sudden imposition of the institutions of this uncultivated and unfamiliar march-state of Ts'in upon Sinic communities who had been conquered by her through force of arms, without ceasing to regard her as a semi-barbarian stepdaughter of the Sinic family of cultivated peoples, was bound to arouse violent resentment among the *ci-devant* feudal aristocracy of the extinguished states. After having lost the power and status that had been theirs under the régime of parochial independence, they were now deprived of all hope of retaining some vestige of their former position through being taken into the service of the newly established Sinic universal state. In these days of their adversity and impotence, these *chün tze* rallied under the standard of the Confucian school of philosophy whose founder's theories and counsels had been ignored during his lifetime by their predecessors; but Ts'in She Hwang-ti's only retort to this *union sacrée* between the aristocratic and the philosophical devotees of conservatism was to take the offensive against philosophy as well as against feudalism. A petition from the conservatives for the re-establishment of feudal principalities under princes of the House of Ts'in seems to have given the occasion for the famous measure of cultural *Gleichschaltung* known as 'the Burning of the Books'.[1]

In thus recklessly closing every safety-valve, Ts'in She Hwang-ti was inviting an explosion, and the first Ts'in emperor's death in 210 B.C. was followed in 209 B.C. by the outbreak of a general revolt, and in 207 B.C. by the capture of the capital of the Ts'in empire[2] and extinction of the Ts'in dynasty itself by one of the rebel leaders, Liu Pang.[3] Ts'in She Hwang-ti's radicalism had thus defeated its own ends; yet this victory of the violent reaction against the revolutionary work of the founder of the Sinic universal state did not, after all, result in a restoration of the *ancien régime*. It was significant that both Ch'êng Shê, the bold initiator of the revolt, and Liu Pang, the rebel who gave the Ts'in Power its *coup de grâce* by capturing its capital, were peasants from outlying southern provinces,[4] not feudal aristocrats from the centre of the Sinic World; and, in the subsequent struggle among the victorious rebels for possession of the spoils of their joint victory, the peasant Liu Pang again emerged as the victor over his cultivated aristocratic opponent Hsiang Yü, whose ancestors had held an hereditary office in the military hierarchy of the former parochial state of Ch'u.

Liu Pang, unlike either Hsiang Yü or Ts'in She Hwang-ti, succeeded

---

[1] The connexion is pointed out by Fitzgerald, op. cit., p. 141. 'The Burning of the Books' has been cited already in this Study, as an illustration of Futurism, in V. vi. 111.

[2] The seat of government had remained at Hsien Yang, the city 'within the passes' that had been the parochial capital of Ts'in before her conquest of the rest of the Sinic World in 230–221 B.C.

[3] In this context English students of history will recall that the restoration of the monarchy in England in A.D. 1660 followed within two years of Oliver Cromwell's death and within five years of his remapping of the Kingdom, in A.D. 1655, into ten military commands under major-generals in place of the traditional feudal organs and institutions of English local self-government.

[4] Ch'êng Shê (*alias* Ch'êng Shêng) was a native of the former state of Ch'u in the Middle Yangtse Basin; Liu Pang came from a coastal district, north of the mouth of the Yangtse, in the northern part of the latter-day province of Kiangsu.

in founding a stable and enduring régime because he did not attempt to re-establish either the anachronistic feudal order or Ts'in She Hwang-ti's revolutionary substitute for it. Liu Pang's policy was to feel his way gradually towards Ts'in She Hwang-ti's Caesarean goal through an Augustan semblance of compromise.

In the short interval between the collapse of the Ts'in Power in 207 B.C. and the general recognition of Liu Pang as sole master of the Sinic World in 202 B.C. the experiment of attempting to restore the *ancien régime* had been tried and proved unworkable.[1]

Under Hsiang Yü's auspices, a legitimate scion of the House of the former parochial state of Ch'u had been invested with the oecumenical style and title and ceremonial prerogatives of the ancient Imperial House of Chóu, which Ts'in She Hwang-ti's grandfather had suppressed in 256–249 B.C.; and the other extinguished states, with the exception of Ts'in, had likewise nominally been restored. In order to make sure that Ts'in should not again establish its domination over the rest of the Sinic World, it had been broken up, as a measure of security, into four fragments.[2] Three of these, covering between them the ancient domain of the state, had been granted to high officers of the Ts'in army who had deserted to Hsiang Yü in good time. The fourth, consisting of recently annexed ex-barbarian territories on the north-western fringes of the Yangtse Basin (in the latter-day provinces of Southern Shensi and Ssechuan) had been assigned by Hsiang Yü to Liu Pang as a scurvy reward for his embarrassingly valuable services.[3] Naturally the other rebel leaders had also had to be rewarded with grants of territory, and these new lordships had had to be carved out of the historic dominions of the nominally restored states of the previous era. The parvenu war-lords, as well as the restored representatives of the old houses, had taken the title of king (*wang*), and the king-maker, Hsiang Yü, had styled himself 'suzerain king' (*pa wang*), with the intention of managing this travesty of the pre-Ts'in dispensation in the name of the nominal emperor of the parochial House of Ch'u.

This makeshift arrangement had been neither a genuine restoration of the old régime nor an alternative instrument for furnishing the Sinic World with the sorely needed oecumenical peace that Ts'in She Hwang-ti had effectively provided at an exorbitant price. On the surface the cause of the immediate breakdown of Hsiang Yü's attempt at a settlement had appeared to be the personal antagonism between Hsiang

[1] For the details see Franke, op. cit., vol. cit., pp. 257 and 259–61; Fitzgerald, op. cit., pp. 149–50.

[2] Compare the Romans' experiment of breaking up the Kingdom of Macedon into four autonomous republics in 167 B.C., after the Third Romano-Macedonian War (see Livy, Book XLV, chaps. 29–30). It was not till after the Macedonian insurrection of 149–148 B.C. that the Romans resigned themselves to the necessity of converting Macedon into a province under direct Roman administration.

[3] As this new 'Kingdom of Han' (so called after the Han River which flows into the Yangtse at Hankow) lay 'within the passes', Hsiang Yü was nominally honouring the preliminary agreement that had been made between the restored King of Ch'u and the rebel leaders that whichever of the latter should be the first to penetrate the passes and overthrow the Ts'in Power on its home ground should become King of 'the Country within the Passes'. Liu Pang had qualified for winning this prize by his capture of Hsien Yang, and by rights he should have received the entire territory of the state of Ts'in within its frontiers of 230 B.C., and not merely an outlying semi-barbarian march.

Yü and Liu Pang. A deeper cause had been the bankruptcy of the old
feudal aristocracy who had been the mainstay of the historic parochial
states. They had not only been decimated in the particularly murderous
last round of fratricidal wars that had ended in the victory of Ts'in
over all her competitors; their spirit had been further broken by Ts'in
She Hwang-ti's subsequent massacres and deportations;[1] and, above
all, they had been discredited in the eyes of the vast peasant majority
of the population of the Sinic World by the plight to which the anarchy
of the Contending States had brought the Sinic Society in the last
phase of its Time of Troubles.

With both Ts'in She Hwang-ti's and Hsiang Yü's failures in mind,
Han Liu Pang and the succeeding emperors of his dynasty followed
a Fabian policy of hastening slowly.[2] In the first act Liu Pang duly
conferred fiefs on his most deserving lieutenants, and even left undisturbed the existing fief-holders of Hsiang Yü's régime who had managed
to come to terms with the victor. But, one by one, the enfeofed generals
were degraded and put to death, while other fief-holders were frequently
transferred from one fief to another and readily deposed, without ever
being given a chance of establishing any dangerously close personal
relation with their temporary subjects. In 144 B.C. Liu Pang's successor
Hsiao Ching changed the law of succession for fief-holders by abolishing
primogeniture and decreeing that their fiefs should be divided among
their sons, and the consequent rapid subdivision of their domains
reduced them to final impotence.

Meanwhile Liu Pang had taken effective measures for maintaining
and progessively increasing the preponderance of the Imperial Power.
The parochial kingships, though they were now no more than shadows
of their former selves, were strictly reserved, nevertheless, for members
of the Imperial House; the entire 'Country within the Passes' was kept
by the Emperor under his own direct administration; and, in the rest
of the Han Empire, he retained enough of Ts'in She Hwang-ti's provincial organization to reduce the autonomous kingdoms and fiefs to
the position of dwindling enclaves within a steadily expanding network
of imperial provinces. Thus, in effect, Ts'in She Hwang-ti's ideal of
a universal state controlled from the centre through a hierarchy of artificially mapped out units of local administration was once more translated into fact within a hundred years of Ts'in She Hwang-ti's death
and this time the achievement was definitive, because the Fabian statesmanship of Han Liu Pang and his successors had given the Imperial
Government time to create the human instrument for lack of which
the first Ts'in emperor's grandiose design for an oecumenical provincial
organization had come to grief.

A centralized government cannot be operated without a professional
civil service, and, in contrast again to Ts'in She Hwang-ti,[3] the Han
Dynasty succeeded in building up a civil service that was acceptable,

---

[1] See pp. 116–17, above.
[2] For the details see Franke, op. cit., vol. cit., pp. 270–2 and 276; Fitzgerald, op. cit.,
pp. 152–3.
[3] See pp. 351–3, below.

and therefore effective,[1] by entering into an alliance with the Confucian
school of philosophy, which had originally associated itself with the
feudal régime and had been driven still farther in that direction by
Ts'in She Hwang-ti's intransigence.[2] The failure of Ts'in She Hwang-
ti's régime had discredited the Legist school of philosophy, in whose
spirit it had been conceived, without rehabilitating the prestige of the
Confucian advocates of the old feudal order, and Han Liu Pang, who
shared the anti-Confucian feelings of Ts'in She Hwang-ti, inclined,
during the *laisser faire* overture to his long-term policy, towards the
passive philosophy of Taoism.[3] Yet, before the close of his reign, Liu
Pang (*imperabat* 202–195 B.C.) had thought better of his earlier hostility
towards Confucianism and had himself initiated[4] that *rapprochement*
between the Han Dynasty and the Confucian School which was consummated when his successor Wuti (*imperabat* 140–87 B.C.) made the
somewhat debased Confucianism of the day into the official philosophy
of the Sinic universal state.[5]

Han Liu Pang and his successors weaned the Confucian philosophers
from their former alliance with the old narrow military aristocracy of
birth by opening the public service to a new and broader-based aristocracy of cultural merit as measured by proficiency in the Confucian
lore. This historic innovation was introduced in a decree promulgated
by Liu Pang in 196 B.C.[6] The result was the creation of a new class of
public servants—the Confucian litterati—with as strong a vested interest
in the preservation of the Empire of the Han as the hereditary feudal
nobility had had in the maintenance of the former parochial states. The
transition was made so gradually and was managed so skilfully that the
new aristocracy inherited the old aristocracy's historic appellation—
chün tze—without any overt recognition that a momentous social and
political revolution was taking place.

Administrative Policy in 'the Middle Empire' and in 'the New Empire' of Egypt

Our relatively abundant information about the vicissitudes of the
political struggle which ended in the definitive victory of bureaucracy
over feudalism in the Sinic World may help us to piece together the fragmentary surviving record of the similar struggle, in the Egyptiac World,
between the nomarchs and the central government of 'the Middle
Empire'.

There is, to begin with, a remarkable parallel between the external
careers of the respective founders of the Sinic and the Egyptiac universal state, Ts'in She Hwang-ti and one of the Mentuhoteps. Either
achieved a dramatic personal success—starting as the ruler of a parochial
principality and ending as an oecumenical emperor. Both of them enjoyed long reigns: Ts'in She Hwang-ti was on the throne for thirty-six

---

[1] For the details see Franke, op. cit., vol. cit., pp. 272–6; Fitzgerald, op. cit., p. 153.
See also the present Study, pp. 355–7, below.
[2] See p. 171, above.
[3] See the passage from a paper by Dr. Hu Shih quoted in V. v. 418.
[4] See the anecdote quoted from Hu Shih, op. cit., in V. v. 654.
[5] See V. v. 655.
[6] German translation in Franke, op. cit., vol. cit., pp. 274–5.

years (246–210 B.C.) all told, and this Mentuhotep for fifty-one (*circa* 2061–2010 B.C.).[1] Yet their deaths were followed, after brief intervening reigns of one or two nonentities, by the extinction of their houses and the foundation of new dynasties;[2] and thus, in spite of achievements that might have been expected to make the fortune of the empire-builder's race for many generations to come, either monarch was virtually the last of his line. This apparent paradox is explained in Ts'in She Hwang-ti's case by the known facts that have been considered above; and, on this analogy, we might hazard the guess that a Mentuhotep brought the same catastrophe upon his house by making the same mistake of trying to force the pace too fast in asserting the authority of his newly established oecumenical government over the defeated yet still formidable representatives of a previous parochial régime. At any rate, we find the founder of the succeeding Twelfth Dynasty Amenemhat I (*imperabat circa* 1991–1962 B.C.) and his successors apparently avoiding a frontal attack on the status of the parochial nomarchs, yet at the same time working steadily to reduce their power by stages.

The deposition of particular nomarchs who found themselves on the losing side in the civil war through which Amenemhat I appears to have won the Imperial Crown[3] may have set a precedent for his subsequent practice of overriding the customary right of hereditary succession and transferring the government of nomes from the old princely houses to his own nominees.[4] Historic families that retained their principalities were tactfully allowed to save their face by keeping up their state, and the most magnificent of their tombs are the last in the series.[5] But Modern Western archaeologists had not discovered any such tombs that were of later date than the reigns of Senwosret II (*imperabat circa* 1897–1879 B.C.) and Senwosret III (*imperabat circa* 1878–1843 B.C.), and the inference was that the power of the nomarchs had been finally broken, at the latest, by the reign of Amenemhat III (*imperabat circa* 1842–1797 B.C.). The administrative vacuum created by this progressive reduction in the power of the nomarchs was perhaps[6] filled by the organization of 'the Middle Empire' into three provinces: 'the North' embracing the Delta, 'the South' embracing the Nile Valley from the head of the Delta to the northern boundary of the Theban march, and 'the Head of the South' embracing the Theban march itself within the boundaries of the principality which Mentuhotep had inherited from

---

1 See Winlock, H. E.: *The Rise and Fall of the Middle Kingdom in Thebes* (New York 1947, Macmillan), p. 22. This Mentuhotep's conquest of Heracleopolis—which had the effect of uniting the Egyptiac World, as the Sinic World was united by Ts'in She Hwang-ti's conquest of Ts'i in 221 B.C.—is dated 1252 B.C. by Winlock in op. cit., p. 28. Winlock's reconstruction of this passage of Egyptiac history is commended by J. A. Wilson in *The Burden of Egypt* (Chicago 1951, University of Chicago Press), p. 127. On the other hand, E. Drioton and J. Vandier, in *L'Égypte* (Paris 1946, Presses Universitaires de France), pp. 234 and 271–2, contest the identification of a Nebhapetre Mentuhotep who united the Egyptiac World with a Nepkherure Mentuhotep who enjoyed a long reign over an Egyptiac universal state.
2 Compare the similar sequels to the deaths of Alexander the Great and Oliver Cromwell.
3 See Meyer, E.: *Geschichte des Altertums*, 3rd ed., vol. i, Part II (Stuttgart and Berlin 1913, Cotta), p. 265.   4 See ibid., p. 269.   5 See ibid., p. 276.
6 Eduard Meyer's reconstruction, followed here, had been challenged by some later scholars.

his forebears before he had brought the rest of the Egyptiac World under his rule.[1]

When this Mentuhotep's empire-building work was repeated some five hundred years after his day by the founder of 'the New Empire', Amosis, the seat of power, which the Twelfth Dynasty had quickly transferred from Thebes to the neighbourhood of Memphis, remained this time at Thebes for two hundred years,[2] and this different location of the political centre of gravity seems to have been reflected in a difference in the grouping of provinces. Under 'the New Empire' two out of the three former provinces of 'the Middle Empire', the Delta and the Nile Valley to the north of the Theban march, which had been united under the rule of the Hyksos, were perhaps brigaded by their Theban 'liberators' in a single province governed by 'the Intendant of the North' or 'of Memphis', while the Theban march was placed under an officer of equal rank, styled 'the Intendant of the Southern Capital', and was divided, perhaps for symmetry's sake, into two sub-provinces, one to the north of the imperial city and the other to the south of it.[3]

Administrative Policy in the Napoleonic Empire

The Napoleonic Empire was overthrown by external forces at so early a stage of its existence that there was little time for the consequences of Napoleon's internal administrative policy to begin to work themselves out. This policy was identical with Ts'in She Hwang-ti's. Starting his career by becoming the ruler of an empire-building parochial state, and finding the home territory of this state newly remapped into artificial administrative divisions in place of the historic territorial units of a past feudal age, Napoleon proceeded to remap the Belgian, Dutch, German, Italian, and 'Illyrian' territories that had been annexed to France outright, or been externally associated with her like the Napoleonic Kingdom of Italy, into departments on the pattern of those of Revolutionary France herself. Before the reaction to this drastic policy had time to declare itself, the Napoleonic Empire came to a premature end because Napoleon was not content with the immense achievement of having won for France that hegemony over the derelict domain of an abortive Medieval Western cosmos of city-states[4] for which she had been contending inconclusively with the other Great Powers of an Early Modern Western World for some three hundred years past.[5]

Napoleon insisted on setting France the further and more formidable task of establishing her supremacy over the whole of an expanding Western World that had come to include the overseas economic dependencies of Great Britain in one direction and the continental hinterland of the Russian Empire in the other; and this task proved too heavy for

---

[1] For these three provinces, see Meyer, op. cit., vol. cit., pp. 274–5. The march-state of Thebes in the Egyptiac World, like the march state of Ts'in in the Sinic World, had played no part in the history of the civilization during its growth stage and had emerged from its original obscurity only in the course of a Time of Troubles which it had eventually brought to an end by imposing its own rule upon all its rivals.

[2] See pp. 215–16, below.

[3] See Meyer, E.: *Geschichte des Altertums*, vol. ii, Part I, 2nd ed. (Stuttgart and Berlin 1928, Cotta), pp. 59–60. This reconstruction, too, had subsequently been challenged.   [4] See III. iii. 344–7.   [5] See III. iii. 311 and IV. iv. 283.

France's strength.[1] We are left to conjecture whether, in the Napoleonic Empire, the same revolutionary administrative policy would have provoked the same explosive reaction as in the empire of Ts'in She Hwangti if Napoleon had not brought his empire to grief by invading Russia in A.D. 1812; and, in the nature of the case, such facts as we have to go upon are insufficient to yield us a conclusive answer; yet, such as they are, they do strongly suggest—for a reason that has been considered at earlier points in this Study[2]—that, even if the Napoleonic Empire had avoided bringing destruction on itself at the hands of foreign Powers, it would have failed sooner or later to secure the acquiescence of its non-French subjects in a thoroughgoing administrative assimilation of the annexed or dependent territories to the French core of the Napoleonic body politic.

The governing fact in the situation was that France herself was not one of those dead-alive successors of the city-states of Medieval Western Christendom which she had just succeeded in gathering together under her rule; the vigour and enterprise which France had displayed in this notable piece of empire-building work were characteristic of the lively Modern Western World in which these mouldering débris of an unsuccessful medieval experiment were embedded. Napoleonic France was a member of this wider and more energetic society, and her membership in it not only led her on into over-ambitious military adventures that resulted in the loss of her newly established dominion over a smaller and tamer world; it also made France the carrier of Modern Western political ideas and ideals that ran clean counter to the spirit and objective of her empire-building enterprise.

The political service that France was performing for the wreckage of an abortive new order in Medieval Western Christendom, which had missed its destiny and broken down as far back as the fourteenth century, was to build the fragments of that shattered world into a universal state; and this service was not unacceptable to Germans, Flemings, and Italians of the generation and outlook of Goethe, who felt themselves stifled by the atmosphere of a Frankfurt, Bruges, or Venice in decay and were eager to escape from it by becoming citizens of the World, without shedding a tear over the extinction of decrepit statelets whose parochial independence had long since lost all meaning and value for their subjects. On the other hand, the political gospel to which France had given her own allegiance, and which she was preaching to her non-French subjects by example, was not Oecumenicalism but Nationalism, and this was the political lesson that the younger generation of Germans, Italians, and Belgians learnt—through both attraction and repulsion—from their intercourse with the very Frenchmen who were the agents of French imperialism. The portent of the German national uprising against French imperial rule in A.D. 1813 makes it evident that, even if the Napoleonic Empire had escaped or survived Napoleon's Russian adventure, the uniform departmental organization of the Napoleonic French administration would have provoked—in the name of the very principles of the French Revolution—the same disruptive national

[1] See V. v. 626–33.   [2] In IV. iv. 283–4 and V. v. 633–42.

movements that were to break a post-Napoleonic Hapsburg hegemony over Italy and Germany within little more than half a century after the Battle of Leipzig. Indeed, the nationalist reaction against a continuance of the drastic process of absorption into the French body politic might have been more vehement than the actual reaction in the 'liberated territories' against a rickety post-Napoleonic restoration of a sluggish *ancien régime*.

Administrative Policy in the Achaemenian Empire

In the administrative history of the Achaemenian Empire the sequence of policies was the inverse of the course of events in the Sinic universal state under the successive régimes of Ts'in and Han. The policy of the first founder, Cyrus II, was not unlike that of Han Liu Pang. He styled his empire 'the Realm of the Lands', and he made it his endeavour to reconcile the conquered peoples to Achaemenian rule by governing each of them as far as possible, at least in outward form, through its own peculiar political institutions.[1] Even the demonic Cambyses, who rode rough-shod over the Egyptians' religious susceptibilities, showed extreme consideration towards the Phoenicians.[2] This policy of deliberate administrative *laisser faire* was proved inadequate by the widespread and obstinate insurrections that broke out in 522 B.C. at the news of the assassination of Cambyses' successor on the imperial throne, who had professed himself to be Cambyses' brother Smerdis; for Smerdis had been the last male representative of the Cyran branch of the Achaemenidae; and, when the assassin Darius, representing the Ariaramnan branch of the house, had succeeded in restoring order and re-establishing the Empire at the cost of almost superhuman exertions, he sought to insure himself and his successors against a repetition of a catastrophe in which the Empire had all but perished by organizing his dominions, behind the façade of the Cyran dispensation, into twenty artificial taxation districts[3] under central control.

The easy-going genius of the Achaemenidae refrained from pushing this new Darian dispensation to the degree of uniformity and centralization that was aimed at in the departmental organization of the Napoleonic Empire or in the network of *chün* and *hsien* into which the Sinic World was remapped by Ts'in She Hwang-ti. Though Darius's successor Xerxes put an end to the constitutional existence of the Babylonian monarchy in form as well as in fact by refusing to repeat, on New Year's Day 484 B.C., the annual ceremony of 'taking the hands of Bel' that was the traditional warrant and sanction of legitimate sovereignty over Marduk-Bel's city,[4] Darius and his successors were as careful as the

---

[1] See p. 582, below.

[2] As is illustrated by the anecdote quoted on p. 149, n. 2, above.

[3] This was the original number according to the list in Herodotus, Book III, chaps. 89–94. See further pp. 582–4, below.

[4] See Meyer, E.: *Geschichte des Altertums*, vol. iii (Stuttgart 1901, Cotta), pp. 129–30, cited in the present Study, V. v. 123, n. 2. Darius himself had long-sufferingly observed the traditional procedure, in spite of Babylon's having revolted twice during the period of anarchy after Cambyses' death. Xerxes' deliberate discontinuance of the traditional rite was followed immediately by the third and last revolt of Babylon against Achaemenian rule.

Ptolemies and the Caesars were, after them, to rule Egypt in the style of a legitimate Pharaoh;[1] and, though, in the interior of the empire as reorganized by Darius, Cilicia[2] was the only surviving client state that was allowed to retain a juridical status of sovereign independence,[3] there were many smaller principalities, temple-states, and city-states that retained their autonomy as enclaves within the territories under direct administration. Indeed, within the taxation district labelled 'Athurā' ('Syria'), the Phoenician city-states were invested with minor empires of their own.[4]

It was likewise characteristic of the spirit of the Achaemenian régime that the viceroys (satraps) retained extensive powers even under the stricter Darian dispensation.[5] An imperial secretary who presumably reported direct to the Central Government was, however, attached to each of them[6] and appears to have been a member, *ex officio*, of the provincial council, mainly consisting of local Persian notables, whose concurrence the governor had to obtain in the more important of his acts of state. Moreover, in some of the more inveterately nationalist-minded viceroyalties—e.g. in Media, Armenia, Babylon-cum-Beyond the River, and West Anatolia—the likelihood of either a traitorous viceroy or an insurgent pretender being able to carry the whole country with him must have been decidedly diminished by the dissection of these four viceroyalties into four, three, two, and two taxation districts respectively.[7]

Administrative Policy in the Arab Caliphate

In contrast to the four instances, examined above, in which a provincial organization was introduced in a universal state as a means of combating persistent parochial opposition to the establishment of an oecumenical régime, a classical example of the opposite situation, in which a provincial organization was required for the filling of an administrative vacuum, is afforded by the Arab Caliphate. The Arab conquests were comparable, in point of speed, to Ts'in She Hwang-ti's, Mentuhotep's, Napoleon's, and Cyrus's; for it took the Arabs only nineteen years (A.D. 633–51)[8] to conquer the whole of the Sasanian Empire up to Merv, inclusive, on the north-east, as well as not much less than half of the surviving dominions of the Roman Empire up to

---

[1] It must be added that the tactfully treated Egyptians remained as irreconcilable to Achaemenian rule as the unceremoniously treated Babylonians.

[2] Erroneously reckoned in the Herodotean list as the fourth taxation district. The effects of this error on Herodotus's presentation of the administrative geography of the Achaemenian Empire are discussed on pp. 594–7, below.

[3] Beyond the frontiers of the territory under direct imperial administration there were friendly peoples in treaty relations with the Imperial Government who were allowed to retain a juridical status of equality with their imperial ally in consideration of their service to the Empire in screening it from the assaults of outer barbarians. Two such allied peoples were 'the Hauma-(?)drinking Saka' in Farghānah and the Arabs astride the road up the Euphrates from Babylonia to Syria and along the shore of the Mediterranean Sea from Syria to Egypt (see pp. 644–5 and 658–9, below).

[4] See V. v. 123, n. 2.

[5] For their powers and functions see Meyer, op. cit., vol. cit., pp. 52–54.

[6] See p. 82, above.　　　　　　　　　　　　　　　　　[7] See pp. 582–3, below.

[8] The Arab conquests are here reckoned to have begun with the campaigns of A.D. 633, and not with the reconnaissance of A.D. 629 which ended so disastrously for the Muslims at Mu'tah.

the Amanus Range on the north and up to the approaches to Carthage on the west.[1] Yet, in spite of the abruptness of the imposition of their rule, the Arab empire-builders were not confronted with any widespread vigorous movements to restore pre-existing régimes.[2]

The Arabs' administrative task was easy in this respect because the vast populations which they had so swiftly subjugated had by that time been broken in by more than eleven centuries' experience of being ruled by successive foreign empire-builders,[3] till they had grown accustomed to submitting passively to any new masters who might assert their title to rule by overthrowing their predecessors. Moreover, throughout this long period of time in most parts of this wide area, the dominant tendency had been for local self-government and parochial autonomy to give place to direct imperial rule, and this imperial administration itself had tended to become more and more centralized. This tendency had been only partially and temporarily counteracted by the break-up of the Achaemenian Empire and the planting of autonomous city-states on provincial territory by the successors of Alexander and by the Romans in their wake. The Sasanian Persian and Diocletianic Roman régimes which were the Arab Caliphate's immediate predecessors had been more highly centralized, not only than their own respective immediate predecessors the Arsacid hegemony and the Roman Principate, but than any of the other imperial régimes that had followed one another in South-West Asia and Egypt since the days of the Achaemenidae. Thus the mapping out of the Arab Caliphate into provinces was called for, not to meet the challenge of any rival political order, but to carry on an oecumenical system of government which, in virtue of its long monopoly, was the only practical possibility in the field. It is not surprising that the provincial organization of this resuscitated Syriac universal state should have borne, in its best days under the early ʿAbbasid Caliphs, a striking resemblance to the provincial organization with which the original Syriac universal state had been endowed by Darius the Great.[4]

---

[1] Carthage itself was momentarily occupied by the Arabs for the first time in A.D. 697 and was not definitely conquered by them till perhaps as late as A.D. 703, though they had established themselves in Tripolitania as early as A.D. 647 (see Becker, C. H.: *Islamstudien*, vol. i (Leipzig 1924, Quelle & Meyer), p. 118).

[2] Successful resistance to the imposition of Arab rule was put up only in a few natural fastnesses: in the ex-Sasanian territories between the Elburz Range and the south coast of the Caspian Sea; in the coastal highlands of Syria; and, after the later Arab conquest of the Visigothic successor-state of the Roman Empire in the Iberian Peninsula, in a strip of territory between the Asturian Mountains and the south coast of the Bay of Biscay which was a miniature counterpart of Daylam and Tabaristan (the physiographical similarity of these two regions has been noticed already in II. ii. 446–7). The most sensational of these resistance movements was that of the Mardaïtes in Syria, who managed to hold their own within short range of the four or five Arab cantonments there and within a stone's throw of the Umayyads' capital city, Damascus, itself. The Mardaïtes, however, seem to have drawn their strength and their *moral* largely from the support which they received from the Roman imperial authorities. Their movement was one of infiltration from a base in unconquered Roman territory, and they were sufficiently under the Roman Government's control for it to be able to undertake to withdraw them as part of the *modus vivendi* into which it entered with the Caliph ʿAbd-al-Malik in A.D. 688.

[3] Reckoning from the date of Darius's administrative reorganization of the Achaemenian Empire in the last quarter of the sixth century B.C.—but Syria and Egypt had had a still longer training in the hard lesson of political submissiveness (see V. v. 118 and IX. viii. 90–97).

[4] A statistical comparison of the areas and assessments of the provinces of the ʿAbbasid

Financial Functions of Provinces

A synoptic view of the provincial systems of the divers universal states that have come under consideration in the present chapter brings to light three main functions—a financial, a judicial, and a military—for which a province may serve as the local agency of an oecumenical government. The relative importance of these different functions will be found to vary widely from case to case, in accordance with historic differences in the policies of the respective empire-builders, in the degree of their ability to carry their policies into effect, and in the temper and traditions of their subjects; and there are cases in which one or more of these normal functions has been altogether in abeyance.

The essential and never dormant function is the financial one. Even the Primitive Muslim Arab conquerors of Roman and Sasanian territory, barbarians though they were, appreciated from the outset the importance, in their own interests, of maintaining as a going concern the existing financial administrative machinery—built up gradually through a continuous practice extending over many generations—of surveys, censuses, assessments, collections, and, above all, trained personnel for carrying all these administrative procedures out. Accordingly the Arabs left undisturbed at their posts the host of inland revenue officials whom they found in operation on either side of the former Romano-Persian frontier; and they wisely allowed them to continue to keep their books in Greek and Pehlevi till the reign of the Caliph 'Abd-al-Malik (*imperabat* A.D. 685–705),[1] by when the lapse of half a century had made the conquerors' language and alphabet sufficiently familiar to their subjects to make it possible to transpose the official book-keeping into Arabic without throwing the financial service into confusion and bringing the collection of revenue to a standstill.[2]

Yet, although the provincial organization of a universal state seems always to be used for some financial purpose, the respective roles of the provincial administration and the central government in the control of finance vary within very wide limits. In both the Arab Caliphate and its prototype the Achaemenian Empire each province was financially autonomous. The provincial government not only carried out the collection of all revenue within its own boundaries; it retained, for provincial use, all receipts beyond a fixed tribute payable to the imperial treasury. On the other hand the financial administration of the British Indian Empire and the Roman Empire was highly centralized, and the imperial treasury here kept in the hands of its own revenue service both the collection of revenue in the provinces and the payment of charges for provincial administration—thus using the provinces as mere organs of the central government for financial purposes.

Caliphate, as recorded by the classical Arab geographers, with those of the taxation-districts of the Achaemenian Empire, as recorded by Herodotus, might yield interesting results.

[1] See V. v. 501, with n. 3, and p. 242, below, where an error in vol. v, p. 501, n. 3, is corrected.

[2] See Ahmad al-Balādhurī: *Kitab Futūh-Al-Buldān*, English translation by Hitti, P. Kh., vol. i (New York 1916, Columbia University Press), pp. 301 and 465–6.

Judicial Functions of Provinces

The judicial function of provincial governors had likewise varied in importance. This was a prominent feature of a provincial governor's duties in both the Achaemenian and the Roman Empire. Indeed, in the acts of Christian martyrs, in which this aspect of a Roman provincial governor's duties is in the foreground in the nature of the case, the governor is frequently referred to simply as *iudex*. In the government of British India the criminal law was administered, above the level of the petty cases dealt with by village headmen or *panchayats*, by salaried magistrates who, *more Romano*, were usually revenue and administrative officers as well as judges; but civil law at the same level, and criminal as well as civil law at all levels higher than that, was here administered, in accordance with a principle already established in the government of the United Kingdom, by a judiciary separate from, and independent of, the administrative service.[1] Even in the loosely organized Achaemenian Empire there appears to have been a bench of imperial judges whose importance in the scheme of imperial government is indicated by the facts that they were recruited from the leading Persian noble houses and that, if they were discovered to have taken bribes, they were arraigned before the Emperor himself and were punished by him with the utmost severity.[2] In the Roman Empire, again, the judicial discretion of a provincial governor in cases to which Roman citizens were parties was limited by the citizens' right of appeal to Caesar; and this procedure had the curious result that the Praetorian Prefect, who had originally been simply the Commander of the Emperor's bodyguard, in course of time became the president of a central court of final appeal through which the Emperor's prerogative was exercised.[3] Under the Diocletianic constitution this court of appeal was decentralized like the imperial office itself, and the Empire was divided into four praetorian prefectures, each presided over by a prefect of its own who had the last word in all judicial business within his area.

Military Functions of Provinces

The military function of provincial governors had varied in scope and character even more widely than the judicial and the financial.

In the Achaemenian Empire the standing army maintained and controlled by the central government was very small by comparison with the size of the total population and area of the Achaemenian dominions. It consisted merely of a bodyguard attached to the emperor's person and of garrisons stationed at key points along the imperial lines

---

[1] See the *Report of the Indian Statutory Commission*, vol. i (London 1930, H.M. Stationery Office = Cmd. 3568), pp. 292–7.

[2] See Herodotus, Book V, chap. 25, and Book VII, chap. 194.

[3] Compare the analogous evolution in the Achaemenian Empire by which the Hazarapatiš (*Graecè* Chiliarch), who had originally been the commander of the Emperor's bodyguard of a thousand men, became something like the president of a council of ministers (see Meyer, E.: *Geschichte des Altertums*, vol. iii (Stuttgart 1901, Cotta), p. 43, and Junge, P. J.: 'Hazarapatiš: Zur Stellung des Chiliarchen der Königlichen Leibgarde im Achämenidenstaat', in *Klio*, vol. xxxiii (Neue Folge, vol. xv) (Leipzig 1940, Dietrich), pp. 13–38).

of communication.[1] The title 'hazarapatiš' (commander of one thousand troops'), borne by the imperial officer who eventually came to perform the functions of a head of the civil administration,[2] indicates that the imperial bodyguard had originally been only 1,000 men strong; and, even if the *corps d'élite* known as 'the Immortals', who served in Xerxes' expeditionary force in 480–479 B.C., were a standing professional force and not merely the cream of a Persian national militia, their number was in any case fixed at no more than 10,000.[3] Allowing for the partial recruitment of the imperial garrisons from non-Persian sources[4] and further for the possibility that the original 1,000 Persian picked troops were included in the eventual 10,000 and that these were not all Persians,[5] it will still seem improbable that any considerable number of additional Persian troops can ever have been raised from the thinly populated home territory of the ruling nation in the highlands of Pārsa (*Graecè* Persis, the latter-day Fars) after more than one half of its area, and perhaps not much less than one half of its population, had been detached from Pārsa by Darius I through his act of degrading the dissident Asagartiyā in Kirmān and dissident Yautiyā and Maciyā in Lāristān to the status of subject peoples.[6] Accordingly, when the Achaemenian Imperial Government was called upon to make a serious war effort, it had to draw very largely on provincial militias, and these again were recruited not merely from the local Persian settlers but from the native populations as well.

The training, inspection,[7] and command of these provincial militias were responsibilities of the provincial governors, and the military power which these prerogatives placed in their hands was not effectively kept in check by the presence, within their domains, of a few imperial garrisons under the central government's control—as was demonstrated by the ever-increasing frequency and formidableness of the rebellions on which provincial governors ventured. The Mughal Empire paid the same penalty for lapsing into the slovenly practice—against which Akbar had set his face in vain—of providing for the payment of the imperial officers (*mansabdārs*), charged with the maintenance of contingents of troops, by assigning to them provincial land revenue which they were empowered to collect for themselves, instead of collecting the revenue on its own account and paying the *mansabdārs* out of the Imperial Treasury.[8] In the Ottoman, unlike either the Mughal or the Achaemenian, Empire the central government had at its disposal a

---

[1] For these garrisons see p. 123, above.

[2] See p. 182, n. 3, above, and p. 344, below.

[3] See Herodotus, Book VII, chap. 83.   [4] See p. 119, with n. 7, above.

[5] On the evidence of the friezes at Susa, A. T. Olmstead holds (see *A History of the Persian Empire* (Chicago 1948, University of Chicago Press), p. 238) that the Ten Thousand were recruited from among the Medes and the Elamites as well as the Persians.   [6] See pp. 583, 622–3, and 637, below.

[7] There would appear to have been periodic musters—presumably for inspection and perhaps also for manœuvres—to judge by the formula 'commander of all the forces whose appointed place of assemblage is the Plain of Castolus', which was part of the terms of appointment issued by Darius II to his son Cyrus in 408 B.C. according to Xenophon: *Expeditio Cyri*, Book I, chap. ix, § 7 (cp. op. cit., Book I, chap. i, § 2, and eundem: *Historia Graeca*, Book I, chap. iv, § 3). See further this Study in the present volume, p. 674, with n. 3, and IX. viii. 548, n. 1.

[8] See p. 127, above.

professional army which, in its best days, was admirably disciplined, mobile, and efficient;[1] yet in wartime the Ottoman Empire, too, had to draw heavily upon provincial forces, and, though, as we have seen,[2] the central government exerted itself to keep under its own control the assignment of the fiefs by which the provincial feudal cavalry was maintained, the feudal contingent of each province was commanded in wartime by the provincial governor.

In the Roman Empire during the Principate, all units of the professional army except the Emperor's Praetorian Guard and the so-called *Cohortes Urbanae* ('Metropolitan Battalions')[3] were under the command of provincial governors; but, in the Augustan constitution, this arrangement did not carry with it that decentralization of military power which was a dangerous weakness of the Achaemenian, Mughal, and Ottoman Empires. At this stage of its history the Roman Empire enjoyed such a decided ascendancy over both the enemy beyond the frontiers[4] and recalcitrant tribesmen in patches of the interior that it was able to keep its troops concentrated in a small fraction of the imperial territory, and this mainly along the borders. In his division of the control over the provinces between himself and the Senate, Augustus was careful to retain in his own hands all provinces in which troops had to be stationed, and the governors of these provinces were the Emperor's own appointees and military subordinates. Constitutionally, therefore, the whole Imperial Army, wherever stationed, remained under the Emperor's own undivided command, and normally this control was effective—though the civil wars of A.D. 69 and A.D. 193-7, in which governors of different imperial provinces who were *ex officio* deputy chiefs of rival army-groups fought one another for the prize of the vacant imperial office, were portents of the greater bout of anarchy, arising from this inherent weakness in the constitution of the Principate, in which the Empire itself was to come within an ace of destruction in the third century of the Christian Era.

By the time when Diocletian (*imperabat* A.D. 284-305) undertook the reorganization of the Roman Empire, the terrible experience of the two preceding generations had demonstrated the danger of combining the civil government of a province with the local military command, even when local commands were constitutionally subordinate to an imperial commander-in-chief and when this dangerous combination of powers was confined to one of two categories of provinces. In Diocletian's day it was no longer practically possible to maintain the distinction between military and civilian provinces which had been of the essence of Augustus's system, for by this time the frontier defences of the Empire had broken down and, in the new military situation, if the Empire could be defended at all, it could be defended only in depth by mobile forces which might need to operate in any part of the imperial territory. These two considerations led Diocletian and his successors to take a radical new departure. They set up a small number of high military commands each embracing a wide area and covering, between them, the whole of

---

[1] See III. iii. 32-44.   [2] See pp. 125-6, above.
[3] For these see p. 123, above, and pp. 321-2, below.   [4] See p. 320, below.

the Empire,[1] but they confined the powers of this professional military hierarchy to military affairs and placed the civil administration—from governorships of provinces[2] up to praetorian prefectures inclusive—in the hands of a professional civil service. This division of powers continued till the break-up of the Empire in the fifth century of the Christian Era in the west and in the seventh century in the east and centre.[3]

In the Sinic World the experience of the last and most appalling round of the warfare between the Contending States led Ts'in She Hwang-ti, in founding a Sinic universal state, into the path that was to be followed in another society by Diocletian when he refounded the Roman Empire. Though Ts'in She Hwang-ti chose an historic institution of military government—the *chün*—as the major unit of provincial administration for his dominions,[4] he separated the civil administration of his *chün* from the military command and placed the two offices in different hands, while the *hsien*—which in Ts'in She Hwang-ti's system became a subdivision of the *chün*—seems to have been under exclusively civilian control.[5] This division of civil and military powers was, of course, the antithesis of the traditional Sinic feudal régime, yet, like other radical and provocative innovations introduced by the first Ts'in emperor, it ultimately prevailed. The permanent victory of this new principle of Sinic administration was assured when, in consequence of the eventual alliance between the Han Dynasty and the Confucian school of philosophy, the Confucian scholar, selected individually for intellectual merit, replaced the feudal warrior, inducted by right of birth, as the typical representative of the Sinic governing class. And a principle thus established in the Sinic Society in the last chapter of its history was resuscitated—after the social interregnum in which the Han Empire foundered—in the affiliated Far Eastern Society in China.

The Utilization of Provincial Organizations by Alien Civilizations

Who had been the principal ultimate beneficiaries from the systems of provincial administration which universal states had set up?

Conspicuous benefits had been secured by intruders of alien culture. The provincial organization of the Achaemenian Empire, for instance, was taken over and turned to good account by the Hellenic successor-states into which the Achaemenian dominions were partitioned at the turn of the fourth and third centuries B.C. after the overthrow of the Empire by Alexander the Great; and when, in the second decade of

---

[1] See pp. 322–3, below.

[2] Under the Diocletianic régime the provinces were reduced in size and were increased in number, by comparison with the administrative map of the Roman Empire under the Principate, owing to a progressive transfer of business that had once been handled by local organs of municipal self-government to the shoulders of imperial officials.

[3] When a ghost of the Roman Empire was conjured up in the Orthodox Christian World by Leo Syrus in the eighth century of the Christian Era, this division of civil and military powers was not one of the imperial institutions that were revived. It had proved too complicated an arrangement to weather the storms of a political interregnum, and, even before the crash had come in the centre and the east, the first steps towards a reversal of the Diocletianic policy had been taken here and there by Justinian (*imperabat* A.D. 527–65). See Bury, J. B.: *A History of the Later Roman Empire* (London 1889, Macmillan, 2 vols.), vol. ii, chap. 13.   [4] See p. 169, above.

[5] See Bodde, D.: *China's First Unifier* (Leiden 1938, Brill), p. 135.

the second century B.C., an Hellenic ruler of the ex-Achaemenian province of Bactria emulated Alexander's feat by overrunning the Indic
universal state that had been established by Chandragupta Maurya, the
provincial organization that had been worked out during the preceding
137 years (322–185 B.C.) by Chandragupta himself and his Mauryan
heirs[1] was no doubt similarly serviceable to the Hellenic princes who
ruled North-Western India for the next hundred years.[2]

The British Rāj in India was indebted in the same way to the foregoing Mughal Rāj, particularly in the financial sphere;[3] for, though so
many Mughal institutions, good and bad alike, had perished during
the century of anarchy that had followed Awrangzīb's death in A.D. 1707,
the military adventurers—Indian, Afghan, and West European—who
had since been contending for the spoils of a derelict Mughal heritage
had all been careful—like the barbarian Arab conquerors of the Sasanian
and Roman Empires—to preserve an imperial administrative machine
for the collection of revenue that was the irreplaceable source of pay
for their troops. Accordingly the British empire-builders, when they
came on the scene, were not faced with the task of rebuilding from the
foundations in the revenue department. Thanks to the legacy which
they here inherited from their Mughal forerunners, the organization,
information, experience, and, above all, the habits which are indispensable conditions for success in the administration of finance were to
a large extent at British disposal as going concerns; and one of the most
effective of the devices by which the British made themselves masters
of India was the employment of a financial leverage for bringing into
British hands the command of the troops and the administration of
the territories of successor-states of the Mughal Empire that became
the Honourable East India Company's allies.

'Our participation in Indian wars began when the English lent a military
contingent to assist some native potentate. The next stage came when we
took the field on our own account, assisted usually by the levies of some
prince who made common cause with us, and whose soldiery were un-
disciplined, untrustworthy, and very clumsily handled. . . . What was
needed was a body of men that could be relied upon for some kind of tacti-
cal precision and steadiness under fire; but for this purpose it was of little
use even to place sepoys under European officers unless they could be
regularly paid and taught to obey one master. So the system soon reached
the stage when the native ally was required to supply not men but money,[4]
and the English undertook to raise, train, and pay a fixed number of troops
on receiving a subsidy equivalent to their cost. . . . Large sums had been

[1] The fragmentary information about this aspect of the Mauryan Empire is presented
in Smith, V. A.: *The Early History of India*, 3rd ed. (Oxford 1914, Clarendon Press),
pp. 163–4.
[2] The scanty information about the provincial organization of the Greek successor-
states of the Mauryan Empire is sorted out, with a masterly hand, by Tarn, W. W.:
The Greeks in Bactria and India (Cambridge 1938, University Press), pp. 230–43
and 259.
[3] The administrative and financial organization set up by the Mughal Darius, Akbar
(*imperabat* A.D. 1556–1605), is set out in Moreland, W. H.: *India at the Death of Akbar*
(London 1920, Macmillan), p. 33.
[4] In the Hellenic World of the fifth century B.C. the requirement of money instead of
ships was the process by which the Athenians converted a Delian League under Athens'
leadership into an Athenian Empire under Athens' thumb.—A.J.T.

hitherto spent by the native princes in maintaining ill-managed and in-subordinate bodies of troops, and in constant wars against each other; they might economise their revenues, be rid of a mutinous soldiery, and sit much more quietly at home, by entering into contracts with a skilful and solvent administration that would undertake all serious military business for a fixed subsidy. But, as punctuality in money matters has never been a princely quality, this subsidy was apt to be paid very irregularly; so the next stage was to revive the long-standing practice of Asiatic governments: the assignment of lands for the payment of troops.'[1]

This method of extending direct British rule in India was applied by Lord Wellesley (*proconsulari munere fungebatur* A.D. 1798–1805) with special vigour to the two important successor-states of the Mughal Empire whose respective rulers were the Wazīr of Oudh and the Nizām of Hyderabad, and the territory thus acquired by the British Rāj from Oudh was of crucial importance.

'The result of Lord Wellesley's somewhat dictatorial negotiations was that the Wazīr ceded all his frontier provinces, including Rohilcund, to the Company, the revenue of the territory thus transferred being taken as an equivalent to the subsidy payable for troops. . . . Oudh was thenceforward enveloped by the English dominion. This most important augmentation of territory transferred to the British Government some of the richest and most populous districts in the heart of India, lying along the Ganges and its tributaries above Benares to the foot of the Himalayan Range. It con-solidated our power on a broader foundation, brought a very large in-crease of revenue, and confronted us with the Marattha chief Sindia along the whole line of his possessions in Upper India.'[2]

While the British in India were entering into the heritage of an empire that had collapsed a hundred years before, and the Hellenic supplanters of the Mauryan and Achaemenid empires overthrew régimes that were already in decay, the Spanish *conquistadores* of the Andean World seized an Incaic Empire that was still intact, and they profited from this piece of good fortune notwithstanding the blind brutality and pride which moved them to destroy so many Inca institutions that were valuable in themselves and would have also served the interests of the new masters of the Andean World. The paternal totalitarian êthos of the Inca régime had been faithfully reflected in its system of provincial administration. A hierarchy of administrative units—based on the natural social unit of the family and the natural geographical unit of the valley—ascended through communes, departments, and provinces to the four viceroyalties, reminiscent of the praetorian prefectures of a Diocletianic Roman Empire, from which this Andean 'Realm of the Four Quarters' took its name.[3] Though this elaborate system was too delicate a tool to fit the alien conqueror's rough hand, the habit of obedience that had been inculcated into the population of the Empire by the minutiae of Incaic administration made these subjects most accommodatingly submissive

---

[1] Lyall, Sir A.: *The Rise and Expansion of the British Dominioni n India* (London 1894, Murray), pp. 244–5.
[2] Lyall, op. cit., p. 247.
[3] For the administrative map of the Inca Empire, see Baudin, L.: *L'Empire Socialiste des Inka* (Paris 1928, Institut d'Ethnologie), pp. 118–19; and the present Study, xi, map 68.

to the more rudimentary administrative methods of the Inca's Spanish supplanters.

The inability of the Spanish *conquistadores* to derive substantial advantage from the administrative system which they found on their hands is characteristic of barbarian conquerors. The German and Sarmatian invaders of the western provinces of the Roman Empire were similarly unable to take advantage of the Diocletianic organization. The signal exception which proves the rule is the success of the Arab invaders of Roman Syria and Egypt in preserving the Roman financial system as a going concern, and this goes far to explain the Arabs' unparalleled achievement of transforming one of the barbarian successor-states of the Roman Empire into an avatar of the Syriac universal state that had once been embodied in the Empire of the Achaemenidae. The administrative receptivity of the Primitive Muslim Arabs has its counterparts in the less striking achievements of the Arsacid 'Parthian', Saka, and Kushan barbarian supplanters of Hellenic empire-builders on former Achaemenian ground in South-West Asia east of Euphrates and on former Mauryan ground in North-West India.[1] But these were all exceptional cases, and, for the most part, the barbarian invaders of universal states had failed to profit from their victims' work in the field of provincial administration.

The Utilization of Provincial Organizations by Churches

On the other hand, the provincial organization of a universal state had more than once been turned to ecclesiastical account.

When the Egyptiac Emperor Thothmes (Tuthmosis) III (*imperabat circa* 1490–1436 B.C.) organized the priests of the parochial divinities of the nomes into a Pan-Egyptiac ecclesiastical corporation under the presidency of the Chief Priest of Amon-Re at Thebes,[2] we may guess that he was extending to the ecclesiastical field the existing political structure of 'the New Empire' of Egypt; for 'the New Empire' was a resuscitation of 'the Middle Empire' after an interregnum of Hyksos barbarian ascendancy, and, as we have seen,[3] 'the Middle Empire' had succeeded, step by step, in extinguishing the autonomy of the once virtually independent nomarchs and eventually bringing the nomes under the direct administration of the imperial government. One of the moves made by the emperors of the Twelfth Dynasty on their road to this objective had been to enter, over the heads of the nomarchs, into direct relations with the priests of the local shrines and to purchase their alliance by sending officials of the Imperial Office of Works to repair and improve their temple buildings at the charge of the Imperial Treasury.[4] Thothmes' historic act set the coping-stone on the construction of this mutually profitable partnership between the local priesthoods and the Imperial Crown.

The hierarchical organization of the local Egyptiac priesthoods into a

---

[1] See V. v. 442–3.   [2] See I. i. 145, n. 5; IV. iv. 421; and V. v. 530–1.
[3] On pp. 174–6, above.
[4] See Meyer, E.: *Geschichte des Altertums*, vol. i, Part II, 3rd ed. (Stuttgart and Berlin 1913, Cotta), p. 274.

Pan-Egyptiac ecclesiastical corporation under a supreme pontiff, on the initiative and under the patronage of the secular Imperial Power, has a parallel in the position accorded to the Magi in the Sasanian Empire (*stabat* A.D. 224[1]-641 or 642[2]). The fundamental difference in structure between the Sasanian Persian Monarchy and the Arsacid 'Parthian' régime which it supplanted lay in the Sasanids' effective assertion of the central government's authority. Provincial governors, appointed by the Sasanian Emperor, now replaced the hereditary local kinglets[3]—seldom effectively under the control of their Arsacid overlord and often in overt rebellion against him—of whom the founder of the Sasanian Empire, Ardashir I, had himself been one before he carried a successful rebellion to its logical conclusion by slaying his master and seizing his throne. This Sasanian centralization of the civil administration of South-West Asia east of Euphrates was reflected in the corresponding organization of the Zoroastrian Church under Ardashir I's auspices and, according to tradition, on his initiative. Ardashir not only made Zoroastrianism the established church of his empire; he organized the Magian priesthood of the imperial religion into a hierarchy[4] rising from the local Magi (*Mōghān*), through the Chief Magi (*Mōghān Mōghān*) of eminent shrines and their superiors the Archimagi (*Mōbadhān*), to a supreme Archimagus (*Mōbadhān Mōbadh*) who was the ecclesiastical counterpart of the Sasanian Emperor himself.[5] This organization had a territorial basis: the empire was divided and subdivided into the equivalents of Christian archbishoprics, bishoprics, and parishes, each under the jurisdiction of an ecclesiastic of the corresponding rank.

Though Ardashir's and Thothmes' acts of state wear the appearance of creations *ex nihilo*, this is doubtless partly an illusion arising from the scantiness of our information about their antecedents. We do know that the Egyptiac priesthood to which Thothmes gave an oecumenical organization had previously ensured its own survival by coming to terms with the perhaps intrusive Sumeric worship of Osiris in an *union sacrée* against the alien religion of the Hyksos;[6] and the Magi—an ancient ecclesiastical caste which had originated in the pre-Zoroastrian age of Iranian paganism—had shown a similar resourcefulness in capturing the revolutionary higher religion founded by Zarathustra after they had come to the conclusion that they could neither stamp it out nor prevent its spread.[7] The Magi had also succeeded in commending Zoroastrianism (in the hardly recognizable form in which it had emerged from the Magian crucible) to

[1] The probable date of the overthrow of the last Arsacid king of kings, Artabanus V by Ardashir I of the House of Sāsān.

[2] The date of the Battle of Nihāwand, after which the Sasanian Government was virtually non-existent, though the last Sasanian Emperor, Yazdagird III, survived as a fugitive in Khurāsān till A.D. 651 or 652.

[3] This unbridled local autonomy had been so characteristic a feature of the Arsacid régime that this whole episode of South-West Asian history came to be known, in the Arabic version of the Sasanian tradition, as the age of the *mulūk-at-tawā'if* (the parochial princelings who were mere 'kings of shreds and patches').

[4] See Christensen, A.: *L'Iran sous les Sassanides* (Copenhagen 1936, Levin & Munksgaard), pp. 112-13.

[5] A second order of ecclesiastics, the *Hērbadhōn*, who were specialists in ritual, were similarly brigaded together under a supreme *Hērbadhān Hērbadh* (Christensen, op. cit., p. 114).

[6] See I. i. 140-5.   [7] See V. v. 542 and 705, n. 1; and V. vi. 43, n. 4.

the Arsacid princes of the Azerbaijānī line (*regnabant* A.D. 10/11–224), who had been the Sasanids' immediate predecessors; and, though these latter-day Arsacids had not gone to the length of making Zoroastrianism the official religion of their state, the captivation of these ex-barbarians by the Magi was a more remarkable achievement than this ecclesiastical corporation's alliance with the Sasanidae. In the act of supplanting the Arsacids, the Sasanidae had virtually committed themselves to Zoroastrianism in advance by claiming to be the legitimate successors of the Achaemenidae, since the personal adherence of the great emperors of the Achaemenian Dynasty to the religion of Zarathustra was one of the few facts of pre-Alexandrine Iranian history of which a lively recollection had been preserved in the folk-memory of the Iranian people during the long ascendancy of an alien Hellenic culture.

Thus both the Magi and the Egyptiac Priesthood had known how to help themselves before their fortunes were made by a stroke of the secular arm, and, in the sequel, both ecclesiastical corporations demonstrated their capacity to survive the state that had called them into existence. The Chief Priest of Amon-Re at Thebes, Hrihor,[1] actually took over the Egyptiac Imperial Crown in the eleventh century B.C. from the last decrepit secular pharoahs of 'the New Empire';[2] and, though nothing came of this attempt to keep 'the New Empire' in being through a personal union of the supreme temporal and ecclesiastical offices, the Pan-Egyptiac ecclesiastical corporation instituted by Thothmes III did continue to maintain itself—and, in doing so, to preserve the distinctive character of the Egyptiac Society—for some fifteen hundred years after the Theban priest-king Hrihor's day, under successive alien ascendancies and native Egyptiac reactions against them, until at last, under Roman rule, its close-grained fabric yielded to the solvent of Christianity. As for the Zoroastrian Church, it failed to emulate the tenacity of the Egyptiac priesthood on its native soil; when the Sasanian Empire was overthrown, the Magian hierarchy fell with it; yet, though Zoroastrianism did not succeed in holding its own at home, it did achieve the even more difficult feat of preserving its identity in diasporá, and the credit for this was largely due to the perennial adaptability of the Magi, who retained their hold over their flock, and thereby kept this flock together, by making the most of their role as executants of a ritual and doctors of a religious law after they had lost their ecclesiastical lordship over a territorial empire.[3]

---

[1] According to recent findings of Modern Western Egyptologists, Hrihor himself was not a priest by profession but was a military adventurer who had usurped the Chief Priesthood of Amon-Re of Thebes without being properly qualified to hold it (see Edgerton, W. F.: 'The Government and the Governed in the Egyptian Empire', in the *Journal of Near Eastern Studies*, vol. iv, July 1947, No. 3 (Chicago 1947, University Press), pp. 152–60). Edgertᴏn makes this statement on p. 153 on the authority of Kees, H.: 'Hrihor und die Aufrichtung des Thebanischen Gottesstaates', in *Nachrichten von der Gesellschaft der Wissenschaften zu Göttingen*, Phil.-Hist. Klasse, Neue Folge, Fachgruppe I, 2. Band (1936–8), pp. 1–20). If this is the fact, it is a further testimony to the potency of the office in Hrihor's day. If it had not been the most favourable 'jumping-off ground' within Hrihor's reach for going on to usurp the Pharaonic Crown, the Chief Priesthood of Amon-Re would hardly have excited the cupidity of a soldier of fortune.

[2] See II. ii. 116, n. 1; IV. iv. 421 and 515–17; and p. 692, below.

[3] There was, of course, a remarkable similarity between the Zoroastrian and the Jewish response to the identic challenge of exile and dispersion.

The Christian Church showed still greater initiative and independence in turning to its own account the provincial organization of the universal state within whose framework it arose.[1] In building up its body ecclesiastic it availed itself of the city-states that were the cells of the Hellenic body social and of the Roman body politic. From the days of Saint Paul and his fellow pioneers in the Christian mission field, city-states were the primary units of the Church's territorial structure, and, as the traditions of the Hellenic Civilization gradually died out, a city came to mean a town that was the seat of a Christian bishop, instead of meaning a town possessing institutions of civil self-government and chartered as a municipality of the Roman Commonwealth. A local bishop whose see was the administrative centre of a Diocletianic Roman province came to be recognized by the bishops of the other cities of the same province as their superior; such metropolitans or archbishops, in their turn, acknowledged as their primate the bishop whose see was the administrative centre of one of those groups of provinces which, in the Diocletianic system, were known as *diœceses*;[2] and bishops, metropolitans, and primates alike paid ecclesiastical allegiance to regional patriarchs, who corresponded hierarchically to the Diocletianic praetorian prefects, though there was no correspondence at this level, as there was at the lower levels, between the areas of ecclesiastical and civil jurisdiction. In the Diocletianic Empire the west and centre were partitioned between three praetorian prefectures, while the east, from the Lower Danube to the First Cataract of the Nile, and from Thrace and Cyrenaica to Mesopotamia, was united in a single vast circumscription. In the Christian ecclesiastical organization, on the other hand, the Diocletianic Praefecture of the East was eventually divided between the four patriarchates of Alexandria, Jerusalem, Antioch, and Constantinople, while the circumscriptions of the other three praefectures were united in the single vast ecclesiastical domain of the Patriarchate of Rome.

This territorial organization of the Christian Church was not called into existence by the fiat of any Roman Thothmes or Ardashir; it was built up by the Church itself in the days when, in Roman official eyes, Christianity was a *religio non licita*; and all but the top story—whose architecture was implicit in the structure of the lower tiers—was in existence by the time of the conversion of Constantine. In virtue of this original independence of the secular imperial régime whose territorial organization it had thus adapted to its own purposes, the Roman-inspired territorial structure of the Christian Church was able to survive the Roman Empire's disappearance. In Gaul, for example, where a tottering Roman imperial régime had sought at the eleventh hour to rehabilitate itself on a novel basis of local support by instituting periodic regional congresses of notables, the Church, after the Empire had faded

[1] The preservation of the lineaments of an obsolete Roman political map in those of a surviving Christian ecclesiastical map is examined further on pp. 693–5, below.

[2] Though this technical term of Diocletianic Roman administration had been adopted as the designation of the 'diocese' of a Christian bishop, this usage was historically incorrect, since the standard domain of a bishopric was the territory of a city-state or canton, whereas the *diœceses* of the Roman Empire each contained several hundreds of territorial units of that order of magnitude.

out of existence, took its cue from this secular precedent by convening regional congresses of bishops;[1] and, though in many regions once in-included in the Roman Empire the Church's structure had eventually weathered away like its secular prototype, the indebtedness of the Church to the Roman Empire in this administrative sphere, as well as its ability to survive its Roman model, was apparent on the face of a latter-day map.

On the medieval ecclesiastical map of France, for example, an historian could discern in the mosaic of bishoprics the boundaries of the city-states of Gallia Togata and the cantons of Gallia Comata, while the arch-bishoprics preserved the outlines of the Diocletianic subdivisions of the four Augustan provinces Narbonensis, Aquitania, Lugdunensis, and Belgica. Even the five patriarchates, which were the precarious super-structure of the Christian ecclesiastical pyramid, were all still in existence —four in Eastern Orthodox hands and one in Western Catholic hands— at the time when these lines were being written; and, though the areas of their circumscriptions, and the distribution and nationality of their ecclesiastical subjects, had undergone vast changes during the fifteen centuries that had elapsed since the date of the Fourth Oecumenical Council (*sedebat Calchedone*, A.D. 451), their mortifying losses had been partially offset by gains that could never have been foreseen at the time when the patriarchates had first taken shape.

For example, the Patriarchate of Rome had lost its African sees to Islam, its South-East European sees to Eastern Orthodoxy, and its North European sees to Protestantism, but it had won hundreds of new bishoprics and millions of new subjects overseas in the Americas and the Indies. The four Eastern Patriarchates within their own historic bounds had suffered losses—to Monophysitism first and to Islam in the sequel— that were far more severe than the corresponding reverses of the Papacy; yet, in drawing up the balance-sheet of fifteen centuries of chequered history, they could still take heart from two signal achievements. They had preserved, as between themselves, their unity of rite and creed with-out sacrificing their independence of one another as units of ecclesiastical administration; and they had jointly called into existence a number of new sister churches that in rite and creed were at one with the four patriarchates and with one another, while enjoying in the sphere of ecclesiastical administration the same independence as the patriarchates themselves. Thanks to this liberality, this ecclesiastical commonwealth of Eastern Orthodox churches had never yet provoked a secession such as the ecclesiastical autocracy of the Roman Church had brought upon itself in a Protestant Reformation or the secular British Empire in an American Revolutionary War. The British Empire might indeed take credit for having learnt its lesson and converted itself into a common-wealth of fully self-governing communities of equal status; but this wisdom after the event could merely exorcise the danger of further

---

[1] See Burns, C. Delisle: *The First Europe* (London 1947, Allen & Unwin), pp. 541–2, for an illuminating comparison between an imperial rescript, issued at Constantinople on the 17th April, 418, in the names of the Emperors Honorius and Theodosius II, and a letter, dated the 23rd August, 546, written by Pope Vigilius.

secessions; it could not induce an independent United States to return
to the British fold. The Commonwealth of Eastern Orthodox churches
had risen to a higher level of statesmanship in being wise in time and
thereby managing to retain within its circle the giant Church of Russia
to champion the cause of Eastern Orthodoxy in an age when the onset of
Western Nationalism, following the inroads of Islam and Monophysitism, had reduced to shadows of their former selves the once mighty
patriarchates of Constantinople, Alexandria, Antioch, and Jerusalem.

4. Capital Cities

'Laws' governing the Migration of Capital Cities

The seats of the central governments of universal states show a
decided tendency to change their locations in course of time, and this is
one of the clearest indications that, whatever may have been the motives
and intentions of the founders of a universal state, the true raison d'être
of their handiwork is not the kingdom, power, or glory of the empire-
builders but the welfare of their subjects.

Empire-builders usually begin by ruling their dominions from a seat
of government convenient to themselves: either the established capital
of their own fatherland, which they have transformed from a parochial
into a universal state by overthrowing its rivals and imposing its peace
on an entire society; or else some new site on the fringe of the subjugated territories, at a point where these are particularly accessible from
the empire-builders' home country. But, as time goes on, the experience
of imperial administration or the pressure of events is apt to lead either
the original empire-builders or successors of theirs who take their empires
over or rebuild them after a temporary collapse to transfer the imperial
capital to a new site which is commended by its convenience, not for the
original empire-building Power, but for the empire itself as a whole.
This new oecumenical outlook will, of course, suggest different new
locations in different circumstances. If the first consideration is administrative convenience, the capital is likely to shift to some point, enjoying
good facilities for communication, that is geographically central.[1] On the
other hand, if the most urgent demand is for defence against some barbarian or alien aggressor, the new capital may gravitate towards the
particular sector of the imperial frontiers on which the hostile pressure is
heaviest at the time.[2]

We have seen that the founders of universal states are not always of
the same origin. Sometimes they are representatives of a civilization
which is foreign to the society for whose political needs they are providing. Sometimes the empire-builders are barbarians who have become
morally alienated from the society which they are supplying with a
universal state, but have nevertheless continued to gravitate towards it.
Frequently the empire-builders are marchmen who have vindicated
their claim to be members of the society by defending its borders

[1] This point is made by Ibn Khaldūn: Muqaddamāt, translated by de Slane,
Baron McG. (Paris 1863–8, Imprimerie Impériale, 3 vols.), vol. ii, pp. 308–9.
[2] This last-mentioned determining factor in changes in the locations of capitals of
universal states has been examined already in II. ii. 112–208.

against outer barbarians before turning their arms against the interior of their own world and forcibly endowing it with an oecumenical peace. Such marchmen empire-builders are indeed true heirs of the civilization which they salvage from a Time of Troubles; yet, in the sight of their co-heirs for whom they have performed an invidious social service, they are sometimes hardly distinguishable from those outer barbarians with whom the marchmen have become familiar through the intercourse of border warfare. Lastly there are cases—apparently rather rare—in which the empire-builders have been neither aliens nor barbarians nor marchmen but 'metropolitans' from the interior of the world on which they have conferred the boon of political unity.

In universal states founded by aliens or barbarians the imperial capital is apt to start on the edge of the empire and to travel towards the interior. When the empire-builders are marchmen the same tendency sometimes asserts itself, but in this situation there are sometimes counter-pulls which tend to hold the capital in its original location. A margrave-emperor may find himself still tied to his ancestral base of operations in the back-woods by the continuance of pressure from the barbarians whom it is his first duty to keep at bay; and, if he does now succeed in disposing of this barbarian menace once for all by mobilizing against it the total resources of the society which he has united under his imperial rule, this very success may have the effect of extending his dominions so far afield into former barbarian territory that his seat of imperial government at the headquarters of his former march is consequently relegated to the interior of his expanded empire. In universal states founded by metropolitans the capital is, of course, likely to be located from the beginning at some point in the interior which is convenient for oecumenical administration, but nevertheless it may be drawn away towards a frontier if a threat of aggression from that quarter comes to be the imperial government's paramount concern. It is evident that the changes in the location of the seats of government of universal states are subject to certain 'laws' of political geography, but that the operation of these 'laws' is modified, in practice, by such complicated combinations of historical contingencies that particular cases have to be examined and analysed *ad hoc*.

Migrations of the Capital Cities of Alien Empire-builders

The operation of the 'law' governing the location of capitals of universal states founded by alien empire-builders is illustrated in the history of the British Rāj in India.[1] Reaching India, as they did, from overseas, and coming there to trade with the inhabitants before they ever dreamed of ruling over them, the English established their first footholds on Indian ground in the seaports Calcutta, Madras, and Bombay; and, of these three British maritime commercial settlements, Calcutta became the first political capital of British India because the East India Company happened to acquire the political dominion over the two great provinces Bengal and Bihar, in the hinterland of Calcutta, some forty or fifty years before they began to make any comparable acquisitions of territory in the

[1] See xi, map 53.

hinterlands of Madras and Bombay. Calcutta continued to be the capital of British India for more than a hundred years after the design of bringing all India under British rule had been first conceived by Wellesley (*proconsulari munere fungebatur* A.D. 1798–1805) and for more than sixty years after this ambition had been achieved. But the gravitational pull of a politically unified sub-continent eventually proved strong enough to draw the seat of the British Indian central government away from Calcutta, where it had been located for the convenience of a British thalassocracy, and to attract it to Delhi,[1] which was the natural site for the capital of a continental empire including the basins of both the Ganges and the Indus.

Delhi was, of course, not merely a natural site; it was also an historic one. The Mughal predecessors of the British rulers of India had governed India from Delhi since the days of Shāh Jahān (*imperabat* A.D. 1628–59),[2] and before Shāh Jahān's day they had governed it from the neighbouring city of Agra,[3] which was situated, like Delhi, on the banks of the Upper Jumna. The Mughals, like the British, had been aliens in the Hindu World on which they had imposed a universal state, but, unlike the British, they had never tried to govern India from a site on the threshold across which they had made their entry. It is true that the Mughals had arrived in India as fugitives from their own country; yet, when once they had placed the barrier of the Hindu Kush between themselves and their Uzbeg pursuers, they might have been tempted to establish their seat of government on some site in the highlands of North-Eastern Iran, where the climate, scenery, and fruits would have resembled those of their lost but lovingly remembered Farghānah. It is noteworthy that Bābur and his successors never in fact cast Kābul for the role of an imperial capital. As soon as they found themselves strong enough to descend upon the plains of the Panjab and Hindustan, they not only conquered them; they also immediately planted their seat of government on the sultry banks of the Jumna, in the heart of their newly acquired dominions. On the administrative map of the Mughal Empire, Kābul was merely the local capital of the north-western march and was never the overland equivalent of the maritime capital at Calcutta from which India was ruled by British hands for a century.

The Spanish *conquistadores* who established a universal state in Central America and took possession of a universal state in the Andean World were alien intruders from overseas like the British conquerors of India,

---

[1] The transfer of the capital of the British Indian Empire to Delhi in A.D. 1912 has already been touched upon in II. ii. 132.

[2] See II. ii. 131, with n. 3, for the establishment of the capital of the Mughal Empire at Delhi from the reign of Shāh Jahān onwards and for the previous history of Delhi, first as a frontier fortress of the Hindu World against Muslim aggression and afterwards as the capital of successive Muslim rulers of Hindustan from the Muslim conquest of the Ganges Basin at the turn of the twelfth and thirteenth centuries of the Christian Era down to the replacement of a Lōdī Afghan by a Mughal Turkish rāj in the sixteenth century.

[3] Akbar's attempt to establish a new capital *ex nihilo* at Fātihpūr Sīkrī was no more successful than his attempt to launch a new higher religion, the Dīn Ilāhī (for these two failures of Akbar's, see II. ii. 131, n. 3, and V. v. 699–704). It is noteworthy that Ikhnaton, who likewise tried and failed to launch a new religion of his own invention, also made a similarly unsuccessful attempt to establish a new capital city at Tall-al-'Amarnah (see p. 215, below).

but, in the location of their seats of government, the Spaniards did not make the move from an original capital on the coast to a subsequent capital in the interior; in this matter they went to opposite extremes in the two new worlds of which they made themselves masters. In the Andean World they laid out a maritime capital at Lima which they never abandoned in favour of the inland capital at Cuzco from which the Andean Realm of the Four Quarters had previously been ruled by the Incas. In Central America, on the other hand, they never attempted to govern their dominions from the seaport which they laid out at Vera Cruz. They immediately located their seat of government in the interior on the site of Tenochtitlan—the highland capital of the Aztecs who were in the act of building a Central American universal state when the Spaniards suddenly came on the scene and usurped the Aztecs' role.

Why did the Spaniards thus adopt opposite policies in two at first sight similar situations? The Mexican Plateau may have attracted them by its resemblance to their native plateau of Castile; yet, if that was the decisive consideration, why did it not lead them to pass over Lima, as they passed over Vera Cruz, and locate their Andean seat of government in the highland city of Cuzco, which was the existing capital from which the Andean universal state was actually being governed by the Incas at the time of the Spaniards' arrival? The explanation of this apparent inconsistency may lie in a difference in the previous historical roles of the respective environs of Vera Cruz and Lima. The lowlands lying between the Mexican Plateau and the shores of the Gulf were no longer playing a great part in the life of the Mexic Civilization. By contrast, the lowlands lying between the Andean Plateau and the shores of the Pacific Ocean had been the cradle of the Andean Civilization and had lost none of their economic or cultural importance since their political incorporation into an Andean universal state established by Inca empire-builders from the highlands.[1] Thus, in consulting their own convenience by abandoning the highland capital of the Incas at Cuzco and establishing their own seat of government in the seaport of Lima, the Spaniards were at the same time selecting a site in the cultural heart of the Andean World.

We may even raise the question whether the Incas themselves might have been impelled to transfer their seat of government from their ancestral capital at Cuzco to some site in the coastal lowlands if their dominion had endured for its natural term instead of having been abruptly brought to an end by the Spanish conquest not more than a hundred years after the establishment of an Andean universal state by the Inca Pachacutec (*imperabat circa* A.D. 1400–48). The decisive act in the elevation of the Inca Empire into an Andean universal state had been Pachacutec's conquest of the lowland states along the seaboard; and, with the passage of time, this epoch-making addition to the Empire's domain might well have affected its administrative structure. In the empire which Pachacutec put together and Pizarro took over, Cuzco was not more centrally situated than Lima; for the Incas had won their way by serving as marchmen, and their ancestral city had become an imperial capital without ceasing to be a frontier fortress guarding the eastern brow of the Andean Plateau against the fierce and aggressive barbarians of the Amazonian tropical forest.[1] If the Incas had been given a longer time to harvest the experience of administering an empire in which highlands and lowlands were linked together, it seems not unlikely that they might have followed up their scientific redistribution of population[2] by a transfer of the seat of their central government. Indeed, before the Spaniards arrived, the Incas had already built two imperial palaces on the coast.[3]

The Ottoman dominion over Orthodox Christendom and the Mongol dominion over China were established, like the Mughal Rāj in India, by invasion overland, and not, like the British Rāj in India or the Spanish Empire in the New World, by assault from across the sea; yet, in the location of their capital cities, their histories followed the British and not the Mughal pattern.

The 'Osmanlis started their empire-building operations from a base just beyond the eastern borders of the Orthodox Christian World within the limits to which Orthodox Christendom had been reduced by the turn of the thirteenth and fourteenth centuries of the Christian Era,[4] and, as the 'Osmanlis' dominions expanded, their seat of government travelled *pari passu*. First it moved from Eskishehr, 'the old city' just within the north-western rim of the Anatolian Plateau, to Yenishehr, 'the new city' in the lowlands within range of the Sea of Marmara. In A.D. 1326 it moved on to Brusa. In A.D. 1366 it leapt the Dardanelles and entered the Balkan Peninsula, into which the centre of gravity of the Orthodox Christian World had already shifted since the Saljūq Turkish conquest of the interior of Anatolia in the later decades of the eleventh century of the Christian Era.[5] The first location of the Ottoman capital in the Balkan Peninsula was at Adrianople, but this was only a halting-place and not its final destination.[6] The Ottoman Sultan Mehmed the Conqueror (*imperabat* A.D. 1451–81), who completed the political unification of the main body of the Orthodox Christian World under Ottoman rule, was also the statesman who brought the Ottoman seat of government to its final resting-place at Constantinople, the former capital of the East Roman Empire and the cultural metropolis of Orthodox Christendom. Constantinople did not lose the status which Mehmed the Conqueror had conferred upon her till after the Ottoman Empire itself had been snuffed out of existence through the reconstitution of an Anatolian remnant of Mehmed the Conqueror's realm into a Republic of Turkey on the 29th October, 1923. In virtue of Article 2 of the Constitution of the 20th April, 1924, Constantinople forfeited juridically to Ankara the role of being the official seat of government of this Turkish successor-state.[7]

[1] See II. ii. 207.   [2] For this, see pp. 114–15, above.
[3] See Markham, Sir C.: *The Incas of Peru* (London 1910, Smith Elder), p. 238.
[4] See II. ii. 151.   [5] See II. ii. 79–80 and 152.
[6] See p 135, n. 1, above.
[7] Since the autumn of 1919 Ankara had, of course, been the *de facto* provisional seat of the revolutionary Kemalist movement out of which the Republic of Turkey had sprung.

The progressive advance of the capital of the Ottoman Empire towards the heart of the Orthodox Christian World has a parallel in the series of stages by which the capital of the Mongol Khāqāns followed the China-ward course of Mongol conquest. The first signal successes in Chingis Khan's career were his conquests of the Karāyits and Naimans,[1] the two Nestorian Turkish Nomad peoples whom the Mongols found in occupation of the choicest portion of the High Steppe[2] in the basin of the River Orkhon. By a long-established tradition the Orkhon Basin was the domain of the paramount Nomad community on the High Steppe,[3] and, when the Mongols acquired this paramountcy in their turn by the customary right of conquest, and then proceeded to extend their rule over a number of sedentary societies round about, their first essay in living up to their newly attained dignity and making use of their newly acquired wealth was to lay out a permanent capital for themselves in the Orkhon Basin at Qāraqorum.[4] For the translation of this dream into reality, skilled artificers were uprooted from their distant homes in China, Russia, and Western Christendom and were carried away captive to beautify the Khāqān's rising city on the Steppe;[5] but before the work was finished it was made of no avail by the triumph of Mongol arms on the Chinese front.

The Mongol Khāqān Qubilāy (*imperabat* A.D. 1259–94) achieved what had proved beyond the strength of the Mongol conquerors' Kin and Khitan forerunners. He conquered not merely Northern China but the whole continental domain of the Far Eastern Society, including the Yangtse Basin and the southern seaboard; and the gravitational pull of this Far Eastern sub-continent, now once more politically united, im-mediately made itself felt in the location of the Mongol Khāqān's capital. In A.D. 1264 Qubilāy began to recondition Peking—the site in the north-east corner of China, just inside the Great Wall, where the previous Kin conquerors of Northern China had placed their seat of government[6]—and in A.D. 1267 he moved his own capital to Peking from Qāraqorum.[7] Though Qubilāy's head dictated this move, his heart remained homesick for its ancestral pastures, and the semi-Sinified

---

[1] See V. v. 250 and 309.

[2] The Great Eurasian Steppe consisted of two areas which were geographically distinct, though both had been theatres of one uniform Nomad way of life. There was the High Steppe (the Alexandrian Hellenic geographer Ptolemy's Scythia extra Imaum) on the immense plateau which was bounded on the west by the Altai and Tien Shan Mountains, and there was the Low Steppe (Ptolemy's Scythia intra Imaum) which extended westward from the Tien Shan to the Carpathians. The two areas were in communication with one another through the Zungarian Gap between Tien Shan and Altai.

[3] This position had been occupied in succession by the Hiongnu, the Juan Juan, the Northern Turks, and the eastern Turkish successors of the united Turkish steppe-empire of the sixth and seventh centuries of the Christian Era. The eighth-century Turkish masters of the Orkhon Basin had left there a memorial of themselves in their celebrated inscriptions. It was not an accident that the seat of government of a latter-day Soviet Socialist Republic of Outer Mongolia was located in the same neighbourhood, at Urga.   [4] See III. iii. 397 and V. v. 312–15.

[5] See Olschki, L.: *Guillaume Boucher, A French Artist at the Court of the Khans* (Baltimore 1946, The Johns Hopkins Press).

[6] The Kin themselves had taken the site over from their own predecessors the Khitan, who had laid the foundations of Peking's political fortunes by choosing this hitherto obscure spot for the location, not of their central seat of government, but of their southern residence.   See II. ii. 121, n. 3.

Mongol statesman indulged his unregenerate Nomad feelings by building himself a subsidiary residence at Chung-tu, a point on the south-eastern rim of the Mongolian Plateau where the Steppe approached nearest to the new imperial city.[1] But Qubilāy's 'Xanadu' was a 'pleasure dome' and no more; his serious business of state was transacted at Peking. The requirements of a conquered world had won a pacific victory over the inclinations of its conqueror which was to have a more lasting effect than the Mongols' mere military victory over the Empire of the Sung.

When the Manchus followed in the Mongols' footsteps by conquering the whole of China and reconstituting a Far Eastern universal state in the seventeenth century of the Christian Era after an interlude of some two centuries during which China had managed to keep herself free from barbarian rule, history duly repeated itself in the location of the imperial capital. Before the Manchus set about the conquest of China within the Wall, they had already made a new capital for themselves at Mukden,[2] the South Manchurian meeting-point of the Manchus' native forests, the Mongols' pastures, and the arable land, beyond the shelter of the Wall, which had been won for the plough by Chinese peasant pioneers in the course of ages. The Manchus were more firmly planted at Mukden than the Mongols had been at Qāraqorum. Their leaders, at any rate, were already half Sinified before they crossed the Great Wall, and Mukden had become a seat not merely of Manchu government but of Chinese culture. Yet the Manchu conquerors of China took the same decision as the Mongol Qubilāy. The guardians of the Manchu boy-king Shun Chih (*imperabat* A.D. 1644–61), when they proclaimed him Emperor, transferred the Manchu seat of government to Peking[3] and allowed Mukden—which had been 'the education of' the Manchus—to sink to a subordinate status.[4] The Manchu rulers of China made the same concession to their own home-sickness as their Mongol forerunners. They built for themselves a counterpart of Qubilāy's Chung-tu in the shape of a magnificent holiday resort at Jehol, a highland paradise on the road back from Peking to the dynasty's original home in the hill-country of North-Eastern Manchuria. Yet, in spite of this backward gesture, the requirements of a conquered China had overcome the inclinations of her conquerors once again.[5]

---

[1] See vol. cit., loc. cit.

[2] Mukden was founded by the second prince of the Manchu Dynasty, T'ai Tsung (*extra Murum regnabat* A.D. 1625–43).

[3] See II. ii. 123.

[4] Mukden (*Sinicè* Shêngking) did retain some vestiges of its former status. For instance, the Manchu Emperor Ch'ien Lung (*imperabat* A.D. 1736–96) directed in A.D. 1782 that one of four fair copies of the manuscript of his Ssu-k'u Ch'üan Shu ('The Four Treasuries') which were designed for official use was to be lodged at Mukden in a building specially erected to hold it (see Mayers, W. F.: 'Bibliography of the Chinese Imperial Collections of Literature', in the *China Review*, vol. vi (1877–8), No. 5, p. 295). The writer of this Study had the privilege of being taken to see this building, the Wên So Ko, with Ch'ien Lung's immense *corpus scriptorum Sinarum* still safely housed in it, on the 17th November, 1929. The corresponding buildings for housing the other three official fair copies were located respectively in the precincts of the Imperial Palace at Peking, at Yüan-ming Yüan, and at Jehol (see further X. ix. 56).

[5] When the gravitational pull of a united China had drawn the Mongols' capital to Peking from Qāraqorum and the Manchus' capital to Peking from Mukden, why, in both cases, did the change of location go thus far and no farther? Why did the seat of imperial

We may conclude this survey of the histories of the capital cities of alien empire-builders by considering one of those exceptions that sometimes prove a rule.

When the successors of Alexander were contending for the spoils of the Achaemenian Empire, Seleucus Nicator made his fortune by concentrating his efforts on gaining possession of the vast interior. There was less keen competition for this prize than for provinces with seaboards on the Mediterranean that offered their Macedonian holders an easy access to the heart of the Hellenic World round the shores of the Aegean Sea; yet the prize on which Seleucus had set his heart was attractive for an empire-builder with the vision to divine its possibilities. Babylonia, which Seleucus had selected for his base of operations, had been both the granary and the industrial workshop of the Achaemenian Empire,[1] and, apart from its economic value, it was the strategic key to the political control of all the ex-Achaemenian provinces to the north-east of it, up to the southern borders of Nomads' Land in Central Asia and the western borders of Chandragupta's Indic Empire in Eastern Iran.[2] Seleucus saw this prize, won it, and made statesmanlike provision for retaining it by laying out, and stamping with his own name, a new metropolis in Babylonia on the right bank of the Tigris at the point where Tigris and Euphrates approached nearest to one another. Seleucia-on-Tigris was a better site than Babylon both for the administration of Babylonia itself and for the command of the great North-East Road linking the Lower Tigris–Euphrates Basin with the Upper Oxus–Jaxartes Basin over the crown of the Iranian Plateau. Thanks to the skill which Seleucus displayed in its location,[3] Seleucia-on-Tigris remained an important city and a flourishing centre of Hellenic life and culture for more than five centuries after its foundation towards the end of the fourth century B.C.[4] But it missed its political destiny through an error of political judgement committed by the founder himself.

The sagacity of Seleucus's original design for constructing a successor-state of the Achaemenian Empire out of its dominions east of Euphrates was conclusively demonstrated after the Seleucid Dynasty's demise by

government come to rest at Peking, instead of travelling on to Loyang on the Yellow River or to Nanking on the Yangtse? Loyang and Nanking had been historic imperial capitals in the past. Why did History fail to repeat itself to this extent on these two occasions? And why did it eventually repeat itself to this extent in A.D. 1928? An attempt to find the answers to these questions has been made in II. ii. 121–7.

[1] According to Herodotus, Book I, chap. 192, Babylonia supplied the Achaemenian court's and mobile army's requirements in kind for four months out of every twelve (cp. p. 205, n. 4, below).

[2] For the analogy between the Seleucid and the Umayyad control over the Iranian Plateau from a base on the plains of the Land of Shinar (alias Babylonia, alias 'Irāq 'Arabī), see p. 137, n. 4, above. This portion of the former Achaemenian Empire lying east of Euphrates, which Seleucus marked out for his own share, was the portion which the last Darius had proposed to retain for himself when, during the interval between the battles of Issus and Arbela, he had offered to divide the Empire with Alexander.

[3] Whereas Seleucia was an artificial foundation deliberately located with an eye to its possibilities as an oecumenical capital, Babylon had become an oecumenical capital through the accident that the Amorite marchmen of the Sumeric World, who had established themselves there on the borders between the Desert and the Sown, had eventually played the part of restorers of a Sumeric universal state (see II ii. 133, and pp. 226–8, below).

[4] The exact date of the foundation of Seleucia-on-Tigris is not known (see Bouché-Leclercq, A.: Histoire des Séleucides (Paris 1913–14, Leroux, 2 vols.), vol. ii, pp. 524–5.

the histories of the Arsacid and Sasanian Powers, each of which lasted for some four hundred years within these limits, whereas the Sasanian Empire came to grief still more quickly than its Seleucid predecessor when it seriously attempted, under the misguided impulsion of Khusrū Parwīz, to extend its dominions westward to the shores of the Mediterranean and the Bosphorus. Seleucus was enticed to his own death and his dynasty's eventual undoing by the completeness of the triumph of two successive coalitions of Macedonian war-lords in which Seleucus found himself each time on the winning side. In 301 B.C. at the Battle of Ipsus, Seleucus of Babylonia, in alliance with Ptolemy of Egypt and Lysimachus of Thrace, succeeded in overthrowing their common adversary Antigonus, who, from his commanding central position in Syria and Anatolia, had aspired to reassemble all the fragments of the Achaemenian Empire under his own rule at the expense of his fellow successors. Thereafter, in 281 B.C., at the Battle of Corupedium, Lysimachus, in his turn, was overthrown by Seleucus and Ptolemy. The cumulative effect of these two decisive successes was to give Seleucus Nicator, who had originally made his way without access to the western seas, both a Syrian seaboard on the Mediterranean and an Ionian seaboard on the Aegean; and this westward expansion of his empire exposed Nicator and his successors to temptations which they failed to resist.

Nicator himself took over Antigonus's half-built capital city Antigoneia-on-Orontes, within one short day's march from the northeast corner of the Mediterranean, and removed it to a more commanding adjacent site to become the capital of his own monarchy under the name of Antioch,[1] and he met his death on his road to Macedon by way of his newly acquired and precariously far-flung dominions in Western Anatolia and Thrace.[2] In the sequel, Seleucus's successors drained away the resources of Babylonia and the Iranian provinces on the farther side of Babylonia in an inconclusive struggle with a mobile and elusive Ptolemaic sea-power for the command of the coasts of the Levant all the way round from Gaza to the Hellespont;[3] and even the ultimate success of the Seleucidae in this warfare between the elephant and the whale was fraught with disaster. When, in 200–198 B.C., Antiochus the Great conquered Coele Syria from Ptolemy Eurgetes' feeble successor Ptolemy Epiphanes, he was bequeathing to his successors the insoluble problem of dealing with the Jewish temple-state in the hill-country between the two branches of 'the King's Highway';[4]

---

[1] See p. 94, above.   [2] See p. 94, above.
[3] One object of this misguided Seleucid policy was to keep open an overland pipe-line through which soldiers and settlers from the heart of the Hellenic World round the shores of the Aegean could be pumped into the interior of the Seleucid dominions; but these reinforcements of Greek manpower could assuredly have been obtained even if the Seleucid Monarchy had not spent its resources in trying to maintain a maritime frontage. The dominant consideration was the prestige attaching to suzerainty over historic Greek city-states, however insignificant. We may recall the equally misguided Hapsburg policy of spending the resources of the Danubian Monarchy during the eighteenth century of the Christian Era in efforts to retain possession of Silesia, the Southern Netherlands and the Breisgau, at the cost of letting slip a golden opportunity for wresting from the Ottoman Empire the whole of South-Eastern Europe between Vienna and Constantinople (see II. ii. 180–6 and cp. III. iii. 301–6).
[4] See pp. 100–2, above, and xi, maps 11, 14, 20, and 21A.

and, when he proceeded to reassert the claim of his house to Seleucus Nicator's acquisitions on both sides of the Hellespont, the result was an irretrievably disastrous collision with the overwhelmingly superior power of Rome.

While the Seleucidae were absorbed in gaining or losing some canton, city-state, or islet on the western fringes of their expanded dominions, they were losing one province after another in the neglected, exploited, but indispensable East. By 248–247 B.C., fifty-four years after Seleucus Nicator's ill-omened victory at Ipsus, the Parnian Nomads had established themselves in the Seleucid province of Parthia astride the Great North-East Road at the point where it descended from the Iranian Plateau towards the Oxus, and the consequent insulation of the Oxus–Jaxartes Basin from the main body of the Seleucid Monarchy quickly resulted in the establishment of an independent state by the Greek 'ascendancy' there.[1] When the Arsacid war-lords of the Parni went on to occupy Media, where the Great North-East Road[2] made its way through the western mountain ramparts of the Iranian Plateau, and when they proceeded, through this open gate, to descend upon Babylonia itself in 142 B.C., they were tearing out the Seleucid Monarchy's heart; and, after Demetrius Nicator's and Antiochus Sîdêtês' successive attempts in 140 and 130 B.C. to reconquer Babylonia and Media had ended in repeated disaster, the remnant of the Seleucid Empire in Syria was doomed to extinction at an early date. The Seleucid Monarchy met its ignominious end when Tigranes King of Armenia—a hitherto obscure non-Hellenic successor-state of the shattered empire of Antiochus the Great[3]—unconsciously avenged the overthrow of Antigonus Monophthalmus by occupying Antioch-on-Orontes in 83 B.C.

Such was the nemesis of Seleucus Nicator's momentous decision to establish the seat of his central government on a site adjoining his defeated rival Antigonus's abortive capital at Antigoneia-on-Orontes instead of establishing it in a metropolis of his own creation at Seleucia-on-Tigris.[4] Nicator could not conjure away inexorable geographical facts which had once been apparent to him by disguising a virtual reconstruction of Antigoneia under a family name of his own;[5] for a site command-

---

[1] See II. ii. 143–4. This Greek Power in Bactria seems to have established its independence gradually between 246 and 228 B.C. (see Tarn, W. W.: *The Greeks in Bactria and India* (Cambridge 1938, University Press), pp. 72–74).   [2] See xi, map 20.

[3] The creation of the Kingdom of Armenia Major by the House of Artaxias—a former lieutenant of Antiochus the Great's who declared his independence after his suzerain's disastrous defeat by the Romans in 190 B.C.—is touched upon on p. 626, below.

[4] It is worth noticing that the corresponding false step was avoided by both the Arsacid and the Sasanian successor-states of the Seleucid Monarchy, each of which lasted nearly twice as long as the Seleucid Monarchy itself. The Arsacidae, and the Sasanidae after them, unhesitatingly established their seat of government at Ctesiphon, a suburb of Seleucia-on-Tigris which was presumably called after the name of the Greek who had originally laid it out, and which was situated on the farther side of the river, on its Iranian bank. The Arsacidae did not attempt to govern Babylonia from Hecatompylos, their previous capital at the north-eastern exit of the Caspian Gates between the central desert of Iran and the Elburz Range; and the Sasanidae did not attempt to govern it from Istakhr, their previous capital in Fars. Istakhr and Hecatompylos both gave way to Ctesiphon, as, in the Far Eastern World, Mukden gave way to Peking after the Manchu conquest of China (see p. 199, above).

[5] Seleucus named his new capital in the neighbourhood of Antigoneia 'Antiocheia after his own father Antiochus.

ing the landward end of the gorge down which the River Orontes forced its way through a coastal range of mountains to the Mediterranean was as unsuitable for the capital of an empire whose heart lay in Babylonia and whose eastern provinces extended across the Iranian Plateau into the Oxus–Jaxartes Basin as it had been felicitous for the capital of an empire which, like Antigonus's empire in its last phase, had been virtually confined to Anatolia and Syria and had not extended farther into the interior of Asia than the western bank of the Euphrates in the section of the river's course in which it approached nearest to the Mediterranean. When eventually the founder's descendants Demetrius Nicator (*imperabat primum* 145–139 B.C.) and Antiochus Sîdêtês (*imperabat* 139/8–129 B.C.) were made keenly aware of the indispensability of Babylonia by the painful experience of the consequences of its loss, the elder brother forfeited his liberty and the younger his life in vainly seeking to undo the untoward effects of the century and a half that had elapsed between the establishment of the capital at Antioch by their ancestor the first Seleucus in 300 B.C. and their own ill-fated expeditions on the forlorn hope of recovering Seleucia. If the change made by Seleucus I in his focus of geographical interest had been the other way about—from the banks of the Orontes, on the western edge of the Achaemenian dominions, to the banks of the Tigris in their heart—the Seleucid Monarchy might have had a longer and a happier history.

Migrations of the Capital Cities of Barbarian Empire-builders

Having now surveyed the shifts in the seats of administration of universal states founded or captured by aliens, we may turn to a consideration of the cases in which the empire-builders were barbarians or marchmen.[1] We may begin with the Persian barbaro-marchmen who gave the Syriac World its universal state, and the Arab barbarians who reconstituted the Empire of the Achaemenidae after a thousand-years-long interlude of Hellenic intrusion.

'The homeland of the Persians lies out of the way of the theatres of historical life. The great highroad that links the West with the Eastern World[2] runs, from Babylon towards the interior, up the valley of the Gyndes [Diyālah] and out of it into the valley of the Upper Choaspes [Karkhah], past the rock of Behistan [*alias* Bisitun], to Ecbatana [Hamadan], and from here it proceeds along the northern rim of the Iranian Plateau. And so we find that, although the Persians, like the Arabs, have repeatedly launched far-sweeping movements, their country has never been able to become the permanent centre of a great state. As soon as the reaction sets in, Persis [Pārsa, Fars] once more disappears, for centuries on end, from the stage of historic life.'[3]

According to a story with which Herodotus concludes his work,[4] Cyrus the Great deprecated a suggestion that the Persian people, now

---

[1] The Manchu Empire, whose founders were barbaro-marchmen, has been considered already, by anticipation, in connexion with the Mongol Empire in China, whose founders were barbarians with a tincture of alien culture; and the Inca Empire, whose founders were marchmen, in connexion with the Spanish Empire by which it was supplanted.

[2] See xi, map 20.—A.J.T.

[3] Meyer, E.: *Geschichte des Altertums*, vol. iii, 1st ed. (Stuttgart 1901, Cotta), p. 22.

[4] The passage has been quoted in the present Study in II. ii. 21.

that they had become masters of the World, should evacuate their bleak highland homeland and settle in one of the many more agreeable countries that were now at their disposal. But, whether or not it was the Achaemenian Government's policy to discourage the Persian people as a whole from migrating to more genial tracts of their newly acquired empire, it is an historical fact that, more than a hundred years before the Empire was established through Cyrus II's overthrow of his Median suzerain Cyaxares, the Achaemenian Dynasty had transferred its own seat of government from its ancestral highlands—which stood not in Fars (Pārsa) but in Lūristān (Parsuwaš)—to the first piece of lowland territory of which it had gained possession. King Teispes of Parsuwaš (*regnabat circa* 675–640 B.C.), the son and first successor of Achaemenes the dynasty's founder and eponym, figures in the Assyrian records as 'King of the city of Anšan';[1] and Anšan was believed by twentieth-century Western scholars to have lain somewhere in the neighbourhood of both the Babylonian district of Der and the city of Susa, the capital of Elam—perhaps at some point where a fortress would command the corridor of lowland territory linking the plains of Elam with the plains of Babylonia between the south-eastern extremity of the Kabīr Kuh Range's Pusht-i-Kuh foothills and the northern extremity of the swamps through which, in that age, the rivers Kārūn, Tigris, and Euphrates made their separate exits into the Persian Gulf.[2] The importance attached to this earliest acquisition of the Achaemenids in the lowlands is attested in the retention of the title 'King of Anšan' by Teispes himself and by his first three successors in the elder branch of his house—Cyrus I, Cambyses I, and Cyrus II the Great[3]—even after Teispes had taken the opportunity to make himself master of Pārsa, on the far side of Elam, while Elam and Assyria were engaged in the last and most exhausting of the Assyro-Elamite wars (*gerebatur circa* 663–638 B.C.), and even after the reunion of the two portions of Teispes' dominions in the hands of the elder branch of Teispes' line—which seems to have come to pass, in or shortly before the year 547 B.C., through the deposition of King Arsāmês (Aršāma), the son of Cyrus I's younger brother Ariaramnes (Ariyāramna) and the heir of Ariaramnes' appanage Pārsa, by Cambyses I's son and Cyrus I's grandson Cyrus II the Great.[4]

For more than a hundred years after the Achaemenidae had acquired their footing in the lowlands of Anšan, just to the west of Susa, and for not much less than a hundred years after they had gone on to acquire the highlands of Pārsa, to the south-east of Elam, Susa remained in non-Achaemenian hands. The former capital of Elam was annexed by Assyria after she had erased Elam from the political map[5] and was inherited

---

[1] See Cameron, G. G.: *A History of Early Iran* (Chicago 1936, Chicago University Press), p. 180; Olmstead, A. T.: *A History of the Persian Empire* (Chicago 1948, Chicago University Press), p. 23.   [2] See p. 621, below.
[3] See König, F. W.: *Älteste Geschichte der Meder und Perser* (Leipzig 1934, Hinrichs), p. 10; Cameron, op. cit., pp. 212 and 218.
[4] According to F. H. Weissbach in Pauly–Wissowa: *Realencyclopädie der Classischen Altertumswissenschaft*, Neue Bearbeitung, Supplementband iv, cols. 1141-2, s.v. 'Kyros', followed by Kent, R. G., in his *Old Persian: Grammar, Texts, Lexicon* (New Haven, Conn. 1950, American Oriental Society), p. 159.
[5] See Cameron, op. cit., p. 211.

from Assyria by Assyria's Neo-Babylonian successor-state. There was archaeological evidence that Susa was included in the Neo-Babylonian Empire in Nebuchadnezzar's day (*imperabat* 605–562 B.C.);[1] and it was not till after his death[2] that the Achaemenian Kingdom managed to gain possession of a city which, ever since Teispes' acquisition of Pārsa, had insulated the dynasty's major new dominion from its minor original patrimony as awkwardly as, from A.D. 1466 to A.D. 1772, the two sections of the Hohenzollern dominions were insulated from one another by a city-state of Danzig under Polish suzerainty marching with a corridor of Polish territory extending to the shore of the Baltic Sea and thereby cutting East Prussia off from Prussian Pomerania and Brandenburg.

After Susa had at last fallen into Achaemenian hands, it was as inevitable that the capital of the Achaemenian Empire should be transferred to Susa from Anšan as it was that the capital of the Ottoman Empire should be transferred to Constantinople from Adrianople after Sultan Mehmed II's capture of the Second Rome in A.D. 1453; and this step was duly taken by Darius I before the end of the year 521 B.C.[3] It will be seen that the geographical situation of Susa *vis-à-vis* the highlands of Fars, the highlands of Lūristān, and the great plain of Shinar was comparable to the position of Peking *vis-à-vis* the highlands of Eastern Manchuria, the Orkhon High Steppe and the great plain of Northern China. The site lay between the semi-barbarian empire-builders' two main reservoirs of military man-power in a corner of the lowlands that were the Empire's main granary and workshop; and the site's proximity to the military reservoirs was the reason for its selection and retention notwithstanding the inconvenience of its location for the purpose of administering the Empire as a whole.

In Darius's reorganization of the Achaemenian Empire it proved not impossible to lead into Susa both the Great North-East Road and the Great North-West Road; yet this achievement of the Achaemenian ministry of works remained something of a *tour de force*, and the awkwardness, even of Susa, as a seat of government for an empire extending to the Jaxartes, Indus, Nile, and Danube, is attested by the fact that the Achaemenian Imperial Court did not reside in the official capital of the Achaemenian Empire year in and year out, but moved round in an annual migration between Susa and two other imperial residences.[4] The winter residence was Babylon, which was far better placed than Susa, though not quite so well placed as the future Seleucia-

---

[1] 'Bricks [identical in make with bricks of Nebuchadnezzar's found at Babylon, and stamped] with his name were used to erect buildings in that city, while an alabaster vase with his inscription and a weight with his legend are further witnesses of his control' (Cameron, op. cit., pp. 219–20).

[2] According to Cameron, op. cit., p. 221, Susa, together with the rest of the lowlands of Elam, was lost by the Neo-Babylonian Empire to the Achaemenidae before Nabonidus's accession in 556 B.C. According to Olmstead, op. cit., p. 43, it was lost when, in 546 B.C., the Neo-Babylonian Government's commandant of the citadel of Susa, Gobryas, turned traitor and joined forces with Cyrus II.   [3] See Olmstead, op. cit., p. 119.

[4] According to Xenophon: *Expeditio Cyri*, Book III, chap. v, § 15, and *Cyropaedia*, Book VIII, chap. vi, § 22, the Achaemenian Court used to spend seven winter months in Babylon, two summer months in Ecbatana, and only three spring months out of every twelve at Susa (cp. p. 200, n. 1, above).

on-Tigris, for serving as the point of junction of the two main imperial highways.[1] The summer residence was Ecbatana (Hamadan), the former capital of the Median Power, which lay at the strategically important point on the Great North-East Road where this highway dropped down to the level of the Iranian Plateau after surmounting the Zagros Range that walled in the plateau on the west.[2]

The significant point here for the purpose of our present investigation is that the Achaemenian Court's fixed annual time-table of circulation from one imperial residence to another does not appear to have allowed for any regular annual residence at any site in the Persian homeland of the imperial people. The Achaemenian emperors showed their reverence for Pārsa by being crowned there and their affection for it by being buried there. Cyrus built for himself a tomb (still standing at the time of writing) in the Persian canton of Clan Pasargadae,[3] near the latter-day village of Murghāb; and, lower down the course of the little River Pulvār, Darius and his successors hewed out their sepulchres in the face of a cliff at the point latterly known as Naqsh-i-Rustam.[4] Cyrus is said also to have built for Clan Pasargadae in the course of the years 559–550 B.C. a city called by the clan name;[5] and between 512 and 494 B.C.[6] Darius I

[1] Seleucia-on-Tigris was skilfully sited by its Macedonian founder to serve as the point of junction not only between the Great North-East Road and the Great North-West Road, but also between the two alinements of the latter. The north-eastern aline-ment of the Great North-West Road, as described by Herodotus (Book V, chaps. 52–3), ran from Susa to Ephesus to the east of the middle course of the Tigris and to the north of the central desert of Anatolia. The south-eastern alinement ran from Susa to Ephesus via Babylon and the east bank of the middle course of the Euphrates through the Cilician Gates. The north-eastern alinement traversed the derelict capitals of both Assyria and the Hittite Power. The south-western alinement was followed by Cyrus the Younger in 401 B.C. and by Alexander in 434–433 B.C., and it became the life-line of Seleucus Nicator's dominions after he had extended them to the shores of the Mediterranean and the Aegean, since the more southerly of the two Iranian successor-states of the Achae-menian Empire in Cappadocia succeeded in maintaining itself astride of the north-eastern branch.

[2] The choice of Ecbatana for the summer residence of the Achaemenian Court was doubtless partly due to the coolness of its climate and partly to its historic prestige as the former capital of the Median Power which the Achaemenian Empire had supplanted. Under the Achaemenian régime, even after its reorganization by Darius I on a narrower political basis, the Medes were second only to the Persians in the hierarchy of imperial peoples. At the same time the selection of this site at a key-point on the Great North-East Road is also evidence of the high priority of the North-East Frontier among Achaemenian cares of state.

[3] According to Herodotus, Book I, chap. 125, the House of Achaemenes was one of the septs of this Clan Pasargadae. Are we to infer that the Pasargadae had migrated from Lūristān to Fars either at the time of the acquisition of Fars by the Achaemenid king of Parsuwaš-and-Anšan, Teispes, or else at the time of its acquisition by Teispes' great-grandson the Cyran Achaemenid King of Parsuwaš-and-Anšan, Cyrus II?

[4] The shock administered to the Persian people by their sudden overthrow from their high estate through the prowess of their Macedonian conquerors was so severe that it broke the continuity of their folk-memory; and, after forgetting that these sepulchres had been hewn and occupied by the greatest potentates of their own race, they expressed their continuing sense of wonder at the mightiness of these ancient monuments by naming the locality after a parvenu hero of an epic cycle which was perhaps of Saka origin (see V. v. 602–4). Even the crushing experience of 334–330 B.C. could hardly have produced so extreme a lapse of memory as this if the association of the Persian people in their homeland with the universal state which Persian hands had built had not been rather tenuous.

[5] For a description see Herzfeld, E. E.: Archaeological History of Iran (London 1934, Milford), pp. 27–28. 'Such a plan cannot be called exactly a town. It looks more like the first settlement of nomads, and such in fact was the case.'

[6] The imperial archives disinterred at Persepolis by twentieth-century Western archaeologists indicated that Persepolis had been built between these dates, and that the

constructed at the point where the gorge of the Pulvār opens out into
the plain of Marv-Dasht[1] an imperial centre for the Persian people as a
whole which, like the civic centres of the cantons of Gaul under the
Roman Empire, came to be known by the name of the nation itself[2] and
not of the locality in which it happened to have been laid out. The layout
of this artificial capital was dominated by a magnificent audience hall,[3]
but the visits paid by Achaemenian emperors to Persepolis and Pasargadae were as rare and brief as those paid by Hapsburg king-emperors
to their royal palace at Buda or by sovereigns of the United Kingdom to
their royal palace at Holyrood. The unusualness of the spectacle of an
Achaemenian emperor giving audience in the stupendous *apadāna* looking out on to the plain of Marv-Dasht is attested by the handsomeness
of the rare imperial visitor's customary atonement for his necessary misdemeanour of being a chronic absentee. Whenever an emperor did, for
once, set foot on Persian ground, he used to give a gold piece to every
woman of Pasargadae[4] or, as some Greek men of letters reported,[5] to
every man and woman in the whole of Fars.

The munificence of this largesse could be afforded thanks to its
infrequency. Persepolis remained unknown to the Hellenes before Alexander fought his way to the spot through a barrage of brigand tribesmen.
Its name is not mentioned in the Babylonian, Jewish, Phoenician, or
Egyptian records either;[6] and the only indication that Persepolis may
after all have been of some political importance is the fact that Alexander
felt it worth while to burn the place down. If the intention of this
unworthy act of vandalism was to break the prestige and efface the
memory of the imperial dynasty that Alexander was aspiring to supplant, he would have employed his destructive energies to better effect
on the more arduous task of defacing the gigantic bas-relief and trilingual
inscription, recording the mighty deeds of Darius the Great, which the
second founder of the Achaemenian Empire had graven on the face of
a precipitous cliff far up above the reach of any ordinary saboteur. But,
if the Macedonian usurper had set out to destroy this all but impregnable
monument, he would not have found it in Fars, but on a crag overhang-

---

work of construction had been most actively pressed forward between the years 503 and
497 B.C. (see Olmstead, op. cit., p. 176).

[1] Olmstead (in op. cit., p. 172) conjectures that Darius's reason for abandoning
Pasargadae was its association with the rival Cyran branch of the Imperial House.

[2] 'Pārsa-tya', in an inscription of Xerxes'. From this usage the Greeks coined the word
'Persepolis', but, in current Greek parlance, to go to this imperial centre of the Persian
people was expressed simply as going ἐς Πέρσας (as a Gallo-Roman would say 'Parisios'
instead of 'Lutetiam'). On this point see Meyer, E.: *Geschichte des Altertums*, vol. iii,
1st ed. (Stuttgart 1901, Cotta), pp. 31–32.

[3] The Sasanidae followed the policy of the Achaemenidae in adorning their native
Fars with magnificent monuments as a compensation for the removal of their seat of
imperial government to a more convenient site. Eighteen out of twenty surviving
Sasanian rock-sculptures were in Fars (Herzfeld, E.: *Archaeological History of Iran*
(London 1935, Milford), p. 79).

[4] 'Whenever the Emperor of the Persians visits Pasargadae, he distributes a largesse of
gold to the Persian women. The value of this donative amounts to twenty Attic drachmae
per head' (Ctesias: *Persica*, Books IV–VI, p. 116 in J. Gilmore's edition (London 1888,
Macmillan). Cp. Nicolaus of Damascus, fr. 65, in *Historici Graeci Minores*, ed. by
Dindorf, L., vol. i (Leipzig 1870, Teubner), p. 63).

[5] Xenophon: *Cyropaedia*, Book VIII, chap. v, § 21, and chap. vii, § 1; cp. Plato:
Leges, Book III, 695 D, and Plutarch: *Life of Alexander*, chap. 69.

[6] See Olmstead, op. cit., p. 162.

ing one of the stations on the Great North-East Road in the section where the imperial highway climbed the Zagros Range *en route* from Babylon to Ecbatana. In choosing a site for his own sepulchre, Darius might indulge his personal sentiment for the Persian crownland of his Ariaramnan Achaemenid ancestors, and in deciding where to lay out an imperial palace he might feel it politic to flatter the vanity of the imperial people on whose loyalty to his throne and house the stability of his empire and dynasty depended. But, in the location of a monument that was to serve neither piety nor policy but publicity, Darius showed the shrewdness of his judgement by putting his finger on the rock of Behistan, where his record would force itself on the attention of the maximum number of his subjects as they travelled on their lawful occasions along the busiest thoroughfare in his empire.

When the universal state that had been originally provided for the Syriac World by Persian empire-builders from the south-west corner of the Iranian Plateau was eventually reconstituted by Hijāzī empire-builders from the western rim of the Arabian Plateau, history repeated itself with emphasis. Thanks to the intuition of the discordant oligarchs of an oasis-state in the Hijāz, who had invited the rejected prophet of a rival community to make himself at home with them and try his hand at being their ruler, in the hope that he would bring them the concord which they had failed to attain by themselves, Yathrib became, within thirty years of the Hijrah, the capital of an empire embracing not only the former Roman dominions in Syria and Egypt but the entire domain of the former Sasanian Empire.[1] Yathrib's title to remain the seat of government for this vast realm was indisputable on its juridical merits. This remote oasis-state was the territorial nucleus out of which the Muslim Arab world-empire had burgeoned in its miraculously rapid growth, and it was now also hallowed as *Madīnat-an-Nabī*, the City of the Prophet which had recognized his mission and had furnished him with home, throne, and sepulchre. This title was so impressive that *de jure* Medina remained the capital of the Caliphate—at any rate until the foundation of Baghdad by the 'Abbasid Caliph Mansūr in A.D. 762.[2] Yet *de facto* the swiftly expanding dominions of the Prophet Muhammad and his successors were governed from Medina for no longer than thirty-four years; for the fact was that this oasis hidden away in the interior of the Arabian Plateau—a vaster, wilder, barer, emptier counterpart of the Plateau of Iran—had condemned itself to political nullity by the immensity of its political success.

It would have been still less practicable to rule 'the Fertile Crescent' and the Lower Nile Valley and the Upper Basin of the Oxus and Jaxartes from Medina than to rule them from Istakhr or Persepolis or Pasargadae. The last event in Medina's brief career as an operative

---

[1] Ibn Khaldūn suggests that the Primitive Muslim Arabs' success in conquering the whole of the Sasanian Empire was a consequence of their conquest of the Sasanian imperial capital Ctesiphon, and that their contemporary failure to conquer more than a portion of the Roman Empire was a consequence of their inability to conquer the Roman imperial capital Constantinople (see the *Muqaddamāt*, translated by de Slane, Baron McG. (Paris 1863–8, Imprimerie Impériale, 3 vols.), vol. i, p. 333).
[2] See pp. 148–50, above.

imperial capital was the assassination there of Muhammad's third Caliph Uthmān in A.D. 656. Thereafter, 'Alī (*imperabat* A.D. 656–61) tried to rule the Caliphate from Kūfah, one of the cantonments of Arab tribal troops on the borderline between the Arabian Steppe and 'Irāq, and Mu'āwīyah (*imperabat* A.D. 661–80) succeeded in ruling it from Damascus, on the borderline between the Arabian Steppe and Syria. Under the Umayyad régime Medina was never the *de facto* seat of government; it was the academic fastness of embittered orthodox exponents of the Islamic Law; and the usurping dynasty, in its wary handling of this impeccable hornet's nest, seldom allowed itself to be provoked into committing invidious acts of repression; it was usually able to dispose of the fulminations of the Medinese doctors of theology by the more elegant and baffling riposte of a mock-respectful disregard.

When the Umayyad usurpers were supplanted by the semi-legitimate 'Abbasids, orthodox Medina's situation did not improve but deteriorated, for the road (if it could be called a road) from this West Arabian oasis to the 'Abbasids' metropolitan territory in 'Irāq was longer and more arduous than the road from Medina to Damascus. Moreover, the downfall of the Umayyads had put an end to that Arab hegemony in the Caliphate which, under the Umayyad régime, had been a link between the Desert and the Sown. The change of dynasty in the Caliphate was accompanied by a virtual secession of the badu of the Arabian Steppes;[1] and, though this break-away was less overt than the insurrection which had broken out after the death of the Prophet Muhammad, it was, unlike the *Riddah*, enduring in its effects. Medina was insulated from Baghdad by a Nomad no-man's-land; and, while the 'Abbasid Caliphs might occasionally advertise their piety by visiting the Haramayn as pilgrims,[2] these imperial pilgrimages to a couple of oases at World's End, where a Commander of the Faithful had no political business to transact, were as infrequent as they were hazardous.

To judge by the experience of later, less august and, by the same token, less opulent Muslim pilgrims to the two principal holy cities of Islam, we may assume that the badu made Hārūn-ar-Rashīd and his ever more degenerate successors pay toll for the right of way across their steppes. Recalcitrant tribesmen are no respecters of persons; and we know for a fact that, when the Achaemenian emperors paid their occasional visits of family piety to Persepolis and Pasargadae from Susa, they had to pay toll to the wild highlanders commanding the mountain passes on their route for the privilege of travelling through to scatter their largesse among their own Persian kinsfolk in Fars. When these impudent Uxii[3] imprudently notified Alexander, on his arrival at their borders in

---

[1] See p. 149, n. 3, above.

[2] The stations on the two pilgrimage routes of the 'Abbasid Age from 'Irāq to the Hijāz—one route taking off into the Arabian steppe from Kūfah and the other from Basrah—are plotted out in Spruner-Menke: *Hand-Atlas für die Geschichte des Mittelalters und der Neueren Zeit*, 3rd. ed. (Gotha 1880, Perthes), Map 81.

[3] This was a Greek version of the name of a people which appears as Ūvjiyā (standing for Hūjiyā) in Old Persian. In the Achaemenian official lists of *dahyāva*, the land name Ūvja or Ūja (standing for Hūja) denotes Elam in the widest sense, including the Susian lowland as well as its highland hinterland. In a later age the same country continued to be known by the same name in the form Hūzistān (or Khūzistān), while its latter-day

331 B.C., that they would not let him pass either unless he paid them their customary fee, the conqueror gave the blackmailers the surprise of their lives;[1] and thereafter, in the winter of 324–323 B.C., he diverted himself by conducting a miniature lightning campaign against the Uxians' north-western neighbours and fellow brigands the Kassites,[2] who had likewise acquired a customary right of levying blackmail—presumably also, like the Uxii, from the Achaemenian Emperor himself, since the Kassites' highland fastness lay astride the direct road from Susa to Ecbatana.[3]

Migrations of the Capital Cities of Marchmen Empire-builders

We may now pass from empires founded by barbarians like the Primitive Muslim Arabs, or by barbaro-marchmen like the Persian henchmen of the Achaemenidae and the Manchu conquerors of China, to empires

capital (the provincial successor of an imperial Susa) was called Ahwāz, the Arabic plural of Hūz, which was the singular of an ethnikon corresponding to the old Persian Hūjiyā.

[1] See Arrian: *Expeditio Alexandri*, Book III, chap. xvii. If these uncouth brigands of the Southern Zagros had been as ready-witted as the accomplished Tyrrhenian pirate, they might have taken a verbal revenge for their military discomfiture by pointing out to Alexander that he was engaged in a larger way in the same trade that they were practising on a petty scale (see the story as told by Saint Augustine: *De Civitate Dei*, Book IV, chap. 4, and translated in XI. ix. 223, n. 1).

[2] See Arrian: *Expeditio Alexandri*, Book VII, chap. xv, §§ 1–3.

[3] The Kassites' customary right to take toll from august travellers seeking passage through their country was flouted in 317 B.C. by Antigonus, as the Uxians' had been by Alexander in 331 B.C., but the sequel was not the same, for this time it was the Macedonian war-lord who was given the surprise of his life by the Iranian mountaineers. Antigonus, confronted with the problem of rapidly extricating his troops from a precarious military situation and a formidably high summer temperature in the lowlands of Elam, had decided to evacuate them to Media—the nearest quarter of the Iranian Plateau—to recuperate and refit. For reaching this destination, he had a choice of two alternative routes: a detour, estimated to involve a forty days' march, for the most part through sultry lowlands, or a short cut, amounting to no more than a nine days' march, through the cool highlands of the Kassite country. The detour would have taken him from Susa along the north-east alinement of the Great North-West Road to a point where this road crossed the Babylon–Ecbatana section of the Great North-East Road, and from there he would have marched to Ecbatana, past the rock of Behistan, along the main highway of the Achaemenian Empire. Diodorus Siculus's source rightly characterizes the detour as being καλὴ καὶ βασιλική. The short cut through the Kassite country was presumably the Ecbatana–Susa diversion of the Great North-East Road of which the proper south-western terminus was not Susa but Babylon. Against advice, Antigonus insisted both on taking the short cut through the Kassites' country and on trying to force his passage without purchasing the tribesmen's acquiescence. The Kassites did not get their money, but they made their redoubtable visitor pay dear in soldiers' lives (Diodorus Siculus: Book XIX, chap. 19). So much for the effect of Alexander's flamboyant chastisement of the Kassites only five and a half years before! It is easier to chastise wild tribesmen than to break their spirit or change their habits, as empire-builders have discovered in many different areas and ages. Tribesmen, like bayonets, are awkward to sit on.

When the Ūvjiyā and the Kassites felt the disconcerting weight of Alexander's arm, they could hearten themselves by recalling that they and their ancestors had survived many previous punitive expeditions of the kind (ignorant though they were of Naramsin's stele portraying him chastising the Gutaeans). The Kassites had, indeed, been sitting, unscotched, in their local fastness in the Zagros since at least as early as the eighteenth century B.C., and a detachment of their braves had made history by descending on a Land of Shinar which Hammurabi had just exhausted in the act of re-establishing the Empire of Sumer and Akkad by main force. This momentarily resuscitated Sumeric universal state had come and gone, but the Kassites had battened on their Babylonian prey for five or six hundred years (see I. i. 1-11). At the time of writing the social condition of this corner of Iran was much like what it had been in the eighteenth century B.C. and in the fourth. In the twentieth century of the Christian Era the Kassites called themselves 'Lūrs' and the Uxii 'Bakhtīyārīs'.

founded by marchmen who were genuine, though rustic, members of the society which they furnished with a universal state. In such cases likewise the normal tendency, as we have noted by anticipation,[1] is for the seat of imperial government to travel from the site of the former parochial capital of the empire-building march-state to some new site nearer the heart of the civilization whose whole domain has now been united politically. A classical illustration of this tendency is afforded by the course of Sinic history.

The cradle of the Sinic Civilization had been the great plain which lay between 'the Country within the Passes' on the west and the hill-country of Shantung on the east, and which was inundated by the waters of the Yellow River in the lower part of its course;[2] but, at an early date, a secondary centre had arisen in the little plain watered by the lower course of the River Wei,[3] the principal right-bank tributary of the Yellow River, which joins the main stream just at the point where the Yellow River bends, in an acute angle, from a south-by-westerly to an east-by-northerly course and forces its way through the mountain barrier that separates the little western plain 'within the passes' from the Great Eastern Plain which was the heart of the Sinic World.

The empire-building march-state Ts'in had started its career as a western outpost of the Sinic World far up the Wei Valley, but, after centuries of progressive expansion, its capital had come—by the time when Ts'in She Hwang-ti united the Sinic World politically by con-quering and annexing Ts'in's six rivals[4]—to be located at Hsien Yang, on the left bank of the Lower Wei near the western end of the little western plain 'within the passes'; and Ts'in She Hwang-ti retained this existing capital of his hereditary kingdom as the seat of government for his newly established universal state.[5] Upon the overthrow of the Ts'in régime after Ts'in She Hwang-ti's death and the capture of Hsien Yang by Liu Pang,[6] the former capital of the Ts'in Power was laid waste in cold blood by the arch-rebel Hsiang-yü.[7] This aristocrat had inherited an implacable hatred of Ts'in and all its works from forebears who had been hereditary dignitaries of the state of Ch'u, Ts'in's principal rival.[8] The peasant-born founder of the Han Dynasty had no such vested interest in the vendettas of a dead feudal past. When he had occupied Hsien Yang in 207 B.C. and thereby brought the Ts'in régime to an end, he had achieved this *coup* by the combination of a politic clemency with military force, and had been content to spare the stones and timbers of the city as well as the life of the last Ts'in emperor, when once the latter had resigned the insignia of the imperial office.[9] When, after his success-ful issue from his inevitable settlement of accounts with Hsiang-yü, Han Liu Pang found himself sole master of the Sinic World, he followed in the footsteps of his Ts'in forerunners, not only in keeping the whole of 'the Country within the Passes' under his own direct administration,[10]

---

[1] On p. 194, above.
[2] See I. i. 90 and 318–21, and xi, map 25.
[3] See II. ii. 118–19, and xi, map 26.
[4] See p. 167, above.
[5] See p. 171, n. 2, above.
[6] See p. 171, above.
[7] See Franke, O.: *Geschichte des Chinesischen Reiches*, vol. i (Berlin and Leipzig 1930, de Gruyter), p. 259.
[8] See p. 171, above.
[9] See Franke, op. cit., vol. cit., p. 258.
[10] See p. 173, above.

but in locating his seat of government at the western end of the little plain of the Lower Wei. Ch'ang Ngan, where Han Liu Pang laid out his new capital, lay near the right bank of the Wei just opposite the devastated site of Hsien Yang on the farther side of the river.

This avatar of the capital of Ts'in remained the capital of the Han Empire for the duration of the Prior Han Dynasty (*imperabant* 202 B.C.–A.D. 9). When, however, after the interregnum arising from the usurpation of Wang Mang (*dominabatur* A.D. 9–23),[1] the Empire was reinstated by the Posterior Han Dynasty (*imperabant* A.D. 25–221), the seat of government was transferred by them from Ch'ang Ngan in the Lower Wei Valley, just 'within the passes', to Loyang, just outside the passes, on the western verge of the Great Eastern Plain, in the lower valley of the River Lo, which was the next right-bank tributary of the Yellow River below the Wei.[2]

This site, just within the plain that was the heart of the Sinic World, was already historic ground by the time when the Posterior Han decided to plant their capital there. The transfer of the seat of government of the Han régime that was made in A.D. 25 had been anticipated in 770 B.C.,[3] when the Chóu Dynasty had evacuated their previous capital 'within the passes' at Tsung Chóu (a few miles to the south-west of the subsequent site of Ch'ang Ngan) after it had been sacked in 771 B.C. by barbarian raiders from the west, and had taken refuge at Loyang, which had previously been no more than a secondary seat of theirs.[4] Moreover, before the Chóu had established this at first subsidiary

---

[1] See V. vi. 295.   [2] See II. ii. 119.
[3] See Hirth, F.: *The Ancient History of China* (New York 1908, Columbia University Press), p. 176.
[4] The political sequels of these two coincident shifts in the location of the seat of government of the Sinic World were not the same. When made in A.D. 25, the transfer of the capital gave the Han régime a new lease of life; when made in 770 B.C., it resulted in the Chóu Dynasty's becoming *rois fainéants* who lingered on, in a miniature imperial domain and with merely ceremonial functions, till they were snuffed out by Ts'in She Hwang-ti's grandfather Kung Chao Hsiang of Ts'in in 256–249 B.C. The histories of the Chóu and Ts'in dynasties had, however, run almost exactly parallel in an earlier chapter, and, even in the last chapter, the two denouements resembled one another in being, both of them, ironic.
    Either dynasty had started its career as a western outpost of the Sinic World in the upper reaches of the Wei Basin. Both of them had subsequently moved their seat of government down into the little plain of the Lower Wei (Chóu perhaps in 1150 B.C., Ts'in after 770 B.C.). Both had then broken out of their western march-state 'within the passes' and had conquered the heart of the Sinic World on the Great Eastern Plain: Ts'in She Hwang-ti's overthrow of Ts'in's six eastern rivals in 230–221 B.C. had its precedent in Chóu Wu Wang's overthrow of the Shang (*alias* Yin) Power on the Great Eastern Plain at some date, not precisely determinable, between 1122 B.C. (the traditional dating) and about 1050 B.C. In the next chapter the two histories diverged. The Chóu Dynasty attempted to organize the government of its eastern conquests by devolution on feudal lines, and thereby reduced itself, by stages, to impotence: the first shock was suffered by the Chóu Power in 841 B.C., the second in 771–770 B.C., and the end came in 249 B.C. Warned (we may guess) by the miscarriage of the Chóu Dynasty's policy, Ts'in She Hwang-ti sought to confirm his hold on his eastern conquests by a policy of extreme *Gleichschaltung* and centralization, and thereby defeated his own personal and dynastic ends by provoking a violent reaction which extinguished the Ts'in Power for ever within three years of the First Ts'in Emperor's death. Thanks, however, to the genius of Han Liu Pang and to the hardly less notable statesmanship of the founder of the Posterior Han Dynasty, Kwang Wuti, Ts'in She Hwang-ti's empire and system of government lasted, in a modified and on that account more practically effective form, for nearly four hundred years—from Ts'in She Hwang-ti's death in 210 B.C. to the decay of the Posterior Han Power towards the close of the second century of the Christian Era (see II. ii. 118–19).

western seat of theirs at Loyang, the neighbourhood had already been a focus of political power. A site a few miles farther down the course of the Lo River, not far from its junction with the Yellow River, had been one of the successive capitals of the Shang (*alias* Yin) Dynasty, which had ruled in the Great Eastern Plain before the Chóu had descended from 'the Country within the Passes' and had brought this Shang régime to an end.[1]

In the history of the main body of the Far Eastern Society that was affiliated to the Sinic Civilization, this episode of the transfer of a seat of government from the little western plain in the Wei Basin to the Great Eastern Plain repeated itself after the evocation of a ghost of the Sinic universal state by the Sui Dynasty.[2] The Sui, and the T'ang after them, located the capital of a politically united China at Si Ngan (the latter-day Sian-fu),[3] on a site adjoining that of Ch'ang Ngan; and the capital of this resuscitation of the Ts'in and Han Empire remained at this spot as long as the Sui and T'ang dynasties endured (*imperabant* A.D. 589–907). But, after an interregnum following the decay of the T'ang Power that had set in before the close of the ninth century of the Christian Era, the reunion of all but a fraction of the former dominions of the T'ang[4] by the Sung Dynasty in A.D. 960 was accompanied by an eastward shift in the seat of government[5] along the historic west–east axis. This time, Loyang was not the beneficiary; under the Sung régime she did not re-emerge from the secondary position that she had occupied under the T'ang.[6] The Sung laid out their capital more than a hundred miles farther to the east, at Kaifêng, in the middle of the Great Eastern Plain, and not on its western verge.

The course of empire in the Yellow River Basin had had a parallel in

---

[1] By the time of writing, archaeological discoveries had confirmed the Sinic literary tradition by producing independent evidence for the existence of the Shang culture (see xi, map 25) on the Great Eastern Plain in the second millennium B.C. (The authenticity of the Hsia Dynasty, which was the traditional precursor of the Shang, still remained to be proved.) The capital of the Shang Power was traditionally recorded to have lain in the Lower Lo Valley from 1386 to 1198 B.C. During the last phase of the Shang régime, traditionally dated 1198–1122 B.C., the seat of government was recorded to have lain farther to the north-east, at Mo (see xi, map 25), on the main northern arm of the Lower Yellow River itself. After the overthrow of the Shang Empire, the dynasty survived as hereditary princes of the parochial state of Sung (see xi, map 25) to the east of Loyang in the upper basin of the Huai River. During the Sinic Time of Troubles that resulted from the decay of the Chóu Power, Sung was one of those little states in the centre of the Sinic World which were the stakes in the contest for hegemony between the great states on the fringes.

[2] For this achievement of the Sui Dynasty, and its prolongation by their successors the T'ang, see II. ii. 120; pp. 19–21, above; and X. ix. 16.

[3] See II. ii. 120.

[4] Though inconsiderable in area compared with the total extent of the main body of the Far Eastern World, this fragment of former T'ang territory which the Sung failed to reincorporate into the reunited empire was strategically and historically important. The sixteen districts of which it consisted (see II. ii. 121) lay just within the Great Wall and included the site of the future imperial city of Peking at the northern extremity of the Great Eastern Plain. The Khitan Nomad barbarians, to whom this fragment of territory had been ceded, *circa* A.D. 927–37, during the post-T'ang interregnum, chose this site for their southern residence and thus prepared the way for it to become the capital of their successors the Kin, after these had shifted the centre of gravity of their dominions southward by conquering the Yellow River Basin from the Sung in A.D. 1124–42 (see V. vi. 307). [5] See II. ii. loc. cit.

[6] At the time of writing, Loyang was serving, under the name of Honan-fu, as the local centre of administration of the central province of Northern China.

the Nile Valley below the First Cataract.[1] In Egyptiac as in Sinic and
Far Eastern history, political unity was conferred—or imposed—on the
society no less than three times over by a march-state starting from
a base of operations up-river;[2] and in Egyptiac history likewise the
aggrandisement of a march into a universal state was followed on each
occasion by a shift in the location of the seat of government from the
former parochial capital of the empire-building marchmen to a new
site nearer to the heart of the domain of the politically unified society.

The foundation, *circa* 3100 B.C., of a united kingdom of Upper and
Lower Egypt was achieved by empire-builders from the extreme south
of the Egyptiac World of the day, in the neighbourhood of the modern
Al-Kāb,[3] between Thebes and the First Cataract. The political union,
from this base of operations, of the whole of the Lower Nile Basin
between the First Cataract and the Mediterranean was immediately
followed by a northward shift of the seat of power. The Hieraconpolite
empire-builders established their imperial residence at Thinis, and their
necropolis at Abydos on the opposite bank of the Nile, down-stream from
their ancestral canton; and the *de facto* centre of imperial administration
seems soon to have moved on still farther down-stream to Memphis.[4]
Thereafter, this ideally convenient site, at the point of junction between
the mouth of the Nile Valley and the head of the Delta, remained the
seat of government of 'the Old Kingdom' to the end. The *de facto* capital
of its spring-time became the *de jure* capital of its summer, when the
Thinites were followed by the pyramid-builders of the Third and Fourth
Dynasties;[5] and, when summer passed over into autumn, Memphis was
still the place from which the demonic pyramid-builders' pious Helio-
politan successors attempted to exert their gradually diminishing
authority.[6]

After the Time of Troubles following 'the Old Kingdom's' collapse,
the establishment, *circa* 2052 B.C., of an Egyptiac universal state by
a prince of the southern march-state of Thebes was similarly followed,
in the reign of the Emperor Amenemhat I (*imperabat circa* 1991–
1962 B.C.), by a transfer of the capital of 'the Middle Empire' from
Thebes to a site, only a few miles up-stream from Memphis, which its
founder named 'the Conqueror of the Two Lands' (*Egyptiacè* 'Iz-
Taui').[7] Though Thebes was slightly less remote than Al-Kāb had been

---

[1] This parallel has been pointed out, in another connexion, in II. ii. 118.

[2] See I. i. 140, n. 2, and II. ii. 112–13.

[3] The nucleus of the 'nome' (canton) which was the original domain of these Horus-
worshipping empire-builders consisted of a pair of cities facing one another across the
Nile: Necheb (*Graecè* 'Eileithuia') on the site of the modern Al-Kāb on the east bank of
the Nile, and Nechen (*Graecè* 'Hieracônpolis', in allusion to the hawk ('hierax') which
was both the heraldic emblem of the city and the symbol of its god Horus) on the west
bank). (See Hall, H. R.: *The Ancient History of the Near East* (London 1913, Methuen),
pp. 93–94; Meyer, E.: *Geschichte des Altertums*, vol. i, Part II, 3rd ed. (Stuttgart and
Berlin 1913, Cotta), pp. 80 and 111).

[4] See Hall, op. cit., pp. 108–9; Meyer, op. cit., vol. cit., ed. cit., p. 134.

[5] See Meyer, ibid., p. 169.

[6] It is significant that, whereas the Thinites were buried at Abydos, far up the Nile
Valley though not so far as Al-Kāb, the Heliopolitans as well as the pyramid-builders
chose the neighbourhood of Memphis for the site of their sepulchres (see ibid. pp. 132
and 202–3).

[7] See ibid., p. 267.

from the heart of the Egyptiac World, the gravitational pull of the body
social which Theban prowess had reunited proved once again so strong
that Thebes on this occasion, like Al-Kāb before her, had to pay for her
political achievement by ceasing to be the seat of government of the
oecumenical polity which she had called into existence. When, however,
after an abortive interregnum,[1] the Egyptiac universal state was restored
circa 1570 B.C. by another prince of Thebes, as a result of his triumph in
a holy war of liberation against the hated alien Hyksos conquerors of
Lower Egypt, the power and prestige of Thebes stood so high that
this time she was able to resist successfully, for more than two hundred
years,[2] the gravitational pull which made itself felt again now that the
Egyptiac World was for the third time politically united.

'[The] structure of "the New Empire" presents a very peculiar picture:
the seat of government lies far away from the geographical centre in the
southernmost part of the [Egyptiac] Civilization's domain, 700 kilometres
above Memphis and only 200 kilometres below the frontier at the First
Cataract, as the Nile flows [and not as the crow flies]. This makes the
impression of a defiance of the conditions set by Nature. . . . In terms of
the Kingdom of Prussia,[3] it is as though the seat of government had lain at
Königsberg [instead of at Berlin]. . . . The distortion is not appreciably
abated by the fact that Nubia has now once again been incorporated into
the permanent domain of the empire. This unnaturalness of "the New
Empire's" structure bears striking testimony to the truth that the
[Eighteenth] Dynasty's hereditary dominions were, and continued to be,
the source of the dynasty's strength.'[4]

In this instance, Nature proved unable to reassert herself till a man
of genius came to her aid. Applying his revolutionary philosophy consistently, as he did, to every side of life, the Emperor Ikhnaton (imperabat circa 1380–1362 B.C.)[5] not only deposed the god Amon-Re of Thebes
from his established primacy in the Egyptiac pantheon in favour of an
etherialized sun-disk; he also transferred his capital from Thebes to
Tall-al-'Amarnah, about half-way, as the Nile flows, from Thebes to
Memphis. Ikhnaton, like Ts'in She Hwang-ti and Akbar, defeated his
own ends by going to extremes that provoked an overwhelming reaction.[6]
What can a solitary philosopher-king achieve against the cumulative
momentum of a cultural tradition? Ikhnaton's Tell-el-Amarna suffered
the fate of Akbar's Fātihpūr Sīkrī. Yet Ikhnaton's discomfiture did not
enable Thebes to recapture her geographically unnatural prerogative of
serving as the seat of imperial government for a united Egyptiac World.
Under Horemheb (imperabat de facto circa 1349–1319 B.C.) a still united
Egyptiac World was ruled once again from its geographical centre at

[1] See I. i. 137–9.
[2] See p. 176, above. It is worth noticing that this was about the length of time for
which, in a Sinic World politically united under the Han régime, Ch'ang Ngan 'within
the passes' succeeded in resisting the gravitational pull on the seat of government which
eventually caused the capital to travel to Loyang, on the verge of the Great Eastern
Plain.
[3] Presumably the writer is thinking of Prussia within the frontiers of A.D. 1866–
1918.—A.J.T.
[4] Meyer, E.: Geschichte des Altertums, vol. ii, Part I, 2nd ed. (Stuttgart and Berlin
1928, Cotta), p. 60.   [5] Or, on another reckoning, circa 1370–1352 B.C.
[6] See I. i. 145–6 and V. v. 695–6.

Memphis; but this time the victory of the interior over the marches was as short-lived as it had been long-delayed. In the next chapter of Egyptiac history the seat of imperial government was prised out, split, and polarized by pressures of unequal magnitude from beyond the frontiers. Two major pressures from the north-east and the north-west drew the principal capital away into the Delta, while a secondary capital arose at Napata, near the foot of the Fourth Cataract, which, under 'the New Empire', had superseded Thebes and Al-Kāb as the southern bulwark of an Egyptiac World that had now expanded southward to take in Nubia.[1]

In Hellenic history the fortunes of Rome are reminiscent of those of Egyptiac Thebes. Rome had won her spurs by taking over from the Etruscans the wardenship of the Italian marches of the Hellenic World over against the Gauls,[2] as Thebes had won hers by taking over from Al-Kāb the wardenship of the First Cataract of the Nile over against the barbarians of Nubia. Like Thebes, again, Rome had afterwards turned her arms inwards and imposed political unity on the society of which she was a member. At the same time the geographical location of Rome in the empire which she eventually gathered round her was so much more central than that of Thebes in either 'the Middle Empire' or 'the New Empire' that Rome might have been expected to remain the seat of the Roman imperial government as long as the Roman Empire lasted. The Roman Empire was, in geographical terms, a Pan-Mediterranean 'thalassocracy', and Rome's own situation at the mid-point of the west coast of Italy, on the banks of a river which was navigable up to Rome by the sea-going vessels of the day, was not far from being the geographically ideal site for the capital of an empire embracing all the shores of the Mediterranean and holding this ring of continental provinces together by a network of maritime communications.[3] As a Greek man of letters, writing in the age of the Antonines, expressed it in an invocation to Rome and the Romans,

'The sea stretches in a belt across the middle of the Inhabited World and across the middle of your empire; and round the sea the continents extend "grand and grandly"—continually supplying your needs with consignments of their products.'[4]

Nevertheless, Rome, like Thebes, did eventually lose her imperial pre-

---

[1] See II. ii. 113–15.   [2] See II. ii. 161.

[3] In a Pan-Mediterranean 'thalassocracy' the ideal seat of imperial government, corresponding to Memphis in the fluvial Egyptiac World, would be one or other of two sites in Sicily—Messina and Marsala—which command respectively the narrower and the wider of the two straits through which the south-eastern and the north-western basins of the Mediterranean communicate with one another. The despots who imposed an imperfect and precarious political unity on the Greek city-states in Sicily and the toe of Italy in the fifth and fourth centuries B.C. (see III. iii. 357, n. 1) had never possessed a sufficient surplus of power to enable them to unite the whole Hellenic World, not to speak of the whole circumference of the Mediterranean, round a Sicilian political centre. Syracuse was the capital of a Mediterranean thalassocracy for the first and last time during the residence there of the Roman Emperor Constans II in the years A.D. 663/4–8 (see IV. iv. 330–1 and 589–91).

[4] Aristeides, P. Aelius: In Romam, §§ 10–11 (Aelii Aristidis Quae Supersunt Omnia, edidit B. Keil (Berlin 1898, Weidmann, 2 vols.), vol. ii, p. 94), quoted on p. 81, n. 2, above.

rogative of serving as the seat of government for an empire which she herself had created.

While Rome lay not far from the centre of the Mediterranean Basin, she was by no means so centrally situated from the standpoint of an Hellenic World of which she was ostensibly the mistress but in the last resort the servant. The Hellenic Civilization had grown up round the shores, not of the Mediterranean, but of the Aegean, which was a north-eastern bay of the larger sea that, for the Romans, was *mare nostrum*; and, though, by the time when the Roman Empire was established, Continental European Greece had lost its former military, political, and economic pre-eminence, the Hellenic and Hellenized provinces of the Empire in Anatolia and Syria were gaining steadily in population and wealth, while Italy, which had conquered the Mediterranean Basin largely in virtue of her then abundant man-power, began, under the *Pax Augusta*, to fall into the same decline as Greece.[1] Accordingly, under the Roman Empire, though Greek influence continued to radiate into Italy, and Rome herself became for a time a predominantly Greek-speaking city,[2] the centre of gravity of the Hellenic World travelled away from the Aegean Basin, not north-westward towards Rome, but south-east-ward towards Antioch and Alexandria. At the same time the centre of gravity of the Empire—which was a hollow ring of land encircling the Mediterranean—was travelling northwards owing to the doubling of the thickness of this ring on its northern side through the annexation of Britain, Gallia Comata, the Danubian provinces, and Cappadocia be-tween the years 58 B.C. and A.D. 84.

These two gradual but persistent displacements of the Empire's economic and social centre of gravity were already exerting a gravita-tional pull upon the imperial seat of government when, in the third century of the Christian Era, their effect was suddenly and violently accentuated by pressures from beyond the frontiers: a pressure on the Euphrates from the aggressive Sasanian Power that had replaced the lethargic Arsacidae; a pressure on the Lower Danube from semi-nomadicized North European barbarian intruders on the Great Western Bay of the Eurasian Steppe;[3] and a pressure on the Rhine and on the Rhine–Danube *limes* from local sedentary barbarians who had made themselves more formidable neighbours by learning something of the Roman arts of war and of state-building. Through the play of these divers social forces the seat of government of the Roman Empire, like that of the Egyptiac 'New Empire', was prised up, split, and polarized.

---

[1] This decay of Italy can be traced back to the social effects of the devastation produced by the Hannibalic War (see I. i. 40), and, in Italy south of the Appennines, these effects had already become alarming by the generation of Tiberius Gracchus (*tribunatum plebis gerebat* 131 B.C.). The depopulation of Peninsular Italy was, however, counterbalanced at that stage by the colonization of the Po Basin, and, largely on this account, the relative decline of Italy as a whole, within the Alpine boundaries conferred on her by Augustus, did not begin to become pronounced until about the second century of the Roman Empire's existence, during 'the Indian Summer' of the Antonine Age.

[2] 'Non possum ferre, Quirites, Graecam urbem' (Juvenal: *Satires*, No. III, ll. 60–61, quoted already in V. v. 67) is merely an exaggeration of a truth which is attested, for example, by the extant works of the Christian Father Hippolytus, who lived in Rome and wrote in Greek in the third century of the Christian Era.

[3] See III. iii. 399 and 426–8.

In this case the principal capital was drawn away eastward from the banks of the Tiber to the shores of the Bosphorus. Diocletian was governing the Empire from Nicomedia, at the point where the road from the Asiatic shore of the Bosphorus leaves the sea behind and plunges into the interior of Anatolia, when he gave the signal, in A.D. 303, for the launching of an oecumenical campaign to extirpate the Christian Church. Constantine laid out his New Rome on the European shore of the Bosphorus, on the site of the Greek city of Byzantium,[1] in A.D. 324. Simultaneously a secondary capital likewise detached itself from Rome and then travelled, not eastward, but north-westward—lingering at Milan and coming to a halt at Trier.[2]

Of all the sites open for consideration by any ruler of the Roman Empire who had once shaken himself free from a traditional inhibition against moving the capital from Rome herself, a site on or near the Bosphorus offered the greatest combination of political advantages in the social and strategic circumstances of Diocletian's and Constantine's day. In a city with a harbour opening on to the narrow seas through which the Black Sea communicated with the Aegean, the imperial government would find itself within easier reach of the original heart of a maritime Hellenic World. At the same time it would find itself posted midway between the two frontiers—the Lower Danube and the Middle Euphrates—which in that age headed the list of its military anxieties, while at its doors, in Thrace and Illyricum, would lie the main reservoir of military man-power from which the Empire was now recruiting its armies. The cumulative weight of these considerations was decisive, and a secondary capital in the basin of the Po or the Moselle was necessary merely for looking after those economically backward ex-barbarian provinces in the far west, from Britain to Morocco inclusive, which could not be directly controlled by way of either the sea-routes or the land-routes that radiated out from Constantinople.

At the turn of the third and fourth centuries of the Christian Era the transfer of the principal capital of the Roman Empire from Rome to Constantinople or to some maritime city in that neighbourhood was, in fact, inevitable. But it is remarkable to find evidence that, more than three hundred years earlier, when Rome was towering at the zenith of her power under the auspices of Julius Caesar and Augustus, the Romans were already anxiously foreboding a shift in the seat of the imperial government, and were expecting that the Roman dictator with whom the decision of Rome's destinies now lay would choose his new site in that very region—on or near the shores of the waterway between the Aegean and the Black Sea—which did in fact eventually attract the choice of Diocletian and Constantine.

One of the causes of the unpopularity that gave Julius Caesar's enemies at Rome their opportunity for compassing his death was said to have been a rumour that he was proposing 'to migrate to Alexandria [Troas] or Ilium and at the same time to transfer thither the empire's

---

[1] The navigational advantages which had previously made Byzantium a key-point in the Hellenic system of maritime communications have been examined in II. ii. 43–48.
[2] See II. ii. 164.

resources after exhausting Italy by levies of man-power and leaving friends of his own as his agents for administering the city of Rome'.[1] This anecdote might have been discounted as an echo of a malicious propaganda campaign were it not for a revelation of the same anxiety in a celebrated passage in one of Horace's odes.[2] The Augustan poet must have written these lines not many years after the Battle of Actium had disposed of the Egyptian Alexandria's attempt to challenge, with Roman arms, Rome's title to be the imperial capital of a politically unified Hellenic World. At that moment[3] Rome stood in solitary omnipotence without any rival to dispute her primacy; and Augustus, who had at last succeeded in winning the support of a *consensus Italiae* by defeating Mark Antony's attempt to transfer the seat of government of the Mediterranean World to the Levant, could not readily be suspected, without substantial evidence, of planning to make on his own initiative a move which had proved a fatal false step for his rival and a damaging insinuation against his predecessor. One of the fundamental principles of Augustus's policy was to steer clear of his adoptive father's fate by eschewing provocatively revolutionary acts and pursuing Caesarean aims by Fabian tactics. Yet it is plain that Horace, writing when and as he did, believed a transfer of the capital of the Roman Empire from Rome to some site on the Asiatic shore of the Hellespont to be both a serious possibility and a dangerous subject. Horace tactfully misrepresents a cold-blooded 'geopolitical' calculation as a pious tribute to the legendary derivation of Rome from Troy, and, after cautiously expressing his disapproval in the form of a mythological conceit, he precipitately breaks off with an apology for trespassing on high matters of state in a mere poet's *jeu d'esprit*.

In the political geography of the Roman Empire,[4] Troy or Alexandria Troas were the equivalents in Augustus's day of Nicomedia or Byzantium in Diocletian's and Constantine's;[5] and the whimsical prophecy, put

---

[1] Or 'the cities of Italy' if the correct reading is not 'Urbis' but 'urbium'. This passage occurs in Suetonius Tranquillus, C. : *The Lives of the Caesars*, 'Divus Iulius', chap. 79.

[2] Horace: *Carmina*, Book III, Ode iii, ll. 57–72.

[3] This challenge, and the abiding resentment of the Greek citizens of Alexandria Aegyptiaca at their city's defeat in her audacious trial of strength with her great Italian rival, have been touched upon in V. vi. 37, n. 1, and 217–19.

[4] See xi, maps 28 and 29.

[5] Before the addition to the Roman Empire of the continental northern tier of provinces from Britain to Cappadocia inclusive (see p. 217, above), the main route from the European to the Asiatic territories of the Empire had run from Rome via the Via Appia to Brundisium, had crossed the mouth of the Adriatic by a sea-passage to Dyrrhachium or Apollonia, and had then followed the Via Egnatia, via Thessalonica and Lysimacheia, to the Hellespont. By Diocletian's day the corresponding main route had come to be an unbroken overland highway running from Lyons via Milan and Aquileia (or even north of the Alps, from Trier via Augsburg and Vienna) to Belgrade, and thence south-eastwards, up the valley of the Morava and down the valley of the Maritsa, to the Bosphorus. As late as the year A.D. 360, when the Rhine–Danube *limes* had long since been submerged and when Swabia was in the hands of the independent and aggressive barbarian confederacy of the Alemanni, the Emperor Julian took the route north of the Alps in his march upon Constantinople from Northern Gaul. Yet, although by Constantine's day the Bosphorus had thus supplanted the Hellespont in the role of affording the most convenient passage across the narrow seas between Roman Europe and Roman Asia, Constantine is said to have started to build his new imperial capital on a site commanding the Asiatic shore of the Hellespont, at a point between Alexandria Troas and Ilium, before arriving at his eventual decision in favour of a site commanding the European shore of the Bosphorus (see Zosimus: *Historiae*, Book II, chap. xxx, §§ 2–3).

by Horace into the goddess Juno's mouth, that, if Troy were to be refounded by the Romans, she would infallibly be recaptured by the Greeks, did in fact come true of Byzantium after her refoundation as a New Rome by Constantine. Though the Latin-speaking Dardanian founder of Constantinople and his successors down to his Latin-speaking fellow countryman Justinian were resolved to make and keep their new Rome a Latin-speaking city,[1] the Greek language had captured the New Rome by the close of the sixth century of the Christian Era, as it had captured the Old Rome in Juvenal's time, some four hundred years earlier; and at Constantinople, with its Greek-speaking hinterland, the Latin language had no chance of repeating the victorious counter-attack by which at Rome it eventually overwhelmed what had never been more than a Greek-speaking enclave in an elsewhere Latin-speaking Italy.

Unlike Rome and Thebes, both Moscow and Yedo successfully avoided the fate of seeing the imperial throne removed from their precincts and permanently transferred to another site, and in both cases this difference of fortune was due to the same cause. Though Moscow and Yedo were on a par with Rome and Thebes in starting their careers as capitals of march-states which became the nuclei of universal states, and, though again, in both pairs of cases alike, the former march was afterwards relegated to the interior in consequence of a victorious expansion of the society into what had previously been barbarian territory beyond the pale, the eventual sequel was not the same. After Moscow and Yedo had thus changed their relative positions in their respective worlds from a former situation near the edge to a latter-day situation much nearer the centre, the advantage of this change for the purpose of serving as the seat of an oecumenical government was not counteracted in either case by the pressure of hostile forces from beyond the new frontiers which the expansion of the society had called into existence. Neither the Japanese World in its northward expansion up the Main Island of Japan and over the Tsugaru Straits into Hokkaido nor the Russian World in its eastward expansion across the Ural Mountains into Siberia ran into such formidable military commitments as those which Rome, for example, eventually incurred as a result of having expanded her dominions from the line of the Appennines to the line of the Rhine and the Danube.

For this reason the locus, half-way up the eastern seaboard of the Main Island of Japan, which became a seat of abortive oecumenical government at the site named Kamakura during the Japanese Time of Troubles and a seat of effective oecumenical government at the site named Yedo after the foundation of the Tokugawa Shogunate, succeeded in retaining its prerogative for the duration of the Tokugawa régime; and, thanks to Japan's being an archipelago in which Yedo, like every other important centre of population, lay almost within a stone's throw of the sea, the site which had proved itself a convenient seat of government for an insulated Japanese universal state did not forfeit its prerogative when Commodore Perry's expedition, by demonstrating that Japan no longer had it in her power to go on living in isolation as

[1] See V. vi. 224.

a self-contained social universe, precipitated a revolution which sought to transform Japan into a parochial state member of a world-wide society within a Western framework. Yokohama, the port of Yedo, was as handy for sea communications with North America or Western Europe as Kobe or Nagasaki; and therefore Japan's decision to open her doors to the West did not confront her with a geographical as well as a cultural problem. The cultural volte-face of the Meiji Revolution did not require any change in the existing capital except a ceremonial change of name from Yedo to Tokyo to signify the inauguration of a new era.

On the other hand in a land-locked Russia the desirability of providing the seat of government of a Westernizing régime with easy access to a maritime Western World raised a geographical problem for which it was difficult to find a satisfactory solution; and, unlike Yedo, Moscow was temporarily deprived of her prerogative as a result of her rulers' decision to open their doors to the West. So far from being able to retain her historic status at the cheap price of a change of name, Moscow was compelled, for more than two hundred years, to see her empire governed from a capital which was not only given a new name but was planted on virgin soil on a far-distant site.[1]

When Seleucus Nicator chose for the capital of his newly carved-out successor-state of the Achaemenian Empire an Antioch-on-Orontes within a stone's throw of the Mediterranean in preference to a Seleucia-on-Tigris in the heart of South-Western Asia, he was acting in accordance with the feelings of the Hellenic ruling element in his dominions and was ignoring the feelings of a subject population which in his day was politically impotent. The transfer of the capital of the Russian Empire by Peter the Great from Moscow in the heart of Holy Russia to Saint Petersburg on the banks of the Neva, within a stone's throw of the Baltic, is comparable to Nicator's choice in its cultural and geographical aspects.[2] In this case, as in that, the seat of government of a land-locked empire was planted in a remote corner of the empire's domain in order to provide the capital with easy access by sea to the sources of an alien civilization which the imperial government was eager to introduce into its dominions. In its political aspect, however, Peter's act was much more audacious than Nicator's; for, in seeking to supplant Moscow by Saint Petersburg, Peter was ignoring the feelings of the Orthodox Christian ruling element in Muscovy with a brusqueness reminiscent of the revolutionary acts of Julius Caesar and Ts'in She Hwang-ti. The Russians whose capital Peter uprooted and transplanted were not a defeated people; on the contrary, they were at that time in process of defeating their Swedish Western enemy under Peter's own auspices; and the site of the new capital which Peter laid out to take the place of Moscow and to serve as a window for letting in Western cultural influence lay in territory wrested from a Western Sweden by Russian force of arms. In the light of this political situation it is astonishing that Saint Petersburg should have remained the capital of the Russian

[1] See pp. 690–1, below.
[2] This comparison has been suggested already in II. ii. 157.

Empire for more than two hundred years (A.D. 1712[1]–1918[2]). The length of this interlude in Moscow's reign is a testimony both to the force of Peter's personality and to the potency of the alien Western Civilization of which Peter had constituted himself a missionary.[3]

Yet even this combination of forces in Saint Petersburg's favour could not avail either to maintain the seat of government there permanently or to avert the untoward effects of its remaining there as long as it did. In the Russian Empire under the Petrine régime the location of the capital at the extreme north-western corner accentuated the tendency, inherent in the imperial government's Westernizing policy, for a Westernized official class to become alienated, like the Hellenic and Hellenized ruling element in the Seleucid Monarchy, from the unassimilated mass of the population. This social schism was the price paid by the Russian Empire for a reception of the alien civilization of the West which never went far enough on the technological plane to achieve Peter the Great's ambition of making Russia capable of holding her own in war against the strongest Western antagonist who might enter the field

[1] This was the date on which Saint Petersburg officially became the capital of the Russian Empire; but the site of the new city had already been the seat of government *de facto* since May 1703, when Peter the Great had started work on the building of Saint Petersburg; for, though the task of conjuring a great city out of a wilderness of waterway and marsh was naturally a labour of many years, the Tsar had at once planted himself on the spot to direct the work in person; and the Tsar, wherever resident, was the Imperial Government incarnate.

[2] The seat of government was moved back from Saint Petersburg to Moscow in A.D. 1728, but was retransferred to St. Petersburg in A.D. 1732 (see Sumner, B. H.: *Peter the Great and the Emergence of Russia* (London 1950, English Universities Press), p. 199).

[3] There was also a feature in the past domestic history of Russian Orthodox Christendom which may have helped Saint Petersburg to maintain itself as the capital of the Russian Empire for as long as it did. The Empire had been brought into existence through the imposition of the rule of the Grand Duchy of Muscovy upon the city-state of Novgorod between A.D. 1471 and 1479. At that date Novgorod represented one half of Russian Orthodox Christendom, and this not merely in the extent of her territory but also in the complexion and orientation of her culture. The Russian state which had been converted to Eastern Orthodox Christianity by the cultural influence of the East Roman Empire at the close of the tenth century of the Christian Era had been founded by pagan seafarers who had made their way into Russia at her opposite extremity, from Scandinavia. Their port of entry had been Novgorod, on the River Volkhov, which the sea-going ships of the Vikings were able to ascend via the River Neva and Lake Ladoga. When the Scandinavians in their homelands were converted to Western Catholic Christianity—a conversion which was simultaneous with that of the Russians to Eastern Orthodoxy—Novgorod became a point of contact between Russia and Western Christendom, and it continued to perform this function till its subjugation by Muscovy. The heavy hand of Muscovite autocracy extinguished both Novgorod's overseas trade with the West and the self-governing institutions that were her heritage from the pagan Viking Age and that had been favoured by the cultural effects of Novgorod's subsequent commercial intercourse with the Hansa towns. In crushing Novgorod and what she stood for, the Muscovite empire-builder Ivan III and his successors were depriving Russian Orthodox Christendom of a valuable cultural asset, and conversely Peter the Great, in founding Saint Petersburg, was in a sense merely restoring to Russia this treasure of which his predecessors had robbed her. In purely geographical terms, Saint Petersburg was the eighteenth-century counterpart of a medieval Novgorod, taking into account the increase in the size and draught of sea-going ships that had taken place in the meantime. In cultural terms the effect of the removal of the capital of the Russian Empire to Saint Petersburg from Moscow was to create at that stage the situation which would have been created in the fourteen-eighties if at that date the political unification of Russia had been brought about through the city-state of Novgorod's conquering the Grand Duchy of Moscow instead of through Moscow's conquering Novgorod. In the light of this historical background, Peter the Great's act of transferring his capital from Moscow to Saint Petersburg appears somewhat less perverse than Seleucus Nicator's act of transferring his from a site in Babylonia to Antioch.

against her. Peter's successors thus fell between two stools; and this was one of the causes of the progressive decay of an always unsound Petrine régime after the assassination of the Tsar Alexander II in A.D. 1881.

In the War of A.D. 1914–18 the Russian Empire narrowly escaped the fate of the Seleucid Monarchy in 83 B.C. Indeed, Saint Petersburg had come near to proving as fatal to the Russian Empire as Antioch proved to be to the Seleucid Monarchy before the empire-building work of Tsar Ivan III and Tsar Ivan IV was salvaged at the eleventh hour by the Bolsheviks. The Bolsheviks snatched the Russian Empire out of the jaws of destruction in order to transform it into a Union of Soviet Socialist Republics, and the general tendency of the Russian Communist Revolution was to carry the process of Westernization, initiated by Peter the Great, a long stage farther, albeit, at this stage, along a line which was heretical from the orthodox Western standpoint of the day. But in one vital point the Bolsheviks made a change which was unquestionably a return to the Pre-Petrine Muscovite tradition. They retransferred the seat of government from Saint Petersburg to Moscow;[1] and this was perhaps the most effective single step that they could have taken to ensure that the results of their salvaging work should be lasting.

As for the capitals of the Danubian Hapsburg Monarchy and the Napoleonic Empire, we can do no more than speculate about the changes of location that might have taken place if the Napoleonic Empire had been less short-lived and if the Danubian Monarchy had either made good its academic pretensions or seized its golden opportunity. If in the eighteenth century of the Christian Era the Hapsburg Power had not allowed itself to be diverted, by inconclusive contests with rival Western Powers for the possession of relatively small and unimportant morsels of territory, from achieving its manifest destiny of entering into the heritage of the Ottoman Empire in the whole of South-Eastern Europe from the eastern outworks of Vienna to Adrianople and Yannina,[2] it is conceivable that in such circumstances the seat of government might have travelled down the Danube from Vienna to Budapest, or even as far as Belgrade. On the other hand, if by some miracle the Hapsburg Monarchy had succeeded in becoming in reality the oecumenical power, embracing the whole of Western Christendom in a single polity, which it purported to be in its style and title and which it was pictured as being in the imaginations of its own Catholic subjects and of its Orthodox Christian and Muslim neighbours and adversaries on the south-east[3], it is conceivable that in such circumstances the capital might have travelled in the opposite direction—up the Danube from Vienna to Ratisbon or Ulm, or even farther afield to either Milan or Frankfurt. It is likewise conceivable that one or other of the two last-mentioned cities might have eventually superseded Paris as the capital of the Napoleonic Empire if the French empire-builders had known how to perpetuate their momentary success in achieving their own less impracticable task of

---

[1] Petrograd, as Saint Petersburg had been rechristened in a fit of Slavophil fervour after the outbreak of war between Russia and Germany in A.D. 1914, was poorly compensated for ceasing to be the seat of government by having its name changed once again—this time from Petrograd to Leningrad.

[2] See II. ii. 179–80 and 182, n. 4.   [3] See V. v. 326–7.

unifying politically the debris of an abortive medieval cosmos of city-states in Northern Italy, Flanders, and Western Germany.

Migrations of the Capital Cities of Metropolitan Empire-builders

If we take, in conclusion, a glance at those universal states that had been founded neither by aliens nor by barbarians nor by marchmen but by some metropolitan power, we shall observe here a general tendency for the seat of government to start in a central position and subsequently to travel towards the frontiers of a politically unified world.

The classical example of this tendency is afforded by the history of the Indic universal state, which was both originally founded and subsequently re-established by dynasties whose ancestral domain was the centrally situated state of Magadha. The Mauryas and the Guptas alike retained their seat of government at Pataliputra (the latter-day Patna), which had previously been Magadha's parochial capital. Standing, as it did, at the junction of the Ganges with the Jumna and with two other tributaries, Pataliputra was the natural administrative centre for the Ganges Basin;[1] yet, in spite of the practical advantageousness of the site, which worked together with the imponderable forces of tradition and prestige to preserve Pataliputra's prerogative, the seat of government eventually travelled north-westward in both these two parallel chapters of Indic history, and in both cases alike it was drawn in that direction by politico-military pressures from beyond the frontier in that quarter.

After the derelict domain of an enfeebled Mauryan Empire had been overrun by the Euthydemid Bactrian Greek prince Demetrius in the second decade of the second century B.C., the conqueror transferred the seat of government from Pataliputra to a new site far along the Great North-West Road[2] connecting the former Mauryan capital with Demetrius's own former capital at Bactra (Balkh) on the Central Asian side of the Hindu Kush.[3] Demetrius's New Taxila[4] lay near the old city of the same name, in the neighbourhood of the latter-day Rawalpindi, which, before the foundation of the Mauryan Empire, had been the capital of a parochial Indian state; and it commanded the approaches, on the Indian side, to the difficult section of the highway in which a traveller had to negotiate the three successive obstacles of the River Indus, the Khyber Pass, and the main chain of the Hindu Kush.

This neighbourhood was the natural location for the capital of a Power which was seeking to 'abolish the Hindu Kush' by uniting the Ganges–Jumna Basin with the Oxus–Jaxartes Basin.[5] The Greek war-lord Demetrius's pioneering essay in this audacious defiance of physical

---

[1] See II. ii. 130.   [2] See xi, maps 23 and 24.
[3] For this road, which ran into the Great North-East Road of the Achaemenian Empire on the steppe of Türkmenistan, between the left bank of the Oxus and the north-eastern edge of the Iranian Plateau, see Tarn, W. W.: *The Greeks in Bactria and India* (Cambridge 1938, University Press), pp. 61–62.   [4] See Tarn, op. cit., p. 179.
[5] This 'geopolitical' *tour de force* which was achieved by the Bactrian Greek prince Demetrius and was repeated by his Kushan barbarian successors had its counterpart in Western history in the long-continuing political union of Piedmont with Savoy in defiance of the intervening physical barrier of the Alps (see IV. iv. 285–6). In this minia-ture Western reproduction of the mountain-bestriding realm of Demetrius and Kanishka, Turin corresponded in location to Taxila (Rawalpindi), Vercelli to Sāgala (Sialkot), Susa to Peshāwar, and Chambéry to Bactra (Balkh).

geography proved ephemeral. The Bactrian Greek Power had no sooner overrun the Mauryan Empire than it was broken up by fratricidal warfare which opened the way for Nomad invasions of its dominions on the Indian as well as the Central Asian side of the Hindu Kush;[1] but, when, after more than two centuries of kaleidoscopic political changes,[2] the momentary achievement of the Greek empire-builder Demetrius was repeated in the first century of the Christian Era by the Kushan empire-builder Kadphises I and was perpetuated by Kadphises' successors, the seat of government of this reconstituted political union of North-Western India with Central Asia came to rest not far from the spot originally selected for it by Demetrius. The capital of the Kushan Empire was planted at Peshāwar, on the Great North-West Road between the Indus and the Khyber Pass.[3]

After the Mauryan Empire had been re-established by the Guptas, history repeated itself. The Guptas, like their predecessors, ruled the Indic World from Pataliputra; but, when the Guptan Empire collapsed in its turn and was momentarily restored by the Emperor Harsha (*imperabat* A.D. 606–47),[4] this last of all the rulers of an Indic universal state placed his seat of government, not at Pataliputra, but at Sthanesvara on the banks of the Upper Jumna, above the site of Delhi, covering the north-western approaches to the Ganges Basin from the quarter from which Hun and Gurjara Nomad invaders had swept down on the Guptan Empire from the Eurasian Steppe in the preceding chapter of Indic history.[5]

Like the Mauryan and Guptan empires, 'the Empire of the Four Quarters', which was the Sumeric universal state, was founded by a power situated in the heart of the world on which it conferred political unity. The founder, Ur-Engur, *alias* Ur-Nammu (*imperabat circa* 2143–2126 or 2079–2062 B.C.), was the ruler of Ur, one of the oldest of the Sumerian city-states in the Tigris–Euphrates Delta; and Ur remained the capital till 'the Empire of the Four Quarters', 118 years after its foundation, was broken up by an Elamite revolt. After an interlude of more than two hundred years, the empire of Ur-Engur was at length partially restored by Hammurabi (*imperabat circa* 1792–1750 or 1728–1686 B.C.);[6] but this Amorite saviour of the Sumeric Society did not

---

[1] During the brief period about half-way through the second century B.C. when Demetrius's dominions were partitioned between one Greek Power in the Oxus–Jaxartes Basin and another in North-Western India, the Greek ruler in India, Menander, placed his capital at Sāgala (Sialkot) on the Great North-West Road a few stages nearer than New Taxila to Pataliputra (see Tarn, op. cit., pp. 247–8).

[2] For this obscure passage in the history of the contact of the Indic, Hellenic, Syriac, and Nomadic civilizations, see V. v. 133, n. 1, following Tarn, W. W., op. cit.

[3] See Smith, V. A.: *The Early History of India*, 3rd ed. (Oxford 1914, Clarendon Press), pp. 261–2. On the political map of the World in A.D. 1952 the role of Taxila (Rawalpindi) in Demetrius's realm and of Peshāwar in Kanishka's was being played by Kābul as the capital of a Kingdom of Afghanistan which had reproduced the structure of the Bactrian Greek and the Kushan Empire by uniting territories lying on opposite sides of the Hindu Kush. The domain of this twentieth-century kingdom of Afghanistan was, of course, much less extensive than those of either of its forerunners. On the north-west it did not extend beyond the left bank of the Upper Oxus, while on the south-east it did not now touch the right bank of the Indus at any point.

[4] See V. vi. 209, n. 3.   [5] See II. ii. 130.

[6] For this chapter of Sumeric history see V. vi. 297–8. For the chronology see the Note in vol. x, pp. 167–212.

reinstate Ur in her former role of serving as the imperial seat of government. Hammurabi governed the empire which he had partially re-established from his own ancestral capital at Babylon—a city which was 'the gate', not only of the Gods, but also of the Amorite barbarians who, during the anarchy following the collapse of the dominion of Ur, had found in Babylon their port of entry from the North Arabian Steppe into the north-west corner of the Land of Shinar.

Regarded from the standpoint of Sumer—the cradle of the Sumeric Civilization in the south-eastern quarter of the Tigris–Euphrates Delta—or even from the wider standpoint of the combined domains of Sumer and its Semitic neighbour and pupil Akkad, Babylon lay on the north-western fringe of the Sumeric World; but the geographical situation had been transformed to Sumer's own detriment, and to Babylon's ultimate profit, by the very success of the Sumeric empire-builder Ur-Engur. The universal state which Ur-Engur had founded and which Hammurabi had partially re-established was not confined to Sumer and Akkad; in its original avatar, at any rate, it embraced the whole of 'the Fertile Crescent', girdling the northern bay of the North Arabian Steppe from the Land of Shinar through Assyria and Mesopotamia as far as Syria and Palestine, which had been opened up during a preceding Time of Troubles by Assyrian traders and Akkadian war-lords; and, in establishing an empire of this extent, Ur had deprived herself and the other cities of Sumer once for all of the central position which they had originally occupied. The expansion of the Sumeric World up-river, north-westward, by commerce and conquest had been an incomparably quicker process than its expansion down-river, south-eastward, by the gradual silting-up of the head of the Persian Gulf.

Thus Ur's empire-building work made Babylon's fortune; and, though Babylon's first innings as the capital of a universal state did not outlast the final collapse of 'the Empire of the Four Quarters' which followed Hammurabi's death, the parvenu Amorite imperial city lived on to enjoy a second innings and a third. After she had recovered her prestige and renewed her youth by bringing the ancient sedentary population of the Land of Shinar into a fraternal union with the interloping Chaldaean tribesmen in an heroic resistance to Assyrian militarism,[1] Babylon was the inevitable capital of Nabopolassar's and Nebuchadnezzar's Neo-Babylonian Empire, which provided a universal state for the Sumeric Civilization's Babylonic successor. And, after the life of this Neo-Babylonian Empire had been cut short by an Achaemenian conquest, the city of Babylon once again survived a political catastrophe to become, as we have seen,[2] the principal capital, de facto, of its alien conquerors.

This virtual retention of an onerous imperial status never reconciled Babylon to Achaemenian rule. No doubt the Babylonians were aware that they owed their dubious good fortune, not to their alien masters' goodwill, but to the felicitousness of their city's geographical position, which constrained the Achaemenidae to use her as a political centre, however much political trouble she might give them. No doubt the Babylonian priesthood were quick to regret their folly in having facilitated

Cyrus's task by turning against their own emperor Nabonidus; and indeed it is remarkable that Nabonidus's unpopularity should have been so extreme as to inveigle the opposition in his own household into cutting off its nose to spite its face. One cause of this unpopularity was the archaeologist-emperor's tactlessly pedantic religious policy;[1] another cause may have been a fear that his penchant towards awkward innovations might inspire him to transfer the capital from Babylon to some other site. Nabonidus showed a marked interest in the North-West Mesopotamian city of Harrān, which not only happened to be his own home town (if this inference from the evidence is correct),[2] but was well placed for serving as a northern bulwark for the Neo-Babylonian Empire against the Achaemenian successor-state of an expansive Median highland Power which had been encircling 'the Fertile Crescent' from the Zagros to the Antitaurus.[3] Was Nabonidus planning to move the seat of government of his threatened empire to this distant outpost?[4] Or was he perhaps planning to move it to his yet more distant asylum at Taymā in the Hijāz?[5] Nabonidus's hostile Babylonian contemporaries may have had no better intelligence than twentieth-century Western scholars had about what was really brewing in their cranky emperor's mind; but we may guess that their conjectures and anxieties on this score played some part in the prompting of their suicidal policy.

In the event, Babylon succeeded in preserving her imperial prerogative in despite of Nabonidus's caprice as well as the Achaemenids' hostility, and the blow which was to deprive her not only of her status but of her existence was dealt her by her Macedonian deliverers from Achaemenian domination. Seleucus Nicator put Babylon out of court by planting his new foundations of Seleucia-on-Tigris[6] on a site still more convenient than the site of Babylon itself for the oecumenical purpose that Babylon had been serving since the days of Hammurabi. The location of Seleucia-on-Tigris was indeed so well chosen that, as we have seen,[7] the Seleucids' barbarian Arsacid successors and the Arsacids' militantly anti-Hellenic Sasanian supplanters made Ctesiphon, the east-bank suburb of Seleucia, into the seat of government of their dominions; and, under the 'Abbasid Caliphs, Ctesiphon had an avatar in the shape of Baghdad.[8] As for Babylon herself, she had dwindled to vanishing-point by the first century of the Christian Era. Yet, after she had forfeited to Seleucia-Ctesiphon the imperial role which Hammurabi had first conferred on her, her site once more demonstrated its felicity by reverting

---

[1] See V. vi. 30 and 94–95.

[2] See Thompson, R. Campbell, in *The Cambridge Ancient History*, vol. iii (Cambridge 1925, University Press), pp. 218–19; Smith, Sidney: *Isaiah, Chapters XL–LV* (London 1944, Milford), pp. 24–25.

[3] The political fortunes of Harrān during the seventy years between the fall of the Assyrian Empire in 610–609 B.C. and the fall of the Neo-Babylonian Empire in 538 B.C. are discussed further on pp. 655–6, below.

[4] After having served as an outpost of the Babylonic Society, Harran became a fastness in which a fossil of the Babylonic Civilization survived the fall of the Neo-Babylonian Empire for some fourteen hundred years (see IV. iv. 101, n. 1, and IX. viii. 408, n. 5).

[5] For the road to Taymā, see p. 101, above. The Neo-Babylonian Emperor Nabonidus's 'funk-hole' at Taymā had its counterpart in the Roman Emperor Honorius's at Ravenna. [6] See p. 200, above.

[7] See p. 202, n. 4, above. [8] See p. 150, with n. 3, above.

to the part which it had played under Hammurabi's own ex-Arabian Amorite ancestors. Both Hīrah, the capital of the Lakhmid Arab principality that stood on guard over the Arabian marches of the Sasanian Empire, and Kūfah, the cantonment of the Primitive Muslim Arab conquerors of 'Irāq and Iran,[1] were virtually west-bank suburbs of Babylon-on-Euphrates.[2]

As a final example of the tendency for the capital of a universal state to travel from the centre towards the fringes when the empire-building Power has been a metropolitan community, we may observe how in Minoan history the imperial sceptre passed from Cnossos to Mycenae. Cnossos was the natural capital for a 'thalassocracy of Minos' ruling the waves of the Aegean from a Cretan base of operations; but, in extending her dominion to the coasts of Continental Greece, Cnossos paved the way for Mycenae to supersede her.

Who are the Beneficiaries?

Having now cursorily surveyed the histories of the capitals of universal states, we may go on to inquire who were the beneficiaries of the insight and will-power that called these capitals into existence. These seats of imperial governments served the divers purposes of both violent and gentle interlopers. Barbarians swooped down on them in quest of mere plunder. Conquerors bred in an alien culture occupied them as a step towards reigning in the stead of a legitimate régime whose inheritance they aspired to usurp. Restorers of dilapidated empires, and revivers of empires that had completely disintegrated, were aided in their reconstruction work by the lingering prestige of the ancient seat of imperial government. Alien cultures, either forcibly imposed by conquerors or voluntarily imported by native 'Herodians',[3] found the capitals of universal states convenient stations for the radiation of their influence. Higher religions found them equally convenient for their own more audacious missionary enterprise of seeking to convert, not merely a cultural élite, but Mankind in the mass. During the Babylonish captivity of Nebuchadnezzar's deportees from Judah the capital city of a secular oecumenical empire actually served an embryonic higher religion as the incubator in which it found its soul by exchanging a parochial for an oecumenical outlook.

The seat of government of a universal state is indeed good ground for

---

[1] See p. 131, above.

[2] If the Primitive Muslim Arab cantonment at Kūfah may be regarded as an avatar of an earlier Amorite cantonment at Babylon, Kūfah's sister foundation at Basrah may similarly be regarded as an avatar of Obolla (Latinè Apologus). Obolla had been one of the cities of Mesênê, a successor-state of the Seleucid Monarchy in the extreme south-east of Babylonia, skirting the head of the Persian Gulf; and this Mesênê was an avatar of the Sea Land which had been a successor-state of the Empire of Sumer and Akkad. The political secession of the Sea Land from the rest of the Land of Shinar after the death of the Emperor Hammurabi may be interpreted as a political expression of a Sumerian national consciousness which had survived the replacement of the Sumerian by the Akkadian language as the living speech of the population of the former territory of Sumer. The special function of the city of Obolla—if its name is derived from the Sumerian word for 'door'—was to serve the Sea Land, as Babylon, 'the Gate', served Akkad, by providing a port of entry from 'the Desert' into 'the Sown'.

[3] The contrast between alternative 'Herodian' and 'Zealot' reactions to the impact of an alien civilization is discussed in IX. viii. 580–623.

spiritual seeds to fall into;[1] for a city that is performing this oecumenical function is the epitome of a wide world in small compass. Its walls enfold, at close quarters, representatives of all nations and classes, speakers of all languages, and adherents of all religious connexions and persuasions, while its gates lead out on to highways running in all directions to the World's end. The same missionary can preach on the same day to the populace in the slums and to the Emperor in his palace; and, if, in the power of the spirit, he does gain the Emperor's ear, he may hope to see the mighty machine of imperial administration set in motion in the cause of the Church. Nehemiah's key-position in the Achaemenian imperial household at Susa gave him his opportunity for enlisting the effective patronage of the Emperor Artaxerxes I for a temple-state at Jerusalem which was still the emotional focus of a world religion in the making; and the Jesuit Fathers who sought and won a footing in the imperial court at Agra and the imperial court at Peking in the sixteenth and seventeenth centuries of the Christian Era dreamed of winning India and China for Catholicism by the Nehemian strategy of converting the Great Mogul and the Son of Heaven. Had not the Mongol Khāqān Qubilāy been half-converted by Tibetan missionaries of the Tantric Mahāyāna?

The Pillage of Capital Cities by Barbarians

The barbarian's appetite for plunder was sated in the looting of Delhi by the Marāthās; of Tenochtitlan and Cuzco by the Spaniards; of Susa, Persepolis, and Ecbatana by the Macedonians; of Ctesiphon by the Primitive Muslim Arabs; of Baghdad by the Mongols; of Loyang by the Hiongnu; of Kaifêng by the Kin; of Thebes by the Assyrians; of Rome by the Visigoths and Vandals; of Babylon by the Hittites; of Cnossos by her Mycenaean marchmen; and of Mycenae, in her turn, by her continental backwoodsmen. An imperial capital in which the tribute of a subject world has silted up for centuries is an irresistibly tempting material prize for invaders who have no subtler or more abiding objective; but the seed sown by covetousness so crude as this bears a vindictive karma. The unsophisticated barbarian squanders his ill-gotten gains as quickly as he snatches them; the more cultivated alien conqueror who, in behaving as a barbarian, is sinning against the light of his own higher moral law, brings a more ironic retribution on the society that has bred him. The ill-gotten gains of the Macedonian and Spanish *conquistadores* slipped through their fingers no less quickly than those of the Vandals and the Mongols; but in these two heinous cases the barren harvest was followed by a calamitous aftermath. The Hellenic Society of the fourth century B.C. and the Western Society of the sixteenth century of the Christian Era were not only put to shame by the barbarism into which their militant apostles had relapsed; they were also devastated by it. For a crime which primitive barbarians can commit with economic impunity does not go unpunished in societies that have risen to a money economy. The rifling of the treasure-houses of the Americas and South-Western Asia put into sudden circulation an

[1] Matt. xiii. 8.

avalanche of bullion which produced a catastrophic inflation, and the sins of Spanish plunderers at Cuzco and Macedonian plunderers at Persepolis were expiated by German peasants in Swabia and by Ionian artisans in the Cyclades.[1]

The Exploitation of the Prestige of Capital Cities by Empire-builders

A less barbarous use has been made of imperial capitals by conquerors or successors who have looked beyond the immediate indulgence of crude appetites towards the more constructive aim of supplanting, re-conditioning, or reviving the régimes into whose heritage they have entered. Thanks to the camouflaging mirage of immortality that is apt to glimmer round the grave of even a long since defunct universal state,[2] a *ci-devant* imperial capital may retain its prestige long after it has ceased to perform its function; and this prestige may stand an interloping empire-builder in good stead if he inherits or adopts the hallowed site as his own seat of government.

When a usurper takes over his victim's former capital as a going concern, the effect is to lighten his task of hoisting himself into the saddle and keeping himself there. Though Peking was first promoted to be a seat of imperial government by the intruding barbarian Khitan, and not by any thoroughbred Chinese dynasty whose choice of the site might have stamped it with the hall-mark of legitimacy in Chinese eyes, the subsequent domination of the Chinese people by the Kin in place of the Khitan and by the Mongols in place of the Kin was undoubtedly facilitated by the retention, under each of these successive barbarian régimes, of a capital from which a subject Chinese population had gradually grown accustomed to receiving a barbarian master's word of command. *A fortiori*, in a later passage of Far Eastern history, the retention of Peking as the seat of imperial government must have facilitated the usurpation of the Manchu barbarians when they took the imperial city over, not from barbarian predecessors, but from the thoroughbred Chinese dynasty of the Ming.

A similar advantage was secured by the Spaniards when they established the seat of government of the universal state which they imposed on the Central American World on the site of Tenochtitlan, which had been the capital of the Spaniards' Aztec forerunners. The political value of the accumulated prestige of an existing imperial capital was rated so high by the Japanese statesmen who engineered the Meiji Revolution that they kept the seat of government at Yedo and induced the Imperial House to migrate thither from Kyoto, although Yedo was the seat of a 'forcèd power'[3] which had been in the saddle for not much longer than a quarter of a millennium, while Kyoto had been for more than ten centuries (A.D. 795–1869) the seat of the legitimate dynasty which was now being rehabilitated. The decisive consideration in the sagacious revolutionaries' minds was no doubt the hard fact that the Japanese

---

[1] For the inflation of prices that was inflicted on the Hellenic World by the Macedonians' looting of the Achaemenian treasuries, see Tarn, W. W.: 'The Social Question in the Third Century', in *The Hellenistic Age* (Cambridge 1923, University Press).
[2] See pp. 7–46, above.
[3] Marvell, Andrew: *An Horatian Ode upon Cromwell's Return from Ireland.*

people had by that time become accustomed to being governed from Yedo *de facto*, whereas Kyoto, for the greater part of its long and venerable history, had been an historical museum and political lumber-room.

The restorer of a universal state likewise finds his task eased if his own initial seat of government happens to be the former capital of the prostrate empire which he is seeking to re-erect. When Amosis successfully repeated the achievement of a Mentuhotep by restoring 'the Middle Empire' of Egypt in the form of 'the New Empire', the founder of the Eighteenth Dynasty was assuredly assisted, and conceivably inspired, by the fact that, like his Eleventh-Dynasty predecessor, he had started his career as prince of Thebes. In the history of the Indic Society a corresponding service was rendered by Pataliputra to the Guptas when they set out from the Mauryas' historic capital to restore the Mauryas' imperial régime.

Dethroned imperial capitals have sometimes been deliberately re-instated by empire-builders who have not had the good fortune either to find these seats of imperial government still at their disposal as going concerns or to inherit them as the local capitals of parochial successor-states of ruined universal states which they have set out to restore.

We have seen[1] that, when Han Liu Pang had made himself sole master of the Sinic World, he laid out a new oecumenical capital in the imme-diate neighbourhood of the Ts'in Power's historic seat of government at Hsien Yang, which had been wantonly destroyed by Hsiang Yü after it had been carefully spared by Liu Pang himself. When, some eight hundred years later, Han Liu Pang's Ch'ang Ngan was reinstated by the Sui Dynasty, under the new name of Si Ngan, as the capital of an empire which was intended by its founders to be an avatar of the Empire of Ts'in and Han, this act of Sui statesmanship bore witness to the vitality of the prestige that clings to a site which has once been a seat of oecumenical dominion; for by that date nearly six hundred years had passed since Ch'ang Ngan had been dethroned. When the Posterior Han Dynasty had re-established the Han Power after its momentary collapse in A.D. 9, they had not reinstated the Prior Han Dynasty's capital. They found Ch'ang Ngan in ruins; for in the anarchy of A.D. 9–25 the city laid out by Liu Pang had suffered the fate of Hsien Yang in the anarchy after the death of Ts'in She Hwang-ti; but in choosing a new site the second founder of the Han Power, Kwang Wuti, did not overlook the value of historic associations. His substitute for Ch'ang Ngan was Loyang, which had been the last seat of the Ts'in Power's predecessors the Chóu. The Chóu, as we have seen,[2] had been extin-guished by Ts'in She Hwang-ti's grandfather in 249 B.C.; and, for more than five centuries before that, their authority had been as shadowy as was that of the Japanese Imperial House during the ten centuries pre-ceding the Meiji Restoration. In the tiny enclave round Loyang which was all that then remained of their once extensive patrimony within as well as outside 'the passes', the Chóu had continued to perform certain customary ritual functions without retaining a shred of practical power.

---

[1] On p. 212, above.   [2] On p. 212, n. 4, above.

It is remarkable that this simulacrum of an imperial past should have invested Loyang with a prestige so abiding as to make its fortune more than 250 years after even a nominal primacy had been taken from it. Yet this Sinic case, though extreme, is not unique.

The prestige of Delhi, for example, survived the decline and fall of the Mughal Empire after the death of Awrangzīb so triumphantly that, more than two hundred years later, she compelled the British to transfer the seat of government of a rāj which had been rebuilt on a basis of British sea-power to the inland site of the capital of their Mughal predecessors from the maritime site of their own original capital at Calcutta. Moscow, too, possessed sufficient prestige to allow her to wait, as Delhi waited, for more than two hundred years for her eventual triumph over a parvenu competitor. Saint Petersburg was Calcutta's twin in her fate, as well as in her location.

As for Babylon, it was inevitable[1] that she should be the capital of a Neo-Babylonian Empire that was a political embodiment of Babylon's genius, but it is remarkable that her situation and prestige should have compelled her Achaemenian conquerors to perpetuate Babylon's imperial prerogative by making her one of the seats of government of their own dominions in preference to a loyal though unpractical Persepolis. It is even more remarkable that the situation and prestige of Peking should have compelled the Ming Dynasty to reverse a deliberate break with an odious past. When the Ming had succeeded in expelling the Mongols from Intramural China, they had transferred the seat of government to Nanking from a city whose only role in Far Eastern history till then had been to serve as the capital of successive barbarian conquerors. Peking was obnoxious to Chinese sentiment for the reason that had rendered her attractive to the Mongol successors of the Kin and to the Kin successors of the Khitan. Yet she was able to compel the Ming to reinstate her at the risk of stultifying themselves in the eyes of their own militantly anti-barbarian Chinese supporters.[2]

In a Medieval Western World the 'Roman Emperors' of the German nation could not acquire a perfect title to legitimate investiture with their purple shirt of Nessus without paying at least one visit to the ruins of Rome in order to be crowned in the midst of them by the Pope and acclaimed by 'a Roman People' who in their day were, not the *faex*, but the *faex faecis Romuli*.[3] For German potentates whose strength was derived from hereditary dominions lying north of the Alps, this Italian expedition was always as costly and perilous as it was frequently barren and humiliating. Yet the prestige of a dead Rome's shadow was still so great that, for the sake of it, these moth-kings sacrificed a living Germany's substance; and, though the medieval German Kingdom eventually came to grief through a persistent pursuit of this Roman will-o'-the-wisp, Napoleon's subsequent experience was to indicate retrospectively the difficulties in which the medieval Western Emperors might have involved themselves if they had refused to pay their personal homage to the ex-imperial city's imponderable power.

---

[1] The reason has been indicated on p. 226, above.
[2] See II. ii. 121–2.   [3] See Cicero: *Ad Atticum*, II. i, § 8.

When Napoleon set to work to build the débris of a cosmos of medieval Western city-states into an empire founded on the might of the most populous and powerful Western national state of his day, he signalized his intention of providing an effective substitute for 'the Holy Roman Empire' by pointedly breaking with the traditional procedure for investiture with the imperial office. Instead of making a pilgrimage to Rome in the wake of an Austrasian Charlemagne and his Saxon and Franconian successors, Napoleon summoned the Pope from Rome to Paris and required him to assist at his coronation in his own imperial capital. Though 'the Corsican usurper' himself was neither Roman nor French, Napoleonic Paris might well feel that she could look contemporary Rome in the face. Had not Paris been the intellectual centre of the Western World since the twelfth century and its cultural centre as well since the seventeenth? And was not her new imperial master now doing for Paris what Augustus had done for Rome when—finding her a city of brick and leaving her a city of marble[1]—he gave her the physical presence that befitted the capital of the World? For the drily rational intelligence of a Napoleon, such considerations might be conclusive; yet the event was to prove that, in the Year Thirteen of the New Era of the French Revolution, Napoleon had under-estimated the longevity of traditional pieties. By flouting Rome and bullying her sovereign pontiff, he won, not respect for his own political power, but sympathy for the helplessness of his venerable victim.

While the Old Rome in the days of her physical impotence thus compelled a series of Western war-lords to reckon with her during a thousand years running from the date of Charlemagne's coronation to the date of Napoleon's, the New Rome gave proof of a comparable power by hypnotizing first the Palaiológhi and then the 'Osmanlis.

When Michael Palaiológhos took Constantinople from its unhappy Western occupants in A.D. 1261, he was relieving them of an untenable position at the cost of creating one for himself and his heirs. In concentrating his efforts on the capture of the ex-imperial city he had let slip through his fingers the best part of his dominions in Anatolia;[2] and, in thus exchanging a countryside that had been the source of his strength for a city that was a liability, he found himself constrained to seek support against the Turkish enemy whom he had neglected from the Latin enemy whom he had affronted. An Eastern Orthodox Christian principality in these straits could not hope to buy military assistance from Western Catholic Christendom except at the price of ecclesiastical submission to the Papacy; and this payment was repeatedly offered by the Palaiológhi, to be invariably rejected by a fanatically Orthodox Greek clergy and people.[3] This insoluble problem of reconciling incompatible terms of appeasement was the rock on which the Palaeologan ship of state eventually foundered:

> Und das hat mit ihrem Singen
> Die Lorelei getan.

---

[1] Suetonius Tranquillus, C.: *The Lives of the Caesars*, 'Divus Augustus', chap. xxviii, § 3.
[2] See V. vi. 298, n. 7, and p. 30, above.
[3] See IV. iv. 615–19.

The Palaiológhi obtained a posthumous revenge; for, in attracting the 'Osmanlis into their wake and drawing them out of Asia into Europe,[1] they exposed these conquerors and supplanters of theirs to the lure of the siren-city by whom they themselves had been brought to shipwreck. The 'Osmanlis could not resist the temptation of seizing a prize that had twice eluded the grasp of their Arab co-religionists and ensamples. They were beckoned forward by the legendary figure of the martyr Seyyid Battāl.[2] Yet, when in A.D. 1453 Mehmed 'Osmanli the Conqueror repeated Michael Palaiológhos's feat, he too was yielding to the magic of the imperial city against the dictates of a sober *raison d'état*. In impelling Sultan Mehmed to conquer her, Constantinople succeeded at last in retrieving her own long-adverse fortunes. By the time of the Conqueror's descendant Suleymān the Magnificent's death in A.D. 1566, Constantinople found herself the capital of a larger empire than she had been ruling in A.D. 565, at the death of Justinian the Prodigal. Yet, by the same token, the commonwealth of which she was the ornament and incubus was by that time once more on the verge of a calamitous decline; and in Ottoman history this decline was to be consummated by a fall before the revolutionary architects of the Ottoman Empire's Turkish successor-state could summon up the courage to transfer the seat of government from Constantinople to Ankara.

This defiance of Constantinople's magic power was indeed the Turkish nationalists' only alternative to committing national suicide; yet even then they could not bring themselves to throw away the millstone that the Ottoman Conqueror of Constantinople had hung about the Turkish nation's neck.[3] Though Atatürk and his fellow revolutionaries dethroned Constantinople, they insisted on retaining possession of her; and in getting their way on this point they did their worst to defeat the governing purpose of all their policy. This governing purpose was to nurse their new-born national state into a vigorous and healthy maturity. The reformers realized in principle that, if they were to give this delicate infant a fair chance of survival, they must allow it to start life free from the grievous burdens that had broken the back of the old Ottoman Empire; and in two cases in point they did not flinch from putting this principle into practice. They renounced bona fide all ambition to re-impose Turkish rule on either the Arabs or the Balkan Christians. Yet, when they had to take their decision about the most formidable burden of all, they opted for clinging to Constantinople and thereby stultified the rest of their acts; for, in burdening the Turkish Republic with Constantinople, they were condemning her, sooner or later, to fall foul of the Soviet Union for the same ineluctable reasons of strategic and commercial geography that had brought the old Ottoman Empire into collision with the old Russia. At the time of writing, it seemed not impossible that Constantinople might once again play her sinister role of luring to destruction a state which had failed to resist the temptation of possessing her.

---

[1] See III. iii. 27 and V. vi. 184.
[2] See V. v. 255 and 256.
[3] Matt. xviii. 6.

The Use of Capital Cities as Transmitting-stations for the Radiation of Cultures

Having now examined certain passages of history in which an ex-imperial city has enchanted some empire-builder into purchasing the asset of her prestige at a prohibitive price, we may go on to consider cases in which an imperial capital has served as a transmitting-station for the diffusion of an alien culture. This was the role of Vienna in the Danubian Hapsburg Monarchy,[1] of Saint Petersburg in the Petrine Russian Empire, of Antioch-on-Orontes and Seleucia-on-Tigris in the Seleucid Monarchy, of Calcutta in the British Indian Empire, of Mexico City in the Spanish Viceroyalty of New Spain, and of Lima in the Spanish Viceroyalty of Peru.

It will be seen that in most of these instances the imperial 'radio city' was a new foundation planted on virgin soil; and in the founding of Seleucia and Antioch and Saint Petersburg this geographical breach with the past was certainly deliberate. Peter the Great realized that the most effective installation for radiating Western culture into Russia would be a seat of Russian government that had no pre-Western associations, and he rejected Moscow, as Seleucus Nicator rejected Babylon, because she was a citadel of the culture which he was planning to replace. Yet this cultural missionary's rule of thumb was broken with impunity by the Spanish foundation of Mexico City and by the Seleucid

[1] Vienna served as a station for the transmission of the Western culture to sub-Western and non-Western receivers, though the province of Lower Austria, in which Vienna lay, was, like the city itself, an integral part of the Western World. Vienna was situated just to the west of the cultural boundary between the heart of Western Christendom and its eastern marches—the lands of the Crown of the Hungarian King Saint Stephen and the United Kingdom of Poland-Lithuania—in which the Western Christian culture was diluted with a tincture of the Nomad culture of the Eurasian Steppe. Vienna's cultural function was to radiate an authentic Western culture, native to Vienna itself and to its western hinterland, into the imperfectly Westernized eastern marches of the Western World and, beyond these again, into Eastern Orthodox Christendom and Dār-al-Islām. Vienna's performance of this cultural task was facilitated by her geographical location; for, while she lay just to the west of the cultural frontier along the line of the River Leitha (where 'the East begins' according to an illuminating Viennese *bon mot*), she lay just to the east of the Austrian Alps, which constituted 'the natural frontier' of Western Christendom in this quarter. Standing, as she thus stood, with her back to the eastern foothills of the Alps, and looking down the course of the River Danube from a point where, after having threaded its way through the Alps, it is heading for the Hungarian Alföld, *en route* for the Iron Gates and for the western tip of the Eurasian Steppe's Great Western Bay, Vienna could not fail to find her missionary field in the sub-Western and non-Western worlds to the east and south-east of her.

Though the writer of this Study did not pay his first visit to Vienna till the summer of A.D. 1929, at a date more than ten years after she had been reduced politically from being the imperial capital of a cosmopolitan empire to being the national capital of an Austrian Republic whose narrow bounds embraced none of the sub-Western or non-Western territories of a now defunct Danubian Monarchy, he found the evidences of Vienna's historic cultural mission still impressively prominent. In A.D. 1929 the names of the subscribers to the Vienna telephone service, as recorded in the book, testified that this city was a melting-pot in which Rumans, Serbs, and Bulgars, as well as Poles, Magyars, and Croats, were being reminted into pure Westerners (see IX. viii. 530); and, when the observer travelled on eastwards to the 'Saxon' cities of Transylvania, which had been under Rumanian rule since the dissolution of the Danubian Hapsburg Monarchy in A.D. 1918, he found these outposts of a Western Civilization, which were now marooned and in peril of being submerged under the resurgent flood of an alien culture, desperately clinging to a traditional link with Vienna which was their cultural lifeline—as the marooned outposts of Hellenism in Western Iran still clung to their traditional link with Antioch-on-Orontes after the military occupation of Media and Babylonia by the Arsacid Power in the sixth decade of the second century B.C.

foundation of Seleucia-on-Eulaeus. Mexico City was not prevented from fulfilling her revolutionary cultural task by any lingering ghost of an Aztec Tenochtitlan; nor was the Seleucid avatar of Susa inhibited from being an active and long-lived focus of Greek life and letters by the more formidable legacy of a site which had been the national capital of Elam before rising to its political apogee as the imperial capital of the Achaemenidae.

The success of this subsidiary transmitting station for the diffusion of Hellenism on an historic site, which, under the Seleucid régime, had ceased to be a capital city, brings out another prevalent feature in the policy of alien empire-builders who use their seats of government for the diffusion of their culture. The Seleucidae were not content to provide for the radiation of Hellenism from a single centre only. When Seleucus Nicator rejected Seleucia-on-Tigris in favour of Antioch-on-Orontes in choosing the location for his imperial capital,[1] he did not deprive the abortive Tigrine seat of government of its cultural role. Seleucia-on-Tigris 'made history' as the local transmitting-station for Hellenism in Babylonia for the next five centuries, and it was the glory of the Seleucidae that, not only on the banks of the Orontes and the Tigris, but throughout their dominions, from Seleucia-on-Eulaeus to Laodicea-on-Lycus, they sowed with a generous hand a star-dust of Greek city-states which continued, long after the disappearance of the missionary dynasty that had called them into being, to shine like a Milky Way across the face of South-Western Asia.[2]

The Spaniards likewise were not content to confine themselves to the use of Mexico City in Central America, or of Lima in the Andean World, as stations for the radiation of the culture that they had brought with them across the Atlantic from Western Europe. As we have already noticed,[3] the Spanish Crown planted its vast new dominions overseas with settlements of Spanish colonists, organized in self-governing municipalities, who, like the Greek colonists in the Seleucid dominions, were to propagate their distinctive way of life by the display of a living example; and, in rural tracts which the radiation of these scattered Spanish municipalities could not reach, the conversion of the subject population was catered for by the Achaemenian expedient of conferring feudal appanages on grandees of the ruling race. In the Spanish Empire such *encomiendas*[4] were granted to their recipients on the condition that, in return for the economic privilege of being furnished by the Crown with a supply of native labour, they must provide for the instruction of their serfs in the Catholic version of the Christian Faith. In the British Empire in India, Madras and Bombay played their part, side by side

---

[1] See p. 201, above.

[2] The cultural idealism of the Seleucidae is thrown into relief by the sharpness of its difference from the narrow-hearted cultural policy of the Seleucids' neighbours and rivals the Ptolemies, whose objective was, not to Hellenize their Egyptiac subjects, but to exploit them. On Egyptiac ground the Ptolemies added only the single Greek community of Ptolemais in Upper Egypt to Alexandria and to the pre-Alexandrine Greek settlement at Naucratis. Yet even the Ptolemies emulated the Hellenizing policy of the Seleucidae in their non-Egyptiac dominions—as is witnessed by the names of the Greek cities in Transjordan and along the Palestinian section of the shores of the Mediterranean.

[3] See pp. 135–6, above.   [4] See p. 145, above.

with Calcutta, in the dissemination of an inflowing alien culture, as the provincial centres in Spanish America and Seleucid Asia played theirs side by side with Lima and Mexico City and Antioch and Seleucia; and Saint Petersburg was singular in serving as the sole centre for the diffusion of Western culture, as well as the sole political capital, in the structure of the Petrine Russian Empire.

The Use of Capital Cities as Seminaries for Higher Religions

We have now made some survey of the divers services that imperial capitals perform for alien cultures, for alien or indigenous empire-builders, and for predatory barbarians; but their historic mission lies in the religious field.

The potent effect on the destinies of Mankind which the Sinic imperial city of Loyang was still exercising at the time when these lines were being written was not a consequence of her former political role as the seat of the Eastern Chóu Dynasty and subsequently of the Posterior Han; she was exercising it in virtue of having been the nursery in which the seeds of the Mahāyāna—wafted by the winds of History from India to China over the Eurasian Steppe—were acclimatized to a Sinic cultural environment and were thus enabled to resow themselves broadcast over the face of the Sinic World. It is true that this historic religious mission would not have fallen to Loyang if the Emperor Kwang Wuti had not previously chosen her for the service of a political purpose; but it was the unforeseen religious consequence of the Posterior Han states-man's political choice that gave Loyang her opportunity to make a lasting mark on history.

The abiding significance of other seats of a transitory political power was likewise due to their religious associations. Si Ngan, for example, was still influencing the life of Mankind in the twentieth century of the Christian Era not because, from A.D. 589 to A.D. 907, she had been the political capital of the Empire of the Sui and T'ang but because, under the T'ang régime, she had become a centre for the diffusion of the Mahāyāna, Manichaeism, and the Nestorian form of Christianity. The desolate site of Qāraqorum was still invisibly alive because, as an un-designed effect of this ephemeral steppe-city's meteoric political career in the thirteenth century of the Christian Era, she had brought mission-aries of the Roman Catholic Christianity of the West face to face with Central Asian exponents of Nestorianism and Tibetan exponents of Lamaism. Peking, in her turn, had won immortality when, as the poli-tical capital of successive Mongol, Ming, and Manchu régimes, she had fallen heir to Qāraqorum's role as a disseminator of higher religions. In A.D. 1928 the city from which a large portion of the Human Race had been governed in succession by Qubilāy and Yung Lo and Ch'ien Lung was at last deprived for a season by a victorious Kuomintang of the poli-tical prerogative which she had so long enjoyed; yet, twenty years later, before she had yet found her opportunity of constraining the Kuomin-tang's Communist successors to serve her purpose by making her the political capital of China once again, she was still making her mark in the life of the contemporary world as an intellectual centre under the non-committal new name of Peiping;[1] and this cultural role, which had thus survived Peking's fall from her imperial estate, had been conferred on her by a succession of religious missionaries who had preached and practised within her gates: the Tibetan Lamas who had gained the ear of Qubilāy; the emissaries of the Roman Church who, twice over,[2] had won a footing in this distant base of operations; and the Protestant educator-evangelists who had followed in the Jesuits' footsteps and had prepared the way for Peiping to fulfil her latter-day function.

In the year A.D. 1952 it was manifest that Peter and Paul, not Romulus or Augustus, had been the true authors of the immortality of Rome. By that date, more than sixteen centuries had run their course since Rome had forfeited to Constantinople and Trèves the prerogative of serving as the political capital of a united Hellenic World; and the paltry political consolation prize which the former imperial city had tardily received when, in A.D. 1870, she had been turned into the national capital of a Modern Western parochial state had been written down to its true value by the humiliation of the Kingdom of Italy in the world war of A.D. 1939–45. The world-wide influence which Rome was nevertheless still exercising—unaffected by political vicissitudes—was a consequence of the work and death, in Rome, of the two Apostles nineteen hundred years before. It was also a consequence of Christianity's subsequently displayed genius for assimilating and transmuting vital elements of other alien religions which had made themselves at home in Rome before the seeds of Christianity had been sown there. The Great Mother who was to play so distinctive a part in the Roman version of Christianity had been escorted in pomp by the Roman Senate and People from Tiber-side to the Palatine[3] 265 years before Paul, after landing at Puteoli, had slipped unnoticed into Rome in the company of the little party that had gone out along the Appian Way to meet him at the Three Taverns.[4]

As for Constantinople, her religious mission was manifest from the moment of her birth; for this New Rome was founded by Constantine the Great, as Saint Petersburg was founded by Peter the Great, with a spiritual as well as a 'geopolitical' purpose.[5] When the first Christian Emperor laid out his new capital on ground that had been cleared by his pagan predecessor Septimius's vindictive erasure of Byzantium, he was founding a city that was to be Christian from the start; and in A.D. 1952 it was apparent that this religious function was of more lasting significance than the superb geographical location[6] that had prompted Constantine to plant his new Christian capital on that particular site. In the course of the following sixteen hundred years, Constantinople had lost and won and lost again the political prerogative of serving as an imperial capital for the Roman Empire, the East Roman Empire, and the Ottoman Empire in turn; and, at the time of writing, such influence

---

[1] Pei-ping meant merely 'northern city', in contrast to Pei-king, which meant 'northern capital'.
[2] In the fourteenth century of the Christian Era and again in the sixteenth.
[3] See V. v. 685–7.   [4] See Acts xxviii. 15.
[5] This comparison had been suggested, by anticipation, in V. vi. 343.
[6] See p. 218, above.

as she was still exercising in the World of the day was due to her being the seat of a Patriarch who was still recognized by the ecclesiastical heads of the other Eastern Orthodox churches—including the mighty Church of Russia—as *primus inter pares*.

(d) THE SERVICEABILITY OF IMPERIAL CURRENCIES

1. *Official Languages and Scripts*

Alternative Possibilities

It can almost be taken for granted that a universal state will have provided itself with official media of mental communication, and that these will include not only one or more languages transmitted viva voce and received by ear, but also some system of visual records that can be preserved and be consulted by the eye after the passing of the minute span of time during which the ear is sensitive to vibrations set in motion by 'winged words'. In the apparatus of nearly all the universal states whose history was within the ken of twentieth-century students, the official system of visual records had taken the form of a visual notation of the meaning of some oral and auditory official language; and, though the Incas had succeeded in creating and maintaining an almost totalitarian régime without the aid of any notational system beyond the wordless semantics of their *quipus*,[1] this *tour de force* was no more than an exception to a general rule that the written word had been an indispensable instrument of oecumenical government.[2]

There had been cases in which some single language and single script had previously driven all other possible competitors off the field throughout the area which the empire-builders had eventually brought under a single government, and in such cases History had virtually decided in advance what the official language and script of the new universal state were to be. In the Egyptiac 'Middle Empire', for example, they were bound to be the Classical Egyptian language and the hieroglyphic characters; in Japan under the Tokugawa Shogunate they were bound to be the Japanese language and the particular selection and usage of Chinese characters that had been worked out already in Japan for conveying the Japanese language visually; in the Russian Empire they were virtually bound to be the Great Russian language and Great Russian variety of the Slavonic version of the Greek Alphabet.[3] This simple situation had not, however, been the usual one; for, in a society that is a 'civilization', more than one language and more than one script are current as a rule, and we have also observed, in another context,[4] that the dominions of universal states are apt to embrace territories of

---

[1] See V. v. 491.

[2] See Myres, J. L.: *The Dawn of History* (London, no date, Williams & Norgate), pp. 68–70.

[3] It was, of course, conceivable that the Muscovite Government might have adopted for its own secular use the 'Church Slavonic', fashioned by the Greek Christian missionaries Cyril and Methodius out of the living Macedonian Slavonic dialect of the ninth century of the Christian Era, which had continued to be the ecclesiastical language of the Slavonic-speaking Orthodox Christian peoples. This would not have been so extreme a *tour de force* as the Guptas' adoption of Neo-Sanskrit (see p. 253, below).

[4] See pp. 62–67, above.

alien culture in addition to the domain of the civilization on which the empire-builders have imposed political unity. More often, therefore, than not, when it comes to deciding what the official language and script of a universal state are to be, the empire-builders find themselves confronted, not with an accomplished fact to ratify, but with a difficult choice to make between a number of competing candidates.

In these circumstances, most empire-builders had given official currency to their own mother tongue, and, if this ancestral language of theirs had hitherto been unprovided with the visual form of presentation which is a necessity for any language that is to be used as an instrument of oecumenical government, they had borrowed or adapted or invented a script for their purpose. There had, indeed, been cases in which empire-builders had passed over their own mother tongue in favour of another language already current in their dominions as a *lingua franca*[1] or even in favour of a classical language which would have been extinct long since if it had not been artificially kept alive or resuscitated.[2] The most usual practice, however, had been for empire-builders to give official currency to their own national language and script without granting these a monopoly. Indeed, in the administration of universal states a plurality of official languages and scripts appears to be the rule; and a medium that enjoys a legal primacy may not in practice be the medium most in use. There may be secondary languages that reign supreme in particular regions of the empire or in particular imperial services; and these may be *lingue franche* that have won this position for themselves *de facto* without having been given recognition *de·jure*. *Lingue franche* that are already going concerns may force their way into official or unofficial use in the service of a universal state that has come into existence after they have already won an established position for themselves; and, conversely, the use of a *lingua franca* in the service of a universal state may be a factor in the making of this language's fortune.

These general propositions may perhaps be usefully illustrated in an empirical survey.

A Monopoly for Some Single Language or Script

In the Sinic World the problem was solved in a characteristically drastic fashion by Ts'in She Hwang-ti.[3] The founder of the Sinic universal state gave exclusive currency to the version of the Chinese characters that had been in official use in his own ancestral state of Ts'in[4] and thereby succeeded in arresting the tendency, which had gone

---

[1] *Lingue franche* are products of social disintegration. A survey of them has been made in V. v. 483–527.

[2] A survey of instances of such archaism in language and literature has been made in V. vi. 62–83.

[3] It would be interesting to know whether, in A.D. 1928, President Mustafā Kemāl Atatürk was aware of this Sinic precedent for his own equally high-handed act of making the use of the Perso-Arabic Alphabet illegal, and the use of the Latin Alphabet obligatory, for conveying the Ottoman Turkish language within the frontiers of the Turkish Republic.

[4] See Fitzgerald, C. P.: *China, A Short Cultural History* (London 1935, Cresset Press), p. 137; Franke, O.: *Geschichte des Chinesischen Reiches*, vol. i (Berlin and Leipzig 1930, de Gruyter), pp. 233–40. Franke gives German translations of the relevant passages in the work of Sse-ma Ts'ien.

far by the end of the foregoing Time of Troubles, for each of the Contending States to develop a parochial script only partially intelligible to litterati outside those parochial limits. Since the Sinic characters were 'ideograms' conveying meanings, not 'phonemes' representing sounds,[1] the effect of Ts'in She Hwang-ti's act was to endow the Sinic Society with a uniform visual language, which would continue—even if the spoken language were to break up into mutually unintelligible dialects— to serve as a means of oecumenical communication by sleight of hand and skill of eye for the very small minority that could learn to read and write so complex a script—just as, in a Western World in A.D. 1952, the Arabic numerals conveyed identical meanings on paper to peoples who, viva voce, called the numbers by different names and wrote these names out in different alphabets.[2] Yet, as this parallel indicates, Ts'in She Hwang-ti's standardization of the Sinic characters would not, in itself, have availed to save the Sinic Society from the curse of a babel of tongues if in the Sinic World there had not been other forces working in favour of uniformity in speech as well as in script.

To begin with, the Sinic World, at the time when the first Ts'in Emperor united it politically under his own rule, happened still to be homogeneous in language to an unusual degree, though by that time it had expanded far and wide from its original nucleus. A great majority of the population even of this vastly extended area spoke some variety of the Chinese branch of the Chinese-Siamese group of the great Asian family of monosyllabic languages,[3] and the heterophone minority largely consisted of speakers of some language of the kindred Tibeto-Burman group. Yet the unifying influence of this original linguistic homogeneity might have been more than counteracted by the combined effect of the geographical expansion and the political disruption of the Sinic Society during its Time of Troubles if Ts'in She Hwang-ti had not opened a new chapter of Sinic history by imposing political unity, and if his Han successors had not underpinned this edifice of oecumenical government by calling into existence, to administer it, the acceptable and therefore effective oecumenical civil service that Ts'in She Hwang-ti had failed to create.[4] These professional civil servants, recruited from all quarters of the Empire and posted in any province except that of their birth, could not conduct their business with one another and with the public solely by brushwork. In addition to the common visual language, provided by Ts'in She Hwang-ti's fiat, which had become the silent shibboleth for admission into the service of the state, the new imperial governing class required a common means of communication viva voce; and it was a standardized official vocalization of a standardized official script that was to save the Sinic Society, and later on the main body of the succeeding Far Eastern Society, from being afflicted with that multiplicity of languages that was to make the Western World an easy prey for the malady of Nationalism.

Ts'in She Hwang-ti's standardization of the Sinic characters may have been anticipated by the founder of a Minoan universal state whose name had not yet been discovered by Modern Western archaeologists in A.D. 1952. Though none of the scripts in use in the Minoan World at divers times and places had yet been deciphered, their sequence gave evidence of a reform in the art of writing that was still more revolutionary than Ts'in She Hwang-ti's. At the transition from 'Middle Minoan II' to 'Middle Minoan III',[1] two separate hieroglyphic scripts, which had made their appearance simultaneously at the beginning of the former period, were suddenly and completely superseded by a single new linear script which was not just one version of the form of writing previously in use, but which drew on its predecessors for the construction of a new form of a different and superior order.[2] In the history of the Syriac Society, we know[3] that Ts'in She Hwang-ti did have a counterpart in the Umayyad Caliph 'Abd-al-Malik (*imperabat* A.D. 685–705), who substituted the Arabic language and script for the Greek in the ex-Roman provinces of the Arab Caliphate, and for the Pehlevi in the ex-Sasanian provinces, as the official vehicle for the public records, including the all-important registers of the inland revenue.[4] When this change was put in hand, there was evidently some anxiety in official circles as to its possible effect on the efficiency of the public administration, particularly in the vital matter of the collection of the land-tax, and there was a corresponding relief when the transition was achieved without the awkward consequences that had been foreboded.

In the Spanish Empire in the Americas, Spanish became both the official language and the unofficial *lingua franca* of the Viceroyalty of New Spain, which provided the Central American World with its universal state, and it was given the same official status in the Andean universal state which the *conquistadores* had converted into the Spanish Viceroyalty of Peru. In the Andean World, however, the Spanish Crown demonstrated the sincerity of its profession to be a devoted secular agent for the propagation of the Catholic Christian Faith by allowing and encouraging the Roman Church to utilize and develop for its own purposes the Quichuan *lingua franca* to which the Spaniards' Inca predecessors had given an oecumenical currency[5] by making its acquisition compulsory for all their subjects.[6]

---

[1] The possibility that the break between 'Middle Minoan II' and 'Middle Minoan III' might be the mark left on the archaeological record by the foundation of a Minoan universal state has been suggested in I. i. 92–93; IV. iv. 64–65; V. v. 236; and V. vi. 312.

[2] See V. v. 491, n. 3.

[3] From the testimony of Ahmad Al-Balādhurī (*Kitāb Futūh al-Buldān*, pp. 300–1 and 465–6 in the English translation by Hitti, P. K., vol. i (New York 1916, Columbia University Press)); Tabarī (2, 1034); and Theophanes (*Chronographia*, ed. by de Boor, C. (Leipzig 1883–5, Teubner, 2 vols.), vol. i, p. 376, *sub Anno Mundi* 6199). Theophanes ascribes the innovation, not to 'Abd-al-Malik, but to his successor Walīd I (*imperabat* A.D. 705–15). Walīd I appears to have completed 'Abd-al-Malik's work by substituting the Arabic language and script for the Coptic in Egypt, where the Coptic had formerly been used side by side with the Greek. This local change in Egypt, which was carried out in A.H. 87 according to Makrizi, *Khitāt*, i. 98, cited by Wellhausen, J.: *Das Arabische Reich und sein Sturz* (Berlin 1902, Reimer), p. 137, n. 1, seems to have been confused by Theophanes with the previous displacement of Greek throughout the ex-Roman provinces of the Caliphate. In the present Study, V. v. 501, n. 3, Theophanes' error has been carelessly reproduced, notwithstanding Wellhausen's elucidation.

[4] See V. v. 501, and p. 181, above.

[5] See Markham, Sir C.: *The Incas of Peru* (London 1910, Smith Elder), p. 165.

[6] See V. v. 523–4, and p. 251, below.

A Partnership between Several Different Languages or Scripts

We may now pass on to consider some instances of the more frequent practice of providing a universal state with several official languages and scripts, including the empire-builders' own.

In the British Rāj in India the English mother tongue of the rebuilders of a Mughal Rāj was, for certain purposes, substituted for Persian, the official language that had been bequeathed by the Mughals to their British and óther successors. In A.D. 1829, for instance, the British Indian Government made English the medium for its diplomatic correspondence, and in A.D. 1835 the medium for higher education in its dominions. But when in A.D. 1837 the final step was taken in the deposition of Persian from its official status in British India, the British Indian Government did not introduce the use of English for all the other purposes that Persian had previously served. In the conduct of judicial and fiscal proceedings, which were provinces of public administration that personally concerned all Indians of every nationality, caste, and class, the British Indian Government replaced Persian, not by English, but by the local vernaculars;[1] and the Sanskritized Hindī vernacular known as Hindustānī was actually manufactured by British Protestant missionaries to provide the Hindu population of Northern India with a counterpart of the Persianized Hindī vernacular, known as Urdu, which the Indian Muslims had already manufactured for themselves.[2] This humane and politic decision to forbear from misusing political power by giving exclusive official currency to the alien empire-builders' own mother tongue perhaps partially accounts for the remarkable fact that when, 110 years later, their descendants voluntarily handed over their rāj to the descendants of their Indian subjects, it was taken as a matter of course, in both of the British Indian Empire's polyglot Indian successor-states, that the English language would remain at least provisionally in use *de facto* for the purposes which it had served under the British régime.

In the Napoleonic Empire in Western and Central Europe, the local vernaculars—Italian, German, and Dutch—which had previously been in use as official languages in parochial states, were allowed to retain their official status side by side with French. In earlier chapters of Western history the French language had made pacific conquests at the expense of Flemish in the Southern Netherlands and of a local High German dialect in Alsace. In both these countries, French had not only become a *lingua franca* but had been accepted as the medium for literature and administration. The Napoleonic Empire had too short a life to furnish any indication whether, if it had endured, its builders' language would have been likely by the same process of peaceful penetration to win for itself over a wider area the position which it had already attained in Alsace and Flanders. The nationalism which the French Revolution had begotten in France, and of which the Napoleonic Empire was inevitably a 'carrier',[3] would in any case have militated against the prestige which the French language and culture had acquired in Central Europe under the *ancien régime*.[1] One thing of which we can be certain is that the French language's prospects, whatever they might otherwise have been, would have been blighted if the Napoleonic régime had attempted, in the manner of the Caliph 'Abd-al-Malik, to impose the use of the empire-builders' own mother tongue on their non-French-speaking subjects.

We can assert this with confidence in the light of the then recent failure of the Emperor-King Joseph II (*res gerebat solus* A.D. 1780–90)[2] to impose the use of German on the non-German-speaking peoples of the Danubian Hapsburg Monarchy. Though economic utility and cultural amenity alike told in favour of this attempted *Diktat* of political authority, Joseph's linguistic policy was a disastrous failure. It not only met with prompt defeat in the territories of the Crown of Saint Stephen, where the vigorous survival of medieval constitutional rights had kept a Magyar and a Croat national consciousness alive, and where the diasporà of German urban and agricultural settlers was very thinly sown; it also evoked the first new stirrings of the long since dormant national consciousness of the Czechs and the Slovenes, who by Joseph's time had been so deeply submerged by a flowing tide of Germanization that, in the judgement of even the sharpest-sighted contemporary observer, their complete assimilation at no distant date might have been taken as a foregone conclusion. The only substantial success which the Josephian policy secured was the retention of German, until the break-up of the Monarchy in A.D. 1918, as the universal language of command in a unitary Imperial-Royal Army. In the Imperial-Royal Navy the language of command had been Italian;[3] and the fact that this Hapsburg fighting service continued during the nineteenth century to employ for this purpose the mother tongue of its principal adversaries in that chapter of its history testifies both to the placidity of the Hapsburg êthos and to the vitality of the Italian language as a maritime *lingua franca* in the Mediterranean.

The Turkish masters of the Ottoman Empire never embarked on the policy which was successfully applied in the Arab Caliphate and unsuccessfully in the Danubian Hapsburg Monarchy. The founders' native Turkish was the official language of imperial administration; but in the heyday of the Ottoman Power in the sixteenth and seventeenth centuries of the Christian Era the *lingua franca* of the Pādishāh's slave-household was Serbo-Croat[4] and the *lingua franca* of the Ottoman Navy Italian[5]— for the same reason that prevailed upon the Hapsburg Navy to employ the same language. Moreover, on the civil side the Ottoman Government, like the British Indian Government, followed a policy of allowing its subjects as far as possible to use languages of their own choice in public affairs that were of personal concern to the individual—though it approached this same statesmanlike objective along a different consti-

---

[1] See V. v. 503, n. 3.
[2] Joseph was Holy Roman Emperor from A.D. 1765 onwards, and from the same date he was also associated with his mother Maria Theresa in the government of the hereditary dominions of the House of Hapsburg; but it was not till after her death in A.D. 1780 that he had a free hand to pursue a policy of his own.
[3] See V. v. 502.   [4] See V. v. 518–19.   [5] See V. v. 502.

tutional avenue. Whereas the British Government in India boldly set aside the previously established Muslim ecclesiastical courts and succeeded in providing an acceptable alternative for its Muslim sub᾿ ᾿cts by applying the Muslim *Sharī*ʿ Law in British courts and by conducting the judicial proceedings in the local vernaculars, the Ottoman Government delegated this great province of public administration to autonomous communal authorities, officially recognized and supported by the Sublime Porte, which conducted their judicial business in languages traditionally employed by them for public purposes.[1] Since these communal authorities were ecclesiastical, the languages which they used for civil as well as for religious affairs were the sacred languages of their respective religions. The law administered in the communal courts of the Muslim community throughout the Ottoman Empire was written in Arabic,[2] the law of the communal courts of the Orthodox Christian community throughout the Empire in Greek, the law of the Gregorian Monophysite community in Armenian, and so on. It will be seen that the ʿOsmanlis in the Orthodox Christian and Arabic worlds showed the same restraint as the British in India in limiting the scope of the official currency which they gave to their own mother tongue.

A similar restraint was shown by the Romans in the imposition of Latin as an official language in provinces of their empire in which Greek was either the mother tongue or the established *lingua franca*. They contented themselves with making Latin the exclusive language of military command for units of the Imperial Army, wherever recruited and wherever stationed,[3] and the principal language of municipal administration for colonies of Italian origin on Greek or Oriental ground. For

---

[1] See IX. viii. 184–6. The non-Muslim autonomous communities were known by the name of *millet*—a word of Arabic origin with a meaning betwixt and between the connotations of the Western words 'nation' and 'church'. Though the dominant Muslim community was not called a *millet*, its constitution and status were in essence the same as those of the Jewish *millet* and of the several Christian *millets* of different denominations. Indeed, the *millet* system, which confounded the traditional Christian distinction between Church and State, was an expression of the Islamic conception of Society which could hardly have taken shape in a predominantly Christian political milieu. In the Ottoman Empire there were two privileged groups within the Muslim community —the kinsfolk of the Prophet Muhammad (*Seyyids*) and the members of the Pādishāh's slave-household (*qullar*)—each of which enjoyed a communal autonomy of its own in the judicial sphere (see Lybyer, A. H.: *The Government of the Ottoman Empire in the Time of Suleiman the Magnificent* (Cambridge, Mass. 1913, Harvard University Press), pp. 116 and 216).

[2] In addition to the *Sherīʿah* the Ottoman ecclesiastical courts did, however, also administer the *qānūns* (imperial rescripts of the Ottoman *pādishāhs*) and *ʿādet* (local customary law). The *qānūns* were written in Ottoman Turkish, while *ʿādet*, if written at all, was not necessarily written in either Turkish or Arabic (see Lybyer, A. H.: op. cit., pp. 152 and 223).

[3] The two policies of giving Latin a monopoly in the Army and paying deference to Greek ran counter to one another in Thrace. In another context (pp. 133–4 and 134–5 above) we have noticed that, when the Romans annexed the client kingdom of the Odrysae, they carried their respect for the Greek language to the point of making Greek, and not Latin, the *lingua franca* and official language of this new Roman province. At the same time Thrace became as prolific a source of recruitment for the Roman Army as the adjoining provinces along the right bank of the Danube. In consequence, Thrace, as well as Moesia and Pannonia, came to be Latinized to a large extent, though in Thrace, unlike the Danubian provinces, the Latinization was not deliberate. For the penetration of Thracians into the Praetorian cohorts from the Severan revolution of A.D. 193 onwards until the disbandment of these units in A.D. 312 by Constantine the Great, see Durry, M.: *Les Cohortes Prétoriennes* (Paris 1938, Boccard), pp. 248 and 255.

other purposes they continued to employ the Attic *koinê*[1] wherever they found it already in official use;[2] and they made its official status in their own empire conspicuous by giving it a place, side by side with Latin, in the central administration as well. At Rome under the Principate the Imperial Chancery was organized in duplicate, with a Greek as well as a Latin side, so that correspondents using either of 'the two languages' (as Latin and Greek were styled *sans phrase*) could be sure of being able to transact their business with the imperial authorities in the language of their choice.

This Roman forbearance towards the Greek language was something more than a tribute to the pre-eminence of Greek over Latin as a medium of culture; it represented a signal victory of statesmanship over *hybris* in Roman souls; for in those far-flung territories of the Empire, extending from Moesia to Mauretania and from Bruttium to Britain, in which Greek was not in competition with Latin on the morrow of the Roman conquest, the triumph of Latin was so sensational that it might have turned the heads of any but the most sober-minded empire-builders. So far from having to impose the use of Latin upon their subjects and allies in territories outside the Greek language's range, the Romans were in the happy position of being able to enhance its attractiveness by treating the use of it as a privilege that had to be sued for.[3] Nor did Latin win its peaceful victories solely at the expense of languages that had never been reduced to writing or enshrined in a literature. In Italy it had to contend with sister Italic dialects like Oscan and Umbrian, and with Illyrian dialects like Messapian and Venetian, which had once been on a cultural par with Latin—not to speak of Etruscan, which was freighted with the cultural heritage of its Anatolian homeland. In Africa, again, Latin had to contend with Punic. Yet, in these contests with non-Greek 'culture languages' already in the field, Latin was invariably victorious; and, although in Africa the wave of Punic speech continued under Roman rule to advance from the coast into the interior, and to penetrate from the upper to the lower strata of society, at the expense of Berber, it now lost ground to a Latin wave, following hard in its wake, as fast as it gained it from a Berber sump. This triumphal progress of the Latin language west of Syrtis and north of Haemus is the setting in which we have to regard the Romans' deference towards the Greek language in order to appreciate this attitude at its full worth.

An even more remarkable restraint was shown by the Sumerian

---

[1] See V. v. 494–5.

[2] In Egypt the Romans continued the Ptolemies' practice of employing, side by side with the Greek language and alphabet, the New Egyptian language and the hieroglyphic and demotic scripts for inscriptions addressed to the native Egyptian population. This practice had been copied by the Ptolemies from the Achaemenidae, who, in Egypt, had employed the Egyptian language and scripts side by side with the Aramaic (see p. 248, below).

[3] For example, in 180 B.C. the municipality of Cumae, whose citizens had possessed the passive rights of Roman citizenship (the Roman *civitas sine suffragio*) since 338 B.C., was allowed, in response to a petition from the municipal authorities themselves, to substitute Latin for the community's native Oscan as its official language ('Cumanis eo anno petentibus permissum ut publice Latine loquerentur et praeconibus Latine vendendi ius esset.'—Livy, Book XL, chap. 42).

founders of 'the Realm of the Four Quarters' when they put the upstart
Akkadian language officially on a par with a Sumerian which was not
only the empire-builders' mother tongue but was the historic vehicle of
the Sumerian culture. This large-minded policy was no doubt inspired
by the practical consideration that in Ur-Engur's (Ur-Nammu's) day
(*imperabat circa* 2143–2126 or 2079–2062 B.C.) Akkadian was gaining
ground[1] while Sumerian was on the ebb; and, in the event, Sumerian
had become almost a dead language by the time when a universal state
which Sumerian-speaking empire-builders had inaugurated reached the
end of its chequered career after the death of Hammurabi (*imperabat
circa* 1792–1750 or 1728–1686 B.C.).[2] The Amorite restorer of a Sumerian
political edifice did 'not strive officiously to keep alive' the moribund
mother tongue of his predecessor Ur-Engur; but it is significant that he
also appears to have made no attempt to fill the Sumerian language's
now all but vacant place with his own ancestral Canaanite dialect, but
to have allowed Akkadian—which in his time stood at its zenith—to
enjoy, unchallenged, the virtual monopoly which by then it had won
for itself *de facto*.

The Achaemenidae gave as modest a place in the government of their
empire to their Persian mother tongue as to their Persian mother country.[3]
Darius the Great's account of his own acts on the rock of Behistan,
overhanging the Great North-East Road, was inscribed in triplicate in
three different adaptations of the cuneiform script conveying the divers
languages of the three imperial capitals: Elamite for Susa, Medo-Persian
for Ecbatana,[4] and Akkadian for Babylon. The same three languages and
scripts were likewise employed in the inscription on Darius's own tomb
at Naqsh-i-Rustam in Fars,[5] and in official inscriptions on imperial
buildings in all parts of the Empire.[6] It is to the credit of the Achaemenidae that they should thus have placed two other languages officially
on a par with their own mother tongue, but this conscientious even-
handedness was too pedantic and too clumsy to meet the practical needs
of current imperial administration. The Elamite tongue, for example,
though it did happen to be the language of Susa, was not a *lingua franca*
and was already moribund even in its own parochial domain;[7] and the
version of the cuneiform script that had been specially devised for the
conveyance of the Medo-Persian language failed—in spite of its technical excellence—to win its way into general use, and consequently
failed to perpetuate itself. The increasing inaccuracy of its use in the
inscriptions of Artaxerxes II (*imperabat* 404–358 B.C.) and Artaxerxes III
(*imperabat* 358–338 B.C.) betrays the truth that its proper usage was

---

[1] See V. v. 496–9.   [2] See V. v. 485.

[3] For the location of the several cities that divided between them the function of
serving as capitals of the Achaemenian Empire, see pp. 203–8, above.

[4] For Ecbatana, the former capital of the Median Monarchy and the actual summer
residence of the Achaemenian Court, see p. 206, above. This Medo-Persian was, of course,
also the language of the Persian imperial people's homeland in Fars, but, at the date
when the Behistan Inscription was carved, the building of Persepolis was certainly not
finished and may not even yet have begun.

[5] See pp. 206–7, above.

[6] See V. v. 499, n. 3, following Meyer, E.: *Geschichte des Altertums*, vol. iii, 1st ed.
(Stuttgart 1901, Cotta), p. 28.

[7] See Meyer, op. cit., vol. cit., p. 29.

being forgotten within perhaps less than two hundred years of its invention.[1]

This infelicity in the Achaemenids' original choice of official scripts and languages was only partially offset by their liberality in the use of unofficial languages and scripts which had a regional currency—for example, the Greek language and alphabet in the neighbourhood of the Aegean, and in Egypt the New Egyptian language conveyed alternatively, for different purposes, in the hieroglyphic and in the demotic form of the Egyptiac characters.[2] It seems, indeed, to have been their regular practice to provide translations, in the local vernaculars, of official documents addressed to their subjects.[3] But the stroke of statesmanship by which they saved a situation which their own pedantry had created was their act of giving official currency to the Aramaic alphabet and language—side by side with the three hyper-official languages and scripts—in all provinces of the Empire to the west of Babylonia.[4]

The sequel showed that commerce and culture may be more potent instruments than politics for making a language's fortune. In the Achaemenian Empire the speakers of Aramaic were politically of no account,[5] whereas the speakers of Medo-Persian were politically dominant; and, apart from this political 'pull', the Medo-Persian language was by no means at a disadvantage in other respects. The area over which it was spoken as a mother tongue was probably not less extensive,[6] though it was of course much less populous, than the area over which Aramaic was current at the time not merely as a *lingua franca* but as the language of daily life. Moreover, the unknown man of genius who had adapted the cuneiform characters for the conveyance of the Medo-Persian language had endowed it with a script that was almost as convenient as the Aramaic Alphabet. Taking his cue, we may suppose, from the Alphabet itself, he had achieved with the cuneiform characters what had never been achieved with them by their Sumerian inventors or their Akkadian, Elamite, and Hittite users: he had contrived to convey visually all the sounds of the Medo-Persian language in an all but alphabetic syllabary

---

[1] See Meyer, op. cit., vol. cit., p. 48.

[2] See Meyer, E.: *Geschichte des Altertums*, vol. iii, 1st ed. (Stuttgart 1901, Cotta), p. 48; eundem: 'Zu den Aramäischen Papyri von Elephantinê', in *Sitz. Kön. Preuss. Ak. Wiss.*, Gesamtsitzung vom 23 November, 1911, Mitth. vom 26 October, p. 1040.

[3] See Meyer, E.: *Geschichte des Altertums*, vol. iii, 1st ed. (Stuttgart 1901, Cotta), pp. 48–49.

[4] See Meyer, E.: *Geschichte des Altertums*, vol. iii, 1st ed. (Stuttgart 1901, Cotta), p. 48; eundem: *Sitz. Kön. Preuss. Ak. Wiss.*, loc. cit.; *Der Papyrusfund von Elephantinê* (Leipzig 1912, Hinrichs), p. 17 (both cited in this Study already in V. v. 123, n. 2). See further Olmstead, A. T.: *A History of the Persian Empire* (Chicago 1948, Chicago University Press), pp. 116–17, 178, 480–1.

[5] Any prospects of political greatness that the Aramaean peoples might ever have been able to look forward to had been blighted when they had lost their long-drawn-out battle with Assyria in the eleventh and tenth centuries B.C. (see II. ii. 134), and the final blow had been the destruction of the south-westernmost of the Aramaean states, the Kingdom of Damascus, in 732 B.C. (see IV. iv. 476). But, at every stage of their military martyrdom, the Aramaeans had snatched cultural victories out of political reverses (see I. i. 79–80).

[6] We do not know the geographical boundaries of the Medo-Persian dialect of the Iranian language in the Achaemenian Age. The dialect of the Oxus–Jaxartes Basin, known in a later form as 'Sogdian', may already have become differentiated from the dialect or dialects of the Iranian Plateau, and we cannot identify the homeland of the Avestan dialect in which Zoroaster composed his *Gathas*.

of not more than thirty-six characters.[1] Yet in the competition between the Medo-Persian and the Aramaic scripts and languages it was the Aramaic that won.

It was not so surprising that the Aramaic language should have beaten the Medo-Persian in a competition for capturing the domain of a faltering Akkadian tongue, for here Aramaic had been the first in the field,[2] and it enjoyed, in addition, the overwhelming advantage of being a sister. Semitic language which an Akkadian-speaker might substitute for his own mother tongue without having to make that conscious and laborious effort to speak an utterly alien language which would be required of him if he were to try to make himself at home with an Indo-European dialect. The really remarkable triumph was achieved by the Aramaic script, which succeeded in replacing the cuneiform as the medium for conveying the Medo-Persian language in its post-Achaemenian phase. This victory must appear the more extraordinary considering that it was accompanied by a lamentably perverse retrogression in the art of writing. Whereas the forgotten inventor of the Achaemenian script for the conveyance of the Medo-Persian language had shown his originality by making an exclusively phonetic use of cuneiform characters that had originated as ideograms, the inventors of the Pehlevi script for the conveyance of the same language in its next phase mishandled a ready-made phonetic Alphabet by coining ideograms out of it. Instead of consistently conveying Persian words by spelling them out in Aramaic letters used phonetically, they lapsed into conveying them by writing Aramaic words that were their equivalents in meaning but were, of course, entirely unrelated to them in sound.[3] This ability of the Aramaic Alphabet to capture the Persian language even in a usage that stultified the Alphabet's own distinctive technical excellence gives some measure of the prestige which it must have acquired, by then, in Persian minds; and one source of this prestige was undoubtedly the official status that had been given to the Aramaic Alphabet and language by Achaemenian Emperors whose mother tongue was not Semitic but Indo-European.

The Manchu restorers of a Far Eastern universal state showed the same liberality, and same touch of pedantry, as the Achaemenidae in placing their own mother tongue and the languages of their Mongol allies and Chinese subjects on a footing of official parity. The Manchus, like the Achaemenidae, inscribed their public records in triplicate: the Chinese text in Sinic characters, the Mongol text in an adaptation of a Uighur version of a Sogdian variant of the Aramaic Alphabet,[4] and the Manchu text in an adaptation of the Mongol Alphabet.[5] In the Manchu, as in the Achaemenian, Empire, two out of the three languages and scripts that had thus been made official on rather formal grounds failed to qualify for this privileged position on the strength of their actual or

---

[1] The inventor of the Medo-Persian cuneiform Alphabet had been anticipated by the inventor of the Phoenician cuneiform Alphabet used at Ras ash-Shamrah on the coast of Northern Syria about a thousand years earlier. But the Ras ash-Shamrah Alphabet had long since fallen into disuse and oblivion, and the inventor of the Behistan Alphabet must have made the same invention independently.

[2] See I. i. 79–80 and V. v. 499.   [3] See I. i. 80 and V. v. 500.
[4] See V. v. 500, n. 6.   [5] See ibid.

prospective currency. The habitat of the Manchus' Mongol-speaking allies was confined to an outlying and sparsely populated glacis of the Manchu Empire; and the northern and north-eastern parts of Manchuria, where, if anywhere, the Manchus' mother tongue had some prospect of surviving, were almost equally remote from the heart of the imperial people's now far extended dominions. In Southern Manchuria the Manchus had entered into a symbiosis with a local Chinese population, and the ruling element among the Manchus had already become half-Sinified before their entry into Intramural China in A.D. 1644. The complete Sinification of the Manchu civil and military 'Bannermen' inside the Wall[1] was manifestly only a matter of time. In fact, the successful achievement of the Manchus' political ambitions had condemned the Manchus' mother tongue to sink *de facto*, whatever its status *de jure*, to the level of a local patois spoken only by the imperial Manchus' country cousins in a 'reservoir' of man-power in the north-eastern marches.[2]

Fortunately for the Manchu Imperial Government, however, the uselessness, for most practical purposes, of two out of the three official languages and scripts of their choice was fully counterbalanced by the all but universal currency, throughout their dominions, of the Sinic characters and the 'mandarin' *lingua franca* of the Chinese civil service.[3] In Eastern Asia in the Manchu Dynasty's day, these two media of visual and oral communication held the field as ubiquitously as the Akkadian language and Akkadian adaptation of the cuneiform characters in South-West Asia in the days of Ur-Engur (Ur-Nammu) and Hammurabi: As compared with the Manchus, the Achaemenidae were unlucky in their generation; for by their time the Akkadian language had lost its former monopoly of serving as a South-West Asian *lingua franca* and was giving way to Aramaic even as the parochial speech of the single province of Babylonia. From Babylon westwards a babel of tongues confronted the Achaemenidae with an administrative problem from which the Manchu rulers of Eastern Asia were exempted by a lucky accident of local linguistic history; and, thanks to this, the Manchus never found themselves compelled like their Achaemenid counterparts to institute a fourth official language in order to redress the inadequacy of three.

In the Mauryan Empire the philosopher-emperor Açoka (*imperabat* 273–232 B.C.) succeeded in reconciling the demands of impartial justice with those of practical convenience by employing a number of different local living vernaculars conveyed in two different scripts, the Brahmī and the Kharoshthī.[4] This happy catholicity in Açoka's choice of media

---

[1] For the Manchu 'Banners', see pp. 128–9, above; for the civil service of the Manchu Empire, see pp. 346–8, below.

[2] The function performed by 'reservoirs' of this kind in universal states established by semi-barbarian or barbarian empire-builders is brilliantly expounded by Lattimore, O., in *Manchuria, Cradle of Conflict* (New York 1932, Macmillan), pp. 31–52.

[3] For the spread of this 'mandarin' dialect of Chinese, see V. v. 512–14.

[4] See Smith, V. A.: *The Early History of India*, 3rd ed. (Oxford 1914, Clarendon Press), pp. 166–70 and 172–4, and the present Study, V. v. 498 and 500. 'Two recensions of the Fourteen Rock Edicts, inscribed on rocks at places near the North-West Frontier of India, were executed in ... Kharoshthī. ... All the other inscriptions [about thirty-two in number] are incised in one or other variety of the early Brahmī Alphabet' (Smith, op. cit., pp. 166–7).

for communication with his subjects was prompted by the single-minded purpose of acquainting them with the way of salvation revealed to Mankind by Açoka's master Gautama,[1] as the Spanish successors of the Incas were moved by their eagerness for the propagation of the Roman Catholic form of Christianity to allow the Gospel to be preached in the Andean World in a Quichuan *lingua franca*.[2] This Quichuan had gained the wide currency that it enjoyed at the time of the Spanish conquest because the Spaniards' Inca predecessors had made the learning of Quichuan compulsory[3] and had imposed this intellectual corvée on themselves as well as on their subjects—if it is a fact that the Incas had an esoteric language of their own which they did not choose to vulgarize.[4]

Empire-builders who have refrained from giving Official Currency to their own Mother Tongue

This Incan self-denying ordinance might have been dismissed as a peculiar product of the Incas' ultra-totalitarian êthos if there were not other examples of imperial peoples refraining from giving any official status to their own mother tongue.

The Mongols, for instance, did not take advantage of their immense conquests in order to propagate the Mongol language from the Pacific to the Euphrates and the Carpathians. The Mongol Khāqāns employed the Sinic characters and the 'mandarin' dialect for the government of China, and the Mongol Il-Khans the New Persian language and the Perso-Arabic Alphabet for the government of Iran and 'Irāq. Even the Khans of Chaghatāy's and Bātū's appanages, who did not transfer their headquarters from 'the Desert' to 'the Sown', nevertheless abandoned the use of their Mongol mother tongue in favour of a Turkish that was current among a majority of their Nomad subjects.

The Turkī dialect that was adopted by the Mongol Chaghatāy Khan's successors from the local Nomads of whom they had taken command in Zungaria had also become the current language of their sedentary subjects in Transoxania; and, when, under the leadership of Timur Lenk (*imperabat* A.D. 1369–1405), the Transoxanians reversed the Mongol political order by force of arms and asserted their own mastery over the Eurasian Nomads,[5] their Turkī tongue was fashioned into a literary language on a Persian model by the Timurid Sultan Husayn's minister Mīr 'Alī Shīr Nawā'ī (*decessit* A.D. 1501).[6] In the next generation Bābur (*vivebat* A.D. 1483–1530)—a scion of the House of Timur who retrieved his family's fortunes by laying the foundations of a new Timurid Empire on the Indian side of the Hindu Kush—made a brilliant use of the vehicle for literary expression that Nawā'ī had provided for him in his own Turkī mother tongue by writing in Turkī his celebrated memoirs.

In the light of these antecedents, it might have been expected that, when Bābur's pioneer empire-building work in India was followed up and completed by his grandson Akbar (*imperabat* A.D. 1556–1605), the Timurid Mughal Dynasty's now literate mother tongue would have

---

[1] See V. vi. 75–76. [2] See p. 242, above. [3] See ibid.
[4] See V. v. 523, n. 2, following Joyce, T. A.: *South American Archaeology* (London 1912, Lee Warner), p. 213.
[5] See II. ii. 144–8. [6] See I. i. 351 and II. ii. 149.

become one of the official languages of the universal state which these Turkī-speaking empire-builders from Central Asia had imposed on the Hindu World. The architects of the Mughal Rāj in India did indeed select for the official language of their empire one of the established literary languages of the Iranic Muslim Society of which they themselves were members, but the language of their choice was not Turkī but Persian;[1] and, in the unofficial hybrid *lingua franca* that was begotten of the social intercourse between a Mughal Court and Army and a Hindu subject population, it was Persian again, and not Turkī, that was infused into Hindustānī.[2] Even in their own household the Mughal Dynasty in India eventually took to speaking Persian instead of their mother tongue. This defeat of Turkī by Persian on all fronts was the more remarkable considering that the discomfited language was the ancestral speech not only of the Timurids themselves but of the most martial contingent of their polyglot henchmen, and also considering that the Emperor Bābur's literary gift reappeared among his descendants. Bābur's daughter Gulbadan Bēgum wrote a history of her brother Humāyūn, and Humāyūn's grandson Jahāngīr emulated his great-grandfather's literary achievement by writing memoirs of his own life and reign;[3] but Gulbadan's *Humāyūn Nāma* and Jahāngīr's *Tuzūk* were written, not in Turkī, but in Persian. When Bābur's pen as well as Bābur's sword had been thrown into the Turkī scale, the balance would hardly have inclined on the Persian side, as it did, if the prestige of the victorious language had not been allowed to pull its weight by a deliberate forbearance on the part of the gifted Turkī-speaking princes with whom the last word lay.

A similar forbearance was shown by the Emperor Hammurabi (*imperabat circa* 1792–1750 or 1728–1686 B.C.) when he refrained[4] from attempting to substitute his living Canaanite mother tongue for a moribund Sumerian as one of the official languages of a momentarily restored Empire of Sumer and Akkad, and thereby left the way open for the Aramaic dialect of a later wave of Semitic-speaking interlopers from the Arabian Steppe eventually to supersede Akkadian as the *lingua franca* of South-Western Asia. It was even more remarkable that in the eighth and seventh centuries B.C., in the hour of the Aramaic language's triumph, when the Akkadian language was manifestly on the wane, as the Sumerian had been in Hammurabi's day, the Chaldaean leaders of an anti-Assyrian resistance movement and founders of a Neo-Babylonian Empire should have followed Hammurabi in making the Akkadian language and Akkadian version of the cuneiform script their official media of communication. The Chaldaeans had been carried into the marshlands of South-Western Babylonia in the same Völkerwanderung that had swept the Hebrews[5] into Southern Syria and the Aramaeans into Damascus and Mesopotamia, and we may infer that, at the time when these three Semitic peoples simultaneously broke out of Arabia, they were all speaking some variety of a common ancestral Aramaic.[6] If there

---

[1] See V. v. 515.   [2] See V. v. 517–18.
[3] See II. ii. 149.   [4] See p. 247, above.
[5] Including under this term Moab and Ammon and Edom and Judah as well as Israel.
[6] On this hypothesis, both the Chaldaeans and the Hebrews were originally Aramaic-speaking peoples who eventually readopted their ancestral speech after an interval during

is substance in this conjecture, it speaks volumes for the prestige of Babylon that the Chaldaeans should have been moved to discard an ancestral Aramaic dialect in favour of the Akkadian speech of their Assyrian oppressors because this Akkadian was also the traditional language of an imperial city and treasure-house of culture which Nabopolassar's Chaldaean followers longed to make their own[1] as eagerly as Mehmed the Conqueror's Turkish followers desired to possess 'the Abode of Felicity' on the shores of the Bosphorus.

The adoption of Akkadian by the Chaldaeans as the official language of the Neo-Babylonian Empire may have prolonged the currency of Akkadian as a living language for perhaps five hundred years. Sanskrit was adopted by the Guptas as the official language of a restored Indic universal state perhaps a thousand years after it had died a natural death.[2] It is one of the curiosities of history that the rebuilders of Açoka's Empire should have chosen for their official medium of communication a language which had been passed over, as obsolete, by Açoka himself some seven hundred years earlier.

Who are the Beneficiaries?

If we now pass from our survey of official languages in universal states to a review of the beneficiaries, we shall find that official languages had been turned to account by restorers of the empires in which these languages had enjoyed official currency; by other latter-day secular agencies, both public and private, political and economic; and by the propagators of higher religions and organizers of universal churches.

Akkadian, for example, as we have seen, was taken over from Ur-Engur's 'Realm of the Four Quarters' by Hammurabi, and again from the Neo-Babylonian Empire by the Achaemenidae. Classical Egyptian was taken over by 'the New Empire' from 'the Middle Empire'; Greek by the Umayyad Caliphate from the Roman Empire; and Persian by the British from the Mughal Rāj in India. It may be observed, however, that in a majority of these cases the inherited official language was not permanently retained. The British Indian Empire discarded Persian in favour of English employed in combination with local Indian vernaculars; the Umayyad Caliphs discarded Greek—and likewise Coptic and Pehlevī—in favour of Arabic; the archaistic-minded 'New Empire' of Egypt acquiesced in Ikhnaton's iconoclasm in the one point of sub-

which—unlike their Aramaean kinsmen and northern neighbours—they had succumbed to the languages of the sedentary peoples among whom they had settled—to Akkadian, that is, in the Chaldaeans' case and to Canaanite (hence miscalled 'Hebrew') in the Hebrews'. In both cases this adoption of the established language of the occupied country was to be expected; for the penetration of the Chaldaeans into Babylonia and of the Hebrews into Palestine was, as we know, a gradual process, and in each case the interlopers were mingling with a sedentary population that was more numerous and more cultivated than they were. On the other hand, it is not surprising that the Aramaean conquerors of the desert-port of Damascus and of the sparsely inhabited Mesopotamian Steppe should have preserved their ancestral language and should have been able, in a key-position at the mid-point of 'the Fertile Crescent', to convert an unextinguished local dialect into an oecumenical *lingua franca*.

[1] The relations between the Chaldaean tribesmen and the citizens of Babylon in the eighth and seventh centuries B.C. have been touched upon in IV. iv. 476–80.

[2] For the artificial revival of Sanskrit which culminated under the Gupta régime, see V. vi. 75–77.

stituting the living Egyptian speech of the day for the now dead classical language; the Achaemenidae found themselves constrained to supplement a waning Akkadian language and script by giving a supernumerary official status to a waxing Aramaic.

Akkadian, again, continued, after the final collapse of 'the Realm of the Four Quarters', to be used as a medium of diplomatic intercourse, commerce, and culture, not only within the former frontiers of the now defunct Sumeric universal state, but also in regions never ruled by either Hammurabi or Ur-Engur, and never even trodden by the great Akkadian war-lords of an earlier age, a Sargon or a Naramsin. In the fourteenth century B.C. the Akkadian language and script were being employed in the archives and libraries of Hittite Kings at Boghazqal'eh, and, *mirabile dictu*, in the correspondence between the Imperial Government of Egypt and its client princes in its own dominions in Syria, as well as in its transactions with such independent Powers as Khatti and Mitanni. A comparable triumph was achieved by the French language after the meteoric rise and fall of the Napoleonic Empire. In the nineteenth century of the Christian Era, French not only retained the role—which, under the *Ancien Régime*, it had already captured from Latin—of serving as the diplomatic language of the Western World; in the less superficial role of a culture-language it now also found new worlds to conquer in the successor-states of a defunct Spanish Empire of the Indies and in an Ottoman Empire that was rapidly going the Spanish Empire's way.[1]

An even more remarkable resilience was shown by Aramaic when, upon the overthrow of the Achaemenian Empire by Alexander, it was brusquely deposed, in favour of the Attic *koinê*, from the official status that the Achaemenidae had conferred on it in their western dominions. Deprived of the imperial patronage which it had enjoyed for two centuries, the Aramaic language succeeded, by the first century of the Christian Era, in completing the process, which it had begun without imperial patronage in the eighth century B.C., of supplanting Akkadian on the east and Canaanite on the west as the living language of the entire Semitic-speaking population of 'the Fertile Crescent'.[2] And, likewise on the strength of its own unaided merits, the Aramaic Alphabet achieved far wider conquests. In A.D. 1599, within less than two thousand years of the Achaemenian Empire's downfall, it was adopted for the conveyance of the Manchu language on the eve of the Manchu conquest of China.[3]

This diffusion of the Aramaic Alphabet was a technological and intellectual conquest which surpassed in its sweep the military and political conquests of the Mongol and Arab herdsmen-warriors, but the ultimate victors in this field were the higher religions which sped the Aramaic Alphabet on its way by taking it into their service. In its 'Square Hebrew' variant it became the vehicle of the Jewish scriptures and

---

[1] In the Ottoman Empire the way had been prepared for the entry of French by the previous currency of the philologically germane Tuscan *koinê* known as the Lingua Franca; and no doubt the adoption of French as the culture-language of Hispanic America was similarly facilitated by the kinship between French and the two locally current Romance languages: Spanish and Portuguese.

[2] See V. v. 499.   [3] See V. v. 500, with n. 6.

liturgy; in an Arabic adaptation of its Nabataean variant it became the Alphabet of Islam; in its Syriac variant it served impartially the two antithetic heresies of Nestorianism and Monophysitism into which Christianity polarized itself south-east of Taurus; in an Avestan adaptation of its Pehlevī variant it enshrined the sacred books of the Zoroastrian Church; in a Manichaean adaptation it laboured for a heresiarch whom Christians and Zoroastrians agreed in execrating; in a Kharoshthī variant it provided the Emperor Açoka with an instrument for conveying the teachings of the Buddha to his subjects in the former Achaemenian province in the Panjab.[1] This latter-day ecclesiastical use of the Aramaic Alphabet had given it an abiding place in history which it would never have won from its ephemeral secular canonization as one of the official scripts of the Achaemenian Empire; and, in this point, its fortunes were by no means peculiar.

In like manner the Latin and Attic Greek official languages and alphabets of the Roman Empire had won their place in history as the liturgical, theological, and administrative vehicles of the Roman Church in the West and the Greek Church in Orthodox Christendom,[2] while the Neo-Sanskrit official language of the Gupta Empire had justified its resurrection by providing a literary medium for both Hinduism and the Mahāyāna.[3] Even the Emperor Ts'in She Hwang-ti's mighty deed of standardizing the Sinic characters might live to be remembered, not for the service that it had done to ethics and politics by providing the Confucian School of Philosophy and the imperial civil service with a common instrument of literary expression, but for its service to religion in preserving in translation certain indispensable scriptures of the Mahāyāna that were no longer extant in the original Sanskrit. The Incas' pedagogic imposition of compulsory Quichuan on their long-suffering subjects would perhaps similarly be commemorated by these pagan Andeans' Catholic Christian descendants for its unintended assistance in furthering the propagation of Christianity in the New World. And it could be predicted that the Buddha's devoted exponent, the Emperor Açoka, would continue to win the blessings of Pālī-reading Hīnayānian Buddhists for his deliberate adoption of the living languages of his subjects as the media for his inscriptions.[4]

2. Law

The Three Provinces of Law

The field of social action which is the domain of Law divides itself into three great provinces: there is an administrative law that lays down the duties of subjects towards a government, and there are a criminal and a civil law, which are alike concerned with acts in which both parties are private persons, but which nevertheless differ, from a government's point of view, in the degree to which they affect governmental interests.

No government, of course, can be indifferent to administrative law;

---

[1] See V. v. 500-1, and p. 250, above.

[2] For the enlistment of a Neo-Attic Greek language, reconstructed by pagan Hellenic archaists, in the service of the Greek Church, see V. vi. 77-78.

[3] See ibid.   [4] See V. v. 498 and V. vi. 76, and p. 251, above.

indeed, it is no exaggeration to say that this province of law is bound to have priority over any government's other concerns; for the first concern of a government is to keep itself in existence; it cannot exist if it does not effectively impose its authority on its subjects by preventing or repressing all those acts of insubordination—ranging from high treason to arrears in the payment of taxes—in which a subject may show himself recalcitrant to a government's will; and the enforcement of governmental authority requires the formulation and execution of a body of administrative law. The same considerations lead governments, in so far as they have the strength, to concern themselves with the criminal law as well; for, though the criminal may not be attacking his government's authority intentionally or consciously in his assaults upon the life, limb, or property of his fellow subjects, he is in fact trespassing on the government's preserves by arrogating to himself, without official licence, a use of force which the Government must jealously preserve as its own monopoly if it is to maintain its authority intact. It will be seen that, in concerning itself with the criminal as well as with the administrative law, a government is primarily actuated by the motive of self-preservation, and for this reason there is in these two provinces of law a close approach to uniformity in the practice of all governments of both the parochial and the universal type. On the other hand, as far as they concern themselves with civil law, governments are acting for Society's and the individual's benefit more directly than for their own; and accordingly we shall not be surprised to find an empirical survey here revealing wide differences in the practice of those universal states which are our subject in the present Part of this Study.

Instances of Failure and Success in Attempts to impose a Uniform Imperial Law

In the domain of law, universal states, by reason of their historical role and their social function, are faced by a special problem of their own which does not confront parochial states—or, at any rate, not ordinarily in so extreme a degree. Universal states do not start life with a clean slate, and they have not time to work out the development of their institutions gradually. They usually establish themselves in place of their parochial predecessors abruptly, as an emergency measure for forestalling a now imminent social collapse. But those predecessors do not perish without leaving—in the domain of law, as in other fields of social action—a legacy with which their destroyer and successor has to reckon.

There had been at least one instance in which the empire-builders had been so abysmally inferior in culture to their conquered subjects that they had found themselves unable to impose on these any part of their own ancestral law. When the Mongols gave the Chinese main body of the Far Eastern Society its universal state and also roped into their empire both a nascent Iranic Muslim Society and a Russian offshoot of the main body of Orthodox Christendom, their leader Chingis Khan naïvely imagined that the legislator's pen would be as puissant an instrument in his hand as the conqueror's sabre.

' "The Great Yasa" was . . . made obligatory on all, including the head of the Empire, the Khāqān, himself. . . . He drew this immutable law neither from the institutions of the more civilised nations with which he came in contact . . . nor from the revelations of a supreme spirit . . . but from the ancient traditions, usages and ideas of his clan and of his nation. He was convinced that . . . he had established eternal norms, good for all time. But . . . "the Great Yasa" has ceased to be law, and the modern Mongols have lost all recollection of it.'[1]

A fortiori, this Nomad code failed to supersede the existing laws of the Mongol Khāqān's sedentary subjects, and, even when it came into head-on collision with them, it did not prevail, though it had the Mongol sword to back it. It conflicted, for example, with the Islamic *Sharī'ah*[2] by prohibiting the washing of hands in running water and by laying down an incompatible ritual procedure for the slaughtering of cattle. Chingis himself recklessly attempted to ride roughshod over the *Sharī'ah* by making it a capital offence to slaughter cattle in the Muslim fashion;[3] but, instead of thereby breaking-in for himself submissive subjects, he found himself inspiring defiant martyrs. This deliberately savage and provocative ordinance was revived by Chingis' successor Qubilāy (*imperabat* A.D. 1259–94)[4] and was not only inflicted on the Muslim diasporà in the Khāqān's own personal domain in Eastern Asia, but was also applied in the Transoxanian subject territories of the Appanage of Chaghatāy,[5] and in the dominions of the Il-Khan Arghūn (*regnabat* A.D. 1284–91)[6] in Iran and 'Irāq, where the Muslims constituted an overwhelming majority of the sedentary population. Yet this third Mongol persecution of Islam[7] was no more successful than its predecessors; and this defeat of the *Yāsāq* by the *Sharī'ah* was typical of the *Yāsāq*'s fortunes in all the Mongols' immense possessions.[8]

The 'Osmanlis—who, unlike the Mongols, found a long-enduring solution for the problem of stabilizing a Nomad empire over a sedentary population[9]—not only dealt summarily with high treason and firmly with the collection of taxes, but also took care to keep in the Ottoman Imperial Government's own hands the administration of the criminal law—to whatever *millet* the criminal or his victims might belong—with the sole, though portentous, exception of the members of the Pādishāh's slave-household, who had extorted from Sultan Bāyezīd II (*imperabat* A.D. 1481–1512) the privileges of being exempted from the jurisdiction of the courts of the Muslim community and of being made amenable exclusively to the judgement of their own officers.[10] On the other hand,

---

1 Vladimirtsov, B. Y.: *The Life of Chingis-Khan*, English translation (London 1930, Routledge), pp. 74–75.
2 See p. 74, above; IX. viii. 355; and X. ix. 36.
3 See Howorth, H. H.: *History of the Mongols*, Part I (London 1876, Longmans Green), pp. 111–12.   4 See ibid., pp. 273–4.
5 See Cahun, L.: *Introduction à L'Histoire d'Asie: Turcs et Mongols des Origines à 1405* (Paris 1896, Colin), p. 412.
6 See Arnold, T. W.: *The Preaching of Islam* (London 1913, Constable), p. 226.
7 There appears to have been a second persecution in the reign of the Khāqān Kuyūk (*imperabat* A.D. 1246–8). See ibid.
8 The eventual utilization of the Mongol Empire by Islam has been noticed on p. 160, above.   9 See III. iii. 22–50.
10 See Lybyer, A. H.: *The Government of the Ottoman Empire in the Time of Suleiman the Magnificent* (Cambridge, Mass. 1913, Harvard University Press), pp. 97, 116, and 216. See also the present Study, IX. viii. 186, n. 2, and X. ix. 37.

as we have seen,[1] the Ottoman imperial authorities showed an equal concern to avoid being implicated in the administration of the civil law, for which the 'peculiar institution' of the Pādishāh's slave-household could not be made to serve as an instrument.

In this province of law the slave-household's only positive concern was its insistence upon enjoying a communal autonomy of its own. As far as other Ottoman Muslims were concerned—apart from the Seyyids (i.e. reputed descendants of the Prophet Muhammad), who enjoyed the privilege of communal autonomy, like the members of the Pādishāh's slave-household[2]—the 'Osmanlis not only conformed to the traditional practice of their adopted Islamic Faith by leaving all matters of civil law to be administered in accordance with the *Sharī'ah* by the Islamic ecclesiastical courts under the authority of the Sheykh-el-Islām; they took the logical further step—which had been taken by other Muslim governments before them, but had never, perhaps, before been carried out so systematically—of granting the same autonomy, on the same ecclesiastical basis, to the non-Muslim communities under their rule. Indeed, they showed an injudiciously light-hearted consistency in conferring corresponding powers on the foreign colonies of Frankish business men of divers nations whom they permitted to reside in the chief commercial centres of their empire—and thereby opened a chink in the curtain-wall of the Ottoman imperial fortress which was eventually to be enlarged into a breach by the lusty application of Frankish diplomatic and military levers.[3]

Thus in the province of the civil law the tendency in the Ottoman Empire was for an initial diversity to become increasingly accentuated with the passage of time, but in this point Ottoman history would appear

---

[1] The Ottoman institution of *millets* has been touched upon on pp. 244–5, above, *à propos* of its linguistic aspect. See further IX. viii. 184–6.

[2] See Lybyer, op. cit., pp. 206, 207, and 216.

[3] Though the name 'capitulations', by which these Ottoman charters to colonies of resident aliens came to be known, meant simply 'articles' and not, of course, 'terms of surrender', they did in fact have the effect of putting the Ottoman Empire at the mercy of the Frankish Powers in the latter days of the Empire's weakness. In origin these instruments were unilateral acts by which the Sublime Porte conferred on Frankish Christian residents the same right to administer their own civil affairs that it granted to its non-Muslim subjects. The 'capitulations' were inspired by the same motive of disinclination towards undertaking the distasteful task of administering the affairs of infidels in a field that did not appear to touch the security either of Islam or of the Ottoman State. Moreover, the 'capitulations', as well as the *millets*, had been a going concern in the parochial states whose place the Ottoman Empire had taken. They had originally been granted by the Western Christian Crusader successor-states of the 'Abbasid Caliphate to colonies of business men from Venice, Genoa, Pisa, Amalfi, and other medieval Italian city-states, and the practice had spread thence both to the dominions of the Egyptian Mamlūks and to the Orthodox Christian successor-states of the East Roman Empire. It was thus easy to understand how the 'Osmanlis slipped into their error of conferring 'capitulations' not only on the old-established Venetian and Genoese residents but on the French, Dutch, and English who now came bustling in at the Italians' heels. The error lay in failing to perceive that the analogy between charters granted to 'millets' consisting of Ottoman subjects and 'capitulations' conferred on resident colonies of the subjects of foreign Powers was one of form without being one of substance. The essential difference was that, in the second case, the rights and powers were accorded, not to Ottoman subjects, but to foreign governments who, unlike the *millet-bāshī* of the *Millet-i-Rum*, were not in the Pādishāh's power, but, on the contrary, wielded power of their own which they could use, in the hour of the Sublime Porte's weakness, for forcing upon the Porte their own interpretation of the 'capitulations' to the advantage of their subjects *in partibus Ottomannorum*.

to have been exceptional. In most universal states the tendency seems to have run contrariwise, towards uniformity. Indeed, even in Ottoman history there was an undercurrent in this direction; for from the fourteenth to the seventeenth century of the Christian Era the dominant Muslim community in the Ottoman Empire was continually gaining adherents at the subject non-Muslim communities' expense, and, if this process had not been checked by a decline in the 'Osmanlis' prestige in the eyes of their Orthodox and Monophysite Christian subjects when the tide turned against 'the Ghāzis of Rum'[1] in their warfare with the Christians of the West,[2] it is conceivable that eventually the Empire might have arrived at uniformity in civil law through attaining uniformity in religion.

In the more frequent cases in which the tendency towards uniformity had prevailed over opposing forces, this common result had not always been reached by the same means or at the same pace.

In the Sinic World, Ts'in She Hwang-ti characteristically imposed an oecumenical uniformity of law at one stroke by decreeing that the legislation in force in his own ancestral kingdom of Ts'in should be applied throughout the territories of the six rival states which he had suddenly conquered and annexed.[3] This act was doubly revolutionary, for these abruptly imposed Laws of Ts'in did not represent the traditional customs even of that outlandish march-state. They were one of those sweeping innovations executed in Ts'in, rather more than a hundred years earlier, by the philosopher-statesman Shang Yang (*decessit* 338 B.C.) which had prepared the way for Ts'in's decisive victory over her competitors in Ts'in She Hwang-ti's generation. Shang Yang had been one of the pioneer exponents of the so-called 'Legist' School of philosophy,[4] which had challenged the sanctity of customary rights and duties and had preached to the receptive ears of sovereigns the Machiavellian doctrine that all means were legitimate for attaining the socially expedient end of breaking the power of a feudal aristocracy for the benefit of parvenu monarchies.

Ts'in She Hwang-ti's revolutionary act had at least two Modern Western parallels. Napoleon introduced his newly minted codification of French law not only in France within her pre-Napoleonic limits, but in Italian, Flemish, German, and Polish annexed territories and client states of the Napoleonic Empire. The British Government of India introduced 'the Common Law' of England—partly in its original form and partly in adaptations embodied in local legislation—throughout the Indian territories over which it established its own direct rule.

This act of British statecraft, as far as it went, was more audaciously revolutionary than either of the other two, for the new law which Napoleon and Ts'in She Hwang-ti imposed on their subjects had, after

---

[1] The title by which the 'Osmanlis are saluted by their Timurid Mughal Turkish kinsman Bābur in his memoirs.

[2] For this change in the relations between the 'Osmanlis and their Orthodox Christian subjects see II. ii. 223-5; III. iii. 47-48; V. vi. 203-4, 299, and 300; and IX. viii. 161-5.

[3] See Franke, O.: *Geschichte des Chinesischen Reiches*, vol. i (Berlin and Leipzig 1930, de Gruyter), p. 233; Fitzgerald, C. P.: *China, A Short Cultural History* (London 1935, Cresset Press), p. 136.

[4] For Shang Yang's doctrine and achievements, see pp. 169 and 170, above.

all, come out of the bosom of the society of which the autocrat and his subjects alike were members, whereas the English 'Common Law' was the outcome of Western religious, political, and economic traditions and influences that were alien to the Muslim as well as to the Hindu subjects of the British Rāj. But, though, in this instance, the wind was not tempered to the shorn Indian lamb, his British shearers tactfully made the operation tolerable for him by shaving him only partwise, like a Parisian poodle.

The civil province of law can be divided into two departments, one concerned with what, in laymen's language, may be described as the 'business relations' between private individuals, and the other with what, in the language of the art, is known as 'personal statute'. 'Business relations' are a broad field in which the pocket is touched without deeply affecting the heart; 'personal statute' is a relatively narrow field, but it touches the quick, for its agenda are the intimacies of social life—marriage, wills, inheritance, wardship, and the like. The 'Osmanlis, as we have seen, consigned both these departments of the civil province of law to be dealt with in the separate communal courts of the Muslim community and of the non-Muslim *millets* of the Ottoman Empire in accordance with their respective communal laws. In the derelict domain of a defunct Mughal Empire in India, the British found a *macédoine* of religions, cultures, and peoples closely resembling the contemporary hotch-potch in the Ottoman dominions, but they worked out a different solution for a similar problem. They gave jurisdiction over the whole field to their own newly instituted British Indian courts, but, in prescribing the law that was to be applied in these courts, they confined the application of the English 'Common Law' and its British Indian derivatives to the department of 'business relations', and laid down that cases concerning 'personal statute' should continue to be governed by the communal law of the parties.[1]

Like the British in India, the Incas in their Andean Empire partitioned the field of law—apparently on somewhat similar lines.

'The customary rules, varying from one clan to another, [under which their subjects had lived,] were subordinated by the Incas to their own law, which was rigorous and uniform. The customary rules survived in great numbers, as was natural, in the domain of private law. The Incaic Law, which was by far the more important of the two, constituted a civil and criminal law of very wide scope.'[2]

The Romans were slower than the Incas or the British or Napoleon or Ts'in She Hwang-ti in achieving uniformity of law in their empire.

[1] This was done, not by drawing up any general definition of the field covered by 'personal statute', but by enumerating in each case the subjects in respect of which the existing communal law of the parties was to be applied in the British Indian courts. The area of the field was different in different cases. The legal institution enabling an owner of property, by making a will which, if valid, is recognized and made enforceable by the law, to determine during his lifetime how his property shall be disposed of after his death, was a feature of Islamic Law, as it was of Western Law, but was unknown to Hindu Law. As a consequence of this historical fact, the testamentary province of personal law came, for Hindus, to fall within the field of the English 'Common Law' or its British Indian derivatives, while for British Indian Muslims it continued to be administered in accordance with the *Sharī'ah*.

[2] Baudin, L.: *L'Empire Socialiste des Inka* (Paris 1928, Institut d'Ethnologie), p. 182.

To live under Roman Law was one of the reputed privileges of Roman citizenship, and the progressive conferment of the citizenship on the Empire's subjects was not carried to its completion till the reign of Caracalla (*imperabat* A.D. 211–17).[1] As and when they received the citizenship, however, the inhabitants of the Roman Empire automatically came under the rule of Roman Law in all its provinces and departments, and thus the universal reign of Roman Law, when it did come, was all-embracing. In the parallel history of the Arab Caliphate the reign of the Islamic Law was progressively extended by conversions of non-Muslim subjects of the Caliphate to the empire-builders' religion, and, though the non-Muslim residue in the Caliphate was never reduced to the same infinitesimal fraction of the population as the non-citizen residue in the Roman Empire in its latter days, the mass-conversion to Islam that took place in the Caliphate and its successor-states from the ninth to the thirteenth century of the Christian Era gained in momentum as the effective power of the Caliphate progressively decayed, and this produced a far more homogeneous result than the corresponding process in the Ottoman Empire, which, as we have seen, was checked, instead of being stimulated, by the political decline of the universal state.[2]

The Attempt to stabilize the Law in Japan under the Tokugawa Régime

In the Roman Empire and other universal states in the days of their decline, attempts were made to arrest the course of deterioration by 'freezing' an existing legal or social situation. The Tokugawa Shogunate in Japan was perhaps unique among universal states in applying this prescription of 'freezing' from first to last and in achieving the *tour de force* of arresting change in the outward forms of social life (though not, of course, in the inward realities) over a span of more than 250 years.

In the domain of law the Tokugawa régime, so far from regarding equality before a uniform law as being a desirable ideal, exerted itself to accentuate and perpetuate a caste division between the feudal aristocracy and their retainers on the one side and the rest of the population on the other which was one of the worst of the wounds that the Japanese Society had inflicted on itself during a foregoing Time of Troubles. The cue was given by Tokugawa Ieyasu's predecessor and patron Hideyoshi in an edict of A.D. 1587 (popularly known as 'the Taikō's Sword Hunt') ordering all non-samurai to surrender any weapons in their

[1] See V. v. 446–7, and pp. 155–6, above, and p. 375, below.
[2] This at first sight puzzling difference is to be explained by a difference in the character of the external enemies by whom a declining Ottoman Empire and a declining 'Abbasid Caliphate were respectively menaced. The most formidable assailants of the 'Abbasid Caliphate were pagan Turkish and Mongol Eurasian Nomads who were as terrifying to the Caliphate's Zoroastrian and Christian subjects as to the ruling Muslim community. In these circumstances the subjects found salvation in adopting Islam themselves and helping their former masters to convert to their now common religion the barbarian conquerors of both parties alike (as the ex-Roman citizen body in Gaul dealt with their pagan Frankish conquerors by converting them to their own recently adopted Catholic Christianity). By contrast, the most formidable assailants of the Ottoman Empire were Western Christians whose culture became extremely attractive to the Ottoman Christians in the secularized version of it that was placed on the international market towards the close of the seventeenth century of the Christian Era, at the very time when the tide of war was turning against the 'Osmanlis.

possession.[1] The recently and arduously established central government further sweetened the pill for the feudal lords whom it had deprived of their long-abused *de facto* local independence by leaving them a very free hand to maintain and develop as they pleased, in all matters that the central government did not consider pertinent to the preservation of its own authority, the variegated 'house laws' which the ruling family of each fief had gradually hammered out and enforced, within the limits of its own parochial jurisdiction, during the later stages of the foregoing Time of Troubles, particularly during the fifteenth and sixteenth centuries of the Christian Era.[2] The edict entitled 'the Laws of the Military Houses' which Tokugawa Ieyasu promulgated in A.D. 1615, on the morrow of his crushing retort to the last challenge to his absolute authority,

'is a document which, like the formularies and "house laws" of earlier times, is not so much a systematic collection of specific injunctions and prohibitions as a group of maxims, in somewhat vague language, supported by learned extracts from the Chinese and Japanese classics.'[3]

'This "Constitution" . . . was regarded by the Shogunate as fundamentally unchangeable. It was re-affirmed by each shogun on his succession, in a solemn ceremony attended by all his vassals; and, though circumstances sometimes forced them to alter it in detail, they never admitted or even contemplated any deviation from its essential principles, and they punished without mercy any breach of its commands.'[4]

It is noteworthy that under this ultra-conservative régime a tendency towards the standardization of local laws did nevertheless declare itself.

'Within their own fiefs the barons enjoyed a very full measure of autonomy. . . . But the Shogunate, without interfering, used to keep a sharp watch on the conduct of the feudatories, and it was one of the chief duties of the censors (*metsuke*) and their travelling inspectors to report upon affairs in the fiefs. For this and similar reasons there was a general tendency among the *daimyō* to assimilate their administrative and judicial methods to those of the central authority, and the legislation in which the Shoguns freely indulged soon began to displace the "house laws" of the fiefs where it did not clash with local sentiment and habit.'[5]

The Expedient of Codification

In universal states in which a progressive standardization of the law had resulted in the attainment of approximate uniformity, there had sometimes been a further stage in which a unified imperial law had been codified by the imperial authorities.

In the history of the Roman Law, the first step towards codification was the 'freezing', in A.D. 131, of the *Edictum Perpetuum* that had hitherto been promulgated afresh by each successive Praetor Urbanus at the beginning of his year of office,[6] and the final steps were the promulgation

---

[1] Sansom, Sir G.: *Japan, A Short Cultural History* (London 1932, Cresset Press)' pp. 422 and 450.
[2] For these local 'house laws', see ibid., pp. 418–20.
[3] Ibid., p. 450.   [4] Ibid., p. 438.   [5] Ibid., p. 449.
[6] Since *circa* 367–366 B.C.—the traditional date at which the practice of annually electing a governing college of three magistrates had been reinstituted (or perhaps in reality introduced for the first time)—or at any rate since 243 B.C., when the number

of the Justinianean *Code* in A.D. 529[1] and *Institutes* and *Digest* in A.D. 533[2] and the subsequent abrogation of the legal validity of all previous legislation and learned comment except in so far as it was reproduced in one or other of the three components of the new *Corpus Iuris Romani*. In the Spanish Empire in the Americas, after two abortive attempts at codification, a Creole Tribonian was found at last, in the person of Antonio León Pinelo, to codify the existing laws of the Indies in a *corpus iuris*, entitled *Recopilación de Leyes de los Reynos de las Indias*, which was completed in A.D. 1635 and eventually published, in a revised version, in 1681.[3] Thereafter the stream of legislation continued to flow till the *Recopilación* had fallen out of date. But a project, first for revising and then for replacing it, which was launched in A.D. 1765, was never carried through.[4] In the Sumeric 'Realm of the Four Quarters' an earlier code compiled under the Sumerian emperors who had ruled this Sumeric universal state from a seat of government at Ur during the first chapter

of annually elected Roman magistrates of the rank of 'praetor' (the next highest rank to the supreme magistracy represented by the two consuls) had been increased from one to two, one praetor had always been detailed to take charge of the conduct of legal business in the metropolis, and hence had come to be known as the Praetor Urbanus. The transformation of a once socially simple peasant community first into one of the Great Powers, and finally into the imperial mistress, of a complicated and sophisticated Hellenic Society had gradually made it necessary for the Praetor Urbanus to interpret— and, by interpreting, to extend—the existing Roman Law in order to make it applicable to an ever-increasing range and complexity of cases. In order to cope with this problem, it had become customary for each successive Praetor Urbanus, on his accession to office, to draw up, in consultation with the best living legal authorities whose advice he could obtain, a declaration of the lines on which he proposed to administer the law during his own term of office. This practice had been regularized by a *Lex Cornelia* of 67 B.C., which had made it thenceforward obligatory, and no longer merely customary, for the Praetor Urbanus to adhere to the terms of his own edict when once he had posted it up, in order that jurymen, judges, litigants, and the general public might know in advance the terms on which the law was going to be administered during the current year (Strachan-Davidson, J. L.: *Problems of the Roman Criminal Law* (Oxford 1912, Clarendon Press, 2 vols.), vol. i, pp. 72–73). From 67 B.C. to A.D. 131 it had still been theoretically open to each successive Praetor Urbanus to ignore the edicts of his predecessors and to draft an entirely new annual edict which, though it would be binding on the draftsman, would no more bind his successors than he himself had been bound to follow the drafts of his predecessors. But, though the word *perpetuum*, as used in the *Lex Cornelia*, had thus meant no more than 'valid for twelve months', the effect had been to confirm the practice—no doubt by then already well established—of carrying over the major part of the edict from year to year, since a Praetor Urbanus who had actually exercised his theoretical right to recast it *in toto* would merely have thrown the administration of the law into confusion if he had accomplished the *tour de force* of executing this herculean labour. Thus from 67 B.C. to A.D. 131 the *Edictum Perpetuum* had been a supple instrument in which the benefits of a substantial continuity had been combined with opportunity for the law to grow in response to changes in the social life with which the law was concerned. The Emperor Hadrian commissioned the legal expert Salvius Iulianus to edit, rearrange, and systematize the *Edictum Perpetuum* of the day, and Iulianus's edition was given the force of law, and at the same time made definitive, by a *senatus consultum* of A.D. 131. The effect, of course, was, not to bring the development of Roman Law to an end, but to transfer to the Senate and the Princeps the virtual legislative power which, under the terms of the *Lex Cornelia* of 67 B.C., the Praetor Urbanus had previously been sharing with them *de facto*.

   [1] According to Collinet, P.: 'The General Problems raised by the Codification of Justinian', in *Tijdschrift voor Rechtsgeschiedenis* (Haarlem 1923, Tjeenk Willink), p. 6, there were two editions of the *Code*, of which the first was ordered on the 13th February, 528, and was promulgated on the 7th April, 529, while the second was promulgated on the 17th November, 534.

   [2] According to Collinet, ibid., the *Digest* was ordered on the 15th December, 530, and was promulgated on the 16th December, 533; the *Institutes* were promulgated on the 21st November, 533.

   [3] See Haring, C. H.: *The Spanish Empire in America* (New York 1947, Oxford University Press), pp. 110–15.   [4] See ibid., p. 114.

of its history (*imperabant circa* 2143–2026 or 2079–1962 B.C.) appears[1]
to have been the basis of the later code, promulgated by the Amorite
restorer of the Empire, Hammurabi of Babylon,[2] which was brought to
light in A.D. 1901 by the Modern Western archaeologist J. de Morgan
in the course of his excavations at Susa, whither the stele on which
Hammurabi's code had been engraved had been carried away from
Babylon in the twelfth century B.C. by the Elamite raider Shutruk-Nach-
chunte.[3] In the main body of the Far Eastern World the victory of the
law of the Mongols' sedentary subjects over their Nomad conquerors'
Yāsāq[4] was celebrated in the codification of Chinese law in and after the
reign of Hung Wu (*regnabat* A.D. 1367–98),[5] the Chinese patriot leader
who had founded the indigenous Ming Dynasty by expelling the Mongols from China-within-the-Wall.[6] In the Napoleonic Empire a labour
which elsewhere was usually 'staggered' over a span of many generations
was crowded, for once, into the compass of a single lifetime.

The Historical Background of Codification in the Spanish Empire of the Indies

In all these otherwise diverse instances the work of codification was
an urgently needed social service. Hung Wu and Hammurabi were confronted with the problem of conjuring order out of the confusion to
which the law, like the rest of the apparatus of oecumenical government,
had been reduced by the respective intrusions of alien Mongol and alien
Elamite conquerors. In the Andean World, where the Incaic Law had
been as strictly administered as it had been sternly conceived,

'Things changed completely when the Spaniards arrived. The swift and
inexorable justice of the Inca disappeared, there was a multiplication of

---

[1] See *The Cambridge Ancient History*, vol. 1, 1st ed. (Cambridge 1924, University
Press), pp. 435 and 461; Rostovtzeff, M.: *Caravan Cities* (Oxford 1932, Clarendon
Press), p. 9; Hrozný, B.: *Die Älteste Geschichte Vorderasiens und Indiens* (Prague 1943,
Melantrich), p. 113. Hrozný ascribes the first essay in codification to the revolutionary
reformer Uru-kagina of Lagash, who lived in the third quarter of the twenty-sixth
century B.C., or in the first quarter of the twenty-fifth century (see the Note on Chronology in vol. x.).

[2] English translations of Hammurabi's Code are given in Smith, J. M. P.: *The Origin
and History of Hebrew Law* (Chicago 1931, University of Chicago Press), pp. 181–222,
and in Pritchard, J. B.: *Ancient Near Eastern Texts* (Princeton 1950, University Press),
pp. 163–80. A convenient summary of the contents will be found in *The Cambridge
Ancient History*, vol. cit., ed. cit., pp. 516–21. Pritchard, in op. cit., pp. 159–63, gives
translations of fragments of codes promulgated at Isin and at Eshnunna during the
interval between the fall of Ibbi-Sin of Ur and the rise of Hammurabi.

[3] See Hrozný, op. cit., p. 113.   [4] See pp. 256–7, above.

[5] 'The first Emperor of the Ming Dynasty, immediately following the capture of
Wuchang, ordered a revision of the existing law. In the tenth month of the first year of
his reign as King Wu, Li San-Chang was appointed Head of the Law Codification Commission, assisted by Yang Shien, Liu Chi and Dao An. The Code was completed in the
twelfth month. In the sixth year of the reign of Hung Wu, Liu Wei-chien was designated
to compile the Code of Great Ming, which was submitted by Sung Lien to the Emperor
for approval the following year. The Code underwent modifications from time to time
after that, and was finally completed and revised by Wu Wei-yung and Wang Kwong
Yang. It was promulgated in the thirtieth year of the same reign.' (Note communicated
to the writer on the 12th December, 1947, by the kindness of the Chinese Ambassador
at the Court of St. James's, Mr. F. I. Cheng, from the record in the official History of
the Ming Dynasty.)

[6] The retransfer of the capital of China from Nanking to Peking by Hung Wu's son
and second successor Yung Lo has been discussed in II. ii. 122–3 and on p. 237, above.

interminable suits, the judges were full of tenderness towards criminals and debauchees, and in the markets of the great cities there were Indians to be found who gained their livelihood by serving as witnesses.'[1]

Moreover,

'Under an absolute and paternalistic [Spanish] monarchy, legislation for the Indies soon became very voluminous, touching every aspect of the duties, rights and responsibilities of the colonists and of the officials set to rule over them. This legislation was intended to carry over into America the spirit and intent of the law of the metropolis, as Philip II explicitly declared in A.D. 1571. It implied the transplanting of society and institutions from an Old World to the New. Yet the legislation of Castile itself had in the colonies the force only of supplementary law. From the very first the Crown had to "adapt the distinct physiognomy acquired by traditional institutions" to circumstances, both geographical and historical, which were radically different from those in the metropolis. The peculiar conditions prevailing in America called for the elaboration of a new legislation with a distinct character of its own. Moreover, in spite of the centralist and unifying tendencies of Hapsburgs and Bourbons, the Crown was forced to take into account, both in legislation and in its application by viceroys and governors, the great differences between one region in America and another. A surprising amount of autonomy was often permitted to colonial authorities. There likewise grew up a substantial amount of customary law in the overseas dominions derived from the jurisprudential practices of the times, which had a recognized legal force if accepted by the Crown and if no written legislation was applicable. Much of this customary jurisprudence developed from the modifications of royal orders by viceroys and captains-general to meet the exigencies of a local situation. Finally, the Crown tried to incorporate into its American legislation some of the juridical customs of the aborigines—especially of those, such as the Incas and the Aztecs, who had evolved a strong political and economic organization—customs which were not in contradiction to the fundamental precepts of Spanish organization and control.'[2]

In the *Recopilación de Leyes de los Reynos de las Indias*, 'León Pinelo reduced the laws of the Indies to over 11,000, extracted from some 400,000 royal *cédulas*.'[3] It is little wonder that this clearance of an Augean stable took even that 'zealous and indefatigable' labourer ten years. But it reflects some discredit on the Spanish imperial administration that the task should not have been placed in Pinelo's competent hands until after A.D. 1624, considering that an abortive preceding essay in codification had been commissioned as far back as A.D. 1582. It is perhaps still more discreditable to the authorities that, though Pinelo's draft was completed in A.D. 1635 and was approved by them within the next seven months, the eventual revised version was not published until A.D. 1681.[4]

The Historical Background of Codification in the Roman Empire

This complexity of the historical background of Pinelo's *Recopilación* is surpassed by that of Tribonian's *Corpus Iuris*. The Law of the Twelve Tables, which, according to the traditional chronology, had been pro-

---

1 Baudin, L.: *L'Empire Socialiste des Inka* (Paris 1928, Institut d'Ethnologie), p. 186.
2 Haring, op. cit., pp. 109–10.
3 Ibid., p. 113.   4 See ibid.

mulgated in 451–450 B.C. by the Board of Decemvirs appointed to draft it, had equipped the still archaic Roman community of the age with an instrument that, by that time, would already have been out of date in the heart of an Hellenic World on whose outskirts Rome then lay. The subsequent progressive and cumulatively enormous revolution in Rome's social and political position demanded, and duly evoked, a flood of new legislation which flowed for ten centuries in a number of different channels: laws enacted by the Populus Romanus; votes, possessing the force of law, passed by the Plebs; the *Edictum Perpetuum* of the Praetor Urbanus; the resolutions of the Senate; and the acts, decisions, and decrees of Caesar after the Republic had been succeeded by the Principate. When the stream of often capricious and inconsequent acts of Plebs and Populus had ceased to flow, the new stream of imperial legislation became, as time went on, even more inconsequent, capricious, and voluminous till, in the western half of the Empire during the century ending in A.D. 476, a climax was reached in a spate of decrees reiterating the same commands on a rising note of hysteria, with threats of ever more savage penalties for disobedience which merely advertised the truth that the imperial legislators in that part of the Empire had by that stage become impotent to enforce their authority. 'Et septemgemini turbant trepida ostia Nili.'[1] The ancient river of Roman legislation had dispersed its waters into a mazy delta on its way to losing them in an 'unharvested sea'.

Yet this maze of legislation was not so formidable as the jungle of learned comment that had sprung up on its marge. Law is by nature conservative, and its ineradicable resistance to change calls always and everywhere for the services of skilled interpreters to ensure that it shall continue to serve the practical needs of social life in spite of perpetually losing its unequally matched race with changing circumstances. In the administration of the Roman Law during the thousand years following the promulgation of the Twelve Tables, the lag—to be made up by interpretation—between the formal state of the law and the social task required of it was enlarged to an unusual degree of magnitude in consequence of the extraordinary political career through which a rustic city-state had grown into an oecumenical empire. If the Roman jurisconsults were to succeed in bridging this formidable gulf,[2] they stood in need of all the intellectual building-materials on which they could lay hands; and, after the reception of Hellenic philosophy at Rome in the second century B.C., the ethics of the Stoic School gradually came to supply the interpreters of the Roman Law with those comprehensive maxims, logical principles, and imaginative vistas that were required for transforming the peculiar local customs of a primitive-minded peasantry into a system acceptable to the Hellenic World.

Under the early Principate as well as under the late Republic, a still persisting aristocratic tradition kept the study and interpretation of the

---

[1] Virgil: *Aeneid*, Book VI, l. 800.
[2] The archaic title *pontifices* would have described the functions of these secular Roman jurisconsults more aptly than those of the Christian bishop who eventually took it over from the college of pagan priests who were its original bearers.

law in the hands of a governing class—confined to the senatorial and
equestrian orders—whose members were expected to be men of action
as well as men of culture and would not have been allowed by their
superiors or their peers to rise to high positions of political responsibility
exclusively in virtue of eminent legal ability, without having also shown
at least some aptitude for military command and public administration.
This aristocratic way of public life, with its obvious merits and its equally
obvious limitations, was abandoned, in the field of law, in the reign of
the Emperor Hadrian (*imperabat* A.D. 117–38),[1] whose personal policy
was consciously inspired by a zeal for efficiency but at the same time
served the purposes of a *Zeitgeist* that was already up in arms against
social privileges and political monopolies.[2] Hadrian converted his predecessors' informal and indefinite entourage of advisers into an imperial
council of salaried jurisconsults of senatorial and equestrian rank, and he
also created a panel of eminent legal authorities (*iuris prudentes*) whom
he invested with powers of replying officially to legal queries (*ius respon-
dendi*) and, in effect, of acting corporately as a legislative body, since
he provided that their opinion, when unanimous, should have the force
of law. By these measures, Hadrian called into existence a professional
class of legal specialists; and the consequent lawyers' 'Golden Age' out-
lasted the Antonine 'Indian Summer' and survived—though not unscathed—the intermittent frosts of the ensuing Severan overture to
winter.[3]

The virtues and abilities of Papinian—whom Posterity regarded as
the brightest link in all the golden chain of the Roman legal tradition[4]—
found a lawyer's mind to appreciate them and a soldier's arm to protect
them combined in the person of Septimius Severus, who had been
Papinian's predecessor in the office of Advocatus Fisci before becoming
his imperial master and patron. Yet even the grim founder of the Severan
Dynasty could not save Papinian from paying the extreme penalty for
his probity to the savagery of Septimius's brutal son and successor
Caracalla; and Papinian's disciple Ulpian was assassinated in his turn,
by the praetorian guards, in the presence of his impotent imperial friend
and admirer the gentle Alexander Severus. Paul, and Paul only, was left;
and when, seven years after the murder of Ulpian, the last Emperor of
the House of Severus himself succumbed to the tragic fate from which
he had failed to rescue an esteemed and beloved public servant, this
culminating political crime heralded a blizzard of anarchy in which
liberal legal studies were blasted and seared. Yet, even so, the golden
century of Roman legal studies, from the 'freezing' of the Urban Praetor's Perpetual Edict in A.D. 131 to the 'revolt of Caliban' in A.D. 235, had
produced a volume of output so enormous that for Tribonian and his
colleagues, three hundred years later, the compression of this matter

---

[1] See p. 262, with n. 6, above.   [2] See pp. 152–8, above.
[3] See *The Cambridge Ancient History*, vol. xi (Cambridge 1936, University Press),
pp. 314–15 and 816–26.
[4] A rescript of Galla Placidia's, dated the 7th November, A.D. 426, gave Papinian
the casting vote in any conflict of authority between two or more of the five classical
jurists (Papinianus, Paullus, Gaius, Ulpianus, Modestinus) in which the authorities,
including Papinian, were ranged in equal numbers on either side (*Cod. Theod.* I. iv. 3).

into the *Digest* was the heaviest of their three titanic tasks, though they virtually confined their selection of materials to the contents of treatises produced within this relatively short period in the long history of Roman Law.

'Seventeen lawyers, with Tribonian at their head, were appointed by the Emperor [Justinian] to exercise an absolute jurisdiction over the works of their predecessors. If they had obeyed his commands in ten years, Justinian would have been satisfied with their diligence; and the rapid composition of the Digest or Pandects in three years (15th December, A.D. 530—16th December, A.D. 533) will deserve praise or censure according to the merit of the execution. From the library of Tribonian they chose forty, the most eminent civilians of former times; two thousand treatises were comprised in an abridgement of fifty books; and it has been carefully recorded that three millions of lines or sentences were reduced, in this abstract, to the moderate number of one hundred and fifty thousand.'[1]

By comparison with this second of his labours, Tribonian's first feat of compiling the *Code* was easy. In codifying within a term of fourteen months (13th February, A.D. 528–7th April, A.D. 529) the decrees that had been promulgated by successive emperors in the course of the four centuries that had elapsed between the accession of Hadrian[2] and the current year of Justinian's reign, Tribonian could avail himself of the existing works of three forerunners: the unofficial codes compiled by Gregorius (later than the 19th October, A.D. 294, and probably in A.D. 297) and by Hermogenianus (later than the 21st March, A.D. 295)[3] and the official supplement to them promulgated, on the 15th February, A.D. 438, by the Emperor Theodosius II (*imperabat* A.D. 408–50),[4] which covered the years A.D. 312/13–437 for the Eastern Half of the Empire and the years A.D. 312/13–432 for the Western Half.[5] By comparison, again, with the arduousness of compiling the Code, it was child's-play for Tribonian to round off his threefold enterprise by enucleating the elements of Roman Law in the Institutes.

The Historical Background of Codification in the Napoleonic Empire

The *Corpus Iuris Iustinianeum* had a worthy counterpart in the Napoleonic array of codes in respect of both the speed and the immensity of the labours of which it was a monument.

'The difficulties of this undertaking consisted mainly in the enormous

---

[1] Gibbon, E.: *The History of the Decline and Fall of the Roman Empire*, chap. xliv.

[2] The series did not begin before Hadrian's reign because Hadrian was the initiator of the practice of promulgating imperial decrees undisguisedly as such. 'From Augustus to Trajan, the modest Caesars were content to promulgate their edicts in the various characters of a Roman magistrate; and, in the decrees of the Senate, the epistles and orations of the Prince were respectfully inserted. Hadrian appears to have been the first who assumed, without disguise, the plenitude of legislative power' (Gibbon, op. cit., loc. cit.). This new departure of Hadrian's was at variance with the spirit of the Principate as inspired by Augustus.

[3] A second edition of Hermogenianus's code was published (probably by Hermogenianus himself) in the reign of Constantine the Great (*imperabat* A.D. 306–37), and a third during the joint reign of Valentinian and Valens (A.D. 364–75).

[4] The Theodosian Code had taken just under nine years to compile, since the commissioners had been appointed on the 26th March, 429.

[5] See Seeck, O.: *Geschichte des Untergangs der Antiken Welt* (Stuttgart: Metzler), vol. vi (1920), pp. 164–83, and vol. vi, Anhang (1921), pp. 428–32.

mass of decrees emanating from the national assemblies, relative to political, civil and criminal affairs.'[1] This amorphous product of more than eleven years of French revolutionary legislation[2] was comparable with the spate of decrees of the Roman Emperors, from Hadrian to Justinian, which Papinian had to confine within the dykes of the Justinianean *Codex*. The resemblance extended beyond the sheer volume to the intrinsic nature of the materials. 'Many of these decrees, the offspring of a momentary enthusiasm, had found a place in the codes of laws which were then compiled; and yet sagacious observers knew that several of them warred against the instincts of the Gallic race.'[3] The French legislators had been attempting, like the Roman jurists, to transfigure a litter of ancient local customary laws by suffusing it with a modern philosophy; but they had sought to achieve at a stroke what their Roman ensamples had been content to accomplish in the course of three or four hundred years, and they had gone to work with an inferior intellectual instrument; for the self-confident iconoclastic humanism of Rousseau or Voltaire was a jejune spiritual elixir by comparison with the ripe and rueful wisdom of a Stoicism that had been refined by many generations of suffering.

The Napoleonic codifiers were therefore well advised in rejecting their revolutionary heralds' academic ideal of making a clean break with the past; yet they could not contemplate reinstating the antediluvian law as it had stood.

'Old French law had been an inextricable labyrinth of laws and customs, provincial privileges, ecclesiastical rights, and the later undergrowth of royal decrees; and no part of the legislation of the revolutionists met with so little resistance as their root-and-branch destruction of this exasperating jungle. Their difficulties only began when they endeavoured to apply the principles of the Rights of Man to political, civil and criminal affairs.'[4]

The revolutionary legislators' axes had cleared away the primeval forest to force a rank second growth in the name of simplicity and reason, and it was left for the Napoleonic codifiers to produce a blend of old and new which could serve the practical needs of the Western Society of the day.

In putting this hard but urgent task in hand, Napoleon did not have to start entirely *de novo* or unaided. Before the expiration of the *Ancien Régime* the industry and sagacity of pre-revolutionary French jurists had already gone far towards distilling a common essence out of the divers provincial varieties of French customary law; and, in following up their work, Napoleon had at his elbow, in the Second Consul Cambacérès, a learned and clear-headed lawyer who had stumbled upon the pitfalls of the revolutionary attitude and method in failing, in A.D. 1793, to obtain the approval of the Convention for a draft of a civil code which he and his fellow committeemen had taken six weeks to prepare instead of the month which the Convention had assigned for the completion of the

---

1 Rose, J. H.: *The Life of Napoleon I* (London 1904, Bell, 2 vols.), vol. i, pp. 287–8.
2 Reckoning from the opening session of the States-General on the 5th May, 1789, to the appointment, on the 12th August, 1800, of a commission to draft a civil code.
3 Rose, op. cit., vol. cit., p. 288.   4 Ibid., p. 288.

work. The four commissioners appointed on the 12th August, 1800, by Napoleon, to try again where the Convention's committee had failed, succeeded in carrying out their instructions to produce a first draft in four months. It was printed on the 1st January, 1801; and, though it then still had to run the gauntlet of the Court of Cassation, the Courts of Appeal, the Legislative Section, and the General Assembly of the Council of State, and thereafter the Tribunate, a civil code of 2,281 articles, embodying the amendments of these successive critics, was duly promulgated between the 15th March, 1803, and the 30th March, 1804, and was thus completed only three and a half years after the drafting commission had been nominated. Within nine and a half years of the same initial date, the entire gigantic task of producing not only a civil code but also a code of civil procedure, a criminal code, a code of criminal procedure, and a commercial code had been completed by the promulgation of the fourth and last book of the criminal code on the 2nd March, 1810.

The extent of Napoleon's own personal contribution to the shaping of these five Napoleonic codes may continue to be disputed. We may believe contemporary reports that, in some episodes of the thirty-five sittings, out of eighty-seven in all, at which the First Consul was present and in the chair while the draft of the Civil Code was being debated in the General Assembly of the Council of State, Napoleon 'fatigued the attention of his audience by the confused abundance and the unexpected turns of his thought'.[1] We may follow a recent English master of Napoleonic studies in his verdict that 'the Civil Code was a hasty piece of work, and' that 'the First Consul imported a strong gust of passion and of politics into the laboratory of legal science'.[2] But any student of history who, at however low a level, has had dealings with both scholars and men of action, and has also had it laid upon him to induce them to co-operate with one another on a common task, will not be blind to the significance of Napoleon's decisive intervention, on the 1st April, 1802, to shorten, simplify, and improve the procedure for passing the draft of the Civil Code at a moment when the cumbrous wheels of an academic constitution had almost stopped turning. And he will readily be convinced that, 'without [Napoleon's] driving power, [the Civil Code] would certainly not have come into existence so soon, and might not have come into existence at all'.[3]

The Price of Codification

Who had been the principal beneficiaries of the empire-builders' legal heritage and of their successors' codifying labours?

The victims of codification would hardly have reckoned themselves among the beneficiaries if they could have risen from the dead to inspect their successors' handiwork. Among the codifiers whom we have just passed in review, the Napoleonic team alone could have contemplated with equanimity a personal encounter with predecessors who, in this

---

[1] Fisher, H. A. L., in *The Cambridge Modern History*, vol. ix (Cambridge 1906, University Press), p. 152.
[2] Ibid., p. 162.
[3] Ibid., p. 163.

exceptional case, would have been compelled, on confrontation, to confess that these deft and elegant surgeons had improved, out of all recognition, the uncouth build of a *corpus vile*. By contrast, the ghosts of Papinian and Ulpian might have protested in all sincerity that they would liefer have felt again, in their own flesh, the agonizing edge of their assassins' swords than have voluntarily submitted the exquisite products of their masterly intellectual labours to be butchered by the rough-and-ready workmanship of Tribonian and his colleagues.

'Instead of a statue cast in a simple mould by the hand of an artist, the works of Justinian represent a tesselated pavement of antique and costly, but too often incoherent, fragments.'[1]

And it is possible that a twentieth-century historian might have felt moved to apply Gibbon's dictum to the Code of Hammurabi if the extant fragments of the underlying work of Hammurabi's Sumerian predecessors[2] that had been preserved independently had been sufficient to enable the latter-day student to extract and reconstruct the copious borrowings from the same source that were to be looked for in Hammurabi's redaction.

The Exceptional Service rendered by the 'Code Napoléon' to a Late Modern Western Society

In their high-handed treatment of their predecessors' work, are the codifiers performing a valuable service for their contemporaries and successors? In the judgement of an eminent post-Gibbonian Western student of Roman Law,

'Justinian's intention was to promulgate legislation applicable to the peoples of diverse race who were living under the law of the Empire of the East, using as his materials the texts of the Roman Law as he found it— first and foremost, the texts of the classical jurists. The basis thus given to his work was the best that he could have taken; for, in the decadent state of the science of Law in his day, he could never have succeeded in obtaining a codification comparable in merit to the system with which his name is actually associated if he had instructed his commissioners to do the drafting themselves. Just because, however, he chose the basis that he did choose, the materials that entered into the composition of his codification, and particularly into the Digest, had to be transformed—as stones from an old building that are being used in a new one are re-cut and re-mortared—in order to be brought into harmony with the exigencies of a civilization that was younger by three centuries at the least, and with the needs of an empire—the Empire of the East—whose boundaries were no longer identical with those of the *Orbis Romanus* of the generation of Gaius or Ulpian.[3] This task of adaptation required the constant employ-

---

[1] Gibbon, E.: *The History of the Decline and Fall of the Roman Empire*, chap. xliv.

[2] Twenty-five laws, in all, of the code compiled in the Sumerian language by the Emperor Ur-Engur and succeeding sovereigns of the Third Dynasty of Ur had been preserved on two clay tablets from Nippur and one from Uruk (*The Cambridge Ancient History*, vol. i, 1st ed. (Cambridge 1924, University Press), p. 461). Whatever might be the respective merits of the draftsmanship, there seemed to be no doubt that, in the penalties prescribed, the Sumerian emperors' code was superior to Hammurabi's in point of humanity.

[3] According to Collinet, P., *Études Historiques sur le Droit de Justinien*, vol. i, 'Le

ment of an adequate instrument, [and this instrument was found in the device of] interpolation.'[1]

The claim made in this passage on behalf of the authors of the *Corpus Iustinianeum* could undoubtedly be substantiated by the authors of the *Code Napoléon*; but this may be one of those exceptions that prove a contrary rule; for the *Code Napoléon* was the work of empire-builders to whom History, as we have seen, had assigned the peculiar task of providing a universal state for a moribund sub-society within a larger body social that had not yet lost its vitality; and these unusual circumstances, which condemned the Napoleonic Empire itself to an early death, ensured a brilliant career for the code that was its offspring. The *ci-devant* city-state cosmos in Italy, the Low Countries, and Germany, whose incorporation into a universal state was the Napoleonic Empire's historical *raison d'être*, did duly dissolve with the downfall of the Napoleonic political edifice that had housed it in its last phase; but in this unique case the sequel was not the catastrophe of a social interregnum but a 'happy ending' in which an abortive sub-society that had failed to make a success of its deliberate departure from the standard pattern of the Western Civilization now at last succeeded in divesting itself of a separate identity which had long since ceased to be anything but a handicap and an embarrassment to it by re-entering the main stream of Western life from which it had once self-consciously sought to part company. It had been the mission of the French empire-builders to draw their non-French subjects back into a flowing current of·life which was the imperial people's own native element, and from which their legal tradition and êthos were derived; and for this reason the successful accomplishment of a French political task, which made the Napoleonic Empire superfluous, launched the *Code Napoléon* on a flood-tide leading on to fortune.

Caractère Oriental de l'Œuvre Législative de Justinien' (Paris 1912, Recueil Sirey), the *Corpus Iustinianeum* was intended to serve the current needs of the Greek and Oriental provinces of the Roman Empire (p. 14). The work is a monument of 'the transformation of Oriental elements, that had previously been merely provincial, into imperial elements [during the interval] between [the generations of] Constantine, who is a Roman emperor reigning in a Roman city, and Justinian, who is an Oriental emperor reigning over an Empire of the East' (ibid., p. 16). Justinian's board of commissioners was composed of representatives of four parties: Constantinopolitan officials, Constantinopolitan professors, Berytan professors, and advocates practising in the court of the Praefectus Praetorio per Orientem at Constantinople (ibid., p. 23)—i.e. the law schools of Constantinople and Bayrūt alone were represented, to the exclusion of those of Rome, Alexandria, Caesarea, and Athens (ibid., p. 23). According to Collinet, the Code was wholly, and the Institutes were mainly, the work of the Constantinopolitan commissioners, while the Berytan commissioners were perhaps principally responsible for the Digest (ibid., p. 24). The *Corpus Iustinianeum* is a codification of the living law of the Roman East (ibid., p. 28); and this was a fusion of Hellenic Law with a Roman Law which had been adapted to Oriental requirements by an abandonment of some of its original native Roman elements (ibid., p. 29). In Justinian's day a Roman Law that, by then, had already become static in the West was still evolving in the East on Oriental lines (ibid., pp. 34, 159, and 314); and, in order to bring the *Corpus Iustinianeum* into conformity with the living Roman Law of the East, a number of traditional Roman legal institutions were jettisoned in the compilation of it (ibid., pp. 213–14). The *Corpus Iustinianeum* was distinguished from contemporary Western Roman Law in two ways: it was more *savant*; and, instead of being stagnant, it embodied the results of regional progress (ibid., pp. 314 and 317).—A.J.T.

[1] Collinet, P.: *Études Historiques sur le Droit de Justinien*, vol. i: 'Le Caractère Oriental de l'Œuvre Législative de Justinien' (Paris 1912, Recueil Sirey), pp. xxv–xxvi.

On the day of its promulgation the Napoleonic Civil Code automatically became law, not only for all inhabitants of France within her pre-Revolutionary frontiers, but for Walloons and Flemings in the Southern Netherlands and Germans west of the Rhine, who on the 21st March, 1804, were already fellow citizens of the French in a Republic that, on the 18th May, was to be converted into an Empire. Thereafter, from A.D. 1804 to A.D. 1811, the Code's domain was being constantly enlarged. It gained ground partly through the enlargement of the French Empire itself, which continued to swallow up satellite states and conquered territories till it stretched north-eastwards as far as Lübeck and south-eastwards as far as Terracina,¹ and partly through the 'reception' of the Code in satellite states that survived or that were increased in stature or that were enlisted as new recruits. On the 30th March, 1806, the Code was promulgated in the Napoleonic Kingdom of Italy, which by that time had been enlarged to include almost all the former dominions of Venice;² and, before the Napoleonic edifice collapsed, the Code had become law throughout Continental Italy, including the satellite Kingdom of Naples. It seeded itself in several Swiss cantons. It was promulgated in Holland on the 18th October, 1810. And it made a triumphal progress across Napoleonic Germany, where it was received in the Kingdom of Westphalia on the 15th November, 1807; in the Free City of Danzig on the 19th November, 1807; in Arenburg on the 28th January, 1808; in the Grand Duchy of Baden on the 5th July, 1808; in the Grand Duchy of Frankfurt on the 15th September, 1809; in the Grand Duchy of Berg on the 1st January, 1810; in the newly constituted Lippe and Hanseatic Departments of the French Empire on the 29th May and the 10th December, 1810, respectively; in the Duchy of Köthen on the 28th December, 1810; and in the Duchy of Nassau on the 1st and 4th February, 1811.³

The most distant and exotic of the Code's pacific conquests was the Grand Duchy of Warsaw, where it was received in A.D. 1808 in the ex-Prussian nucleus, and in A.D. 1810 in the ex-Austrian annex.⁴ In A.D. 1928 it was still in force in a fragment of territory, wedged in between the left bank of the River Niemen and the eastern frontier of East Prussia, which had once constituted the north-eastern extremity of the Duchy of Warsaw and its successor the 'Congress Kingdom' of Poland, but which in 1928 formed part of the *Saisonstaat* of inter-war Lithuania.⁵

This widespread 'reception' of the Code was brought about by a

---

¹ Without reckoning in the Illyrian Provinces, insulated geographically from the main body of the French Empire by the breadth of the satellite Kingdom of Italy, which France acquired from Austria in the Peace Treaty of Schönbrunn (14th October, 1809).

² All, indeed, except the Ionian Islands. The Kingdom of Italy obtained these acquisitions through the Franco-Austrian Peace Treaty of Pressburg (26th December, 1805). In the territorial rearrangements following the conclusion of the subsequent Franco-Austrian Peace Treaty of Schönbrunn (14th October, 1809) the Kingdom of Italy lost Dalmatia but acquired the Trentino.

³ This calendar of the progressive reception of the Code in Germany is taken from Fisher, H. A. L.: *Studies in Napoleonic Statesmanship in Germany* (Oxford 1903, Clarendon Press), p. 380, n. 2.

⁴ See ibid.

⁵ This curiosity of legal history was imparted to the writer of this Study one day in that year when he was standing in Kovno and gazing across the Niemen towards its once Napoleonic western bank.

variety of means, ranging from a more or less genuine free choice to sheer and undissimulated coercion.

'The transplantation from one country to another of a code of laws, and of a system of judicial organisation, must in all cases be a delicate proceeding, for, though the elementary principles of justice are universally appreciated, nation differs from nation in the principles of their application. . . . The immediate introduction of the French codes into the Grand Duchy of Berg seemed to the conservative mind of Count Beugnot [the French Imperial Commissioner] to savour of indiscretion. "Germany", as he reminded his Government, "had not, like France, been levelled by the legislation of iconoclastic assemblies." It would require time and instruction before she could properly attune herself to the new melodies of the Code. Nor was there any danger in delay. . . . These representations were received and rejected. On the 12th November, 1809, an imperial decree ordered that the *Code Napoléon* was to have the force of law in the Grand Duchy of Berg from the 1st January, 1810, and at the same time the Imperial Commission was requested instantly to furnish a draft scheme for judicial organization. Beugnot had no option but to obey.'[1]

In the Kingdom of Westphalia, likewise, the *Code Napoléon* was made law, as from the 1st January, 1808,[2] by the terms of a constitution, promulgated from Paris on the 15th November, 1807, which 'may be considered either in the light of a treaty or in that of a guarantee'.[3] But here the peremptoriness of the imperial dictate was mitigated by the tender-handedness of its local application. In the crucial matter of feudalism, for example, a declaration of 'the unconditional abolition of serfage passed through the crucible of successive legal refinements';[4] and when

'some proprietors complained of these proceedings as too revolutionary, the Government replied with justice that, according to the liberal principles of the *Code Napoléon* and of the Act constituting the Kingdom of Westphalia, all rights of serfage and feudalism might have been suppressed. . . . ; that the suppression had been general in Genoa, Parma, Piacenza and Tuscany; but that the Westphalian Government had preferred an equitable temperament between the rigour of the laws and the respect due to long possession. They had kept everything which they could keep without violating principle.'[5]

In any case, whatever the political circumstances of its local 'reception' might have been, the intrinsic merits of the *Code Napoléon* were such as to secure its survival when the Napoleonic Empire was overthrown through an irresistible reaction of its non-French subjects and victims against an intolerable abuse of French military and political power.

'When the project for the German Civil Code came before the Reichstag in 1900, it was stated that seventeen per cent of the fifty million inhabitants of the German Empire were still ruled by French law. In the Prussian, Hessian and Bavarian Rhine provinces, and in Alsace-Lorraine, the *Code Napoléon* was administered in its original tongue; while a German translation, only slightly differing from its French prototype, was current in

---

[1] Fisher, op. cit., pp. 197–8.
[3] Ibid., p. 231.
[4] Ibid., p. 257.
[2] See ibid., p. 232.
[5] Ibid.

Baden. That the Code should have persisted in any portion of Germany, when all the circumstances of the War of Liberation are taken into account, is a remarkable tribute to its merits. We may admit that its preparation was hurried, that the discussions in the Council of State were often unsatisfactory, and that it is based upon an imperfect survey of practical contingencies. There is doubtless great weight in Savigny's contention that Germany was not ripe for a code, and that the legal system of a country should be the natural result of its historical development. But the choice in 1807 and in 1815 did not lie between pure German and pure French law. It lay between the *Code Napoléon* on the one hand, sketchy, no doubt, and over-simplified, but lucid, intelligible and portable,[1] and an "endless waste of contradictory, conjectural and motley ordinances. . . ." We cannot wonder that, in comparison with this hybrid miscellany, the French Code seemed to many Germans to be the utterance of Reason herself.'[2]

Even in territories where, upon the downfall of the Napoleonic Empire, the *Code Napoléon* was abrogated, along with all other Napoleonic innovations, by the 'Zealotism' of a momentarily restored *Ancien Régime* that was too uncertain of its tenure to venture to be discriminating in its policy, the imported French law was not in every case rescinded *in toto*, while in other cases it crept back, unacknowledged yet effectively operative, in a non-French disguise, when the mounting pressure of nineteenth-century Industrialism and Democracy compelled even unrepentant reactionary régimes to overhaul the antiquated law that they had reinstated in the *Code Napoléon's* place. This happened in several of the temporarily re-erected pre-Napoleonic statelets in Italy; and, when, in belated response to Napoleon's trumpet-call,[3] an Italian Risorgimento

---

[1] The portability of the *Code Napoléon* proclaims its success; its lucidity and intelligibility account for its portability; and this trinity of virtues was heaven-sent; for the substitution of one system of law for another, *in toto* and at one stroke, is, at best, a formidable undertaking. Even when the substitute exists, ready-made, and has merely to be translated and enacted in order to give it the force of law on paper, it cannot become practically operative without the introduction of a corresponding new code of procedure and without the training up of a new generation of judges, barristers, and solicitors who have familiarized themselves with the new law and new procedure by daily practice in the courts. When the writer of this Study visited Lithuania at Eastertide, 1928, he found that, in their enthusiasm for reorganizing their life on a Lithuanian national basis, the Lithuanians had taken two steps which, in their combined effect, were producing serious practical difficulties. On the one hand they had set themselves to draft a unitary national Lithuanian system of law to replace both the *Code Napoléon*, which was in force in the fragment of Lithuanian territory on the left bank of the Niemen, and the Imperial Russian Law, which was in force in the rest of the country. Simultaneously, in their educational system, they had deposed the Russian language from its former position of being the first foreign language to be learnt by Lithuanian children, and had replaced it by a choice between the leading Western languages. This replacement of the Russian language in the Lithuanian schools was, of course, as quick and easy a step as the replacement of the Imperial Russian Law in the Lithuanian Courts was slow and difficult. By A.D. 1928 the Lithuanians had realized, too late, that their self-imposed task of introducing a new national Lithuanian system of law was not going to be fulfilled as a going concern within any foreseeable period of time; but by 1928 a time could already be foreseen when the Imperial Russian Law would have to be administered in Lithuania by a rising generation of Lithuanian judges and lawyers who would have been brought up without having been taught the Russian language. To tide over the awkward interim stage that could thus be seen ahead, could not the Imperial Russian Law be translated into Lithuanian? Alas, no; for this was not a code but a congeries of 'case law', and the use of it demanded a familiarity with decisions of the Imperial Russian Senate running into hundreds of volumes. In such a situation the merits of the *Code Napoléon* were conspicuous. Happy that small minority of Lithuanian judges, lawyers, and litigants whose business was transacted on the River Niemen's Napoleonic bank.
—A.J.T.   [2] Fisher, op. cit., p. 379.   [3] See V. v. 642.

had swept this political lumber away, to make room for an Italian national state that aspired to be liberal as well as united, Italian codifiers frankly took the *Code Napoléon* as their model in drafting the Italian Civil Code that was adopted on the 25th June, 1865, and was brought into force on the 1st January, 1866.

The *Code Napoléon*'s most remarkable triumphs, however, were its conquests of alien worlds on which the claws of the Napoleonic eagle had never fastened. During Napoleon's trial of strength with Great Britain, British sea power had foiled his attempt to conquer Egypt and Syria, forced him to sell Louisiana to the United States,[1] and prevented him from following up his military occupation of Spain and invasion of Portugal by pouncing upon these decrepit Powers' great possessions in the Americas. Yet the *Code Napoléon* struck roots both in the Americas and in the Levant. It became an important constituent of the local law of the State of Louisiana within the North American Union;[2] it influenced the development of the established variety of pre-Revolutionary French customary law in the anti-Revolutionary Canadian Province of Quebec;[3] while in the successor-states of the Spanish Empire of the Indies it came as a god-send to fill the legal vacuum left by the failure of the Spanish Bourbon régime to bring up to date the worthy Pinelo's long-since antiquated *Recopilación de Leyes de Los Reynos de las Indias*.[4]

As for Egypt, it would hardly be an exaggeration to say that the *Code Napoléon* found a second home in this stronghold of Islam after the process of Westernization, foreshadowed in the shattering but transitory visitation of Napoleon's expeditionary force, had been put in hand in good earnest by Mehmed 'Alī. In the whole field of civil law outside the communal preserve of Personal Statute, the *Code Napoléon* was 'received' in Egypt in A.D. 1876 as the law for the new Mixed Courts and in A.D. 1883 (a sensational triumph, this!)[5] as the law for the new system of civil and criminal jurisdiction,[6] applying to Ottoman subjects in Egypt,

---

[1] French land power had enabled Napoleon, in a secret convention signed at Saint Ildefonso on the 7th October, 1800, to extort from the Spanish Crown the retrocession to France of the originally French possession of Louisiana, which the French Crown had ceded to Spain in the peace settlement of A.D. 1763; but Napoleon missed his opportunity for seizing this Transatlantic prey during his momentary enjoyment of the freedom of the seas after the conclusion of the Anglo-French Peace Treaty of Amiens on the 25th March, 1802; and the naval war was in full swing again by the 20th December, 1803, when the sale of Louisiana by the French Empire to the United States was completed.

[2] The state law of Louisiana was a blend of several different elements: the local French customary law of the *Ancien Régime*, the law of the Spanish Indies, introduced after the cession of Louisiana by France to Spain in A.D. 1763, and the English 'Common Law' introduced after the retrocession of Louisiana by Spain to France in A.D. 1800 and its purchase from France by the United States in A.D. 1803. The Napoleonic codes were grafted on to the existing local French law *pari passu* with the introduction of the 'Common Law' current in the United States.

[3] This influence was manifest in the Quebec Civil Code of A.D. 1867.

[4] See p. 263, above.

[5] Sensational in view of the gulf between the *Code Napoléon* and the communal systems of law which it was replacing. It did, however, share one vital common source with the Islamic *Sharī'ah* as well as with the communal laws of the several Christian *millets*. All these legal systems alike were derived in large measure from varieties or transmutations of Roman Law. The influence of Roman Law on Islamic Law is discussed on pp. 288–91, below.

[6] The traditional *Sharī'* courts retained their jurisdiction in matters of 'personal statute'.

that was introduced in that year. This naturalization of French Law in Egypt goes far to account for the strength of the hold which French culture obtained in Egypt notwithstanding the ultimate discomfiture of France in her military and political struggle with Great Britain for ascendancy there. The French military occupation of Egypt had lasted for little more than three years (reckoning from the landing of Napoleon's expeditionary force on the 1st July, 1798, to the ignominious surrender of 'Abdallah Menou on the 2nd September, 1801); the second and single-handed British occupation[1] had lasted for fifty-four years (reckoning from the landing of a British expeditionary force on the 20th August, 1882, to the ratification of the Anglo-Egyptian Treaty of Alliance signed on the 26th August, 1936), and in A.D. 1952 the vestiges of British occupation which the terms of the Treaty had preserved had not yet been entirely removed. Yet on the morrow of the General War of 1939–45 the by this time penetratingly Westernized governing class of Egypt bore its Western imprint in the French and not in the British variety of the pattern.

One of the most remarkable episodes in the history of the dissemination of the *Code Napoléon* was the role that it was called upon to play in Japan during the Meiji Era. In embarking on a general programme of Westernization the authors of the Meiji Revolution showed their wisdom in the field of law by hastening slowly. Their first step, taken in A.D. 1870, was to have the French Codes translated into Japanese. Law schools for French, English, and German Law were successively established in A.D. 1872, 1874, and 1887. In A.D. 1875 a commission was appointed to compile a civil code, and, after its draft, which followed the Napoleonic Civil Code very closely, had been submitted to the Japanese Government in A.D. 1878 and had been rejected, a member of the commission, the French jurist Boissonade, was asked in 1880 to prepare a new draft. His draft was published on the 27th March, 1890, and a complementary draft by Japanese jurists, covering the province of 'personal statute', on the 16th October of the same year, and the whole code was to come into force on the 1st January, 1893.

This apparent acceptance, in Japan, of a Napoleonic *Code Boissonade* was the high-water mark in the flow of the *Code Napoléon*'s influence over the face of the globe; and a turn in the tide was not slow to follow. Before the arrival of the date fixed for bringing the *Code Boissonade* into operation, the newly created Japanese Imperial Diet voted, on the 16th May, 1892, for postponing the date till the 31st December, 1896. Thereupon, a third draft was commissioned, and this draft, which was published in instalments in 1896 and 1898 and was brought into force in July 1899, was inspired, not by the *Code Napoléon*, but by the second draft of a German Civil Code, which had been published in 1895.[2]

The controversy in Japan which resulted in this victory of German

---

[1] In response to the challenge of the French occupation, British troops had already set foot on Egyptian soil from the 8th March, 1801, to March 1803; but on this first occasion they had come by invitation of the lawful sovereign of Egypt, the Ottoman Pādishāh, and in the company of a Turkish expeditionary force.

[2] In the German Empire this draft was subsequently adopted on the 16th August, 1896, and was brought into force on the 1st January, 1900.

over French law had not arisen over the respective merits of two variant Western schools of jurisprudence, but had been

'a deep-seated conflict between two fundamental ideas of law. The immediate enforcement party contended for the juristic idea embodied in the theory of the school of Natural Law, namely that Law was based upon Human Nature, that it is of a universal character, and that, inasmuch as the codification of a civilised country like France was a refined expression of Human Nature or of the universal character of Law, it could be adopted by Japan. The postponement party stood for the juristic idea of the historical school, that Law, like Language, was an expression of national character and a product of History, and that the introduction of a foreign code into Japanese Society was absurd and preposterous.'[1]

On the 16th May, 1892, the majority in the Japanese Diet showed their impartial hostility towards exotic law of all varieties by voting for the postponement of the coming into force, not only of a French-inspired civil code, but of a German-inspired commercial code, which they had already condemned to a first period of postponement in a previous vote on the 16th December, 1890. Nevertheless, in the Japanese civil code that was eventually brought into force in 1898, as well as in the commercial code brought into force in 1899, it was a German, not a Japanese, influence that replaced the French; and this eventual adoption, in Japan, of a German instead of a French model might be read as the opening of a new chapter in the history of the dissemination of Western Law. For the German Civil Code was likewise taken as the basis for the Swiss Civil Code adopted on the 10th December, 1907, and brought into force on the 1st January, 1912; and the Turkish Civil Code, adopted on the 17th February, 1926, was, in its turn, virtually a translation of the Swiss.

The German Civil Code was, indeed, a more scientifically executed piece of work than its famous French forerunner; yet, even if the outlook for German cultural influence abroad had not been blighted by the sinister military and political events of A.D. 1914–45, the ghosts of Napoleon's draftsmen might, not unjustly, have booked the German Civil Code's successes to the credit of their French account. The workmanlike instrument that saw the light in Germany in A.D. 1895 could never have emerged out of the 'hybrid miscellany' of German customary law if the *Code Napoléon* had not pegged out a drove-road for ruminant German jurists to follow; and it would have been surprising, after all, if this German cud had not been well digested when it had been chewed for more than ninety years.

The Normal Failure of Codification to arrest Decay

In any case, whatever verdict History might eventually pronounce on the respective merits and achievements of the Revolutionary French Code and its slow-footed German competitor, our glance at the *Code Napoléon's* nineteenth-century history has perhaps made it evident that

---

[1] Takayanagi, Kenzo: *Reception and Influence of Occidental Legal Ideas in Japan* (Tokyo 1929, The Japanese Council, Institute of Pacific Relations), p. 11.

this ninety-years-long triumphal progress from Paris to New Orleans and Buenos Aires and Cairo and Tokyo was the exceptional result of peculiar historical circumstances. As a rule—and this rule is inherent in the very nature of the declines and falls of civilizations—the demand for codification reaches its climax in the penultimate age before a social catastrophe, long after the peak of achievement in jurisprudence has been passed, and when the legislators of the day are irretrievably on the run in a losing battle with ungovernable forces of destruction. Justinian himself had no sooner turned at bay against Fate, and thrown up in her face the imposing barricade of his *Corpus Iuris*, than he was driven by the Fury's relentless hounds to sprint on again in a paper-chase in which he was constrained to strew the course with the tell-tale sheets of his *Novellae*. Yet in the long run Fate is apt to deal kindly with the codifiers, even when they have not shared Napoleon's fortune in being moved to do their work at an exceptionally auspicious hour; for the meed of admiration which their outraged predecessors would have refused, with indignation, to accord to them has been offered to their *manes*, in full and overflowing measure, by a Posterity that has been too remote, too barbarous, or too sentimental to be capable of arriving at a soberly correct appraisal of the codifiers' work.

Even this uncritically admiring Posterity, however, finds the consecrated codes impossible to apply in real life until they have suffered a sea change; for it is the tragedy of the codifiers that, in reducing the law of a happier and more cultivated past age to the social, moral, and intellectual level of their own melancholy generation, they have still pegged it so high that it is bound to pass forthwith beyond the reach[1] of a herd running violently down a steep place into the sea.[2]

'In the parts in which they were borrowing from the classical law—of which they preserved many useful rules—as well as in Justinian's own personal constitutions and in the interpolations, the [Justinianean] commissioners succeeded, notwithstanding the difficulties of their task, in producing a work which, without being free from contradictions and obscurities, was better suited to the needs of the populations of their countries than were the admirable classical masterpieces. One might even say that, in itself, this work was still too strong meat for the juridically uncultivated minds to which it was addressed. In the East it does not appear to have succeeded in dethroning the Syro-Roman Custumal, which was unquestionably less scientific. In the West its only effect on legal practice was by way of glosses which were never more than mediocre before the study of the Justinianean Law received its impulsion from the School of Bologna.'[3]

In the last phase of the Roman Empire in its last strongholds, Justinian's reign was promptly followed by a deluge of Lombard, Slav, and Arab barbarian invasion; in the last phase of the Empire of Sumer and Akkad, Hammurabi's strenuous work of political and social reclamation on the plains of Shinar was no less promptly waterlogged by a Kassite

---

[1] See V. vi. 224, with n. 3.
[2] Matt. viii. 32; Mark v. 13; Luke viii. 33.
[3] Collinet, P.: *Études Historiques sur le Droit de Justinien*, vol. i: 'Le Caractère Oriental de l'Œuvre Législative de Justinien' (Paris 1912, Recueil Sirey), p. xxix.

inundation from the hills; in the Andean World the rule of the Inca law-givers was brought to a sudden end by the calamity of the Spanish conquest. Even in the Anatolian core of Justinian's empire, when Leo the Restorer and his successors set to work, after a virtual interregnum of 150 years, to replace the wreckage of Justinian's pretentious imperial edifice by something more modest, more practical, and, above all, more firmly based, they found apter materials in the Mosaic Law than in the Justinianean *Corpus Iuris* for meeting the simple needs of a new society that was struggling to be born under their aegis.[1] In Italy, whom Justinian succeeded in 'liberating' momentarily from barbarian rule at the cost of finally wrecking her social structure and her cultural life, the immediate future lay, not with the secular *Corpus Iuris*,[2] but with the monastic rule of Saint Benedict,[3] which was conceived during the agony of the Great Romano-Gothic War (*gerebatur* A.D. 537–53) and was disseminated to Ultima Thule before Monte Cassino was laid desolate by the Lombards. In the former Transalpine provinces of the Roman Empire that Justinian neither inherited from his imperial predecessors nor reconquered from barbarian war-bands, the Justinianean *Corpus Iuris* did not, of course, obtain even the short-lived currency that it enjoyed in Italy and North-West Africa pending the undoing of Justinian's work there by the Lombards and the Arabs.[4]

The Decay of the Roman Law in the Roman Empire's Teutonic Barbarian Successor-states

In these lost and never even temporarily recovered Transalpine dominions of Rome a Roman subject population was permitted, by the indulgence or indifference of its new barbarian masters, to continue to live under Roman civil law in its locally prevalent pre-Justinianean embodiments; and the milder and more statesmanlike of the emperors' barbarian successors went so far as to anticipate Justinian by promulgating local codes of Roman Law—a *Lex Romana Burgundionum* and a Visigothic *Breviarium Alarici*—for the use of their Roman sheep without a jurisprudent shepherd. The *Breviarium* of the Visigoth King Alaric II, which was mainly based on the Theodosian Code, had also actually preserved extracts from the *Sententiae* of the Severan jurist Paulus which would have been lost to latter-day scholars if the sole surviving

---

[1] See III. iii. 276 and X. ix. 21–27.

[2] Collinet, in op. cit., vol. cit., points out that Italy had not yet come under Justinian's rule at the time—A.D. 528–34—when Justinian's *Corpus Iuris* was being compiled (p. 11); and that no Italian jurists were included in the board of commissioners by whom the work of codification was carried out (p. 13). Justinian's legislation did not apply to Italy automatically; it was made applicable there by express provisions, and this only *pari passu* with the progress of the reconquest (p. 12). At the same time, Collinet suggests elsewhere that an already formed design of reconquering Italy may have been one of Justinian's motives in compiling his *Corpus Iuris*. While he did not draw upon the local Italian version of the Roman Law, he did wish to provide himself with a *Corpus Iuris* that would be applicable in Italy (Collinet: 'The General Considerations raised by the Codification of Justinian', in *Tijdschrift voor Rechtsgeschiedenis*, vol. iv (Haarlem 1923, Tjeenk Willink), pp. 7–8).

[3] See III iii. 265–7 and V. vi. 224, n. 3.

[4] This point is brought out by Burns, C. Delisle: *The First Europe* (London 1947, Allen & Unwin), p. 326.

official anthology of the masterpieces of Roman jurisprudence had been
Tribonian's *Digest*. In the first phase of the Visigothic régime in
Southern Gaul and Spain, King Euric I (*regnabat* A.D. 466–84) enlisted
the services of Sidonius Apollinaris' friend and correspondent the Roman
jurist Leo of Narbonne.[1] Yet this precarious survival of Roman Law in
the West was limited in its range and, even within those limits, was a
wasting asset. Roman subjects of Teutonic barbarian successor-states
were subjected, it would seem, from the outset, to a regressive barbarian
criminal law providing for the payment of a *wergeld* to the injured party
or his heirs, in lieu of punishments imposed and exacted by the state;[2]
and, though, in the deliberately conciliatory common law for Romans
and Burgundians that was embodied in the Burgundian war-lord Gundobad's *Liber Constitutionum*,[3] the invidious differentiation of scales of
wergeld was based on differences of class and not of community, in the
wergeld tariff of the ultra-barbarous Frankish *Lex Salica* 'the life of an
ordinary Frank' was 'reckoned worth double that of a Roman'.[4] What
is still more significant, the Roman Law was now in retreat even in the
tolerated departments of business relations and 'personal statute'.

'The Roman Law survived, but it sank to the level of custom.[5] Since

---

[1] See Apollinaris, Sidonius: *Epistulae*, Book VIII, Letter iii, § 3.

[2] See Lot, F.: *Les Invasions Germaniques* (Paris 1935, Payot), pp. 166–8.

[3] In Southern Gaul at the turn of the fifth and sixth centuries of the Christian Era the
subject Romans gained a notable improvement in their legal status from the play of power
politics between their barbarian masters of the moment—the Nomadicized East German
Burgundians and Visigoths—and the neighbouring Frankish backwoodsmen from the
Lower Rhineland, who, under Clovis' leadership, were now showing themselves formidably aggressive. In the preface to the Burgundian *Liber Constitutionum* it is declared to be
the king's benevolent intention to secure justice, unalloyed by either corruption or communal inequality, for Burgundians and Romans alike, by providing a common law for
cases between a Burgundian and a Roman, and a separate code for cases in which both
parties are Romans (see Dill, Sir S.: *Roman Society in Gaul in the Merovingian Age*
(London 1926, Macmillan), p. 65). This Burgundian profession of virtue is borne out
by the sixth-century Gallic Roman historian Gregory of Tours. '[Gundobadus] Burgun-
dionibus leges mitiores instituit, ne Romanos opprimerent' (*Historia Francorum*, Book
II, chap. 9, *ad fin.*); and the evidence is impressive when a Roman and Francophil
Catholic ecclesiastic testifies in favour of a barbarian and Arian Burgundian war-lord
whose dynasty had been suppressed by Gregory's Frankish patrons by the time when
Gregory was writing. Dill (op. cit., p. 63) dates the first edition of Gundobad's *Liber
Constitutionum* about A.D. 501; Burns (op. cit., p. 330) about 503 (the dating turns on an
article, dated the 28th May, 502, which appears in the final edition). The *Breviarium* of
the Burgundian Gundobad's Visigoth contemporary Alaric II (*regnabat* A.D. 484–507) is
dated by Dill (op. cit., p. 94) and by Burns (op. cit., p. 330) *circa* A.D. 506, on the eve of
the Battle of Vouillé. This battle, which was fought in A.D. 507, resulted in the conquest
of all Southern Gaul save Septimania from the Visigoths by the Franks (see II. ii. 166,
380, and 428; V. v. 217, n. 1, and 221, 222, 225–6). The Burgundian principality had
suffered its first Frankish invasion in A.D. 500. These coincidences of date bear out the
view that at the turn of the century the Visigothic and Burgundian governments were
attempting to offset the odium of their heretical Arian faith by granting genuine equality
before the law to their Catholic Roman subjects. Though their conciliatory policy did
not induce the Catholic Roman clergy in their dominions to cease working for the victory of their own barbarous Frankish convert Clovis, some of the Roman laity felt
differently. A grandson of Sidonius Apollinaris fell at Vouillé fighting for the Visigoths;
and, though, when the converted Franks conquered Aquitaine and Burgundy, they left
in force the liberal *Breviarium Alarici* and *Lex Romana Burgundionum* and *Liber Constitutionum Gundobadi* that had been enacted by their Visigoth and Burgundian victims, the
Aquitanians chafed under the Frankish yoke for centuries thereafter. The Catholic
clergy, however, were privileged in all contingencies. Under the barbarian law of the
Ripuarian Franks it cost four times as much to kill even a sub-deacon, and nine times as
much to kill a bishop, as to kill an ordinary Roman layman (Burns, op. cit., p. 336).

[4] Dill, op. cit., p. 47; cp. Lot, op. cit., p. 195.

[5] Cp. Collinet, op. cit., vol. cit., pp. 312–13.—A.J.T.

the Empire had disappeared, there was no longer any legislation to put fresh life into the old law by adapting it to new necessities.'[1]

'In the sixth century [of the Christian Era] in the West, the destinies of Roman Law were dominated by one key phenomenon: an arrest in the development of the classical law. When we analyse this phenomenon in order to examine it in its diverse aspects, we can see that there are three elements in it: a traditional persistence of the classical institutions;[2] an evolution of these institutions in which there is nothing creative; and, as an inexorable consequence of these first two facts, a general regression in legal standards. . . .

'The full measure of the feebleness of the evolution comes to light when one measures it by this sixth-century Western World's needs. In the troubled period that marks the end of the Ancient World and ushers in the Middle Ages, the new needs were numerous and pressing. In whatever direction one turns one's eyes—towards the political, the economic, the moral or the religious situation—one sees nothing but the overthrow of the ancient traditional order, the Roman order, of things. At this decisive moment in history, did Italy and Gaul, to confine our attention to them, make any attempt to satisfy these needs in so far as they affected private law? When it had become clear that the barbarian conquest had come to stay, the accomplishment of [legal] reforms that would have sufficed to bring the law in force into harmony with the new way of life— a harmony that was imperatively required—called for energetic and intelligent men (such as were the feudal jurists of a later age) who would labour diligently to bring the [necessary] evolution to pass. Evolution does not take place without effort, and is never automatic. The times called for someone with the courage to apply the pick-axe to the dilapidated edifice of law, and with the authority and ability to build up a new edifice [in place of the old one]. But this was something beyond the powers of the men of [sixth-century] Italy and Gaul. Their impotence is attested by the decadence which had brought them under the yoke of their new masters and had opened the way for the profound transformation of economic life. . . .

'The West [in the sixth century] was "a static society in which nothing could die because nothing was coming to birth there any longer". In this static world, stagnation and decadence had incontestably gained the upper hand over progress. This is the spectacle presented by Roman Law in Italy and Gaul at the very moment when the names of Constantinople and Justinian were lighting up the World with their lustre.'[3]

Thus, in the last chapter of the history of Roman Law in the West, the Theodosian Code played a dwindling part and the Justinianean Corpus no part at all. In Western and Orthodox Christendom alike, the Justinianean Corpus eventually came into its own, not by showing itself proof against death, but by surmounting a *vitai pausa*[4] through a feat of hibernation. Though in Italy as a whole the Corpus had an innings of no more than fifteen years (reckoning from the end, in

[1] Lot, op. cit., p. 166.
[2] e.g. *mancipatio*, which was abolished by Justinian, persisted in Italy down to the ninth century of the Christian Era (Collinet, op. cit., vol. cit., p. 216). *Dictio dotis*, which was likewise abolished by Justinian, was retained by Alaric in his *Breviarium* (ibid., p. 220). See further ibid., p. 308.—A.J.T.
[3] Collinet, P.: *Études Historiques sur le Droit de Justinien*, vol. i: 'Le Caractère Oriental de l'Œuvre Législative de Justinien' (Paris 1912, Recueil Sirey), pp. 309–14.
[4] Lucretius: *De Rerum Natura*, Book III, l. 930.

A.D. 553, of the Ostrogoths' last stand to the beginning, in A.D. 568, of a piecemeal Lombard conquest), it came to life again, some four hundred years later, in an eleventh-century juristic renaissance at Bologna, the principal city in the bridgehead which the Constantinopolitan Government's Italian exarchs had maintained till A.D. 751 in the hinterland of Ravenna. From there from that time onwards, Tribonian's work radiated its influence into extremities and extensions of an expanding Western World that had lain beyond the political horizon not only of Justinian but of Trajan; and, thanks to Bologna's capacity, in the Dark Ages, for intellectual cold storage, a version of Roman Law was eventually 'received' in Modern Holland, Scotland, and South Africa. In Orthodox Christendom the Justinianean *Corpus Iuris* survived, with greater ease, the less exacting ordeal of hibernating for three centuries at Constantinople, and re-emerged in the tenth century of the Christian Era in the Imperial Code (*Vasiliká*) by which the Emperors of the Macedonian Dynasty replaced the Mosaistic legislation of their eighth-century Syrian predecessors. These parallel juristic renaissances in Orthodox and in Western Christendom will occupy our attention in a later Part of this Study.[1] In the present place we are inquiring into cases in which the juristic legacy of a defunct universal state has been inherited direct, not rediscovered as a treasure-trove.

The Failure of the Spanish Empire of the Indies to profit by the Law of the Incaic and Aztec Empires

In the broken history of the Andean universal state, we have seen[2] that some vestiges of the oecumenical law of the Incas did find their way into the heterogeneous and ill-digested *corpus iuris* of the Spanish Empire of the Indies, but the greater part of this precious Incaic legal heritage, which had been so carefully adapted by its authors to the social needs of the Andean World, was sacrificed by the destructiveness of the *conquistadores* and the unimaginativeness of their more reputable successors the *licenciados*. It is true that among the legal advisers of the Spanish Crown in the Indies there were individuals who saw that

'the most difficult problems . . . were those arising from the government of an Indian population which could not be reduced to the norms of Spanish law. Juan Matienzo, judge in the Audiencia of Charcas and intimate adviser to [the Viceroy] Toledo (*proconsulari munere fungebatur* A.D. 1569–81), in his celebrated text-book of Peruvian administration, *Gobierno del Perú* (*circa* A.D. 1570), warns the Spanish authorities not "to try and change the customs abruptly and make new laws and ordinances, until they know the conditions and customs of the natives of the country and of the Spaniards who dwell there; for, as the country is large, so customs and tempers differ. One must first accommodate oneself to the customs of those one wishes to govern and proceed agreeably to them until, having won their confidence and good opinion, with the authority thus secured one may undertake to change the customs." '[3]

---

[1] See X. ix. 27–34.
[2] On p. 265, above.
[3] Haring, C. H.: *The Spanish Empire in America* (New York 1947, Oxford University Press), p. 110.

But the indigenous customs that were incorporated into Spanish colonial law on the strength of such considerations as those set forth by Matienzo

'had to do, naturally enough, with the life of the lower orders of society: the regulation of labour, the succession and the privileges of native chiefs, Indian village organisation, agricultural practices, etc. . . . Basically . . . people in the Indies, especially in the domain of private law, lived according to the same judicial criteria as in Spain.'[1]

The Infusion of a Decadent Roman Law into the Customary Law of the Roman Empire's Teutonic Barbarian Conquerors

In the more usual situation in which the aggressors who have snatched the sceptre out of the hands of the rulers of a universal state are not the representatives of some alien civilization, but are barbarians, we should expect *à priori* to see the governments of the barbarian successor-states take over much more of the juristic heritage of a former oecumenical Power which has eventually succumbed to force of barbarian arms without having lost its cultural prestige in barbarian eyes. We have, indeed, noticed already[2] that in the Teutonic barbarian successor-states of the Roman Empire the new masters were ready to allow their Roman subjects to continue to live under Roman Civil Law. On the other hand the barbarians' impulse to maintain a distinctive communal culture of their own in the alien social environment in which they have placed themselves through their conquests is apt to declare itself in the field of law, as well as in the fields of religion and poetry in which we have studied it in another context.[3]

The extant collections of the laws of divers Teutonic war-bands on ex-Roman ground gave a latter-day student the impression that these barbarians wanted to accommodate themselves to their new social environment with as little change in their own traditional life as local circumstances might allow. The most archaic of these collections was the Frankish *Lex Salica*;[4] but the same imperviousness to Roman influence was displayed in the rather more sophisticated provisions of the other law-books which had been put into their final form at a later date: for instance, the laws of the Ripuarian Franks, the Alamanni, the Bavarians, the Frisians, the Lombard conquerors of Italy, and the English conquerors of Britain. The backbone of these laws consisted of such utterly un-Roman institutions as ordeal by battle and the atonement for crimes of violence by the payment of compensation to the injured party or his heirs.[5] This contrast in character between the sophisticated Roman Law of a moribund Hellenic World and the archaic barbarian law of the Teutonic war-bands who had settled on the Roman Empire's derelict provinces had its counterpart in a corresponding contrast between the Sumerian Law, as mirrored in Hammurabi's Code, and the law of the

---

[1] Haring, op. cit., loc. cit.   [2] On pp. 280–1, above.
[3] See V. v. 194–337, *passim*.
[4] See the *aperçu* of it in Dill, Sir Samuel: *Roman Society in Gaul in the Merovingian Age* (London 1926, Macmillan), pp. 43–62.
[5] An illuminating survey and analysis of the history of this institution among the Teutonic barbarian invaders of the Roman Empire and their successors is given by Phillpotts, B. S.: *Kindred and Clan* (Cambridge 1913, University Press).

Hittite barbarians who had settled on a moribund Sumeric World's
Anatolian fringes. The difference in the spirit of the law was here twofold. From one point of view the Hittite Law gave the impression of
being more advanced than the Sumerian; for, whereas in Hammurabi's
Code the punishments prescribed were savage and, in particular, the
lex talionis was worked out to forbiddingly pedantic extremes,[1] the
Hittite law substituted fines for Hammurabi's sentences of death or
mutilation as the penalty for a number of offences.[2] From another point
of view, however, the Hittite Law represented a regression; for, in
dealing with crimes against persons, it substituted a tariff of *wergeld* for
the punishments, to be imposed and exacted by the state, that had been
prescribed for the same crimes by Hammurabi.[3]

What were the prospects of life for these barbarian systems of law on
the alien ground of a decadent civilization whose domain the barbarians
had overrun? The Hittite Law, in the redaction in which it happened
to have been disinterred by twentieth-century Western archaeologists,
dated from the later days of the second phase of Hittite history, for
which the Carolingian Age of Western history would be the Frankish
equivalent both in cultural terms of the contemporary state of society
and in chronological terms of the passage of time since the emergence
of a nascent new civilization out of a cultural interregnum.[4] Here we
have an historical example of a law of barbarian origin successfully
providing for the needs of a civilization in the first chapter of its history.
Beyond this point, however, Hittite history does not carry us; for, not
long after the date at which the Hittite Code was promulgated in the
redaction that had been unearthed, the homeland of the Hittite Society
in Eastern Anatolia was overwhelmed by a barbarian Völkerwanderung
from the Balkan Peninsula and the Aegean which had been set in motion
by the catastrophic dissolution of the neighbouring Minoan Society, and
thereafter the Hittite Civilization lingered on only in refugee communities, beyond the Taurus in Northern Syria and overseas along the

---

[1] The articles in which it was applied are set out in Smith, J. M. P.: *The Origin and
History of Hebrew Law* (Chicago 1931, University of Chicago Press), p. 24, n. 2.
[2] See Hrozný, B.: *Die Älteste Geschichte Vorderasiens und Indiens* (Prague 1943, Melantrich), pp. 114 and 167; Götze, A.: *Hethiter, Churriter und Assyrer* (Oslo 1936, Asche-
houg), pp. 64–65; Delaporte, L.: *Les Hittites* (Paris 1936, La Renaissance du Livre),
p. 231.
[3] See Cavaignac, E.: *Le Problème Hittite* (Paris 1936, Leroux), p. 105. The institution
of *wergeld* thus turns out to be a common feature of Teutonic and Hittite barbarian law.
'The idea of settling conflicts by a money indemnity is not peculiar to the Germans. It is
found among other peoples and is of a high antiquity. We come across it already, fourteen centuries before the beginning of our Era, among the Hittites of Asia Minor' (Lot,
F.: *Les Invasions Germaniques* (Paris 1935, Payot), p. 166).
[4] This Hittite law, as latter-day Western students had it, was a code drafted in the
language of the Power that had exercised political hegemony over the Hittite World from
the sixteenth century B.C. onwards. It was written in the Akkadian cuneiform script on
two clay tablets, containing one hundred paragraphs each, which were discovered on the
site of the Hittite Empire's capital, Boghazqal'eh, in A.D. 1906–7. This redaction dated
from the fifteenth century B.C. according to Hrozný, op. cit., pp. 166–7; from the
thirteenth century according to Cavaignac, op. cit., p. 105. According to Delaporte, op.
cit., p. 214, there were three successive redactions, of which the second was made in the
fifteenth or fourteenth century B.C. English translations of the disinterred text will be
found in Smith, J. M. P.: *The Origin and History of Hebrew Law* (Chicago 1931, University of Chicago Press), pp. 247–74, and in Pritchard, J. B.: *Ancient Near Eastern Texts*
(Princeton 1950, University Press), pp. 188–97.

west coast of Italy, which were eventually absorbed by the Syriac and
the Hellenic Society respectively.[1] It was as if, in the ninth century of
the Christian Era, the collapse of the Carolingian Empire had resulted
in the destruction of the nascent Western Christian Civilization at the
hands of Scandinavian, Eurasian Nomad, and Muslim Arab invaders.
If we are to follow the fortunes of barbarian law in a growing civilization
farther than this point, we must turn from Hittite to Western history,
where we find the law of the English barbarian settlers on ex-Roman
ground in Britain succeeding, without any deliberate or systematic
'reception' of Roman law at any stage,[2] in developing sufficiently, out of
its own resources, to be able to provide for the needs of a civilization
that has arrived at a high degree of social sophistication and economic
complexity.

This unique ability of the English Common Law to keep pace with
the growth of the Western Civilization could be explained as the effect
of three distinct causes. In the first place, at the time of the post-Hellenic
Völkerwanderung, the barbarian law of the English invaders of Britain
was largely relieved of such hampering archaic institutions as *wergeld*
thanks to the exceptionally rapid disintegration of the kin-group organization of society in a migration across the sea.[3] In the second place the
ex-Roman population did not, in Britain, survive under barbarian rule
as a distinct community, continuing to live under its own Roman law,
as it survived in the Continental Teutonic successor-states of the Roman
Empire. In Britain the provincials were exterminated, expelled, or
assimilated by the English settlers. In the third place, at the opening of
the second chapter of Western history towards the close of the eleventh
century of the Christian Era the English law was carried forward and,
above all, was effectively enforced, thanks to the exceptionally strong
and efficient monarchy that was imposed on a politically united England
by a Norman conquest. The survival of the English Common Law,
however, was an exception that proved a rule; for the ancestral law of
the other Teutonic barbarian invaders of the Roman Empire failed to
stay the course. In all other cases we find Roman influence seeping in
from an early date.

To begin with, the earliest versions of all the Teutonic law-books,
with the significant exception of the English, were drafted in Latin; and,
when we turn our attention from this point of form to matters of substance, we catch glimpses of Teutonic custom fighting a stubborn rearguard action against the moral pressure of Roman concepts and Christian
standards. The comparatively enlightened King Liutprand of the ultra-
barbarian Lombards declares frankly, in a law promulgated in A.D. 731,
163 years after the Lombards' eruption into the comparatively highly
cultivated social environment of Italy, that ordeal by battle is a Lombard

---

[1] See I. i. 114–15; III. iii. 139; IV. iv. 109; V. v. 88; and IX. viii. 438–9.

[2] This is not, of course, to say that 'the Common Law' of England remained impervi-
ous to the influence of Roman Law after this influence had become prevalent in Western
Christendom as a whole in consequence of the Justinianean juristic renaissance at
Bologna in the eleventh century of the Christian Era (see X. ix. 31–34).

[3] On this point, see the passage quoted from Phillpotts, op. cit., pp. 257–65, in the
present Study, II. ii. 90–91.

custom which it is beyond his power to ban, though he is 'uncertain of
the judgment of God and' has 'heard that many litigants have unjustly
lost their case through' this practice.[1] On the other hand the genial
Burgundians had mellowed under Roman influence within less than a
hundred years of their crossing the Rhine.

'There is hardly a trace of German ideas or institutions in the legislation of Gundobad.[2] He has no resemblance to the old German chief, surrounded by his assembled warriors. His type and model is the political
authority wielded by the Emperor or the great Praetorian Prefects. . . . In
the Salian Law pecuniary compensation is almost universal: other punishments are almost unheard of. In Burgundy, besides the pecuniary sanction, there are many and various punishments for crime, some of them
even harsh and cruel. This, however, it has been observed, does not prove
a less civilised social tone, but rather the reverse.[3] The Burgundian
legislator, in fact, is striving to abolish the vindictiveness of private conflicts by making the state the avenger of personal wrongs.'[4]

The Burgundian *Liber Constitutionum* marked a radical departure
from archaic Teutonic law not only in its character but in its application;
for, while the *Lex Salica* and other Teutonic law-books of that type were
merely communal prescriptions for the exclusive use of an intrusive
barbarian war-band, Gundobad and Sigismund were enacting, as we
have observed already, a 'common law' for their barbarian Burgundian
followers and their Roman subjects. The *Edictum Theodorici*,[5] which was
promulgated in the Ostrogothic dominions at about the same date,
either *circa* A.D. 500 or *circa* A.D. 511–15,[6] was a 'common law' in the
same sense of applying alike to Theodoric's Ostrogoth followers and to
the Roman population under his rule; and in this case the scales already
incline heavily in the Romans' favour. The contents of this barbarian
war-lord's edict are drawn from Roman sources—the Theodosian Code
and the *Sententiae* of Paulus—and the Ostrogoth masters of Italy are
referred to as 'barbarians' throughout the document. It is even more
remarkable that the Visigothic *Breviarium Alarici*, which was promulgated within a few years of Theodoric's *Edictum* and Gundobad's *Liber
Constitutionum* and was compiled, from the same sources as Theodoric's
work, avowedly for the benefit of the Visigoths' Roman subjects, declares
in its preamble that its prescriptions apply to 'both Romans and barbarians'.[7]

The promulgation of these three codes of 'common law' by Teutonic
war-lords on ex-Roman ground at the opening of the sixth century of

---

[1] *Liutprandi Leges*, cxviii: 'Incerti sumus de iudicio Dei, et multos audivimus per
pugnam sine iusticiam [*sic*] causam suam perdere, sed, propter consuetudinem gentis
nostrae Langobardorum, legem ipsam mutare non possumus.'

[2] i.e. in his 'common law' for Burgundians and Romans (see p. 281, above). His
version of Roman Civil Law for the use of his Roman subjects among themselves is not
in question here.—A.J.T.

[3] Compare the corresponding contrast between the salutary severity of Hammurabi's
Code and the inexpedient laxity of the Hittite Code, to which attention has been drawn
above.—A.J.T.   [4] Dill, op. cit., p. 66.

[5] See Hodgkin, T.: *Italy and Her Invaders*, 2nd ed. (Oxford 1892-9, Clarendon Press,
8 vols), vol. iii, pp. 276–7 and 309–14.

[6] See Collinet, P.: 'The General Problems raised by the Codification of Justinian', in
Tijdschrift voor Rechtsgeschiedenis, vol. iv (Haarlem 1923, Tjeenk Willink), pp. 6–7.

[7] Burns, C. Delisle: *The First Europe* (London 1947, Allen & Unwin), pp. 329–30.

the Christian Era was only the beginning of the transfusion of Roman
law into the body of Teutonic custom. In the unstable social situation
produced by the establishment of barbarian rule over Roman populations, legislation could not stand still. The rulers of the Teutonic barbarian successor-states followed the example of their Imperial Roman
predecessors, from the Emperor Hadrian onwards, by issuing a spate of
decrees; and these decrees, in their turn, were inevitably coloured by
the legal traditions of their Roman social setting. The classic example
is the corpus of rescripts, issued in Theodoric's name, which were
largely drafted, besides being collected and published, by the Ostrogoth
war-lord's Roman minister Cassiodorus. The Ostrogothic régime in
Italy, however, met with an early violent end at Roman hands, and the
Iberian Peninsula under Visigothic rule was the place where the natural
course of events had time to work itself out before the Visigothic Power
was overthrown, in its turn, by the more competent rival hands of the
Visigoths' fellow barbarian invaders the Primitive Muslim Arabs.

The Visigothic King Receswinth (*regnabat* A.D. 649–72) restored to
the former Roman territories under his rule the uniformity of law that
they had enjoyed from the time of Caracalla until the Visigothic conquest. In A.D. 654 he put out of commission the *Breviarium* of his predecessor Alaric II (*regnabat* A.D. 484–507) and gave sole force of law to
a code[1] compiling the decisions of the Visigothic Kings from Euric
down to Receswinth himself.

'These decisions are thoroughly imbued with the spirit of Roman Law.
. . . Where else [in the field of Teutonic barbarian legislation] can one
find anything comparable to Book I [of Receswinth's *Forum*], entitled *De
Legislatore, De Lege*, in which an effort is made to formulate general
principles of legislation?'[2]

The end of the story was the blending of Roman with Teutonic law in
as many different mixtures[3] as there were local customary laws[4] in
Medieval Western Christendom.[5]

The Infusion of a Decadent Roman Law into the Islamic Sharī'ah

This infusion of Roman Law into the custom of Teutonic barbarians
who had no future was, however, neither so important an event nor so
striking a feat as its surreptitious and unavowed yet unmistakable infiltration into the Islamic law of the Arab barbarian conquerors of other
ex-Roman territories. The two elements that blended here were even
more incongruous, and the result of their blending was the creation, not

---

[1] Known under the alternative names of *Liber Iudicum* and *Forum Iudiciorum*, and
eventually translated into Castilian as the *Fuero Juezgo*.

[2] Lot, F.: *Les Invasions Germaniques* (Paris 1935, Payot), pp. 182–3.

[3] The close resemblance of medieval Spanish customary law to Scandinavian law
leads Lot (op. cit., p. 183) to surmise that, in the Visigothic dominions, an unwritten
Gothic customary law survived both the *Breviarium Alarici* and Receswinth's *Forum
Iudiciorum*.

[4] In France, this diversity of local customary laws survived even the effective political
unification of the kingdom and was only ironed out by the legislation of the 'iconoclastic
assemblies' convened by the Revolution.

[5] The main contributions of Roman Law on the one side and Teutonic Law on the
other are set out by Lot, op. cit., pp. 245–7.

just of a parochial law for a barbarian successor-state of the Roman Empire, but of an oecumenical law which was to serve the needs of a restored Syriac universal state and, after surviving the break-up of this political framework, was to govern and mould the life of an Islamic Society that, after the fall of the Caliphate, was to continue to expand until, at the time of writing, its domain had come to extend from Indonesia to Lithuania and from South Africa to China.

Unlike their pagan and Arian Teutonic counterparts, the Primitive Muslim Arabs had been roughly shaken out of their archaic traditional way of life before they administered to themselves the additional shock of a sudden change of social environment by bursting out of the deserts and oases of Arabia into the fields and cities of the Roman and Sasanian empires. A long-continuing radiation of Syriac and Hellenic cultural influences into Arabia had produced a cumulative social effect which had declared itself dramatically in the personal career of the Prophet Muhammad;[1] and his achievements had been so astonishing and his personality so potent that his oracles and acts, as recorded in the Qur'ān and the Traditions, were unquestioningly accepted by his followers as the source of law for regulating, not only the life of the Muslim community itself, but the relations between the Muslim conquerors and their at first many times more numerous non-Muslim subjects. The speed and sweep of the Muslim conquests—which brought half of what remained of the Roman Empire and the whole of the Sasanian Empire under the rule of Muhammad's successors within less than twenty years of the Prophet's death—conspired with the irrationality of the accepted basis of the Muslim empire-builders' new-laid law to create a problem which was hardly more awkward for the non-Muslim population of the Caliphate than it was for their Muslim masters; for, even when the Qur'ān was eked out by the Traditions, the task of wringing out of these unpromising materials an oecumenical law for a sophisticated society was as preposterous as the demands for welling water in the wilderness that the Children of Israel were said to have addressed to Moses.[2]

For a jurist in search of legal pabulum for sustaining social life, the Qur'ān was indeed stony ground. The chapters dating from the non-political Meccan period of Muhammad's mission, before the *Hijrah*, offered far less matter for the practical jurist than he would find in the New Testament; for this literary legacy of the politically disinterested first phase of the Prophet's career contained little beyond a patently sincere and monotonously reiterated declaration of the unity of God and denunciation of the moral and intellectual error of polytheism and idolatry. The chapters afterwards delivered at Medina might look, at first sight, more promising; for at the *Hijrah* Muhammad achieved in his own lifetime a position that was not attained by any follower of Jesus till the fourth century of the Christian Era;[3] he became the head of a state, and his utterances during this Medinese period were mainly concerned with public business. Yet it would be at least as difficult to elicit

---

[1] See III. iii. 276–7.   [2] Exod. xvii. 1–7.
[3] The difference between the respective political environments in which Christianity and Islam came to birth has been noticed in III. iii. 466–72.

a comprehensive system of law for a sophisticated society from the Medinese *surahs*, unsupplemented, as it would be to perform the same juristic conjuring trick with the Epistles of Saint Paul. Like the apostle-missionary, the apostle-podestà found that the flurry of improvising provisional solutions, *ad hoc*, for a ceaseless succession of emergencies, serious or trivial,[1] left him no breathing-space for attempting to sort out these stray sibylline leaves into anything like a comprehensive or systematic code. Yet, even if Muhammad had succeeded, where Paul had failed, in performing this superhuman labour, the result would have been of less practical use to the Arabian prophet's successors than a Pauline code would have been to the Christian Roman Emperors; for the private business of religious congregations in important cities of the Roman Empire in Paul's day actually had more in common with the public business of the Roman Empire in the fourth century of the Christian Era than had the public business of the agricultural, non-commercial, oasis-state of Medina under Muhammad's rule during the years A.D. 622–32 with the public business of the universal state, embracing all but a fraction of the Syriac World, of which Muhammad's thirty-third successor Mu'tamid found himself master upon his accession in A.D. 870.[2]

In these compelling circumstances the men of action who built the Arab Caliphate let theory take its chance and resorted to self-help. In a legal no-man's-land where the oracles of the Qur'ān were dumb and where even the beaten track (*Sunnah*) of concordant Tradition faded out, they found their way through by the aid of common sense, analogy, consensus, and custom.[3]

'In the oldest period of the development of Islam the authorities entrusted with the administration of justice and the conduct of the religious life had in most cases to fall back on the exercise of their own *ra'y* (common-sense personal judgment) owing to the scarcity of legislative material in the Qur'ān and the dearth of ancient precedents. This was regarded as a matter of course by everyone. . . . Corresponding to this recognition of *ra'y* as an approved source of law are the instructions ascribed to the Prophet and the early Caliphs, which they gave to the officials sent to administer justice in the conquered provinces. . . . In the digests which were developed from these simple origins we find deduction from decisions in allied cases expressly mentioned, i.e. the application of analogy (*qiyās*) as a methodical adjustment of equity (*ra'y*). . . .

'We have—there is evidence for it at a very early period—a kind of popular element adopted among the constitutive sources for the deduction

---

[1] For these characteristics of Muhammad's personal legislation in the Medinese *surahs*, see Margoliouth, D. S.: *The Early Development of Mohammedanism* (London 1914, Williams & Norgate), pp. 5 and 12. 'It has been noticed that the word which we ordinarily render "reveal", and which literally means "send down", is properly applied to royal rescripts; the suppliant "raises" a petition and the sovereign "sends down" the reply. The faithful at Medinah used to await fresh revelations each day somewhat as we in these days are on the look out for the morning paper.'

[2] i.e. three hundred years after the birth of Muhammad in A.D. 570.

[3] 'It is likely that [Muhammad] meant current practice to continue except where his legislation had abrogated it' (Margoliouth, op. cit., p. 66). To begin with, the custom which counted for most was that of the Arabian oasis-dwellers and Nomads whose conquests re-established a Syriac universal state. The custom which eventually prevailed was that of the Arab empire-builders' converted subjects.

of laws: the conception of consensus (*ijmā'*), i.e. the general usage of the community which has been established by agreement in the larger circles of believers independent of the written, traditional or inferred law. . . .

'It was quite natural, from the changed conditions after the conquests, that the formation of the law, not only in its special provisions, but particularly in the point of view they adopted in their method of deductive operation as laid down in *fiqh* (Islamic jurisprudence), was greatly influenced by what the authorities on the development of law in Syria and Mesopotamia were able to learn of Roman Law, sometimes of the special laws for the particular provinces. It was obvious that a quite uncultured people, coming from a land in a primitive stage of social development into countries with an ancient civilization where they established themselves as rulers, would adopt from among their new surroundings as much of the customary law of the conquered lands as could be fitted in with the conditions created by the conquest and be compatible with the demands of new religious ideas. . . . The comparative study of one chapter of private law has yielded the most conclusive proofs of the thorough-going adoption of Roman Law by the jurists of Islam.[1] . . . Roman Law, however, does not exhaust the sources drawn upon in the development of Muslim Law. The receptive character that marks the formation and development of Islam also found expression, naturally first of all in matters of ritual, in borrowings from Jewish Law. According to [von] Kremer,[2] even many of the provisions of Roman Law that have been adopted by Islam only found a place in *fiqh* through the intermediary of the Jews.'[3]

The Mosaic Law's Debt to the Codification of the Sumeric Law by Hammurabi

This Jewish Law, which had so long a history behind it already by the time of Muhammad's *hijrah* from Mecca to Medina, had originated, like the Islamic *Sharī'ah*, as the barbarian customary practice of Nomads who had broken out of the steppes of Northern Arabia into the fields and cities of Syria; and, for meeting the same emergency of an abrupt and extreme change of social environment, the primitive Israelites, like the Primitive Muslim Arabs, had recourse to the existing law of a sophisticated society which they found in operation in the Promised Land.

While the Decalogue—at any rate in a pristine form, in which all the Commandments were couched in the lapidary style still preserved in the Sixth, Seventh, and Eighth[4]—would appear, on the face of it, to be a native Hebrew product, the next piece of Israelite legislation, known to scholars as 'the Covenant Code',[5] betrays its debt to the Code of Ham-

---

[1] Schmidt, F. F.: *Die Occupatio im Islamischen Recht*, reprinted from *Der Islam*, i (Strassburg 1910).

[2] Kremer, A. von: *Culturgeschichte des Orients* (Vienna 1875–7, Braumüller, 2 vols.), vol. i, p. 535; English translation by Khuda Bukhsh, S.: *The Orient under the Caliphs* (Calcutta 1920, University Press), chap. viii, 'The Origin and Development of Muslim Law', Section 6, 'The Sources of Muslim Law'.

The influence of local Medinese Jewish jurisprudence on the early school of Islamic jurisprudence at Medina is emphasized by Margoliouth, op. cit., p. 74: 'There is no evidence that Roman Law penetrated into this primitive city.'

[3] Goldziher, I., in the *Encyclopaedia of Islam*, vol. ii (London 1927, Luzac), s.v. Fiḳh, quoted with the permission of the publishers.

[4] A conjectural reconstruction of the whole Decalogue in this presumably original style will be found in Smith, J. M. P.: *The Origin and History of Hebrew Law* (Chicago 1931, University of Chicago Press), pp. 6–7.

[5] The Covenant Code 'exists in two forms: one very short, viz. Exodus xxxiv, 17–26;

murabi more patently than the *Sharī'ah* reveals its corresponding debt
to a Syrian Roman law-book.

'It has been calculated that, out of forty-five, or possibly fifty-five,
judgments preserved in this old Hebrew Law, thirty-five have points of
contact with the Hammurabi Code, and quite half are parallel.'[1]

This masterful influx of a code of Sumerian Law into legislation
enacted at least nine centuries later in one of the local communities of
a latter-day Syriac Society testified to the depth and tenacity of the
roots which the Sumeric Civilization had struck in Syrian soil during
the millennium ending in Hammurabi's generation. A First Syriac
Civilization, affiliated to the Sumeric, had miscarried as a result of the
insatiable aggressiveness of the Hyksos barbarians, who, not content
with carving out for themselves a successor-state in the Syrian provinces
of the Empire of Sumer and Akkad, had driven on into the Egyptiac
World and had thereby eventually brought down upon Syria an Egyptiac
counter-invasion.[2] On the political plane, Syria had been included, for
two centuries, in a reinstituted Egyptiac universal state and thereafter
been partitioned, for two further centuries, between this Egyptiac Power
and a rival Hittite Empire. On the cultural plane the subject Syrian
peoples, while continuing, down to the reign of the Egyptiac Emperor
Ikhnaton (*imperabat circa* 1380–1362 B.C.), to employ as their medium
of literary expression the Akkadian language, conveyed in the cuneiform
characters according to the Akkadian usage, had experimented in working out an Alphabet for the conveyance of their native Canaanite speech,
and, after testing the adaptability of the cuneiform characters for alphabetic use,[3] had discarded them in favour of the notation—possibly of
Minoan origin—which they immortalized by creating the historic Alpha-

the other more extended, viz. Exodus xx, 23—xxiii, 33. This code is incorporated in two
of the documents which compose the Hexateuch: Exodus xxxiv, 17–26, in the J document, and Exodus xx, 23—xxiii, 33, in the E document. These two documents arose
in the latter part of the ninth century or the early part of the eighth century B.C., J being
probably a half-century or so older than E' (Smith, op. cit., p. 15).

  [1] Johns, C. H. W.: *The Relations between the Laws of Babylonia and the Laws of the
Hebrew Peoples* (London 1914, Milford), p. 49. In the third of the three lectures composing this book, the writer takes up the question whether the indubitable and, indeed,
striking points of similarity between Hammurabi's Code and the Covenant Code are to
be accounted for as products of a uniformity of Human Nature, in virtue of which we
find different individuals or communities independently making similar responses to
similar challenges, or whether these particular similarities are to be traced to a process of
diffusion through which the Covenant Code has borrowed from Hammurabi's Code or
both have borrowed from some common source. Johns' conclusion is that most of the
matter which the Covenant Code shares with Hammurabi's Code has been borrowed by
the Covenant Code from the earlier of the two compilations. He argues from the similarity, down to arbitrary details, of the provisions in the two codes concerning (i) debt
slavery (Johns, op. cit., pp. 56–60; cp. pp. 39–46) and (ii) the prescription of the penalty
of burning alive for two particular offences (op. cit., pp. 60–61), and from the grouping
of the laws, in both codes, in sets of fives and tens (op. cit., pp. 26–27 and 61). Thus, in
Johns' view, Sumerian Law, as finally codified by Hammurabi, is the main common
element in the two codes. He does, however, allow for a subsidiary common element in
the shape of a primitive customary law of the Semite Nomads of Arabia which may have
been imported independently by Hammurabi's Amorite ancestors into Shinar and by the
Hebrews, in their turn, into Palestine, and have been injected, in both cases, by the
Nomad conquerors into the existing law of the conquered sedentary population (op. cit.,
pp. vi-vii, 28, and 32–33).   [2] See II. ii. 388–91.
  [3] In this experiment, they were anticipating the work of the creator of the Medo-
Persian cuneiform Alphabet, which was invented—to all appearance, quite independently—about a thousand years later (see p. 247, above).

bet out of it. Finally, the Syrians had struck out for themselves, in all departments of life, a new civilization of their own which was affiliated to the Minoan, and not to either the Sumeric or the Egyptiac. Yet the Israelite Covenant Code is evidence that, through all these political and cultural revolutions in Syria, the Sumerian Law, as embodied in Hammurabi's Code, had remained in force among the descendants of Hammurabi's Syrian subjects—and this in such vigour as to impress itself imperiously upon the callow legislation of the Canaanites' Hebrew barbarian conquerors.[1]

In thus entering into the law of barbarians who happened, exceptionally, to be incubators of a higher religion, the Sumerian Law, like the Roman Law, made a greater mark on history than when it was influencing barbarians whose destiny was the usual inglorious exit of their kind. At the time of writing, the Sumerian Law was still a living force in virtue solely of its Mosaic offprint. On the other hand, the Islamic *Sharī'ah* was neither the sole nor the liveliest living carrier[2] of the Roman Law at the same date. In the twentieth century of the Christian Era the chief direct heirs of the Roman Law were the canons of the Eastern Orthodox and Western Catholic Christian Churches. In the domain of law, as in other fields of social action, the master institution created by the internal proletariat was the universal state's principal beneficiary.

3. *Calendars; Weights and Measures; Money*

The Concern of Governments with Standard Measures

Generally accepted and effectively operative standard measures of time, distance, length, volume, weight, and value are necessities of social life at any level above the most primitive. They are needed not only by manufacturers, stock-breeders, and agriculturists, but by hunters of the higher type that does not simply wait passively for game to turn up, but pursues a strategy dependent on ability to forecast and anticipate its

---

[1] The Covenant Code was a selection from the Code of Hammurabi. 'There are 282 laws in the Code of Hammurabi, and only 50 in the Covenant Code' (Smith, op. cit., p. 18); and the selection had been made to suit the requirements of a much more backward society than that for which Hammurabi was legislating. 'The provisions in the case of each law in Hammurabi's Code are much more detailed and elaborate and presuppose a much greater experience with the practices of an advanced social and economic order' (ibid., p. 18). 'It would . . . seem that wages for service were higher in Hammurabi's day than when the Covenant Code was drawn up' (ibid., p. 19). The legislation in Hammurabi's Code on the subject of runaway slaves has no counterpart in the Covenant Code as we have it (ibid., p. 29). 'The Code of Hammurabi is much the more severe of the two and uses the penalty of capital punishment to a much greater extent' (ibid., p. 20), but, as we have seen in comparing the Hittite Code with Hammurabi's and the Teutonic barbarian laws with Roman Law, the absence of severe penalties may be evidence, not of humane feeling, but merely of impotence, on the legislator's part. Moreover, the law concerning the working off of debt by the enslavement of the debtor or members of his household to the creditor is less harsh in Hammurabi's Code than in the Covenant Code. Hammurabi's Code frees male and female debt-slaves alike after three years' service; the Covenant Code exacts six years' service from males and enslavement for life (with certain reservations and exceptions) from females (ibid., pp. 18–19). The Israelite laws prescribing the punishments for divers unnatural forms of sexual practice are likewise harsher than the corresponding provisions in the Hittite Code (see the comparative table in Cavaignac, E.: *Le Problème Hittite* (Paris 1936, Leroux), p. 109, n. 1).

[2] The continuous carriers of an institution are, of course, to be distinguished from reconverted renegades who have adopted the same institution *de novo* in a 'renaissance'.

victims' movements and behaviour. Social currencies of these kinds are older—perhaps far older—than governments; and they become matters of concern to governments as soon as these come into existence in their turn. The positive *raison d'être* of governments is to provide central political leadership for common social enterprises, and common enterprises cannot be operated without standard measures. Again, the negative *raison d'être* of governments is to ensure at least a modicum of justice in the private relations between their subjects, and, in most private issues of a 'business' kind, standard measures of some sort are involved. While governments thus find themselves implicated *ab initio* in the maintenance and enforcement of standard measures as one of their essential functions which they cannot afford to neglect, they also eventually discover that the administration of these institutions—for example, of the calendar at one end of the scale and of a coinage at the other—can be turned to account by them incidentally for the secondary purpose of moving their public in the direction of their policy.

In these various ways, standard measures concern governments of every species; but they are of particular concern to the governments of universal states for two reasons. In the first place, such governments start life as parvenus who have to take active steps to win the obedience, respect, and loyalty of subjects whom they have taken over, without consulting their wishes, from the former parochial states that they have overthrown and replaced by force. In the second place, universal states, by their very nature, are confronted with the problem of holding together far greater numbers of subjects and far wider areas of territory than any single one of their parochial predecessors; and for this reason, again, they have a special interest in the social unity and uniformity that standard measures promote when effectively enforced.

Calendrical Cycles

Of all the standard measures here in question, a standard system of registering time is the earliest felt and the most persistently imperative need; and the first necessity here is a measurement of the seasons of the year-cycle, which continues, even in technically advanced societies, to be the indispensable basis of Man's unceasing struggle to win a livelihood from Non-Human Nature.[1] But the problem of measuring the seasons soon carries the pioneer chronometrist into calculations of vastly longer aeons of Time than the single year-period within which the seasons revolve. The measurement of the seasons requires a harmonization of the three different natural cycles of the year, the month, and the day; the discovery that the ratios between these three cycles are not

[1] At first sight it might look as if Man's primeval servitude to the seasons had been thrown off in a Modern Western factory in which the temperature and atmosphere were 'conditioned' by artificial regulation and in which the machinery was worked by shifts of operatives for 24 hours in the day and for 365 days in the year. But this appearance of successfully contracting out of the tyranny of Nature was, of course, an illusion. Factories were fed by raw materials, and factory-workers by food, and in a Westernizing Modern World, no less than in the Higher Palaeolithic Society, the ultimate constituents of both food and raw materials had to be wrested from Nature. Moreover, this continuing war with Nature was still being waged, even in this technologically precocious society, by such 'higher hunters' as the trawler and the whaler, as well as by their younger brothers the husbandman and the shepherd.

simple fractions but surds leads a would-be harmonizer into thinking in terms of vaster cycles—the products, not of observation, but of reasoning—in which the elusive correspondences between the beginnings or between the ends of days, months, and years are found, by a mathematical computation, to recur after a formidably long lapse of time; and, when the habit of reckoning with these ampler periods leads the budding astronomer to take into his account the real or apparent cyclic movements of the planets and the 'fixed' stars, besides those of the Sun, Moon, and Earth, the chronological horizon recedes to a distance which is not easy to express and is still less easy to imagine—narrow-verged though it may seem to a latter-day cosmogonist in whose eyes our particular solar system is no more than one speck of star-dust in the Milky Way, and the Milky Way itself no more than one *ci-devant* nebula out of myriads of nebulae on their way from a flaming birth towards a deathly incineration.

Short of this latest stage in the mental exploration of chronological magnitudes, the 'least common measure' of the recurrent coincidences between the apparent movements of the Sun and those of a single one of the 'fixed stars' had generated the Egyptiac 'Sothic Cycle' of 1,460 years,[1] and a recurrent common cycle of the Sun, the Moon, and five planets the Babylonic *Magnus Annus*[2] of 432,000 years,[3] while, in the

[1] These 1,460 years were 'Sothic' years: i.e. years reckoned from heliacal rising to heliacal rising of the star Sothis (Sirius), its heliacal rising being the first occasion in the year on which the star is visible above the horizon before dawn. Throughout the life-span of the Egyptiac Civilization the Sothic-year was virtually coincident in length with the Julian year of $365\frac{1}{4}$ days, whereas the Egyptiac official year was a conventional one of 365 days. Thus a period of 1,460 Sothic years was exactly equal to a period of 1,461 official years, and in the course of a 1,460-years-long Sothic cycle the New Year's Day of the official year would travel right round the Sothic year-clock. The mathematical device of controlling the palpably inaccurate conventional year by relating it to the much more nearly accurate Sothic year must have been inaugurated in—or been based retrospectively on—some year in which the New Year's Day of the official year actually coincided with the heliacal rising of Sirius. In the latitude of Memphis in the fifth and fourth millennia B.C. this astronomical event occurred on the 19th July of the Julian Calendar, which in that age corresponded to the 15th June of the Gregorian Calendar—a date approximate to the Summer Solstice and also to the beginning of the annual rising of the Nile in the Lower Nile Valley and the Delta. It seems a fairly safe guess that, at the time when the official year of 365 days was first put into commission, it was set to begin on a date which was of such paramount importance for the whole life of the Egyptiac World. The Egyptiac official year did actually open on the 19th July of the Julian Calendar in each of the four-year periods A.D. 140/1–143/4, 1321/1320–1318/1317 B.C., 2781/2780–2778/2777 B.C., and 4241/4240–4238/4237 B.C. Since the Egyptiac Calendar, with its Sothic correction, is known to have been in use at both the two first-mentioned of these dates, the inaugural year—or retrospectively calculated starting-point—must fall within one or other of the two last-mentioned four-year periods. Eduard Meyer opts for the earlier of the two alternatives, i.e. 4241/4240–4238/4237 B.C., on the ground that, by the time of the Old Kingdom, the Calendar was already a long since established institution (see Meyer, E.: *Geschichte des Altertums*, vol. i, Part II, 3rd ed. (Stuttgart and Berlin 1913, Cotta), pp. 28–30).

[2] See IV. iv. 23–24 and 37, and V. v. 56–57.

'Quarum [stellarum] ex disparibus motionibus magnum annum mathematici nominaverunt, qui tum efficitur cum Solis et Lunae et quinque errantium ad eandem inter se comparationem confectis omnium spatiis est facta conversio. Quae quam longa sit, magna quaestio est; esse vero certam et definitam necesse est' (Cicero: *De Natura Deorum*, Book II, chap. 20).

'Homines . . . populariter annum tantummodo Solis, id est unius astri, reditu metiuntur; cum autem ad idem, unde semel profecta sunt, cuncta astra redierint, eandemque totius anni descriptionem longis intervallis retulerint, tum ille vere vertens annus appellari potest—in quo vix dicere audeo quam multa saecula hominum teneantur' (Cicero: *Somnium Scipionis*, chap. 7 = *De Republica*, Book VI, chap. 22, in Cardinal Angelo Mai's edition (Rome 1823, Mawman)).

[3] This appears to have been the estimate that was traditional in the Babylonic school

stupendous Mayan Grand Cycle of 374,440 years, no less than ten distinct constituent cycles were geared together.[1]

Governmental Methods of Keeping Count of Time

Governments, like astronomers, find themselves concerned with computations of terms of years, as well as with the seasonal articulation of the recurrent year-cycle. Their interest in the seasonal calendar is obvious, for it is the key not only to the livelihood of their subjects, for which governments are held responsible in the last resort, but also to their own ability to command the resources without which they cannot perform a government's recognized functions. Even in a technically advanced and highly industrialized state of society the parochial governments of a Westernized World in the year A.D. 1952 were having their policies dictated to them by the results of the last harvest and the prospects of the next one; and in simpler states of society this domination of weather over policy had made itself felt *a fortiori*. Governments had not been able to mobilize and maintain armies without a sufficient surplus of food stocks with which to feed them, and they had been constrained to time their military campaigns to coincide with the slack season of the agricultural year (whichever of the seasons this might happen to be in the particular climate in which their dominions were situate and under the particular system of agricultural production that was practised there).

In a state of society in which a money economy is either unknown or else only partially operative, the government even of a sedentary agricultural community may have to make an annual round of seasonal migrations to draw on food-supplies which, under the technological conditions of the time and place, are less mobile than even august human bodies. We have already taken note of the Achaemenian Court's regular distribution of its time between three different imperial residences.[2] The Merovingian Frankish rulers of the most barbarous of the Continental Teutonic successor-states of the Roman Empire in one of the most backward of the Empire's former territories used to roam from one estate to another of their royal domain in order to browse on the fat of the land. Where the government has been of Nomad origin and has brought with it, out of 'the desert' into 'the sown', a war-band of Nomad empire-builders who persist, *in partibus agricolarum*, in following their ancestral way of life, this migratory dance of attendance on the

of astronomers (see Cumont, F.: *Les Religions Orientales dans le Paganisme Romain*, 4th ed. (Paris 1929, Geuthner), pp. 164 and 289). Macrobius, in his commentary on the *Somnium Scipionis*, II. 11, rushing in where Cicero had feared to tread, ventures on an estimate of his own in which he reckons the span of the Magnus Annus at 15,000 solar years, and Cicero himself had proposed a figure of 12,954 years in his *Hortensius* (inaccessible in A.D. 1952), according to Tacitus in his *Dialogus de Oratoribus*, chap. 16. Cicero's and Macrobius's shots fell much nearer the mark than their Babylonic predecessors' conscientious calculations, if the true figure is 25,817 solar years (see Pickman, E. M.: *The Mind of Latin Christendom* (London 1937, Oxford University Press), p. 119).
[1] See Morley, S. G.: *The Ancient Maya* (Palo Alto, California 1946, Stanford University Press), pp. 262 and 289; Thompson, J. E. S.: *Maya Hieroglyphic Writing: Introduction* (Washington, D.C., 1950, Carnegie Institution of Washington), pp. 141–56. Like the Egyptiac Sothic Cycle, the Mayan Grand Cycle was a device for correcting the inaccuracy of an official year of 365 days.
[2] See pp. 205–6, above.

seasons is, of course, a still more conspicuous feature of public business. Yet even the most primitive and rudimentary government cannot allow its enslavement to a tyrannous annual round to preoccupy its attention to the exclusion of all provision for reckoning in terms exceeding the length of a single year; for the first concern of every government is to keep itself in existence; the most incompetent government may last for a whole lifetime, and perhaps for a term spanning a number of successive generations; and the most naïve administration soon discovers that it cannot remain in business without keeping some permanent record of its acts.

For this purpose the gigantic astronomical cycles evolved by the chronometrists were, however, as useless as the miniature calendar of the annual round, since the spans of time to which the continuous acts of even the longest-lived governments had run had, in human history up to date, been of a lesser order of magnitude than even the relatively modest length of the Sothic period. Consequently, governments had had to work out methods of their own for dating events over a series of years.

One of their methods had been based on the distinctiveness of every individual human being and on the personal names in which this distinctive individuality was expressed. They had taken to dating their acts by the names of magistrates with an annual term of office, such as the Assyrian *limmu*, the Athenian *archôn epônymus*, and the Roman pair of consuls; alternatively they had dated them by the series of regnal years of successive sovereigns ruling (short of accidents) for life. This system of dating does effectively distinguish every year in the count from every other; its weakness is that, when the continuous life of the institution employed as a time-measure happens to be prolonged for 1,050 years, as the life of the Roman consulate was from the reputed date of its institution in 509 B.C. to its abolition by the Emperor Justinian in A.D. 541,[1] a list of eponymous magistrates becomes far too long to be retained in the memory with the ease with which it is possible, for example, to learn by heart the twenty-six letters of the Latin Alphabet in their arbitrary sequence; and in these circumstances the denotation of a date by the citation of the consuls of the year no longer suffices to call the date to mind without a tiresome search through a list of perhaps a thousand pairs of names. The reckoning by reigns is ultimately open to the same objection, even when the names of individual sovereigns are grouped together under the names of dynasties, and when each individual reign is articulated, not only into single regnal years but into tax-assessment periods each extending over a number of years (the fifteen-yearly 'indictions' of the Later Roman Empire). The difficulty is not overcome by inventing an artificial cycle of official years with 'fancy' names, such as the Sinic cycle in which the years are named after animals (real and mythical) and other objects with auspicious associations; for, if the cycle is kept within the manageably short compass of

---

[1] See V. vi. 111 and 224. The life-span of the consulate would have to be reckoned as having been 990 years if we were to take as the initial date the traditional year, not of the inauguration of the institution itself (509 B.C.), but of its first restoration (449 B.C.).

the Latin Alphabet, it will recur so frequently that confusion will arise between one of its occurrences and another, while, if such confusion is to be avoided, this can only be done by drawing out the series towards the unmanageable length which the Roman consular *fasti* had reached by the year A.D. 541.

The only satisfactory way out is to adopt the different method of choosing some particular year as an initial date and reckoning subsequent years from that date onwards in a numerical sequence which can, if necessary, be continued *ad infinitum* without in any way diminishing the convenience of the system for ready reckoning.[1] The dates chosen as the starting-points for new eras had in some cases been those of events of which the authenticity and the time of occurrence had been established beyond dispute. Classical examples were the eras starting from the Fascist occupation of Rome on the 28th October, 1922; from the establishment of the First French Republic on the 22nd September, 1792; from the Prophet Muhammad's *hijrah* from Mecca to Medina on the 15th July, A.D. 622;[2] from the assumption of a formal claim to oecumenical authority in the Indic World by the Gupta Dynasty on the 26th February, A.D. 320; from the definitive establishment of the Seleucid Empire's Hasmonaean successor-state in Judaea in 142 B.C.; and from the triumphal re-entry of the founder of the Seleucid Monarchy, Seleucus Nicator, into Babylon in 312 B.C. (an event which, for chronometrical convenience, was retrospectively equated with the 1st of the Macedonian month Dius (October) of that year).

There were other cases in which eras had been reckoned from events of which the precise date had been disputable. For example, there was no evidence that Jesus had in fact been born in the first year of a Christian Era that did not become current in divers provinces of Western Christendom till divers dates in and after the sixth century from the birth of Christ according to this computation;[3] there was likewise no evidence that the city of Rome had in fact been founded in the year 753 B.C. from which later generations of Romans had reckoned their era *post urbem conditam*; and the year 776 B.C., which figured as the first year of 'the First Olympiad' quadriennium, was admittedly not the ascertained first year in which the Olympian Festival had been celebrated, but merely the first year in which there was a record of the name of a victor in the games at the chronometrist's disposal for use as an eponym. In the third place there were cases in which eras had been reckoned from an imaginary event in the cosmogonical scheme of some particular school of theology: for example, the supposed instantaneous creation of the World by the fiat of a unique and omnipotent personal God, which had been discrepantly dated the 7th October, 3761 B.C., by the Jews, the 1st September, 5509 B.C., by the Eastern Orthodox Christians,[4] and

---

[1] 'New eras' have already been discussed, as symptoms of 'Futurism', in V. vi. 339–45.

[2] This is the proper correction for the popular traditional date 16th July, 622. D. S. Margoliouth dates the *Hijrah* the 20th September, 622 (*Mohammed and the Rise of Islam* (3rd ed.: London 1905, Putnam), p. xx).

[3] The traditional Christian Era is said to have been instituted in A.D. 525 at Rome, by the Abbot Dionysius Exiguus, at the instance of the Pope. Even within the limits of Western Christendom it did not become generally prevalent till the ninth century.

[4] The Eastern Orthodox Christian reckoning by 'Years of the World' appears to have

6.0 p.m. on the evening before the 23rd October, 4004 B.C., Old Style, by the Anglo-Irish chronologist-archbishop Ussher (*vivebat* A.D. 1581–1656).[1]

The Inability of New Eras to establish themselves without Religious Sanctions

In the two preceding paragraphs the eras passed in review have been marshalled in a descending order of the cogency of the evidence for the events chosen by their originators for setting their initial dates; but, if we now resurvey these same eras from the standpoint of their relative success or failure in gaining a wide and lasting currency, we shall observe that the talisman by which their destinies had been decided had not been the touchstone of historical attestation, but the presence or absence of a religious sanction. In A.D. 1952 the historically dubious Western Christian Era was in the ascendant in the World on the unexpended strength of its ancient appeal to the former religious sentiment of its once Christian Western disseminators. The Islamic Era of the Hijrah, which was now on the defensive against the Christian Era, was still holding its own, in so far as it was succeeding in doing so, in virtue of its living appeal to the surviving religious sentiment of a majority of its hereditary adherents, and not at all in virtue of its being, as it was, as impeccable historically as the Christian Era was vulnerable to assaults of the higher criticism. At the same date the Jews were still persistently reckoning by their hallowed version of the date of the Creation. The vitality that was thus being displayed by the religious eras in A.D. 1952 was thrown into sharp relief by its contrast with the mortality rate of these consecrated eras' unhallowed secular counterparts. The Era of the First French Republic had been discarded by Revolutionary France herself in its fourteenth year on the 1st January, 1806; the Era of the Italian Fascist Revolution had shared the downfall of Fascism itself; and even the Seleucid and Gupta eras, after remaining in use for centuries, and being adopted or imitated by successive epigoni and supplanters of their originators, had long since fallen out of use.[2]

It is also significant that other secular events which, in the minds of contemporaries and Posterity, were no less epoch-making than those cited above, were never taken as the starting-points of new eras—not even of new eras that were abortive. Cases in point are the beginning, in May 1703, of the building, at St. Petersburg, of a new capital for Russia that was to be Western from the start;[3] the landfall of the Pilgrim Fathers in New England on the 21st December, 1620; the

arisen at Constantinople in the seventh century of the Christian Era. In Russia, it was abrogated by Peter the Great, in favour of the Western Christian reckoning by 'Years of Our Lord', as from the 1st January, 1700. The celebration of New Year's Day thenceforward on the 1st January, in lieu of the 1st September, was made obligatory (see Brückner, A.: *Peter der Grosse* (Berlin 1879, Grote), p. 227).

1 See XI. ix. 178. Bishop Ussher's chronology found its way into the margin of the Church of England's Authorized Version of the Bible.

2 'The tenacity of the Seleucid calendar was remarkable: Doura used it when under Roman rule and Jews down to the eleventh century, and it is said to have still been in use among Syrian Christians at the beginning of the present century' (Tarn, W. W.: *The Greeks in Bactria and India* (Cambridge 1938, University Press), p. 65).

3 See p. 221, above.

opening of a new chapter in Western history towards the close of the fifteenth century of the Christian Era (an event which could have been dramatically symbolized either in the crossing of the Alps by King Charles VIII of France in A.D. 1494, or in da Gama's landfall at Calicut on the 20th May, 1498, or in Columbus's landfall on one of the Antilles on the 12th October, 1492, or in the publication of the first Western printed book in A.D. 1445–6). We might add to this catalogue the beginning, in the year A.D. 324, of the building, at Constantinople, of a new capital for the Roman Empire that was to be Christian from the start,[1] and the crossing of the Hellespont by Alexander the Great in 334 B.C.

Evidently the recognition of the authenticity and the importance of an event is not enough, in itself, to make such an event eligible for serving as a mark for the measurement of Time. If the historic event is not consecrated by some religious sanction, its intrinsic merits as a starting-point for an era may count in practice for little or nothing. There is indeed a traditional association, which cannot be dissolved with impunity, between the measurement of Time by human intellects and the hold of Religion over human souls, and the ground for this is not difficult to descry. Religion dominates every side of life or aspect of the Universe that is recognized by Man as being out of his control, and in this respect there is·a striking contrast between Man's relation to the heavenly bodies whose cyclic movements give him his measures of Time and the divers objects which he subjects to measurements of length, volume, weight, and value. Man has at least an illusion of being master of the flour that he metes out in a man-made vessel after having ground it from grain produced by a harvest that Man himself has sown and reaped; he has a still greater sense of mastery over the piece of metal that he strikes into a coin after having smelted it from ore that he has detected in, and extracted from, the bowels of the Earth; but the stars in their courses overawe him by their inexorable aloofness, though in truth the astronomer's intellectual mastery over them is a more wonderful achievement than any physical feats of miner, miller, husbandman, or metallurgist.

> In caeloque deûm sedes et templa locarunt,
> per caelum volvi quia nox et luna videtur—
> luna, dies et nox et noctis signa severa,
> noctivagaeque faces caeli flammaeque volantes . . . .
> nam cum suspicimus magni caelestia mundi
> templa super stellisque micantibus aethera fixum,
> et venit in mentem solis lunaeque viarum,
> tunc aliis oppressa malis in pectora cura
> illa quoque expergefactum caput erigere infit,
> nequae forte deûm nobis immensa potestas
> sit, vario motu quae candida sidera verset.[2]

So far from readily falling into the delusion that he can affect the move-

---

[1] See pp. 218 and 238, above. The dedication date of the completed city was the 11th May, 330.

[2] Lucretius: *De Rerum Natura*, Book V, ll. 1188–91 and 1204–10.

ments of the heavenly bodies, Man has found it difficult to shake off the contrary delusion that these movements influence human destinies.

The persistence of this superstition in the inaccessible subconscious depths of the Psyche, even in societies that had attained a degree of sophistication at which Astrology had been professedly discredited and repudiated, was attested by the rarity of the instances in which a revolutionarily rational reform of the Calendar had succeeded in establishing itself. The French Revolution, whose rationalized codes of law went forth, conquering and to conquer, to the ends of the Earth[1] and whose pedantically new-fangled weights and measures—grammes and kilogrammes and milligrammes, metres and kilometres and millimetres —enjoyed a *succès fou* and ran like wildfire round the globe, was utterly defeated in its attempt to supersede a pagan Roman calendar that had been rejuvenated through being consecrated by the Christian Church, though the substitute which the lucid French Reason offered was the attractive one of a neatly proportioned new series of picturesquely renamed months—a Brumaire, a Ventôse, a Germinal, a Fructidor— each cut to a uniform length of thirty days grouped in three ten-day weeks. The batch of five supernumerary days that made up the tale of the ordinary (non-leap) year 'hardly marred the most sensible calendar ever invented—too sensible for a country which calls the tenth, eleventh and twelfth months of the year October, November and December'.[2] Yet, while the fantastically erroneous lunar year of an archaic Meccan oasis-state had been adopted, as the calendar of Islam, by hundreds of millions of people over a vast area extending almost from end to end of the Old World, the 'sensible' calendar devised by French votaries of Reason did not manage to outlive its fourteenth year, and the shortness of its life testified that, after all, the French revolutionaries had been less wise in their generation than the Roman conservatives.

The Roman misnomers pointed out by a distinguished Modern Western historian in the passage quoted just above were neither casual nor imbecile but deliberate and sagacious. The six months originally denoted in the Roman calendar by numerals, and not by the names of gods, had not, of course, been wrongly numbered when their names had first been bestowed on them. Originally the Roman official year had begun on the 1st March, in the spring of the solar year, and this month had been a convenient starting-point for the annual round of administration and warfare, as well as agriculture, so long as the Roman Government's range of action had extended no farther afield than a few days' march from the Pomoerium; for, under those conditions, an annual magistrate elect who had entered on his term of office on the 15th March could still take up the local command, assigned to him by the Senate, in time to take advantage of the spring campaigning season. When, however, in and after the Hannibalic War, the field of Roman military operations expanded out of Italy overseas into the Balkan Peninsula and the still more distant Iberian Peninsula, a magistrate,

---

[1] See pp. 271–8, above.
[2] Thompson, J. M.: *The French Revolution* (Oxford 1943, Blackwell), p. ix.

appointed to one of these distant commands, who had to wait till the 15th March before setting out from Rome might find himself unable to get into action before the summer was at its height and the autumn was approaching.

During the half-century immediately following the end of the Hannibalic War, this hampering loss of the best part of each annual campaigning season, with which the Roman state was threatened now that it had come to be fighting its wars in theatres at a distance of as much as several months' journey from the Italian homes of a Roman peasant soldiery, was at first largely offset by a discrepancy between the Roman official calendar and the actual cycle of the seasons resulting from the Pontifical College's cumulative neglect to keep the official year in step with the solar year by inserting intercalary months of the requisite length at the requisite intervals. For example, in the year 190 B.C., in which a Roman army inflicted a decisive defeat upon a Seleucid army on the Asiatic battlefield of Magnesia, the legions found time to arrive on the threshold of Sardis before the current season was over, because in that year the official 15th March fell on a day that was in reality the 16th November of the preceding solar year, while in the year 168 B.C., in which another Roman army inflicted an equally decisive defeat on a Macedonian army at Pydna, the official 15th March fell on a day that was in reality the 31st December of the solar year 169 B.C.[1] In these two militarily critical years the campaigning season was thus salvaged for Roman military operations thanks to a calendrical error; but, whether this error had been dictated by military considerations or by superstition, its efficacy diminished as the Roman calendar was progressively brought back nearer to correspondence with the solar year. The additional time now needed for arriving at a theatre of war before the campaigning season would be too far advanced had therefore to be provided by some alternative means; and, with this eminently practical consideration in mind, the Roman Government secured the passage of a law providing that, as from the year 153 B.C. onwards, the date on which the annually elected magistrates were to enter on their term of office was to be advanced, by two and a half months, from the 15th March to the 1st January,[2] and in consequence January instead of March became the first month of the year.[3]

Finding themselves thus constrained by *raison d'état* to call upon their

---

[1] In these two cases the magnitude of the Roman calendar's deviation from the current solar year can be calculated because Livy has recorded the dates of eclipses in terms of the day of the official Roman month (see Bouché-Leclercq, A.: *Histoire des Séleucides* (Paris 1913–14, Leroux, 2 vols.), vol. i, p. 205).

[2] The original provision in the United States for a four months' interval between the election of a President's electors and the President Elect's assumption of office was made with the similar practical purpose of ensuring that he should have sufficient time to convey himself to Washington by horse-traction from his home state, even if this happened to be Georgia or New Hampshire. Within half a century of the year in which the Constitution had been adopted, the invention of steam-traction by railroad had stultified the practical purpose which this provision had originally been designed to serve, but it was not till the 6th February, 1933, that the interval was shortened by 36 days through the coming into force of the Twentieth Amendment to the Constitution (see XII. ix. 496).

[3] The definitive replacement of the 1st March by the 1st January as the Roman New Year's Day seems to have taken place on the 1st January 45 B.C. as part of Julius Caesar's reform of the Roman Calendar.

public to put up with one shock to its habits and prejudices, the Roman authorities forbore to aggravate an already somewhat vexatious demand upon the Roman People's capacity for adaptation by simultaneously asking them to alter the traditional names of six of their twelve months merely out of respect for a different kind of reason which would have been, not political, but sheerly pedantic. Satisfied with their success in meeting the bare practical need of the day, the Conscript Fathers let the names of the months alone, and more than a century was allowed to pass before two out of the six resultant misnomers were corrected. At length the architects of the Principate took the bold step of renaming the first two of those six months which a Roman poverty of imagination had hitherto left unanimated and unhallowed by the names of gods. The month that was now the seventh, though still called 'the fifth' (*Quinctilis*), was renamed after Divus Iulius, and the following month (previously *Sextilis*) after Divus Augustus. The audacious innovation caught on, and in A.D. 1952 the calendars of both the Orthodox Christian and the Western World were still bearing the superscription of those two Roman statesmen in the month-names 'July' and 'August'.

Such currency is indeed apotheosis, if not immortalization; yet, in thus achieving a nomenclatory *tour de force* that proved beyond the capacity of French revolutionary enthusiasts, the astute authors of the Julian Calendar were exceptionally successful. In the United Kingdom in the supposedly enlightened eighteenth century of the Christian Era, disturbances were caused by an Act of Parliament, passed in A.D. 1751, for replacing the inexact Julian by the virtually perfect Gregorian calendar. This amended calendar had first been introduced by Pope Gregory XIII as far back as A.D. 1582, and in the meantime it had been adopted in most of the leading states of the Western World. But, in the sacrosanct sphere of the Calendar, religious susceptibilities long inhibited English Protestants from embracing a Papistical innovation, even if it were astronomically correct; and, sure enough, when the Act was published, it became suspect of having a catch in it. By the year 1752, in order to bring the current Julian reckoning into line with the Gregorian reckoning when this was substituted for it, it was necessary to drop eleven days out of the calendar year in which the change was being inaugurated. In their superstitious fear of calendrical magic, the British public were impervious to the simple truth that the eleven days which were to be dropped were only theoretical days on paper; they jumped to the conclusion that they were being cheated of eleven days' pay,[1] or perhaps even being docked of eleven days of life, and vociferous crowds went about demanding to have their stolen eleven days given back to them.

The Conservation of Pagan Calendars by Churches

Who had been the beneficiaries of calendars inherited by universal states from a dim religious past and rationalized by them at their peril?

---

[1] In fact, of course, everyone who was paid by the year or the month stood to gain, while anyone who was paid by the week or the day did not stand to lose, by the omission of eleven days in the month of September, 1752.

The marvellously exact, though formidably complex, Mayan calendar was bequeathed by 'the Old Empire' of the Mayas to the Yucatec and Mexic societies that were affiliated to the Mayan Civilization. The Sinic calendar was similarly bequeathed by the Empire of Ts'in and Han to the Far Eastern society affiliated to the Sinic Civilization. The Sumerian calendar, after having been bequeathed by 'the Realm of the Four Quarters' to the Babylonic Society affiliated to the Sumeric Civilization, and having survived to serve the Neo-Babylonian and Achaemenian Empires in their turn,[1] acquired at this stage a new lease of life through being adopted by the Jewish Church that was the endur- ing monument of Judah's fifty-years' exile by the waters of Babylon. The Roman calendar was bequeathed by the Roman Empire to the Christian Church and was transmitted[2] by this original legatee to secondary recipients—in the first place to the Orthodox Christian and Western societies, and thereby eventually to a number of universal states founded by Orthodox Christian and Western empire-builders: e.g. the Muscovite Empire in the Russian offshoot of Orthodox Christen- dom; the Danubian Hapsburg Monarchy; the Spanish Empire of the Indies; the British Rāj in India. By a still stranger caprice of Fortune the archaic lunar calendar of Mecca, thanks to its adoption by Islam and by the Caliphate, became the calendar of the Iranic and Arabic Muslim societies and hence the calendar of the Ottoman Empire and of the Timurid Mughal Empire on Indian ground.

This brief survey shows that in the histories of calendars the function most frequently performed by a universal state had been to take over a calendar from a primitive pagan past and to transmit it to a higher religion. In the process of transmission the universal state had some- times stamped the pagan calendar with its own political imprint; yet, when once a calendar had been adopted from a universal state by a 'higher religion', it was apt, notwithstanding the patent evidence of its unhallowed origin, to acquire the sacrosanctity with which the higher religions had been tempted to invest their casually acquired external accessories as well as their inner spiritual essence; and a calendar that had received this consecration had to be taken as it had been found by civilizations and universal states of a later generation who had inherited it from some higher religion that had incubated them. The accoutre- ments of a church usually cannot be refurbished by any party except the Church's own recognized supreme authority, whatever that authority may be. In Northumbria in the seventh century of the Christian Era the abandonment of a traditional method of reckoning the date of Easter, which had survived in a Far Western Christendom, in favour of a

[1] In the Jewish garrison-community at Elephantinê under the Achaemenian régime, the Babylonian calendar was current officially and the Egyptiac unofficially (Meyer, E.: 'Zu den Aramäischen Papyri von Elephantinê', in Kön. Preuss. Ak. Wiss., Gesammt- sitzung vom 23 November, 1911: Mitt. vom 26 October, pp. 1040–1).

[2] With the important addition of a reckoning by Jewish weeks as well as by Roman months. The Jewish community's original count of weeks—from the forgotten initial date at which this had been started—was still being kept, in A.D. 1952, in all living com- munities with a Jewish, Christian, or Muslim background. This was an historically notable common practice of the three religions—though Christianity and Islam had taken care to differentiate their practice from the Jews' and from one another's by choosing a different day of the week for their own equivalent of the Jewish Sabbath.

novel method which was a Roman innovation, implied a recognition of
the Roman Church's supremacy over the churches of 'the Celtic Fringe'.[1]
In a Western Catholic Christendom in the sixteenth century of the
Christian Era the Julian Calendar—work of pagan genius though it was—
could not have been reformed by any other authority than the Papacy;
and the act of Pope Gregory XIII was as effective as it was uncharac-
teristic of the normally conservative êthos of an established universal
church.

The Defeat of a Duodecimal by a Decimal System of Reckoning

When we pass from calendars and eras to weights and measures and
money, we enter a province of the field of social currencies in which
the rationalizing intellect holds sway uncensored by those religious
scruples that had sometimes welled up forcefully from the subconscious
depths of the Psyche when Reason had sought to extend her rule over
the reckoning of Time.

The French Revolutionaries, who suffered such a shattering defeat
in their attempt to inaugurate a rational new calendar and new era
unfortified by an augur's indispensable religious prestige, scored with
their new weights and measures an oecumenical success that eclipsed
even the triumph of the Napoleonic Codes. And a kindred spirit, Ts'in
She Hwang-ti, the revolutionary founder of a Sinic universal state,
succeeded in imposing the current weights and measures of his own
hereditary parochial state of Ts'in upon the conquered remainder of the
Sinic World[2] without, apparently, provoking in this case the stultifying
reaction by which, in other fields, his work, like that of his French
confrères, was so largely undone within a few years of its recklessly
sweeping execution.

Though it is evident that weights and measures are a sphere in which
the revolutionary intellect can disport itself with an unusual impunity,
a comparison of the respective fortunes of the French and the Sumeric
new model metric system suggests that the dazzling success of the
French reformers' work was due, above all, to their judicious moderation
in setting common-sense bounds to their pursuit of their ideal. They
were uncompromising in reducing the bewilderingly variegated tables
of the *Ancien Régime* to one single system of reckoning; but they showed
their practical good sense in irrationally following for this purpose the
inconvenient decimal system which had been unanimously adopted by
all branches of the Human Race, neither on its merits nor as the result
of some laboriously achieved diplomatic compromise between conflict-
ing better plans, but simply because the normal human being was born
with ten fingers and ten toes.

It was one of Nature's unkind practical jokes that she had furnished
some of the tribes of her vertebrate brute creation with six digits apiece
for each of their four limbs without endowing the possessors of this

[1] See II. ii. 326, 332, and 335.
[2] See Fitzgerald, C. P.: *China, A Short Cultural History* (London 1935, Cresset Press),
pp. 136–7; Franke, O.: *Geschichte des Chinesischen Reiches*, vol. i (Berlin and Leipzig
1930, de Gruyter), p. 233.

admirable natural abacus with the intellectual capacity for mathematical calculation, while she had dealt out to the *Genus Homo* a niggardly allowance of appendages that added up, not to dozens and double dozens, but only to decades and scores. Given the human anatomy, a decimal notation of Man's mathematical affairs was as inevitable as it was unfortunate. It was unfortunate because, on a decimal count, the basic scale of reckoning is divisible only by the low-powered number Two and the not very useful number Five, while the lowest number divisible alike by all the three key-factors Two, Three, and Four is Twelve. The decimal notation was nevertheless inevitable because, by the time when any wits in any society had come to appreciate the intrinsic superiority of the number Twelve over the number Ten, the decimal notation had become ineradicably entrenched in practical life, in language, and perhaps even already in written records.

The reformers of the French weights and measures forbore to kick against these ten-pronged pricks, but they had Sumerian predecessors who had been less wise in their generation. The Sumerian discovery of the virtues of the number Twelve was a stroke of pure intellectual genius, for there were no obvious sets of twelve articulations on the surface of the human body to guide a pioneer mathematician to the ideal choice for a scale of reckoning. The Sumerians not only saw the advantages of the number Twelve; they took the revolutionary step of recasting their system of weights and measures on a duodecimal basis; but apparently they did not realize that, unless they could also achieve the further, and far more difficult, step of leading their fellow men to substitute a duodecimal for a decimal basis of reckoning for all purposes,[1] the convenience of acquiring, for the simple purpose of weighing and measuring, a basic scale divisible by both the numbers Three and Four would be far more than offset by the inconvenience of having two incommensurable scales in operation side by side. This hopeless irreconcilability of an ideally convenient Twelve with a practically ineradicable Ten foredoomed an intrinsically superior duodecimal system of weights and measures to ultimate defeat, and assured a whole-hogging decimal system of a rapid victory. In the course of the four thousand years preceding the inauguration of the French decimal metric system the Sumeric duodecimal metric system had spread, notwithstanding its inherent handicap, to the ends of the Earth. Yet this long start in Time and Space did not save it from being almost entirely supplanted by its latter-day decimal competitor within 150 years of this rival system's promulgation. By A.D. 1952 the twelve ounces constituting a troy-weight pound and the twelve pence constituting a shilling in the antediluvian

---

[1] Technically the step would be simple enough in a society employing the originally Hindu 'Arabic' numerals or any other application of the device of making the numerical value of a figure depend on its relative location in a group. All that would be needed would be the invention of two new figures to represent the numbers Ten and Eleven. The notations 10 and 11 would then be released to stand respectively for Twelve and Thirteen. Twelve would be represented by 10, Twenty-four by 20, One Hundred and Forty-four by 100, and so on. The difficulty would lie, of course, not in cyphering, but in thinking, duodecimally; for in the common cultural tradition of the Human Race the decimal count was so immemorially old a piece of mental furniture that it had come to be virtually a fixture.

metronomy of the United Kingdom were almost the last surviving monuments of an unpractical stroke of Sumerian genius; and in an obstinately decimal-minded world it could not be maintained that this piously conservative loyalty to a provedly unsuccessful intellectual experiment was anything but a hindrance to the dispatch of business.

The Invention of Coinage

As soon as it has come to be recognized and accepted that honest dealing in weights and measures is a matter of social concern transcending the personal interests of the parties directly involved, and that therefore any government that aspires to be worthy of the name must make the giving of false weight and measure a prosecutable and punishable offence at law, the invention of money lies just round the corner. Yet this corner can only be turned by the taking of certain precise successive steps, and the requisite combination of moves in fact remained unachieved in the history of any society in process of civilization before the seventh century B.C., though by that time the species of societies called civilizations had already been in existence for perhaps as long as three thousand years.

The first step was the invention of the commercially useful expedient of giving some particular commodity or commodities the special function and status of serving as media of exchange and thereby acquiring a secondary use independent of their intrinsic utility. But this step did not, in itself, lead on to the invention of money when the commodities selected as media of exchange were multifarious and not exclusively metallic. In the Mexic and Andean worlds, for example, by the time of the Spanish conquest, the substances known and coveted in the Old World as 'the precious metals' existed in quantities that seemed fabulous to the Spanish *conquistadores*, and the natives had long since learnt the art of extracting, refining, and working this local gold and silver; but, though they valued it as material for works of art and ornaments, they had not thought of turning it to account as an exclusive medium of exchange,[1] though they, too, had hit upon this secondary use of com-

---

[1] Chronological facts forbid the otherwise almost irresistible conjecture that some report of this Mexic and Andean practice (so strange to the ears of denizens of the Old World) of estimating gold and silver, like any other commodity, at a valuation based on their mere intrinsic utility inspired a famous passage of More's *Utopia*:

'They keep an inestimable treasure, but yet not as a treasure. . . . Gold and silver . . . they do so use as none of them doth more esteem it than the very nature of the thing deserveth. And then who doth not plainly see how far it is under iron—as without the which, men can no better live than without fire and water, whereas to gold and silver Nature hath given no use that we may not well lack, if that the folly of men had not set it in higher estimation for the rareness' sake. . . . Whereas they eat and drink in earthen and glass vessels, which indeed be curiously and properly made, and yet be of very small value, of gold and silver they make commonly chamber-pots and other vessels that serve for most vile uses. . . . Furthermore, of the same metals they make great chains, fetters and gyves, wherein they tie their bondmen. . . . Thus by all means possible they procure to have gold and silver among them in reproach and infamy' (More, Sir Thomas: *Utopia*, English version, Book II: 'Of their Journeying or Travelling Abroad').

Utopia, however, was published before the end of A.D. 1516, and 'it is important to remember that the Inca Empire of Peru, which in more than one detail had a likeness to Utopia, was not known till some fourteen years later; Cortés had not yet conquered Mexico' (Chambers, R. W.: *Thomas More* (London 1935, Cape), p. 143). Evidently these dates rule out the possibility that the passage in *Utopia*, quoted above, could have been inspired by reports of Central American or Andean institutions. It may, however,

modities independently of the Old World and perhaps also independently of one another.

In the Mexic World the Spaniards found cacao beans, cotton cloths, T-shaped pieces of copper, and quills stuffed with gold dust circulating as media of exchange;[1] in the Andean World they found pimento, dried fish, cotton, maize, chuño, birds' feathers, salt, coca, and copper being used for the same purpose.[2] There was also at least one instance in which they found sea-shells being employed in this way, as the cowrie shell likewise was employed round the shores of the Indian Ocean.[3] It will be seen that the civilizations of the New World came near to employing standard units of metal in the fashion which, in the Old World, had led to the invention of money more than two thousand years earlier, while the employment of shells—a commodity without any intrinsic value of its own—was an anticipation of that use of paper money which in the Old World had already arisen, before the Spaniards' conquest of the Americas, as a sequel to the use of metallic coin.[4] Yet, though the civilizations of the New World thus came within an ace of inventing money, they failed to take the final step, and the verdict of History on their achievements in this sphere is that 'a miss is as good as a mile'.

In the commercially interwoven Egyptiac, Babylonic, Syriac, and Hellenic worlds by the date of the invention of money in the Hellenic World in the seventh century B.C.,

'the use of the precious metals in bar form as measures of value had been a regular institution for thousands of years past. They circulated, not in the form of coin minted by a state and guaranteed as legal tender, but as units of weight which passed from hand to hand in established forms such as rings, plaques, ornaments and so on, but which, in the act of payment, had to be verified by being weighed like any other commodity.'[5]

This usage had perhaps become customary in the Sumeric World in the time of its universal state;[6] but a regular metallic medium of exchange was the raw material of money without being the thing itself.

have been inspired by reports of already discovered fringes of the Americas where 'the precious metals' were given the same valuation by the inhabitants as in Mexico and Peru—whether in consequence of the radiation of one or other or both of these indigenous civilizations of the New World, or because even the more backward among the 'native' peoples had arrived independently, by the light of Nature, at the same common-sense valuation of gold and silver as their more progressive neighbours. 'We can only understand *Utopia* if we remember the Europe for which it was written; . . . the travels of Vespucci in every man's hands: Vespucci, who had found folk holding property in common and not esteeming gold, pearls or jewels' (ibid.).

Though the historic institutions of the Incaic Empire did not inspire *Utopia*, the imaginary institutions of More's ideal society did inspire one of the more beneficent and successful attempts, on the part of the Spanish conquerors of the New World, to fill the social vacuum which they themselves had produced by brutally shattering the fabric of Central American and Andean society. The Spanish philanthropist Vasco de Quiroga, who arrived in the Indies in A.D. 1530 as an enthusiastic disciple of More, succeeded in founding Indian *pueblos* on lines that were a deliberate attempt to reproduce *Utopia* in real life (Haring, C.: *The Spanish Empire in America* (New York 1947, Oxford University Press), p. 193). The present writer visited some of these on the 23rd–26th April, 1953.

[1] See Gann, T.: *Mexico from the Earliest Times to the Conquest* (London 1936, Lovat Dickson), p. 174; Vaillant, G. C.: *The Aztecs of Mexico* (London 1950, Penguin), p. 132.
[2] See Baudin, L.: *L'Empire Socialiste des Inka* (Paris 1928, Institut d'Ethnologie), p. 174.
[3] See ibid.   [4] See pp. 312–13, below.
[5] Meyer, E.: *Geschichte des Altertums*, vol. iii, 1st ed. (Stuttgart 1901, Cotta), p. 79.
[6] See Rostovtzeff, M: *Caravan Cities* (Oxford 1932, Clarendon Press), p. 11.

The decisive steps which conjured money into existence were taken in the seventh century B.C. by some Greek city-state, or perhaps by several of the commercially foremost Greek city-states of the day simultaneously, when their governments went beyond the existing practice of putting metallic media of exchange on a par with other commodities and thereby including them under the common ruling that made it an offence at law to give false weight and measure in the transfer of any commodity from hand to hand. These pioneer city-states now took the two revolutionary steps of making the issue of these metallic units of value a government monopoly and of stamping this exclusive governmental currency with a distinctive official image and superscription as a guarantee that the coin was an authentic product of the governmental mint and that its weight and quality were to be accepted as being what they purported to be on the face of them. When a government had assumed this prerogative, the clipping or filing of authentic coins became a political crime against the state and not merely an offence in civil law against some private individual on whom the fraudulently reduced lump of metal had been palmed off, and counterfeit coining by private individuals became a crime of the same order—a crime which would be not a whit less heinous if the unauthorized coiner's politically bad money happened to be as good in weight and quality as the legitimate coinage of the realm.[1]

The Diffusion of the Use of Coinage

Since the management of a coinage is evidently least difficult in a state with a minimum area and population, it was perhaps no accident that city-states should have been the political laboratories in which the invention was made. At the same time it is equally evident that the utility of a coinage increases with every enlargement of the area and population in which it circulates as legal tender. Such Greek city-states as Phocaea, Lampsacus, Miletus, Aegina, and Corinth, which were pioneers in minting coin, were of miniature material dimensions; and the narrow range of currency of these city-state issues was not appreciably extended when, as happened in several notable instances, two or three city-states situated in different quarters of the Hellenic World—one, perhaps, in Ionia or on the Hellespont, a second in Continental European Greece, and a third in Sicily or Magna Graecia—went into commercial partnership and arranged to issue uniform coinages which could all circulate *de facto*, if not *de jure*, throughout the issuing governments' combined domains. In the wide world beyond, where the writ of these petty governments did not run, their minted coinage was not accepted at its face value but was still treated like any unminted standard unit of metal whose value had to be assayed by weighing, every time the piece changed hands.[2]

[1] It will be seen that the invention of coinage is analogous, in the field of commerce, to the epoch-making change that takes place in the field of criminal law when a government takes to treating crimes as political offences against itself instead of regarding them merely as personal injuries to be avenged by the private self-help of the victim or his surviving kinsmen, in regard to which the government's own responsibility, at its widest, is limited to promulgating a tariff of *wergelds*.

[2] In out-of-the-way places with no coinage of their own, this practice of treating

A regional jump in scale was achieved when, in the earlier decades of the sixth century B.C., the Lydian Monarchy conquered all the Greek city-states round the western coasts of Anatolia except Miletus, as well as the interior of the peninsula as far east as the River Halys, and issued a coinage of electron (gold alloyed with silver), based on the local standard of the subjected Greek city-state of Phocaea, which was given a general currency throughout the Lydian dominions. The last and decisive step was taken when the Kingdom of Lydia, with its subject Greek city-states, was incorporated, in its turn, into the Achaemenian Empire. The Achaemenidae had the imagination to perceive the value, for a universal state, of this new invention which they had stumbled upon on the far western fringe of their South-West Asian World. They issued a gold coinage superior to the Lydian both in weight and in purity of metal, with a subsidiary silver coinage to supplement it, and they made the coining of gold an imperial monopoly. At the same time, with characteristic liberality, they permitted autonomous Greek and Phoenician city-states, client principalities, and even the Persian viceroys of imperial provinces, to issue, on their own account, not only small change in copper, but also silver money to circulate side by side with the silver issues of the imperial mints.[1]

In a more jealous vein the Roman Imperial Government in its day monopolized, throughout its dominions, the coining of silver as well as gold, and left nothing but copper cash to be issued by autonomous and allied states members of the Roman Commonwealth.[2] The prerogative, asserted by the Roman Imperial Government, of monopolizing the coining of gold was tacitly respected by the Arsacid Government, in spite of an insistence on their political independence which they vindicated successfully by force of arms on several critical occasions; and, when the easy-going Arsacidae were supplanted by militant Sasanidae who asserted, not merely their independence of Rome, but a political parity with her, these self-conscious successors of the Achaemenids in the Cis-Euphratean portion of the former Achaemenian dominions found themselves debarred by economic inability from emulating their Achaemenian ensamples and flouting their Roman contemporaries by taking to coining in gold as well as in silver.

After the Primitive Muslim Arabs had achieved the unfulfilled ambitions of the Sasanidae by reuniting under a single oecumenical régime, for the first time since the death of Alexander the Great, the bulk of the

---

foreign coins as if they were pieces of uncoined metal lasted for at least twelve hundred years after the invention of coinage on the shores of the Aegean. For example, 'at Mecca in Muhammad's day Roman gold pieces and Persian dirhems were already in circulation, but in commercial transactions they were valued by their weight' (Kremer, A. von: *Culturgeschichte des Orients* (Vienna 1875–7, Braumüller, 2 vols.), vol. i, p. 169).

[1] See Meyer, E.: *Geschichte des Altertums*, vol. iii, 1st ed. (Stuttgart 1901, Cotta), pp. 80–82. A viceroy who presumed to issue a silver coinage with as low a content of alloy as the alloy content of his Achaemenian imperial master's gold coinage was, however, found guilty of high treason by Darius *ipso facto*, according to Herodotus, Book IV, chap. 166.

[2] A provincial silver coinage was issued at Alexandria, and for a time at Antioch as well, by local branches of the Imperial Mint; on the other hand, in the western provinces even the copper cash in circulation was mostly of Roman and not of local mintage (see Rostovtzeff, M.: *The Social and Economic History of the Roman Empire* (Oxford 1926, Clarendon Press), p. 171).

former Achaemenian dominions, including the latterly Roman provinces in Syria and Egypt as well as the entire domain of the Sasanian Empire,[1] successive attempts were made by the Umayyad Caliphs Mu'āwīyah I (*imperabat* A.D. 661–80) and 'Abd-al-Malik (*imperabat* A.D. 685–705) to restore the long-lost monetary unity of the Syriac World.[2] There are indications,[3] however, that, in the matter of coinage, weights, and measures, the Caliphate did not in practice succeed in re-establishing a unity which was so triumphantly re-established under its aegis on the social, cultural, and spiritual planes.

The Invention of Paper Money

The oecumenical Achaemenian gold coinage had given the then still recent invention of money an impetus that had sped it—as the Revolutionary French decimal metric system and the Napoleonic Codes were to be sped in a later age—on an irresistible and almost ubiquitous course of conquest. Coined money was launched on its historic career in India by the temporary annexation of the Panjab to the Achaemenian Empire itself.[4] The more distant Sinic World became ripe for adopting the new institution after Ts'in She Hwang-ti's revolutionary empire-building work had been salvaged through being tempered by the tactful hands of Han Liu Pang. In its first fumblings with this puzzling alien device, the Prior Han régime betrayed its failure to apprehend one of the essential principles involved when in 175 B.C. the Emperor Hsiao Wên (*imperabat* 180–157 B.C.) sought to make up a shortage of currency by abandoning the imperial monopoly of issue and giving licences to local governors and princes of the Imperial House to mint copper cash.[5] The consequent inflation was eventually cured in 113 B.C. by the drastic steps of demonetizing all current coins and issuing a new imperial currency minted exclusively at Ch'ang Ngan under the direct control of imperial officials,

---

[1] See I. i. 76–77.

[2] See Wellhausen, J.: *Das Arabische Reich und Sein Sturz* (Berlin 1902, Reimer), pp. 135–6. According to Ahmad Al-Balādhurī: *Kitāb Futūh-al-Buldān* (English translation by Hitti, P. K., and Murgotten, F. C. (New York: Columbia University Press), vol. i (1916), pp. 383–4, and part ii (1924), pp. 263–6, 'Abd-al-Malik started coining gold (in ex-Roman territory) at Damascus in A.H. 74, and his eastern viceroy Al-Hajjāj silver (in ex-Sasanian territory) at Kūfah at the end of A.H. 75. The same authority reports that the occasion was a quarrel between the Umayyad and Roman Governments over a delicate question of images and superscriptions. According to Al-Balādhurī, the Caliphate had been selling to the Roman Empire Egyptian papyrus (which the Romans could not do without) in exchange for Roman gold coin (for circulation in the ex-Roman part of the Umayyad dominions). The water-mark on the papyrus (which was processed in Egypt before export) had been provocatively changed by 'Abd-al-Malik from the sign of the Cross to the Qur'anic text 'Say: He alone is God'. The Romans had threatened to retaliate by inscribing their—as they believed, indispensable—gold pieces with strictures on the Prophet Muhammad. This threat moved the Caliph 'Abd-al-Malik to start coining gold for himself. According to the East Roman chronicler Theophanes, *sub* A.M. 6183 (*Theophanis Chronographia*, ed. C. de Boor, vol. i (Leipzig 1883, Teubner), p. 365), the Roman Imperial Government refused to accept these new Damascene gold pieces in payment of the tribute which had been one of the stipulations in the treaty of A.D. 688 prolonging the peace settlement of A.D. 685, and this was the occasion of the recrudescence of war between the Umayyad Power and the Roman Empire in A.D. 692 (see Bury, J. B.: *A History of the Later Roman Empire* (London 1889, Macmillan, 2 vols.), vol. ii, p. 322; von Kremer, op. cit., vol. i, pp. 168–70.

[3] See Wellhausen, op. cit., loc. cit.

[4] See Meyer, op. cit., vol. cit., p. 80.

[5] See Fitzgerald, C. P.: *China, A Short Cultural History* (London 1935, Cresset Press), p. 161.

while at the same time granting an amnesty to the host of convicted coiners[1] who had continued to mint cash without licence in defiance of the Imperial Government's reassumption of its monopoly. But in 119 B.C., in the reign of the Emperor Wuti, in the course of preliminary gropings after some less arduous method of reinstituting a sound currency, the Imperial Government redeemed its compromised reputation for financial acumen by a quaint expedient based on a brilliant intuition of the hitherto undiscovered truth that metal is not the only stuff of which good money can be made.

'In the imperial park at Ch'ang Ngan the Emperor had a white stag, a very rare beast, which had no fellow in the empire. On the advice of a minister the Emperor had this animal killed, and made a kind of treasury note out of its skin, which, he believed, could not be copied. These pieces of skin were a foot square, and were made with a fringed border and decorated with a pattern. Each piece was assigned the arbitrary value of 400,000 copper coins.[2] The princes, when they came to pay their respects to the Throne, were compelled to buy one of these pieces of skin for cash, and present their gifts to the Emperor upon it. This precaution ensured the circulation of "the White Stag Notes". The skin of the white stag was, however, a limited quantity, and the time soon came when this device ceased to supply the Treasury with much needed money.'[3]

Leathern money—in this case apparently made from sable pelts—turns up again in Russia in the thirteenth century of the Christian Era, at a time when she was politically associated with China under a common Mongol domination;[4] but the invention of currency notes did not become effectively applicable till it had become associated with the two subsequent inventions of paper (invented in the penultimate chapter of Sinic history under the Posterior Han Dynasty)[5] and printing (invented in the early summer of the affiliated Far Eastern Society under the T'ang Dynasty).[6]

Negotiable paper ('flying money'), in the form of cheques tallying with stubs retained by the Imperial Treasury at Si Ngan, was issued by the T'ang Government in the years A.D. 807 and A.D. 809;[7] but there is no evidence that the inscriptions on these cheques were printed. Paper money on which there was probably an imprint was issued in the Chinese province of Szechwan—first by a group of private men of business, and later by the local government through the agency of a bank established for the purpose—during the interval (durabat A.D. 907–60) of political disunity in China between the extinction of the T'ang Dynasty and the re-establishment of an all but oecumenical régime by the Sung.[8] In A.D. 970 the invention of printed paper money was taken up by the Sung Government, and in China and its dependencies from that date onwards until the reign of the third Ming sovereign Yung Lo

---

[1] See Fitzgerald, op. cit., p. 165.
[2] Not 400,000 but 40,000, according to Ma Tuan-Lin: Wên Hsien T'ung K'ao, quoting from the Dynastic History of the Prior Han, as translated in Carter, T. F.: The Invention of Printing in China and its Spread Westward, revised edition (New York 1931, Columbia University Press), pp. 222–3.—A.J.T.
[3] Fitzgerald, op. cit., pp. 164–5.
[4] See Carter, op. cit., pp. 76 and 225.
[5] See ibid., pp. 1–6 and 190–1.
[6] See ibid., pp. 28–32 and 201–4.
[7] See ibid., pp. 70–71 and 223.
[8] See ibid., pp. 71–72 and 223–4.

(*regnabat* A.D. 1403–25) paper money was continuously and ubiquitously current.[1] In the latter part of the twelfth century of the Christian Era the practice was taken over from the Sung by the Kin barbarian invaders who had wrested the Yellow River Basin out of the hands of the Sung in A.D. 1124–42; and from the Kin it was taken over in succession by their more redoubtable supplanters the Mongols.[2]

The Mongols' sweeping conquests round all the shores of the Great Eurasian Steppe carried the western frontiers of an empire based on China up to the Euphrates and the Carpathians and thereby made China momentarily accessible to Iranic Muslim and Western Christian observers; and the paper money current in China at the time is mentioned by Marco Polo[3] and at least seven other pre-Renaissance Western authors, as well as by a number of Muslim authorities.[4] In Hūlāgū Khān's appanage of the Mongol Empire in Iran and 'Irāq, in the reign of his descendant Gaykhātū Khān (*dominabatur* A.D. 1291–5), in the year A.D. 1294, an issue of printed paper notes, with a bilingual inscription in Chinese and Arabic, was uttered in the commercial capital, Tabrīz. The local business community did not take kindly to the innovation, and their protests were so violent that the issue had to be withdrawn after two or three days' trial. It has been conjectured that some of this historic but unprofitable printed paper money may have been unloaded on to the hands of the Venetian and Genoese merchants residing in Tabrīz at the time.[5]

The Utility of a Monetary Currency as a Medium for Governmental Propaganda

Who had been the principal beneficiaries from this institution of money in the divers material media in which it had been issued by innumerable governments—parochial and oecumenical, ephemeral and rather longer-lasting—since its invention in the Hellenic World in the seventh century B.C.? Undoubtedly this device had proved, on balance, a convenience in the private transactions of the issuing governments' subjects—in spite of the socially subversive fluctuations of inflation and deflation, and temptations to borrow and lend at usurious rates, which the invention had brought in its train. But a greater benefit had assuredly accrued to the issuing governments themselves; for the issue of money is an *acte de présence* which brings a government into direct and constant contact with at least an active, intelligent, and influential minority of its subjects, even where the circulation does not extend through the entire population; and this monetary epiphany—which does not cease to be

[1] Yung Lo withdrew it from circulation (no doubt in view of the inflation that had occurred in the latter days of the Mongol régime in China, and, before that, in the latter days of the Sung). No further issues of paper money were made in China till A.D. 1851, when the Manchu Dynasty, in its turn, was declining towards its fall (see Carter, op. cit.; p. 76).

[2] See Carter, op. cit., pp. 72–76 and 224–5.

[3] An English translation of the passage, accompanied by valuable notes, will be found in *The Book of Ser Marco Polo*, translated into English and edited by Sir Henry Yule, 3rd ed., revised by Henri Cordier (London 1903, Murray, 2 vols.; 1920, supplementary volume), vol. ii, pp. 423–30.

[4] See Carter, op. cit., pp. 76–79 and 225–6.

[5] See ibid., pp. 128–9 and 238.

impressive by becoming familiar—not only automatically fosters a government's prestige and authority; it also gives a government a magnificent opportunity for deliberately indoctrinating its subjects with sentiments, beliefs, and views.

The hypnotic effect of a coinage even on the minds of a population under alien rule who resent this political yoke and abominate the Power by whom it has been imposed, is conveyed in a classic passage of the New Testament.

'They send unto Him certain of the Pharisees and of the Herodians, to catch Him in His words. And when they were come, they say unto Him: "Master, we know that thou art true, and carest for no man; for thou regardest not the person of men, but teachest the way of God in truth. Is it lawful to give tribute to Caesar, or not? Shall we give, or shall we not give?"'

'But He, knowing their hypocrisy, said unto them: "Why tempt ye me? Bring me a penny, that I may see it." And they brought it, and He saith unto them: "Whose is this image and superscription?" And they said unto him: "Caesar's". And Jesus answering said unto them: "Render to Caesar the things that are Caesar's, and to God the things that are God's".'[1]

'And they could not take hold of His words before the people, and they marvelled at His answer, and held their peace.'[2]

This automatic moral profit which the prerogative of issuing money yielded, even in a formidably adverse political and religious environment, was of incomparably greater value to the Roman Imperial Government than any mere financial gains which the management of the mint might incidentally bring in. The Emperor's likeness on a coin gave the Imperial Government a certain status in the minds of a Jewish population which not only regarded Rome's dominion as illegitimate but treasured, as the second of ten commandments believed to have been received by Moses from Yahweh viva voce, the explicit injunction:

'Thou shalt not make unto thee any graven image or any likeness of anything that is in Heaven above or that is in the Earth beneath or that is in the water under the Earth. Thou shalt not bow down thyself to them nor serve them; for I the Lord thy God am a jealous god.'[3]

When in 167 B.C. the Seleucid sovereign Antiochus IV Epiphanes had placed a statue of Olympian Zeus in the Holy of Holies of Yahweh's temple at Jerusalem, the horror and indignation of the Jews at seeing the 'abomination that maketh desolate'[4] 'standing where it ought not'[5] were so intense that, thenceforward, they could not rest until they had thrown off every vestige of Seleucid rule. Again, when in A.D. 26 the Roman procurator Pontius Pilate smuggled into Jerusalem, draped and under cover of night, Roman military standards bearing the Emperor's image in medallions, the reaction of the Jews was so vehement as to compel Pilate to remove the offensive emblems from the precincts of the Holy City.[6] Yet in their holy land the Jews had schooled themselves

---

[1] Mark xii. 13–17. Cp. Matt. xxii. 15–21; Luke xx. 20–25.
[2] Luke xx. 26. Cp. Matt. xxii. 22; Mark xii. 17.
[3] Exod. xx. 4–5. Cp. Deut. v. 8–9.   [4] Dan. xi. 31 and xii. 11.
[5] Mark xiii. 14. Cp. Matt. xxiv. 15.
[6] Josephus: *Antiquitates*, Book XVIII, chap. iii, § 1; *Bellum Iudaïcum*, Book II, chap. ix, §§ 2–3.

meekly, not only to seeing, but to handling, using, earning, hoarding, and by all these compromising actions progressively countenancing, the abominable image on Caesar's coinage, and had thereby anticipated in action the observation of their future Roman chastiser Vespasian that sordid money does not smell.[1]

The Roman Government was not slow to perceive the value of an oecumenical coinage as an instrument of policy.

'From the middle of the first century onwards the Imperial Government had appreciated, as few governments have done before or since, not only the function of coinage as a mirror of contemporary life—of the political, social, spiritual and artistic aspirations of the age—but also its immense and unique possibilities as a far-reaching instrument of propaganda. Modern methods of disseminating news and modern vehicles of propaganda, from postage-stamps to broadcasting and the press, have their counterpart in the imperial coinage, where yearly, monthly—we might almost say, daily—novelties and variations in types record the sequence of public events and reflect the aims and ideologies of those who control the state.'[2]

The designers of the Roman imperial coinage could make play with a combination of image and superscription for giving visual form to the issuing government's political directives. The Umayyad successors of the Roman Empire in Syria, Egypt, and North-West Africa, and the innumerable Muslim governments that had succeeded the Umayyads in their turn down to the time of writing, were required to perform the still more skilful feat of conveying their messages to their subjects by superscription alone, since the Jewish tabu on graven images had been adopted by the Prophet Muhammad. In this inverted Psyche's task of spinning straw out of gold, they were fortunate in operating with a version of the Alphabet whose beauty, like that of the Sinic characters, when displayed by a master of calligraphy, could still be appreciated even by an eye whose owner's mind was illiterate. This capacity of a superscription, even when unsupported by an image, to transmit to the users of a coinage the message impressed on it by its makers was attested by the variety and abundance of the issues uttered by Muslim states.

The User's Demand for Conservatism in the Reproduction of Coin Types

There is, however, one golden rule that has to be rigidly observed if a coinage, iconic or aniconic, is to produce its psychological effect. A type that has once caught the imagination of its clientèle will not retain its hold unless it is reproduced in successive issues with blind fidelity.

The abortive first essay in an Umayyad gold and silver coinage— made by the founder of the dynasty, Mu'āwīyah, himself—is recorded

[1] 'Reprehendenti filio Tito, quod etiam urinae vectigal commentus esset, pecuniam ex primâ pensione admovit ad nares, sciscitans num odore offenderetur; et, illo negante, "Atquin", inquit, "e lotio est"' (Suetonius Tranquillus, C.: *The Lives of the Caesars*, 'Divus Vespasianus', chap. xxiii, § 3).
[2] Toynbee, J. M. C.: *Roman Medallions* (New York 1944, The American Numismatic Society), p. 15. See further eandem: *The Hadriânic School: A Chapter in the History of Greek Art* (Cambridge 1934, University Press), pp. 2–5 and 24–159, for the 'province' coin series; p. 5 for the 'exercitus' coins; and Sutherland, C. H. V.: *Coinage in Roman Imperial Policy, 31 B.C.–A.D. 68* (London 1951, Methuen).

to have been boycotted by the public because it did not bear on its face
the reassuringly familiar symbol of the Cross which was the hall-mark
of the antecedent Christian Roman mintage.[1] Vexatious experiences of
this kind no doubt explain the rigid conservatism of the Attic and
Achaemenian mints, which continued to strike their primitive Athenian
'owls' and Daric 'archers' in latter days when the artificers' fingers must
have itched to replace these stiff archaic types by something in a more
lifelike modern style. Such sedulously mummified coin-types may indeed
continue not only to pass current but to be uttered for centuries after
the disappearance of the government whose image and superscription
they bear. Silver *dirhems* (drachmae) bearing the image of Athena's owl
were still circulating in the highland fastness of the Yaman[2] down to the
date of the Umayyad Caliph 'Abd-al-Malik's (*imperabat* A.D. 685–705)
new oecumenical gold and silver issue, though by that time more than
nine centuries had gone by since the native Attic issues of silver 'owls'
from an Athenian mint had been discontinued by the Athenians
themselves.[3]

After a brief taste of the novel experience of being a province of a
universal state, the Yaman promptly took advantage of the weakening
of the Caliphate's hold in the latter days of the 'Abbasid régime in order
to revert to her familiar way of life as a 'hermit kingdom'; and in A.D.
1952 the most popular monetary medium of exchange in the dominions
of the Imām of San'ā, as well as in the adjoining Arabian regions of the
Hadramawt and the hinterland of Aden, was the Maria Theresa dollar
of an extinct Danubian Hapsburg Monarchy which, in the Hapsburg
dominions themselves, had ceased to be legal tender as long ago as
A.D. 1858.[4] The writer of this Study, when he was travelling on foot in

---

[1] See Wellhausen, J.: *Das Arabische Reich and Sein Sturz* (Berlin 1902, Reimer),
p. 136.

[2] See ibid., p. 136. During the interval between the annexation of the Yaman to the
Medinese nucleus of the Arab Empire, in the last days of the Prophet Muhammad's lifetime, and the Caliph 'Abd-al-Malik's new issues, these Himyarite silver 'owls' were
actually in circulation, in small numbers, throughout the Arab dominions, side by side
with Sasanian silver and with Roman silver and gold.

[3] This change of Attic coin types appears to have been made soon after the liberation
of Athens from Macedonian occupation in 229 B.C. (see Ferguson, W. S.: *Hellenistic
Athens* (London 1911, Macmillan), p. 245).

[4] See Hans, J.: *Zwei Jahrhunderte Maria-Theresien-Taler, 1751–1951* (Klagenfurt
1950, Hans), p. 16.
Of the 320 million MTT that had been minted since A.D. 1751, more than 150 million
had been minted within the thirty years ending in A.D. 1950 (see ibid., pp. 3 and 10).
Between A.D. 1751 and A.D. 1866, 82,727,621 had been minted in divers Hapsburg mints;
between 1867 and 1935, 163,202,763 had been minted at Vienna; between 1935 and
1949, 72,326,022 had been minted at Vienna, Rome, London, Paris, Brussels, and
Bombay (see ibid., pp. 14–15). The number minted at Vienna and exported to the Levant
had been 15 million in 1925 and 15½ million in 1927 (see ibid., pp. 3 and 22); and, during
the years 1935–9, 19,445,000 MTT, minted at Rome, had been imported by the Italian
authorities into Abyssinia (p. 34).
The type of the MTT which thus made its fortune so far afield from the Queen-
Empress' dominions was the issue minted at Günsburg in A.D. 1780, which was the last
year of Maria Theresa's reign (p. 7). More than a hundred years later, in the last decade
of the nineteenth century of the Christian Era, MTT of this type were circulating in a
vast area extending in Africa from Algeria to the Upper Niger and to Madagascar and in
South-West Asia as far as Maskat and Trebizond (according to a map, cited by Hans, p.
16, in Peez, C., and Raudnitz, J.: *Geschichte des Maria-Theresien-Thalers* (Vienna 1898)),
and they were also circulating in China, side by side with Mexican dollars, *circa* A.D.
1900, according to Kann, E.: *The Currencies of China* (Shanghai 1928), cited ibid. In
Abyssinia the MTT was the officially recognized coin of the realm from about the begin-

out-of-the-way districts of the Kingdom of Greece in A.D. 1911–12 found that gold 'Napoleons' of the French Second Empire were the most convenient coins to carry in his stocking; for the image and superscription of a bankrupt French political adventurer then still retained all their prestige in the eyes of Greek peasants and Vlach shepherds, though forty years had passed already since Napoleon III's capture by the Prussians and deposition by his own French subjects. On this showing, it might be anticipated that the English gold 'sovereign', of which Englishmen saw the last in A.D. 1914, might still be circulating in Albania for generations, and in Arabia for centuries, after that portentous date.[1]

ning of the nineteenth century until the Italian occupation in the years A.D. 1936–41 (Hans, p. 24).

For more than a hundred years, dating from the Ottoman Government's unsuccessful attempt in and after A.D. 1837 to replace the MTT by the Mejidīyeh in its Arabian provinces as well as in the rest of the Empire (p. 21), the MTT triumphantly resisted repeated attempts to drive it out of circulation by the substitution of alternative metallic currencies. It did not begin to lose its hold upon the loyalty of its Abyssinian and Arabian addicts until after the liberation of Abyssinia from Italian occupation in A.D. 1941, and then it succumbed, not to any more attractive metallic currency, but to a belated adoption of the latter-day Western institutions of paper money, cheques, and bonds. In A.D. 1867 a British expeditionary force in Abyssinia had found itself compelled to import large quantities of MTT, specially minted at Vienna for its use, because the Abyssinian public had been unwilling to take payment in gold sovereigns (p. 20); in A.D. 1941 another British expeditionary force in Abyssinia found the public eager to surrender MTT in exchange for British East African paper money (see Hans, op. cit., p. 41, citing Lord Rennell of Rodd: *British Military Administration of Occupied Territory in Africa during the years 1941–1947* (London 1948, H.M. Stationery Office): see pp. 365–7, 370–1, 373–4, 379). Yet there were indications (see Hans, op. cit., pp. 50–51 and 53–54) that in A.D. 1950 the MTT was still being hoarded in large quantities in its old domain. A fine silver coin was, after all, proof against the two dangers, to which a paper note was exposed, of being eaten by termites and being devalued by politicians.

[1] During the general war of 1914–18, both the Albanians and the Arabs welcomed the opportunity of being paid by the belligerents for continuing to conduct their own intertribal feuds in the role of their respective foreign paymasters' partisans. So long as they might go on fighting one another, they did not greatly care whether it was the Entente Powers or the Central Powers that were financing their customary activity, but they were unanimous and intransigent in insisting that they must be paid for their services in gold, cash down—not because they foresaw a coming catastrophic depreciation of paper money with a prescience denied to the wily financiers of Lombard Street and Wall Street, but for the simpler reason that, in Albania and Arabia, an invention that had been made in China only a thousand years back (see pp. 312–13, above) had not succeeded in acclimatizing itself yet by the beginning of the twentieth century of the Christian Era. The European belligerent governments—fighting, as they were, for their lives, and therefore clutching at straws—could not resist purchasing the nominal support of rival Albanian and Arab war-bands, and, to buy this dubious asset, they ruefully disgorged some of the gold that they had so ruthlessly withdrawn from circulation at home. An amusing sequel to this war-time tragi-comedy was witnessed by the writer of this Study at the Paris Peace Conference of A.D. 1919–20. The moving spirit of the Hashimite Hijāzī Arab delegation was Colonel T. E. Lawrence, and, when he was on his delegation's official business, he used to make a point of wearing the highly distinctive uniform of an officer of the Hijāzī Army. One day, in a corridor of the Hotel Majestic, the present writer had the good fortune to see this picturesque and animated figure run into a weary-looking official of the British Treasury. In a flash, Lawrence had whipped out from under the folds of his robe a magnificent dagger with a head of chased gold, and was holding it under the Treasury official's nose, saying: 'Do you know what that is made of?' 'No, I don't,' said the Treasury official rather testily. 'A hundred and fifty of your sovereigns,' Colonel Lawrence retorted; and the intended shock was duly registered by his victim. During the antecedent hostilities, while Colonel Lawrence had been having the fun of carrying bags of 'sovereigns' on camel-back and dispensing them to the Hijāzī allies of His Britannic Majesty's Government, the Treasury official had been saddled with the vexatious task of trying in vain to induce these Arab recipients of 'sovereigns' to part with them again in exchange for Indian piece goods, which he had dangled, like carrots, before a knowingly irresponsive donkey's nose. The Arabs had found a better use for British sovereigns' than that. So long as the gold remained in the form of minted coin, it might

1. Standing Armies

The Difficulty of Creating and Maintaining a Mobile Standing Army

Our survey of imperial installations and imperial currencies has indicated that these had been features in the life of all the universal states that had come into existence down to the time of writing; and indeed it is difficult to imagine any universal state establishing or maintaining itself without roads and postal arrangements, garrisons and colonies, a provincial organization, a capital city, one or more official languages and scripts, a code of law, a calendar, a set of weights and measures, and the rudiments or equivalents of money. By contrast, imperial corporations—standing armies, civil services, and citizenships—were to be found in the life of different universal states in various degrees of development ranging over the whole gamut between the rudimentary bud and the full-blown flower; and, because of this, they provided criteria for arranging the score of universal states on our panel in a tentative order of comparative maturity.[1]

In the role played in the lives of universal states by organized military force, the extent of the variation had been particularly great.

In the history of 'the Old Empire' of the Mayas there was no certain evidence for the existence of armed forces even in the form of a police cordon to keep out barbarians from beyond the imperial frontiers. The Spanish Empire of the Indies had been almost equally innocent of armaments on land during the two centuries and more that had elapsed between the domestication of the epigoni of the *conquistadores* and the establishment of a common land-frontier between the Spanish and the British dominions in the New World in the territorial settlement after the Seven Years War. During the intervening age the only permanent professional troops in the Indies had been the few hundred halberdiers in the ceremonial bodyguards of the Viceroys of New Spain and Peru. It had not been till A.D. 1762 that the Spanish Empire in the Americas had found it necessary to provide itself with a standing army and a militia.[2]

In the Achaemenian Empire, the Caliphate, and the Mughal Rāj the

---

(they felt) slip through their fingers; so they had converted it into dagger handles, which were not only more beautiful but more secure, since they could be carried more snugly on the person and were riveted to an automatic caretaker in the shape of a formidable steel blade.

[1] Of our twenty-one civilizations, the Hittite, Iranic, Arabic, Mexic, and Yucatec had apparently failed to produce universal states. On the other hand, the Egyptiac, Syriac, Indic, and Far Eastern societies had produced recurrent universal states, while, in the histories of the Sumeric, Hindu, Andean, and Russian universal states, there had been a break of continuity which not only permitted but constrained a student of History to treat as separate instances the Sumerian régime at Ur and the Amorite régime at Babylon; the Mughal Rāj and the British Rāj; the Incaic Empire of the Andes and the Spanish Empire of the Indies; and the pre-Petrine dispensation and the post-Petrine dispensation in Russia. See the table of contents of the atlas in vol. xi.

[2] Haring, C. H.: *The Spanish Empire in America* (New York, 1947, Oxford University Press), pp. 124, 125, and 145. The Empire of the Indies was not, of course, as defenceless as it might appear to have been, for down to A.D. 1763 it was more or less effectively insulated by the Spanish Navy from direct contact with the dominions of any other Power except France in Louisiana.

standing army included garrisons at strategic points along the frontiers[1] and in the interior[2] as well as the emperor's personal bodyguard at the headquarters of the imperial administration;[3] the 'small but efficient standing army', which even the later Mughal emperors managed to keep up 'consisted of cavalry and matchlockmen, and its kernel was the imperial park of artillery, without which no great fortress could be forcibly reduced';[4] but, when there was a call for mobile armies of any considerable strength, all three empires depended upon levies *ad hoc*. In all three the first ban was furnished by the imperial people itself. The Mughal and Achaemenian empires could call up their feudal cavalry, and the Caliphate its henchmen quartered in the cantonments (Arabs under the Umayyad Caliphs and Khurāsānīs under the 'Abbāsids). When, however, it was a question of a major military enterprise, these empires had to call upon the population at large.[5] When Xerxes invaded European Greece in 480 B.C., he not only mobilized his personal bodyguard and his Persian fief-holders and the rest of the manhood of the Perso-Median imperial people; he also raised levies from the subject population of all the provinces.[6] The regular spring and autumn raids from Cilicia into the East Roman Empire which were one of the institutions of the Caliphate for some two hundred years, until the tide of war turned in the East Roman Empire's favour at last in the second quarter of the tenth century of the Christian Era, were made by Muslim volunteers from all over the Caliph's dominions who assembled and dispersed behind the double screen of fortresses known as the Thughūr and the 'Awāsim.[7]

On the other hand, standing armies capable of providing mobile forces for campaigns, besides imperial bodyguards and provincial garrisons, were maintained by the Roman, Han, Manchu, Ottoman, Danubian Hapsburg, and Napoleonic empires, by the British Rāj in India, and by the post-Petrine Russian imperial régime.[8] The histories of these standing armies show that mobility is difficult to maintain. With the lapse of time a mobile professional force tends to degenerate into a sedentary militia.

The Danubian Hapsburg Monarchy and the British Rāj counteracted this tendency by deliberately organizing a local militia, distinct from the mobile army, to man chronically restless *limites*. There were the Croat

---

[1] See pp. 120–1, above.

[2] See pp. 123–4 and 130–1, above.

[3] See pp. 182–3, above.

[4] Spear, T. G. P.: *Twilight of the Mughuls* (Cambridge 1951, University Press), pp. 7–8. 'The Mughul train of artillery, in maintaining internal security, had something of the potency of the Tudor monopoly of gunpowder. The artillerymen were generously paid, Europeans were freely engaged at high rates, and even supplied with servants so that they should be relieved of all labour save that of aiming the guns' (ibid., p. 8).

A detailed account of the Mughal artillery is given in Irvine, W.: *The Army of the Indian Moghuls* (London 1903, Luzac), chaps. 10–12.

[5] See p. 183, above.

[6] See the army list in Herodotus, Book VII, chaps. 61–99.

[7] See II. ii. 368, with n. 1, and the present volume, p. 121, above.

[8] After the Russian Empire had been equipped with a Western-model professional army by Peter the Great, efforts continued to be made to improve this army's professional standards. In A.D. 1731 an officer's cadet corps was founded, with places for 150 Russian nobles and 50 Livlanders. In A.D. 1732 garrison schools were started (see Mettig, C.: *Die Europäisierung Russlands im Achtzehnten Jahrhundert* (Gotha 1913, Perthes), pp. 82 and 314).

and Serb territorial regiments which, in the eighteenth and nineteenth centuries of the Christian Era, held the line of the Save for the Hapsburg King-Emperor against their Bosniak and Turkish hereditary adversaries;[1] and there were the Pathan militias whom the British Indian military authorities on the North-West Frontier of India recruited during the century beginning in A.D. 1849 from among the wild tribesmen on the principle of setting a thief to catch a thief. These Danubian Hapsburg and British Indian sedentary *limitanei* were of minor importance compared to the mobile armies which they supplemented, whereas in the Ottoman military system the Kurdish *foederati* who, under the command of their own tribal chiefs, held the Ottoman frontier over against Persia,[2] and the Turkish feudal cavalry whose fiefs were sown thick over the Empire except in the more remote of the Arab provinces,[3] together considerably outnumbered the Pādishāh's Slave-Household. Yet the existence of this border militia and provincial feudal array did not preserve the Janissaries, after the death of Suleymān the Magnificent, from losing their mobility and changing, in their turn, into a militia, cantoned in Constantinople and the provincial capitals, which became ever more unwarlike and ever more seditious *pari passu*, till there was nothing to be done with this once magnificently soldierly force except to annihilate it in order to rebuild an Ottoman professional army from the foundations—this time on an alien new model derived from the West.[4] In the Manchu and Roman empires the originally mobile 'banners' and legions likewise struck root through vegetating in fixed stations —the 'banners' in the interior of China and the legions on the frontiers of the Roman World.

The Creation of a Mobile Standing Army in the post-Diocletianic Roman Empire

In the history of the Roman Imperial Army this loss of mobility—of which the danger did not become apparent so long as the prestige of the Empire stood so high that no outsider ventured seriously to attack it[5]— was one of the causes of the catastrophe in which the Empire all but came to grief in the third century of the Christian Era. The improvisation of a new mobile army was the creative act of that desperate age; and, though it was achieved in adverse circumstances at the eleventh hour, it proved so great a success that it prolonged the life of the Empire for one and a half centuries even in the West and for three and a half centuries in the East and the Centre.[6]

---

[1] See pp. 117–18, above.   [2] See I. i. 389–90, and pp. 121–2, above.
[3] See pp. 124–6, above.
[4] For Sultan Selīm III's tragic failure, and Sultan Mahmūd II's grim success, in coping with the task of superseding the Janissaries, see III. iii. 48–50 and IX. viii. 239.
[5] See p. 184, above.
[6] This impressive chronological evidence of the success of the Diocletiano-Constantinian reorganization of the Roman system of imperial defence would seem, to a layman's eyes, to suffice in itself to refute Zosimus's savage critique of it in his *Historiae*, Book II, chap. xxxiv. Zosimus submits that the withdrawal of units from the frontiers to create a mobile reserve in the interior exposed the Empire to uncontested invasion, located the troops in places not requiring defence, brought ruin upon the cities in which they were stationed, and demoralized the troops themselves in the process. Zosimus does not mention the telling truth that, during the century ending in A.D. 284, when the

The truth that a military force can be kept mobile only by relieving it of sedentary tasks had been perceived and translated into action by the genius of Julius Caesar. Out of the thirty-two legions that he had in hand at the close of his civil wars, he posted twenty-six on the frontiers and kept six in reserve.[1] Thereafter, Augustus posted all his twenty-eight legions[2] on the frontiers[3]—whether from lack of his adoptive father's strategic insight or because a further bout of civil wars had left him with that amount less of man-power and sinews of war at his command.[4] Apart from the 4,500 men in the nine praetorian cohorts constituting the Emperor's personal bodyguard[5] and the 1,500 men in the original three urban cohorts,[6] which—as their designation ('Metropolitan Battalions') pointedly proclaimed—were a semi-civic force, Augustus's army possessed no striking force, no field army, no reserves, and the only means of reinforcing the garrison of one sector of the imperial frontier was the drafting of a detachment (*vexillatio*) from the garrison of another sector.[7] Domitian carried the process of immobilizing the legions one stage farther by ruling that each legion was to have a camp of its own.[8] After Hadrian had made a rule of the already prevailing tendency for the legions, like the *auxilia*, to be recruited locally,[9]

Augustan system of frontier defence had still been in operation, the Empire had suffered far more grievously from barbarian invasion than it suffered thereafter, under the new system, during the century ending in A.D. 378. His flagrantly incorrect ascription of the Augustan system to Diocletian, the pagan innovator whose reforms a Christian Constantine had merely carried through to completion, seems to indicate that Zosimus's critique of a policy which he falsely attributes to Constantine's initiative was at least partly prompted by religious animus.

[1] See Grosse, R.: *Römische Militärgeschichte von Gallienus bis zum Beginn der Byzantinischen Themenverfassung* (Berlin 1920, Weidmann), p. 55.

[2] This appears to have been the establishment of Augustus's standing army in 16 B.C. The number was reduced to 25 by the loss of three legions in Varus's disaster in Germany in A.D. 9. This number was raised to 27 by Gaius or (more probably) by Claudius. By the end of the civil wars of A.D. 69 the number had perhaps risen to 31. It was reduced to 29 by Vespasian, but had been raised again to 30 by A.D. 83; and this seems to have been regarded as the standard establishment for the next 110 years. To maintain this figure, Trajan appears to have replaced one legion lost by Domitian in Sarmatia in A.D. 92, and another lost by himself, and Marcus Aurelius to have replaced two lost (perhaps) by Hadrian in Britain and in Palestine respectively. Thereafter, Septimius Severus raised the standing army to a higher strength than it had ever yet possessed by adding his three *Legiones Parthicae* to Marcus's thirty (see Parker, H. M. D.: *The Roman Legions* (Oxford 1928, Clarendon Press), chaps. 3 and 4, pp. 72–117, and compare the *Cambridge Ancient History*, vol. x (Cambridge 1934, University Press), pp. 123 and 221).

[3] See p. 184, above.

[4] At the moment when this final bout of civil wars was brought to an end by the overthrow of the last of Augustus's competitors for the mastery of the Roman World, the victor had on his hands perhaps as many as sixty legions. In his *res gestae*, Augustus claims to have replanted 300,000 discharged soldiers in civilian life by either repatriating them in their original communities or settling them in new colonies. Twenty-eight legions was presumably the maximum establishment that, in Augustus's view, an exhausted world could be expected to support.

[5] The original strength of both a praetorian and an urban cohort was 500 men. The strength of the praetorian cohorts was raised from 500 to 1,000 momentarily during the crisis of A.D. 69 and then permanently in A.D. 193 by Septimius Severus. Septimius also raised the strength of the urban cohorts from 500 to 1,500 (see Durry, M.: *Les Cohortes Prétoriennes* (Paris 1938, Boccard), pp. 82–87).

[6] For these, see pp. 123 and 184, above. By Vespasian's time (*imperabat* A.D. 70–79) the number of urban cohorts appears to have risen to four stationed in Rome and the two posted in the provinces at Lyons and at Carthage respectively (see the *Cambridge Ancient History*, vol. xi (Cambridge 1936, University Press), p. 135).

[7] See Grosse, op. cit., p. 55.

[8] See Suetonius Tranquillus, C.: *The Lives of the Caesars*, 'Domitianus', chap. 7.

[9] See Durry, op. cit., p. 246.

and had carried to completion the Augustan system of fixed frontier defences, the whole Roman Army was degraded into being a bevy of gendarmes and customs officials'.[1] In the third century, 'when the whole empire became one single gigantic fortress assaulted simultaneously from all sides, the old method of frontier-defence inevitably proved totally inadequate, and the need for a strong field army that could be brought into action rapidly at any point inevitably declared itself ever more insistently'.[2] Before the third century was over, this need had been met. Gallienus (*imperabat* A.D. 260–8) made a beginning by detaching the cavalry from the legions and grouping them under an independent command,[3] and the work of reorganization was continued by Aurelian (*imperabat* A.D. 270–5)[4] and was completed by Diocletian (*imperabat* A.D. 284–305).

Out of the best of the battered units of the Augustan Army, without any discrimination between legionary *vexillationes*[5] and auxiliary cohorts and *alae*, the third-century reformers built up a mobile army of all arms; and, within this category of troops trained and equipped to accompany the emperors on campaign (*Comitatenses*),[6] there were gradations of mobility, proficiency, and privileged proximity to a throne that dire necessity of state had now transformed into a portable camp-stool which was pitched from day to day wherever the need for the emperor's presence might happen at the moment to be the greatest.[7] Within the *Comitatenses* there came to be an *élite* of *Palatini*,[8] an inner guard composed of the *Scholae*[9] and the *Candidati*, and a personal bodyguard of *Protectores* and *Domestici*[10] who provided the new mobile army with the

---

[1] Grosse, op. cit., p. 56.   [2] Ibid., p. 56.
[3] See ibid., pp. 15, 18, and 56.   [4] See ibid., pp. 56–57.
[5] By Diocletian's time the Augustan legions seem to have been already broken up into detachments (*vexillationes*) of the strength of the cohorts which had always been the units of the *auxilia* and had also been the principal subdivisions of the legions themselves since the reforms of Marius. At the same time the auxiliary cohorts of infantry and *alae* of cavalry had become detached from the legions with which they had been brigaded under the Principate. After this dissolution of the Augustan legion of 10,000 to 12,000 men (including its complement of *auxilia*), the name legion came to denote a *vexillatio* of perhaps no more than 500 men. The fifth-century *Notitia Dignitatum* catalogues 174 legions, as against the 33 in the army of the Principate after the addition of three to the previous total by Septimius Severus (see Grosse, op. cit., pp. 30–32).
[6] A Latin inscription (*C.I.L.* vi. 2759) witnesses that the *Comitatenses* were in existence at latest by A.D. 301 (see Grosse, op. cit., p. 59).
[7] After the foundation of Constantinople on a site where the new political capital of the Roman Empire could simultaneously serve as a military base for the defence, in depth, of both the Lower Danube and the Upper and Middle Euphrates frontier (see pp. 217–18, above), the Imperial camp-stool was pitched here more often than not; and this gravitation of the Imperial headquarters to the shores of the Bosphorus is reflected in the distribution of the standing cantonments of the Comitatensian infantry legions (excluding the *Palatini*) according to the *Notitia Dignitatum*. No less than twenty of these units were cantoned in Thrace, as compared with nine apiece in Oriens and Gaul, eight apiece in Eastern Illyricum and Africa, and five apiece in Western Illyricum, Italy, and Spain (see Grosse, op. cit., p. 90).
[8] First heard of in A.D. 365 (see ibid., p. 61). The name was, of course, by that time an anachronism; for it was more than a century since the Roman Empire had been governed from the Palatine Hill.
[9] The *Scholae*, once unofficial clubs organized by officers, in the Empire's halcyon days, to provide amenities for their leisure hours, had become part of the working organization of the Army in consequence of their feat of surviving the general dissolution of institutions in the third century.
[10] The Praetorian Cohorts had perished in the last gusts of the hundred-years-long social tornado by which the Roman Empire had been ravaged. Diocletian had depressed

equivalent of a much-needed staff college.[1] The leavings of the Army, when the mobile *Comitatenses* had been formed out of it, were assigned to a frontier force (*Ripenses, Riparienses, Limitanei*)[2] which was frankly permitted to be the sedentary militia[3] that the Army of the Principate had tended to become *sub rosa*[4] ever since it had been cantoned along the frontiers by Augustus, while the mobile standing army embodied in the *Comitatenses* constituted at last, after a dearly paid-for delay of nearly 350 years, that mobile reserve which had been designed, on a smaller scale, by *Divus Iulius*.[5]

Esprit de corps

The superiority of a mobile standing army over a sedentary militia in professional technique is surpassed both in degree and in importance by its superiority in *esprit de corps*. A militiaman tends to be drawn back into civilian life and êthos by a fixed domicile, by marriage, and by the pressure on him to engage in gainful occupations in order to support a family which cannot live on a soldier's pay. This masterful process of demilitarization overtook the Roman Army of the Principate after the removal, by Septimius Severus, of the ban on marriage while with the colours,[6] and it overtook the Janissary Corps after the relaxation of its discipline upon the death of Suleymān the Magnificent. By contrast, a professional soldier in a mobile standing army is 'conditioned' by an insulating way of life and a differentiating discipline into being first and

their status and reduced their importance by keeping them at the long since evacuated seat of imperial government at Rome (Grosse, op. cit., p. 59, citing Aurelius Victor, 39, 47, and Lactantius, *De Mortibus Persecutorum*, 26). Thereafter, Constantine the Great had abolished them after they had fought on the losing side at the Battle of the Milvian Bridge on the 28th October, A.D. 312 (see Durry, op. cit., pp. 170 and 393; Grosse, op. cit., p. 60).

[1] See ibid., pp. 61–63 and 93–96.   [2] See ibid., pp. 66 and 68.

[3] We are ignorant of the date at which the soldiers of the frontier garrisons became *adscripti glebae* by being given personal and hereditary holdings of land to cultivate, but there is no doubt that, from the fourth to the sixth century of the Christian Era, the frontier troops were in fact 'a militia of sedentary peasants' (ibid., pp. 64–65).

[4] In theory the Army of the Principate was always mobile, and the symbol of this theory was the legal inability of the serving soldier to contract a valid marriage so long as he was with the colours. Considering, however, that, upon a soldier's honourable discharge, a permanent illicit union could be converted into a legal marriage and children already born of it be legitimized retrospectively (see p. 132, above); that the soldiers' families were allowed to live in civilian *canabae* adjoining the camps; and that the men were free, while still on active service, to cultivate the *prata legionum*, it is evident that the difference *de facto* between the pre-Severan legionary and the post-Diocletianic *limitaneus* was not by any means as great as the difference in theory. The rights of contracting a legal marriage while on active service and of leasing plots in the *prata legionum* were granted to soldiers by Septimius Severus (see Grosse, op. cit., p. 248; *The Cambridge Ancient History*, vol. xii (Cambridge 1939, University Press), p. 32).

[5] Not the least part of this price of a long delay was a formidable increase in the total strength of the Army in an age when the economic resources of the Empire were dwindling. Even after Septimius Severus had increased the number of the legions from 30 to 33, the Army of the Principate had amounted to not much more than 300,000 men. Diocletian raised the figure by perhaps something like two-thirds, from about 300,000 to about 500,000 (see Grosse, op. cit., p. 253). Within this total, the field army may have had a nominal strength of 148,000 infantry and 46,500 cavalry (see ibid., p. 254).

[6] See Grosse, op. cit., p. 248. In the post-Diocletianic Army, both the soldier and his wife (if he were married in lawful wedlock) were tax-free after he had completed five years' service (see ibid., p. 202). Nevertheless, private soldiers as well as officers were still apt to get entangled in civilian business concerns in the sixth century of the Christian Era (see ibid., p. 278).

foremost a member of his corps and paying only a secondary and conditional allegiance to the civilian community which bears the cost of keeping him under arms; and, if and when the interests of community and corps diverge, the professional soldier is apt to become, in relation to the community, that portentous creature, the unsocial human being, who, as Aristotle sees him, is 'either a beast or a god'.[1] In this predicament the professional soldier can, indeed, either sink to a depth of inhumanity or rise to a height of heroism that are alike beyond the range of his brethren who have not put themselves outside the pale of civilian life through being initiated into a professional military fraternity.

In sacrificing himself to his professional duty the soldier is, of course, happiest when *esprit de corps* gives the same orders as patriotism.

> Ὦ ξεῖν᾽, ἄγγειλον Λακεδαιμονίοις ὅτι τῇδε
> κείμεθα, τοῖς κείνων ῥήμασι πειθόμενοι·

and this famous epitaph by Simonides on the Three Hundred Spartans who fell, to the last man but one,[2] at Thermopylae was to inspire a worthy counterpart in Housman's epitaph on a British army of mercenaries that likewise faced and met certain death in pitting itself against overwhelming odds in order to purchase eventual victory for its cause by checking the first onset of a formidable invader.

> These, on the day when Heaven was falling,
>   The hour when Earth's foundations fled,
> Followed their mercenary calling
>   And took their wages and are dead.
>
> Their shoulders held the sky suspended;
>   They stood, and Earth's foundations stay;
> What God abandoned, these defended,
>   And saved the sum of things for pay.

No doubt, in all situations, the professional soldier's First Commandment is

> Theirs not to reason why,
> Theirs but to do and die;

yet there are degrees of heroism which can be measured by the desperateness of the situation in which the soldier obeys the call to give his life. The Spartan soldier who died in 480 B.C. and the British soldier who died in A.D. 1914 in the act of saving a civilization was not confronted with so severe an ordeal as the Assyrian soldier who, in 610–609 B.C.,[3] made the same supreme personal sacrifice in the baneful cause of striving to undo the World's accomplished deed of liberating itself from the scourge of Assyrian militarism; for the *moral* of Assyria's last army, which took the field again and perished in that last campaign, had been proof against the shock of seeing Assyria herself laid desolate and her fortress-capital Nineveh taken by storm and put to the sack two years

---

[1] Aristotle: *Politics*, Book I, chap. i, §§ 9–12 (p. 1253A), quoted in I. i. 173, n. 3.
[2] The tragic story of the sole survivor Aristodâmus has been told, with sympathetic insight, by Herodotus, Book VII, chaps. 229–31, and Book IX, chap. 71 (see III. iii. 63, n. 3).
[3] See IV. iv. 475 and 480.

earlier.[1] In 610 B.C. Assyria still lived within a defeated but undismayed army's lines at Harrān, as in A.D. 1848 Austria survived in Radetsky's camp within the Quadrilateral of Hapsburg fortresses in Lombardy.

> In deinem Lager ist Österreich,
> Wir Andern sind einzelne Trümmer.[2]

While manfully standing to arms for a new trial of strength with adversaries who had won the preceding round, the Assyrian army in 610 B.C. hoped as sanguinely against hope as Radetsky's army in A.D. 1848 that, this time, they would retrieve their country's fortunes by rescuing her from the very jaws of destruction. While the Assyrians duly failed in their forlorn hope, Radetsky's army played a capital part in winning for the Danubian Hapsburg Monarchy a seventy years' reprieve from her eventually inevitable doom of disruption by the mounting force of Nationalism.[3] Yet, though Radetsky's success might be less romantic than the Assyrians' failure, it was the fruit of a greater *tour de force* in the art of leadership.

The Assyrian army of 610 B.C., like the British Light Brigade of A.D. 1854 and Expeditionary Force of A.D. 1914, was a military formation of a homogeneous national texture fighting in its own national cause without any conflict of mutually incompatible loyalties, whereas the Austria that, in A.D. 1848, was incarnate in Radetsky's camp on the banks of the Po was a miniature reproduction of the house divided against itself in the valley of the Danube. The troops who in that year held together in Lombardy under Radetsky's command had to withstand a twofold psychological assault upon their *esprit de corps*. They were being asked to go on fighting for a state which not only appeared to have dissolved already in their rear, but which, for many of them, was not their own country but was, rather, their country's hereditary oppressor whose yoke had just been broken, not by their Italian opponents in the field, but by their own kinsmen on the home front in a revolutionary upheaval that was threatening to rankle into an outright civil war. Radetsky's army in the Quadrilateral was a mixed multitude in which German

---

[1] This steadfastness of Assyrian military *moral* in 610–609 B.C. will appear the more remarkable when it is recalled that, although by that date the Assyrian state had been in serious adversity for no longer than about sixteen years, since the death of Asshurbanipal in 626 B.C., the Assyrian soldier had been living under a severe personal strain for more than a hundred years past, ever since the opening of the fourth and final bout of Assyrian militarism in 745 B.C. (see IV. iv. 476–7) had first carried him away from home on distant, protracted, and consecutive campaigns. In the fragments of Assyrian law, dating from an earlier chapter of Assyrian history, that Modern Western archaeologists had recovered, a significantly high proportion of the legislation was concerned with situations arising from a soldier's return home from foreign service after so long an absence that his wife had given him up for dead. (Convenient English translations and commentaries will be found in Smith, J. M. P.: *The Origin and History of Hebrew Law* (Chicago 1931, University of Chicago Press), pp. 233–45, and in Pritchard, J. B.: *Ancient Near Eastern Texts* (Princeton 1950, Princeton University Press), pp. 180–8.) An Englishman who had lived through the World War of A.D. 1939–45 would be reminded of the similar marital troubles arising from the absence of British troops from home for years on end in the Middle East and Burma. A student of Roman history would be reminded of the personal strain on the Roman peasant-soldier during the four generations that elapsed between the beginning of the Hannibalic War and the creation of a professional army by Marius.

[2] Grillparzer, Franz: *Feldmarschall Radetzky* [written at the beginning of June 1848].

[3] See II. ii. 182–6.

Austrians found themselves cheek by jowl with Magyars whose kinsmen at home were repudiating a German ascendancy, and with Slavs whose kinsmen—in the hope of winning Imperial-Royal support in their struggle to throw off the ascendancy of German and Magyar alike—were rallying to a refugee King-Emperor whose flight from Vienna had been as humiliating as Radetsky's ejection from Milan. When full allowance has been made for the momentum of a habit of co-operation that had been inculcated by more than two centuries of professional military discipline, it will still seem little less than a miracle that Radetsky's troops did not turn their arms against one another when their spirits, already depressed by the experience of defeat at the front, were further unsettled by the news of national uprisings in their rear.[1]

> Die Gott als Slav' und Magyaren schuf,
> Sie streiten um Worte nicht hämisch,
> Sie folgen, ob deutsch auch der Feldherrnruf,
> Denn: Vorwärts! ist ung'risch und böhmisch.[2]

A greater miracle of the same kind was worked by the *esprit de corps* that, in the Tropical African theatre of the World War of A.D. 1914–18, kept von Lettow-Vorbeck's Bantu askaris in the field for more than four years in a cause that was not their own, with no hope at all of reinforcements, and none of fresh supplies except such as they might succeed in capturing from the enemy. Yet the armistice imposed on them by Ludendorff's failure of nerve in a reverse that had not yet carried the war on to German territory in Europe found these mercenary askaris still fighting gamely for their German masters in Portuguese East Africa after having been driven out of German East Africa by the tardy pressure of a decisively superior enemy force. Equally noteworthy was the loyalty to the British Rāj, during the mutiny of the East India Company's older sepoy-troops in A.D. 1857–8, of the regiments then daringly recruited from a warrior community of Sikhs who, only nine years before, had

---

[1] The *esprit de corps* of the Austrian Army, which gave such a good account of itself in Radetsky's camp in Lombardy in A.D. 1848, eventually succumbed to the ordeal of the World War of A.D. 1914–18. In that war, Czech regiments deserted *en masse* to their Russian fellow Slavs, and after the armistice of 1918 the Army of the Isonzo, as it drifted back from a defensive campaign which, with German help, it had carried on to enemy territory, dissolved into mutually hostile national elements. This end of an army that had been called into existence, four hundred years back, to defend the eastern flank of Western Christendom against the 'Osmanlis, had been described to the writer of this Study by an Austrian friend of his who, being at that moment a civilian, had been caught in the eastward-ebbing tide of self-demobilizing troops as he was trying to make his own way, across the current, from Graz to Innsbruck. The Imperial-Royal comrades-in-arms of yesterday, as they sorted themselves out into Czechs, Germans, Magyars, Poles, Ukrainians, Rumans, and Yugoslavs, were eyeing one another suspiciously, with forebodings of the fratricidal conflicts into which they were to be drawn on the morrow. Since Radetsky's day the unitary tradition of a once professional Austrian Army had been undermined by the introduction of universal compulsory short-term military service, which, in a general mobilization, inevitably filled the cadres to bursting-point with men who were civilians and nationalists at heart while they were soldiers and servants of the King-Emperor against the grain. Yet, even in this war that was the old Austrian Army's death, the Hungarian, German, and Polish subjects of the Dual Crown, whose national interests happened to coincide with the interests of the Monarchy, still gave a good account of themselves; and the Croats, among whom a military tradition of personal loyalty to the Dynasty was still alive, fought valiantly against their Serb fellow Yugoslavs.

[2] Grillparzer, op. cit.

fought the British for the second time and, this time, had paid for a second defeat the penalty of forfeiting, at one stroke, their ascendancy over the other communities in the Panjab and their own political independence. Yet all these signal triumphs of professional *esprit de corps* were surpassed by the unsung achievement of the sepoy mutineers themselves, in which the honours had to be divided between the British officers who had once inculcated the discipline and the Indian noncommissioned officers and privates who succeeded in maintaining it in spite of the deadly wounds which they had dealt to their own *moral*. The mutineers had committed the militarily and morally unforgivable sin of breaking faith with their employers and murdering their superiors; and by this treachery they had deprived themselves of an alien leadership which had held together a mixed multitude of mutually antipathetic Hindus and Muslims and had welded them into a professional army that had not met its match east of Indus. Yet, disabled though they were by these self-inflicted handicaps, they had the spirit to challenge their British makers, and in the ensuing struggle they came within an ace of repeating the feat of those Mamlūks who, in Egypt six hundred years earlier, had wrested the sceptre irrevocably out of the hands of their Ayyūbid masters.[1]

The Problem of Controlling Alien or Barbarian Troops

This professional military *esprit de corps* is both more necessary and more notable in a universal state than it is in a parochial state; for, in contrast to the standing armies of parochial states, which are usually homogeneous in their personnel, the armies of universal states are usually composed of heterogeneous elements that have to be inspired by artificial influences of discipline and tradition with a community of feeling which the recruit does not bring with him, ready-made, from civilian life. While one of these artificially associated elements, and this the leading one, had generally, though not invariably, been the imperial people itself, the empire-builders, however generous they might have been in taking outsiders into their ranks, had seldom had the numbers or the strength to win and hold their empire unaided. In most of the universal states that had come into existence up to date, the rulers had found it expedient to take into military partnership in their standing armies the military *élite* of their subjects within their frontiers or of the barbarians beyond their pale, or even to enlist representatives of an alien civilization.

The unpopularity of the Napoleonic Empire, which was one cause of its premature fall, was due in large measure to the 'blood-tax' which Napoleon imposed not only on the French but on the non-French populations incorporated into the Empire and on the peoples of the client states. When he invaded Russia in A.D. 1812, he compelled even Prussia and Austria to furnish contingents—if only as hostages to ensure that these two discomfited Great Powers should not rise and attack him in the rear after he had traversed their dominions on his eastward march. In the Grand Army that started to cross the Niemen on the

[1] See III. iii. 30–31.

24th June, 1812, only about 120,000 out of 363,000 men were Frenchmen.

The Mongols swiftly won and momentarily held their far-flung dominion over the sedentary peoples round the periphery of the Great Eurasian Steppe by first taking into partnership all but a small fraction of the rest of the Eurasian Nomads and then drafting troops from one conquered sedentary sub-continent to assist in the conquest of another. In the Mongols' service Chinese military engineers played their part in the capture of Transoxanian cities, while Muslim troops from Transoxania, and Orthodox Christian Alan cavalry from the northern slopes of the Caucasus,[1] were brought into action in China against the recalcitrant Empire of the Sung.

The Mughal conquerors of India reinforced their own scanty numbers with drafts of fellow Muslims from an Iranic World out of which they themselves had issued; and in their dearth of martial man-power they did not hesitate to accept recruits from among the barbarous Uzbegs who had driven Bābur out of Farghānah and the heretical qyzyl-bāshīs with whom he had allied himself, against his conscience, in a vain attempt to recover the Transoxanian heritage of his ancestor Timur from the Uzbeg invader.[2] Yet even the most generous-handed sharing of the spoils of India with fellow Iranic Muslims enlisted at the eleventh hour did not give the Mughals the strength to complete the conquest of the peninsula, or even to hold securely what they had already won, against the obstinate resistance of the epigoni of earlier Muslim conquerors; and they found themselves constrained to sin against the spirit and tradition of Islam by enlisting the services of the infidel chivalry of their Rājpūt client states in their fratricidal wars against their True Believing rivals.

The Achaemenian Empire, which on the military plane was perhaps the least efficient of all the universal states in our catalogue, exposed its own incompetence to the World and to itself by embarking on the formidable enterprise of trying to conquer European Greece. The humiliating outcome of the thirty years' war (480–450 B.C.) that Xerxes had wantonly brought upon himself and his successors convinced the Achaemenian Government of their need for a mobile standing army; but, instead of building up one of their own out of the excellent military man-power and abundant economic resources that the Empire could afford, they contented themselves with the unimaginative, slovenly, expensive, and dangerous makeshift of hiring Greek to meet Greek. After the break-down of the Hellenic Civilization had been signalized by the outbreak of the Atheno-Peloponnesian War, the daric could purchase any number of seasoned soldiers from among the uprooted citizens of the faction-ridden city-states of Hellas; but, of course, the latter-day Achaemenids' Greek mercenary army, so far from arresting the Hellenic Society's counter-offensive, invitingly blazed a trail for their fellow Hellenes into the heart of South-Western Asia. After ten thousand Greek mercenary troops in an Achaemenid pretender's

---

[1] See the passages of Marco Polo quoted in V. v. 350–1.
[2] For this episode in Bābur's history, see I. i. 375–80.

service had demonstrated their ability to march unhindered from Ephesus to Cunaxa and back again from Cunaxa to Trebizond, it was evident that the thirty-six thousand Greeks whom Alexander led across the Hellespont would suffice to overthrow the Achaemenian régime and to conquer the Empire from the Aegean to the Pamirs.

The fate of the Arab Caliphate shows that a standing army of barbarians from beyond the pale may be almost as great a political danger as one recruited from the *déracinés* of an alien civilization. When, on the Khurasanian frontier of the Umayyad Power, the local garrisons of Arab empire-builders had fraternized and blended with comrades-in-arms enlisted from the local Iranian subject population,[1] the ruling element in the Caliphate had been strengthened by this broadening of its basis. But when, after the revolution that had brought the 'Abbasids into power, the Khurāsānī henchmen of the new régime were supplanted, in their turn, by Turkish mercenaries from beyond the Oxus, the mastery of the Caliphate passed first to these Transoxanian Turkish praetorians and eventually to the Nomad Turkish Saljūqs from the Eurasian Steppe. In 'the New Empire' of Egypt a similar consequence followed from the recruitment of a mercenary army of Minoan *déracinés* and Achaean and Libyan barbarians. Though this hazardous expedient appeared to have vindicated itself when, at the turn of the thirteenth and twelfth centuries B.C., the barbarians in the Egyptian service loyally assisted their native Egyptian comrades-in-arms to repel successive waves of barbarian invasion,[2] the policy stood condemned when, in the event, the discomfited Libyans sauntered back, unopposed, into the Egyptiac World and settled down upon the land as an incubus-militia.[3]

The 'Osmanlis in their heyday were unique among empire-builders in debarring the imperial people itself from participation in either the defence or the government of their empire, and in relying exclusively on the services of subjects and aliens. In a different context[4] we have seen how they achieved this *tour de force* by detaching their recruits from all previous ties of family, nationality, and religion, and reconditioning them through a strenuous course of broadly conceived and skilfully devised education. The system was so efficient that it produced its transforming effect not only upon tribute-children subjected to it at a tender age but also upon adult prisoners-of-war and renegades; but, when the system broke down owing to the defiance of human nature which was the price at which its efficiency had been purchased, and the free Muslim population of the Empire was grudgingly admitted to a long-overdue participation in public power and responsibility, the Ottoman Empire began to go the way of the 'Abbasid Caliphate and 'the New Empire' of Egypt.

When the long military retreat that had started under the walls of Vienna in A.D. 1683 was converted into a rout by the disastrous outcome of the Great Russo-Turkish War of A.D. 1768–74, both the Sublime

---

[1] See V. v. 450, and pp. 140–1, above.
[2] See I. i. 93 and 101; IV. iv. 85 and 422; V. v. 269 and 352; and V. vi. 207.
[3] See IV. iv. 422; V. v. 269–70, 352–3, and 463.   [4] In III. iii. 31–44.

Porte and its increasingly independent lieutenants in the provinces found themselves leaning on a broken reed in their belated reliance on a free Turkish squirearchy and peasantry that were untutored alike in the old Ottoman school of warfare followed by the Pādishāh's now demoralized Slave-Household and in the new Western school that had originally been inspired by an Ottoman ensample. In these straits the distracted rulers of a tottering empire turned, in their desperate search for martial man-power, to the rude but still untarnished valour of barbarian Albanians and Bosniaks.[1] In Continental European Greece they even authorized the enrolment of a militia of Christian Greek highlanders, under native captains, to guard the passes.[2] And, on the analogy of what happened in other universal states in similar situations in which the process was not checked by the intervention of a third force, we may guess that these and other barbarians would have duly entered into the Ottoman heritage if the Ottoman World had not fallen, at that juncture, under the shadow of the West.[3] As a result of this new turn in their fortunes, the 'Osmanlis succeeded in building up a new Western-model Ottoman Army which put the pashas' Albanian house-carls out of business, brought the Kurdish tribes to heel, saved the Turkish core of the Empire from being partitioned by the European Powers, and eventually shepherded their country into the fold of Western political life as an independent Turkish national republic.[4]

The ruling element in the British Rāj in India, like the rulers of the Spanish Empire of the Indies, were peculiar in being a company of pilgrims and sojourners who were neither born nor educated nor super-annuated nor buried within the bounds of the universal state that they garrisoned and governed during the prime of their working lives;[5] and in British India, which, unlike the Spanish Indies, found itself unable to dispense with a standing army, this permanent geographical and social segregation of a West European imperial people from an Indian subject population was a military safeguard, though in some ways a political stumbling-block.

The standing army of the British Rāj in India was composed of three elements: West Europeans from the United Kingdom, Indians from British Indian territory and from the Indian client states, and barbarians recruited mainly from the independent Gurkha states of Nepal and Bhutan and from the autonomous Pathan tribes in the zone between the north-western boundary of British-administered Indian territory and the Indo-Afghan political frontier. The British troops, the Gurkhas, the Pathan *limitanei* in the North-West Frontier militias, and the Indian troops maintained by the client states were organized in separate units,

---

[1] See IV. iv. 76.
[2] See V. v. 297–9.
[3] See IV. iv. 76–78 and V. v. 299–302.
[4] For the Westernization of Turkey and the part played in the process by the new Western-model Ottoman Army, see further IX. viii. 234–9.
[5] In the Spanish Indies there was, of course, a considerable Creole population of Spanish blood, descended from the *conquistadores*, and both there and in British India there was a half-caste population (the *mestizos* and the 'Eurasians', latterly renamed 'Anglo-Indians'). But in both empires power and responsibility remained in the hands of thoroughbred West Europeans born and brought up in the European countries of which these two universal states were political dependencies.

each of which was homogeneous in its personnel;[1] the Hindu and Muslim British Indian troops and the Pathans in the mobile regular army (as distinct from sedentary Pathan militiamen) all served together in the same regiments, though not usually in the same companies or squadrons. From A.D. 1849 onwards, when the British Rāj took over the North-West Frontier of the Panjab from the Sikhs and thereby established direct contact with the Pathans, there was a tendency for the ratio of soldiers of transfrontier barbarian origin in the British Indian Army to increase;[2] but down to A.D. 1947, when the British authorities withdrew the last British troops from India and handed over the former British Indian Army to the governments of the Indian Union and Pakistan, this increase in the relative numerical strength of the barbarian contingent in the armed forces of the Rāj had not seemed to be preparing the way for an eventual barbarian domination over India such as had threatened to overtake the Ottoman Empire and had actually overtaken the 'Abbasid Caliphate and 'the New Empire' of Egypt.

If in British India this danger had been successfully kept at arm's length, the success may have been due to a combination of causes which were all bound up with the special character of the British Rāj. There were no Gurkha or Pathan units in the British Indian Army that were furnished to the British authorities *en bloc*, under national or tribal commanders of their own, by the Gurkha states or the Pathan tribes themselves. The only units that were permitted that degree of corporate individuality and autonomy were the contingents furnished by the Indian client princes, of whose loyalty the British Indian authorities were sure. The Gurkha and Pathan soldiers enrolled in units of the British Indian Army were recruited, not corporately, but individually, and were commanded, not by leaders drawn from their own community, but by British officers. A further safeguard was that the British troops in India, consisting, as they did, exclusively of soldiers born and bred in the United Kingdom, and being segregated, as they were, from their Indian, Pathan, and Gurkha comrades-in-arms in self-contained units of their own, retained their pristine martial qualities from one generation to another—in contrast to their immediate predecessors the Mughals and other earlier alien empire-builders in India, who, by making India their home and by intermarrying with the native inhabitants, had merged themselves in the mighty mass of the Indian people and, in thus losing their alien identity, had forfeited their ascendancy over their Indian subjects. In A.D. 1952, when these former British counterweights to the menace of a barbarian preponderance in a now divided Indian Army had all been removed, the outlook was still obscure, but it was

---

[1] After A.D. 1858, when the British Crown took over the administration of British India from the British East India Company, there were no units of British troops in India that were not part of the Royal Army of the United Kingdom. Under the Company's régime the Company had maintained an army of its own which had included British as well as Indian units. The Gurkha and British Indian regular units and the Pathan militias were under British command and had a complement of British officers—though they also had non-British commissioned officers of special grades. The forces maintained by the Indian client states were officered by Indians but were uniform with the British Indian Army in their training and equipment.

[2] See II. ii. 128, n. 1.

evident that the Pathans had a brighter prospect of capturing the army of Pakistan, and the Gurkhas of capturing the army of Hindu India, than either of these two barbarian peoples—martial though both of them were—had ever had of capturing the army of the British Rāj.

The success of the British Rāj in India in employing with political impunity the military services of barbarians beyond its pale, as well as those of its own Indian subjects, was emulated by the Manchu restorers of a Far Eastern universal state in China. As we have noticed in another context,[1] Chinese and Mongol battalions were brigaded with Manchu battalions in varying numbers and ratios in the Manchu Power's army corps known as 'banners'. Even when the Manchu Government's domain was still confined to territories lying outside the Great Wall, the Chinese members of the community outnumbered the Manchus and Mongols;[2] and, after their passage of the Wall in A.D. 1644, it was the South Manchurian Chinese contingent in the banners that gave the invaders the man-power requisite for completing the conquest of Intra-mural China. While the Manchus thus succeeded in enlisting Chinese to help them win and hold China for a Manchu régime, they were no less successful in dealing with the equally delicate problem presented by the Mongols, martial barbarians with memories of a great imperial past of their own and with a tincture of alien culture[3] that made them no less difficult to assimilate than the intensely cultivated Chinese.

The Manchus attacked their Mongol problem from two directions. On the one hand, in the organization of the Mongol battalions of the banners they anticipated the policy of the British military authorities towards the Gurkhas and Pathans by recruiting their Mongol soldiers individually, and not in tribal *blocs*, and by placing them under the command of Manchu officers. On the other hand, they handled the Mongol tribes on the Steppe as the 'Osmanlis had handled the Kurdish tribes in the Zagros Mountains. Without attempting to destroy their tribal organization, they contented themselves with dividing the tribes up into tribal atoms of a minimum size, and with imposing a strict delimitation of the boundaries between their respective pastoral ranges. The Mongol tribes, thus reduced in size and penned within fixed limits, were allowed to remain autonomous under the rule of their own tribal chiefs, while, to save appearances, these Mongol tribal chieftainships were nominally given the status of 'banners', as the Kurdish tribal chieftainships had been officially classified as Ottoman fiefs in the books of the Pādishāh.[4] The political success of this Manchu military organization is attested by the fact that, when the Manchu régime in China was liquidated in A.D. 1911, the revolution was not the work of the Manchus' comrades-in-arms in the Chinese and Mongol battalions of the banners.

The success of the Manchus in China and the British in India in

[1] See pp. 128–9, above.
[2] See Michael, F.: *The Origin of Manchu Rule in China* (Baltimore 1942, Johns Hopkins University Press), p. 71.
[3] See II. ii. 237–8; III. iii. 451; V. v. 309 and 348.
[4] See Michael, op. cit., pp. 96–97. It will be seen that, in post-Diocletianic Roman terminology, these Mongol and Kurdish tribes were *foederati* of the Manchu and the Ottoman Empire respectively.

employing the professional military services of barbarians with political impunity was eclipsed by the Carthaginian architects of a colonial Syriac universal state in the area opened up by Phoenician maritime enterprise in the western basin of the Mediterranean. Though the citizens of Carthage never exempted themselves entirely from serving personally in the field, they did not hesitate, in the heyday of their wealth and power, to enrol Libyans and Iberians—and these not only from among their own subjects, but also from among the untamed barbarians beyond their pale—on a scale which quite dwarfed the Carthaginians' own citizen force. This, on the face of it, perilous policy did, sure enough, bring the Carthaginian Empire, and Carthage herself, to the verge of destruction when, at an hour in which Carthage's prestige was at a low ebb owing to her defeat in the First Romano-Punic War (*gerebatur* 264-241 B.C.), the Carthaginian Government imprudently, though characteristically, exasperated their mercenaries by proposing to interpret their agreed terms of service on lines so niggardly as, in the mercenaries' view, to create a breach of contract. Yet Carthage did succeed in quelling the Great Mutiny of 240-237 B.C.; and this discreditable incident in her military annals apparently did so little permanent damage to her mercenary army's discipline and *moral* that in the next generation the successors of the discomfited mutineers, when led by a captain of genius who inspired them with a personal devotion to himself, all but succeeded in inflicting on Rome the fate that Carthage herself was eventually to suffer at Roman hands.[1]

The Consequences of the Enlistment of Barbarians in the post-Diocletianic Roman Army

The problem which was solved by the Carthaginians in the Western Mediterranean, by the Manchus in China, and by the British in India, but which defeated the Ramsids and the 'Abbasids, overtook the Roman Empire likewise in its post-Diocletianic age.

Though, in all ages, able-bodied adult Roman citizens were legally liable to be called up compulsorily for military service, the standing army of the Principate had in fact been recruited by voluntary enlistment; for, though service in the Army was confined to Roman citizens for the legions and to free Roman subjects for the *auxilia*, to the exclusion of both slaves and aliens, the strength of the Army in that age was a very low percentage of the total man-power available in the two eligible categories. This easy state of affairs was brought to an end once for all by Diocletian's military reforms, involving, as they did, an increase in the strength of the Army by perhaps as much as two-thirds, from about 300,000 men to about 500,000.[2] From that time onwards there was perpetual difficulty in finding suitable recruits in sufficient numbers.[3]

The civil authorities, whose responsibility it was to produce the men

---

[1] See V. v. 465-6. [2] See p. 323, n. 5, above.

[3] Vegetius complains (probably with reference to conditions in the western provinces of the Empire in the fifth century of the Christian Era) of the difficulty of filling the cadres—especially in the legions, to which the *auxilia* were preferred by recruits (see Vegetius, Book I, chap. 5, and Book II, chap. 3, quoted by Grosse, op. cit., p. 266).

for their military colleagues,[1] dealt with the Roman citizen-body—which, since the *Constitutio Antoniniana* of A.D. 212, embraced nearly the whole of the native-born free population of the Empire[2]—by sifting it, for military purposes, into different categories which received differential treatment ranging between the two extremes of compulsion to serve and prohibition to enlist.[3] In the conscription of agricultural serfs, which was by far the largest reservoir of citizen man-power at the recruiting authorities' disposal, there were elaborate arrangements—unfortunately frustrated to a large extent by fraud, bribery, and pressure—for distributing the burden equitably between province and province and between estate and estate.[4] Conscripted serfs, however, were naturally apt to be of poor martial quality, even if they had been forthcoming in sufficient numbers to cover Diocletian's formidable increase in the Army's strength, and the recruiting authorities therefore looked for an additional source of supply. The ban on the enlistment of slaves was not lifted, and it was still in force in Justinian's day (*imperabat* A.D. 527–65).[5] From Diocletian's reign (*imperabat* A.D. 284–305) onwards, however, all barriers to the recruitment of aliens were removed,[6] and barbarian alien recruits were now the more highly esteemed the more barbarous they were.[7]

For Roman military purposes an unreclaimed barbarian had the double attraction of bringing with him a native martial tradition and of being a volunteer who had not had the edge taken off his zest for military service through being pressed into it,[8] as were the majority of the post-Diocletianic recruits of Roman origin.[9] Even barbarian prisoners-of-war, if distinguished by rank or prowess in their native social environment, were able to bargain with the Roman recruiting authorities, as a condition of enlistment in the Roman Army, that they should start their career as officers;[10] and the number of high officers of barbarian origin in the post-Diocletianic Roman Army indicates either that this privilege of a flying start was frequently secured by barbarian recruits or else that high promotion was frequently earned by men who

---

[1] See Grosse, R.: *Römische Militärgeschichte von Gallienus bis zum Beginn der Byzantinischen Themenverfassung* (Berlin 1920, Weidman), p. 158. We may conjecture that this task was assigned to the civil authorities in the post-Diocletianic Roman Empire for the reason that led the Government of the United Kingdom, during the World War of A.D. 1939–45, to assign it to the Ministry of Labour and National Service. Whereas the military authorities were bound to think of their own needs first, the civil authorities might be expected to look at the problem of man-power as a whole, and to do their best to keep the Army up to strength with the least possible detriment to civilian services, such as the production of foodstuffs and the manning of the merchant marine, which, on a comprehensive view, might be seen to be not less essential than military defence itself for the welfare, or even for the survival, of the community.

[2] See V. vi. 7, n. 4, and p. 156, above.

[3] See Grosse, op. cit., pp. 202 and 204–6.

[4] See ibid., pp. 210–15.

[5] See ibid., p. 198.

[6] See ibid., p. 200.

[7] See ibid., pp. 200–1.

[8] See ibid., pp. 201–2.

[9] A majority, but not all; for, as late as the sixth century of the Christian Era, in what remained of the Illyrian provinces of the Empire, there was a native Latin-speaking rural population of Roman citizens in which an historic local martial tradition was still sufficiently alive to inspire two Dardanian peasants—the future Emperor Justin I and his brother—to seek their fortunes by coming to Constantinople to enlist (see Grosse, op. cit., p. 203).

[10] See ibid., p. 203.

started as privates.[1] Conversely, the citizen recruit came to be rated so low that in A.D. 440, at a date when, in the West, the Empire was at its last gasp, Roman citizens were freed from all military obligations save for taking part in the manning of city-walls in an emergency.[2]

The increasingly numerous and important barbarian intake into the post-Diocletianic Roman Army was recruited and organized on two systems, each of which had its own disadvantages and dangers. Besides the barbarian soldiers who enlisted individually in Roman military formations, there were national units, commanded by officers of their own nationality, that were furnished to the Roman Army by autonomous barbarian communities with the status of *foederati*.[3] On the face of it, the system of individual enlistment might seem the less hazardous of the two—the more so, in view of the success of the Manchus in China and the British in India in keeping in order the barbarian soldiers whom they enrolled in this way. If the Romans ran into disaster where the British and the Manchus steered clear of it, the explanation of this difference in the outcome perhaps lies in a difference in the extent to which the dilution of regular units with barbarian personnel was carried; and, if, in this delicate matter, the Roman military authorities trespassed beyond the margin of safety, the culprit is to be found in the Emperor Theodosius I (*imperabat* A.D. 378-95).[4] Theodosius tipped the hazardous balance in the post-Diocletianic Roman Army in the barbarians' favour.[5] He drafted them into the Roman regular formations in a ratio so high as to produce a break in the Roman military tradition and discipline.[6] The disastrous consequences are reflected in Vegetius's picture[7] of the Army going to pieces. The troops can no longer be induced to submit to training,[8] drill,[9] or assaults at arms;[10] they are unwilling to carry burdens;[11] they are slack in the performance of their military duty in general;[12] and they are unwilling to undertake the hard labour of fortifying camps.[13] 'The Roman Army had ceased to exist. It had never succumbed to the Germans; it had simply been supplanted by them.'[14]

The Roman Army, and consequently the Roman Empire itself, was thus confronted, by Theodosius's ill-judged abandonment of all restrictions on the admission of barbarian recruits, with the imminent threat of a barbarian ascendancy. This doom was not accepted by the Roman

[1] See ibid., p. 196. [2] See ibid., p. 202.

[3] Strictly, *foederati dediticii* (see Grosse, op. cit., p. 206), presumably because, since the *Constitutio Antoniniana*, *dediticii* were the only category of inhabitants of the Roman Empire who did not possess the Roman franchise.

[4] See Grosse, op. cit., p. 262, n. 2.

[5] See Zosimus: Book IV, chaps. xxx and xxxi, cited by Grosse, op. cit., p. 260.

[6] The effect, according to Zosimus, chap. xxxi, §§ 1-2, was a dissolution of military discipline and a breakdown of the system of registering effectives—with the result that the professed 'deserters' from barbarian tribes beyond the Roman imperial *limes* who had been registered as serving soldiers in the Roman regular army took to going home, sending substitutes to fill their places, and falling into the ranks again whenever it took their fancy.

[7] Cited as evidence by Grosse, op. cit., p. 261.

[8] Vegetius: Book I, chaps. 20 and 28. Compare Book I, chap. 26, Book II, chaps. 18 and 24, and many other passages.

[9] Ibid.: Book I, chap. 8. [10] Ibid., chaps. 11, 12, and 18.

[11] Ibid., chap. 19. [12] Ibid.: Book III, chap. 8.

[13] Ibid.: Book I, chap. 21; Book III, chap. 10.

[14] Grosse, op. cit., p. 262.

element in the Army without a struggle; but, while the Roman reaction was ubiquitous, the results were quite different in different sections of the Empire. In the East and Centre the untoward effects of Theodosius's error were reversed in the nick of time, while in the West the vantage surrendered by him to the barbarians was not, in the end, retrieved.

In the East the coming conflict was heralded, before Theodosius's death, by a clash at Philadelphia between Egyptian and barbarian troops which was provoked by the barbarians' intolerable treatment of the civilian population and in which the barbarians suffered more than two hundred casualties;[1] but the crucial trial of strength in the East—in which the utter discomfiture of the barbarians made history by producing a permanent parting of the ways between the fortunes of the eastern and western sections of the Empire[2]—came in A.D. 400. In the East in that year there was a general civil war between the Roman and barbarian soldiery in which 35,000 Gothic troops were wiped out;[3] and the victors confirmed and enhanced the effects of their signal triumph by taking advantage of the breathing-space that they had thereby won for themselves in order to introduce effective measures for precluding, in the East, a recurrence of the barbarian peril. In the East the imperial authorities had the courage thenceforward to dispense with a barbarian instrument whose dangerousness had proved greater than its value. Almost all the surviving names of military officers in the East in the records of the next fifteen years are Graeco-Roman;[4] and, though this resolute purge of barbarian military man-power may have had adverse short-term military effects, its long-term political result was that the Empire managed, in the East, to stave off for two centuries longer the final catastrophe that now swiftly descended upon the West.[5]

Before the close of the fifth century of the Christian Era the East had tapped a native source of martial man-power by making serviceable Roman soldiers out of the wild highlanders of the Taurus;[6] and these Isaurian troops showed themselves a match for the barbarians from beyond the pale in the Great Romano-Gothic War of A.D. 537–53.[7] At the same time the Roman military authorities in the East continued to draw recruits from the general population, even in the least warlike of the eastern provinces. In the documents preserved on Egyptian papyri dating from the sixth and seventh centuries, none of the soldiers there mentioned bear barbarian names,[8] and, according to a Modern Western scholar who was an eminent authority on the subject, the first mention of *foederati* serving in Egypt was to be found in the chronicle of John of Nikiû, who lived to record the Arab conquest.[9] By that time

---

[1] See Zosimus: Book IV, chap. xxx, §§ 4–8, cited by Grosse, op. cit., p. 263.
[2] The historic importance of this event has been pointed out already in IV. iv. 324.
[3] See Grosse, op. cit., p. 264. [4] See ibid.
[5] See ibid., pp. 264–5. [6] See IV. iv. 324–5.
[7] In the Modern Western World the Government of the United Kingdom pursued the same policy with similar success when it enrolled the wild highlanders of Scotland in the British Army after their last outbreak in A.D. 1745.
[8] See Grosse, op. cit., p. 277.
[9] The authority for this statement is Grosse, op. cit., p. 281, but the page (p. 531) of Zotenburg's edition of the chronicle of John of Nikiû which he cites as his reference does not exist in Zotenburg's definitive edition: *Chronique de Jean, Evêque de Nikiou*, texte éthiopien publié et traduit par H. Zotenberg (Paris 1883, Imprimerie Nationale),

the *foederati* in the East had been transformed from national contingents furnished by autonomous barbarian communities under native commanders into units of the Roman regular army which were, indeed, still barbarian in their personnel but were of mixed nationality and were under the command of Roman officers.[1] These sixth-century barbarian regulars to whom the name *foederati* now attached were a mobile cavalry force which was the cream of Justinian's army.[2] In fact, by Justinian's day the Roman Army of the East had learnt the secret of how to employ barbarian troops with military profit[3] without political risk. The only non-Romans whom Justinian enrolled were prisoners-of-war[4] or deserters.[5] His barbarian troops were relatively few in numbers, but it was they who won his victories for him.[6]

This Roman military recovery in the East was not reproduced in the West. The anti-barbarian reaction that had started in Constantinople in A.D. 400 did indeed have repercussions on the farther side of the Adriatic. It made its influence felt in the assassination of the Vandal generalissimo Stilicho in A.D. 408 and in the ineptly brutal accompanying massacre of the families of barbarian soldiers, domiciled in Italy, by Roman troops.[7] Moreover, for the next half-century the perilously dictatorial western military office of generalissimo (*magister peditum in praesenti*)[8] was held by five successive incumbents, from Constantius to

and the reference is presumably to the preliminary edition published in the *Journal Asiatique* in 1879. In the French translation accompanying the definitive edition, it is mentioned (p. 421, chap. cvii) that, when Heraclius in Africa revolted against Phocas, he raised mercenary troops from the barbarians of Tripolitania and Pentapolis and that a strong contingent of these was included in the expeditionary force which marched on Egypt under the command of Nicetas. These barbarian mercenaries are mentioned subsequently on three occasions in the chronicler's account of the ensuing military operations in Egypt (pp. 426–7, chap. cvii; p. 428, chap. cviii; p. 431, chap. cix). Again, in the account of the military operations arising out of the invasion of Egypt by the Arabs, there is a reference to 'toutes les troupes d'Égypte et les troupes auxiliaires' (p. 434, chap. cix). If these are the passages that Grosse has in mind, he is presumably taking it for granted that Nicetas' 'barbarians' and Theodore's 'auxiliaries' were *foederati* in the then current technical meaning of the term.

[1] See Grosse, op. cit., pp. 280–1.   [2] Ibid., pp. 282–3.

[3] One index of the re-establishment of discipline in the Roman Army of the East, after the *dégringolade* following the dilution of the Army with barbarians in the reign of Theodosius I, may be found in the survival, in Justinian's day, of the laborious practice of fortifying camps (as described by the 'Anonymus Köchly', chaps. 26–29 (Köchly, H., and Rüstow, W.: *Griechische Kriegschriftsteller*, Zweiter Theil, Zweite Abtheilung, pp. 136–47) cited by Grosse, op. cit., p. 302). As Grosse points out (op. cit., pp. 305–6), this survival of the tradition of camp-making in the Roman Army of the sixth century of the Christian Era is the more noteworthy considering that camp-making was an infantry technique, whereas by this time the principal arm of the Roman Army had long since come to be the cavalry.

[4] e.g. Vandals.   [5] See Grosse, op. cit., pp. 277–8.

[6] See ibid., pp. 279–80.

[7] See Zosimus: Book V, chap. xxxv, §§ 7–8, cited by Grosse, op. cit., p. 265.

[8] The *magistri militum* of the post-Diocletianic Empire were the commanders of the mobile army (the *Comitatenses*) that Diocletian had called into being. Since the *Comitatenses* were divided into an infantry and a cavalry arm, there was originally a pair of *magistri*—a *magister peditum* and a *magister equitum*—attached to the Emperor, or one pair to each of the emperors at times when the imperial office was in commission. In this college of commanders-in-chief the *magister peditum* ranked senior to his colleague commanding the cavalry (see Grosse, op. cit., p. 183). When an Empire that had been re-united in the hands of Theodosius I was divided again, upon his death, between his sons Arcadius and Honorius, the *magister peditum* at the imperial headquarters (*in praesenti*) in the West came to overshadow his junior colleague the *magister equitum in praesenti* so completely as to become virtually a permanent military dictator within the western emperor's domain (see ibid., pp. 188–9)—a situation which was recognized in

Aëtius inclusive,[1] who were Roman in nationality. When, however, with the accession of Ricimer to the generalissimate in A.D. 456, an army which in the West was still overwhelmingly barbarian in its personnel[2] found itself once more under the supreme command of an all-powerful barbarian war-lord, the fate of the Empire in the West was sealed,[3] and Ricimer's death in A.D. 472 could not prevent his fellow barbarian Odovacer from taking his place and completing his work by making appearances in the West more nearly conform with realities.[4]

The Roman Army's Legacy to the Christian Church

If we now ask ourselves who had been the beneficiaries of the institution of mobile standing armies in universal states, we can answer at once that these military corporations had been apt to make the fortunes of

the practice that grew up of investing him, almost *ex officio*, with the title of *patricius* (see Grosse, op. cit., p. 182).

'This dominance of the office of imperial generalissimo was one of the principal factors in the fall of the West Roman Empire; the German *magister militum* eventually supplanted the Emperor. Ricimer laid the foundations of the German supremacy in Italy and thereby prepared the way for Odovacer's usurpation. Theodoric, in the next chapter of history, was, from the Roman standpoint, simply the East Roman Emperor's *magister militum utriusque militiae* [i.e. area commander, in Italy, of both arms of the mobile branch of the Roman Imperial Army]'—(ibid., p. 190).

This development, which worked itself out in the West with such fatal consequences for the Empire, was avoided in the East thanks to precautions taken there by Theodosius I to prevent the concentration of military authority in a single pair of hands. In the first place the two *magistri praesentales* at Constantinople were given equal and coordinate rank with one another, and the command of the mobile troops of both arms at the eastern imperial headquarters was divided equally between them. In the second place, under the co-ordinate commandership-in-chief of the two eastern *praesentales*, the army groups of *Comitatenses* stationed in the eastern and central provinces were divided between three different area commands—per Orientem, per Thraciam, per Illyricum— under the regional command of three subordinate *magistri equitum* who were styled *magistri utriusque militiae* because they were in command of the infantry as well as the cavalry units of the mobile army within their respective areas (see ibid., pp. 185-6). Since the area command per Orientem was still dangerously large, Justinian reduced its size by carving out of it a fourth eastern area command per Armeniam (see ibid., p. 190). This institution of subordinate area commands *utriusque militiae* was not confined to the East. In the West there was, for example, an area command per Gallias. In the West, however, this decentralization did not avail to curb the power of the senior *magister militum praesentalis*.

Though Zosimus lived to see the western provinces of the Roman Empire overtaken by a disaster from which the central and eastern provinces were saved by Theodosius's precautions, the pagan historian professes (in Book IV, chap. xxvii, §§ 3–5) to see no more in the Christian Emperor's statesmanlike division of commands than a wantonly extravagant inflation of the imperial budget for military salaries.

[1] For the career and the significance of Aëtius, see V. v. 471–2.

[2] See the rhetorical, yet nevertheless revealing, catalogue, given by Sidonius Apollinaris (*Carmen* V, ll. 474–9), of the barbarian peoples represented in the army with which the unhappy emperor Majorian crossed the Alps from Italy into Gaul in A.D. 458.

[3] There were, of course, other, and perhaps more potent, causes of the dissolution of the Roman Empire in the West at this juncture. One underlying cause, from which all the rest derive in some measure, was the general social and economic backwardness and feebleness of the western provinces by comparison with those of the Centre and the East. One symptom of this was an unhealthy concentration of such wealth as there was in the West in the hands of great rural landowners who in the fifth century of the Christian Era virtually escaped the control of the imperial authorities and, in particular, defied the efforts of the inland revenue authorities to collect from them the taxes which they alone had the means to pay. (On this point see Grosse, op. cit., p. 269.)

[4] The conformity achieved was far from being complete, for, though Odovacer did depose the puppet-emperor Romulus Augustulus in whose name he had been ruling Italy, he did not venture to assume authority in his own name by naked right of his *de facto* power, but sought and obtained investiture as the vicegerent, in Italy, of the Imperial Government at Constantinople.

the aliens or barbarians who had been enrolled in them. The latter-day Achaemenids' recruitment of a mobile professional force of Greek mercenaries led to the conquest of the Achaemenian Empire by Alexander and its partition between a number of Macedonian Greek successor-states. The enrolment of barbarians in the bodyguard of the 'Abbasid Caliphs and in the standing armies of the Roman Empire and 'the New Empire' of Egypt led to the establishment of barbarian rule in the dominions of the Caliphate, in the Egyptiac World, and in the western provinces of the Roman Empire. We can also espy cases in which the beneficiary had been an alien secular culture. The Hellenic culture made its entry into the Hittite, Syriac, Egyptiac, Babylonic, and Indic worlds at the heels of the Macedonian *conquistadores*. The creation of a new army on a Western model in the Russian Empire by Peter the Great, and in the Ottoman Empire by Selīm III and Mahmūd II, led to the progressive Westernization of other sides of Russian and Ottoman life.[1] The enrolment of Italian, Flemish, and West German troops in the Napoleonic army expedited the re-absorption of the debris of a city-state cosmos in Northern Italy, Western Germany, and Flanders, which had differentiated itself from the rest of Western Christendom in the medieval age of Western history,[2] into a Modern Western body social represented by contemporary French society. It is more surprising to see the mantle of an army descending upon the shoulders of a church—and the more so when the recipient of this military inspiration is a church with an anti-military tradition and êthos.

In their conscientious objection to the shedding of blood, and consequently to the performance of military service, the Primitive Christians were at variance with both the Jewish and the Roman tradition.

'In the last resort, the Jew literally drew the sword and forestalled the Messiah. . . . The Christian, on the other hand, was instructed to await the coming of his victorious Christ.'[3]

In striking contrast to the series of Jewish insurrections against first Seleucid and then Roman rule during the three hundred years running from 166 B.C. to A.D. 135,[4] the Christians never once rose in armed revolt against their Roman persecutors during the approximately equal period of time that elapsed between the beginning of Jesus' mission and the conclusion of peace and alliance between the Roman Imperial Government and the Church in A.D. 313.[5] As for service in the Roman Army, this was a stumbling-block for Christians because it involved not only the shedding of blood on active service but also, among other things, the passing and execution of death sentences, the taking of a military oath of unconditional loyalty to the Emperor, the worship of the Emperor's genius and offer of sacrifice to it, and the veneration of military standards as idols.[6] Service in the Army was, in fact, expressly

[1] The penetration of an alien culture through a military door is examined further in IX. viii. 126–53.
[2] See III. iii. 344–7 and V. v. 619–42.
[3] Harnack, A. von: *Militia Christi: Die christliche Religion und der Soldatenstand in den Ersten Drei Jahrhunderten* (Tübingen 1905, Mohr), p. 9.
[4] See V. v. 68. [5] See Harnack, op. cit., p. 44.
[6] See ibid., p. 46.

declared to be unlawful for Christians by successive Early Christian Fathers—by Origen,[1] by Tertullian,[2] and even by Lactantius in a work published after the conclusion of the Constantinian peace between the Christian Church and the Roman State.[3] In his downright assertion—'We do not march with the Emperor, not even if he presses us'—Origen retrospectively justified Celsus's complaint (of which the record has been preserved by Origen himself) that the Christians refuse to perform military service.[4]

It is significant that this ostracism of the Roman Army by the Christian Church broke down, and this through developments in the position and outlook of the Christian community at a time when the Army of the Principate was still being recruited by voluntary enlistment—indeed, more than a hundred years before the issue was raised on the Roman Government's side through the reintroduction of compulsory military service as a corollary to the expansion of the Army by Diocletian.

Down to about the year A.D. 170, occasions for conflict over this issue were, it would seem, avoided; for down to that time Christian civilians apparently abstained as a matter of course from enlisting in the Army, while, if a pagan serving soldier became a convert, the Church tacitly acquiesced not only in his serving out his term with the colours but in his continuing to perform all acts that the Army expected of him, including those requirements that deterred Christians from enlisting. Possibly the Church justified to herself this laxity on a question of principle on the same ground on which, in this first chapter of her history, she tolerated other social anomalies or enormities in her bosom, such as the continuance of the institution of slavery even when master and slave alike were members of the Christian community. In the Church's expectation in this age, the time remaining before Christ's Second Coming was so short that the Christian soldier-convert might just as well pass it under arms as the Christian slave convert in bondage.[5]

'The incompatibility [of Christian principles] with the State, the social order, public life and the like, first impinged upon the Christians' conscience in its full force when the Christians began to suspect and to recognise that they were going still to have to do with these affairs for quite a long time to come, and were also going to incur their share of responsibility for them.[6]

In the third century of the Christian Era, when the Christians did begin to make their way in rapidly increasing numbers into the politically responsible classes of Roman society—partly by themselves rising in the world, and partly by winning upper-class converts—they answered in practice the question raised for them by the social impor-

---

[1] *Contra Celsum*, Book VIII, chap. 73 (see Harnack, op. cit., pp. 31, 72, and 104).
[2] See the passages cited by Harnack, op. cit., pp. 58–68, especially those from the *De Coronâ*.
[3] *Institutes*, Book VI, chap. 20, § 16 (see Harnack, op. cit., p. 72).
[4] See Harnack, op. cit., p. 54.
[5] For this possible application of the eschatological outlook on life to the delicate case of the soldier-convert, see Harnack, op. cit., pp. 49–50.
[6] Harnack, op. cit., pp. 50–51. Compare p. 69.

tance of the Roman Army without ever solving it in theory and without waiting for the conversion of the State of which this army was an organ. In Diocletian's army the Christian contingent was already so large, so conspicuous, and so influential that the persecution launched in A.D. 303 was directed against Christianity in the Army in the first instance.[1] The Army was, in fact, the testing ground of the issue between the Imperial Government and the Church.[2] The strength of the Christians in the Army even in the West, where at the opening of the fourth century the percentage of Christians in the population was very much lower than in the contemporary East, is indicated by Constantine's manifesto in the Church's favour in A.D. 312, on the eve of the critical battle at the Milvian Bridge.[3] The future pioneer of Christian monachism, the Egyptian Pachomius, was converted to Christianity as a soldier in the expeditionary force with which Constantine was then marching against Maxentius.[4] The completeness of the eventual identification of Church and Army in an age when the names 'Christian' and 'Roman' had become virtually synonymous is symbolized in the record that, when, in the fifth century, the flood of barbarian invasion finally engulfed the Upper Danubian *limes*, and the last unit of local *limitanei* dissolved, their commanding officer found alternative service as a bishop.[5]

Still more significant than this breakdown of the Christian Church's original boycott of the Roman Army is the influence of the Army on the Church in the age in which the ban was still in force.

' "War" is one of the fundamental forms of Life, and there are inalienable virtues that find their highest, or at any rate their symbolic, expression in the warrior. . . . Accordingly, no higher religion can do without imagery derived from war, or, in consequence, do without "warriors" [of its own].'[6]

In the Jewish tradition, which the Christian Church had retained as a treasured part of its own heritage when it had parted company with Judaism, war was consecrated both in the literal sense as an indispensable means of realizing the messianic hope and in a symbolic sense in the metaphorical language of the authors of the Books of the Prophets and the Psalms;[7] and, though the Church dropped the literal application, she retained the symbol.[8] While, however, the Jewish martial tradition was thus a potent literary influence on the life of the Primitive Christian Church, the Roman martial tradition presented itself to Christians as a living and impressive reality. Baneful and hateful though the Roman Army of the Republic had been to the population of the Hellenic World in the cruel age of the Roman conquests and the still more cruel age of the ensuing Roman civil wars, the Roman Army of the Principate, which lived on its pay instead of lining its pockets by looting,

---

[1] See Harnack, op. cit., p. 80.   [2] See ibid., p. 82.
[3] This point is made by Harnack, op. cit., pp. 86–87.
[4] See Harnack, op. cit., p. 85.
[5] Eugippius: *Vita Sancti Severini*, chap. iv, § 2, and chap. xx, § 1, cited by Grosse, op. cit., pp. 269–70.
[6] Harnack, op. cit., p. 2.   [7] See ibid., pp. 8–9.
[8] This abandonment, by the Christian Church, of Jewry's literal militancy was perhaps originally sub-conscious, or at any rate tacit. Origen, however, frankly admitted a change of principle, on this point, as between the New Testament dispensation and the Old (see Harnack, op. cit., pp. 26–27 and 72).

and which was stationed on the frontiers, to defend Civilization against the barbarians, instead of infesting and devastating the civilized interior, came to win the involuntary respect, admiration, and even affection of Rome's subjects, as an oecumenical institution that ministered to their welfare and that was a legitimate object for their pride.

'Let us observe', wrote Clement of Rome, about the year A.D. 95, in his First Epistle to the Corinthians,[1] 'the conduct of the soldiers who serve our rulers. Think of the orderliness, the pliancy, the submissiveness with which they carry out their orders. Not all of them are legates or tribunes or centurions or options or officers of the grades below these. But each serving soldier in his own unit carries out the commands of the Emperor and the Government.'

In thus commending the discipline of the contemporary Roman Army as an exemplar for his Christian correspondents, Clement was seeking to establish a rule of organization for the Church. Obedience, he was saying, is due from Christians, not only to God, but to their ecclesiastical superiors. '*All* Christians are soldiers; but, just for that reason, they have to obey their leaders the presbyters.'[2] This equation of 'soldier of God' with 'member of the Church' would have seemed a matter of course to Mithraists; for, of the seven grades of initiation in the Mithraic Church, the third from the bottom was *miles*, and it is probable that most initiates never rose higher than that level.[3] In the evolution of the Christian Church's military imagery, however, the original equation of 'soldier' had been not with 'convert' but with 'missionary'; and from this equation its author, Saint Paul, had drawn two inferences: the missionary must disencumber himself from the impedimenta of civilian life, and the missionary has the same claim to be supported by his flock as the soldier has to receive his pay out of the contributions of the tax-payer.[4]

'The two military axioms that were adopted by the Christian community in its earliest phase—that the Christian missionary and teacher should receive his maintenance from others, and that on the other hand he should not entangle himself in civilian business life—are in a relation of polarity to one another and just on that account already contain in themselves the germs of a whole hierarchical system.'[5]

Yet, whatever influence the Roman Army may have had on the development of the Church's institutions, the Church owed more in that sphere to the influence of the Roman civil service,[6] and the Army's example produced its principal effect on the life of the Church in the more elusive but more intimate realm of ideas and ideals. The Roman military imagery that was introduced into the Christian Church's terminology by Saint Paul, and that was adopted and developed by Clement of Rome, was extended by Saint Ignatius, whose letters, written early in the second century of the Christian Era in Greek, bristle

---

[1] Chap. 37.　　　　　　　　　　　　[2] Harnack, op. cit., pp. 18–19.
[3] See ibid., pp. 37–8.
[4] See ibid., pp. 14–16, citing 1 Tim. i. 18 and 2 Tim. ii. 3.
[5] Harnack, op. cit., p. 17. Compare pp. 17–18.
[6] See pp. 191–3, above, and pp. 369–70, below.

with transliterated Latin military technical terms.[1] Tertullian (*vivebat circa* A.D. 155–222), who was the son of an army officer, worked out the simile of the *militia Christi* consistently and thoroughly,[2] and in this he was followed up by his North-West African compatriot Saint Cyprian.[3]

The Christian initiation-rite of baptism is equated by Cyprian with the military oath (*sacramentum*) required of the recruit upon his enrolment in the Roman Army.[4] Once enrolled, the Christian soldier must wage his warfare 'in accordance with the regulations' ($\nu o\mu i\mu\omega s$).[5] He must eschew the unpardonable offence of desertion,[6] and likewise the grave misdemeanour of dereliction of duty.[7] 'The pay of delinquency is death', as Tertullian translates the phrase in Saint Paul's Epistle to the Romans[8] which appears as 'the wages of sin' in the Authorized English Version of the Bible. The ritual and moral obligations of the Christian life are equated by Tertullian with military fatigues. In his terminology a fast is a stint of sentry-go (*statio*),[9] and the Christian duty which is declared in the Gospel according to Saint Matthew to be so well within the compass of human powers is 'the Lord's light pack' (*levem sarcinam Domini*).[10] Moreover, the Christian soldier's faithful performance of his duty is duly recompensed. If 'the pay of sin is death', it must be reckoned on the other side of the account between the spiritual soldier and his heavenly paymaster that 'God's gratuity is life' (*donativum autem Dei vita*).[11] And, short of receiving a gratuity, the soldier can look forward to drawing his rations so long as he gives satisfaction to the master with whom he has taken service.[12] 'Your deposits [of deferred pay] are your works, [and you bank them] in order that you may [eventually] draw your receipts on an appropriate scale.'[13] The Cross is a military standard ($\sigma\dot{v}\sigma\sigma\eta\mu o\nu$) which Jesus has raised to inspire his troops.[14] The Christian soldier's general (*imperator*) is Christ,[15] and the soldier must never forget that he is under his general's eye.[16] Thus inspired, led, and disciplined, Christ's army can challenge comparison with Caesar's. If Christians are civilians (*pagani*) from the standpoint of Caesar's army, so are Caesar's

---

[1] See Harnack, op. cit., pp. 19–20.
[2] See ibid., pp. 32–33 and 35.
[3] See ibid., p. 41.   [4] See ibid.
[5] 2 Tim. ii. 3–5, cited by Harnack, op. cit., p. 17.
[6] $\Pi o\hat{i}os\ \delta\grave{e}\ \kappa\acute{o}\sigma\mu os\ \delta\acute{e}\xi\epsilon\tau a\acute{i}\ \tau\iota\nu a\ \tau\hat{\omega}\nu\ a\dot{v}\tau o\mu o\lambda o\acute{v}\nu\tau\omega\nu\ \dot{a}\pi'\ a\dot{v}\tau o\hat{v};$ (1 Clem. ad. Cor., chap. 28). $M\acute{\eta}\tau\iota s\ \dot{v}\mu\hat{\omega}\nu\ \delta\epsilon\sigma\acute{e}\rho\tau\omega\rho\ \epsilon\dot{v}\rho\epsilon\theta\hat{\eta}$ (Ignatius ad. Polycarpum, chap. 6). These passages are printed in Harnack, op. cit., pp. 94–95.
[7] $\Delta\acute{\iota}\kappa a\iota o\nu\ o\dot{v}\nu\ \dot{e}\sigma\tau\grave{\iota}\nu\ \mu\grave{\eta}\ \lambda\iota\pi o\tau a\kappa\tau\epsilon\hat{\iota}\nu\ \dot{\eta}\mu\hat{a}s\ \dot{a}\pi\grave{o}\ \tau o\hat{v}\ \theta\epsilon\lambda\acute{\eta}\mu a\tau os\ a\dot{v}\tau o\hat{v}$ (1 Clem. ad. Cor., chap. 21, printed in Harnack, op. cit., p. 94).
[8] Rom. vi. 23.
[9] See Harnack, op. cit., pp. 35–36.
[10] Matt. xi. 30, as translated into Latin by Tertullian: *De Monogamiâ*, chap. 2 (Harnack, op. cit., p. 36).
[11] Rom. vi. 23, as translated into Latin by Tertullian.
[12] $'A\rho\acute{e}\sigma\kappa\epsilon\tau\epsilon\ \hat{\omega}\ \sigma\tau\rho a\tau\epsilon\acute{v}\epsilon\sigma\theta\epsilon,\ \dot{a}\phi'\ o\dot{v}\ \kappa a\grave{\iota}\ \tau\grave{a}\ \dot{o}\psi\acute{\omega}\nu\iota a\ \kappa o\mu\acute{\iota}\zeta\epsilon\sigma\theta\epsilon$ (Ignatius *Ad Polycarpum*, chap. 6, printed in Harnack, op. cit., p. 95).
[13] $T\grave{a}\ \delta\epsilon\pi\acute{o}\sigma\iota\tau a\ \dot{v}\mu\hat{\omega}\nu\ \tau\grave{a}\ \dot{e}\rho\gamma a\ \dot{v}\mu\hat{\omega}\nu,\ \dot{\iota}\nu a\ \tau\grave{a}\ \dot{a}\kappa\kappa\epsilon\pi\tau a\ \dot{v}\mu\hat{\omega}\nu\ \dot{a}\xi\iota a\ \kappa o\mu\acute{\iota}\sigma\eta\sigma\theta\epsilon$ (Ignatius, op. cit., loc. cit.).
[14] Ignatius *Ad Smyrnaeos*, chap. i, cited by Harnack, op. cit., p. 20. (N.B. This phrase occurs in the Septuagint Greek translation of Isaiah v. 26 and xlix. 22, and it therefore seems more likely that Ignatius is here quoting from the Septuagint than that he is employing a Roman military term current in his own day.—A.J.T.)
[15] Cyprian (see Harnack, op. cit., p. 41).
[16] 'Spectat militem suum Christus' (Cyprian, Ep. lviii, ch. 4, cited by Harnack, op. cit., p. 42).

soldiers from the standpoint of Christ's.[1] Justin Martyr (*florebat circa* A.D. 150) goes so far as to claim that the Christians' devotion to their service is greater than the Army's is to theirs.[2]

With a great Modern Western scholar's aid, enough evidence has now been cited to show that the Roman Army's impress on the Christian Church had cut deep. The mark that it had made had been enduring; and, in virtue of it, a mundane military organization which had finally lost its own identity in wars to the death with Persian and Arab adversaries in the seventh century of the Christian Era was still a living force in the World in A.D. 1952.

2. Civil Services

The Difficulty of Creating a Professional Civil Service

The variety which our survey of imperial standing armies has brought to light in the degree of development of the institutional organization of the universal states in our catalogue makes itself apparent again when we pass to the consideration of imperial civil services.

These vary, in degree of development, between two extremes illustrated by the Achaemenian Empire at the lower end of the scale and by the Ottoman Empire at the upper end. The Achaemenian professional civil service always remained rudimentary. Its most important representatives were the imperial secretaries who were resident at the headquarters of the provincial governors but were independent of the satraps and reported directly to the Central Government. As a further check, the satraps were also kept under observation by itinerant inspectors, expressively nicknamed 'the Emperor's eyes'.[3] The need for a central authority to gather together, hold, and manipulate these widely ramifying threads of administrative control seems to have been met, in the organization of the Imperial Court, by the evolution of an officer who was known in Old Persian as 'the Hazarapatiš' and in Greek as 'the Chiliarch', because he had begun by being simply the commander of an inner imperial bodyguard of one thousand men, into an Imperial Chancellor or Minister of State performing some, at any rate, of the functions that, in the Roman Empire, through a parallel process of evolution, came to be performed by the commandant of the Emperor's praetorian guards (*praefectus praetorio*).[4] While the Achae-

---

[1] Tertullian: *De Coronâ, passim*, cited by Harnack, op. cit., pp. 68–9, who points out that *paganus* is likewise used in the sense of 'civilian' in *Digest*, XLIX. xix. 14.

[2] See Harnack, op. cit., p. 21.

[3] The Achaemenian network of imperial communications, which made this system of inspection a practical possibility, has been noticed on p. 82, above.

[4] See p. 182, n. 3, and p. 183, above, and Junge, P. J.: 'Hazarapatiš: Zur Stellung des Chiliarchen der königlichen Leibgarde im Achämenidenstaat', in *Klio*, vol. xxxiii (Neue Folge, vol. xv) (Leipzig 1940, Dietrich), pp. 13–38. The Hazarapatiš could not have performed his duties without being served by a skilful, organized, and numerous administrative and clerical staff. The scale of his Chancery is indicated by the quantity of the imperial archives. By A.D. 1940 no less than 30,000 clay tablets, inscribed in the Elamite language, had been discovered at Persepolis alone by Modern Western archaeologists (see Junge, op. cit., p. 14, n. 2), and the collection at Susa, the principal seat of the Achaemenian imperial administration, must have been far larger (see ibid., p. 30, n. 3). These bulky, heavy, and brittle records on clay, together with the staff whose duty it was to keep them up to date and to consult them for administrative purposes, must have

menian civil service never developed beyond this point,[1] the Ottoman Government provided for its corresponding administrative needs by doing everything that human ingenuity could devise, and human determination accomplish, to produce a civil service that was to be no mere professional fraternity but a secular equivalent of a religious order, so rigorously segregated, austerely disciplined, and potently 'conditioned' as to be transfigured into a super-human, or sub-human, race —as different from the ordinary run of human kind as a thoroughbred and broken-in horse, hound, or hawk is from the wild life that has been the breeder's and trainer's raw material.[2]

At divers points between these two extremes we may place the professional civil services that were taken over by the Umayyad Caliphate from the Roman and Sasanian empires and by the Manchus from the Ming; those that were inherited from the pre-imperial past of the empire-building state by the Ts'in Empire in the Sinic World, the Mongol Empire in the Far Eastern World, and the Spanish Empire of the Indies; those that were modelled in the British Rāj in India, in the Napoleonic Empire, and in the Danubian Hapsburg Monarchy on home-grown institutions of the metropolitan countries that were themselves new creations; those that were worked out more or less *ab initio* in the Han Empire, the Roman Empire, and 'the Middle Empire' of Egypt; and those that, like the professional civil service of the Petrine Russian Empire, were fashioned on a last of an alien mould.

The Taking Over of an Existing Civil Service by a Barbarian Conqueror

The taking over of the existing civil service of a conquered polity is an expedient that almost forces itself upon empire-builders when these are barbarians who have won their empire by a sudden stroke and when the conquered polity itself has been a universal state whose imperial civil service has still been a going concern at the time of the conquest. Yet, though, in this situation, the main lines of action may be dictated by circumstances, there will still be some room for the free play of statesmanship. The barbarian empire-builders may be more or less receptive, and the subjugated civil servants more or less pliant; and it is a question of judgment how far the conquering ex-barbarian imperial

---

remained, year in and year out, in the administrative centre, whichever one it might be, where they had originally been inscribed and deposited; they cannot have accompanied the Emperor and his Court on their seasonal migration between Susa, Babylon, and Ecbatana, or on their occasional state visits to Persepolis (see pp. 205–7, above). Junge conjectures (ibid., p. 33 and p. 34, n. 4) that, besides being responsible for the Imperial Chancery, the Hazarapatiš was invested with the command over the imperial garrisons in the provinces.

[1] The differentiation from one another of the Imperial Household, the Imperial Treasury, and the Imperial Chancery, which was a feature of the subsequent Sasanian régime, was still unknown to the Achaemenidae (see Junge, op. cit., p. 30, n. 4). The Emperor's Bow-Bearer and Lance-Bearer served, no doubt, as his adjutants (see ibid., p. 22), and perhaps as his private secretaries. The post of Cup-Bearer, which came to be frequently, and in the end perhaps exclusively, held by eunuchs, seems to have carried with it the comptrollership of the Corps of Pages and of the whole personnel of the Household (see ibid., pp. 19–21). The Book of Nehemiah indicates how well placed the Cup-Bearer was for winning the Emperor's ear, and there seems to have been a tendency for him to gain in power at the Hazarapatiš's expense (see Junge, ibid., p. 37).

[2] For the ideal inspiring the creation of the Ottoman Pādishāh's Slave-Household, see the passage quoted from Lybyer in III. iii. 32–34.

people is to resign itself to taking over the conquered ex-imperial civil service lock, stock, and barrel as a permanent solution for its own problem of having to administer an empire, and how far it shall venture to reject or modify the institution that has so providentially fallen into its hands, for the sake of trying to preserve at any rate the more valuable elements in its own native communal tradition and êthos.

The Umayyad princes, on whom the sweeping conquests of the Primitive Muslim Arabs had conferred an unexpected dominion over ex-Roman and ex-Sasanian territories, compelled their Christian and Zoroastrian civil servants in the third generation to substitute Arabic for Greek, Coptic, and Pehlevi as the official language of the public records,[1] without attempting to take over the business of administration themselves; and, though under the ensuing 'Abbasid régime—especially from the ninth century of the Christian Era onwards, when the 'Abbasid Caliphate was declining towards its fall—the process of conversion to Islam became a landslide which carried into the Islamic fold a majority of the population of the Caliphate of all classes and occupations, the residual unconverted Christian minority continued to play a part in the civil service, and especially in the revenue administration, that was out of proportion to its eventual numbers.

In the less abrupt course of the establishment of the Manchu Empire over China, the reciprocal relations of Manchu and Chinese administrative institutions came to be adjusted more subtly.

In the Manchu polity a Chinese-inspired bureaucracy had already prevailed over both the original clan system and the subsequently engrafted feudal system, that had been the Manchus' own communal heritage, in the organization of the Manchu 'banners'[2] that had been created in A.D. 1601, forty-three years before the Manchus had embarked on the conquest of Intramural China.[3] To staff a bureaucratic administration of their newly established banners, the Manchu Central Government commandeered Chinese scholar-serfs from the Manchu feudal lords,[4] and, if a new element had not entered into the situation thereafter, the Manchu Power might have followed independently the path that the Ottoman Power took when it provided for the government of its empire by building up the Pādishāh's Slave-Household. In the history of the Manchu Empire, however, this embryonic servile civil service never came to maturity; for the Manchu empire-builders soon came to recognize the expediency, and indeed necessity, of taking Chinese civil servants into the Manchu service as free men enjoying the status that was traditionally theirs under an indigenous Chinese régime.[5]

---

[1] See p. 242, n. 3, above.   [2] See p. 129, above.
[3] See Michael, F.: The Origin of Manchu Rule in China (Baltimore 1942, Johns Hopkins University Press), pp. 61 and 64.   [4] See Michael, op. cit., pp. 58 and 68.
[5] See ibid., p. 68. While the Manchus took the Chinese into their service on these generous terms at an early date and of their own free choice, the 'Osmanlis did not take the corresponding step of employing Greeks as freemen, unconverted to Islam, until they were constrained by the breakdown of the Pādishāh's Slave-Household and by a turn in the tide of war, in favour of the Western Christian Powers, which for the first time made the Ottoman Government feel the need for diplomacy and consequently appreciate the qualifications of their Greek Christian ra'īyeh for negotiating with Western diplomats on their Ottoman masters' behalf (see II. ii. 223–5; III. iii. 47–48; and V. vi. 299).

The epoch-making event that produced this change in the Manchus'
attitude and policy towards Chinese litterati was the desertion in A.D.
1618, from the Ming to the Manchu service, of Li Yung-fang, the
Chinese commandant of Fushun, a strategic point just inside the Great
Wall at its eastern extremity on the coast of the Gulf of Chihli. The
possibility of Li's adhesion to their cause promised the Manchus so
important an advantage that they offered him admission to their service
on terms of equality. He accepted the offer, and this bargain created a
precedent by which Li's compatriots benefited from that time onwards.[1]
In fact, 'the Chinese forced their standards on the invader'.[2] In A.D.
1631, thirteen years before the Manchus' passage of the Great Wall,
a conference of Manchu feudal lords and high officials decided in favour
of adopting the traditional Chinese bureaucratic organization for the
central government;[3] and the Manchu administrative system was duly
Sinified by Prince Dorgon, the son of the founder of the Manchu
Power, Nurhachi (*regnabat* A.D. 1618–25), and the younger brother of
Nurhachi's successor T'ai Tsung (*regnabat* A.D. 1625–43).[4]

'Feudalism had given the Manchus their first integrating power. The
acceptance of bureaucracy in the banner and central administration made
them a state. It was the Chinese system, Chinese officials and Chinese
ideas that enabled the Manchus to conquer China.'[5]

The tottering Ming régime was given its *coup de grâce*, not by the
Sinified Manchu Power beyond the Great Wall which was to succeed,
in the event, to the fallen Ming régime's heritage, but by a rebel who
had raised his horn in the interior of China. As against the Manchus, Li
Tse-chêng, after occupying Peking, had the double advantage of being
in possession and being Chinese. In the revolutionary breaks in the
history of the Chinese state, native Chinese rebels, no less than barbarian
invaders, had found themselves unable to gain possession of the Empire
without the use of force,[6] and for this reason the aspirants to supreme
power in times of anarchy, whether barbarians or Chinese, had usually
been men who had little to lose and who had had to fight to hold even
what they had.[7] Li Tse-chêng, the extinguisher of the Ming, conformed
to the historic type of successful Chinese rebel in being an illiterate
proletarian. On the other hand, the *ci-devant* barbarian Manchus were
by this time in the second generation of Sinification and, in the process,
had become men of substance with something to lose and therefore
with a motive for hesitating to put their fortunes to the touch by playing
for the greater but more hazardous prize of oecumenical dominion.[8]
In the circumstances, that prize might have remained in the bandit
Li Tse-chêng's hands if the issue had depended on him and the

---

[1] See Michael, op. cit., pp. 69–72.

[2] Ibid., p. 75. As has been noticed in III. iii. 31, n. 1, Chinese litterati at the Manchu
Court were styled 'officials' (*ch'en*), whereas Manchu officials were styled 'slaves' (*nu*).
This distinction of nomenclature lasted down to the fall of the Manchu régime in
A.D. 1911 (see ibid.).   [3] See ibid., pp. 76–77.

[4] See ibid., pp. 78 and 92–93.   [5] Ibid., p. 79.

[6] See ibid., p. 9.   [7] See ibid., p. 41.

[8] The Manchu Government had even waited till A.D. 1636 to repudiate the suzerainty
of the moribund Ming over their extramural principality (Michael, op. cit., pp. 100 and
103).

Manchus alone. In the history of the antecedent Sinic Civilization, Liu Pang had become the founder of the Han Dynasty through a very similar career. In the crisis of A.D. 1644, however, the issue was decided otherwise by the suffrages of a third party. The Chinese civil service, and the scholar-gentry from whose ranks they were drawn, could not stomach the illiterate usurper, while they felt that there was a future for them under an ex-barbarian Power which had already given practical proof of its esteem for the Confucian culture by Sinifying itself of its own accord.[1] The Manchus crossed the Great Wall with at least the hint of a mandate to make the Empire safe for the Chinese scholar-gentry against the barbarian from within; and, though there proved to be nationalist-minded elements in the South of China which refused to recognize the Manchus' cultural mission and which remained unreconciled to the Manchu domination to the end of the story, the unenthusiastic yet efficacious support of the Chinese cultivated class enabled the Manchus to make themselves masters of China and to hold their prize for more than a quarter of a millennium.

'The Manchu State was growing in the Chinese World at the edge of the Chinese Empire. Its development can only be understood in its relationship to the Chinese Empire, as it was—though a conquering force —still a part of China all the time.'[2]

At the same time the Manchus did not become Chinese altogether without reservations. While they adopted the Confucian philosophy and educated their young men in it, they interpreted Confucian virtue in military terms[3] that would have been more acceptable to the Sinic hereditary feudal nobility of Confucius's day than to Confucius himself or to the latter-day *chün tze* of the Han Age who bore the by then extinct feudal class's historic name, while teaching and practising what they believed to be Confucius's philosophy.[4] T'ai Tsung warned his Manchus against assimilation to the Chinese civilian way of life.[5] 'The banners had at first been the Manchu state. Now'—as a consequence of the Manchu Power's momentous act of taking over the Chinese State as a going concern under the administration of the established Chinese professional civil service—the banners 'became a state within a State'.[6] In this equivocal position they did, however, maintain their existence and retain their identity till the Manchu régime in China fell, in its turn, in A.D. 1911.

Experiments in Recruiting a Civil Service from an Existing Aristocracy

The Manchus and the Primitive Muslim Arabs were exceptional among empire-builders in the scantiness of the indigenous cultural and institutional heritage that they brought with them. Most of their peers had come into the saddle better equipped, and, in addressing themselves to the unfamiliar and formidable task of governing an empire, they had naturally been apt to turn to account as far as possible, for

---

[1] See Michael, op. cit., pp. 113-14.
[3] See ibid., pp. 104-6.
[5] See Michael, op. cit., p. 107.

[2] Ibid., p. 99.
[4] See pp. 355-6, below.
[6] Ibid., p. 118.

this new purpose, the social heritage of the pre-imperial age of their own national history.

The Manchus themselves, as we have seen, had developed the rudiments of a tribal and feudal aristocracy before they embraced the Confucian culture and virtually put themselves in the hands of the Chinese civil service as the price of their acquisition of the Chinese Empire. Longer-established national aristocracies were in existence, by the time of their accession to oecumenical power, among the Persian henchmen of the Achaemenidae and among their Macedonian supplanters; among the clansmen of the Inca Emperors and among their Spanish supplanters; and in the hereditary dominions of the Hapsburg founders of the Danubian Monarchy. There was an incapable aristocracy in Muscovy at the time when Peter the Great took her Westernization in hand, and a highly capable one in the Roman Republic at the date of the foundation of the Principate.

In each of these cases the aristocracy descending from a previous age was drawn upon by the founder or reorganizer of a universal state as material for the building of an oecumenical administrative structure. The motives prompting an identical policy were, however, widely diverse. While Peter the Great tried to dragoon the old-fashioned Muscovite nobility into becoming the cultivated, efficient, and industrious administrators in the contemporary Western style whom he needed urgently in large numbers, Augustus took the politically experienced Roman Senatorial Order into a cautiously regulated partnership with his own new dictatorial régime, not so much because he needed or desired their collaboration as because he judged this policy of appeasement to be a prudent measure of insurance against suffering his adoptive father's fate at the hands of an old governing class whose thirst for power was still unsatiated, and because he realized that, in spite of their shameful and notorious betrayal of their trust during the last 150 years of their government of the Roman body politic, the Senatorial Order had not yet exhausted the credit of an accumulated prestige.

These antithetical problems that confronted respectively Augustus and Peter the Great are the horns of a dilemma that is apt to catch the architect of a universal state who finds himself with an imperial people's pre-imperial aristocracy on his hands. If the aristocracy is capable and experienced, it will probably be resentful of the change in its fortunes that has left it no opening, except the unpalatable service of a dictator, for still exercising those administrative capacities which it has developed through having been in power on its own account before losing its old political supremacy to its new master. Conversely, if the aristocracy is easy-going, the dictator who seeks to make use of its services will probably find that the innocuousness of his tool is offset by the bluntness of its edge. After Peter the Great's attempt to turn Muscovite nobles into Western-style administrators had been tried for two generations,[1] the Petrine Imperial Government gave it up as a bad

---

[1] Peter and his successors tried to use the Russian nobility in the provincial, as well as the central, administration by enrolling them in colleges of Landrats modelled on those

job[1] and granted the hereditary nobility a conditional exemption from public service in A.D. 1762.[2] On the other hand, Augustus, who was as anxious to dispense with his *viri senatorii* as Peter was to make use of his *boyars*, had to be content with making them ineligible for the single governorship of Egypt (a province that was a personal conquest of his own, and whose resources were so extensive and so efficiently concentrated in government hands that no Roman emperor could afford to see a Roman senator in control of them). The best part of three centuries was to pass before Augustus's successor Gallienus (*imperabat* A.D. 260–8) could venture, in the equalitarian revolutionary atmosphere of the third century of the Christian Era,[3] to set about excluding the senatorial class systematically from key positions of public responsibility and power; and, even then, nearly half a century elapsed before Gallienus's work was completed by Diocletian (*imperabat* A.D. 284–305).[4]

Among the other national aristocracies, mentioned above, whose fortune it was to be called upon to share in the administration of a universal state, the Macedonian, like the Roman, nobility was competent but recalcitrant. In the generation of anarchy in Macedon preceding the accession of Philip II these spirited and turbulent Macedonian rural barons had enjoyed as great a licence as the Polish nobility in the age preceding the Partition of A.D. 1772, and they fiercely resented being called upon to become the devoted humble servants, *more Persico*, of a once constitutional king of their own blood who had formerly been proud to recognize them as his social peers (ἑταῖροι). They rebelled against this demand even when it was made of them by a legitimate king of the Argead line who had won a position of unique eminence by overthrowing and supplanting the last Achaemenid. Still less willing were the Macedonian nobility to serve a despotic master when their lawful King Alexander was replaced by a batch of noble-born usurpers of the royal title, in whose shoes any other Macedonian noble military adventurer might have found himself standing if the luck of the game, in the scramble for power after Alexander's death, had happened to come his way instead of playing into the hands of his peers the Ptolemies, Antigoni, and Seleuci. In these psychological circumstances it was no wonder that the Seleucids and the Ptolemies had to look for ministers and administrators for their successor-states among the adaptable

---

that were a going concern in the Baltic Provinces that Peter had conquered from Sweden (see Brückner, A.: *Peter der Grosse* (Berlin 1879, Grote), p. 505).

[1] Peter found himself constrained, by an effective passive resistance, to revoke, after a two years' trial, his edict of A.D. 1714, ordering all landowners and civil servants to send their children, between the ages of ten and fifteen, to his newly founded secular elementary schools. Peter vainly tried to enforce this edict by making a school-leaving certificate a pre-requisite—in the case of all persons subject to the edict—for a licence to marry (see Sumner, B. H.: *Peter the Great and the Emergence of Russia* (London 1950, English Universities Press), p. 153, and the present Study, III. iii. 282, n. 2). A would-be bridegroom had to satisfy the examiners in arithmetic, geometry, and navigation (see Mettig, op. cit., p. 412).

[2] See Mettig, C.: *Die Europäisierung Russlands im Achtzehnten Jahrhundert* (Gotha 1913, Perthes), p. 413; Sumner, op. cit., pp. 197–8.

[3] For this revolutionary movement and its triumph, see pp. 152–8, above.

[4] See Grosse, R.: *Römische Militärgeschichte von Gallienus bis zum Beginn der Byzantinischen Themenverfassung* (Berlin 1920, Weidmann), pp. 4–9. Between Augustus's day and Gallienus's, Septimius Severus (*imperabat* A.D. 193–211) had followed the precedent set by Augustus in Egypt when he enlarged the Roman Empire by adding the new

citizens of the city-states of the Hellenic World rather than among their intractable fellow noblemen from Hellas' Macedonian march.

By contrast, the grandees of Spain were ready enough to serve the Spanish Crown as viceroys and captains-general of the kingdoms of the Indies, even though the crown was worn by foreign Hapsburg and Bourbon heads, while, in the Danubian dominions of the eastern branch of the House of Hapsburg, the nobility of the dynasty's Austrian hereditary dominions was likewise willing to serve an Imperial-Royal-Archiducal master in the task of attempting to knit into a unity the congeries of kingdoms and lands which had been shaken into the lap of the *Caesarea Maiestas* by the shock of the Ottoman victory at Mohacz in A.D. 1526.[1] These Austrian and Spanish aristocrats, however, were as sluggish as they were loyal. In fine, of all the aristocracies to whom Fortune had offered an opportunity for distinguishing themselves by sharing in the administration of a universal state, the Persian *megistânes* and the Inca *orejones* alone had risen to the occasion—and, in rising to it, had redeemed the credit of their caste by acquitting themselves so well that, in the hour of their defeat and humiliation, they extorted a posthumous tribute of praise from the mouths of the very adversaries who had beaten and supplanted them.[2]

Experiments in Recruiting a Civil Service from Novi Homines

Such pre-imperial aristocracies were the principal, but not the only, national administrative material that empire-builders had brought with them for setting about their oecumenical task. The blue-blooded viceroys whom the Spanish Crown sent out to New Spain and Peru would hardly have succeeded in turning the offspring of the unmanageable *conquistadores* into governable Creoles if they had not had the assistance of middle-class lawyers whose natural ability was fortified by a professional training and tradition. As for the Mongols, they would assuredly have failed to retain, even for one lifetime, their hold on China, Russia, Iran, and 'Irāq if they had not had the good sense to enlist the secretarial services of Nestorian Christian Uighurs whom they took over from their Karāyit and Naiman predecessors in the hegemony of the High Steppe.[3] But the most formidably—though, as it turned out, fatally—well equipped of all empire-builders was Ts'in She Hwang-ti.[4]

While the six rival contending states that succumbed to the last king of Ts'in and first emperor of a Sinic universal state were still living under the traditional feudal régime of the Chóu dispensation, the corresponding régime in the State of Ts'in had been liquidated by the revolutionary reforms of the Lord of Shang nearly a hundred years before the future First Emperor's accession to the parochial throne of

province of Mesopotamia and enlarged the Roman Army by adding the three new *Legiones Parthicae*. Members of the Senatorial Order were disqualified from holding either the governorship of Mesopotamia or any of these three new legionary commands (see Grosse, op. cit., p. 4).

[1] The Danubian Hapsburg Monarchy was created and kept in being by Ottoman military pressure, as has been noticed in II. ii. 177–88.

[2] See V. v. 50–52.

[3] See II. ii. 237–8; III. iii. 451; V. v. 309 and 348.

[4] See pp. 169–74, above.

Ts'in in 246 B.C.[1] as King Chêng. In place of the liquidated aristocracy of Ts'in the reformer had installed a professional bureaucracy, and the concentration of power in the royal government's hands as a result of this drastic administrative reorganization was the secret of Ts'in's subsequent advance from strength to strength which culminated in King Chêng's feat of overthrowing all his competitors and thereby making himself master of the entire Sinic World in 230–221 B.C. The cause of Ts'in's dramatic triumph was, however, likewise the cause of the equally dramatic reversal of her fortunes on the morrow of the First Ts'in Emperor's death.

The unimaginatively revolutionary-minded conqueror had committed the fatal blunder of trying to hold his conquests by the use of the same instrument that had won them. Not content with subduing and annexing the six rival states, he deposed their feudal aristocracy as well as their royal houses, and put their administration in the hands of bureaucrats from his own hereditary kingdom of Ts'in, without realizing that he was imposing on his victims a sharper affliction than they could bear. Even in Ts'in a century back, Lord Shang might have failed to carry through his revolution at the local aristocracy's expense if Ts'in had not been a rude and backward march-state where tradition had less strong a hold than in more mellow countries nearer the heart of the Sinic World. The abrupt imposition of the rule of the bureaucracy of Ts'in upon the people of these other countries a hundred years later brought the loss of their independence home to them in a direct personal way. It was a misfortune for the ambitions of Ts'in She Hwang-ti that, owing to Lord Shang's revolutionary service to his royal predecessors, he found himself in possession of the means to carry out the intolerably sweeping administrative revolution which his own successful successor Liu Pang deliberately forbore to emulate on the morrow of the swift undoing of Ts'in She Hwang-ti's revolutionary work.

The builders of two other universal states had drawn, with happier results, upon the practice and personnel of a civil service which the empire-building community had not inherited from the past but had created to meet its own domestic needs at home in the same generation in which the task of imperial administration had descended on its shoulders. This was the means by which the French equipped themselves for administering the Napoleonic Empire in a politically stagnant Central Europe, and the British for reconstructing a derelict Mughal Rāj in India.

The character and achievements of the British Indian civil service can hardly be understood without being looked at against the background of an immediately preceding chapter of administrative history in the United Kingdom.

'The institution of factory inspection by the Act of 1833 was a stage in the development of a new kind of civil service. . . . Bentham's passion for substituting science for custom, his view of administration that it was a

---

[1] In 246 B.C. according to Fitzgerald, C. P.: *China, A Short Cultural History* (London 1935, Cresset Press), p. 70; in 247 B.C. according to Franke, O.: *Geschichte des Chinesischen Reiches*, vol. i (Berlin and Leipzig 1930, de Gruyter), p. 226.

skilled business, had in this instance results that were wholly satisfactory: under his inspiration England created a staff that brought to its work training and independence; unlike the English Justice of the Peace, the new Civil Servant had knowledge; unlike the French *intendant*, he was not the mere creature of a government. The English people learnt to use educated men on terms that preserved their independence and their self-respect. . . . For the moment, the chief occupation of this educated class was to throw a searchlight on the disorder of the new world. Nobody can study the history of the generation that followed the passing of the first Reform Bill without being struck by the part played by lawyers, doctors, men of science and letters in exposing abuses and devising plans.'[1]

The new fraternity of middle-class professional administrators which took a passage to India, after having thus made its way peacefully to the front in England, had, in France, to force an outlet for itself by an explosive outbreak of its artificially dammed-back energies.

'The French bourgeoisie of '89 belonged to a class proud of its economic independence and of its social standing. Its members had earned or inherited a competence derived from honest toil. They cherished a self-respect that set them no further from the *aristos* above them than from the *sansculottes* below. Yet they resembled the English aristocracy, and differed from that of their own country, in being a class, not a caste. Their ranks were not fixed, but fluid. There was always an element in them surging up from *roturier* to *bourgeois*, and from *bourgeois* to noble. . . . Hitherto they had been kept out of the government of a country which they enlightened and enriched. But nothing had been able to exclude them from the management of its trade, its agriculture, or its administration. Here they had become apprenticed to political power. Here, during half a century of political outlawry, they had been educating themselves for 1789.'[2]

The new field of action that the French *bourgeoisie* now opened up for themselves was a bureaucratic public service, which was called for to fill an institutional vacuum created in France by the Revolution itself before the French conquests abroad, which the Revolution set in motion, enlarged this vacuum to embrace Flanders, Italy, and Western Germany and to give a French bureaucracy *in partibus peregrinis* a different function from that which it had recently been called into existence to perform at home.

'The French had long lost the feeling for local autonomy, and the efforts to decentralise the government of the *Ancien Régime* had not had time to fructify before the Revolution supervened. That catastrophe eliminated the aristocracy, sowed hate and jealousy in every village, and prevented any further development of the constitution on the lines laid down by Turgot and Necker. A centralized bureaucracy was a necessity for France, being, as it were, not only a kind of anaesthetic or healing drug, but also the elementary condition for the preservation of all that was precious in the revolutionary movement. Among the lethargic inhabitants of West-phalia the mission of the bureaucracy was not to calm but to excite, not to preserve but to communicate. . . .[3]

[1] Hammond, J. L. and Barbara: *The Rise of Modern Industry* (London 1925, Methuen), pp. 256–7.
[2] Thompson, J. M.: *The French Revolution* (Oxford 1943, Blackwell), p. 26.
[3] Fisher, H. A. L.: *Studies in Napoleonic Statesmanship in Germany* (Oxford 1903, Clarendon Press), pp. 269–70.

'It was not merely by their laws that the French left a permanent mark upon the Duchy [of Berg]. Their administration was a pattern and a precedent. The Prussians, indeed, had done good bureaucratic work in Mark and in Münster before the French occupation, but it was the French who first adequately expounded the arts of finance and administration to the whole region. To the slovenly government of the Bavarians in Berg, the French methods, combining, as they did, strict control with prompt, orderly and intelligent action, and distinguished always for their clear definition and distribution of functions, were related as the railway train is related to the stage coach.'[1]

Napoleon was seeking to carry out in a subjugated Central Europe the long overdue administrative reformation that Ts'in She Hwang-ti had tried to impose upon the subjugated states of the Sinic World 'outside the passes', and the great demonic French innovator's tragedy was the same as his Sinic counterpart's. In forcing the pace of revolutionary change without mercy on Human Nature, he defeated his reformatory purpose and brought his own work to grief.

'There has been no greater master in the art of using, driving, and inspiring men. He found great disorder and demoralisation; he created a bureaucracy more competent, active, and enlightened than any which Europe had seen. But, as the Consulate passed into the Empire, and as the growing palsy of despotism spread over France, the quality of the work declined. The best men hated the never-ending wars and saw insanity written in large tokens over their master's schemes. . . . All criticism, all independent political thought, expired. Resolutely closing his eyes to unpleasant facts, Napoleon insisted that his servants should be blind also, and, being despotic and irritable, he was able to exact a constant supply of nutriment for his illusions. The men who spoke the truth and thought justly were dismissed or scolded; and, as compliance came to be rated more highly than ability, the most precious qualities were excised from public life.'[2]

The Metamorphosis of an Hereditary Aristocracy into a Professional Civil Service

If Napoleon and Ts'in She Hwang-ti deservedly failed in their attempt abruptly to force an alien bureaucracy on their subjects, Augustus and Han Liu Pang well deserved the success that attended their humane and statesmanlike policy of calling a new civil service into existence to answer to the needs of the devastated, disorganized, and weary world for whose welfare each of them found himself responsible. The administrative systems founded by the Hellenic bourgeois and the Sinic peasant saviour of society were perhaps the two finest secular institutions that, down to the time of writing, had yet been fashioned by the wisdom and benevolence of Man; yet, when they are compared with one another, their merits can be seen to be as unequal as their longevity. The Roman imperial administrative system, which went to pieces in the seventh century after its inauguration by Augustus, was not on a par with the Han system which had been founded 150 years earlier and which lasted, with at least a thread of continuity, down to A.D. 1911.

[1] Fisher, op. cit., p. 222.   [2] Ibid., pp. 374-5.

The defect of the Roman imperial civil service was its reflection of the discord between the old republican senatorial aristocracy and the new imperial dictatorship which an Augustan compromise had glozed over but had not healed. In the Roman imperial civil service under the Principate there were two rigidly segregated hierarchies and two mutually exclusive careers in which the senatorial and the equestrian civil servant went their respective ways. This schism in the heart of the service was, as we have seen, eventually brought to an end in the third century of the Christian Era, not by the achievement of that *concordia ordinum* which the public interest had always required, but by a high-handed elimination of the Senatorial Order from all posts of administrative responsibility. Their discomfiture, however, did not leave their equestrian rivals in enjoyment of a monopoly of the imperial service; for by this time the decay of local civic self-government had so swollen the volume of the imperial service's work[1] that Diocletian found himself compelled to make an inordinate increase in the permanent establishment of the civil service as well as the army; and in a post-Diocletianic Age the entry into the service was open to any Roman citizen possessed of the necessary degree of education, without discrimination between classes. The contrast with the history of the Han imperial civil service[2] is instructive. The opening of careers to talent, which was not achieved in the Roman Empire till more than three hundred years after the establishment of the Augustan Peace, was inaugurated in the Han Empire by Han Liu Pang himself, within six years of his restoration of order in 202 B.C., in an ordinance, issued in 196 B.C.,[3] in which he directed the provincial public authorities to select candidates for the public service on a test of merit, and to send them to the capital for appointment or rejection by the officers of the Central Government.

This new Sinic civil service received its definitive form when Han Liu Pang's successor Han Wuti (*imperabat* 140–87 B.C.) decided that the merit required of candidates should be a proficiency in reproducing the style of the classical literature of the Confucian canon and in interpreting the Confucian philosophy to the satisfaction of the Confucian litterati of the day.[4] Under the skilful handling of the Han emperors the transition from the old feudal order of the Chóu Age to the new bureaucratic order of the Han Age was made so smoothly—notwithstanding the violence of the abortively revolutionary Ts'in interlude—that old names acquired new meanings, and old doctrines new interpretations, by insensible degrees.

'The disappearance of feudalism was rendered possible by the policy of the Han emperors towards a very important and hitherto irreconcilably reactionary class, the *chün tze*. The aristocracy had been virtually destroyed by the revolutionary measures of She Hwang-ti, but they transmitted their ideals and their political outlook to a new class, the scholars and officials of the centralised empire. From this time onwards the *chün tze* cease to be an hereditary nobility distinguished by membership of a

---

[1] See pp. 59–60 and 166, above.   [2] See pp. 173–4, above.
[3] Franke, O.: *Geschichte des Chinesischen Reiches*, vol. i (Berlin and Leipzig 1930, de Gruyter), pp. 274–5, gives a German translation of the text as recorded in the official history of the Prior Han Dynasty.   [4] See V. v. 418–19, 654–5, and 708.

limited number of clans. The revolution had destroyed the territorial and clan basis of the old aristocracy for ever. The *chün tze*, including many of the old aristocratic families, became a class marked off from the mass of the people by education, and only by education. . . . The very meaning of the old terms became obscure. *Chün tze* had meant the son of a lord, member of a noble clan. Under the new régime it gradually came to mean a gentleman in much the same sense as [that in which] that word is used in modern English—one who had received a polite education.

'The later Han emperors adroitly favoured the new educated class. Themselves of peasant origin, with no trace of divine or noble blood to fortify their claim to the throne, it was of vital importance to the new emperors to discover some principle of legitimacy for their power. Noble blood and divine descent they could not claim; force, upon which the Ts'in had relied, had proved to be a double-edged weapon. The master-stroke of the Han emperors was to enlist in support of the centralised state the very school which had upheld feudalism to the last. . . . Their supreme achievement was to persuade the new scholar class, to whom the Feudal Age was personally unknown, that the doctrines of Confucius could be applied to the new political régime. . . .

'She Hwang-ti tried to destroy the memory of the past; the Han sovereigns, more subtle than he, succeeded in distorting it. The interpretation of the Confucian doctrine which gained currency during the Han Dynasty proved one of the most enduring results of the revolution. The ideal of a centralised state became closely associated with the scholar class and the followers of the Confucian School. Henceforward fissiparous movements are always opposed by the scholars, the very class who had defended ancient feudalism.'[1]

The Confucian School of the second century B.C. which was thus tactfully coaxed into partnership with the Han imperial régime would have astonished Confucius himself by the enormity of its intellectual, as well as its political, departure from the founder's own standpoint. The break in scholarly tradition caused by Ts'in She Hwang-ti's burning of the books, and the syncretism in religion produced by the levelling of the former barriers between contending parochial states and by the inclusion of a host of semi-barbarous peoples within the pale of the Sinic Society through their subjugation by force of Ts'in and Han arms, had made of the epimethean philosophy of Confucius a melting-pot for exotic superstitions.[2] To translate the course of this chapter of Sinic social history into Hellenic terms, we should have to imagine the Emperor Marcus Aurelius making the Stoicism of his day[3] into the official philosophy of the Roman civil service,[4] and this Stoically rigged Roman ship of state being freighted with as heavy a cargo of superstition as Neoplatonism eventually took on board.[5]

To complete this imaginary parallel, however, we must picture the Stoic School in the next chapter of its history, after it has become the

[1] Fitzgerald, C. P.: *China, A Short Cultural History* (London 1935, Cresset Press), pp. 153–5. The quotations from this book have been made with the permission of the publishers.   [2] See V. v. 549 and 555–6.
[3] For the flush of religious feeling that suffused the Stoicism of the second century of the Christian Era, see the passage quoted from Dill in V. v. 550–1.
[4] Marcus's conscientious abstention from misusing his political power for the purpose of propagating his philosophic faith has been noticed in V. v. 705.
[5] See V. v. 565–7 and 680–3.

official philosophy of a universal state, deliberately purging its doctrine and practice of the superstitious accretions of the preceding age, and abandoning to its unofficial rival, Neoplatonism, the mission of supplying a demand for a popular religion under a philosophical veneer. In the Sinic World in the course of the last three centuries of the Han régime, the Confucian School did jettison the superstition that it had picked up in its rough passage through a revolutionary last phase of the Sinic Time of Troubles and first phase of the universal state established by Ts'in She Hwang-ti and refounded by Han Liu Pang. Yet, although 'the rather arid doctrines of the Confucian scholars had little appeal for the mass of the people', and in consequence 'the popular religion, which Confucianism had rejected', fell into the hands of 'the principal heterodox philosophy, Taoism',[1] even the dehydrated official philosophy of the Han imperial civil service was a more effective inspiration for a corporate professional way of life than the merely literary archaistic culture that was the shibboleth of a post-Diocletianic Roman civil service.[2]

A comparable vein of literary archaism was, indeed, carried to perhaps even greater lengths of absurdity by the Confucian School in the Han Age,[3] with the same unfortunate effect of cutting off a civil service that plumed itself on this conceit from the realities of contemporary life outside its own charmed circle; but the pedantic canon of literary taste to which the Han imperial civil service had subjected itself was always the handmaid of a rule of conduct which, however pedantic it, too, might be, still gave its followers a social cohesion among themselves, even when they had lost human touch with the rest of Society. This bond of a common traditional ethic was lacking among the Han civil servants' Roman counterparts; and no doubt this was one of the reasons for the difference in the fortunes of these two official corporations during the interregna following the break-up of the universal states whose respective servants they had been.[4]

---

[1] Fitzgerald, op. cit., p. 261.
[2] See V. vi. 71–81.   [3] See V. vi. 81–83.

[4] This difference is explored further on pp. 370–2, below. While one cause of it was the Roman imperial civil service's lack of a corporate philosophy such as the Han imperial civil service acquired in the shape of a purged Confucianism, another cause was the lack of a spacious fastness, impregnable to barbarian attack, such as the Han imperial civil service found for itself in the South of the Sinic World, where the expansion of the Sinic Civilization during its Time of Troubles had been carried forward, by the united forces of the subsequent universal state, until the conquest of Nan Yüeh (the present Chinese provinces of Kwangsi and Kwangtung, together with Tongking) by Han Wuti in 111 B.C. brought an expanding Sinic World to the 'natural frontier' of the sea coast (see Fitzgerald, op. cit., p. 181). The Yangtse Basin and the Southern Seaboard, unlike the Yellow River Basin, were unpropitious terrain for the cavalry of the Eurasian Nomad barbarian invaders of the Sinic World during the post-Han interregnum; and their defeat in A.D. 383 at Fei Shui (see Franke, op. cit., vol. ii, pp. 95–97; the date is given as A.D. 387 by Fitzgerald, op. cit., p. 257) was a decisive battle which may be compared, in respect of the magnitude of its consequences, to the defeats of the Mongols by the Egyptian Mamlūks in A.D. 1260, 1281, 1299–1300, and 1303 (see I. i. 350), since this battle insured the birth of a Far Eastern Civilization, affiliated to the Sinic, as those insured the birth of an Arabic Civilization affiliated to the Syriac. The Roman Empire embraced no fastness of comparable size that was immune against attack by the same Eurasian Nomad barbarian enemy, and in any case the barbarian invaders of the Roman Empire included sedentary peoples—highland Berbers and non-nomadicized West Germans—who were less sensitive to the nature of the terrain than their more highly specialized Nomad fellow aggressors. In the politico-strategic geography of the Roman

In the art of converting an aristocracy of birth into a professional civil service, both Augustus and Han Liu Pang were to be surpassed by Peter the Great; for the wisdom of hastening slowly, which Han Liu Pang had learnt from the fate of Ts'in She Hwang-ti's revolutionary handiwork, and Augustus from the fate of Julius Caesar's, was not only learnt by Peter from his own experience but was taken to heart by him in time to retrieve a first false start.

After having discovered, by trial and error, the unwisdom of attempting either to dragoon feudal nobles into becoming professional administrators[1] or to supersede them by a wholesale substitution of *novi homines* and foreigners, Peter set himself in A.D. 1722 gradually to convert the Muscovite nobility into an effective instrument of Russian Imperial administration by instituting an official hierarchy of military and civil ranks, in fourteen grades.

'Through each of these it was necessary to pass, beginning from the bottom, just as it had been Peter's practice to make his guards officers, like himself, start from the ranks. Promotion from grade to grade was to be partly by length of service and partly by exceptional merit. Standing in the state service took precedence of birth, even in the court and social hierarchy. The privileges of the land-owning class—notably those of owning serfs and of being exempt from the poll-tax—were extended hereditarily to all persons, whether Russians or foreigners, who reached the eighth grade, and in the case of the Army and Navy even from the lowest grade.

'Throughout his life Peter picked men for multifarious duties without regard to birth or class, in the interests of recruitment for military or state service. From this time forward the land-owning class began to receive an influx of newcomers, who in the course of the next two generations broadened its composition and changed its complexion. . . . Despite subsequent alterations, the table of ranks had a profound influence on the future. It set the stamp on the hierarchal, bureaucratic ordering of the upper class in military and state service, which during the next two centuries became so prominent a feature of the social structure of Russia. Rank, in the sense of position in the table of ranks, largely displaced birth or wealth in the administrative and social scale.'[2]

Empire the nearest counterpart to the great southern fastness of the Han Empire was Anatolia; but even Anatolia was constantly overrun by invading and occupying Persian and Arab armies in the seventh century of the Christian Era; and the measure of the break in administrative continuity, even here, is given by the contrast between the Diocletianic administrative organization, as it survived in Anatolia in the reign of Justinian, and the system of local government through army corps districts (*themata*), as it had emerged there within a hundred years of Justinian's death. Only the precincts of Constantinople remained inviolate, and this Constantinopolitan fastness was too small, and too alien in experience and outlook from the exposed and harried countryside, to play the part which the New South of the Sinic World was able to play in the affiliation of a new-born civilization to an extinct one. The administrative continuity between the Roman Empire that foundered in the seventh century of the Christian Era and the ghost of it that was evoked in the eighth century by Leo Syrus was one of form without substance, whereas in the Sinic World 'the flight of the scholars after the fall of Loyang [under the impact of Hiongnu Eurasian Nomad invaders in A.D. 311] brought civilisation into the South, and gave these provinces an importance which they had not possessed in the Han Empire, but which was to grow more and more marked in succeeding ages' (Fitzgerald, op. cit., p. 260). Observers of the Sino-Japanese war of A.D. 1931–45 would have been reminded of the similar effect of a similar migration of a Westernized intelligentsia from Peking and the treaty ports into the south-western provinces of contemporary China. See further X. ix. 649–81.   [1] See IX. viii. 554–7.
[2] Sumner, B. H.: *Peter the Great and the Emergence of Russia* (London 1950, English

In the judgement of an acute and sensitive Russian student of Russian history,

'La noblesse, cette nouvelle élite infiniment plus large, plus agile, plus capable d'avenir que l'ancienne, était sans doute, avec la nouvelle capitale, le don le plus précieux du tsar [Pierre] a la Russie future. Malgré Lomonossov et d'autres "parvenus" de génie, tout ce que la Russie a produit jusqu'au milieu du siècle suivant de grands hommes et de valeurs culturelles vient de cette classe ou du moins n'a pu éclore que dans le milieu formé par elle. ... L'ascension culturelle, politique et sociale de la Russie, de Pierre 1er a Alexandre 1er, est l'œuvre de la noblesse.'[1]

Experiments in Providing an Education for New Recruits

While the Han Empire and the Roman Empire created their magnificent civil services[2] out of their own respective social and cultural heritages, Peter the Great and his successors in Russia, when they were in search of administrative support for their enterprise of Westernizing their empire and had found the hereditary Muscovite nobility a broken reed,[3] forced the pace in the first stage of the manufacture of their new bureaucratic 'nobility of service' by copying Western institutions and even enlisting Western personnel.[4] The Cabinet Secretary instituted by Peter on a contemporary Western model[5] performed for the autocrat of a Westernizing Muscovy the service that an Achaemenian emperor received from his hazarapatiš and a Roman Emperor from his praetorian prefect. The contemporary organization of Western governments likewise suggested the Senate that was established by Peter on the 22nd February, 1711, and was endowed with far-reaching executive powers,[6] and the Administrative Colleges that were set up in A.D. 1717–18. Most of these colleges started life with Russian presidents and foreign vicepresidents to induct the Russians into new-fangled Western methods of administrative work.[7] To provide the staff, Swedish prisoners-of-war were roped in, and Russian apprentices were sent to acquire a Prussian training at Königsberg.[8] In A.D. 1722 the office of Procurator-General was created for the purpose of keeping a 'king's eye'[9] (to use the Achaemenian term) on both the colleges and the Senate.[10] An historian who was a Westerner himself would like to believe—against the presumptive

---

Universities Press), pp. 155–6. See also Brückner, A.: *Peter der Grosse* (Berlin 1879, Grote), p. 506, and the present Study, III. iii. 282, n. 2. Though the creation of this professional civil service was Peter's personal achievement, he did not have to start entirely from the beginning. For the pre-Petrine rudiments, see Mavor, J.: *An Economic History of Russia*, 2nd ed. (London 1925, Dent, 2 vols.), vol. i. p. 73.

1 Weidlé, W.: *La Russie Absente et Présente* (Paris 1949, Gallimard), p. 68.
2 See V. v. 38–39.   3 See pp. 349–50, above.
4 The first wave of immigrant Western bureaucrats consisted of German aristocrats from the Baltic Provinces after the conquest of these from Sweden by Peter the Great (see Sumner, B. H.: *Peter the Great and the Emergence of Russia* (London 1950, English Universities Press), p. 119). The second wave came from Germany itself during the sixteen years (A.D. 1725–41) immediately following Peter's death (see ibid., p. 192). During Peter's reign, however, there were no non-Russians in the taxation service, the provincial governorships, or the Senate, and very few in the Ministry of Foreign Affairs and in the diplomatic service (see ibid., pp. 204–5).
5 See Brückner, op. cit., p. 497; Sumner, op. cit., pp. 64 and 131.
6 See Brückner, op. cit., pp. 499–500; Sumner, op. cit., pp. 123–5 and 127.
7 See Brückner, op. cit., pp. 501–2; Sumner, op. cit., pp. 125–7.
8 See Brückner, op. cit., pp. 501–2.   9 See p. 82, above.
10 See Sumner, op. cit., pp. 127–8.

evidence of contemporary Venetian practice—that this official organization of espionage on the new Westernizing Russian civil service[1] was not likewise inspired by Western models.

Where, as in the Petrine Russian Empire, an imperial civil service is thus called into existence in conscious imitation of alien institutions, the need for special arrangements for the training of personnel is, of course, particularly evident.[2] At the same time, this need arises in some degree in all the divers situations in which an imperial civil service has to be provided, since it is inherent in the nature of a universal state and in the invariable circumstances of its advent in history.

An oecumenical polity of this type normally takes shape rather suddenly out of a cluster of contending parochial states that have brought a Time of Troubles to its climax and conclusion by an obstinate refusal to adapt themselves to the necessities of a new age. The problems, experience, institutions, and êthos of these anachronistic predecessors are manifestly unlikely to be of much use to the new polity that has at last belatedly superseded them. A fledgling universal state nearly always has, in the main, to supply its own needs for itself; and it cannot afford to imitate its parochial forerunners' comfortable habit, in the spacious days of their long-since vanished youth, of waiting upon experience to give them the necessary instruction; for the universal state has been brought into being as a response to the urgent challenge of its parochial predecessors' protracted failure to meet the World's political requirements; its mission is to grapple at once with the troubles of a society on the verge of dissolution; and, if it cannot draw profitably on its predecessors' experience and cannot wait to learn by experience of its own, it must take a leaf out of the book of Utopia[3] and must improvise the education of a new type of administrator for a new form of government. Most universal states will be found to have worked out arrangements of some kind for educating the administrators that they need.

In the Incaic, Achaemenian, Roman, and Ottoman empires the Emperor's personal household was both the hub of the wheel of imperial government and the training-school for the administrators required for making the machinery of government work, and in a number of cases this educational function of an imperial household had been catered for by the creation, within it, of the special institution of a corps of pages.

At the Inca Emperor's court at Cuzco there was a regular course of education—with tests and ordeals at successive stages of initiation—in which the young men of the Inca's own imperial clan were brigaded

---

[1] See Brückner, op. cit., p. 504.

[2] Peter the Great sought to meet this need *quam celerrimè* by sending batches of young Russians to be educated abroad from A.D. 1697 onwards. In A.D. 1697–8 he voluntarily performed, himself, a task that he was imposing on his subjects when he went abroad for eighteen months on 'the Great Embassy' in the suite of his Swiss-born ambassador Lefort (see Brückner, A.: *Peter der Grosse* (Berlin 1879, Grote), pp. 174–5; Sumner, B. H.: *Peter the Great and the Emergence of Russia* (London 1950, English Universities Press), pp. 34–41; and the present Study, III. iii. 281 and IX. viii. 556–7).

[3] We have seen that Utopias are products of Times of Troubles. They are attempts to arrest the decline of a disintegrating civilization by 'pegging' it at the highest level still attainable. The price of this bid for survival is a sacrifice of plasticity; but, in a chapter of history in which plasticity represents a danger of disintegration rather than an opportunity for growth, rigidity comes to seem a blessing and not a curse (see III. iii. 88–111).

with the sons of the chiefs and notables of the subject peoples.[1] In the Achaemenian Empire 'all Persian boys of noble birth' were 'educated at the Emperor's court ($\epsilon\pi\grave{\iota}\ \tau\alpha\hat{\iota}\varsigma\ B\alpha\sigma\iota\lambda\acute{\epsilon}\omega\varsigma\ \theta\acute{\upsilon}\rho\alpha\iota\varsigma)$',[2] 'from the age of five to the age of twenty, in three things and three only: riding, shooting, and telling the truth'.[3] This Achaemenian method of breaking in noblemen for the public service was copied in the Hellenic kingdom of Macedon, which, on the political map of the Achaemenian world order, was a barbarian principality lying just beyond the pale of the universal state; and the borrowed institution proved its efficacy, to its Persian inventors' detriment, first in the service of the historic Macedonian Monarchy by which the Achaemenian Empire was eventually overthrown, and thereafter in the service of upstart Macedonian successor-states whose domains were carved out of a defunct Achaemenian Empire's carcass. The Petrine Russian Empire, whose relation to the Western World was not unlike Macedon's relation to the Achaemenian Empire, was likewise imitating its neighbours when it instituted a corps of pages.[4]

The Ottoman Court made similar provision for the education of pages in its early days at Brusa,[5] and it was still treading a well-worn path when Sultan Murād II (*imperabat* A.D. 1421–51) established a school for princes at Adrianople, which was the capital of the Empire in his time;[6] but his son and successor, Sultan Mehmed II Fātih (*imperabat* A.D. 1451–81), struck out a new line of his own when, after the conquest of Constantinople, he built his father's foundation at Adrianople into a new educational edifice, centred in his own palace in the conquered metropolis of Orthodox Christendom, which was not only laid out on a larger scale but was designed for the different purpose of staffing the Ottoman imperial administrative service, no longer with independent-minded princes of the Imperial House and sons of 'Osmanli Muslim noblemen, but with Christian slaves—including renegades and prisoners-of-war from Western Christendom, as well as 'tribute children' levied from the Pādishāh's Orthodox Christian subjects[7]—whose status of servitude, and still more, perhaps, their segregation from their ancestral environment, would make them peculiarly susceptible to the skilful process of 'conditioning' to which they were to be subjected as cadets in the Pādishāh's Slave-Household. This 'peculiar institution' of the Ottoman Empire[8] has been described in a previous passage of this

[1] See Joyce, T. A.: *South American Archaeology* (London 1912, Lee Warner), pp. 106 and 112–16; Markham, Sir Clements: *The Incas of Peru* (London 1910, Smith Elder), pp. 128–34 and 142.

[2] Xenophon: *Expeditio Cyri*, Book I, chap. ix, § 3.

[3] Herodotus, Book I, chap. 136. See Meyer, E.: *Geschichte des Altertums*, vol. iii, 1st ed. (Stuttgart 1901, Cotta), pp. 35–36.

[4] In A.D. 1759, according to Mettig, Č.: *Die Europäisierung Russlands im Achtzehnten Jahrhundert* (Gotha 1913, Perthes), p. 83; in A.D. 1730, according to Sumner, B. H.: *Peter the Great and the Emergence of Russia* (London, 1950, English Universities Press), p. 153.

[5] See Miller, B.: *The Palace School of Muhammad the Conqueror* (Cambridge, Mass. 1941, Harvard University Press), p. 20.　　　　[6] See Miller, op. cit., p. 22.

[7] Though the 'tribute children' accounted for less than half the total intake of imperial slaves, they were in a great majority among the *élite* selected for training and service in the Palace, which was the avenue to subsequent employment in the administrative service instead of employment in the standing army (see Miller, op. cit., p. 75).

[8] The Ottoman Pādishāh's Slave-Household was a characteristic product of the Eurasian Nomad Society out of which the original nucleus of the Ottoman community had

Study[1] which need not be recapitulated here. At its zenith the Ottoman public slave-education system for entry into the administrative service was a graded pyramidal edifice of nine colleges ranged in four tiers, rising to the Hall of the Imperial Bedchamber at the apex.[2]

This establishment for training recruits for the administrative branch of the Slave-Household was built on such solid foundations of *esprit de corps*[3] that, when in the last quarter of the sixteenth century of the Christian Era the free Muslim subjects of the Empire at last succeeded in forcing an entry into the military branch,[4] the colleges composing the Palace School managed for another century and a half to keep their doors closed to boys of free birth and to continue to supply the Ottoman civil service with admirably trained slave-administrators.[5] Even after Sultan Mahmūd II (*imperabat* A.D. 1808–39), in his thoroughgoing replacement of obsolete indigenous Ottoman institutions by substitutes of a Western pattern, had swept away the six colleges inside the palace precincts after his destruction of the Janissaries in A.D. 1826,[6] he spared the Galata Seray, which in Mahmūd's day was the sole survivor of the former three extramural schools;[7] and an abortive attempt, made by Mahmūd himself in A.D. 1828, to put the Galata Seray on a Western basis was eventually carried through successfully in A.D. 1868.[8] As a *lycée* recog-

come, but it was a revolutionary innovation in the life of the Orthodox Christian sedentary society on which the Ottoman conquerors had imposed their rule. The Ottoman Sultans Murād II and Mehmed II were not the first Turkish-speaking empire-builders of Eurasian Nomad origin to found schools of public administration. When the Saljūq Turkish barbarian invaders of the dominions of the 'Abbasid Caliphate took over responsibility for carrying on the government of their august protégé-puppet, their gifted Minister of state, the Nizām-al-Mulk, included a division for training in public administration, as well as one for instruction in Islamic theology, in the celebrated *madrasah* which he founded at Baghdad in A.D. 1065–7 (see Miller, op. cit., p. 12). His Nizāmīyah was a resident college (see ibid., p. 16). Was this Saljūq precedent in the minds of the Ottoman Sultans Murād II and Mehmed II (see ibid., p. 20)?

[1] In III. iii. 35–45. Since the publication of that volume of this Study, the Western World's understanding of the Pādishāh's Slave-Household, and of the educational institutions embedded in it by which it had provided for its own self-perpetuation, had been increased by the publication of two works of Western scholarship in addition to those mentioned in vol. iii, p. 32, n. 1. These subsequent published works were Penzer, N. M.: *The Harēm* (London 1936, Harrap); Miller, B.: *The Palace School of Muhammad the Conqueror* (Cambridge, Mass. 1941, Harvard University Press).

[2] The component institutions of this educational pyramid were, to enumerate them in ascending order: (i) three schools outside the precincts of Mehmed II's Palace at Constantinople, namely Murād II's school at Adrianople; a school in the Galata Seray on the opposite side of the Golden Horn from Istanbul; and Ibrāhīm Pasha's school in Istanbul, near the Hippodrome, which catered for cadets of Bosniak and Albanian origin. These three outside schools were preparatory for (ii) the Great and Small Halls inside the Palace. These, in turn, were preparatory for (iii) three vocational schools inside the Palace: the Hall of the Expeditionary Force (*Seferli Oda*) and the Halls of the Commissariat and the Treasury. The three vocational schools were preparatory for (iv) the Hall of the Imperial Bedchamber (see Miller, op. cit., pp. 43–44 and 126).

[3] The pages of the Palace School displayed a steady loyalty that was in strong contrast with the turbulence of the Janissaries (see Miller, op. cit., p. 8).

[4] See III. iii. 45.   [5] See Miller, op. cit., p. 174.

[6] See ibid., p. 182.

[7] See ibid., p. 80. Compare the present Study, III. iii. 49, n. 4.

[8] See Miller, op. cit., pp. 182–3; Engelhardt E.: *La Turquie et le Tanzimat*, vol. ii (Paris 1884, Pichon), pp. 12–15; Davison, R. H.: *Reform in the Ottoman Empire, 1856–1876* (thesis submitted to Harvard University for degree of D.Phil., 1st April, 1942, typescript copy in the Harvard University Library). The lines on which the Galata Seray was to be reconstructed were laid down in March 1867 in consultations between Fu'ād Pasha and a French mission, and it was decided that it should be transformed into a secondary school on a Western model in which French was to be the language of instruction. This *lycée*

nized by the Ministry of Education in Paris, the Galata Seray came, in the last chapter of the history of the Ottoman Empire, to be once again the *alma mater* of men of mark, not only among the Muslim ruling class of a truncated Turkey, but also among the Orthodox Christian elder statesmen of Turkey's Bulgarian successor-state.

While the Ottoman Pādishāhs deliberately expanded their personal slave-household into an instrument for the government of a rapidly enlarged empire to the exclusion of the free 'Osmanlis who were the Ottoman imperial people, the Roman emperors, when they found themselves driven to make a similar use of Caesar's slave-household in an administrative emergency arising from the bankruptcy of the Roman republican régime, took steps first to limit and then to reduce the role of the imperial freedmen in the task of world government.

We have already noticed that Augustus reserved for members of the Senatorial Order the posts of highest dignity and heaviest responsibility in the service of the Princeps, quite apart from the senatorial monopoly of the administration of those provinces that the founder of the Principate handed back to the Senate under his system of 'dyarchy'.[1] No imperial freedman was ever appointed to the governorship of a major imperial province or to the command of a legion; and, when members of the Senatorial Order were eventually disqualified from holding these high posts,[2] it was the Equestrian Order that entered into their heritage. The freedmen's stronghold in the administration of the Roman Empire in the early days of the Principate was the central government, in which five administrative offices in Caesar's household—*ab epistulis, a rationibus, a libellis, a cognitionibus*, and *a studiis*[3]—had grown into imperial ministries of state;[4] and even in these posts, which were traditionally the freedmen's preserve, the freedmen became politically impossible as soon as they had impoliticly made themselves conspicuous. The scandal caused by the spectacle of Claudius's and Nero's freedmen-ministers exercising inordinate power led, under the Flavian emperors and their successors, to the transfer of one of these key posts after another from the hands of imperial freedmen to those of members of the Equestrian Order,[5] which was the equal of the Emperor's slave-household in

was to be open to members of all Ottoman communities, and students who were successful in passing the leaving examination were thereby to acquire a right of entry into the Ottoman public service. The text of the Imperial Firman in which this project was given effect will be found in G. M. Young: *Corps de Droit Ottoman* (Oxford 1905–6, Clarendon Press, 7 vols.), vol. ii, pp. 377–80. The new-model Galata Seray was opened on the 1st September, 1868. Out of the 341 students enrolled, 147 were Muslims, 48 were Armenian Gregorian Monophysite Christians, 36 were Greek Eastern Orthodox Christians, 34 were Bulgar Eastern Orthodox Christians, 34 were Jews, 23 were Roman Catholics of the Latin rite, 19 were Roman Catholics of the Armenian rite. By December 1869 there were 622 students, including 277 Muslims, 91 Gregorian Armenian Christians, 85 Greeks, 65 Roman Catholics of the Latin rite, 40 Bulgars, 29 Jews, 28 Roman Catholic Uniat Armenian Christians, and 7 Protestant Christians. The Armenians and the Bulgars proved to make the best students.

[1] See pp. 349–50, above.   [2] See p. 350, above.
[3] See *The Cambridge Ancient History*, vol. x (Cambridge 1934, University Press), pp. 687–8.
[4] See V. v. 452–3.
[5] The first equestrian secretary of state *a rationibus* was appointed by Trajan (*imperabat* A.D. 98–117) according to *The Cambridge Ancient History*, vol. xi (Cambridge 1936, University Press), p. 220.

business ability, and which could be placed in charge of the central administration of the Empire without offence to other free-born Roman citizens.

Thus in the history of the Roman civil service under the Principate the equestrian middle class gained ground at the expense of the slave underworld and the senatorial aristocracy alike. The Equestrian Order's victory over its rivals on either hand was justified by the efficiency and integrity with which the equestrian civil servants performed their official duties, and this redemption of a class which, during the last two centuries of the republican régime, had risen to wealth and power by a predatory exploitation of army contracts, tax-farming, and usury, was perhaps the most remarkable of the Principate's moral triumphs. The British Indian civil servants, whose record during the last four or five generations of the British Rāj, in the service first of the East India Company and afterwards of the Crown, could bear comparison with the record of the Roman equestrian civil servants at their best, were conjured out of much the same unpromising human materials as their Roman counterparts.

The antecedents of these British Indian civil servants likewise were commercial. They had originated as the employees of a private trading organization whose purpose had been pecuniary profit; one of their original incentives for taking employment far from home in an uncongenial climate had been the possibility of making money for themselves by personal trading on the margin of their work for their employers; and, when the break-up of the Mughal Rāj had suddenly transformed the East India Company from a mere commercial concern into the virtual sovereign of the Mughals' largest and most lucrative successor-state, the Company's servants had yielded to the temptation to make illegitimate and inordinate pecuniary profits out of the political power that Fortune had thrust into their hands,[1] with much the same shamelessness and irresponsibility as the Roman equites had shown when they had found a prostrate Hellenic World at their mercy after Rome's victory over Carthage in the Hannibalic War. In the British, as in the Roman, case, this start might have seemed so bad as to be beyond hope of retrieving;[2] yet in the British, as in the Roman, episode of administrative history a predatory band of harpies was converted in a surprisingly short time into a body of public servants whose incentive was not personal pecuniary

[1] See IV. iv. 511–12. The metamorphosis of the East India Company's servants 'from pettifogging traders . . . into imperialistic swashbucklers and large-scale extortionists' was accomplished between A.D. 1750 and A.D. 1785 (see Spear, T. G. P.: *The Nabobs* (London 1932, Milford), p. 23). 'The transformation of factors into soldiers and statesmen . . . meant that soldiers and officials brought commercial minds to their new duties, in which, if they were not always over-careful of the Company's coffers, they never forgot their own' (ibid., p. 28). In Bengal the European adventurers' reign of terror was at its height from A.D. 1761 to A.D. 1771–2, when it was curbed by Warren Hastings' reforms (see ibid., pp. 32–33).

[2] In the early years of the nineteenth century of the Christian Era the highest reasonable hope might well have been thought to be the conversion of a piratical Clive into a chicken-livered Jos. Sedley (see IV. iv. 641). At Calcutta, where the transition from a respectable obscurity to a corrupt ascendancy had taken place between A.D. 1756 and 1765, there was a reversion towards respectability under Cornwallis' régime (*pro-consulari munere fungebatur* A.D. 1786–93). The nineteenth-century era of virtuous aloofness was inaugurated by Wellesley (*fungebatur* A.D. 1798–1805). See Spear, op. cit., p. 26.

gain and who had come to make it a point of honour to wield enormous political power without abusing it.[1]

This redemption of the character of the British administration in India was due in part to the East India Company's decision to educate their servants for bearing the new political responsibilities that had fallen upon their shoulders. The Company acquired the financial administration of Bengal, Bihar, Orissa, and the Northern Circars in A.D. 1765; it opened its college in Hertfordshire for probationer-appointees to its administrative service in India in A.D. 1806; and the college played an historic role during the fifty-two years (A.D. 1806–57) for which it performed this function.[2]

The influence of an educational tradition and environment on the professional êthos of a civil service may be no less profound when the aspirants for admission to its ranks are educated in non-official institutions. In the history of the British Indian civil service, this was shown when in A.D. 1853–5, on the eve of the transference of the Government of India from the Company's hands to the Crown's, Parliament's decisions to recruit the service in future by competitive examination and to close the Company's vocational school for cadets opened the door to candidates drawn from the wider field offered by such non-official institutions as the universities of the United Kingdom and the so-called 'public schools' from which the English universities were almost exclusively recruited at that date.

In making this new departure in educational policy for the English contingent in the personnel of a British Indian civil service, Her Britannic Majesty's Government were unconsciously following the precedent set by Han Wuti when he decided to place the education of a Sinic imperial civil service in the hands of the Confucian school of philosophy.[3]

---

[1] See V. v. 47–48.

[2] The East India Company's College was installed in Hertford Castle at its opening in February 1806, but was moved into new buildings at Haileybury in A.D. 1809. There were about 100 students; the length of the course was two years; and the age of admission ranged between 16 and 19. A student obtained admission through a nomination by one of the Directors of the East India Company which assured him not only of a place in the college but of a post in India thereafter. This method of admission was abolished by an Act of Parliament, passed in A.D. 1853, which provided for the future recruitment of the Indian Civil Service by open competitive examination. The first examination of the kind was held in London in A.D. 1855, and the College was closed, by an Act of A.D. 1855, as from the end of the calendar year 1857.

Besides the contribution that it made to the improvement of British administration in India, the College had the distinction of contributing to the advancement of the science of human affairs through the work of Malthus, who was a professor on its staff from A.D. 1806 until his death in A.D. 1834.

[3] In the histories of the Confucian and the British Indian civil services the experiments in official and unofficial education of aspirants for admission were made in an inverse order. While the British began by setting up a vocational college and then, on second thoughts, decided to rely, instead, on a traditional system of higher education in non-governmental institutions, Han Wuti entrusted the education of civil servants to the Confucian school of philosophy, and the alternative method of training them in a state college was not introduced until the renaissance of the Han Empire, in the shape of the Sui and T'ang régimes, in the history of a Far Eastern Civilization, affiliated to the Sinic, which arose after the social interregnum following the Han Empire's dissolution. When the political unification of the main body of the Far Eastern World by the short-lived Sui Dynasty had been repeated by the second sovereign, but actual founder, of the T'ang Dynasty, T'ai Tsung, one of his measures for placing his political achievement on enduring foundations was to give his unified empire a unitary civil service of Confucian scholars on the Han model. During the interregnum the Confucian scholar-

The indigenous Indian contingent in the personnel of the British Indian civil service—which always vastly outnumbered the handful of Europeans occupying the key posts at the top—was recruited, both under the Company and under the Crown, from the alumni of Western Christian missionary schools and colleges in India, and of Indian universities built up round them or founded side by side with them, whose curricula and standards were largely governed by those of the universities of the United Kingdom, particularly the University of London.[1] On the whole, it would seem that, the less direct the hand that a government finds it necessary to take in the training of candidates for its civil service, the more satisfactory the results are likely to be. The limits to the possibility of compulsory training and enrolment are illustrated by the experience of Peter the Great and his successors in Russia. Peter himself, as we have seen,[2] debarred Russian noblemen from contracting a legal marriage without having passed examinations in arithmetic, geometry, and navigation; and in A.D. 1736 a course of compulsory education from the age of seven to the age of twenty was imposed on noblemens' sons, with a series of three examinations in which a failure entailed the penalty of serving in the Army as a common soldier.[3] Yet, as we have also seen,[4] the disappointing experience of two generations of unprofitable coercion led the Russian Imperial Government in A.D. 1762 to grant an unsuccessfully dragooned hereditary nobility a conditional exemption from compulsory public service.

Our survey of the methods and sources of recruitment of imperial civil services suggests that neither a pre-imperial hereditary nobility nor an imperial slave-household provides the best human materials for the purpose. Neither the attractiveness of the Persian *megistânes* and Inca *orejones* nor the impressiveness of the Ottoman Pādishāh's *qullar* can obscure the manifest truth that the most promising recruiting ground for an imperial civil service is a middle class which has served an apprenticeship in the responsible management of important and intricate non-official business. It was no accident that, in the history of the Roman imperial civil service, the Equestrian Order steadily gained ground at

administrator had survived in a fastness in the South (see p. 357, n. 4, above, and X. ix. 667). But, though the South was united politically with the North under the Sui and T'ang régimes, as it had been under the Han, the remnant of the scholar-administrator class in the South could not be expected suddenly to provide the personnel for staffing the whole of T'ai Tsung's united empire. Like the Ottoman Sultan Mehmed II after his conquest of Constantinople, T'ai Tsung filled an awkward vacuum by enlarging an existing imperial college and using it for the training of professional administrators. The new faculty of Confucian studies was instituted by him in A.D. 628, and in A.D. 630 he took action to provide the Confucian cadets for his resuscitated imperial civil service with the requisite means of instruction and examination by giving orders for the preparation of an official standard edition of the Confucian classics and—what was perhaps of still greater practical convenience—an official digest and elucidation of the existing commentaries (see Fung Yu-lan: *A Short History of Chinese Philosophy* (New York 1948, Macmillan), p. 266). As it emerged from T'ai Tsung's hands, the imperial college at Si Ngan had a student body of 8,000, of whom 3,260 were residents. T'ai Tsung further increased the Imperial Government's control over its intake of recruits into the imperial civil service by instituting a system of public examinations which was afterwards perfected by the Sung and later dynasties (see Fitzgerald, op. cit., pp. 304, 312, and 381–2).

[1] The nature, genesis, and unhappiness of an intelligentsia have been touched upon in V. v. 154–9.

[2] On p. 350, n. 1, above.

[3] See Mettig, op. cit., p. 412.

[4] On p. 350, above.

the expense of the Senatorial Order on the one hand and of the imperial freedmen on the other. Nor, perhaps, again, is it an accident that the Roman 'knight' and the English 'gentleman', drawn, as they both were, from an ex-commercial class fumigated with an aristocratic literary culture, should have to yield the palm to a Chinese scholar-administrator educated in an aristocratic philosophy without any skeleton of a commercial past in the cupboard of his family history.

Who are the Beneficiaries?

If we turn now to consider who had been the principal beneficiaries from the imperial civil services that universal states had called into existence for their own purposes, we shall see that the most obvious benefits had been obtained by these empires' non-barbarian successor-states:[1] the Latin American successors of the Spanish Empire of the Indies; the Central and East European successors of the Napoleonic Empire and the Danubian Hapsburg Monarchy; the Soviet Union that had succeeded the Petrine Russian Empire; the two British Dominions —an Indian Union and a Pakistan—that had succeeded the British Indian Rāj; and the indigenous successor-states of the Han Empire in the Yangtse Basin and along the southern seaboard of an expanded Sinic World, where a remnant of the Confucian scholar-administrator class had been able to hibernate until the evocation of a ghost of the Han Empire by the Sui and the T'ang had given this academic Rip van Winkle an opportunity to play his professional part again on the old oecumenical scale in the life of a new Far Eastern Civilization.[2] A fledgling successor-state that is struggling to establish itself is seldom inhibited by political animosity from taking over from its imperial predecessor a vital administrative technique or even an existing professional personnel that knows how to make the wheels of administration keep on revolving. The British Rāj in India, which was perhaps unique among universal states in having voluntarily liquidated itself, had taken pains during the transitional thirty years 1917–47 to prepare the way for its successors by progressively Indianizing the previously European-manned higher ranks of the Indian civil service, and the Napoleonic French administrators in Central Europe had been equally conscious of having an educational mission, though perhaps not equally aware that it was of the essence of their task to educate their non-French flock to a level of administrative efficiency at which these pupils would be able to do without the services of their blandly self-assured masters.

'If, as Napoleon said, experience is everything in administration, faith also goes for something. The French administrators in Westphalia were not only experienced, but they had faith in their own value. It is only necessary to read the letters of Beugnot or the speeches and circulars of Siméon to see how saturated men can become with the belief in the superiority of the language and civilization of their own country. They

---

[1] Barbarian hands are seldom gentle and deft enough to make effective use of so subtle and delicate an administrative implement as a professional civil service.

[2] See p. 357, n. 4, above, and X. ix. 667.

speak kindly, considerately, condescendingly to the poor Westphalians, explaining everything in the lucid French manner, as a master might expound a beautiful text to a class of stupid and backward boys, now calling attention to a grace of phrase, now to its inner logical coherence, now to its bearing on life. The official letters and documents of this time have all the air of being written by men who regarded themselves as missionaries of Civilisation, and who wish to impart the mysteries of their creed.'[1]

A characteristic exposition of this condescending outlook is given in the following passage from the pen of an eminent representative of the French missionary-administrator fraternity:

'It was then a position in Europe to be a Frenchman, and it was a great position to represent the Emperor anywhere; save that I should not have abused my office with impunity, I was in Germany what the proconsuls were in Rome. . . . We were at that time under the charm of the Peace of Tilsit, the invincibility of the Emperor had not yet received a wound. I came from Paris, where I had passed my life at his Court, that is to say, in the midst of the memorable works and miracles of his reign. In his councils, I had admired this genius who dominated human thought; I believed that he was born to chain up Fortune, and it seemed to me quite natural that people should be prostrate at his feet. . . . I presented myself in the Grand Duchy [of Berg] under the empire of these ideas. . . . I worked from morn to night with a singular ardour, and astonished the natives of the country, who did not know that the Emperor exerted upon his servants, however distant, the miracle of the Real Presence.'[2]

This radiation of the demonic influence of Napoleon's personality was as fruitful at long range in raising administrative standards in the Napoleonic Empire's non-French successor-states as it was fatal at short range to the perpetuation of French rule over non-French populations for whom, at close quarters, the upsetting effect of a genially high-handed re-education in the administrator's art decidedly outweighed the stimulus.

While serving the administrative needs of its imperial creators and their successors, a professional civil service may also be performing the historically more important function of propagating a culture. In the minds of Beugnot and his colleagues, their political and cultural missions were manifestly inseparable; and the Western culture that these Napoleonic French missionary-administrators were dispensing, on their own doorstep, to a still semi-medieval Central Europe, was likewise being propagated farther afield, in various forms and divers degrees of maturity, by Spanish administrators in the Central American and Andean worlds; by Austrian administrators among semi-Western Magyars, Croats, and Poles and among Orthodox Christian Rumans, Serbs, and Ukrainians; by Petrine administrators (many of them of Baltic German or other Western origin) in Russian Orthodox Christendom; and by British Indian civil servants (of Indian as well as European

---

[1] Fisher, H. A. L.: *Studies in Napoleonic Statesmanship in Germany* (Oxford 1903, Clarendon Press), p. 256.
[2] Beugnot, Count: *Mémoires*, vol. i, pp. 312–13, as translated in Fisher, op. cit., pp. 191–2 (the original French text will be found on pp. 263–4 in the single-volume 3rd ed.: Paris 1889, Dentu).

blood) among the variegated population of a sub-continent. As for the Confucian scholar-administrators who found asylum in the South after the break-up of the Han Empire, they succeeded—during a social interregnum in which the homeland of the moribund Sinic Civilization in the Yellow River Basin was submerged by the influx of barbarian conquerors and of an alien higher religion—in raising a recently incorporated and hitherto backward southern fringe of the Sinic World in its last phase to a cultural level that could compare with that prevailing in the northern focus of the Sinic Civilization under the Han.

The most important beneficiaries from imperial civil services had, however, been neither successor-states nor secular civilizations but churches. In surveying in an earlier chapter the provincial structure of universal states and its after-effects, we have noticed a number of cases in which the hierarchical organization of a church had been based on that of an empire.[1] This basis was provided by 'the New Empire' of Egypt for the Pan-Egyptiac Church that was organized by Thothmes III under the presidency of the Chief Priest of Amon-Re at Thebes; by the Sasanian Empire for the Zoroastrian Church; and by the Roman Empire for the Catholic Christian Church. The ecclesiastical pyramid reproduced the features of its secular model from base to apex. At the summit, the Chief Priest of Amon-Re at Thebes was created in the image of a Theban Pharaoh; the Zoroastrian Chief Mōbadh (Mōbadhān Mōbadh) in the likeness of a Sasanian Shāhinshāh; the Pope in the likeness of a post-Diocletianic Roman Emperor.[2] Secular administrative corporations had, however, performed more intimate services for churches than the mere provision of an organizational last. They had also influenced their outlook and êthos, and in some cases these intellectual and moral influences had been conveyed, not merely by example and mimesis, but by the social translation of a personality, in whom they had been incarnate, from the secular to the ecclesiastical sphere.

Three historic figures, who each gave a decisive turn to the development of the Catholic Church in the West, were recruits from the secular Roman imperial public service. Ambrosius (*vivebat circa* A.D. 340–97) was the son of a civil servant who had reached the peak of his profession by attaining the office of praetorian prefect in the Gauls; and the future Saint Ambrose was following in his father's steps as a young and promising governor of the two North Italian provinces of Liguria and Aemilia when in A.D. 374, to his astonishment and consternation, he was dragged out of the rut of an assured official career and was hustled into the episcopal see of Milan by a popular impetus that did not wait to ask his leave. Flavius Magnus Aurelius Cassiodorus Senator (*vivebat circa* A.D. 490–585) spent his working life on the thankless—and, as his colleague Boethius's fate proved, perilous—task of administering a Roman Italy in the service of a barbarian war-lord. It was only after his retirement from secular public life that Cassiodorus found a creative use for a literary archaism that had been an impediment to his draftsmanship as

[1] See pp. 188–93, above.
[2] See Toynbee, J. C. M.: 'Catholicism and the Roman Imperial Cult', in *The Month*, vol. clviii, November 1931, pp. 390–2.

a Minister of State. In his latter days he turned a rural property of his in the toe of Italy—the Vivarium, in the district of Squillace—into a monastic settlement that was the complement of Saint Benedict's foundation at Monte Cassino. Saint Benedict's school of monks broken-in, by the love of God, to hard physical labour in the fields[1] could not have done all that it did do for a nascent Western Society if it had not been wedded, at the start, to a Cassiodoran school that was inspired by the same motive to perform the mentally laborious task of copying the Classics and the Fathers.[2] As for Gregory the Great (*vivebat circa* A.D. 540–604),[3] he abandoned the secular public service, after serving as *Praefectus Urbi*, in order to follow Cassiodorus's example by making a monastery out of his ancestral palace in Rome, and he was thereby led, against his expectation and desire, into becoming one of the makers of the Papacy.

After citing the names of these three great luminaries, we may single out, among the lesser lights, two country gentlemen, Gaius Sollius Modestus Apollinaris Sidonius of Auvergne (*vivebat* A.D. 430–83) and Synesius of Cyrene (*vivebat* A.D. 370–415), who were both drawn out of a life of innocent but uncreative literary dilettantism when their local countryside was engulfed in the oecumenical catastrophe of their age. Both of them responded nobly to this personal challenge by taking on their shoulders the burdens, anxieties, and perils of local leadership; and each found that he could best perform an arduous duty, that he would not shirk, by allowing himself to be made bishop of his local community.[4]

Diverse as the origins and histories of these five personalities were, they had four things in common. For all of them except, perhaps, Cassiodorus, their ecclesiastical career went against the grain. Ambrose was aghast at being made a bishop, while Synesius and Sidonius half-whimsically acquiesced in a role which evidently struck them as being, to say the least, incongruous. Gregory was as reluctant to be made seventh deacon, apocrisiarius, and pope, and even to become abbot of his own monastery, as he had been eager to enrol himself as an ordinary monk. The second common feature in these five ecclesiastical careers was that all these *ci-devant* lay notables were constrained, willy-nilly, to employ their secular administrative gifts and experience in the Church's service. In the third place, they found a scope for the use of this mundane faculty in the ecclesiastical field which they had not found in secular life.[5] And, finally, they eclipsed their own performance as ecclesiastical administrators by their prowess on the spiritual plane.

Thus, when the break-up of the universal state for whose administrative service they had been educated had deprived these Roman *honestiores* of the possibility of following secular public careers, they responded to this formidable challenge by entering the service of the Christian Church and devoting all their powers to assisting in the creation of a new order of society. An instructive contrast is presented

---

[1] See III. iii. 266.   [2] Ibid., p. 267.
[3] Ibid., p. 267–9.
[4] Synesius was made metropolitan bishop of the Cyrenaic Pentapolis *circa* A.D. 410; Sidonius was made bishop of Auvergne in A.D. 469 or 470.
[5] See IV. iv. 55.

by the very different reaction of their Sinic counterparts. Under the same ordeal the Confucian scholar-administrator did not paradoxically save his life by losing it;[1] he kicked obstinately against the pricks;[2] he put up a stouter fight than the Roman civil servant against overwhelmingly powerful forces of disintegration;[3] he declined to confess that 'we have no armour against Fate'; and, if he can be said to have performed any service at all for any church, it was the negative and unintentional service of leaving to Buddhist scholar-monks and Taoist philosopher-medicine-men the thankless task of carrying on a secular administration for the Eurasian Nomad war-lords of the defunct Han Empire's barbarian successor-states.

'The fall of the Han Empire, and the partitions and barbarian invasions which followed, opened the road to Buddhism and effected a religious revolution which was the most significant development in what the historians of Confucian tradition describe as an "Age of Confusion". . . . The northern Tatar dynasts extended their favour to Buddhist monks in the conquered provinces. The Confucian scholars had for the most part fled south when Loyang fell [in A.D. 311]. Those who remained in the North were not favoured by the invaders, who rightly suspected this class of secret loyalty to the Chinese Emperor and hostility to the new conquerors. The new sovereigns, needing the assistance of a literate class, found in the Buddhists and Taoists, who had been the opponents of the orthodox Confucians, a body of scholarly men who were trustworthy and loyal. . . . In A.D. 405[4] the [Confucian] historians confess that nine out of every ten families in the northern empire had embraced the Buddhist faith. The proportion is significant, for the non-Buddhist tenth fairly represents the educated class of Confucian scholars and Taoist sectaries who alone remained detached from the new religion. . . . A hundred years later, in A.D. 500, it is admitted that the whole of China, North and South alike, was Buddhist. . . . A few Confucian scholars refused for themselves the salvation which their own families, and particularly the women, eagerly embraced.'[5]

For this uncreative obstinacy, the epigoni of the Han imperial civil service had their reward.[6] Though, by the end of the interregnum between the disappearance of the Sinic and the emergence of an affiliated Far Eastern Civilization, 'the Han civil service based on scholarship was almost forgotten',[7] the Confucian scholar never abdicated. The tide was running all against him, for

'these melancholy conditions and the apparently incurable anarchy of the times tended to encourage the progress of Buddhism. . . . The doctrines

---

[1] Matt. x. 39 and xvi. 25; Mark viii. 35; Luke ix. 24; John xii. 25.
[2] Acts ix. 5 and xxvi. 14.
[3] In the last phase of the dissolution of the Han Empire, in A.D. 166, the Confucian civil servants founded an association for combating the pernicious influence of the eunuchs, and thereby drew down upon themselves a crushing counterstroke in A.D. 168, partly because they were not sufficiently adaptable to succeed in co-operating with the fighting service, even in this supreme common cause (see Fitzgerald, op. cit., pp. 248–9).
[4] According to Sir Charles Eliot: *Hinduism and Buddhism* (London 1921, Edward Arnold, 3 vols.), vol. iii, p. 250, this religious landslide in the North of a disintegrating Sinic World had already taken place by the year A.D. 381.—A. J. T.
[5] Fitzgerald, C. P.: *China, A Short Cultural History* (London 1935, Cresset Press), pp. 275–6.
[6] Matt. vi. 2, 5, and 16.   [7] Fitzgerald, op. cit., p. 259.

of the new religion offered comfort to men living in a world of violence and instability. To renounce society, abandon possessions, and seek peace in a monastery among the mountains became the fashion among thoughtful men. Those who could not take the extreme step contributed to the building of temples and pagodas and their enrichment with artistic treasures.'[1]

If, in these psychologically propitious circumstances, Buddhism eventually failed after all to anticipate Christianity's triumphant success in making the future decisively her own, the explanation lies in the Confucian scholar's feat of holding out in a situation in which the Roman civil servant at last despaired of the republic.

The Confucian civil service produced no Buddhist or Taoist equivalent of an Ambrose or a Gregory the Great. So far from giving the Buddhist Church wings to fly with, it sullenly bided its time for clipping the wings that she had.

'Even at the height of Buddhist fervour, the political power remained in the hands of laymen who were Confucian in training, even if Buddhist in sympathy and the practice of daily life.'[2]

The Confucian scholar's monopoly of a literary culture that was indispensable for the practice of a latter-day Sinic administrative technique, in combination with his cult of a family solidarity which was as close-knit as it was narrow-hearted, armed him with two weapons that enabled him not only to retain his power in the South but actually to recover it in the North by eventually establishing his ascendancy over the epigoni of the barbarian conquerors.[3] By the persistent exercise of these prosaic arts at the price of closing his eyes to the vision of an Other World which the disintegration of his own world might have revealed to him, the Confucian scholar lived to achieve in the end his blinkered mundane ambition of reanimating a defunct universal state with which he had come to identify his own existence so completely that he had ceased to be able to imagine the possibility of felicity in any other social setting.

3. Citizenships

The Initial Gulf between Subjects and Rulers

Since a universal state usually arises in the first instance[4] from the forcible unification of a number of contending parochial states at the end of a Time of Troubles in the history of a disintegrating civilization, it is apt to start life with a great gulf fixed between rulers and ruled. On the one side of this sharp political dividing line stands an empire-building community representing the survivors of a dominant minority in a protracted struggle for existence between the rulers of the com-

[1] Fitzgerald, op cit., p. 259.   [2] Ibid., p. 286.
[3] An illuminating study of the Confucian recovery in the North, in which the evidence latent in the official records of the *ci-devant* barbarian To Pa dynasty is extorted by a brilliant use of 'third-degree' statistical methods, will be found in Eberhard, W.: *Das Toba-Reich Nord Chinas* (Leiden 1949, Brill).
[4] In contrast to the re-establishment of a universal state after a break caused by the intrusion of an alien civilization, as, for example, 'the Middle Empire' of Egypt was re-established in the shape of 'the New Empire,' the Achaemenian Empire in the shape of the Arab Caliphate, and the Maurya Rāj in the shape of the Gupta Rāj.

peting local communities of the preceding age; on the other side lies a conquered population which, in spite of a superiority in numbers that may be very great, finds itself militarily and politically at the mercy of its conquerors. This standard initial political pattern can be detected even in the history of the Ottoman Empire, which afterwards followed the singular course of excluding the free 'Osmanli imperial people themselves from political power in favour of professional slaves recruited from among their subjects and their neighbours. It is also common form—as can be observed in the subsequent history of the Ottoman Empire as well as in the careers of universal states of the standard type —for the effectively enfranchised element in the body politic[1] of a universal state to become, as time goes on, a relatively larger fraction of the total population as a result of the admission of recruits from the subject majority. It had, however, been unusual, in the universal states that had come into existence up to date, for this process to go to the length of completely obliterating the initial division between rulers and ruled by enfranchising politically the whole of the originally subject element.

The Obliteration of the Gulf by the Statesmanship of Han Liu Pang

The outstanding instance in which a comprehensive political enfranchisement had been achieved—and this within a quarter of a century of the foundation of the universal state—was in the Sinic World. In the Sinic universal state established in 230–221 B.C. through the conquest of six other parochial states by their victorious competitor Ts'in, the supremacy of Ts'in was brought to an end when Hsien Yang, the capital of the Ts'in Power, was occupied by Liu Pang in 207 B.C. and was sacked by Hsiang-yü in 206 B.C.[2] The political enfranchisement of the whole population of a Sinic universal state that had collapsed after Ts'in She Hwang-ti's death and had been restored by Han Liu Pang may be dated from the ordinance of 196 B.C.[3] in which the first Han emperor directed that candidates for posts in the imperial civil service should be selected by merit. Though this political act did not, and could not, change at a stroke the fundamental economic and social structure of the Sinic Society, it was, as we have seen, revolutionary in its effects on the political plane. The Sinic Society continued, it is true, to consist of a mass of tax-paying peasantry supporting a small privileged ruling minority, but henceforward the avenue giving entry into the Sinic political paradise was genuinely open to talent, in the sense that admission was no longer confined either by a national restriction to inhabitants of the former state of Ts'in or by a class restriction to scions of the former Sinic hereditary nobility.

The historical explanation of this exceptionally rapid and thoroughgoing political enfranchisement of the originally subject population of a Sinic universal state is to be found in the previous destruction of a

---

[1] In the Greek terminology of Hellenic political science the meaning of this clumsy English periphrasis is accurately conveyed by the single word πολίτευμα.
[2] See pp. 211–12, above.   [3] See p. 355, above.

former monopoly of political power in the hands of the Sinic hereditary nobility. This was accomplished, as we have seen, in the State of Ts'in through the reforms introduced by Lord Shang in the fourth century B.C.,[1] and in the rest of the Sinic World after 221 B.C. through still more drastic measures on the part of Ts'in She Hwang-ti.[2] The sequel indicates that Ts'in She Hwang-ti did his work less effectively than Lord Shang had done his; for there appears to be no record that Han Liu Pang ever had to reckon with attempts on the part of the people of Ts'in to recapture for their state the political dominion over the rest of the Sinic World which, after striving for it for a hundred years, Ts'in had held from 221 B.C. to 207 B.C.—though, if any sense of disappointed imperialism had been alive in the Ts'in people's hearts, it would assuredly have been inflamed by the experience of coming under the rule of a foreign usurper whose home country lay at the farther extremity of the region 'outside the passes', in the borderland between the former territories of Ts'in's conquered rivals Ts'i and Ch'u. The politically dangerous nostalgia for the past that gave Han Liu Pang anxiety was cherished by the dynasties and aristocracies of the former parochial states 'outside the passes' whose hereditary authority their conqueror Ts'in She Hwang-ti had done his utmost to eradicate. To forestall a second outburst, in these quarters, of the political explosion that had shattered the work of Ts'in She Hwang-ti was the main object of Han Liu Pang's carefully planned face-saving policy.

Han Liu Pang's choice of a territory for his own imperial demesne would hardly have fallen on the former parochial domain of Ts'in solely on the ground of the strategic strength of 'the Country within the Passes' unless he had felt the local population to be amenable to his rule; and for this he could hardly have counted on their gratitude to him for his clemency in 207 B.C.—even though this had been thrown into relief by the atrocities committed in Ts'in by Hsiang-yü in the following year. There must be some further explanation of the amenability which the people of Ts'in manifestly displayed in these apparently provocative circumstances, and we may perhaps find the explanation in the political annihilation of the nobility in Ts'in to the profit of the Crown more than a hundred years earlier. This concentration of power in the Crown's hands had made the people of Ts'in a formidably pliant military instrument for the overthrow of all the other parochial states in a war to the death; but it had given the state this military predominance at the cost of depriving it of the political vitality embodied in an experienced and self-conscious aristocracy; and accordingly, when the legitimate hereditary dynasty, in its turn, was extinguished in 207 B.C., the people of Ts'in were left as sheep without a native shepherd, at the mercy of the first competent stranger to arrive on the scene and round them up. The combined effect of Lord Shang's revolutionary work 'inside the passes' and Ts'in She Hwang-ti's outside them would seem to account for Han Liu Pang's success in obliterating, within the span of a single generation, the dividing line between rulers and ruled in the Sinic universal state.

¹ See p. 351, above.
² See p. 352, above.

The Inefficacy of a merely Juridical Enfranchisement

The unifying effect produced by living historical forces, operating over a long period of time, cannot be reproduced by the mere formality of conferring a uniform juridical status. The uniform status of Europeans, Eurasians, and Asiatics under the British Rāj in India, and of Europeans, Creoles, and 'Indians' in the Spanish Empire of the Indies, as subjects, in either case, of one Crown, did not have any appreciable practical effect in diminishing the gulf between rulers and ruled in either of these polities. In the Danubian Hapsburg Monarchy, on the other hand, the common allegiance of the divers religious and national communities to one dynasty, and the opening of careers in the Emperor-King-Archduke's service to talent, wherever this might be forthcoming among the Hapsburg monarch's motley collection of subjects, might in time have had the same effect as the same cause in the Han Empire, if in the Danubian Monarchy the tendency towards political equality had not been overtaken and reversed in the last chapter of its history by a nationalism, derived from Western Europe, which eventually split the Monarchy into pieces.[1] The classical instance in which an initial gulf between rulers and ruled was successfully obliterated by a gradual merger of a once privileged ruling minority in the mass of its former subjects is to be found in the history of the Roman Empire, and here, too, as we have seen,[2] the substance of political equality was not communicated by the mere conferment of the juridical status of Roman citizenship. After the promulgation of the *Constitutio Antoniniana* in A.D. 212 all inhabitants of the Roman Empire were Roman citizens with the possible exception of an inconsiderable residue of *dediticii*; yet, after that, it still required the political and social revolution of the third century of the Christian Era to bring the realities of life into conformity with the law, because the effective governing element ($\pi o \lambda \acute{\iota} \tau \epsilon \upsilon \mu a$) under the Principate had not been coextensive with the Roman citizen body, but had been a narrower oligarchy whose privileges had survived the progressive extension of the status of Roman citizenship to former Roman subjects.

Imperial Citizenships and Ecclesiastical Allegiances

The ultimate beneficiary from the political egalitarianism towards which the Roman Empire was moving in the Age of the Principate and at which it arrived in the time of Diocletian was, of course, the Catholic Christian Church, and this in more than one way.

In the first place, the Catholic Church borrowed the Roman State's master institution of dual citizenship—a constitutional device that had solved the technical and psychological problem of how to enjoy the advantages of membership in an oecumenical community without having to repudiate narrower loyalties or to cut local roots.[3] In the Roman Empire under the Principate, which was the political framework within which the Christian Church grew up, all citizens of the world-city of Rome, except a small minority whose ancestral domicile was the

---

[1] See II. ii. 182–6. [2] On pp. 152–8, above.
[3] See IV. iv. 307–14.

metropolis itself or its immediate environs, were also citizens of some local municipality that, though within the Roman body politic, was an autonomous city-state with the traditional Hellenic form of city-state self-government and the traditional hold of such a local motherland upon the affections of her children. On this Roman secular model a growing and spreading Christian ecclesiastical community built up an organization and a corporate feeling that was both local and oecumenical. The Church to which a Christian gave his allegiance was both the local Christian community of a particular city-state and the Catholic Christian community in which all these local churches were embraced in virtue of a uniform practice and doctrine and a perpetual intercourse through which they kept in touch and in step with one another.

The Catholic Church became, in another sense, a beneficiary of the Roman Empire in its post-Diocletianic phase when—after the conversion of Constantine to Christianity had been followed by Theodosius's proscription of all non-Christian religions[1] except Judaism—the terms 'Catholic Christian' and 'Roman citizen' became almost interchangeable. The politico-ecclesiastical equation thus established in the Roman Empire towards the close of the fourth century of the Christian Era reappeared in the constitutions of those 'ghosts' of the Roman Empire that were afterwards conjured up in Western and in Orthodox Christendom. In the medieval 'Holy Roman Empire', and even in the modern Danubian Hapsburg Monarchy, at least down to the Austro-Hungarian *Ausgleich* of A.D. 1867, it was hardly possible to be a fully approved and privileged subject of the Imperial Crown without at the same time being a Roman Catholic Christian, while in the East Roman Empire and in the Russian Empire, even in its post-Petrine phase, full membership in the political community could hardly be enjoyed without a profession of Eastern Orthodox Christianity. In A.D. 1952 a philological fossil of this once living state of politico-religious affairs was still preserved in the Modern Greek appellation *Rómyós*, to which an unsophisticated Greek peasant or a hyper-sophisticated cultivator of the vulgar tongue would answer rather than to the artificially revived name *Hellên* with which he would have been indoctrinated at school. Though *Rómyós*, in the philologist's ear, merely rang a slight change on the Ancient Greek word ʿΡωμαῖος, it had long since ceased, on the lips of its Modern Greek users, to mean 'Roman' in the historical sense. It had come to mean an Orthodox Christian whose mother tongue was Modern Greek and whose true fatherland was an ideally still existing East Roman Empire with its capital at Constantinople.[2]

In the convergent histories of the Roman Empire and the Catholic Christian Church, the Roman citizen body and the Christian ecclesiastical community had made their *rapprochement* from entirely different origins in extremely diverse social and cultural milieux; and, though, at an early date in the history of Christianity, they had acquired an outstandingly important common member in the person of Saint Paul, they did not coalesce until the Christian Church was nearly four hundred, and the Roman State more than a thousand, years old. In the histories

---

[1] See IV. iv. 226–7.   [2] See pp. 29–31, above.

of the Arab Caliphate and the Sunnī form of Islam, the higher religion that was eventually to be embraced by all but a remnant of the population of the universal state was associated from the outset with the imperial people; and, so far from converging—as the Catholic Christian Church and the Roman citizen body converged, to the point of eventual coalescence—by extending their membership from opposite quarters to include by degrees almost the whole population of the state, the imperial people and the Islamic community ceased to be coextensive as Islam proceeded to convert the Primitive Muslim Arab empire-builders' non-Arab subjects. The revolution that carried the 'Abbasids on to the imperial throne of the Caliphate in place of the Umayyads corresponded, as we have seen,[1] to the revolution in the Roman Empire in the third century of the Christian Era in breaking down a previous political barrier between a dominant minority and a subject majority. Since, however, in the pre-'Abbasid Caliphate, the ruling element had been distinguished from its subjects, not by a secular citizenship to which non-citizens could be admitted by naturalization, but by the incommunicable physical heritage of Arab descent and by a communicable religious allegiance to Islam that did not give a non-Arab convert Arab status,[2] the effect of the 'Abbasid revolution was to open the way towards egalitarianism in the Caliphate, not by making Arabs as well as Muslims out of an increasing number of the Caliphate's non-Arab subjects, but by substituting the Muslim for the Arab community as the imperial people.[3] Thus in the Caliphate, in contrast to the Roman Empire, the political distinction between rulers and ruled was eventually effaced by their merger, not in both a common citizenship and a common religion, but in a common religion alone. In the Caliphate an oecumenical faith had to do duty for an oecumenical citizenship as well.

The role of Islam in the Caliphate in the last phase of the history of the Syriac Civilization recurs in the histories of the Mughal Rāj and the Ottoman Empire, in which Muslim empire-builders imposed universal states on the Hindu World and on Orthodox Christendom respectively. In both these cases, Islam once again served as a unifying and a levelling political force.

In the Ottoman Empire after the death of Suleymān the Magnificent the free Muslim community, who for the best part of two centuries past had been paradoxically excluded from a share in the government, were stimulated by a sense of the incongruity between their profession of Islam and their unfavourable political status into wresting out of the hands of the Pādishāh's infidel-born Slave-Household its monopoly of political power. In the Mughal Rāj, which developed only the rudiments of a counterpart of the 'Osmanlis'' 'peculiar institution',[4] no revolution

---

[1] On pp. 147–52, above.

[2] The most that could be communicated to a non-Arab subject of the pre-'Abbasid Caliphate who embraced Islam and sought to associate himself with an Arab patron was a relation of clientship that was an intolerably inferior status compared with that of the Arab imperial people itself.

[3] The deposition of the Arabs from their former political supremacy in the Caliphate as a result of the fall of the Umayyads was comparable to the deposition of the people of Ts'in from their supremacy in the Sinic World as a result of the fall of the Ts'in Dynasty.　　　　　　　　　　　　　　　　　　　　[4] See III. iii. 31, n. 1.

was needed in order to merge the Transoxanian Turkī henchmen of the Timurid imperial house with their fellow Muslims who had made their way into India before them or who came in afterwards from Central Asia or Iran to reinforce them.

In the Caliphate, the Ottoman Empire, and the Mughal Empire alike, Islam also brought recruits to the imperial people in the form of converts from the non-Muslim subject population, but failed to drive rival religions entirely off the field, as Christianity virtually succeeded in superseding its rivals in the Roman Empire; and for this difference in the outcome we can see two reasons. One is that Islam had to contend with higher religions—Zoroastrianism and Orthodox, Monophysite and Nestorian Christianity in the Caliphate; Hinduism in the Mughal Rāj; Orthodox Christianity in the Ottoman Empire—which were all already well established before Islam's advent, whereas Christianity in the Roman Empire had better chances. She was running a neck-and-neck race with coeval higher religions which, like her, had still to establish their positions, while the older religions that were already established in the Hellenic World of that age had no chance of holding their own against any higher religion that might enter the lists against them, since they were worships either of a Non-Human Nature who had been deprived of her prestige by Man's establishment of his mastery over her, or of some parochial human community which had lost its prestige in losing its sovereign independence. Islam's second handicap, by comparison with Christianity, was its honourable obligation, under one of its own articles of faith, to grant toleration to other 'Peoples of the Book' so long as they accepted Muslim political supremacy and gave practical proof of their acceptance of it by paying tribute; and, though, on a strict interpretation of the Islamic Law (sharī'ah), the Jews and Christians were the only sects that were entitled to claim this status, the same privileges were accorded in practice to both Zoroastrians and Hindus,[1] partly perhaps, owing to an intuitive perception that their faiths, too, were 'higher religions', and partly, no doubt, on account of the sheer political impracticability of proscribing any religion that commanded the allegiance of the solid mass of a numerous subject population —which was the position of Hinduism in the Mughal Rāj in India and of Zoroastrianism in the eastern provinces of the Caliphate down to at least the ninth century of the Christian Era.

While these handicaps were operative in all the three cases under consideration, there was a notable difference in the extent of Islam's success in the conversion of non-Muslim subject populations in the Caliphate on the one hand and in the Mughal and Ottoman empires on the other. In the Caliphate, by the time of the extinction of the last lingering shadow of the 'Abbasid Power by the Mongols in A.D. 1258, the process of conversion had gone so far—particularly during the last two or three centuries, under the spur of successive Eurasian Nomad barbarian invasions—that the non-Muslim residue in the population had been reduced to a numerically insignificant minority.[2] In the Otto-

[1] See IV. iv. 225–6; V. v. 674, n. 2; and V. vi. 204–5.
[2] For the process, see, further, Tritton, A. S.: *The Caliphs and their Non-Muslim*

man Empire and the Mughal Rāj the corresponding missionary activity never made a comparable impression on the non-Muslim mass, and in both states the process was arrested in the course of the seventeenth century of the Christian Era by an increase in the vigour and confidence of the reaction of the Orthodox Christian and the Hindu subject population respectively.

The explanation of this marked difference in results is probably to be found in differences on the non-Muslim side in this competition between Islam and rival faiths. Among Islam's rivals in the Caliphate, Zoroastrianism and Orthodox Christianity had forfeited their popular appeal through their adoption by the Sasanian and Roman Imperial governments as established official religions.[1] The Nestorian Christians in the ex-Sasanian provinces and the Monophysite Christians in the ex-Roman provinces were not disposed to resist a change of masters when their former Zoroastrian and Melchite oppressors were deposed by the Primitive Muslim Arabs, though they were slow to adopt Islam themselves in place of faiths which they had originally embraced of their own accord and not under compulsion. This divided religious opposition to Islam in the Caliphate was evidently less difficult to overcome than the united front that Hinduism opposed to it in the Mughal Rāj and Orthodox Christianity in the Ottoman Empire. In the contest between Islam and Orthodox Christianity for the spiritual allegiance of the Ottoman *ra'īyeh* the scales were eventually weighted against Islam by the impact of Western Christendom after the tide of war between the 'Osmanlis and the Western Powers had begun to flow in favour of the West. This change in military fortunes lowered the prestige of Islam in the Orthodox Christians' eyes and inspired them with the new ideal of remoulding themselves in the cultural image of their heterodox Western co-religionists.[2] The West had impinged on India likewise before Awrangzīb's abandonment of the Islamic tradition of toleration evoked a militant Hindu counter-attack, but in this case Islam's arrest must be ascribed to an error in Mughal statesmanship and not to any influences emanating from Western onlookers who, in India at this date, had not yet acquired prestige by a display of their military strength.

These considerations on oecumenical citizenships, ecclesiastical and secular, conclude our survey of universal states—an institution whose evil genii had been the Ts'in She Hwang-tis and its good genii the Han Liu Pangs.

Subjects (London 1930, Milford), and Browne, L. E.: *The Eclipse of Christianity in Asia from the Time of Muhammad till the Fourteenth Century* (Cambridge 1933, University Press).

[1] For the effect of this on Zoroastrianism, see V .v. 125–6 and 659–61. For the ostracism of the Orthodox Church, as the religion of the Melchites ('Imperialists'), by Syriac and Coptic Christians, see IV. iv. 593, n. 3.

[2] See IX. viii. 161–5.

GALAXY BOOKS

GALAXY BOOKS